Get the eBook FREE!

(PDF, ePub, Kindle, and liveBook all included)

We believe that once you buy a book from us, you should be able to read it in any format we have available. To get electronic versions of this book at no additional cost to you, purchase and then register this book at the Manning website.

Go to https://www.manning.com/freebook and follow the instructions to complete your pBook registration.

That's it!
Thanks from Manning!

TypeScript Quickly

YAKOV FAIN AND ANTON MOISEEV

MANNING
SHELTER ISLAND

For online information and ordering of this and other Manning books, please visit www.manning.com. The publisher offers discounts on this book when ordered in quantity. For more information, please contact

Special Sales Department
Manning Publications Co.
20 Baldwin Road
PO Box 761
Shelter Island, NY 11964
Email: orders@manning.com

Manning Publications Co.
20 Baldwin Road
PO Box 761
Shelter Island, NY 11964

Development editor: Susanna Kline
Technical development editor: Dennis Sellinger
Review editor: Aleks Dragosavljević
Production editor: Lori Weidert
Copy editor: Andy Carroll
Proofreader: Keri Hales
Technical proofreader: George Onofrei
Typesetter: Gordan Salinovic
Cover designer: Marija Tudor

ISBN 9781617295942
Printed in the United States of America

contents

preface

This book is about the programming language *TypeScript,* which is one of the most loved languages, according to the Developer Survey on Stack Overflow (see https://insights.stackoverflow.com/survey/2019). According to the latest issue of the reputable *ThoughtWork's Technology Radar* (http://mng.bz/Ze5P), "TypeScript is a carefully considered language and its consistently improving tools and IDE support continues to impress us. With a good repository of TypeScript-type definitions, we benefit from all the rich JavaScript libraries while gaining type safety."

We use TypeScript daily, and we like it a lot! We really like TypeScript for allowing us to focus on the main problem we're solving and not on typos in an object's property name. In TypeScript programs, the chances of getting runtime errors are substantially lower compared to code originally written in JavaScript. We also like that IDEs offer great TypeScript support and literally walk us through the maze of APIs from third-party libraries we use in our projects.

TypeScript is great, but since it's a compiled-to-JavaScript language, we also need to talk a bit about JavaScript. In May 1995, after 10 days of hard work, Brendan Eich created the JavaScript programming language. This scripting language didn't need a compiler and was meant to be used in the Netscape Navigator web browser.

No compilers were needed to deploy a JavaScript program in the browser. Adding a `<script>` tag with the JavaScript sources (or a reference to a file with sources) would instruct the browser to load and parse the code and execute it in the browser's JavaScript engine. People enjoyed the simplicity of the language—there was no need to declare the types of variables and no need to use any tools. You'd just write your code in a plain text editor and use it in a web page.

When you first start learning JavaScript, you can see your first program running in two minutes. There's nothing to install or configure, and there's no need to compile the program, because JavaScript is an interpreted language.

JavaScript is also a dynamically typed language, which gives additional freedom to software developers. There's no need to declare an object's properties up front, as the JavaScript engine will create the property at runtime if the object doesn't already have it.

Actually, there's no way to declare the type of a variable in JavaScript. The JavaScript engine will guess the type based on the assigned value (for example, `var x = 123` means that `x` is a number). If, later on, the script has an assignment `x ="678"`, the type of `x` will automatically change from a number to a string. Did you really want to change the type of `x` or was that a mistake? You'll know that only at runtime, as there's no compiler to warn you about it.

JavaScript is a very forgiving language, which is not a shortcoming if the codebase is small, and you're the only person working on the project. Most likely, you'll remember that `x` is supposed to be a number, and you don't need any help with this. And, of course, you'll work for your current employer forever, so the variable `x` is never forgotten.

Over the years, JavaScript became super popular and the de facto standard programming language of the web. But 20 years ago, developers used JavaScript to display web pages with some interactive content; today we develop complex web apps that contain thousands of lines of code developed by teams of developers. Not everyone in your team remembers that `x` was supposed to be a number. To minimize the number of runtime errors, JavaScript developers write unit tests and perform code reviews.

To be more productive, software developers get help from IDEs with autocomplete features, easy refactoring, and so on. But how can an IDE help you with refactoring if the language allows complete freedom in adding properties to objects and changing types on the fly?

Web developers needed a better language, but replacing JavaScript with another one that would be supported by all the different browsers was not realistic. Instead, new compile-to-JavaScript languages were created. They were more tool-friendly, but the program still had to be converted to JavaScript before deployment so every browser could support it. TypeScript is one of these languages, and after reading this book, you'll see what makes it stand out.

acknowledgments

Yakov would like to thank his best friend Sammy for creating a warm and cozy environment while he was working on this book. Unfortunately, Sammy can't talk, but like any dog, he loves all his family members more than they love themselves.

Anton would like to thank the authors of and contributors to the open source projects used in this book. Without the numerous hours they regularly dedicate to the projects, and their constant work growing and supporting communities, this book wouldn't be possible. He's also grateful to his family for being patient while he was working on the book.

Special thanks go to multiple book reviewers who provided valuable feedback: Ahmad F Subahi, Alexandros Dallas, Brian Daley, Cameron Presley, Cameron Singe, Deniz Vehbi, Floris Bouchot, George Onofrei, George Thomas, Gerald James Stralko, Guy Langston, Jeff Smith, Justin Kahn, Kent R. Spillner, Kevin Orr, Lucas Pardue, Marko Letic, Matteo Battista, Paul Brown, Polina Keselman, Richard Tuttle, Srihari Sridharan, Tamara Forza, and Thomas Overby Hansen.

about this book

Who should read this book

This book is written for software engineers who want to become more productive developing web or standalone apps. Both authors are practitioners, and we wrote this book for practitioners. Not only do we explain the syntax of the language using basic code samples, but we also develop multiple apps that show how you can use TypeScript with popular libraries and frameworks.

While working on this book, we ran workshops using the code samples from the book, giving us early feedback about the book's content. We really hope that you'll enjoy the process of learning TypeScript with this book.

We expect readers to have a working knowledge of HTML, CSS, and JavaScript that use recent additions from ECMAScript specs. If you are only familiar with the ECMAScript 5 syntax, looking through the appendix first will make it easier to understand the code samples in the book—the appendix provides an introduction to modern JavaScript.

How this book is organized: A roadmap

This book is divided into two parts. In part 1, we cover various syntax elements of TypeScript using small code snippets for illustration. In part 2, we apply TypeScript in several versions of a blockchain app. If your goal is to quickly learn TypeScript's syntax and tooling, part 1 of this book is all you need.

Chapter 1 will get you started with TypeScript development. You'll compile and run very basic programs so you understand the workflow, from writing a program in

TypeScript to compiling it into runnable JavaScript. We'll also cover the benefits of programming in TypeScript versus JavaScript and introduce the Visual Studio Code editor.

Chapter 2 explains how to declare variables and functions with types. You'll learn how to declare type aliases with the `type` keyword and how to declare custom types with classes and interfaces. This will help you understand the difference between nominal and structural type systems.

Chapter 3 explains how class inheritance works and when to use abstract classes. You'll see how TypeScript interfaces can force a class to have methods with known signatures, without worrying about the implementation details. You'll also learn what "programming to interfaces" means.

Chapter 4 is dedicated to enums and generics. This chapter covers the benefits of using enums, the syntax for numeric and string enums, what generic types are for, and how to write classes, interfaces, and functions that support generics.

Chapter 5 covers decorators and mapped and conditional types. It's about advanced TypeScript types, and you should be familiar with the syntax of generics to understand the material in this chapter.

Chapter 6 is about tooling. We explain the use of source maps and TSLinter (although TSLinter is being deprecated, many developers are still using it). Then we show you how to compile and bundle TypeScript apps with Webpack. You'll also learn how and why to compile TypeScript with Babel.

Chapter 7 teaches you to use JavaScript libraries in your TypeScript app. We start by explaining the role of type definition files, and then we present a small app that uses a JavaScript library in a TypeScript app. Finally, we go over the process of gradually upgrading an existing JavaScript project to TypeScript.

In part 2, we apply TypeScript in a blockchain app. You might be thinking to yourself, "None of the companies I've worked for are using blockchain technology, so why should I learn about blockchain when my goal is to master TypeScript?" We didn't want our sample app to be yet another ToDo example, so we looked for a hot technology where you could apply the different TypeScript elements and techniques introduced in part 1. Seeing how TypeScript is used in a not-so-trivial app will make this content more practical, even if you're not going to use blockchain technology in the near future.

In this part of the book, you'll develop several blockchain apps: a standalone app, a browser app, an Angular app, a React.js app, a Vue.js app. Feel free to read only those chapters that interest you, but make sure you read chapters 8 and 10 where the foundational concepts are introduced.

Chapter 8 introduces the principles of blockchain apps. You'll learn what the hashing functions are for, what block mining means, and why the proof of work is required to add a new block to a blockchain. After covering the blockchain basics, we present a project and explain the code that creates a basic blockchain app. Most chapters in part 2 have runnable blockchain projects with detailed explanations of how they were written and how to run them.

Chapter 9 describes how to create a web client for a blockchain. This app will not use any web frameworks; we'll use only HTML, CSS, and TypeScript. We'll also create a small library for hash generation that can be used in both web and standalone clients. You'll also see how to debug your TypeScript code in the browser.

Chapter 10 reviews the code of a blockchain app that uses a messaging server for communications between blockchain members. We create a Node.js and WebSocket server in TypeScript, and we'll show you how the blockchain uses the longest chain rule to achieve consensus. You'll find practical examples of using TypeScript interfaces, abstract classes, access qualifiers, enums, and generics.

Chapter 11 provides a brief introduction to developing web apps in Angular with TypeScript, and chapter 12 reviews the code of a blockchain web client developed using this framework.

Chapter 13 offers a brief introduction to developing web apps in React.js with TypeScript, and chapter 14 reviews the code of a blockchain web client developed using React.

Chapter 15 similarly introduces developing web apps in Vue.js with TypeScript, and chapter 16 reviews the blockchain web client developed with this Vue.

About the code

This book contains many examples of source code both in numbered listings and in line with normal text. In both cases, source code is formatted in a `fixed-width font like this` to separate it from ordinary text. Sometimes code is also **`in bold`** to highlight code that has changed from previous steps in the chapter, such as when a new feature adds to an existing line of code.

In many cases, the original source code has been reformatted; we've added line breaks and reworked indentation to accommodate the available page space in the book. In rare cases, even this was not enough, and listings include line-continuation markers (➥). Additionally, comments in the source code have often been removed from the listings when the code is described in the text. Code annotations accompany many of the listings, highlighting important concepts.

Part 1 is about the syntax of the language, and most of the code samples are published online on the TypeScript Playground—an interactive tool that quickly checks the syntax of a TypeScript code snippet and compiles it into JavaScript. The links to these code snippets are provided in the book as needed.

The second part of the book consists of multiple projects that use TypeScript to develop applications using popular libraries and frameworks (such as Angular, React.js, and Vue.js). The source code of these apps is located on GitHub at https://github.com/yfain/getts.

We thoroughly tested every app that comes with the book, but new versions of TypeScript and other libraries may be released, with breaking changes. If you're getting an error while trying to run one of these projects, please open an issue on the book's GitHub repository.

liveBook discussion forum

Purchase of *Typescript Quickly* includes free access to a private web forum run by Manning Publications where you can make comments about the book, ask technical questions, and receive help from the author and from other users. To access the forum, go to https://livebook.manning.com/#!/book/TypeScriptQuickly/discussion. You can also learn more about Manning's forums and the rules of conduct at https://livebook.manning.com/#!/discussion.

Manning's commitment to our readers is to provide a venue where a meaningful dialogue between individual readers and between readers and the author can take place. It is not a commitment to any specific amount of participation on the part of the author, whose contribution to the forum remains voluntary (and unpaid). We suggest you try asking the author some challenging questions lest their interest stray! The forum and the archives of previous discussions will be accessible from the publisher's website as long as the book is in print.

About the authors

Yakov Fain is a cofounder of two IT companies: Farata Systems and SuranceBay. He has authored and co-authored books such as *Java Programming: 24-Hour Trainer, Angular Development with TypeScript, Java Programming for Kids,* and others. A Java Champion, he has taught multiple classes and workshops on web- and Java-related technologies and has presented at international conferences. Fain has written more than a thousand blog entries at yakovfain.com. His Twitter and Instagram handles are @yfain. He also publishes videos on YouTube.

Anton Moiseev is a lead software developer at SuranceBay. He's been developing enterprise applications for more than a decade with Java and .NET technologies. He has a solid background and a strong focus on web technologies, implementing best practices to make the frontend work seamlessly with the backend. He has taught a number of training sessions on AngularJS and Angular frameworks. He blogs occasionally at antonmoiseev.com, and his Twitter handle is @antonmoiseev.

about the cover illustration

The figure on the cover of *TypeScript Quickly* is captioned "Bourgeoise Florentine." The illustration is taken from a collection of dress costumes from various countries by Jacques Grasset de Saint-Sauveur (1757–1810), titled *Costumes civils actuels de tous les peuples connus,* published in France in 1788. Each illustration is finely drawn and colored by hand. The rich variety of Grasset de Saint-Sauveur's collection reminds us vividly of how culturally apart the world's towns and regions were just 200 years ago. Isolated from each other, people spoke different dialects and languages. In the streets or in the countryside, it was easy to identify where they lived and what their trade or station in life was just by their dress.

The way we dress has changed since then and the diversity by region, so rich at the time, has faded away. It is now hard to tell apart the inhabitants of different continents, let alone different towns, regions, or countries. Perhaps we have traded cultural diversity for a more varied personal life—certainly for a more varied and fast-paced technological life.

At a time when it is hard to tell one computer book from another, Manning celebrates the inventiveness and initiative of the computer business with book covers based on the rich diversity of regional life of two centuries ago, brought back to life by Grasset de Saint-Sauveur's pictures.

Part 1

Mastering the TypeScript syntax

Part 1 starts with explaining the benefits of TypeScript compared to JavaScript. Then, we'll cover various syntax elements of TypeScript using small code snippets for illustration. You'll see how to use built-in and declare custom types. We'll introduce the use of classes and interfaces as well as generics, enums, decorators, mapped and conditional types. You'll learn the tooling used by TypeScript developers (such as compilers, linters, debuggers, and bundlers). Finally, we'll show you how to use the TypeScript and JavaScript code in the same app.

For those of you who like learning by watching videos, Yakov Fain has published a number of videos (see http://mng.bz/m4M8) that illustrate the materials from Part 1 of this book. If your goal is to quickly learn the TypeScript's syntax and tooling, Part 1 of this book is all you need.

1 Getting familiar with TypeScript

This chapter covers

- The benefits of programming in TypeScript over JavaScript
- How to compile the TypeScript code into JavaScript
- How to work with the Visual Studio Code editor

The goal of this chapter is to get you started with TypeScript development. We'll start by paying respect to JavaScript, and then we'll share our own opinion on why you should be programming in TypeScript. To round out this chapter, we'll compile and run a very basic program so you can follow the workflow from writing a program in TypeScript to compiling it into runnable JavaScript.

If you're a seasoned JavaScript developer you'd need a good reason to switch to TypeScript, which would have to be compiled into JavaScript before deployment anyway. If you're a backend developer planning to learn the frontend ecosystem, you'd also need a reason for learning any programming language other than JavaScript, so let's start with the reasoning.

1.1 Why program in TypeScript

TypeScript is a compile-to-JavaScript language, which was released as an open source project by Microsoft in 2012. A program written in TypeScript has to be *transpiled* into JavaScript first, and then it can be executed in the browser or a standalone JavaScript engine.

The difference between transpiling and compiling is that the latter turns the source code of a program into bytecode or machine code, whereas the former converts the program from one language to another, such as from TypeScript to JavaScript. But in the TypeScript community, the word *compile* is more popular, so we'll use it in this book to describe the process of converting TypeScript code into JavaScript.

You may wonder, why go through the hassle of writing a program in TypeScript and then compiling it into JavaScript if you could write the program in JavaScript in the first place? To answer this question, let's look at TypeScript from a very high-level perspective.

TypeScript is a superset of JavaScript, so you can take any JavaScript file, such as myProgram.js, change its file extension from .js to .ts, and myProgram.ts will likely become a valid TypeScript program. We say "likely" because the original JavaScript code may have hidden type-related bugs (it may dynamically change the types of object properties or add new ones after the object is declared) and other problems that will be revealed only after your JavaScript code is compiled.

> **TIP** In section 7.3, we'll provide some tips on migrating your JavaScript code to TypeScript.

In general, the word *superset* implies that the superset contains everything that the *set* has, plus something else. Figure 1.1 illustrates TypeScript as a superset of ECMAScript, which is a spec for all versions of JavaScript. ES.Next represents the very latest additions to ECMAScript that are still in the works.

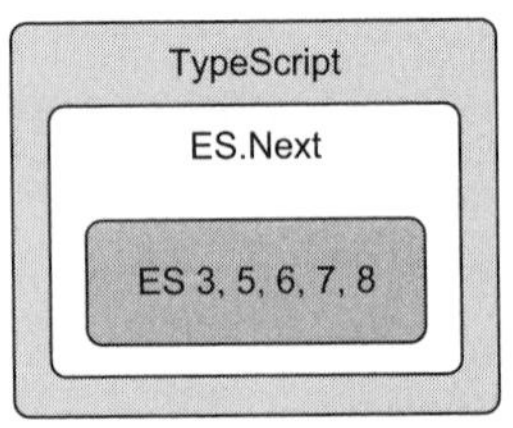

Figure 1.1 TypeScript as a superset

In addition to the JavaScript set, TypeScript also supports *static typing*, whereas JavaScript supports only *dynamic typing*. Here, the word "typing" refers to assigning types to program variables.

In programming languages with static typing, a type must be assigned to a variable before you can use it. In TypeScript, you can declare a variable of a certain type, and any attempt to assign it a value of a different type results in a compilation error.

This is not the case in JavaScript, which doesn't know about the types of your program variables until runtime. Even in the running program, you can change the type of a variable just by assigning it a value of a different type. In TypeScript, if you declare a variable as a `string`, trying to assign a numeric value to it will result in a *compile-time* error.

```
let customerId: string;
customerId = 123;  // compile-time error
```

JavaScript decides on the variable type at runtime, and the type can be dynamically changed, as in the following example:

```
let customerId = "A15BN"; // OK, customerId is a string
customerId = 123;   // OK, from now on it's a number
```

Now let's consider a JavaScript function that applies a discount to a price. It has two arguments and both must be numbers.

```
function getFinalPrice(price, discount) {
  return price - price / discount;
}
```

How do you know that the arguments must be numbers? First of all, you authored this function some time ago, and having an exceptional memory, you may just remember the types of all the arguments. Second, you used descriptive names for the arguments that hint at their types. Third, you can guess the types by reading the function code.

This is a pretty simple function, but let's say someone invoked this function by providing a discount as a string. This function would print `NaN` at runtime.

```
console.log(getFinalPrice( 100, "10%")); // prints NaN
```

This is an example of a runtime error caused by the wrong use of a function. In TypeScript, you could provide types for the function arguments, and such a runtime error would never happen. If someone tried to invoke the function with the wrong type of argument, this error would be caught as you were typing. Let's see it in action.

The official TypeScript web page (www.typescriptlang.org) offers language documentation and a Playground where you can enter code snippets in TypeScript, which will be immediately compiled to JavaScript.

At http://mng.bz/Q0Mm you'll see our code snippet in the TypeScript Playground, with the squiggly red line under the `"10%"`. If you hover your mouse over the erroneous code, you'll see a prompt explaining the error, as shown in figure 1.2.

This error is caught by the TypeScript static code analyzer while you type, even before you compile this code with the Typescript compiler (tsc). Moreover, if you specify the variable types, your editor or IDE will offer an autocomplete feature suggesting argument names and types for the `getFinalPrice()` function.

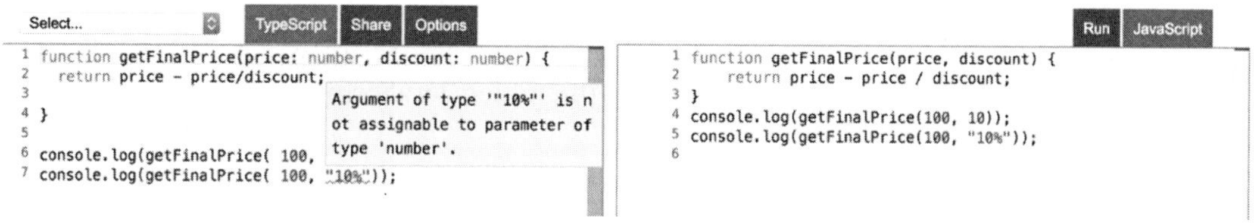

Select... TypeScript Share Options

```
function getFinalPrice(price: number, discount: number) {
  return price - price/discount;

}

console.log(getFinalPrice( 100,
console.log(getFinalPrice( 100, "10%"));
```

Argument of type '"10%"' is not assignable to parameter of type 'number'.

Run JavaScript

```
function getFinalPrice(price, discount) {
    return price - price / discount;
}
console.log(getFinalPrice(100, 10));
console.log(getFinalPrice(100, "10%"));
```

Figure 1.2 Using TypeScript Playground

Isn't it nice that errors are caught before runtime? We think so. Most developers with a background in such languages as Java, C++, and C# take it for granted that such errors are caught at compile time, and this is one of the main reasons why they like TypeScript.

> **NOTE** There are two types of programming errors—those that are immediately reported by tools as you type, and those that are reported by users of your program. Programming in TypeScript substantially decreases the number of the latter.

> **TIP** The TypeScript site (www.typescriptlang.org) has a section called "Documentation and Tutorials." There you'll find useful tips for configuring TypeScript in specific environments, like ASP.NET, React, and others.

Some hard-core JavaScript developers say that TypeScript slows them down by requiring them to declare types, and that they'd be more productive in JavaScript. But remember that types in TypeScript are optional—you can continue writing in JavaScript but still introduce tsc in your workflow. Why? Because you'll be able to use the latest ECMAScript syntax (such as `async` and `await`) and compile your JavaScript down to ES5 so your code can run in older browsers.

But most web developers aren't JavaScript ninjas and can appreciate the helping hand offered by TypeScript. As a matter of fact, all strongly typed languages provide better tool support and thus increase productivity (even for ninjas). Having said that, we'd like to stress that TypeScript gives you the benefits of statically typed languages when and where you want it, without stopping you from using the good old dynamic JavaScript objects when you want them.

More than a hundred programming languages are compiled to JavaScript (as this list shows: http://mng.bz/MO42). What makes TypeScript stand out is that its creators follow the ECMAScript standards and implement upcoming JavaScript features a lot faster than the vendors of web browsers.

You can find the current proposals for new ECMAScript features on GitHub: https://github.com/tc39/proposals. A proposal has to go through several stages to be included in the final version of the next ECMAScript spec. If a proposal makes it to stage 3, it will most likely be included in the latest version of TypeScript.

In the summer of 2017, the `async` and `await` keywords (see section A.10.4 in the appendix) were included in ECMAScript specification ES2017 (a.k.a. ES8). It took more than a year for major browsers to start supporting these keywords, but TypeScript has supported them since November 2015. TypeScript developers were able to start using these keywords about three years before those who waited for browser support. The best part is that you can use the future JavaScript syntax in today's TypeScript code, and compile it down to the older JavaScript syntax (such as ES5) supported by all browsers!

Having said that, we'd like to make a clear distinction between the syntax described in the latest ECMAScript specifications and the syntax that's unique to TypeScript. We recommend you read the appendix first, so you know where ECMAScript ends and TypeScript begins.

Although JavaScript engines do a decent job of guessing the types of variables by their values, development tools have limited ability to help you without knowing variable types. In mid- and large-size applications, this JavaScript shortcoming lowers the productivity of software developers.

TypeScript follows the latest specifications of ECMAScript and adds to them types, interfaces, decorators, class member variables (fields), generics, enums, the keywords `public`, `protected`, and `private`, and more. Check the TypeScript roadmap (https://github.com/Microsoft/TypeScript/wiki/Roadmap) to see what's available and what's coming in future releases of TypeScript. And one more thing: the JavaScript code generated from TypeScript is easy to read, and it looks like handwritten code.

> **Five facts about TypeScript**
>
> - The core developer of TypeScript is Anders Hejlsberg, who also designed Turbo Pascal and Delphi and is the lead architect of C# at Microsoft.
> - At the end of 2014, Google approached Microsoft asking if they could introduce decorators in TypeScript so this language could be used for developing the Angular 2 framework. Microsoft agreed, and this gave a tremendous boost to TypeScript's popularity, given that hundreds of thousands of developers use Angular.
> - As of December 2019, tsc had several million downloads per week from npmjs.org, and this is not the only TypeScript repository. For current statistics, see www.npmjs.com/package/typescript.
> - According to Redmonk, a respectable software analytics firm, TypeScript came in 12th in the programming language rankings of January 2019 (see the rankings here: http://mng.bz/4eow).
> - According to Stack Overflow's 2019 Developer Survey, TypeScript is the third most loved language (see https://insights.stackoverflow.com/survey/2019).

Now we'll introduce the process of configuring and using the tsc on your computer.

1.2 Typical TypeScript workflows

Let's get familiar with the TypeScript workflow, from writing your code to deploying your app. Figure 1.3 shows such a workflow, assuming that the entire source code of the app is written in TypeScript.

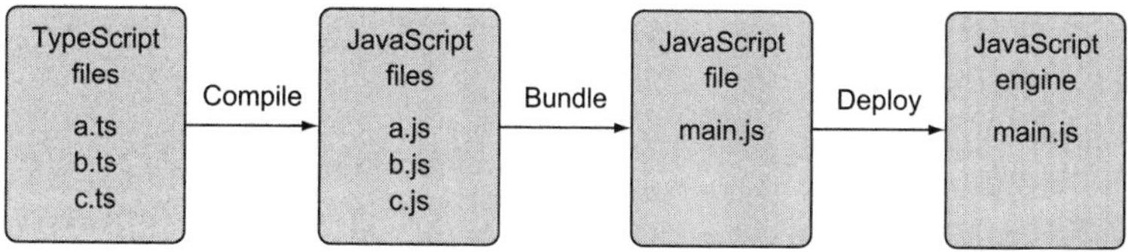

Figure 1.3 Deploying an app written in TypeScript

As you can see, the project consists of three TypeScript files: a.ts, b.ts, and c.ts. These files have to be compiled to JavaScript by the Typescript compiler (tsc), which will generate three new files: a.js, b.js, and c.js. Later in this section, we'll show you how to tell the compiler to generate JavaScript of specific versions.

At this point, some JavaScript developers will say, "TypeScript forces me to introduce an additional compilation step between writing code and seeing it run." But do you really want to stick to the ES5 version of JavaScript, ignoring all the latest syntax introduced by ES6, 7, 8, through to ES.Next? If not, you'll have a compilation step in your workflow anyway—you'll need to compile your source written in a newer JavaScript version into the well-supported ES5 syntax.

Figure 1.3 shows just three files, but real-world projects may have hundreds or even thousands of files. Developers don't want to deploy so many files in the web server or a standalone JavaScript app, so we usually bundle these files (think "concatenate") together.

JavaScript developers use different bundlers, like Webpack or Rollup, which not only concatenate multiple JavaScript files, but can optimize the code and remove unused code (performing tree-shaking). If your app consists of several modules, each module can be deployed as a separate bundle.

Figure 1.3 shows just one deployed bundle—main.js. If this were a web app, there would be an HTML file with a `<script src='main.js'>` tag. If the app were run in a standalone JavaScript engine like Node.js, you could start it with the following command (assuming Node.js is installed):

```
node main.js
```

The JavaScript ecosystem includes thousands of libraries, which won't be rewritten in TypeScript. The good news is that your app doesn't have to be TypeScript-only, and it can use any of the existing JavaScript libraries.

If you just add the JavaScript library to your app, tsc won't help with autocomplete or error messages when you use the APIs of these libraries. But there are special type definition files with the extension .d.ts (covered in chapter 6), and if they're present, tsc will show you errors and offer context-sensitive help for this library.

Figure 1.4 shows a sample workflow for an app that uses the popular JavaScript library lodash.

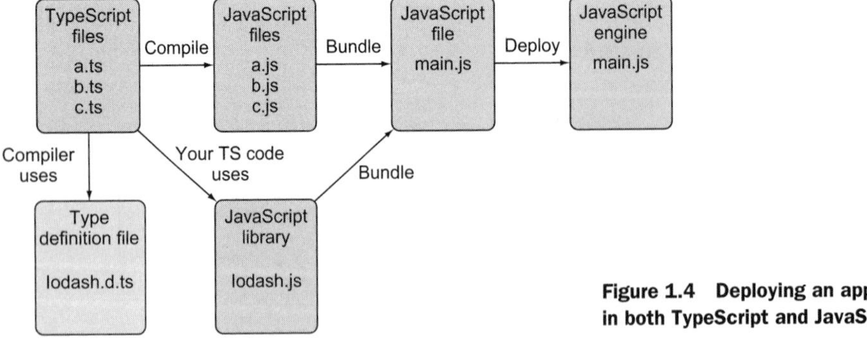

Figure 1.4 Deploying an app written in both TypeScript and JavaScript

This diagram includes the type definition file lodash.d.ts, which is used by tsc during development. It also includes the actual JavaScript library lodash.js, which will be bundled with the rest of your app during deployment.The term *bundle* refers to the process of combining several script files into one.

1.3 Using the Typescript compiler

Now you'll learn how to compile a basic TypeScript program into a JavaScript version. The compiler, tsc, can be bundled with your IDE of choice or can be installed as an IDE plugin, but we prefer to install it independently of an IDE by using the npm package manager that comes with Node.js.

Node.js (or simply *Node*) isn't just a framework or a library—it's a JavaScript runtime environment as well. We use the Node runtime for running various utilities like npm or launching JavaScript code without a browser.

To get started, you need to download and install the current version of Node.js from https://nodejs.org. It will install `node` and `npm`.

Using npm, you can install software either locally inside your project directory, or globally where it can be used across projects. We'll use npm to install tsc and other packages from the npm repository located at www.npmjs.com, which hosts more than half a million packages.

You can install tsc globally (with the `-g` option) by running the following command in your terminal window:

```
npm install -g typescript
```

NOTE For simplicity, we'll use the globally installed tsc in the first part of this book. In real-world projects, however, we prefer to install tsc locally in the project directory by adding it in the devDependencies section of the project's package.json. You'll see how we do that in chapter 8 where we'll start working on a sample blockchain project.

In this book's code samples, we used TypeScript version 3 or newer. To check your tsc version, run the following command from the terminal window:

```
tsc -v
```

Now let's look at how you can compile a simple program from TypeScript to JavaScript. In any directory, create a new main.ts file with the following content.

Listing 1.1 A main.ts file

```
function getFinalPrice(price: number, discount: number) {    <-- Function arguments have types.
  return price - price/discount;
}

console.log(getFinalPrice(100, 10));      <-- Correct function invocation
console.log(getFinalPrice(100, "10%"));   <-- Wrong function invocation
```

The following command will compile main.ts into main.js.

```
tsc main
```

It will print the error message "argument of type '10%' is not assignable to parameter of type 'number'," but it will generate the main.js file with the following content anyway.

Listing 1.2 The resulting main.js file

```
function getFinalPrice(price, discount) {    <-- Arguments have no types.
  return price - price/discount;
}

console.log(getFinalPrice(100, 10));         <-- Correct function invocation
console.log(getFinalPrice(100, "10%"));      <-- Wrong function invocation, but the
                                                 error will be shown during runtime only
```

You may ask, "What's the point of producing the JavaScript file if there's a compilation error?" Well, from the JavaScript perspective, the content of the main.js file is valid. But in real-world TypeScript projects, we won't want to allow code generation for erroneous files.

tsc offers dozens of compilation options, described in the TypeScript documentation (http://mng.bz/rf14), and one of them is `noEmitOnError`. Delete the main.js file and try to compile main.ts as follows:

```
tsc main --noEmitOnError true
```

Now the main.js file won't be generated until that error is fixed in main.ts.

> **TIP** Turning on the `noEmitOnError` option means that previously generated JavaScript files won't be replaced until all errors in the TypeScript files are fixed.

The compiler's `--t` option allows you to specify the target JavaScript syntax. For example, you can use the same source file and generate its JavaScript peer compliant with ES5, ES6, or newer syntax. Here's how to compile the code to ES5-compatible syntax:

```
tsc --t ES5 main
```

tsc allows you to preconfigure the process of compilation (specifying the source and destination directories, target, and so on). If you have a tsconfig.json file in the project directory, you can just enter `tsc` on the command line, and the compiler will read all the options from tsconfig.json. A sample tsconfig.json file is shown here.

Listing 1.3 A tsconfig.json file

```
{
  "compilerOptions": {
      "baseUrl": "src",          <-- Transpiles .ts files located
                                     in the src directory
```

```
        "outDir": "./dist",
        "noEmitOnError": true,
        "target": "es5"
    }
}
```

Saves the generated .js files in the the dist directory

If any of the files have compilation errors, don't generate JavaScript files.

Transpiles TypeScript files into the ES5 syntax

TIP The compiler's `target` option is also used for syntax checking. For example, if you specify `es3` as the compilation target, TypeScript will complain about the getter methods in your code. It simply doesn't know how to compile getters into the ECMAScript 3 version of the language.

Let's see if you can do it yourself by following these instructions:

1. Create a file named tsconfig.json in the folder where the main.ts file is located. Add the following content to tsconfig.json:

   ```
   {
     "compilerOptions": {
         "noEmitOnError": true,
         "target": "es5",
         "watch": true
     }
   }
   ```

   Note the last option, *watch*. The compiler will watch your typescript files, and when they change, tsc will recompile them.

2. In the terminal window, go to the directory where the tsconfig.json file is located, and run the following command:

   ```
   tsc
   ```

   You'll see the error message described earlier in this section, but the compiler won't exit because it's running in watch mode. The file main.js won't be created.

3. Fix the error, and the code will be automatically recompiled. Check to see that the main.js file was created this time.

If you want to get out of watch mode, just press Ctrl-C on your keyboard in the terminal window.

TIP To start a new TypeScript project, run the command `tsc --init` in any directory. It'll create a tsconfig.json file for you with all the compiler's options, most of which will be commented out. Uncomment them as needed.

NOTE A tsconfig.json file can inherit configurations from another file by using the `extends` property. In chapter 10 we'll look at a sample project that has three config files: the first with common tsc compiler options for the entire project, the second for the client, and the third for the server portion of the project. See section 10.4.1 for details.

The REPL environment for TypeScript

REPL stands for Read-Evaluate-Print-Loop, and it refers to a simple interactive language shell that allows you to quickly execute a code fragment. The TypeScript Playground at www.typescriptlang.org/play is an example of a REPL that allows you to write, compile, and execute a code snippet in a browser.

The following example shows how you can use the TypeScript Playground to compile a simple TypeScript class into the ES5 version of JavaScript.

```
class Person {
    name = '';
}
```

```
"use strict";
var Person = /** @class */ (function () {
    function Person() {
        this.name = '';
    }
    return Person;
}());
```

Transpiling TypeScript to ES5

The following image shows how the same code is compiled into the ES6 version of JavaScript.

```
class Person {
    name = '';
}
```

```
"use strict";
class Person {
    constructor() {
        this.name = '';
    }
}
```

Transpiling TypeScript to ES6

The Playground has an Options menu where you can select the compiler's options. In particular, you can select the compilation target, such as ES2018 or ES5.

If you'd like to run code snippets from the command line without the browser, install the TypeScript Node REPL, which is available at https://github.com/TypeStrong/ts-node.

1.4 Getting familiar with Visual Studio Code

Integrated development environments (IDEs) and code editors increase developers' productivity, and TypeScript is well supported by such tools: Visual Studio Code, WebStorm, Eclipse, Sublime Text, Atom, Emacs, Vim. For this book, we decided to use the open source and free Visual Studio Code (VS Code) editor created by Microsoft, but you can use any other editor or IDE to work with TypeScript.

NOTE According to the Stack Overflow 2019 Developer Survey (https://insights.stackoverflow.com/survey/2019), VS Code is the most popular developer environment, and more than 50% of all respondents use it. By the way, VS Code is written in TypeScript.

On real-world projects, good context-sensitive help and support for refactoring are very important. Renaming all occurrences of a TypeScript variable or function name in statically typed languages can be done by IDEs in a split second, but this isn't the case in JavaScript, which doesn't support types. If you make a mistake in a function, class, or a variable name in the TypeScript code, it's marked in red.

You can download VS Code from https://code.visualstudio.com. The installation process depends on your computer's OS, and it's explained in the Setup section of the VS Code documentation (https://code.visualstudio.com/docs).

Once it's installed, start VS Code. Then, using the File > Open menu option, open the chapter1/vscode directory included with this book's code samples. It contains the main.ts file from the previous section and a simple tsconfig.json file. Figure 1.5 shows the "10%" underlined with a red squiggly line, indicating an error. If you hover the mouse pointer over the underlined code, it will show the same error message shown earlier in figure 1.2.

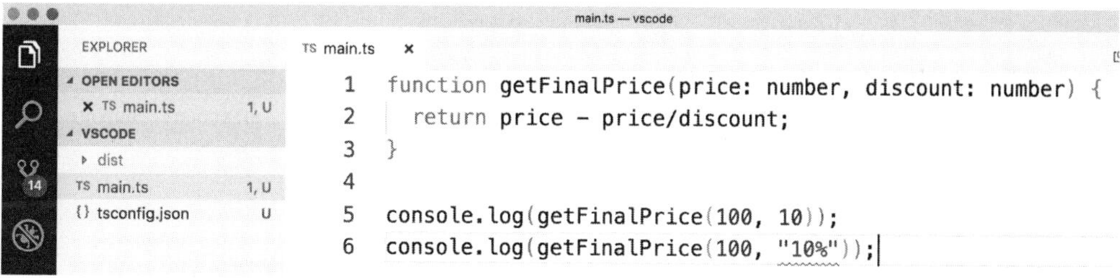

Figure 1.5 Highlighting errors in VS Code

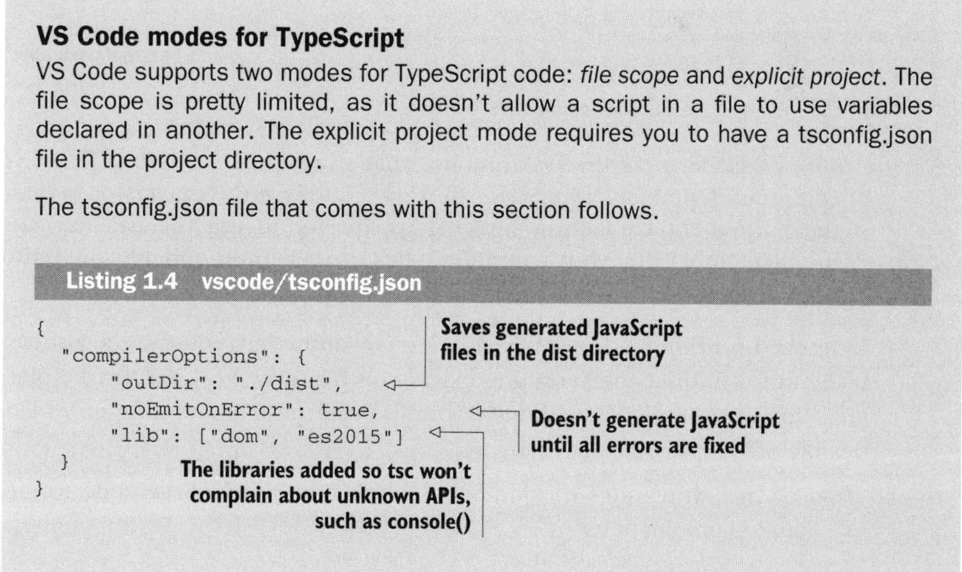

VS Code modes for TypeScript

VS Code supports two modes for TypeScript code: *file scope* and *explicit project*. The file scope is pretty limited, as it doesn't allow a script in a file to use variables declared in another. The explicit project mode requires you to have a tsconfig.json file in the project directory.

The tsconfig.json file that comes with this section follows.

Listing 1.4 vscode/tsconfig.json

```
{
  "compilerOptions": {
      "outDir": "./dist",
      "noEmitOnError": true,
      "lib": ["dom", "es2015"]
  }
}
```

- `"outDir": "./dist"` — Saves generated JavaScript files in the dist directory
- `"noEmitOnError": true` — Doesn't generate JavaScript until all errors are fixed
- `"lib": ["dom", "es2015"]` — The libraries added so tsc won't complain about unknown APIs, such as console()

If you'd like to be able to open VS Code from the command prompt, its executable will have to be added to the `PATH` environment variable on your computer. In Windows, the setup process should do it automatically. In macOS, start VS Code, select the View > Command Palette menu option, type `shell command`, and pick this option: Shell Command: Install 'code' Command in PATH. Then restart your terminal window and enter `code .` from any directory. VS Code will start, and you'll be able to work with the files from the directory you're in.

In the previous section, we compiled the code in a separate terminal window, but VS Code comes with an integrated terminal. This eliminates the need to leave the editor window to use the command prompt window. To open VS Code's terminal window, select View > Terminal or Terminal > New Terminal from the menu.

Figure 1.6 shows the integrated terminal view right after we executed the `tsc` command. The arrow on the right points at the plus icon that allows you to open as many terminal views as needed. We've commented out the last erroneous line, and tsc will generate the main.js file in the dist directory.

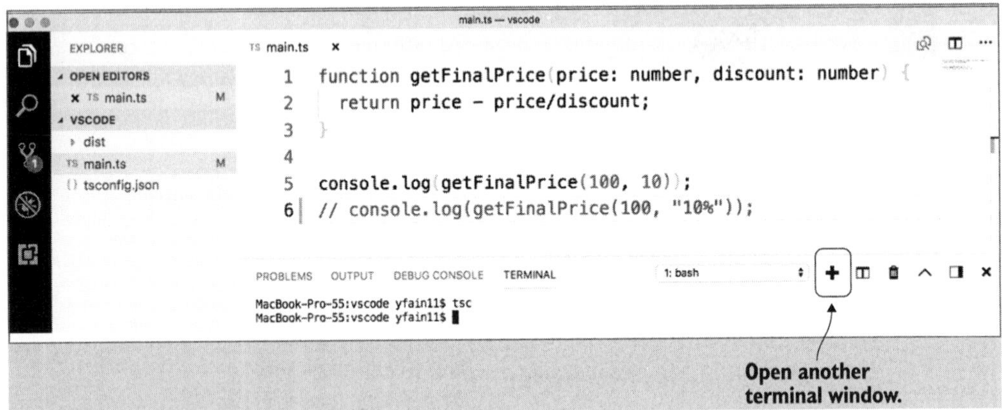

Figure 1.6 Running the `tsc` command in VS Code

> **TIP** VS Code picks the tsc compiler that's included with Node.JS on your computer. Open any TypeScript file, and you'll see the tsc version noted on the bottom toolbar at the right. If you prefer to use the tsc that you've installed globally on your computer, click the version number at the bottom-right corner, and select the tsc compiler of your choice.

In figure 1.6, at the bottom of the black panel at the left, you can see a square icon—it's used for finding and installing extensions from the VS Code marketplace. These are some extensions that will make your TypeScript programming in VS Code more flexible:

- *ESLint*—Integrates the JavaScript linter and checks your code for readability and maintainability

- *Prettier*—Enforces a consistent style by parsing your code and reformatting it with its own rules
- *Path Intellisense*—Autocompletes file paths

For more details about using VS Code for TypeScript programming, take a look at the product documentation at https://code.visualstudio.com/docs/languages/typescript.

TIP There is an excellent online IDE called StackBlitz (https://stackblitz.com). It's powered by VS Code, but you don't need to install it on your computer.

NOTE Part 2 of this book contains various versions of a sample blockchain app. Although reading part 2 is optional, we recommend you read at least chapters 8 and 9.

Summary

- TypeScript is a superset of JavaScript. A program written in TypeScript has to be transpiled into JavaScript first, and then it can be executed in the browser or a standalone JavaScript engine.
- Errors are caught by the TypeScript static code analyzer as you type, even before you compile code with the Typescript compiler (tsc).
- TypeScript gives you the benefits of statically typed languages when and where you want it, without stopping you from using the good old dynamic JavaScript objects when you want them.
- TypeScript follows the latest specifications of ECMAScript and adds to them types, interfaces, decorators, class member variables (fields), generics, enums, the keywords `public`, `protected`, and `private`, and more. Check the TypeScript roadmap at https://github.com/Microsoft/TypeScript/wiki/Roadmap to see what's available now and what's coming in future releases of TypeScript.
- To start a new TypeScript project, run the command `tsc --init` in any directory. It'll create the tsconfig.json file for you, containing all the compiler's options with most of them commented out. Uncomment them as needed.

2 Basic and custom types

This chapter covers

- Declaring variables with types, and using types in function declarations
- Declaring type aliases with the type keyword
- Declaring custom types with classes and interfaces

You can think of TypeScript as JavaScript with types. That's an oversimplified statement because TypeScript has some syntax elements that JavaScript doesn't (such as interfaces, generics, and some others). Still, the main power of TypeScript is types.

Although declaring types of identifiers before their use is highly recommended, it's still optional. In this chapter, you'll start getting familiar with different ways of using the built-in and custom types. In particular, you'll see how to use classes and interfaces to declare custom types; the coverage of classes and interfaces will continue in chapter 3.

NOTE If you're not familiar with the syntax of modern JavaScript, you may want to read the appendix before proceeding with learning TypeScript. This appendix will also help you understand which syntax elements exist in JavaScript and which were added in TypeScript.

2.1 Declaring variables with types

Why declare variable types if, in JavaScript, you can just declare a variable name and store the data of any type in it? Writing code in JavaScript is easier than in other languages mainly because you don't have to specify types for identifiers, isn't it?

Moreover, in JavaScript, you can assign a numeric value to a variable, and later assign a text value to that variable. This isn't the case in TypeScript, where once the type is assigned to a variable, you can't change its type, as shown in figure 2.1.

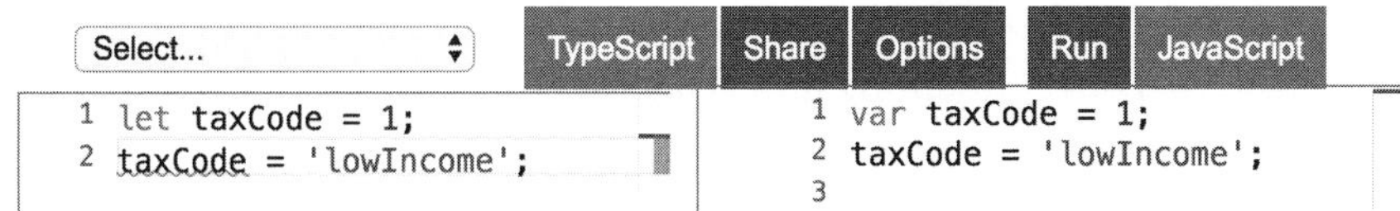

Figure 2.1 Attempting to change a variable's type in TypeScript (left) and JavaScript (right)

On the left of figure 2.1, you see the TypeScript code entered in the Playground section of www.typescriptlang.org. But where did we declare the type of the `taxCode` variable? We didn't do it explicitly, but since we initialized it with a numeric value, TypeScript assigns the type `number` to `taxCode`.

The second line is marked with a squiggly line, indicating an error. If you hover over this squiggly line, the error message will read "'lowIncome' is not assignable to type 'number'." In the TypeScript world, this means that if you declared the variable to store numeric values, you can't assign string values to it. On the right side in figure 2.1, the compiled JavaScript code doesn't show any errors because JavaScript allows you to assign values of different types to a variable at runtime.

Although declaring variable types forces developers to write more code, their productivity increases in the long run because, more often than not, if a developer tries to assign a string value to a variable that already stores a number, it's a mistake. It helps that the compiler can catch such errors during development rather than *not* discovering it until runtime.

A type can be assigned to a variable either explicitly by the software developer or implicitly (an *inferred* type) by the Typescript compiler. In figure 2.1, we declared a `taxCode` variable without providing its type. Assigning the value `1` to this variable lets the compiler know that its type is `number`. This is an example of an inferred type. Most of the code samples in the next section use explicit types, with a couple of exceptions that are marked as inferred types.

2.1.1 Basic type annotations

When you declare a variable, you can add a colon and a *type annotation* to specify the variable type:

```
let firstName: string;
let age: number;
```

TypeScript offers the following type annotations:

- string—For textual data
- boolean—For true/false values
- number—For numeric values
- symbol—A unique value created by calling the Symbol constructor
- any—For variables that can hold values of various types, which may be unknown when you're writing the code
- unknown—A counterpart of any, but no operations are permitted on an unknown without first asserting or narrowing it to a more specific type
- never—For representing unreachable code (we'll provide an example shortly)
- void—An absence of a value

Most of the basic types are self-descriptive and need no further explanation.

Starting with ECMAScript 2015, symbol is a primitive data type that is always unique and immutable. In the following code snippet, sym1 is not equal to sym2:

```
const sym1 = Symbol("orderID");
const sym2 = Symbol("orderID");
```

When you create a new symbol (note the absence of the new keyword), you can optionally provide its description, such as orderID. Symbols are typically used to create unique keys for object properties.

Listing 2.1 Symbols as object properties

```
const ord = Symbol('orderID');        <-- Creates a new symbol

const myOrder = {
    ord: "123"                        <-- Uses the symbol as an object's property
};

console.log(myOrder['ord']);          <-- This line prints "123".
```

Being a superset of JavaScript, TypeScript also has two special values: null and undefined. A variable that has not been assigned a value has a value of undefined. A function that doesn't return a value also has a value of undefined. The value of null represents an intentional absence of value, as in `let someVar = null;`.

You can assign null and undefined values to variables of any type, but more often they're used in combination with values of other types. The following code snippet shows how you can declare a function that returns either a string or a null value (the vertical bar represents the *union type*, discussed in section 2.1.3):

```
function getName(): string | null {
    ...
}
```

As in most programming languages, if you declare a function that returns `string`, you can still return `null`, but being explicit about what a function can return increases code readability.

If you declare a variable of type `any`, you can assign any value to it, whether it's numeric, textual, Boolean, or a custom type like `Customer`. You should avoid using the type `any`, because you're losing the benefits of type checking, and the readability of your code suffers.

The `never` type is assigned to a function that never returns—one that either keeps running forever or that just throws an error. The arrow function in the next listing never returns, and the type checker will *infer* (guess) its return type as `never`.

Listing 2.2 An arrow function that returns the `never` type

```
const logger = () => {
    while (true) {          <-- This function never ends.
        console.log("The server is up and running");
    }
};
```

In the preceding listing, the type assigned to `logger` is `() => never`. In listing 2.9 you'll see another example where the `never` type is assigned.

The `void` type is not something you'd use in a variable declaration. It's used to declare a function that doesn't return a value:

```
function logError(errorMessage: string): void {
    console.error(errorMessage);
}
```

Unlike the `never` type, the `void` function does complete its execution, but it returns no value.

> **TIP** If a function body doesn't have a return statement, it still returns a value of type `undefined`. The `void` type annotation can be used to prevent programmers from accidentally returning an explicit value from the function.

The fact that any JavaScript program is a valid TypeScript program means that using type annotations is optional in TypeScript. If some variables don't have explicit type annotations, TypeScript's type checker will try to infer the types. The following two lines are valid TypeScript syntax:

```
let name1 = 'John Smith';              <-- Declares and initializes a variable without an explicit type

let name2: string = 'John Smith';      <-- Declares and initializes a variable with a type annotation
```

The first line declares and initializes a `name1` variable in JavaScript style, and we can say that the inferred type of `name1` is `string`. Do you think that the second line is a good example of declaring and initializing the name2 variable in TypeScript? In terms of code style, specifying types is redundant here.

Although the second line is correct TypeScript syntax, specifying the type string is unnecessary, because the variable is initialized with the string and TypeScript will infer that the type of name2 is string.

You should avoid explicit type annotations where the Typescript compiler can infer them. The following code snippet declares the variables age and yourTax. There's no need to specify the types of these variables because the Typescript compiler will infer the types.

Listing 2.3 Identifiers with inferred types

```
const age = 25;                    <-- The age constant doesn't declare its type.

function getTax(income: number): number {
    return income * 0.15;
}

let yourTax = getTax(50000);       <-- The yourTax variable doesn't declare its type.
```

TypeScript also allows you to use literals as types. The following line declares a variable of *type* John Smith.

```
let name3: 'John Smith';
```

We can say that the variable name3 has a literal type John Smith. The name3 variable will only allow one value, John Smith. Any attempt to assign another value to a variable of a literal type will result in a type checker error:

```
let name3: 'John Smith';

name3 = 'Mary Lou';  // error: Type '"Mary Lou"' is not assignable to type
➥ '"John Smith"'
```

It's not likely that you'll be using string literals for declaring a type as shown in the name3 variable, but you may use string literals as types in unions (explained in section 2.1.3) and enums (explained in chapter 4).

Here are some examples of variables declared with explicit types:

```
let salary: number;
let isValid: boolean;
let customerName: string = null;
```

TIP Add explicit type annotations for function or methods signatures and public class members.

Type widening

If you declare a variable without initializing it with a specific value, TypeScript uses the internal types `null` or `undefined`, which are converted to `any`. This is called *type widening*.

The value of the following variable would be `undefined`.

```
let productId;
productId = null;
productId = undefined;
```

The Typescript compiler applies type widening and assigns the type `any` to `null` and `undefined` values. Hence, the type of the `productId` variable is `any`.

It's worth mentioning that the Typescript compiler supports a `--strictNullCheck` option that prohibits the assignment of `null` to variables with known types. In the following code snippet, the type of `productId` is `number`, and the second and third lines won't compile if you turn on `--strictNullCheck`:

```
let productId = 123;
productId = null;  // compiler error
productId = undefined;  // compiler error
```

The `--strictNullCheck` option also helps in catching potentially undefined values. For example, a function may return an object with an optional property, and your code might wrongly assume that this property is there and try to apply a function on it.

NOTE TypeScript includes other types that are used in interactions with the web browser, such as `HTMLElement` and `Document`. Also, you can use the keywords `type`, `class`, and `interface` to declare your own types, such as `Customer` or `Person`. We'll show how to do that in the next section. You'll also see how you can combine types using *unions*.

Type annotations are used not only for declaring variable types, but also for declaring types of function arguments and their return values. We'll discuss that next.

2.1.2 Types in function declarations

TypeScript functions and function expressions are similar to JavaScript functions, but you can explicitly declare the types of arguments and return values.

Let's start by writing a JavaScript function (with no type annotations) that calculates tax. The function in the next listing has three parameters and will calculate tax based on the state, income, and number of dependents. For each dependent, the person is entitled to a \$500 or \$300 tax deduction, depending on the state the person lives in.

Listing 2.4 Calculating tax in JavaScript

```
function calcTax(state, income, dependents) {     // The function arguments have no type annotations.
    if (state === 'NY') {
        return income * 0.06 - dependents * 500;   // Calculates the New York tax
    } else if (state === 'NJ') {
        return income * 0.05 - dependents * 300;   // Calculates the New Jersey tax
    }
}
```

Suppose a person with an income of $50,000 lives in the state of New Jersey and has two dependents. Let's invoke `calcTax()`:

```
let tax = calcTax('NJ', 50000, 2);
```

The `tax` variable gets the value of 1,900, which is correct. Even though `calcTax()` didn't declare any types for the function parameters, we guessed how to call this function based on the parameter names.

What if we didn't guess it right? Let's invoke it the wrong way, passing a `string` value for the number of dependents:

```
let tax = calcTax('NJ', 50000, 'two');
```

You won't know there's a problem until you invoke this function. The `tax` variable will have a `NaN` value (not a number). A bug sneaked in just because you couldn't explicitly specify the types of the parameters, and the compiler couldn't infer the types of the function arguments.

The next listing shows a TypeScript version of this function, using type annotations for the function arguments and return value.

Listing 2.5 Calculating tax in TypeScript

```
function calcTax(state: string, income: number, dependents: number) : number {   // The function arguments and its return value have type annotations.

    if (state === 'NY'){
        return income * 0.06 - dependents * 500;
    } else if (state ==='NJ'){
        return income * 0.05 - dependents * 300;
    }
}
```

Now there's no way to make the same mistake and pass a `string` value for the number of dependents:

```
let tax: number = calcTax('NJ', 50000, 'two');
```

The Typescript compiler will display an error: "Argument of type `string` is not assignable to parameter of type `number`." Moreover, the return value of the function is declared as `number`, which stops you from making another mistake and assigning the result of the tax calculation to a non-numeric variable:

```
let tax: string = calcTax('NJ', 50000, 'two');
```

The compiler will catch this, producing the error "The type 'number' is not assignable to type 'string': var tax: string." This kind of type-checking during compilation can save you a lot of time on any project.

> **Fixing the calcTax() function**
>
> This section has JavaScript and TypeScript versions of the `calcTax()` function, but they only process two states: NY and NJ. Invoking either of these functions for any other state will return `undefined` at runtime.
>
> The Typescript compiler won't warn you that the function in listing 2.5 is poorly written and may return `undefined`, but the TypeScript syntax allows you to warn the person who reads this code that the function in listing 2.5 may return not only a number but also an `undefined` value, if you invoke it with any other state but NY or NJ. You should change this function signature to declare such a use case as follows:
>
> ```
> function calcTax(state: string, income: number, dependents: number) :
> ➥ number | undefined
> ```

2.1.3 *The union type*

Unions allow you to express that a value can be one of several types. You can declare a custom type based on two or more existing types. For example, you can declare a variable of a type that can accept either a `string` value or a `number` (the vertical bar means *union*):

```
let padding: string | number;
```

Although the `padding` variable can store the value of either of the two specified types, at any given time it can be only of one type—either a `string` or a `number`.

TypeScript supports the type `any`, but the preceding declaration provides some benefits compared to the declaration `let padding: any`. Listing 2.6 shows one a code sample from the TypeScript documentation (see http://mng.bz/5742). This function can add the left padding to the provided string. The padding can be specified either as a string that will prepend the provided value or as a number of spaces that should prepend the provided string.

Listing 2.6 `padLeft` with the any type

```
function padLeft(value: string, padding: any ): string {
    if (typeof padding === "number") {
        return Array(padding + 1).join(" ") + value;
    }
    if (typeof padding === "string") {
        return padding + value;
    }
    throw new Error(`Expected string or number, got '${padding}'.`);
}
```

- Provides the string and the padding of type any
- For a numeric argument, generates spaces
- For a string, uses concatenation
- If the second argument is neither a string nor a number, throws an error

The following listing illustrates the use of `padLeft()`:

Listing 2.7 Invoking the `padLeft` function

```
console.log( padLeft("Hello world", 4));
console.log( padLeft("Hello world", "John says "));
console.log( padLeft("Hello world", true));
```

- Returns "Hello world"
- Returns "John says Hello world"
- Runtime error

Type guards `typeof` and `instanceof`

An attempt to apply conditional statements to refine a variable's type is called *type narrowing*. In the `if` statement in listing 2.6, we used the `typeof` *type guard* to narrow the type of a variable that can store more than one TypeScript type. We used `typeof` to find out the actual type of `padding` at runtime.

Similarly, the `instanceof` type guard is used with custom types (with constructors), as will be explained in section 2.2. The `instanceof` guard allows you to check the actual object type at runtime:

```
if (person instanceof Person) {...}
```

The difference between `typeof` and `instanceof` is that the former is used with the built-in TypeScript types and the latter with the custom ones.

TIP In section 2.2.4, we'll explain the structural type system implemented in TypeScript. In short, an object created using the object literal syntax (the syntax with curly braces) can be used where an object of a class (such as `Person`) is expected if the object literal has the same properties as `Person`. Because of this, `if (person instanceof Person)` may give you a false negative if the variable `person` points at an object that was not created by the constructor of the class `Person`.

If we now change the type of `padding` to the union of `string` and `number` (as shown in the following listing), the compiler will report an error if you try to invoke `padLeft()` providing anything other than `string` or `number`. This will also eliminate the need to throw an exception.

Listing 2.8 `padLeft` with the union type

```
function padLeft(value: string, padding: string | number ): string {
    if (typeof padding === "number") {
        return Array(padding + 1).join(" ") + value;
    }
    if (typeof padding === "string") {
        return padding + value;
    }
}
```

Allows only a string or a number as a second argument

Now invoking `padLeft()` with the wrong type for the second argument (such as `true`) returns a compilation error:

```
console.log( padLeft("Hello world", true)); // compilation error
```

> **TIP** If you need to declare a variable that can hold values of more than one type, don't use the type `any`; use a union such as `let padding: string | number`. Another choice is to declare two separate variables: `let paddingStr: string; let paddingNum: number;`.

Let's modify the code in listing 2.8 to illustrate the type `never` by adding an `else` clause to the `if` statement. This next listing shows how the type checker will infer the `never` type for an impossible value.

Listing 2.9 The `never` type of an impossible value

```
function padLeft(value: string, padding: string | number ): string {
    if (typeof padding === "number") {
        return Array(padding + 1).join(" ") + value;
    }
    if (typeof padding === "string") {
        return padding + value;
    }
    else {
        return padding;
    }
}
```

This else block is never executed.

Since we declared in the function signature that the `padding` argument can be either `string` or `number`, any other value for `padding` is impossible. In other words, the `else` case is not possible, and the type checker will infer the type `never` for the `padding` variable in the `else` clause. You can see it for yourself by copying the code from listing 2.9 into the TypeScript Playground and hovering the mouse over the `padding` variable.

NOTE Another benefit of using the union type is that IDEs have an autocomplete feature that will prompt you with allowed argument types, so you won't even have the chance to make such a mistake.

Compare the code of the `padLeft()` functions in listings 2.6 and 2.9. What are the main benefits of using the `string | number` union versus the `any` type for the second argument? If you use the union, the Typescript compiler will prevent incorrect invocations of `padLeft()` by reporting an error at compile time.

We just used a union of primitive types (`string` and `number`), but in the next section you'll see how to declare unions of custom types.

2.2 Defining custom types

TypeScript allows you to create custom types with the `type` keyword, by declaring a class or an interface, or by declaring an `enum` (covered in chapter 4). Let's get familiar with the `type` keyword first.

2.2.1 Using the type keyword

The `type` keyword allows you to declare a new type or a type alias for an existing type. Let's say your app deals with patients who are represented by their name, height, and weight. Both height and weight are numbers, but to improve the readability of your code, you can create aliases hinting at the units in which the height and weight are measured.

Listing 2.10 Declaring alias types `Foot` and `Pound`

```
type Foot = number;
type Pound = number;
```

You can create a new `Patient` type and use the preceding aliases in its declaration.

Listing 2.11 Declaring a new type that uses aliases

```
type Patient = {          <-- Declares the Patient type
  name: string;
  height: Foot;           <-- Uses the type alias Foot
  weight: Pound;          <-- Uses the type alias Pound
}
```

Declarations of type aliases don't generate code in the compiled JavaScript. In TypeScript, declaring and initializing a variable of type `Patient` can look like the following.

Listing 2.12 Declaring and initializing a type's properties

```
let patient: Patient = {     <-- We create an instance using
    name: 'Joe Smith',           the object literal notation.
    height: 5,
    weight: 100
}
```

What if, while initializing the `patient` variable, you forget to specify the value of one of the properties, such as `weight`?

Listing 2.13 Forgetting to add the `weight` property

```
let patient: Patient = {
    name: 'Joe Smith',
    height: 5
}
```

TypeScript will complain:

```
"Type '{ name: string; height: number; }' is not assignable to type 'Patient'.
  Property 'weight' is missing in type '{ name: string; height: number; }'."
```

If you want to declare some of the properties as optional, you must add a question mark to their names. In the following type declaration, providing the value for the `weight` property is optional, and there won't be any errors.

Listing 2.14 Declaring optional properties

```
type Patient = {
    name: string;
    height: Height;
    weight?: Weight;        <-- The weight property is optional.
}

let patient: Patient = {    <-- The patient variable is initialized without the weight.
    name: 'Joe Smith',
    height: 5
}
```

> **TIP** You can use the question mark to define optional properties in classes or interfaces as well. You'll get familiar with TypeScript classes and interfaces later in this section.

You can also use the `type` keyword to declare a type alias for a function signature. Imagine you're writing a framework that should allow you to create form controls and assign validator functions to them. A validator function must have a specific signature—it must accept an object of type `FormControl` and return either an object describing the errors of the form control value, or `null` if the value is valid. You can declare a new `ValidatorFn` type as follows:

```
type ValidatorFn =
  (c: FormControl) => { [key: string]: any }| null
```

Here, `{ [key: string]: any }` means an object that can have properties of any type, but the key has to be either of type string or convertable to a string.

The constructor of the `FormControl` can have a parameter for the validator function, and it can use the custom `ValidatorFn` type as follows:

```
class FormControl {

    constructor (initialValue: string, validator: ValidatorFn | null) {...};
}
```

> **TIP** In the appendix, you can see the syntax for declaring optional function parameters in JavaScript. The preceding code snippet shows you a way of declaring an optional parameter using the TypeScript union type.

2.2.2 *Using classes as custom types*

We assume you're familiar with the JavaScript classes covered in the appendix. In this section we'll start showing you additional features that TypeScript brings to JavaScript classes. In chapter 3, we'll continue covering classes in more detail.

JavaScript doesn't offer any syntax for declaring class properties, but TypeScript does. In figure 2.2, on the left, you can see how we declared and instantiated a `Person` class that has three properties. The right side of figure 2.2 shows the ES6 version of this code produced by the Typescript compiler.

TypeScript

```
class Person {
        firstName: string;
        lastName: string;
        age: number;
}

const p = new Person();
p.firstName = "John";
p.lastName = "Smith";
p.age = 25;
```

JavaScript (ES6)

```
"use strict";
class Person {
}
const p = new Person();
p.firstName = "John";
p.lastName = "Smith";
p.age = 25;
```

Figure 2.2 The `Person` class compiled into JavaScript (ES6)

As you can see, there are no properties in the JavaScript version of the `Person` class. Also, since the `Person` class didn't declare a constructor, we had to initialize its properties after instantiation. A constructor is a special function that's executed once when the instance of a class is created.

Declaring a constructor with three arguments would allow you to instantiate the `Person` class and initialize its properties in one line. In TypeScript you can provide type annotations for a constructor's arguments, but there's more.

TypeScript offers the access level qualifiers `public`, `private`, and `protected` (covered in chapter 3), and if you use any of them with the constructor arguments, the

TypeScript

```
1   class Person {
2       constructor(public firstName: string,
3                   public lastName: string, public age: number) {};
4   }
5
6   const p = new Person("John", "Smith", 25);
7
8
9
10
```

JavaScript (ES6)

```
1   "use strict";
2   class Person {
3       constructor(firstName, lastName, age) {
4           this.firstName = firstName;
5           this.lastName = lastName;
6           this.age = age;
7       }
8       ;
9   }
10  const p = new Person("John", "Smith", 25);
```

Figure 2.3 The `Person` class with a constructor

Typescript compiler will generate the code for adding these arguments as properties in the generated JavaScript object (see figure 2.3).

Now the code of the TypeScript class (on the left) is more concise, and the generated JavaScript code creates three properties in the constructor. Note line 6 in figure 2.3 on the left. We declared the constant without specifying its type, but we could rewrite this line explicitly specifying the type of `p` as follows:

```
const p: Person = new Person("John", "Smith", 25);
```

This would be an unnecessary use of an explicit type annotation. Since you declare a constant and immediately initialize it with an object of a known type (`Person`), the TypeScript type checker can easily infer and assign the type to the constant `p`. The generated JavaScript code will look the same regardless of whether you specify the type of `p` or not. You can see how to instantiate the class `Person` without explicitly declaring its type by following this link to the TypeScript Playground: http://mng.bz/zlV1. Hover the mouse pointer over the variable `p`—its type is `Person`.

TIP In figure 2.3, we used the `public` access level with each constructor argument in the TypeScript class, which simply means that the generated corresponding properties can be accessed from any code located both inside and outside of the class.

When you declare properties of a class, you can also mark them as `readonly`. Such properties can be initialized either at the declaration point or in the class constructor, and their values can't be changed afterwards. The `readonly` qualifier is similar to the `const` keyword, but the latter can't be used with class properties.

In chapter 8, we'll start developing a blockchain app, and any blockchain consists of blocks with immutable properties. That app will include a `Block` class, and a fragment of it follows.

Listing 2.15 The properties of the `Block` class

```
class Block {
  readonly nonce: number;
  readonly hash: string;

  constructor (
    readonly index: number,
    readonly previousHash: string,
    readonly timestamp: number,
    readonly data: string
  ) {
    const { nonce, hash } = this.mine();
    this.nonce = nonce;
    this.hash = hash;
  }
  // The rest of the code is omitted for brevity
}
```

- `nonce`, `hash`: This property is initialized in the constructor.
- `index`, `previousHash`, `timestamp`, `data`: The value for this property is provided to the constructor during instantiation.
- `const { nonce, hash } = this.mine();`: Uses destructuring to extract the values from the object returned by the mine() method

The `Block` class includes six `readonly` properties. Note that we don't need to explicitly declare class properties for constructor arguments that have `readonly`, `private`, `protected`, or `public` qualifiers as we would in other object-oriented languages. In listing 2.15, two class properties are declared explicitly and four implicitly.

2.2.3 Using interfaces as custom types

Many object-oriented languages include a syntax construct called `interface`, which is used to enforce the implementation of specified properties or methods on an object. JavaScript doesn't support interfaces, but TypeScript does. In this section, we'll show you how to use interfaces to declare custom types, and in chapter 3, you'll see how to use interfaces to ensure that a class implements the specified members.

TypeScript includes the keywords `interface` and `implements` to support interfaces, but interfaces aren't compiled into JavaScript code. They just help you to avoid using wrong types during development. Let's get familiar with using the `interface` keyword to declare a custom type.

Suppose you want to write a function that can save information about people in some storage. This function should take an object that represents a person, and you want to ensure that it has specific properties of specific types. You can declare a `Person` interface as follows.

Listing 2.16 Declaring a custom type using an interface

```
interface Person {
  firstName: string;
  lastName: string;
  age: number;
}
```

The script on left side of figure 2.2 declares a similar custom `Person` type but using the `class` keyword. What's the difference? If you declare a custom type as `class`, you can use it as a value, meaning you can instantiate it using the `new` keyword, as shown in figures 2.2 and 2.3.

Also, if you use the `class` keyword in the TypeScript code, it'll have the corresponding code in generated JavaScript (a function in ES5, and a class in ES6). If you use the `interface` keyword, there won't be any corresponding code in JavaScript, as seen in figure 2.4.

```
1   interface Person {
2       firstName: string;
3       lastName: string;
4       age: number;
5   }
6
7   function savePerson (person: Person): void {
8       console.log('Saving ', person);
9   }
10
11  const p: Person = {
12              firstName: "John",
13              lastName: "Smith",
14               age: 25 };
15
16  savePerson(p);
```

```
1   "use strict";
2   function savePerson(person) {
3       console.log('Saving ', person);
4   }
5   const p = {
6       firstName: "John",
7       lastName: "Smith",
8       age: 25
9   };
10  savePerson(p);
11
```

Figure 2.4 The custom `Person` type as an interface

There is no mention of the interface on the right side of figure 2.4, and the JavaScript is more concise, which is good for any deployable code. But during development, the compiler will check that the object given as an argument to the `savePerson()` function includes all the properties declared in the `Person` interface.

We encourage you to experiment with the code snippet from figure 2.4 by visiting TypeScript Playground at the following link: http://mng.bz/MOpB. For example, remove the `lastName` property defined in line 13, and the TypeScript type checker will immediately underline the variable `p` with a red line. Hover your mouse pointer over the variable `p`, and you'll see the following error message:

```
Type '{ firstName: string; age: number; }' is not assignable to type 'Person'.
  Property 'lastName' is missing in type '{ firstName: string; age: number; }'.
```

Keep experimenting. Try to access `person.lastName` inside `savePerson()`. If the `Person` interface won't declare the `lastName` property, TypeScript will give you a compiler error, but the JavaScript code would just crash at runtime.

Try another experiment: remove the `Person` type annotation in line 11. The code is still valid and no errors are reported in line 17. Why does TypeScript allow you to invoke the `savePerson()` function with an argument that wasn't explicitly assigned the type `Person`? The reason is that TypeScript uses a structural type system, which means that if two different types include the same members, the types are considered compatible. We'll discuss the structural type system in more detail in the next section.

Which keyword to use: `type`, `interface`, or `class`?

We've shown you that a custom type can be declared using the keywords `type`, `class`, or `interface`. Which of these keywords should you use for declaring a custom type like `Person`?

If the custom type doesn't need to be used for instantiating objects at runtime, use `interface` or `type`; otherwise use `class`. In other words, use `class` for creating a custom type if it should be used to represent *a value*.

For example, if you declare a `Person` interface and there's a function that takes an argument of type `Person`, you can't apply the operator `instanceof` to the argument:

```
interface Person {
   name: string;
}

function getP(p: Person){
      if (p instanceof Person){ // compile error
     }
}
```

The type checker will complain that `Person` only refers to a type but is being used as a value here.

If you are declaring a custom type just for the additional safety offered by TypeScript's type checker, use `type` or `interface`. Neither interfaces nor types declared with the `type` keyword have representations in the emitted JavaScript code, which makes the runtime code smaller (bytewise). If you use classes for declaring types, they will have a footprint in the generated JavaScript.

Defining a custom type with the `type` keyword offers the same features as `interface` plus some extras. For example, you can't use types declared as interfaces in unions or intersections. Also, in chapter 5, you'll learn about conditional types, which can't be declared using interfaces.

2.2.4 Structural vs. nominal type systems

A primitive type has just a name (such as `number`), whereas a more complex type like an object or class has a name and some structure, represented by properties (for example, a `Customer` class likely has name and address properties).

How would you know if two types are the same or not? In Java (which uses a *nominal type system*), two types are the same if they have the same names declared in the same namespace (a.k.a. packages). In a nominal type system, if you declare a variable of type `Person`, you can assign to it only an object of type `Person` or its descendant. In

Java, the last line in the following listing won't compile, because the names of the classes are not the same, even though they have the same structure.

Listing 2.17 A Java code snippet

```
class Person {            <-- Declares the Person
    String name;              class (think "type")
}

class Customer {          <-- Declares the Customer class
    String name;
}
                                 Syntax error: the names of the classes
Customer cust = new Person();  <-- on the left and right are not the same.
```

But TypeScript and some other languages use a *structural type system*. The following listing shows the preceding code snippet rewritten in TypeScript.

Listing 2.18 A TypeScript code snippet

```
class Person {            <-- Declares the Person
    name: string;             class (think "type")
}

class Customer {          <-- Declares the Customer class
    name: string;
}
                                         No errors: the type
const cust: Customer = new Person();  <-- structures are the same.
```

This code doesn't report any errors because TypeScript uses a structural type system, and since both the `Person` and `Customer` classes have the same structure, it's OK to assign an instance of one class to a variable of another.

Moreover, you can use object literals to create objects and assign them to class-typed variables or constants, as long as the shape of the object literal is the same. The following listing will compile without errors.

Listing 2.19 Compatible types

```
class Person {
    name: String;
}

class Customer {
    name: String;
}

const cust: Customer = { name: 'Mary' };
const pers: Person = { name: 'John' };
```

TIP The access-level modifiers affect type compatibility. For example, if we declared the `name` property of the `Person` class as `private`, the code in listing 2.19 wouldn't compile.

Our classes didn't define any methods, but if both of them defined a method with the same signature (name, arguments, and return type), they would again be compatible.

What if the structure of `Person` and `Customer` are not exactly the same? Let's add an `age` property to the `Person` class.

Listing 2.20 When classes are not the same

```
class Person {
    name: String;
    age: number;              ⇽ We've added this property.
}

class Customer {
    name: String;
}

const cust: Customer = new Person(); // still no errors
```

Still no errors! TypeScript sees that `Person` and `Customer` have *the same shape* (something in common). We just wanted to use the constant of type `Customer` (it has the property `name`) to point at the object of type `Person`, which also has the property `name`.

What can you do with the object represented by the `cust` variable? You can write something like `cust.name='John'`. The instance of `Person` has the `name` property, so the compiler doesn't complain.

NOTE Because we can assign an object of type `Person` to a variable of type `Customer`, we can say that the `Person` type is *assignable* to the `Customer` type.

Take a look at this code in TypeScript Playground: http://mng.bz/adQm. Click Ctrl-space after the dot in `cust.` and you'll see that only the `name` property is available, even though the `Person` class has also the `age` property.

In listing 2.20, the `Person` class had more properties than `Customer`, and the code compiled without errors. Would the code in the next listing compile if the `Customer` class had more properties than `Person`?

Listing 2.21 The instance has more properties than a reference variable

```
class Person {
    name: string;
}

class Customer {
    name: string;
    age: number;
}

const cust: Customer = new Person();     ⇽ The types don't match.
```

The code in listing 2.21 wouldn't compile because the `cust` reference variable would point to a `Person` object that wouldn't even allocate memory for the `age` property, and an assignment like `cust.age = 29` wouldn't be possible. This time, the `Person` type is *not assignable* to the `Customer` type.

TIP We'll come back to TypeScript's structural typing in section 4.2 when we discuss generics.

2.2.5 Unions of custom types

In the previous section, we introduced union types that allow you to declare that a variable can have one of the listed types. For example, in listing 2.8 we specified that the function argument `padding` could be *either* a `string` *or* a `number`. This is an example of a union that included primitive types.

Let's look at declaring a union of custom types. Imagine an app that can perform various actions in response to the user's activity. Each action is represented by a class with a different name. Each action must have a type and optionally may carry a payload, such as a search query. The following listing includes declarations for three action classes and a union `SearchActions` type.

Listing 2.22 Using a union to represent actions in the actions.ts file

```
export class SearchAction {
  actionType = "SEARCH";

  constructor(readonly payload: {searchQuery: string}) {}
}

export class SearchSuccessAction {
  actionType = "SEARCH_SUCCESS";

  constructor(public payload: {searchResults: string[]}) {}
}

export class SearchFailedAction {
  actionType = "SEARCH_FAILED";
}

export type SearchActions = SearchAction | SearchSuccessAction |
➥ SearchFailedAction;
```

A class with an action type and payload

A class with an action type but without a payload

A union type declaration

TIP The code in listing 2.22 needs improvement, because just stating that each action must have a property describing its type is more of a JavaScript style of programming. In TypeScript, such a statement can be enforced programmatically, and we'll do that in section 3.2.1.

Discriminated unions include type members that have a common property—the *discriminant*. Depending on the value of the discriminant, you may want to perform different actions.

The union shown in listing 2.22 is an example of a discriminated union because each member has an `actionType` discriminant. Let's create another discriminated union of two types, `Rectangle` and `Circle`.

Listing 2.23 Using a union with a discriminant to tell shapes apart

```
interface Rectangle {
    kind: "rectangle";     <-- The discriminant
    width: number;
    height: number;
}
interface Circle {
    kind: "circle";        <-- The discriminant
    radius: number;
}

type Shape = Rectangle | Circle;     <-- The union
```

The `Shape` type is a discriminated union, and both `Rectangle` and `Circle` have a common property, `kind`. Depending on the value in the `kind` property, we can calculate the area of the `Shape` differently.

Listing 2.24 Using a discriminated union

```
function area(shape: Shape): number {
  switch (shape.kind) {     <-- Switches on the discriminator's value
    case "rectangle": return shape.height * shape.width;     <-- Applies the formula for rectangles
    case "circle": return Math.PI * shape.radius ** 2;     <-- Applies the formula for circles
  }
}

const myRectangle: Rectangle = { kind: "rectangle", width: 10, height: 20 };
console.log(`Rectangle's area is ${area(myRectangle)}`);

const myCircle: Circle = { kind: "circle", radius: 10};
console.log(`Circle's area is ${area(myCircle)}`);
```

You can run this code sample in the Playground at http://mng.bz/gVev.

The `in` type guard

The `in` type guard acts as a narrowing expression for types. For example, if you have a function that can take an argument of a union type, you can check the actual type given during function invocation.

The following code shows two interfaces with different properties. The `foo()` function can take an object `A` or `B` as an argument. Using the `in` type guard, the `foo()` function can check if the provided object has a specific property before using it.

```
interface A { a: number };
interface B { b: string };

function foo(x: A | B) {
    if ("a" in x) {          <-- Checks for a specific property using in
        return x.a;
    }
    return x.b;
}
```

The property that you check has to be a string, such as `"a"`.

2.3 The any and unknown types, and user-defined type guards

At the beginning of this chapter, we mentioned the types `any` and `unknown`. In this section, we'll show you the difference between them. You'll also see how to write a custom type guard, in addition to `typeof`, `instanceof`, and `in`.

Declaring a variable of `any` type allows you to assign it a value of any type. It's like writing in JavaScript where you don't specify a type. Similarly, trying to access a nonexistent property on an object of `any` type may give unexpected results at runtime.

The `unknown` type was introduced in TypeScript 3.0. If you declare a variable of type `unknown`, the compiler will force you to narrow its type down before accessing its properties, sparing you from potential runtime surprises.

To illustrate the difference between `any` and `unknown`, let's assume that we declared the `Person` type on the frontend, and it's populated with data coming from the backend in JSON format. To turn the JSON string into an object, we'll use the method `JSON.parse()`, which returns `any`.

Listing 2.25 Using the any type

```
type Person = {          <-- Declares a type alias
  address: string;
}

let person1: any;          <-- Declares a variable of type any

person1 = JSON.parse('{ "adress": "25 Broadway" }');          <-- Parses the JSON string

console.log(person1.address);          <-- This prints undefined.
```

The last line will print `undefined` because we misspelled "address" in the JSON string. The `parse` method returns a JavaScript object that has an `adress` property, but not `address` on `person1`. To experience this issue, you need to run this code.

Now let's see how the same use case works with a variable of type unknown.

Listing 2.26 The compiler's error with the type `unknown`

```
let person2: unknown;    <-- Declares a variable of type unknown

person2 = JSON.parse('{ "adress": "25 Broadway" }');

console.log(person2.address);
```

Attempting to use a variable of the unknown type results in a compilation error.

This time the last line won't even compile because we tried to use the `person2` variable of `unknown` type without narrowing its type down.

TypeScript allows you to write user-defined type guards that can check if an object is of a particular type. This would be a function that returns something like "thisFunctionArg is SomeType." Let's write an `isPerson()` type guard which assumes that if the object under test has an `address` property, it's a person.

Listing 2.27 The first version of the `isPerson` type guard

```
const isPerson = (object: any): object is Person => "address" in object;
```

This type guard returns `true` if the given object has an `address` property. You can apply this guard as in the following listing.

Listing 2.28 Applying the `isPerson` type guard

Applies the type guard

```
if (isPerson(person2)) {
    console.log(person2.address);    <-- Safely accesses the address property
} else {
    console.log("person2 is not a Person");
}
```

This code has no compilation errors, and it works as expected unless the `isPerson()` guard gets a falsy object as an argument. For example, passing `null` to `isPerson()` will result in a runtime error in the expression `"address" in object`.

The following listing shows a safer version of the `isPerson()` guard. The double-bang operator `!!` will ensure that the given object is truthy.

Listing 2.29 The `isPerson` type guard

```
const isPerson = (object: any): object is Person => !!object && "address"
➥ in object;
```

You can try this code in the TypeScript Playground at http://mng.bz/eDaV.

In this example, we assumed that the existence of the address property is enough to identify the Person type, but in some cases checking just one property is not enough. For example, the Organization or Pet classes may also have address properties. You may need to check several properties to determine if an object matches a specific type.

A simpler solution is to declare your own discriminator property that will identify this type as a person:

```
type Person = {
  discriminator: 'person';
  address: string;
}
```

Then your custom type guard could look like this:

```
const isPerson = (object: any): object is Person => !!object &&
➥ object.discriminator === 'person';
```

OK, we've covered just enough of the TypeScript syntax related to types. It's time to apply the theory in practice.

2.4 A mini project

If you're the type of person who prefers learning by doing, we can offer you a little assignment, followed by a solution. We won't provide detailed explanations about the solution—the description of the assignment should make it clear enough.

Write a program with two custom types, Dog and Fish, which are declared using classes. Each of these types must have a name property. The Dog class should have a sayHello(): string method, and the Fish class should have a dive(howDeep: number): string method.

Declare a new Pet type as a union of Dog and Fish. Write a talkToPet(pet: Pet): string function that will use type guards and will either invoke the sayHello() method on the Dog instance or print the message "Fish cannot talk, sorry."

Invoke talkToPet() three times providing the object Dog first, then Fish, and finally an object that is neither Dog nor Fish.

Our solution is shown in the following listing.

Listing 2.30 The solution

```
class Dog {                                        ◁— Declares a custom Dog type
    constructor(readonly name: string) { };

   sayHello(): string {
     return 'Dog says hello!';
   }
}

class Fish {             ◁— Declares a custom Fish type
```

```
    constructor(readonly name: string) { };

    dive(howDeep: number): string {
     return `Diving ${howDeep} feet`;
   }

}

type Pet = Dog | Fish;            <-- Creates a union of Dog and Fish

function talkToPet(pet: Pet): string | undefined {

  if (pet instanceof Dog) {        <-- Uses a type guard
    return pet.sayHello();
  } else if (pet instanceof Fish) {
    return 'Fish cannot talk, sorry.';
  }
}

const myDog = new Dog('Sammy');     <-- Creates an instance of a Dog
const myFish = new Fish('Marry');   <-- Creates an instance of a Fish

console.log(talkToPet(myDog));      | Invokes talkToPet(),
console.log(talkToPet(myFish));     | passing a Pet
talkToPet({ name: 'John' });       <-- This won't compile—wrong parameter type
```

You can see this script in action on CodePen at http://mng.bz/pyjK.

Summary

- Although declaring variable types forces developers to write more code, their productivity increases in the long run.
- TypeScript offers a number of type annotations, but you can declare custom types as needed.
- You can create new types by declaring a union of existing ones.
- You can declare custom types using the `type`, `interface`, and `class` keywords. In chapter 4, you'll see yet another way of declaring custom types with the `enum` keyword.
- TypeScript uses a structural type system as opposed to languages like Java or C#, which use a nominal type system.

3 Object-oriented programming with classes and interfaces

This chapter covers

- How class inheritance works
- Why and when to use abstract classes
- How interfaces can force a class to have methods with known signatures without worrying about implementation details
- What "programming to interfaces" means

In chapter 2, we introduced classes and interfaces for creating custom types. In this chapter, we'll continue learning about classes and interfaces from the object-oriented programming (OOP) perspective. OOP is a programming style where your programs focus on handling objects rather than on composing actions (think functions). Of course, some of those functions would create objects as well, but in OOP, objects are the center of the universe.

Developers who work with object-oriented languages use interfaces as a way to enforce certain APIs on classes. Also, you can often hear the phrase "program to interfaces" in the conversations of programmers. In this chapter, we'll explain what that means. In short, this chapter is a whirlwind tour of OOP using TypeScript.

3.1 Working with classes

Let's recap what you learned about TypeScript classes in chapter 2:

- You can declare classes with properties, which in other object-oriented languages are called *member variables.*
- As in JavaScript, classes may declare constructors, which are invoked once during instantiation.
- The Typescript compiler converts classes into JavaScript constructor functions if ES5 is specified as the compilation target syntax. If ES6 or later is specified as the target, TypeScript classes will be compiled into JavaScript classes.
- If a class constructor defines arguments that use such keywords as `readonly`, `public`, `protected`, or `private`, TypeScript creates class properties for each of the arguments.

But there's more to classes. In this chapter, we'll cover class inheritance, what the abstract classes are for, and what the `public`, `protected`, and `private` access modifiers are for.

3.1.1 Getting familiar with class inheritance

In real life, every person inherits some features from their parents. Similarly, in the TypeScript world, you can create a new class based on an existing one. For example, you can create a `Person` class with some properties, and then create an `Employee` class that will *inherit* all the properties of `Person` as well as declare additional ones. Inheritance is one of the main features of any object-oriented language, and the `extends` keyword declares that one class inherits from another.

Figure 3.1 is a screenshot from the TypeScript Playground (http://mng.bz/O9Yw). Note that we didn't use explicit types in declaring the properties of the `Person` class. We initialized the `firstName` and `lastName` properties with empty strings and `age` with `0`. The Typescript compiler will infer the types based on the initial values.

> **TIP** In the TypeScript Playground's Config menu, the `strictProperty-Initialization` compiler option is on. With this option, if the class properties are not initialized either when declared or in the class's constructor, the compiler reports an error.

Line 7 in figure 3.1 shows how you can declare an `Employee` class that extends the `Person` class and declares an additional `department` property. In line 11 we create an instance of the `Employee` class.

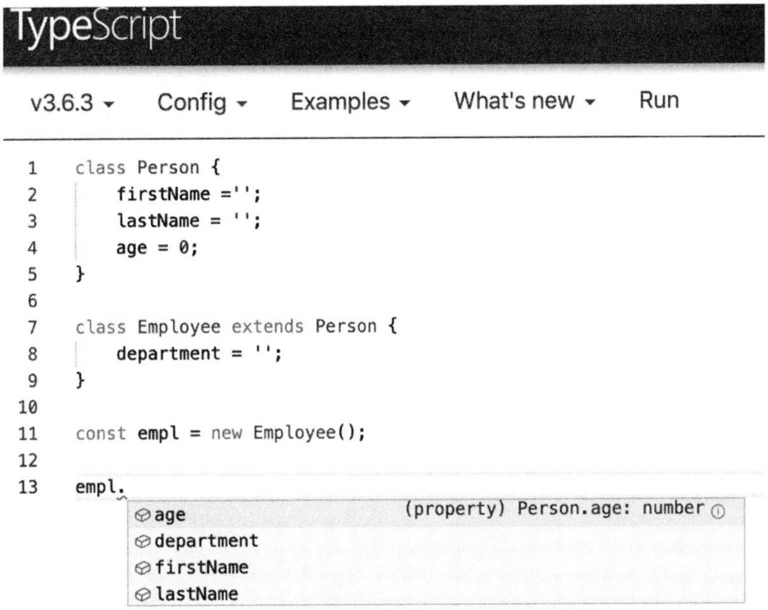

TypeScript

v3.6.3 ▾ Config ▾ Examples ▾ What's new ▾ Run

```
1   class Person {
2       firstName ='';
3       lastName = '';
4       age = 0;
5   }
6
7   class Employee extends Person {
8       department = '';
9   }
10
11  const empl = new Employee();
12
13  empl.
        age                 (property) Person.age: number
        department
        firstName
        lastName
```

Figure 3.1 Class inheritance in TypeScript

This screenshot was taken after we entered `empl.` followed by Ctrl-space on line 13. TypeScript's static analyzer recognizes that the `Employee` type is inherited from `Person`, so it suggests the properties defined in both the `Person` and `Employee` classes.

In our example, the `Employee` class is a *subclass* of `Person`. Accordingly, the `Person` class is a *superclass* of `Employee`. You can also say that the `Person` class is an *ancestor*, and that `Employee` is a *descendant* of `Person`.

> **NOTE** Under the hood, JavaScript supports prototypal *object-based* inheritance, where one object can be assigned to another object as its prototype—this happens at runtime. Once TypeScript code that uses inheritance is compiled, the generated JavaScript code uses the syntax of prototypal inheritance.

In addition to properties, a class can include *methods*—this is how we call functions declared inside classes. And if a method is declared in a superclass, it will be inherited by the subclass unless the method was declared with the `private` access qualifier, which we'll discuss a bit later.

The next version of the `Person` class is shown in figure 3.2, and it includes the `sayHello()` method. (You can find this code in the Playground at http://mng.bz/YeNz.) As you can see in line 18, TypeScript's static analyzer included this method in the autocomplete dropdown.

You may be wondering, "Is there any way to control which properties and methods of a class are accessible from other scripts?" The answer is yes—this is what the `private`, `protected`, and `public` keywords are for.

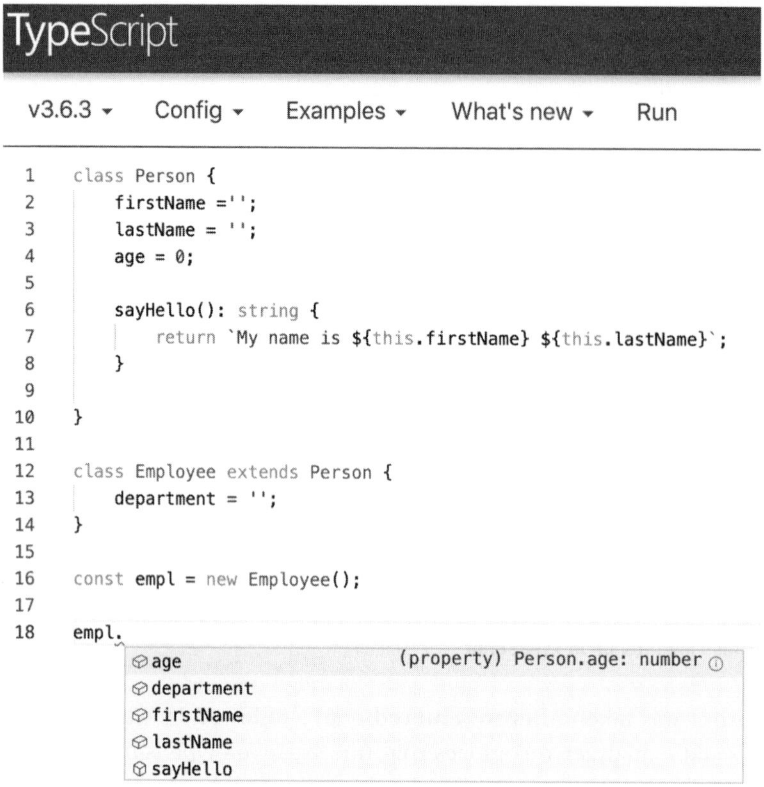

TypeScript

v3.6.3 ▾ Config ▾ Examples ▾ What's new ▾ Run

```
class Person {
    firstName ='';
    lastName = '';
    age = 0;

    sayHello(): string {
        return `My name is ${this.firstName} ${this.lastName}`;
    }

}

class Employee extends Person {
    department = '';
}

const empl = new Employee();

empl.
    age                      (property) Person.age: number
    department
    firstName
    lastName
    sayHello
```

Figure 3.2 The `sayHello()` method from a superclass is visible.

3.1.2 *Access modifiers public, private, protected*

TypeScript includes the `public`, `protected`, and `private` keywords to control access to the members of a class (properties or methods).

- `public`—Class members marked as `public` can be accessed from the internal class methods as well as from external scripts. This is the default access, so if you place the keyword `public` in front of a property or method of the `Person` class shown in figure 3.2, the accessibility of these class members won't change.
- `protected`—Class members marked as `protected` can be accessed either from the internal class code or from class descendants.
- `private`—The `private` class members are visible only within the class.

NOTE If you know languages like Java or C#, you may be familiar with restricting the access level with the `private` and `protected` keywords. TypeScript is a superset of JavaScript, which doesn't support the `private` keyword, so the keywords `private` and `protected` (as well as `public`) are removed during code compilation. The resulting JavaScript won't include these keywords, so you can consider them just a convenience during development.

Figure 3.3 illustrates the `protected` and `private` access level modifiers. In line 15, we can access the `protected` ancestor's `sayHello()` method because we do this from the descendant. But when we clicked Ctrl-space after `this.` in line 20, the `age` variable is not shown in the autocomplete list because it's declared as `private` and can be accessed only within the `Person` class.

This code sample shows that the subclass can't access the `private` member of the superclass (try it in the Playground at http://mng.bz/07gJ). Here, only a method from the `Person` class can access `private` members from this class.

Although protected class members are accessible from the descendant's code, they are not accessible on the class instance. For example, the following code won't compile and will give you the error, "Property 'sayHello' is protected and only accessible within class 'Person' and its subclasses."

```
const empl = new Employee();
empl.sayHello(); // error
```

Let's look at another example of the `Person` class that has a constructor, two `public` properties, and one `private` property, as shown in figure 3.4 (or in the Playground at

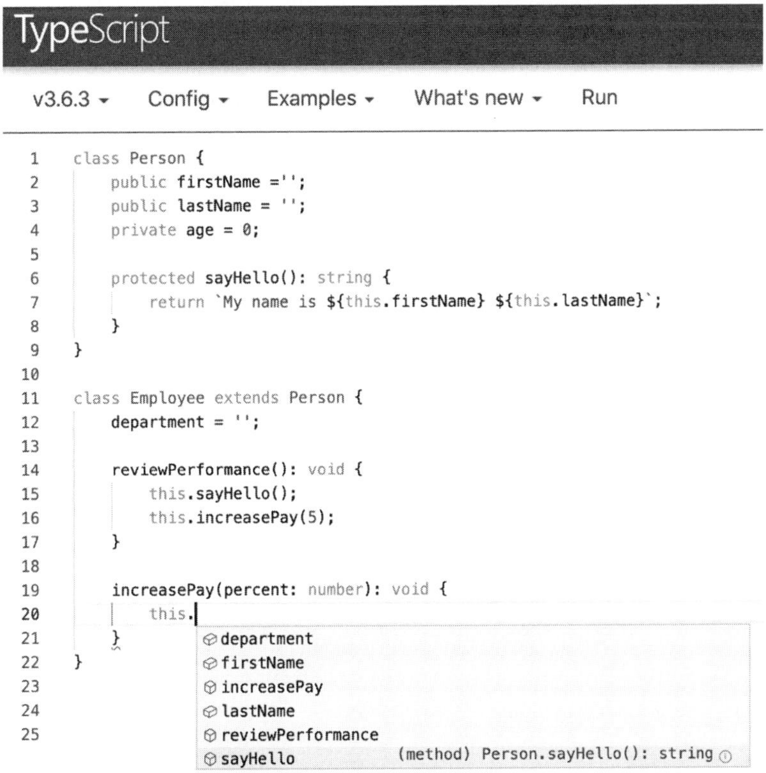

TypeScript

v3.6.3 ▾ Config ▾ Examples ▾ What's new ▾ Run

```
1  class Person {
2      public firstName ='';
3      public lastName = '';
4      private age = 0;
5
6      protected sayHello(): string {
7          return `My name is ${this.firstName} ${this.lastName}`;
8      }
9  }
10
11 class Employee extends Person {
12     department = '';
13
14     reviewPerformance(): void {
15         this.sayHello();
16         this.increasePay(5);
17     }
18
19     increasePay(percent: number): void {
20         this.
21     }
22 }
23
24
25
```

```
department
firstName
increasePay
lastName
reviewPerformance
sayHello          (method) Person.sayHello(): string
```

Figure 3.3 The `age` private property is not visible

TypeScript

v3.6.3 ▾ Config ▾ Examples ▾ What's new ▾ Run

```
class Person {
    public firstName ='';
    public lastName = '';
    private age = 0;

    constructor(firstName: string, lastName: string, age: number) {
        this.firstName = firstName;
        this.lastName = lastName;
        this.age = age;
    }
}
```

Figure 3.4 A verbose version of the `Person` class

http://mng.bz/KEgX). This is a verbose version of the class declaration because we explicitly declared three properties of the class. The constructor in the `Person` class performs the tedious job of assigning values from its arguments to the respective properties of this class.

Now let's declare a more concise version of the `Person` class, as shown in figure 3.5 (or in the Playground at http://mng.bz/9w9j). By using access qualifiers with the constructor's arguments, we can instruct the Typescript compiler to create class properties having the same names as the constructor's arguments. The compiler will autogenerate JavaScript code that assigns the values given to the constructor to class properties.

In line 7 of figure 3.5, we create an instance of the `Person` class, passing the initial property values to its constructor, which will assign these values to the respective object's properties. In line 9 we wanted to print the values of the object's `firstName` and `age` properties, but the latter became marked with a red squiggly line because `age` is private.

Compare figures 3.4. and 3.5. In figure 3.4, the `Person` class explicitly declares three properties, which we initialize in the constructor. In figure 3.5, the `Person` class has no explicit declarations of properties and no explicit initialization in the constructor.

```
1 class Person {
2     constructor(public firstName: string,
3                 public lastName: string,
4                 private age: number) { }
5 }
6
7 const pers = new Person('John', 'Smith', 29)
8
9 console.log(`${pers.firstName} ${pers.lastName} ${pers.age}`);
```

Figure 3.5 Using access qualifiers with the constructor's arguments

So what's better—explicit or implicit declaration of class properties? There are arguments for both programming styles. Explicit declaration and initialization of class properties may increase the readability of the code, whereas implicit declaration makes the code of the TypeScript class more concise. But it doesn't have to be an either-or decision. For example, you can declare `public` properties explicitly and `private` and `protected` ones implicitly. We generally use implicit declarations unless the property initialization involves some logic.

3.1.3 Static variables and a singleton example

In the ES6 version of JavaScript, when a property has to be shared by each instance of a class, we can declare it as `static` (see section A.9.3 in the appendix). Being a superset of JavaScript, TypeScript also supports the `static` keyword. In this section we'll look at a basic example, and then we'll implement the singleton design pattern with the help of a `static` property and a `private` constructor.

Suppose a group of gangsters is on a mission (no worries—it's just a game). We need to monitor the total number of bullets they have left. Every time a gangster shoots, this value has to be decreased by one. The total number of bullets should be known to each gangster.

Listing 3.1 A gangster with a static property

```
class Gangsta {
  static totalBullets = 100;      // Declares and initializes a static variable

  shoot(){
    Gangsta.totalBullets--;       // Updates the number of bullets after each shot
    console.log(`Bullets left: ${Gangsta.totalBullets}`);
  }
}

const g1 = new Gangsta();         // Creates a new instance of the Gangsta
g1.shoot();                       // This gangster shoots once.

const g2 = new Gangsta();         // Creates a new instance of the Gangsta
g2.shoot();                       // This gangster shoots once.
```

After running the code shown in listing 3.1 (it's in the Playground at http://mng.bz/j5Ya), the browser console will print the following:

```
Bullets left: 99
Bullets left: 98
```

Both instances of the `Gangsta` class share the same `totalBullets` variable. That's why no matter which gangster shoots, the shared `totalBullets` variable is updated.

Note that in the `shoot()` method we didn't write `this.totalBullets` because this is not an instance variable. You access `static` class members by prepending their names with the class name, like `Gangsta.totalBullets`.

> **NOTE** Static class members are not shared by subclasses. If you create a `SuperGangsta` class that subclasses `Gangsta`, it will get its own copy of the `totalBullets` property. We've provided an example in the Playground at http://mng.bz/WO8g.

> **TIP** Often we have several methods that perform similar actions. For example, we may need to write a dozen functions for validating user input in different UI fields. Instead of having separate functions, you can group them in a class with a dozen `static` methods.

Now let's consider another example. Imagine you need to store important data in memory representing the current state of the app. Various scripts can access this storage, but you want to make sure that only one such object can be created for the entire app, also known as *a single source of truth. Singleton* is a popular design pattern that restricts the instantiation of a class to only one object.

How do you create a class that you can instantiate only once? It's a trivial task in any object-oriented language that supports the `private` access qualifier. Basically, you need to write a class that won't allow the `new` keyword to be used, because with `new` you can create as many instances as you want. The idea is simple—if a class has a `private` constructor, the `new` operator will fail.

How can you create even a single instance of such a class? If the class constructor is private, you can access it only within the class, and as the author of this class, you'll responsibly create it only once by invoking the `new` operator from the class method.

But can you invoke a method on a class that hasn't been instantiated? You can do it by making the class method `static`, so it doesn't belong to any particular object instance and belongs to the class.

Listing 3.2 shows our implementation of the singleton design pattern in an `AppState` class, which has a `counter` property. Let's assume that the `counter` represents our app state, and it may be updated by multiple scripts in the app. This single instance of `AppState` should be the only place that stores the value of `counter`. Any script that needs to know the latest value of `counter` will get it from this `AppState` instance.

Listing 3.2 A singleton class

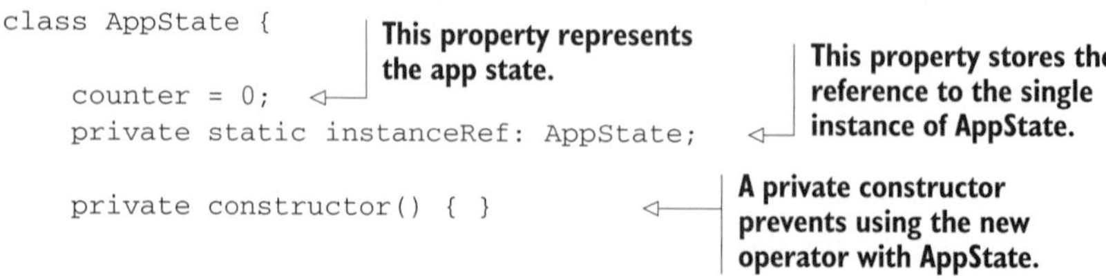

```
class AppState {

    counter = 0;
    private static instanceRef: AppState;

    private constructor() { }
```

This property represents the app state.
This property stores the reference to the single instance of AppState.
A private constructor prevents using the new operator with AppState.

```
    static getInstance(): AppState {          ◁── This is the only method to
      if (AppState.instanceRef === undefined) {    get an instance of AppState.
          AppState.instanceRef = new AppState();  ◁──
      }
                                              Instantiates the AppState
      return AppState.instanceRef;            object if it doesn't exist yet
    }
}

// const appState = new AppState(); // error because of the private
➥ constructor

const appState1 = AppState.getInstance();   This variable gets a reference
const appState2 = AppState.getInstance();   to the AppState instance.

appState1.counter++;
appState1.counter++;            Modifies the counter (we use
appState2.counter++;            two reference variables)
appState2.counter++;

console.log(appState1.counter);       Prints the value of the counter
console.log(appState2.counter);       (we use two reference variables)
```

The `AppState` class has a `private` constructor, which means that no other script can instantiate it using the `new` statement. It's perfectly fine to invoke such a constructor from within the `AppState` class, and we do this in the static `getInstance()` method. This is the only way we can invoke a method in the absence of the class instance. Both `console.log()` invocations will print `4` because there is only one instance of `AppState`. You can see this code sample in the Playground at http://mng.bz/8zKK.

3.1.4 The super() method and the super keyword

Let's continue looking into class inheritance. In figure 3.3 in line 15, we invoked the `sayHello()` method, which was declared in the superclass. What if both the superclass and subclass have methods with the same names? What if both have constructors? Can we control which method is executed? If both the superclass and the subclass have constructors, the one from the subclass must invoke the constructor of the superclass using the `super()` method.

Listing 3.3 Invoking the constructor of the `super` class

```
class Person {

  constructor(public firstName: string,
              public lastName: string,        The constructor of the
              private age: number) {}    ◁──  Person superclass
}

class Employee extends Person {      ◁── The Employee subclass
```

```
  constructor (firstName: string, lastName: string,
               age: number, public department: string)  {   ◁── The constructor of the Employee subclass
      super(firstName, lastName, age);   ◁── Invokes the constructor of the superclass
  }
}

const empl = new Employee('Joe', 'Smith', 29, 'Accounting');  ◁── Instantiates the subclass
```

NOTE We discuss using `super()` and `super` in JavaScript in the appendix, section A.9.2. In this section, we'll provide a similar example, but in TypeScript.

Both classes define constructors, and we must ensure that each of them is invoked with the correct parameters. The constructor of the `Employee` class is automatically invoked when we use the `new` operator, but we'll have to manually invoke the constructor of the `Person` superclass. The `Employee` class has a constructor with four arguments, but only one of them—`department`—is needed to construct the `Employee` object. The other three parameters are needed for constructing the `Person` object, and we pass them over to `Person` by invoking the `super()` method with three arguments. You can play with this code in the TypeScript Playground at http://mng.bz/E14q.

Now let's consider the situation where both the superclass and subclass have methods with the same names. If a method in a subclass wants to invoke a method with the same name that's defined in the superclass, it needs to use the `super` keyword instead of `this` when referencing the superclass method.

Let's say a `Person` class has a `sellStock()` method that connects to a stock exchange and sells the specified number of shares of the given stock. In the `Employee` class we'd like to reuse this functionality, but every time employees sell stocks, they must report it to a compliance department in the firm.

We can declare a `sellStock()` method on the `Employee` class, and this method will call `sellStock()` on `Person`, and then its own method `reportToCompliance()`, as shown in the following listing.

Listing 3.4 Using the `super` keyword

```
class Person {

  constructor(public firstName: string,
              public lastName: string,
              private age: number) { }

  sellStock(symbol: string, numberOfShares: number) {    ◁── The sellStock() method in the ancestor
    console.log(`Selling ${numberOfShares} of ${symbol}`);
  }
}

class Employee extends Person {
```

```
  constructor (firstName: string, lastName: string,
               age: number, public department: string)  {
      super(firstName, lastName, age);                    ◁── Invokes the constructor
  }                                                           of the ancestor

  sellStock(symbol: string, shares: number) {    ◁── The sellStock() method
    super.sellStock(symbol, shares);              ◁──   in the descendant
                                                    Invokes sellStock()
    this.reportToCompliance(symbol, shares);        on the ancestor
  }

  private reportToCompliance(symbol: string, shares: number) {    ◁──
    console.log(`${this.lastName} from ${this.department} sold ${shares}
➥ shares of ${symbol}`);
  }                                          A private reportToCompliance() method
}

const empl = new Employee('Joe', 'Smith', 29, 'Accounting');
empl.sellStock('IBM', 100);      ◁── Invokes sellStock() on
                                     the Employee object
```

Note that we declared the `reportToCompliance()` method as `private` because we want it to be called only by the internal method of the `Employee` class and never from an external script. You can run this program in the Playground at http://mng.bz/NeOE, and the browser will print the following in its console:

```
Selling 100 of IBM
Smith from Accounting sold 100 shares of IBM
```

With the help of the `super` keyword, we reused functionality from the method declared in the superclass and added new functionality as well.

3.1.5 Abstract classes

If you add the `abstract` keyword to the class declaration, it can't be instantiated. An abstract class may include both methods that are implemented as well as abstract ones that are *only declared*.

Why would you want to create a class that can't be instantiated? You may want to delegate the implementation of some methods to its subclasses, and you want to make sure these methods will have specific signatures.

Let's look at how abstract classes can be used. Suppose a company has employees and contractors, and we need to design classes to represent the workers of this company. Any worker's object should support the following methods:

- `constructor(name: string)`
- `changeAddress(newAddress: string)`
- `giveDayOff()`
- `promote(percent: number)`
- `increasePay(percent: number)`

In this scenario, "promote" means giving one day off and raising the salary by the specified percent. The `increasePay()` method should raise the yearly salary for employees but increase the hourly rate for contractors. How we implement the methods is irrelevant, but a method should just have one `console.log()` statement.

Let's work on this assignment. We'll need to create the classes `Employee` and `Contractor`, which should have some common functionality. For example, changing addresses and giving days off should work the same way for contractors and employees, but increasing their pay requires different implementations for these categories of workers.

Here's the plan: we'll create an `abstractPerson` class with two descendants: `Employee` and `Contractor`. The `Person` class will implement the methods `changeAddress()`, `giveDayOff()`, and `promote()`. This class will also include a declaration of the `abstract` method `increasePay()`, which will be implemented (differently!) in the subclasses of `Person`, as shown in the following listing.

Listing 3.5 The abstract `Person` class

```
abstract class Person {            <— Declares an abstract class

    constructor(public name: string) { };

  changeAddress(newAddress: string ) {                      <—┐
    console.log(`Changing address to ${newAddress}`);         │
  }                                                           │ Declares and
                                                              │ implements a
    giveDayOff() { 2((CO5-3))                               <—┤ method
        console.log(`Giving a day off to ${this.name}`);      │
    }                                                         │
                                                              │
    promote(percent: number) {                              <—┘
        this.giveDayOff();
        this.increasePay(percent);              <— "Invokes" the abstract method
    }

    abstract increasePay(percent: number): void;     <— Declares an abstract method
}
```

> **TIP** If you don't want to allow the `giveDayOff()` method to be invoked from external scripts, add `private` to its declaration. If you want to allow it to be invoked only from the `Person` class and its descendants, make this method `protected`.

Note that you are allowed to write a line that looks like it invokes the abstract method. But since the class is abstract, it can't be "instantiated," and there's no way that the abstract (unimplemented) method will actually be executed. If you want to create a descendant of the abstract class that can be instantiated, you must implement all the abstract methods of the ancestor.

The following listing shows how we implemented the classes `Employee` and `Constructor`.

Listing 3.6 Descendants of the `Person` class

```
class Employee extends Person {
    increasePay(percent: number) {
        console.log(`Increasing the salary of ${this.name} by ${percent}%`);
    }
}

class Contractor extends Person {
    increasePay(percent: number) {
        console.log(`Increasing the hourly rate of ${this.name} by
➥ ${percent}%`);
    }
}
```

Implements the increasePay() method for employees

Implements the increasePay() method for contractors

In section 2.2.4, we used the term *assignable* while discussing listing 2.20. When we have `class A extends class B`, this means that `class B` is more general and `class A` is more specific (for example, it adds more properties).

A more specific type is assignable to a more general one. That's why you can declare a variable of type `Person` and assign to it an `Employee` or `Contractor` object, as you'll see in listing 3.7.

Let's create an array of workers with one employee and one contractor, and then iterate through this array invoking the `promote()` method on each object.

Listing 3.7 Running the promotion campaign

```
const workers: Person[] = [];

workers[0] = new Employee('John');
workers[1] = new Contractor('Mary');

workers.forEach(worker => worker.promote(5));
```

Declares an array of the superclass type

Invokes promote() on each object

The `workers` array is of type `Person`, which allows us to store the instances of descendant objects there as well.

> **TIP** Because the descendants of `Person` don't declare their own constructors, the constructor of the ancestor will be invoked automatically when we instantiate `Employee` and `Contractor`. If any of the descendants declared its own constructor, we'd have to use `super()` to ensure that the constructor of `Person` was invoked.

You can run this code sample in the TypeScript Playground at http://mng.bz/DNvy, and the browser console will show the following output:

```
Giving a day off to John
Increasing the salary of John by 5%
Giving a day off to Mary
Increasing the hourly rate of Mary by 5%
```

The code in listing 3.7 gives the impression that we iterate through the objects of type `Person`, invoking `Person.promote()`. But some of the objects can be of type `Employee` while others are instances of `Contractor`. The actual type of the object is evaluated only at runtime, which explains why the correct implementation of `increasePay()` is invoked on each object. This is an example of *polymorphism*—a feature that each object-oriented language supports.

Protected constructors

In section 3.1.3, we declared a `private` constructor to create a singleton—a class that can be instantiated only once. There's some use for `protected` constructors as well. Say you need to declare a class that can't be instantiated, but its subclasses can. You could declare a `protected` constructor in the superclass and invoke it using `super()` from the subclass constructor.

This mimics one of the features of abstract classes. But a class with a protected constructor won't let you declare abstract methods unless the class itself is declared as abstract.

In section 10.6.1, you'll see another example of using an abstract class for handling WebSocket messages in a blockchain app.

3.1.6 *Method overloading*

Object-oriented programming languages like Java and C# support *method overloading*, which means that a class can *declare* more than one method with the same name but with different arguments. For example, you can write two versions of the `calculateTax()` method—one with two arguments, such as the person's income and number of dependents, and the other with one argument of type `Customer` that has all the required data about the person.

In strongly typed languages, the ability to overload methods, specifying the types of arguments and a return value, is important because you can't just invoke a class method and provide an argument of an arbitrary type, and the number of arguments can be different. TypeScript, however, is a sugar coating for JavaScript, which allows you to invoke a function while passing more or fewer arguments than the function signature declares. JavaScript won't complain, and it doesn't need to support function overloading. Of course, you may get a runtime error if the method doesn't properly handle the provided object, but this would happen at runtime. TypeScript offers a syntax for explicitly declaring each allowed overloaded method signature, eliminating the runtime surprises.

Let's see if the following code works.

Listing 3.8 An erroneous attempt of method overloading

```
class ProductService {

    getProducts() {
        console.log(`Getting all products`);
    }

    getProducts(id: number) { // error
        console.log(`Getting the product info for ${id}`);
    }
}

const prodService = new ProductService();

prodService.getProducts(123);

prodService.getProducts();
```

The getProducts() method without arguments

The getProducts() method with one argument

The Typescript compiler will give you an error, "Duplicate function implementation," for the second `getProduct()` declaration, as shown in figure 3.6.

The syntax in the TypeScript code (on the left) is wrong, but the JavaScript syntax on the right is perfectly fine. The first version of the `getProducts` method (line 4) was replaced with the second one (line 7), so during runtime the JavaScript version of this script has only one version of `getProducts(id)`.

Let's ignore the compiler's errors and try to run the generated JavaScript in the TypeScript Playground. The browser console will print the messages only from the `getProducts(id)` method, even though we wanted to invoke different versions of this method:

```
Getting the product info for 123
Getting the product info for undefined
```

In the compiled JavaScript, the method (or function) can have only one body that can account for all allowed method parameters. Still, TypeScript offers the syntax to specify

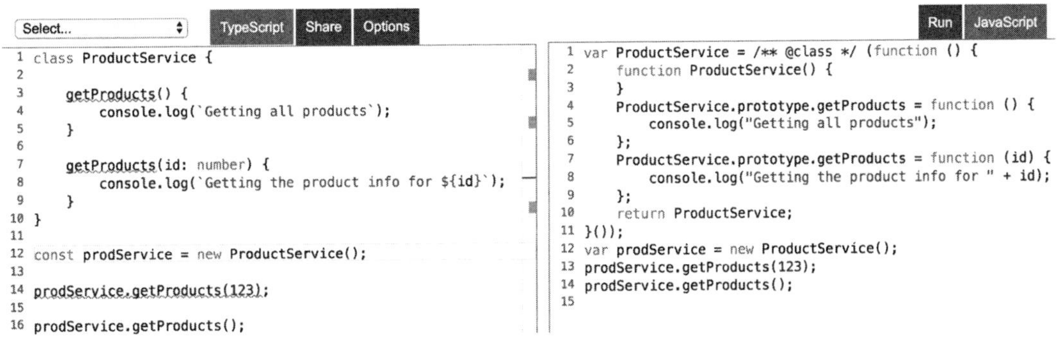

Select... TypeScript Share Options

```
class ProductService {

    getProducts() {
        console.log(`Getting all products`);
    }

    getProducts(id: number) {
        console.log(`Getting the product info for ${id}`);
    }
}

const prodService = new ProductService();

prodService.getProducts(123);

prodService.getProducts();
```

Run JavaScript

```
1  var ProductService = /** @class */ (function () {
2      function ProductService() {
3      }
4      ProductService.prototype.getProducts = function () {
5          console.log("Getting all products");
6      };
7      ProductService.prototype.getProducts = function (id) {
8          console.log("Getting the product info for " + id);
9      };
10     return ProductService;
11 }());
12 var prodService = new ProductService();
13 prodService.getProducts(123);
14 prodService.getProducts();
15
```

Figure 3.6 Erroneous TypeScript but valid JavaScript

method overloading. It comes down to declaring all allowed method signatures without implementing these methods, followed by one implemented method.

Listing 3.9 Correct syntax for method overloading

```
class ProductService {

    getProducts(): void;
    getProducts(id: number): void;
    getProducts(id?: number) {
        if (typeof id === 'number') {
          console.log(`Getting the product info for ${id}`);
        } else {
          console.log(`Getting all products`);
        }
    }
}

const prodService = new ProductService();

prodService.getProducts(123);
prodService.getProducts();
```

Declares the allowed method signature

Implements the method

Note the question mark after the `id` argument in the implemented method. This question mark declares this argument as optional. If we didn't make this argument optional, the compiler would give us the error "Overload signature is not compatible with function implementation." In our code sample, this means that if we declared a no-argument `getProducts()` method signature, the method implementation should allow us to invoke this function without arguments.

> **TIP** Omitting the first two declarations in listing 3.9 wouldn't change this program's behavior. These lines just help IDEs provide better autocomplete options for the `getProducts()` function.

Try this code sample in the TypeScript Playground at http://mng.bz/lozj. Note that the generated JavaScript has just one `getProducts()` function, as shown in figure 3.7.

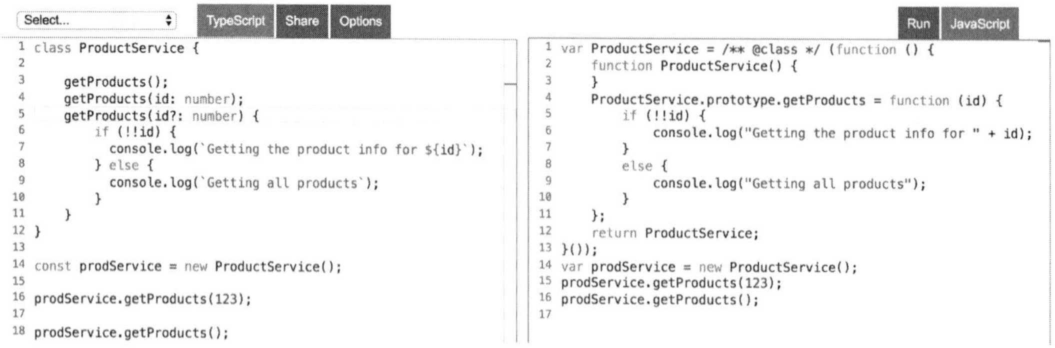

Select... TypeScript Share Options

```
class ProductService {

    getProducts();
    getProducts(id: number);
    getProducts(id?: number) {
        if (!!id) {
          console.log(`Getting the product info for ${id}`);
        } else {
          console.log(`Getting all products`);
        }
    }
}

const prodService = new ProductService();

prodService.getProducts(123);

prodService.getProducts();
```

Run JavaScript

```
var ProductService = /** @class */ (function () {
    function ProductService() {
    }
    ProductService.prototype.getProducts = function (id) {
        if (!!id) {
            console.log("Getting the product info for " + id);
        }
        else {
            console.log("Getting all products");
        }
    };
    return ProductService;
}());
var prodService = new ProductService();
prodService.getProducts(123);
prodService.getProducts();
```

Figure 3.7 Proper syntax for overloading the method

Similarly, you can overload a method signature to indicate that it can not only have different arguments but return values of different types. Listing 3.10 shows a script with an overloaded `getProducts()` method, which can be invoked in two ways:

- Provide the product `description` and return an array of type `Product`.
- Provide the product `id` and return a single object of type `Product`.

Listing 3.10 Different arguments and return types

```
interface Product {                    <— Defines the Product type
  id: number;
  description: string;
}

class ProductService {

    getProducts(description: string): Product[];    <— The first overloaded signature of getProducts()
    getProducts(id: number): Product;               <— The second overloaded signature of getProducts()
    getProducts(product: number | string): Product[] | Product{   <— Implementation of getProducts()
        if (typeof product === "number") {      <— Sees if the method was invoked with product id
          console.log(`Getting the product info for id ${product}`);
                    return { id: product, description: 'great product' };
        } else if (typeof product === "string") {    <— Sees if the method was invoked with product description
          console.log(`Getting product with description ${product}`);
          return [{ id: 123, description: 'blue jeans' },
                  { id: 789, description: 'blue jeans' }];
        } else {
           return { id: -1,
                    description: 'Error: getProducts() accept only number or
➥ string as args' };
        }
    }
}

const prodService = new ProductService();

console.log(prodService.getProducts(123));

console.log(prodService.getProducts('blue jeans'));
```

You can see and run the preceding code sample in the TypeScript Playground at http://mng.bz/BYov. The output in the browser console is shown in figure 3.8.

Now, let's experiment with the code in listing 3.10. If you comment out the two lines that declare signatures of `getProducts()`, the program still works. You can invoke this method providing either the number or string as an argument, and this method will return either one `Product` or an array of them.

The question is, why even declare overloaded signatures if you can simply implement a single method using unions in argument types and return values? Method overloading helps the Typescript compiler to properly map the provided argument types to the types of the return values. When the overloaded method signatures are

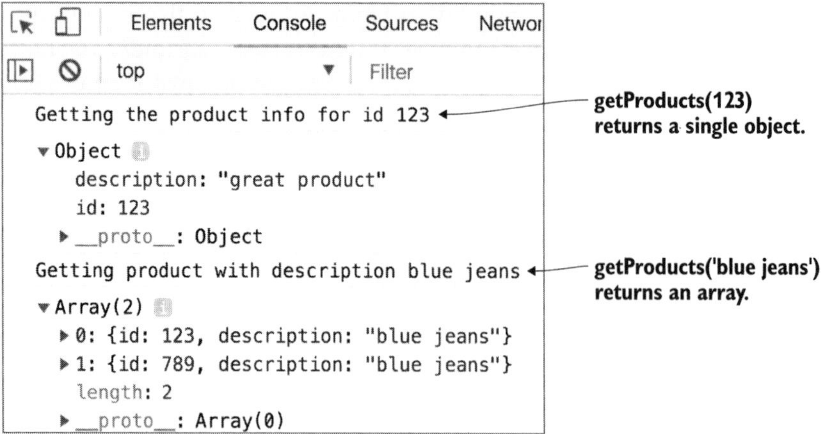

Figure 3.8 Overloading with different returns

declared, the TypeScript static analyzer will properly suggest possible ways of invoking the overloaded method. Figure 3.9 (a screenshot from VS Code) shows the first prompt (note 1/2) for invoking the `getProducts()` method.

```
const prodService = new ProductService();

const product: Product = prodService.getProducts()
```

```
1/2 getProducts(description: string): Product[]
```

Figure 3.9 Prompting the first method signature

Figure 3.10 shows the second prompt (note 2/2) for invoking the `getProducts()` method, with a different parameter and return type.

```
const prodService = new ProductService();

const product: Product = prodService.getProducts()
```

```
2/2 getProducts(id: number): Product
```

Figure 3.10 Prompting the second method signature

If we commented out the declarations of the `getProducts()` signatures, the prompt wouldn't be as easy to reason about. It would be difficult to understand which argument type results in returning a value of which type, as shown in figure 3.11.

```
const prodService = new ProductService();

const product: Product = prodService.getProducts()
```

```
getProducts(product: string | number
): Product | Product[]
```

Figure 3.11 The prompt without overloading

You may argue that the benefits offered by TypeScript's method overloading are not too convincing, and we agree that it may be easier to just declare two methods with different names, such as `getProduct()` and `getProducts()`, without unionizing their argument and return types. This is true except for one use case: overloading constructors.

In TypeScript classes, there's only one name you can give to a constructor, and that's `constructor`. If you want to create a class with several constructors having different signatures, you may want to use the syntax for overloading, as shown in listing 3.11.

Listing 3.11 Overloading constructors

```
class Product {
  id: number;
  description: string;

  constructor();
  constructor(id: number);
  constructor(id: number, description: string);
  constructor(id?: number, description?: string) {
    // Constructor implementation goes here  )
  }
}
```

- A no-argument constructor declaration
- A one-argument constructor declaration
- A two-argument constructor declaration
- An implementation of constructor handling all possible arguments

NOTE Because we wanted to allow a no-argument constructor in the preceding listing, we made all arguments optional in the constructor implementation.

But again, overloading constructors is not the only way to initialize an object's properties. For example, you could declare a single interface to represent all possible parameters for a constructor. The following listing declares an interface with all optional properties and a class with one constructor that takes one optional argument.

Listing 3.12 A single constructor with an optional argument

```
interface ProductProperties {
    id?: number;
    description?: string;
}

class Product {
  id: number;
  description: string;

  constructor(properties?: ProductProperties ) {
    // Constructor implementation goes here
  }
}
```

- A ProductProperties interface with two optional properties
- A class constructor with an optional argument of type ProductProperties

To summarize, use common sense when overloading a method or a constructor in TypeScript. Although overloading provides multiple ways of invoking a method, the logic may quickly become difficult to reason about. In our daily TypeScript work, we rarely use overloading.

3.2 Working with interfaces

In chapter 2, we used TypeScript interfaces only for declaring custom types, and we came up with a general rule: if you need a custom type that includes a constructor, use a class; otherwise use an interface. In this section, we'll show you how to use TypeScript interfaces to ensure that a class implements a specific API.

3.2.1 Enforcing the contract

An interface can declare not only properties but also methods (no implementations though). A class declaration can then include the `implements` keyword followed by the name of the interface. In other words, while an interface just contains method signatures, a class can contain their implementations.

Say you own a Toyota Camry. It has thousands of parts that perform various actions, but as a driver you just need to know how to use a handful of controls—how to start and stop the engine, how to accelerate and brake, how to turn on the radio, and so on. All these controls together can be considered *a public interface* offered to you by the designers of the Toyota Camry.

Now imagine that you have to rent a car, and they give you a Ford Taurus, which you've never driven before. Will you know how to drive it? Yes, because it has a familiar *interface*: a key for starting the engine, acceleration and brake pedals, and so on. When you rent a car, you can even request a car that has a specific interface, such as an automatic transmission.

Let's model some of the car interface using TypeScript's syntax. The following listing shows a `MotorVehicle` interface that declares five methods.

Listing 3.13 The `MotorVehicle` interface

```
interface MotorVehicle {
    startEngine(): boolean;
    stopEngine(): boolean;
    brake(): boolean;
    accelerate(speed: number): void;
    honk(howLong: number): void;
}
```

Declares a method signature that should be implemented by a class

Note that none of the methods of `MotorVehicle` are implemented. Now we can declare a `Car` class that will implement all the methods declared in the `MotorVehicle` interface. By using the keyword `implements`, we declare that a class implements a certain interface:

```
class Car implements MotorVehicle {

}
```

This simple class declaration won't compile. It will give you the error "Class Car incorrectly implements interface MotorVehicle." When you declare that a class implements some interface, you must implement each and every method declared in the interface. In other words, the preceding code snippet states "I swear that the class `Car` will implement the API declared in the interface `MotorVehicle`." The following listing shows a simplified implementation of this interface in the `Car` class.

Listing 3.14 A class that implements `MotorVehicle`

```
class Car implements MotorVehicle {
  startEngine(): boolean {
    return true;
  }
  stopEngine(): boolean{
    return true;
  }
  brake(): boolean {
    return true;
  }
  accelerate(speed: number): void;
    console.log(`Driving faster`);
  }

  honk(howLong: number): void {
    console.log(`Beep beep yeah!`);
  }
}

const car = new Car();
car.startEngine();
```

Implements the methods from the interface

Instantiates the Car class

Uses the Car's API to start the engine

Note that we didn't explicitly declare the type of the `car` constant—this is an example of type inference. We could explicitly declare the type of `car` as follows (although it's not required):

```
const car: Car = new Car();
```

We could also declare the `car` constant of type `MotorVehicle`, because our `Car` class implements this custom type:

```
const car: MotorVehicle = new Car();
```

What's the difference between these two declarations of the `car` constant? Let's say a `Car` class implements eight methods: five of them come from the `MotorVehicle` interface and the others are some arbitrary methods. If the `car` constant is of type `Car`, you can invoke all eight methods on the instance of the object represented by `car`. But if the type of `car` is `MotorVehicle`, only the five methods declared in this interface can be invoked using the `car` constant.

We can say that *an interface enforces a specific contract.* In our example, this means that we force the `Car` class to implement each of the five methods declared in the `MotorVehicle` interface, or else the code won't compile.

Now let's design an interface for James Bond's car. Yes, for agent 007. This special car should be able to fly, and swim as well. Not a problem. Let's declare a couple of interfaces first.

Listing 3.15 `Flyable` and `Swimmable` interfaces

```
interface Flyable {
  fly(howHigh: number);
  land();
}

interface Swimmable {
  swim(howFar: number);
}
```

A class can implement more than one interface, so let's make sure that our class implements these two interfaces.

Listing 3.16 A car with three interfaces

```
class Car implements MotorVehicle, Flyable, Swimmable {
  // Implement all the methods from three
  // interfaces here
}
```

Actually, making every car flyable and swimmable is not a good idea, so let's not modify the `Car` class from listing 3.14. Let's instead use class inheritance and create a `SecretServiceCar` class that extends `Car` and adds more features.

Listing 3.17 A class that extends and implements

```
class SecretServiceCar extends Car implements Flyable, Swimmable {
  // Implement all the methods from two
  // interfaces here

}
```

By implementing all the methods declared in `Flyable` and `Swimmable`, our `SecretServiceCar` turns a regular motor vehicle into a flyable and swimmable object. The `Car` class continues to represent a regular auto with the functionality defined in the `MotorVehicle` interface.

3.2.2 Extending interfaces

As you saw in the previous section, combining classes and interfaces brings flexibility to code design. Let's consider yet another option—extending an interface.

In the prior example, when the requirement to develop the secret service car came in, we already had the `MotorVehicle` interface and the `Car` class that implemented this interface. In listing 3.17, the `SecretServiceCar` class inherited from `Car` and implemented two additional interfaces.

But when you design a special car for the secret service, you may want to implement all the methods in the `MotorVehicle` interface differently as well, so you may want to declare the `SecretServiceCar` class as follows.

Listing 3.18 A class that implements three interfaces

```
class SecretServiceCar implements MotorVehicle, Flyable, Swimmable {
  // Implement all the methods from three interfaces here

}
```

On the other hand, our flyable object is a motor vehicle as well, so we could declare the `Flyable` interface as follows.

Listing 3.19 Extending an interface

```
interface Flyable extends MotorVehicle{     <-- One interface extends another
  fly(howHigh: number);                     | Declares a method signature
  land();                                   | to be implemented in a class
}
```

Now, if a class includes `implements Flyable` in its declaration, it must implement the five methods declared in the `MotorVehicle` interface (see listing 3.13) as well as two methods from `Flyable` (listing 3.19)—seven methods in total. Our `SecretServiceCar` class must implement these seven methods plus one from `Swimmable`.

Listing 3.20 A class that implements `Flyable` and `Swimmable`

```
class SecretServiceCar implements Flyable, Swimmable {

  startEngine(): boolean {                  <--
    return true;
  };
  stopEngine(): boolean{                    <--
    return true;
  };
  brake(): boolean {                        <--  Implements the method
    return true;                                 from MotorVehicle
  };
  accelerate(speed: number) {               <--
    console.log(`Driving faster`);
  }

  honk(howLong: number): void {             <--
    console.log(`Beep beep yeah!`);
  }
```

```
  fly(howHigh: number) {                          ◁─┐
    console.log(`Flying ${howHigh} feet high`);     │ Implements the
  }                                                 │ method from Flyable
                                                    │
  land() {  2((CO16-7))                           ◁─┘
    console.log(`Landing. Fasten your belts.`);
  }

  swim(howFar: number) {                  ◁──── Implements the method
    console.log(`Swimming ${howFar} feet`);      from Swimmable
  }
}
```

TIP Even if `Swimmable` also extended `MotorVehicle`, the Typescript compiler wouldn't complain.

Declaring interfaces that include method signatures improves code readability because any interface describes a well-defined set of features that can be implemented by one or more concrete classes.

However, the interface won't tell you exactly how a class will implement it. Developers who practice the object-oriented approach in programming have a mantra: "Program to interfaces, not implementations." In the next section, you'll see what this means.

3.2.3 Programming to interfaces

To understand the meaning and benefits of programming to interfaces, let's consider a case where this technique wasn't used. Imagine you had to write code that would retrieve information about all products or one product from a data source.

You know how to write classes, so you could start implementing them right away. You could define a custom `Product` type and a `ProductService` class with two methods.

Listing 3.21 Programming to implementations

```
class Product {       ◁── A custom Product type
  id: number;
  description: string;
}
                                   A concrete implementation
class ProductService {   ◁──      of ProductService

  getProducts(): Product[]{             ◁── An implemented method
    // the code for getting products
    // from a real data source should go here

    return [];
  }

  getProductById(id: number): Product {  3((CO17-4))
    // the code for getting products
    // from a real data source should go here
```

```
    return { id: 123, description: 'Good product' };
  }
}
```

Then, in multiple places in your app, you could instantiate `ProductService` and use its methods:

```
const productService = new ProductService();
const products = productService.getProducts();
```

That was easy, wasn't it? You proudly commit this code to the source code repository, but your manager says that the backend guys are delaying implementing the server that was supposed to provide data for your `ProductService`. He asks you to create another class, `MockProductService`, with *the same API* that could return hardcoded product data.

No problem. You write another implementation of the product service.

Listing 3.22 Another implementation of the product service

A concrete implementation of MockProductService

```
class MockProductService {

  getProducts(): Product[]{
    // the code for getting hard-coded
    // products goes here

    return [];
  }

  getProductById(id: number): Product {

    return { id: 456, description: 'Not a real product' };
  }
}
```

An implemented method

> **TIP** You might need to create `MockProductService` not only because the backend guys are running late, but also for use in unit tests, in which you don't use real services.

You've created two concrete implementations of the product service. Hopefully you didn't make mistakes while declaring methods in `MockProductService`. They need to be exactly the same as in `ProductService` or you may break the code that uses `MockProductService`.

We don't like the word *hopefully* in the previous paragraph. We already know that an interface allows us to enforce a contract upon a class—upon `MockProductService` in this case. But we didn't declare any interface here!

It sounds weird, but in TypeScript you can declare a class that implements another class. The better (not the best) approach would be to start writing `MockProductService` as follows:

```
class MockProductService implements ProductService {
  // implementation goes here
}
```

TypeScript is smart enough to understand that if you use a class name after the word `implement`, you want to use it as an interface and enforce the implementation of all public methods of `ProductService`. This way, there's no chance that you'll forget to implement something, or make a mistake in the signature of `getProducts()` or `getProductById()`. Your code won't compile until you properly implement these methods in the `MockProductService` class.

But the best approach is to program to interfaces from the very beginning. When you got the requirement to write `ProductService` with two methods, you should have started by declaring an interface with these methods, without worrying about their implementation.

Let's call this interface `IProductService` and declare two method signatures there. Then declare a `ProductService` class that implements this interface.

Listing 3.23 Programming to an interface

```
interface Product {                         <-- Declares a custom type using an interface
  id: number;
  description: string;
}

interface IProductService {                 <-- Declares an API as an interface
  getProducts(): Product[];
  getProductById(id: number): Product
}

class ProductService implements IProductService {      <-- Implements the interface

  getProducts(): Product[]{
    // the code for getting products
    // from a real data source goes here

    return [];
  }

  getProductById(id: number): Product {
    // the code for getting a product by id goes here
    return { id: 123, description: 'Good product' };
  }
}
```

Declaring an API as an interface shows that you spent time thinking about the required functionality, and only afterwards took care of the concrete implementation. Now, if a new class, such as `MockProductService`, has to be implemented, you'd start it like this:

```
class MockProductService implements IProductService {
  // Another concrete implementation of the
  // interface methods goes here
}
```

Have you noticed that the custom `Product` type is implemented differently in listings 3.21 and 3.23? Use the `interface` keyword instead of `class` if you don't need to instantiate this custom type (for example, `Product`), and the JavaScript footprint will be smaller. Try the code from these two listings in the TypeScript Playground and compare the generated JavaScript. The version where `Product` is an interface is shorter.

> **TIP** We named the interface `IProductService`, starting with a capital `I`, whereas the class name was `ProductService`. Some people prefer using the suffix `Impl` for concrete implementations, such as `ProductServiceImpl`, and to simply name the interface `ProductService`.

Another good example of programming to interfaces is factory functions, which implement some business logic and then return the proper instance of the object. If we had to write a factory function that returned either `ProductService` or `MockProductService`, we'd use the interface as its return type.

Listing 3.24 A factory function

```
function getProductService(isProduction: boolean): IProductService {   // A factory function that uses the interface as a return type
  if (isProduction) {
     return new ProductService();
  } else {
     return new MockProductService();
  }
}

const productService: IProductService;   // A constant of the interface type

...

const isProd = true;   // In a real-world app, this wouldn't be hardcoded.
const productService: IProductService  = getProductService(isProd);   // Gets the proper instance of the product service

const products = productService.getProducts();   // Invokes the method on the product service
```

In this example, we used the `isProd` constant with a hardcoded value of `true`. In real-world apps, this value would be obtained from a property file or environment variable.

By changing this property from `true` to `false`, we can change the behavior of the app at runtime.

Although the actual type of the returned object will be either `ProductService` or `MockProductService`, we used an `IProductService` abstraction in the function signature. This makes our factory function more flexible and easily expandable: if in the future we need to modify this function's body to return an object of the type `AnotherProductService`, we can just make sure that this new class declaration includes `implements IProductService`, and the code that uses our factory function will compile without any additional changes. Program to interfaces!

> **TIP** Chapter 16 has a sidebar titled "Once again about programming to interfaces," and there you'll see another use case where programming to interfaces could prevent a runtime bug.

> **NOTE** In section 11.5, while explaining the specifics of using dependency injection with the Angular framework, we'll come back to the idea of programming to abstractions. There you'll see that TypeScript interfaces can't be used, but you could use abstract classes instead.

Summary

- You can create a class using another one as a base. We call this *class inheritance.*
- A subclass can use `public` or `protected` properties of a superclass.
- If a class property is declared as `private`, it can be used only within that class.
- You can create a class that can only be instantiated once by using a `private` constructor.
- If methods with the same signatures exist in the superclass and a subclass, we call it *method overriding.* Class constructors can be overridden as well. The `super` keyword and the `super()` method allow a subclass to invoke the class members of a superclass.
- You can declare several signatures for a method, and this is called *method overloading.*
- Interfaces can include method signatures but can't contain their implementations.
- You can inherit one interface from another.
- While implementing a class, see if any methods can be declared in a separate interface. Then your class will have to implement that interface. This approach provides a clean way to separate the declaration of functionality from the implementation.

4 Using enums and generics

This chapter covers

- The benefits of using enums
- The syntax for numeric and string enums
- What generic types are for
- How to write classes, interfaces, and functions that support generics

In chapter 2, we introduced unions, which allow you to create a custom type by combining several existing types. In this chapter, you'll learn how to use enums—a way to create a new type based on a limited set of values.

We'll also introduce generics, which allow you to place type constraints on class members, function parameters, or their return types.

4.1 Using enums

Enumerations (a.k.a. enums) allow you to create limited sets of named constants that have something in common. Such constants can be numbers or strings.

4.1.1 Numeric enums

A week has seven days, and you can assign the numbers 1 to 7 to represent them. But what's the first day of the week?

According to ISO 8601, the standard on data elements and interchange formats, Monday is the first day of the week, which doesn't stop such countries as USA, Canada, and Australia from considering Sunday to be the first day of the week. Also, what if someone assigned the number 8 to the variable that stores the day? We don't want this to happen, and using day names instead of numbers makes our code more readable. Using just the numbers 1 to 7 to represent days may not be a good idea. On the other hand, using numbers to store days is more efficient than using names. We want readability, the ability to restrict values to a limited set, and efficiency in storing data. This is where enums can help.

TypeScript has an `enum` keyword that can define a limited set of constants. We can declare a new type for weekdays as follows.

Listing 4.1 Defining weekdays using enum

```
enum Weekdays {
  Monday = 1,
  Tuesday = 2,
  Wednesday = 3,
  Thursday = 4,
  Friday = 5,
  Saturday = 6,
  Sunday = 7
}
```

This listing defines a new type, `Weekdays`, that has a limited number of values. We initialized each enum member with a numeric value, and days of the week can be referred to using dot notation:

```
let dayOff = Weekdays.Tuesday;
```

The value of the variable `dayOff` is now 2, but if you typed the preceding line in your IDE or in TypeScript Playground, you'd be prompted with the possible values, as shown in figure 4.1.

```
let dayOff = Weekdays.Tuesday;
                    Friday        (enum member) Weekdays.Friday = 5
                    Monday
                    Saturday
                    Sunday
                    Thursday
                    Tuesday
                    Wednesday
```

Figure 4.1 Autocomplete with enums

Using the members of the `Weekdays` enum stops you from making a mistake and assigning a wrong value (such as 8) to the variable `dayOff`. Well, strictly speaking, nothing stops you from ignoring this `enum` and writing `dayOff = 8`, but this would be a misdemeanor.

In listing 4.1, we could have initialized only Monday with 1, and the rest of the days values would be assigned using auto-increment: Tuesday would be initialized with 2, Wednesday with 3, and so on.

Listing 4.2 The enum with auto-increment values

```
enum Weekdays {
  Monday = 1,
  Tuesday,
  Wednesday,
  Thursday,
  Friday,
  Saturday,
  Sunday
}
```

By default, enums are zero-based, so if we didn't initialize the `Monday` member with 1, its value would be 0.

Reversing numeric enums

If you know the value of a numeric enum, you can find the name of that enum member. For example, you might have a function that returns the weekday number, and you'd like to print its name. By using this value as an index, you can retrieve the name of the day.

```
enum Weekdays {                  <- Declares a numeric enum
  Monday = 1,
  Tuesday,
  Wednesday,
  Thursday,
  Friday,
  Saturday,
  Sunday
}

console.log(Weekdays[3]);        <- Gets the name of the member that's equal to 3
```

In the last line of the preceding code, we retrieve the name of day 3. It will print "Wednesday" on the console.

In some cases, you won't care which numeric values are assigned to the `enum` members—the following `convertTemperature()` function illustrates this. It converts the temperature from Fahrenheit to Celsius or vice versa. In this version of `convertTemperature()` we won't use enums, but we'll then rewrite it with them.

Listing 4.3 Converting temperature without enums

```
function convertTemperature(temp: number, fromTo: string): number {

  return ('FtoC' === fromTo) ?
        (temp - 32) * 5.0/9.0:
         temp * 9.0 / 5.0 + 32;
}

console.log(`70F is ${convertTemperature(70, 'FtoC')}C`);
console.log(`21C is ${convertTemperature(21, 'CtoF')}F`);
console.log(`35C is ${convertTemperature(35, 'ABCD')}F`);
```

- This function takes two parameters: temperature and conversion direction.
- Converts from Fahrenheit to Celsius
- Converts from Celsius to Fahrenheit
- Converts 70 degrees Fahrenheit
- Converts 21 degrees Celsius
- Invokes the function with a meaningless fromTo

The function in listing 4.3 converts the value from Celsius to Fahrenheit if you pass any value for `fromTo` except `FtoC`. In the last line, we purposely provided the erroneous value `ABCD` as the `fromTo` parameter, and the function still converted the temperature from Celsius to Fahrenheit. You can see it in action on CodePen at http://mng.bz/JzaK. Attempts to invoke a function with erroneous values should be caught by the compiler, and this is what TypeScript enums are for.

In the following listing, we declare a `Direction` enum that restricts the allowed constants to either `FtoC` or `CtoF` and nothing else. We also changed the type of the `fromTo` parameter from `string` to `Direction`.

Listing 4.4 Converting temperature with enums

```
enum Direction {
  FtoC,
  CtoF
}

function convertTemperature(temp: number, fromTo: Direction): number {

      return (Direction.FtoC === fromTo) ?
             (temp - 32) * 5.0/9.0:
             temp * 9.0 / 5.0 + 32;
}

console.log(`70F is ${convertTemperature(70, Direction.FtoC)}C`);
console.log(`21C is ${convertTemperature(21, Direction.CtoF)}F`);
```

- Declares the Direction enum
- The type of the second parameter is Direction.
- Invokes the function using the enum members

Since the type of the second parameter of the function is `Direction`, we must invoke this function providing one of this enum's members, such as `Direction.CtoF`. We're not interested in the numeric value of this member. The purpose of this enum is just to provide a limited set of constants: `CtoF` and `FtoC`. The IDE will prompt you with two possible values for the second parameter, and you won't have a chance for a typo.

> **TIP** Using the `Direction` type for the second argument doesn't prevent another misdemeanor—invoking this function like `convertTemperature (50.0, 99)`.

Enum members are initialized with values (either explicitly or implicitly). All the examples in this section had enum members initialized with numbers, but TypeScript allows you to create enums with string values, and we'll see such examples next.

4.1.2 String enums

In some cases, you may want to declare a limited set of string constants, and for this you can use string enums—enums whose members are initialized with string values. Say you're programming a computer game where the player can move in four directions.

Listing 4.5 Declaring a string enum

```
enum Direction {
    Up = "UP",
    Down = "DOWN",
    Left = "LEFT",
    Right = "RIGHT",
}
```

Initializes the enum member with a string value

When you declare a string enum, you must initialize each member. You might ask, "Why not just use a numeric enum here so TypeScript could automatically initialize its members with any numbers?" The reason is that in some cases you want to give meaningful values to enum members. For example, you'll need to debug the program, and instead of seeing that the last move was `0`, you'll see that the last move was `UP`.

The next question you might ask is "Why declare the `Direction` enum if I can just declare four string constants with the values `UP`, `DOWN`, `LEFT`, and `RIGHT`?" You can, but suppose we have a function with the following signature:

```
move(where: string)
```

A developer could make a mistake (or a typo) and invoke this function as `move("North")`. But `North` is not a valid direction, so it's safer to declare this function using the `Direction` enum:

```
move(where: Direction)
```

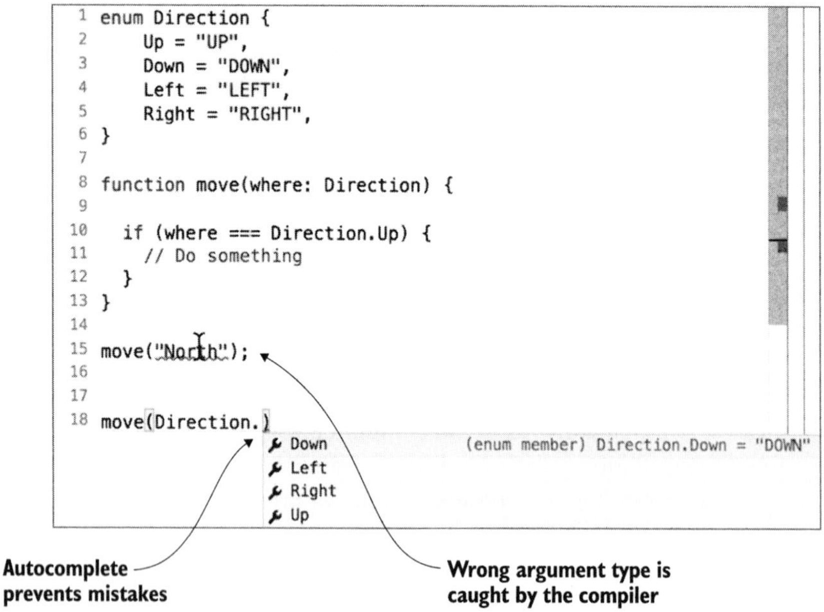

```
1 enum Direction {
2     Up = "UP",
3     Down = "DOWN",
4     Left = "LEFT",
5     Right = "RIGHT",
6 }
7
8 function move(where: Direction) {
9
10   if (where === Direction.Up) {
11     // Do something
12   }
13 }
14
15 move("North");
16
17
18 move(Direction.)
       Down          (enum member) Direction.Down = "DOWN"
       Left
       Right
       Up
```

Autocomplete prevents mistakes

Wrong argument type is caught by the compiler

Figure 4.2 Catching erroneous function invocations

As you can see in figure 4.2, we made a mistake and provided the string "North" in line 15. The compile-time error would read "Argument of type '"North"' is not assignable to the parameter of type 'Direction'." In line 18, which uses the `Direction` enum, the IDE offers you a selection of valid enum members so there's no way you can provide the wrong argument.

You can use the union type as an alternative to enums. For example, the signature of the `move()` function could look like this:

```
function move(direction: 'Up' | 'Down' | 'Left' | 'Right') {  }
move('North'); // compilation error
```

Another alternative to enums is defining a custom type:

```
type Direction = 'Up' | 'Down' | 'Left' | 'Right';
function move(direction: Direction) {}
move('North'); // compilation error
```

Now let's imagine that you need to keep track of the app's state changes. The user can initiate a limited number of actions in each of the app's views, and you want to log the actions taken in the Products view. Initially the app tries to load products, and this action can either succeed or fail. The user can also search for products. To represent the states of the Products view, you might declare a string enum.

Listing 4.6 Declaring a string enum for monitoring actions

```
enum ProductsActionTypes {
  Search = 'Products Search',                       // Initializes the Search member
  Load = 'Products Load All',                       // Initializes the Load member
  LoadFailure = 'Products Load All Failure',        // Initializes the LoadFailure member
  LoadSuccess = 'Products Load All Success'         // Initializes the LoadSuccess member
}

// If the function that loads products fails...
console.log(ProductsActionTypes.LoadFailure);       // Prints "Products Load All Failure"
```

When the user clicks on the button to load products, you can log the value of the `ProductsActionTypes.Load` member, which will log the text `"Products Load All"`. If the products were not loaded successfully, you can log the value of `ProductsActionTypes.LoadFailure`, which will log the text `"Products Load All Failure"`.

> **NOTE** Some state management frameworks (such as Redux) require the app to emit actions when the app's state should change. We can declare a string enum as in listing 4.6 and emit the actions `ProductsActionTypes.Load`, `ProductsActionTypes.LoadSuccess`, and so on.

String enums can easily be mapped to string values coming from a server or database (order status, user role, and so on) with no additional coding, providing you with all the benefits of strong typing. We'll illustrate this at the end of this chapter in listing 4.17.

> **NOTE** String enums are not reversible—you can't find a member's name if you know its value.

4.1.3 Using const enums

If you use the keyword `const` while declaring an `enum`, its values will be inlined and no JavaScript will be generated.

Let's compare the generated JavaScript of `enum` and `const enum`. The left side of figure 4.3 shows an `enum` declared without `const`, and the right side shows the generated JavaScript. For illustration purposes, in the last line, we print the next move.

```
enum Direction {
    Up = "UP",
    Down = "DOWN",
    Left = "LEFT",
    Right = "RIGHT",
}

const theNextMove = Direction.Down;
```

```
var Direction;
(function (Direction) {
    Direction["Up"] = "UP";
    Direction["Down"] = "DOWN";
    Direction["Left"] = "LEFT";
    Direction["Right"] = "RIGHT";
})(Direction || (Direction = {}));
var theNextMove = Direction.Down;
```

Figure 4.3 An enum without the `const` keyword

```
const enum Direction {
    Up = "UP",
    Down = "DOWN",
    Left = "LEFT",
    Right = "RIGHT",
}

const theNextMove = Direction.Down;
```

```
var theNextMove = "DOWN" /* Down */;
```

Figure 4.4 An enum with the `const` keyword

Now, in figure 4.4, we'll add the keyword `const` on the first line before `enum` and compare the generated JavaScript (on the right) with that in figure 4.3.

As you see, no JavaScript code for `enum Direction` was generated in figure 4.4. But the value of the enum member from the TypeScript code (`Direction.Down`) was inlined in the JavaScript.

> **TIP** The earlier sidebar, "Reversing numeric enums," includes a listing where we reversed the third member of the enum: `Weekdays[3]`. This isn't possible with `const enum` as they are not represented in the generated JavaScript code.

Using `const` with `enum` results in more concise JavaScript, but keep in mind that because there is no JavaScript code to represent your `enum`, you may run into some limitations. For example, you won't be able to retrieve a numeric enum member's name with its value.

Overall, using enums increases the readability of your programs.

4.2 Using generics

You know that TypeScript has built-in types, and you can create custom ones as well. But there's more to it. Strange as it may sound, types can be *parameterized*—you can provide a type (not the value) as a parameter.

It's easy to declare a function that takes parameters of specific concrete types, such as a number and a string:

```
function calctTax(income: number, state: string){...}
```

But TypeScript *generics* allow you to write functions that can work with a variety of types. In other words, you can declare a function that works with a generic type, and the concrete type can be specified later by the caller of the function.

In TypeScript, you can write generic functions, classes, or interfaces. A generic type can be represented by an arbitrary letter (or letters), such as `T` in `Array<T>`, and when you declare a specific array, you provide a concrete type in angle brackets, such as `number`:

```
let lotteryNumbers: Array<number>;
```

In this section, you'll learn how to use generic code written by someone else, as well as how to create your own classes, interfaces, and functions that can work with generic types.

4.2.1 Understanding generics

A *generic* is a piece of code that can handle values of multiple types, which are specified when this code is used (during a function invocation or class instantiation).

Let's consider TypeScript arrays, which can be declared as follows:

- Specify the type of the array element followed by `[]`:

  ```
  const someValues: number[];
  ```

- Use the generic `Array` followed by the type parameter in angle brackets:

  ```
  const someValues: Array<number>;
  ```

If all elements of the array have the same type, both declarations are equivalent but the first syntax is simpler to read. With the second syntax, the angle brackets represent a type parameter. You can instantiate this `Array` like any other while restricting the type of allowed values (to `number` in our example). A bit later, we'll show you when declaring an array with a generic type is the better approach.

The next code snippet creates an array that will initially have ten objects of type `Person`, and the inferred type of the `people` variable is `Person[]`.

```
class Person{ }

const people = new Array<Person>(10);
```

TypeScript arrays can hold objects of any type, but if you decide to use the generic `Array` type, you must specify which value types are allowed in the array, such as `Array<Person>`. By doing this, you place a constraint on this instance of the array. If you tried to add an object of a different type to this array, the Typescript compiler would generate an error. In another piece of code, you could use the array with a different type parameter, such as `Array<Customer>`.

The following listing declares a `Person` class, its descendant `Employee`, and an `Animal` class. Then it instantiates each class and tries to store all these objects in the `workers` array using the generic array notation with the type parameter `Array<Person>`.

Listing 4.7 Using a generic type

```
class Person {        <—— Declares the Person class
    name: string;
}

class Employee extends Person {    <—— Declares a subclass of Person
    department: number;
}

class Animal {        <—— Declares the Animal class
```

```
    breed: string;
}

const workers: Array<Person> = [];   <-- Declares and initializes a generic array with a concrete parameter

workers[0] = new Person();
workers[1] = new Employee();
workers[2] = new Animal(); // compile-time error   <-- Adds objects to the array
```

In listing 4.7, the last line won't compile because the `workers` array was declared with the type parameter `Person`, and `Animal` is not a `Person`. But the `Employee` class extends `Person` and is considered a *subtype* of `Person`, so you can use the `Employee` subtype anywhere the supertype `Person` is allowed.

So, by using a generic `workers` array with the parameter `<Person>`, we announce our plans to store only instances of the class `Person` or objects of compatible types there. An attempt to store an instance of the class `Animal` (as it was defined in listing 4.7) in the same array will result in the following compile-time error: "Type `Animal` is not assignable to type `Person`. Property `name` is missing in type `Animal`." In other words, using TypeScript generics helps you avoid errors related to using the wrong types.

Generic variance

The term *generic variance* relates to the rules for using subtypes and supertypes in any particular place in your program. For example, in Java, arrays are *covariant*, which means that you can use `Employee[]` (the subtype) where the array `Person[]` (the supertype) is allowed.

Because TypeScript supports structural typing, you can use either an `Employee` or any other object literal that's compatible with the type `Person` where the `Person` type is expected. In other words, generic variance applies to objects that are structurally the same. Given the importance of anonymous types in JavaScript, an understanding of this is important for the optimal use of generics in Typescript.

To see if type `A` can be used where type `B` is expected, read about structural subtyping in the TypeScript documentation at http://mng.bz/wla2.

TIP We used `const` (and not `let`) to declare the `workers` identifier in listing 4.7 because its value never changes. Adding new objects to the `workers` array doesn't change the address of the array in memory, so the value of the `workers` identifier remains the same (i.e., immutable).

If you're familiar with generics in Java or C#, you may get the feeling that you understand TypeScript generics as well. There is a caveat, though. Whereas Java and C# use a *nominal* type system, TypeScript uses a *structural* one, as was explained in section 2.2.4.

In a nominal type system, types are checked against their names, but in a structural system they're defined by their structure. In languages with a nominal type system, the following line would *always* result in an error:

```
let person: Person = new Animal();
```

With a structural type system, as long as the structures of the types are similar, you may get away with assigning an object of one type to a variable of another. Let's add a `name` property to the `Animal` class.

Listing 4.8 Generics and the structural type system

```
class Person {
    name: string;
}

class Employee extends Person {
    department: number;
}

class Animal {
    name: string;         <-- The only additional line compared to listing 4.7
    breed: string;
}

const workers: Array<Person> = [];

workers[0] = new Person();
workers[1] = new Employee();
workers[2] = new Animal();   // no errors
```

Now the Typescript compiler doesn't complain about assigning an `Animal` object to a variable of type `Person`. The variable of type `Person` expects an object that has a `name` property, and the `Animal` object has one! This is not to say that `Person` and `Animal` represent the same types, but these types are compatible.

Moreover, you don't even have to create a new instance of the `Person`, `Employee`, or `Animal` classes—you can use the syntax of object literals instead. Adding the following line to listing 4.8 is perfectly fine, because the structure of the object literal is compatible with the structure of type `Person`:

```
workers[3] = { name: "Mary" };
```

On the other hand, trying to assign a `Person` object to a variable of type `Animal` will result in a compilation error:

```
const worker: Animal = new Person(); // compilation error
```

The error message would read "Property breed is missing in type Person," and that makes sense, because if you declare a worker variable of type Animal but create an instance of the Person object that has no breed property, you wouldn't be able to write worker.breed. Hence the compile-time error.

NOTE The previous sentence may irritate savvy JavaScript developers who are accustomed to adding object properties like worker.breed without thinking twice. If the breed property doesn't exist on the worker object, the JavaScript engine would simply create it, right? This works in dynamically typed code, but if you decide to use the benefits of static typing, you have to play by the rules.

Generics can be used in a variety of scenarios. For example, you can create a function that takes values of various types, but during its invocation you must specify a concrete type. To be able to use generic types with a class, an interface, or a function, the creator of this class, interface, or function has to write them in a special way to support generic types.

When to use generic arrays

We started this section by showing two different ways of declaring an array of numbers. Let's take another example:

```
const values1: string[] = ["Mary", "Joe"];
const values2: Array<string> = ["Mary", "Joe"];
```

When all elements of the array have the same type, you can use the syntax used to declare values1—it's easier to read and write. But if an array can store elements of different types, you can use generics to restrict the types allowed in the array.

For example, you may declare an array that allows only strings and numbers. In the following code snippet, the line that declares values3 will result in a compilation error because Boolean values are not allowed in this array.

```
const values3: Array<string | number> = ["Mary", 123, true]; // error
const values4: Array<string | number> = ["Joe", 123, 567]; // no errors
```

Open TypeScript's type definition file (lib.d.ts) from the TypeScript GitHub repository at http://mng.bz/qXvJ and you'll see the declaration of the Array interface, as shown in figure 4.5.

The <T> in line 1008 is a placeholder for a concrete type that must be provided by the application developer during the array's declaration, as we did in listing 4.8. TypeScript requires you to declare a type parameter with Array, and whenever you add new elements to this array, the compiler will check that their type matches the type used in the declaration.

```
1008  interface Array<T> {
1009      /**
1010        * Gets or sets the length of the array. This is a number one higher than the h
1011        */
1012      length: number;
1013      /**
1014        * Returns a string representation of an array.
1015        */
1016      toString(): string;
1017      toLocaleString(): string;
1018      /**
1019        * Appends new elements to an array, and returns the new length of the array.
1020        * @param items New elements of the Array.
1021        */
1022      push(...items: T[]): number;
1023      /**
1024        * Removes the last element from an array and returns it.
1025        */
1026      pop(): T;
```

Figure 4.5 A fragment of lib.d.ts describing the Array API

In listing 4.8, we used the concrete type `<Person>` as a replacement for the generic parameter represented by the letter `<T>`:

```
const workers: Array<Person>;
```

But because generics aren't supported in JavaScript, you won't see them in the code generated by the compiler—generics (and any other types) are erased. Using type parameters is just a safety net for developers at compile time.

You can see more generic `T` types in lines 1022 and 1026 in figure 4.5. When generic types are specified with function arguments, no angle brackets are needed—you'll see this syntax in listing 4.9.

There's no `T` type in TypeScript. The `T` here means the `push()` and `pop()` methods let you push or pop objects of the type provided during the array declaration. For example, in the following code snippet, we declared an array using the type `Person` as a replacement for `T`, and that's why we can use the instance of `Person` as the argument of the `push()` method:

```
const workers: Array<Person>;
workers.push(new Person());
```

> **NOTE** The letter `T` stands for type, which is intuitive, but any letter or word can be used when declaring a generic type. In a map, developers often use the letters `K` for key and `V` for value.

Seeing the `T` type in the API of the `Array` interface tells us that its creator enabled support for generics. Even if you're not planning to create your own generic types, it's really important that you understand the syntax of generics when reading someone else's code or TypeScript documentation.

4.2.2 Creating your own generic types

You can create your own generic classes, interfaces, or functions. In this section, we'll create a generic interface, but the explanations are applicable to creating generic classes as well.

Let's say you have a `Rectangle` class and need to add the capability of comparing the sizes of two rectangles. If you didn't adopt the concept of programming to interfaces (introduced in section 3.2.3), you'd simply add a `compareRectangles()` method to the `Rectangle` class.

But armed with the concept of programming to interfaces, you think differently: "Today, I need to compare rectangles, and tomorrow they'll ask me to compare other objects. I'll play it smart and declare an interface with a `compareTo()` function. Then the `Rectangle` class, and any other class in the future, can implement this interface. The algorithms for comparing rectangles will be different than comparing, say, triangles, but at least they'll have something in common, and the method signature of `compareTo()` will look the same."

So you have an object of some type, and it needs a `compareTo()` method that will compare this object to another object of the same type. If this object is bigger than the other, `compareTo()` will return a positive number; if this object is smaller, it returns negative; if they are equal, it returns 0.

If you weren't familiar with generic types, you'd define this interface as follows:

```
interface Comparator {
  compareTo(value: any): number;
}
```

The `compareTo()` method can take any object as its argument, and the class that implements `Comparator` must include the appropriate comparison algorithm (such as for comparing the sizes of rectangles).

The following listing shows a partial implementation of `Rectangle` and `Triangle` classes that use the `Comparator` interface.

Listing 4.9 Using the interface without a generic type

```
interface Comparator {
  compareTo(value: any): number;      <-- The compareTo() method takes
}                                         one parameter of type any.

class Rectangle implements Comparator {
                                          Implementation of
  compareTo(value: any): number {     <-- compareTo() in Rectangle
```

```
    // the algorithm for comparing rectangles goes here
  }
}

class Triangle implements Comparator {

  compareTo(value: any): number {
    // the algorithm for comparing triangles goes here
  }
}
```

Implementation of compareTo() in Triangle

If the developer had a good night's sleep and a cup of double espresso, they'd create instances of two rectangles and then pass one of them to the `compareTo()` method of another:

```
rectangle1.compareTo(rectangle2);
```

But what if the coffee machine wasn't working that morning? Our developer could make a mistake and try to compare a rectangle to a triangle.

```
rectangle1.compareTo(triangle1);
```

`Triangle` fits the `any` type of the `compareTo()` parameter, and the preceding code can result in a runtime error. To catch such an error at compile time, we could use a generic type (instead of `any`) to place a constraint on which types can be given to the `compareTo()` method:

```
interface Comparator<T> {
    compareTo(value: T): number;
}
```

It's important that both the interface and the method use the generic type represented by the same letter `T`. Now the `Rectangle` and `Triangle` classes can implement `Comparator`, specifying concrete types in angle brackets:

Listing 4.10 Using the interface with a generic type

Declares a generic interface that takes one type as a parameter

```
interface Comparator <T> {
    compareTo(value: T): number;
}

class Rectangle implements Comparator<Rectangle> {

  compareTo(value: Rectangle): number {
    // the algorithm of comparing rectangles goes here
  }
}
```

The compareTo() method takes one parameter of the generic type.

In class Rectangle, compareTo() has a parameter of type Rectangle.

```
class Triangle implements Comparator<Triangle> {

  compareTo(value: Triangle): number {
    // the algorithm of comparing triangles goes here
  }
}
```

In class Triangle, compareTo() has a parameter of type Triangle.

Let's say our developer tries to make the same mistake:

```
rectangle1.compareTo(triangle1);
```

The TypeScript code analyzer will underline `triangle1` with a red squiggly line, reporting an error: "Argument of type 'Triangle' is not assignable to parameter of type 'Rectangle'." As you can see, using generic types lowers the dependency of your code quality on the coffee machine.

Listing 4.11 shows a working example that declares a `Comparator<T>` interface that declares a `compareTo()` method. This code shows how this interface can be used for comparing rectangles as well as programmers. Our algorithms are simple:

- If the area of the first rectangle (width multiplied by height) is bigger than that of the second, the first rectangle is bigger. Two rectangles may have the same areas.
- If the salary of the first programmer is higher than that of the second, the first one is richer. Two programmers may have the same salaries.

Listing 4.11 A working example that uses a generic interface

```
interface Comparator<T> {
    compareTo(value: T): number;
}

class Rectangle implements Comparator<Rectangle> {

    constructor(private width: number, private height: number){};

    compareTo(value: Rectangle): number {
        return this.width * this.height - value.width * value.height;
    }
}

const rect1:Rectangle = new Rectangle(2,5);
const rect2: Rectangle = new Rectangle(2,3);

rect1.compareTo(rect2) > 0 ? console.log("rect1 is bigger"):
   rect1.compareTo(rect2) == 0 ? console.log("rectangles are equal") :
➥ console.log("rect1 is smaller");
```

Declares a generic Comparator interface

Creates a class that implements Comparator for the Rectangle type

Implements the method for comparing rectangles

Compares rectangles (the type T is erased and replaced with Rectangle)

```
class Programmer implements Comparator<Programmer> {    <-- Creates a class that implements Comparator for the Programmer type

    constructor(public name: string, private salary: number){};

    compareTo(value: Programmer): number{    <-- Implements the method for comparing programmers
        return this.salary - value.salary;
    }
}

const prog1:Programmer = new Programmer("John",20000);
const prog2: Programmer = new Programmer("Alex",30000);

prog1.compareTo(prog2) > 0 ? console.log(`${prog1.name} is richer`):
      prog1.compareTo(prog2) == 0?
           console.log(`${prog1.name} and ${prog1.name} earn the
➥ same amounts`) :
           console.log(`${prog1.name} is poorer`);    <-- Compares programmers (the type T is erased and replaced with Programmer)
```

Running the script in listing 4.11 prints the following:

```
rect1 is bigger
John is poorer
```

You can see this program in action on CodePen here: http://mng.bz/7zqe.

Default values of generic types

To use a generic type, you have to provide a concrete type. The following code won't compile because we didn't specify a concrete type parameter while using the type `A`:

```
class A <T> {
    value: T;
}

class B extends A { // Compile error

}
```

Adding the type `any` while *using* the class `A` would fix this error:

```
class B extends A <any> {

}
```

Another way to fix that error would be to specify a default parameter while *declaring* the generic type. The following code snippet will compile without any errors:

```
class A < T = any > {  // declaring default parameter type
    value: T;
}

class B extends A { // No errors

}
```

> ***(continued)***
> Instead of `any`, you can specify another dummy type:
>
> ```
> class A < T = {} >
> ```
>
> With this technique, you won't need to specify a generic parameter when you use generic classes. In figure 13.10 you'll see how the `React.FC` type from the React library uses these default types.
>
> Of course, if you create your own generic types and can provide parameter defaults that make some business sense (not just `any`), do that by all means.

In this section, we've created a generic `Comparator<T>` interface. Now let's see how we can create a generic function.

4.2.3 *Creating generic functions*

We all know how to write a function that can take arguments of concrete types and return a value of a concrete type. This time around, we'll write a generic function that can take parameters of multiple types.

But first, let's consider a not-so-good solution where a function can take a parameter of the type `any` and return a value of the same type. The function in the following listing can log objects of different types and return the data that was logged.

Listing 4.12 A function with the type `any`

```
function printMe(content: any): any {     <-- Declares a function expression with any
    console.log(content);
    return content;
}

const a = printMe("Hello");     <-- Invokes printMe() with the string argument

class Person{     <-- Declares a custom Person type
  constructor(public name: string) { }
}

const b = printMe(new Person("Joe"));     <-- Invokes printMe() with an argument of type Person
```

This function works for various types of arguments, but TypeScript doesn't remember the argument type the `printMe()` function was invoked with. If you hover your mouse over the variables `a` and `b` in your IDE, the TypeScript static analyzer will report the types of both variables as `any`.

If we care to know which types of arguments were used in the invocation of `printMe()`, we'd need to rewrite it as a generic function. The following listing shows the syntax for providing the generic type `<T>` for the function, its parameter, and the return value.

Listing 4.13 A generic function

```
function printMe<T> (content: T): T {
    console.log(content);
    return content;
}

const a = printMe("Hello");

class Person{
  constructor(public name: string) { }
}

const b = printMe(new Person("Joe"));
```

Uses the type T for the function, param, and return value

Invokes printMe() with a string argument

Invokes printMe() with an argument of type Person

In this version of the function, we declare the generic type for the function as `<T>` and the type of the parameter and return value as `T`. Now the types are preserved, and the type of the constant `a` is `string` and the type of `b` is `Person`. If later on in the script you need to use `a` and `b`, the TypeScript static analyzer (and compiler) will perform the proper type checking.

> **NOTE** By using the same letter `T` for the function argument type and return type, we place a constraint ensuring that no matter what concrete type is used during invocation, the return type of this function will be the same.

Similarly, you could use generics in fat arrow function expressions. The code sample from listing 4.13 could be rewritten as follows.

Listing 4.14 Using generic types in fat arrow functions

```
const printMe = <T> (content: T): T => {
    console.log(content);
    return content;
}

const a = printMe("Hello");

class Person{
  constructor(public name: string) { }
}

const b = printMe(new Person("Joe"));
```

The signature of this fat arrow function starts with <T>.

You could also invoke these functions specifying the types explicitly in angle brackets:

```
const a = printMe<string>("Hello");

const b = printMe<Person>(new Person("Joe"));
```

But using explicit types is not required here, as the Typescript compiler will infer the type of `a` as `string` and `b` as `Person`.

The preceding code snippet may not look too convincing—it seems redundant to use `<string>` if it's clear that "Hello" is a string. But this may not always be the case, as you'll see in listing 4.17.

Let's write another little script that will provide more illustration of using generics in a class and function. The following listing declares a class that can represent a pair: a key and a value. Both key and value can by represented by multiple types, so we smell generics here.

Listing 4.15 The generic `Pair` class

```
class Pair<K, V> {       // Declares a class with two parameterized types
    key: K;              // Declares a property of generic type K
    value: V;            // Declares a property of generic type V
}
```

When you write a piece of code that introduces generic type parameters represented by letters (such as `K` and `V`), you can declare variables using these letters as if they were built-in TypeScript types. When you declare (and compile) a concrete `Pair` with specific types for `K` and `V`, the `K` and `V` will be erased and replaced with the declared types.

Let's write a more concise version of the `Pair` class, which has a constructor and automatically created `key` and `values` properties:

```
class Pair<K, V> {
  constructor(public key: K, public value: V) {}
}
```

Now let's write a generic function that can compare generic pairs. Is your head spinning yet? The function in the following listing declares two generic types that are also represented by `K` and `V`.

Listing 4.16 A generic `compare` function

```
function compare <K,V> (pair1: Pair<K,V>, pair2: Pair<K,V>): boolean {   // Declares the generic function
    return pair1.key === pair2.key &&
           pair1.value === pair2.value;                                  // Compares keys and values of the pairs
}
```

During the invocation of the `compare()` function you're allowed to specify two concrete types, which should be the same as the types provided for its parameters—the `Pair` objects.

Listing 4.17 shows a working script that uses the generic `Pair` class as well as the generic `compare()` function. First we create and compare two `Pair` instances that use the `number` type for the key and `string` type for values. Then we compare another two `Pair` instances that use the `string` type for both key and value.

Listing 4.17 Using `compare()` and `Pair`

```
class Pair<K, V> {
  constructor(public key: K, public value: V) {}
}

function compare <K,V> (pair1: Pair<K,V>, pair2: Pair<K,V>): boolean {
    return pair1.key === pair2.key &&
           pair1.value === pair2.value;
}

let p1: Pair<number, string> = new Pair(1, "Apple");    // Creates the first <number, string> pair

let p2 = new Pair(1, "Orange");    // Creates the second <number, string> pair using type inference

// Comparing apples to oranges
console.log(compare<number, string>(p1, p2));    // Compares the pairs (prints "false")

let p3 = new Pair("first", "Apple");    // Creates the first <string, string> pair

let p4 = new Pair("first", "Apple");    // Creates the second <string, string> pair

// Comparing apples to apples
console.log(compare(p3, p4));    // Compares the pairs (prints "true")
```

Please note that in the first invocation of `compare()`, we explicitly specified the concrete parameters, and in the second invocation we didn't:

```
compare<number, string>(p1, p2)

compare(p3, p4)
```

The first line is easier to reason about, as we can see what kinds of pairs `p1` and `p2` are. Besides, if you make a mistake and specify the wrong types, the compiler will catch it right away:

```
compare<string, string>(p1, p2) //compile error
```

You can see this code in action in the Playground at http://mng.bz/m454.

The next script shows another example of the generic function. This time we'll map the members of a string enumeration to the user roles returned by a function. Imagine that an authorization mechanism returns one of the following user roles: admin or manager. We want to use string enums and map the user roles to the corresponding members of this enum.

First, we'll declare a custom `User` type:

```
interface User {
    name: string;
    role: UserRole;
}
```

Then we'll create a string enum that lists a limited set of constants that can be used as user roles.

```
enum UserRole {
    Administrator = 'admin',
    Manager = 'manager'
}
```

Next, we'll create a function that loads the object with a hardcoded user name and its role. In real-world apps, we'd make a request to some authorization server, supplying a user ID to get the user's role, but for our purposes, returning a hardcoded object will suffice.

```
function loadUser<T>(): T {
    return JSON.parse('{ "name": "john", "role": "admin" }');
}
```

The following listing shows a generic function that returns the User and then maps the received user role to an action using the string enum.

Listing 4.18 Mapping string enums

```
interface User {                    <— Declares a custom User type
    name: string;
    role: UserRole;
}

enum UserRole {                     <— Declares a string enum
    Administrator = 'admin',
    Manager = 'manager'
}

function loadUser<T>(): T {         <— Declares a generic function
    return JSON.parse('{ "name": "john", "role": "admin" }');
}

const user = loadUser<User>();      <— Invokes the generic function with a concrete User type

switch (user.role) {                <— Switches on the user role with a string enum
    case UserRole.Administrator: console.log('Show control panel'); break;
    case UserRole.Manager: console.log('Hide control panel'); break;
}
```

The script in listing 4.18 uses the User type during the invocation of loadUser(), and the generic type T declared as the return type of this function becomes the concrete type User. Note that the hardcoded object returned by this function has the same structure as the User interface.

Here, `user.role` will always be `admin`, which maps to the enum member `UserRole.Administrator`, and the script will print "Show control panel." You can see this script in action on CodePen at http://mng.bz/5Aqa.

TIP In chapter 10 (listing 10.15), you'll see the code of a `MessageServer` class that uses a generic `<T>` type in several methods.

4.2.4 Enforcing the return type of higher-order functions

If a function can receive a function as an argument or return another function, we call it a *higher-order function.* In this section we'll show you an example that enforces the return type of a higher-order function while allowing arguments of different types.

Let's say we need to write a higher-order function that returns a function with the following signature:

```
(c: number) => number
```

This fat arrow function takes a number as an argument and returns a number. The higher-order function (we'll use fat arrow notation) might look like this:

```
(someValue: number) => (multiplier: number) => someValue * multiplier;
```

We didn't write the `return` statement after the first fat arrow because in single-line fat arrow functions, return is implicit. The following listing shows the use of such a function.

Listing 4.19 Using a higher-order function

```
const outerFunc = (someValue: number) =>
    (multiplier: number) => someValue * multiplier;

const innerFunc = outerFunc(10);

let result = innerFunc(5);

console.log(result);
```

- Declares the higher-order function
- innerFunc is a closure that knows that someValue = 10.
- Invokes the returned function
- This will print 50.

Now let's make our task a bit more complex. We want to allow our higher-order function to be called with arguments of different types, ensuring that it always returns a function with the same signature:

```
(c: number) => number
```

Let's start by declaring a generic function that can take a generic type `T` but returns the function `(c: number) ? number`:

```
type numFunc<T> = (arg: T) => (c: number) => number;
```

Now we can declare variables of type `numFunc`, and TypeScript will ensure that these variables are functions of type `(c: number) ? number`.

Listing 4.20 Using the generic `numFunc<T>` function

```
const noArgFunc: numFunc<void> = () =>
        (c: number) => c + 5;
const numArgFunc: numFunc<number> = (someValue: number) =>
                    (multiplier: number) => someValue * multiplier;
const stringArgFunc: numFunc<string> = (someText: string) =>
                   (padding: number) => someText.length + padding;

const createSumString: numFunc<number> = () => (x: number) => 'Hello';
```

- Invokes the function with no arguments (line 1)
- Invokes the function with a numeric argument (line 3)
- Invokes the function with a string argument (line 5)
- Compiler error: numFunc expects another signature (last line)

The last line won't compile because the signature of the returned function is `(c: number) ? string`, which can't be assigned to the variable of type `numFunc`. You can see this example in the Playground at http://mng.bz/6wqA.

Summary

- TypeScript has an `enum` keyword that can define a limited set of constants.
- TypeScript supports numeric and string enums.
- If you use the `const` keyword while declaring an `enum`, its values will be inlined and no JavaScript will be generated.
- A generic is a piece of code that can handle values of multiple types that are specified when the code is used.
- You can create your own generic classes, interfaces, and functions.

5 Decorators and advanced types

This chapter covers

- What the TypeScript decorators are for
- How to create a new type based on an existing one using mapped types
- How conditional types work
- Combining mapped and conditional types

In previous chapters, we covered the main types, which should be sufficient for most of your coding activities. But TypeScript goes further and offers you additional derivative types that can be quite handy in certain scenarios.

We used the word "advanced" in this chapter's title for a couple of reasons. First, you don't have to know these types to be a productive member of your team. Second, their syntax may not be immediately obvious to a software developer who's familiar with other programming languages.

The title of this book is *TypeScript Quickly*, and the content in the first four chapters deliver on the promise to introduce the main syntax constructs of the language at a fast pace. But you may need to read this chapter more then once.

The good news is that learning the advanced types presented in this chapter is not required to understand the rest of this book. You can skip them if you need to learn the language quickly. You may want to study this chapter if:

- It's time to prepare for your next technical interview, where rarely used knowledge is expected.
- You look at some specific code and have a gut feeling that there should be a more elegant solution.
- You're curious to learn what else is available, as if dealing with interfaces, generics, and enums is not enough.

NOTE In this chapter, we'll use the syntax of *generics* a lot, and we assume that you've read and understand the materials from section 4.2, related to the syntax of generics. That's a must for understanding the mapped and conditional types described in this chapter.

5.1 Decorators

TypeScript's documentation defines a *decorator* as

> *a special kind of declaration that can be attached to a class declaration, method, accessor, property, or parameter. Decorators use the form* `@expression`*, where* `expression` *must evaluate to a function that will be called at runtime with information about the decorated declaration.*
>
> —"Decorators" in the Typescript documentation (www.typescriptlang.org/docs/handbook/decorators.html)

Say you have `class A {…}`, and there's a magic decorator called `@Injectable()` that knows how to instantiate classes and inject their instances into other objects. We could decorate one of our classes like this:

```
@Injectable() class A {}
```

As you can guess, the `@Injectable()` decorator will somehow change the behavior of `class A`. Alternatively, we could change the behavior of `class A` without modifying its code by creating a subclass of `class A` and adding or overriding the behavior there. But simply adding a decorator to the class definition looks more elegant.

We could also say that a decorator adds *metadata* to a specific target, which is `class A` in our example. In general, metadata is additional data about some other data. Take an mp3 file—we can say that the song is the data. But the mp3 file may have additional properties, like the name of the artist and album, an image, and so on—this is the metadata of the mp3 file. Thus you can use decorators to annotate a TypeScript class with metadata describing additional features you'd like this class to have.

Names of TypeScript decorators start with the `@` sign, such as `@Component`. You can write your own decorators, but it's more likely that you'll use the decorators available in a library or framework.

Consider the following simple class:

```
class OrderComponent {
  quantity: number;
}
```

Imagine that you want to turn this class into a UI component. Moreover, you want to declare that the value for the `quantity` property will be provided by the parent component. If you were using the Angular framework with TypeScript, you could use the built-in `@Component()` decorator for a class and `@Input()` for a property.

Listing 5.1 An example of an Angular component

```
@Component({                                         // Applies the @Component decorator
  selector: 'order-processor',                       // This component can be used in HTML as <order-processor>.
  template: `Buying {{quantity}} items`              // The browser should render this text.
})
export class OrderComponent {

  @Input() quantity: number;                         // The value for this input property is provided by the parent component.
}
```

In Angular, the `@Component()` decorator can be applied only to a class, and it supports various properties, such as `selector` and `template`. The `@Input()` decorator can be applied only to the properties of a class. We could also say that these two decorators provided metadata about the `OrderComponent` class and the `quantity` property respectively.

To make decorators useful, there should be some code that knows how to parse them and to do what these decorators prescribe. In the example from listing 5.1, the Angular framework would parse these decorators and generate additional code to turn the `OrderComponent` class into a renderable UI component.

> **NOTE** In chapters 11 and 12, we'll be working with the Angular framework, and you'll see many examples of using decorators there. Decorators are heavily used by the server-side Nest.js framework (https://docs.nestjs.com/custom-decorators), state management MobX library (https://mobx.js.org/refguide/modifiers.html), and Stencil.js UI library (https://stenciljs.com/docs/decorators).

TypeScript doesn't come with any built-in decorators, but you can create your own or use the ones provided by a framework or library of your choice.

The decorators in listing 5.1 allowed you to specify additional behavior for the class and its property in a concise and declarative manner. Of course, using decorators is not the only way to add behavior to an object. For example, the creators of Angular could have created an abstract `UIComponent` class with a particular constructor and forced developers to extend it every time they wanted to turn a class into a UI component. But using decorator components is a nicer, more readable and declarative solution.

Decorators (unlike inheritance) separate the concerns and facilitate easier code maintenance, since the framework is free to interpret them as it wants. In contrast, if a component was a subclass, it could override or just expect or rely on certain behavior of the methods in the superclass.

> **NOTE** There is a proposal to add decorators to JavaScript. The proposal is currently a Stage 2 draft (https://tc39.github.io/proposal-decorators).

Although decorators were introduced back in 2015, they are still considered an experimental feature, and you have to compile your app with the `--experimentalDecorators` tsc option. If you use tsconfig.json, add the following compiler option there:

```
"experimentalDecorators": true
```

A decorator can be used to observe or modify the definition of the target (a class, method, and so on), and the signatures of these special functions (the decorators) differ depending on what the target is. In this chapter, we'll show you how to create class and method decorators.

5.1.1 Creating class decorators

A class decorator is applied to a class, and the decorator function is executed when the constructor executes. A class decorator requires one parameter—a constructor function for the class. In other words, a class decorator will receive the constructor function of the decorated class.

The following listing declares a class decorator that just logs information about the class on the console.

Listing 5.2 Declaring a custom `whoAmI` decorator

Declares the decorator, which takes a constructor function as an argument

```
function whoAmI (target: Function): void {
  console.log(`You are: \n ${target}`)
}
```

Logs the target class information

> **NOTE** If the return type of a class decorator is `void`, this function doesn't return any value (see section 2.1.1). Such a decorator won't replace the class declaration—it'll just observe the class, as in listing 5.3. But a decorator can modify a class declaration, in which case it would need to return the modified version of the class (the constructor function), and we'll show you how to do that at the end of this section.

To use the `whoAmI` decorator, just prepend the class name with `@whoAmI`. The constructor function of the class will be automatically provided for the decorator. In our example, the constructor has two arguments: a string and number.

Listing 5.3 Applying the decorator `whoAmI` to a class

```
@whoAmI
class Friend {

  constructor(private name: string, private age: number){}
}
```

When the TypeScript code is transpiled into JavaScript, tsc checks if any decorators were applied, in which case it will generate additional JavaScript code that will be used at runtime.

You can run this code sample in the Playground at http://mng.bz/omop. You'll need to turn on the `experimentalDecorators` config option and click the Run button. It will run the JavaScript version of the code, producing the following output on the browser's console:

```
You are:
function Friend(name, age) {
  this.name = name;
  this.age = age;
}
```

> **TIP** To see the effect of the `@whoAmI` decorator on the generated code in the Playground, remove the decorator from the `Friend` class declaration and note the difference in the JavaScript that's generated.

You may think that the `@whoAmI` decorator is not overly useful, so let's create another one. Say you're developing a UI framework and want to allow classes to be turned into UI components in a declarative way. You want to create a function that takes an arbitrary argument, such as an HTML string for rendering.

Listing 5.4 Declaring a custom `UIcomponent` decorator

```
function UIcomponent (html: string) {
    console.log(`The decorator received ${html} \n`);

  return function(target: Function) {
      console.log(`Someone wants to create a UI component from \n ${target} `);
  }
}
```

- This decorator factory has an argument.
- Prints the string received by the decorator
- This is a decorator function.

Here you see a decorator function inside another function. We can call the outer function *a decorator factory*. It can take any arguments and apply some app logic to decide which decorator to return. In this case, listing 5.4 has just one `return` statement, and this code always returns the same decorator function, but nothing stops you from conditionally returning the decorator you need based on the parameters provided to the factory function.

NOTE A bit later, in the sidebar titled "Formal declarations of decorator signatures," you'll see that the requirements for decorator signatures depend on what they decorate. So how were we able to use an arbitrary argument in the `UIComponent()` function? The reason is that `UIComponent()` is not a decorator, but a decorator factory that returns a decorator with the proper `function (target: Function)` signature.

The next listing shows the `Shopper` class decorated as `UIcomponent`.

Listing 5.5 Applying a custom `UIcomponent` decorator

```
@UIcomponent('<h1>Hello Shopper!</h1>')       ◁— Passes HTML to the decorator
class Shopper {

  constructor(private name: string) {}         ◁— A class constructor that
                                                   takes a shopper's name
}
```

Running this code will produce the following output:

```
The decorator received <h1>Hello Shopper!</h1>

Someone wants to create a UI component from
function Shopper(name) {
        this.name = name;
}
```

You can see this code in action on CodePen at http://mng.bz/nv62.

So far, all our decorator examples observed the classes—they didn't modify class declarations. In the next example, we'll show you a decorator that does. But first, we'll show you a constructor mixin.

In JavaScript, a *mixin* is a piece of code that implements a certain behavior. Mixins are not meant to be used alone, but their behavior can be added to other classes. Although JavaScript doesn't support multiple inheritance, you can compose behaviors from multiple classes using mixins.

If a mixin has no constructor, mixing its code with other classes comes down to copying its properties and methods to the target class. But if a mixin has its own constructor, it needs to be capable of taking any number of parameters of any type; otherwise it wouldn't be "mixable" with arbitrary constructors of target classes.

TypeScript supports a *constructor mixin* that has the following signature:

```
{ new(...args: any[]): {} }
```

It uses a single rest argument (three dots) of type `any[]` and can be mixed with other classes that have constructors. Let's declare a type alias for this mixin:

```
type constructorMixin = { new(...args: any[]): {} };
```

Accordingly, the following signature represents a generic type `T` that extends `constructorMixin`; in TypeScript, this also means that type `T` is assignable to the `constructorMixin` type:

```
<T extends constructorMixin>
```

You'll use this signature to create a class decorator that modifies the original constructor of a class. The class decorator signature will look like this:

```
function <T extends constructorMixin> (target: T) {
   // the decorator is implemented here
}
```

Now we're prepared to write a decorator that modifies the declaration (and constructor) of a target class. Let's say we have the following `Greeter` class.

Listing 5.6 Undecorated `Greeter` class

```
class Greeter {
  constructor(public name: string) { }
  sayHello() { console.log(`Hello ${this.name} `) };
}
```

We can instantiate and use it like this:

```
const grt = new Greeter('John');
grt.sayHello();  // prints "Hello John"
```

We want to create a decorator that can accept a `salutation` parameter, and add to the class a new `message` property, concatenating the given salutation and name. Also, we want to change the code of the `sayHello()` method so that it prints the `message`.

The following listing shows a *higher-order function* (a function that returns a function) that implements our decorator. We can also call it a *factory function* because it constructs and returns a function.

Listing 5.7 Declaring the `useSalutation` decorator

```
function useSalutation(salutation: string) {      // A factory function that takes one parameter—salutation

  return function <T extends constructorMixin> (target: T) {      // The decorator's body
    return class extends target {      // Redeclares the decorated class
     name: string;
     private message = 'Hello ' + salutation + this.name;      // Adds a private property to the new class

     sayHello() { console.log(`${this.message}`); }      // Redeclares the method
    }
  }
}
```

Starting from the `return class extends target` line, we provide another declaration of the decorated class. In particular, we've added a new `message` property to the original class and replaced the body of the `sayHello()` method so that it uses the salutation provided in the decorator.

In the next listing, we use the `@useSalutation` decorator with the `Greeter` class. Invoking `grt.sayHello()` will print "Hello Mr. Smith."

Listing 5.8 Using the decorated `Greeter` class

```
@useSalutation("Mr. ")      <-- Applies the decorator with an argument to the class
class Greeter {

  constructor(public name: string) { }
  sayHello() { console.log(`Hello ${this.name} `) }
}

const grt = new Greeter('Smith');
grt.sayHello();
```

You can see and run this code in the Playground at http://mng.bz/vlM4. Click the Run button and open the browser console to see the output.

It's great that we have such a powerful mechanism for replacing a class declaration, but use it with caution. Avoid changing the public API of a class, because the static type analyzer won't offer autocomplete for decorator-added public properties or methods.

Say you modified the `useSalutation()` decorator so it would add a public `sayGoodbye()` method to the target class. After typing `grt.`, as in listing 5.8, your IDE would still only prompt you with the `sayHello()` method and the `name` property. It wouldn't suggest `sayGoodbye()`, even though typing `grt.sayGoodbye()` will work just fine.

Formal declarations of decorator signatures

A decorator is a function, and its signature depends on the target. Signatures for class and method decorators won't be the same. After you install TypeScript, it will include several files with type declarations. One of them is called lib.es5.d.ts, and it includes type declarations for decorators for various targets:

```
declare type ClassDecorator =      <-- The signature for a class decorator
      <TFunction extends Function>(target: TFunction) =>
➥ TFunction | void;
declare type PropertyDecorator =      <-- The signature for a property decorator
      (target: Object, propertyKey: string | symbol) => void;
declare type MethodDecorator =      <-- The signature for a method decorator
      <T>(target: Object, propertyKey: string | symbol,
       descriptor: TypedPropertyDescriptor<T>) =>
➥ TypedPropertyDescriptor<T> | void;
declare type ParameterDecorator =      <-- The signature for a parameter decorator
      (target: Object, propertyKey: string | symbol,
➥ parameterIndex: number) => void;
```

In section 4.2.3, we explained generic functions and the syntax for named functions as well as fat arrow functions. That section should help you in understanding the signatures shown in the preceding code. Consider the following line:

```
<T>(someParam: T) => T | void
```

That's right—it declares that a fat arrow function can take a parameter of a generic type `T` and return either the value of type `T` or `void`. Now let's try to read the declaration of the `ClassDecorator` signature:

```
<TFunction extends Function>(target: TFunction) => TFunction | void
```

It declares that a fat arrow function can take a parameter of a generic type `TFunction`, which has an additional constraint: the concrete type must be a subtype of `Function`. Any TypeScript class is a subtype of `Function`, which represents a constructor function. In other words, the target for this decorator must be a class, and the decorator can either return a value of this class's type or return no value.

Take another look at the `@whoAmI` class decorator shown in listing 5.2. We didn't use a fat arrow expression there, but that function had the following signature, which is allowed for class decorators:

```
function whoAmI (target: Function): void
```

Because the signature of the `whoAmI()` function doesn't return a value, we can say that this decorator just *observes* the target. If you wanted to modify the original target in the decorator, you'd need to return the modified class, but its type would be the same as that originally provided in lieu of `TFunction` (a subtype of `Function`).

5.1.2 Creating method decorators

Now let's create a decorator that can be applied to a class's method. For example, you may want to create a `@deprecated` decorator to mark methods that will be removed soon. As you can see in the sidebar titled "Formal declarations of decorator signatures," the `MethodDecorator` function requires three parameters:

- `target`—An object that refers to the instantiated class that defines the method
- `propertyKey`—The name of the method being decorated
- `descriptor`—A descriptor of the method being decorated

The `descriptor` parameter contains an object describing the method that your code is decorating. Specifically, `TypedPropertyDescriptor` has a `value` property that stores the original code of the decorated method. By changing the value of this property inside the method's decorator, you can modify the original code of the decorated method.

Let's consider a `Trader` class that has a `placeOrder()` method:

```
class Trade {

  placeOrder(stockName: string, quantity: number, operation:
➥ string, traderID: number) {
```

```
      // the method implementation goes here
    }
  // other methods go here
}
```

Say there's a trader with the ID 123, and she can place an order to buy 100 shares of IBM as follows:

```
const trade = new Trade();
trade.placeOrder('IBM', 100, 'Buy', 123);
```

This code has worked fine for years, but a new regulation came in: "For audit purposes, all trades must be logged." One way to do this is to go through all methods related to buying or selling financial products, which may have different parameters, and add code that logs their invocations. But creating a `@logTrade` method decorator that works with any method and logs the parameters would be a more elegant solution. The following listing shows the code of the `@logTrade` method decorator.

Listing 5.9 The `@logTrade` method decorator

```
function logTrade(target, key, descriptor) {      // The method decorator must have three arguments.

    const originalCode = descriptor.value;        // Stores the original method's code

    descriptor.value = function () {              // Modifies the code of the method being decorated

      console.log(`Invoked ${key} providing:`, arguments);
      return originalCode.apply(this, arguments);   // Invokes the target method
    };

  return descriptor;        // Returns the modified method
}
```

We stored the original method's code and then modified the received descriptor by adding a `console.log()` statement. Then we used the JavaScript function `apply()` to invoke the decorated method. Finally, we returned the modified method descriptor.

In the following listing we applied the `@logTrade` decorator to the method `placeOrder()`. No matter how `placeOrder()` is implemented, its decorated version will start by printing this message: "Invoked placeOrder providing:".

Listing 5.10 Using the `@logTrade` decorator

```
class Trade {

  @logTrade        // Decorates the placeOrder() method
  placeOrder(stockName: string, quantity: number,
```

```
            operation: string, tradedID: number) {

        // the method implementation goes here
    }
}

const trade = new Trade();
trade.placeOrder('IBM', 100, 'Buy', 123);    <-- Invokes placeOrder()
```

You can run a sample implementation of the preceding code in the TypeScript Playground at http://mng.bz/4e7j.

After invoking the decorated `placeOrder()` method, the console output will look similar to this:

```
Invoked placeOrder providing:
Arguments(4)
0: "IBM"
1: 100
2: "Buy"
3: 123
```

By creating a method decorator, we eliminated the need to update the code of potentially many trade-related methods that require auditing. Besides, the `@logTrade` decorator can work with methods that haven't even been written yet.

We've shown you how to write class and method decorators, which should give you a good foundation for mastering property and parameter decorators on your own.

5.2 Mapped types

Mapped types allow you to create new types from existing ones. This is done by applying a transformation function to an existing type. Let's see how they work.

5.2.1 The Readonly mapped type

Imagine that you need to pass objects of type `Person` (shown next) to the `doStuff()` function for processing:

```
interface Person {
  name: string;
  age: number;
}
```

The `Person` type is used in multiple places, but you don't want to allow the `doStuff()` function to accidentally modify some of the Person's properties, like `age` in the following listing.

Listing 5.11 The unlawful change of the age

```
const worker: Person = {name: "John", age: 22};

function doStuff(person: Person) {

    person.age = 25;          <-- We don't want to allow this.
}
```

No properties of the Person type were declared with the readonly modifier. Should we declare another type just to be used with doStuff(), as follows?

```
interface ReadonlyPerson {
  readonly name: string;
  readonly age: number;
}
```

Do you need to declare (and maintain) a new type each time you need a read-only version of an existing one? There's a better solution. We can use a built-in mapped type, Readonly, to turn all the properties of a previously declared type to be readonly. We just need to change the signature of the doStuff() function to take an argument of type Readonly<Person> instead of Person.

Listing 5.12 Using the mapped type Readonly

```
const worker: Person = {name: "John", age: 22};

function doStuff(person: Readonly<Person>) {    <-- Modifies the existing type with
                                                    the mapped type Readonly
    person.age = 25;          <-- This line generates a compiler error.
}
```

To understand why an attempt to change the value of the age property generates a compiler error, you need to see how the Readonly type is declared, which in turn requires an understanding of the keyof lookup type.

KEYOF AND A LOOKUP TYPE

Reading the declarations of the built-in mapped types in the typescript/lib/lib.es5.d.ts file can help you understand their inner workings, but it requires some familiarity with TypeScript's *index type query* keyof and a *lookup type*.

You can find the following declaration of the Readonly mapping function in lib.es5.d.ts:

Listing 5.13 The declaration of the Readonly mapped type

```
type Readonly<T> = {
  readonly [P in keyof T]: T[P];
};
```

We assume that you've read about generics in chapter 4, and that you know what <T> in angle brackets means. Usually the letter T in generics represents *type*: K for key, V for value, P for property, and so on.

keyof is also called an *index type query*, and it represents a union of allowed property names (the keys) of the given type. If the type Person is our T, then keyof T would represent a union of name and age. Figure 5.1 shows a screenshot taken while hovering the mouse over the propNames custom type. As you can see, the type of propName is a union of name and age.

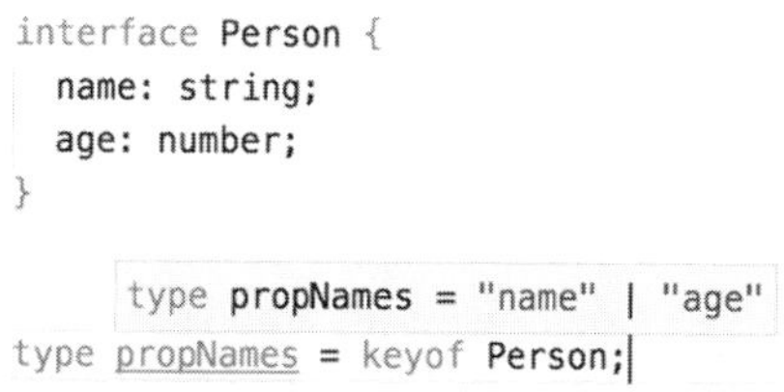

```
interface Person {
  name: string;
  age: number;
}

    type propNames = "name" | "age"
type propNames = keyof Person;
```

Figure 5.1 Applying keyof to the Person type

In listing 5.13, the fragment [P in keyof T] means "give me the union of all the properties of the given type T." This fragment looks as if we're accessing the elements of some object, but actually, this is done to declare types. The keyof type query can be used only in type declarations.

We now know how to get access to the property names of a given type, but to create a mapped type from an existing one, we also need to know the property types. In case of the Person type we need to be able to find out programmatically that the property types are string and number.

This is what *lookup types* are for. The piece T[P] (from listing 5.13) is a lookup type, and it means "Give me the type of a property P." Figure 5.2 shows a screenshot taken while hovering the mouse over the propTypes type. The types of the properties are string and number.

```
type propNames = keyof Person;

    type propTypes = string | number
type propTypes = Person[propNames];
```

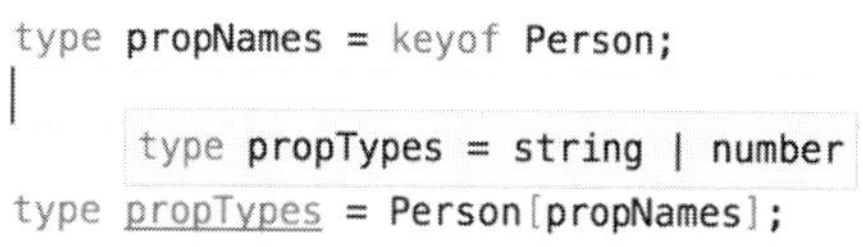

Figure 5.2 Getting the types of Person's properties

Now let's read the code in listing 5.13 one more time. The declaration of the Readonly<T> type means "Find the names and types of the properties of the provided concrete type, and apply the readonly qualifier to each property." In our example, Readonly<Person> will create a mapped type that will look like the following.

Listing 5.14 Applying the Readonly mapped type to the Person type

```
interface Person {
  readonly name: string;
  readonly age: number;
}
```

Now you can see why an attempt to modify the person's age results in the compiler error "Cannot assign to age because it's a read-only property." Basically, we took an existing type, Person, and mapped it to a similar type but with read-only properties. You can see that this code won't compile in the Playground at http://mng.bz/Q05v.

You may say, "OK, I understand how to apply the mapped type `Readonly`, but what's the practical use of it?" Later, in listing 10.16, you'll see two methods that use the `Readonly` type with their message argument, something like this:

```
replyTo(client: WebSocket, message: Readonly<T>): void
```

This method can send messages to blockchain nodes over the WebSocket protocol. The messaging server doesn't know what types of messages will be sent, and the message type is generic. To prevent accidental modification of the message inside `replyTo()`, we use the `Readonly` mapped type there.

Let's consider one more code sample that illustrates the benefits of using `keyof` and `T[P]`. Imagine we need to write a function to filter a generic array of objects, keeping only those that have a specified value in a specified property. In the first version, we won't use type checking and will write the function as follows.

Listing 5.15 A poor version of `filterBy()`

```
function filterBy<T>(
  property: any,
  value: any,
  array: T[]) {

  return array.filter(item => item[property] === value);
}
```

Keeps only those objects that have the provided value in the specified property

Calling this function with a non-existing property name or the wrong value type will result in hard-to-find bugs.

The following listing declares a `Person` type and function. The last two lines invoke the function, providing either a non-existing `lastName` property or the wrong type for `age`.

Listing 5.16 A buggy version of `filterBy()`

```
interface Person {
    name: string;
    age: number;
}

const persons: Person[] = [
    { name: 'John', age: 32 },
    { name: 'Mary', age: 33 },
];

function filterBy<T>(
    property: any,
    value: any,
    array: T[]) {

    return array.filter(item => item[property] === value);
}
```

This function doesn't do any type checking.

Filters data based on the property/value

```
console.log(filterBy('name', 'John', persons));          <-- A correct invocation of the function

console.log(filterBy('lastName', 'John', persons));      <-- An incorrect invocation of the function

console.log(filterBy('age', 'twenty', persons));         <-- An incorrect invocation of the function
```

Both of the last two code lines will return zero objects without any complaints, even though the `Person` type has no `lastName` property and the type of the `age` property is not a string. In other words, the code in listing 5.16 is buggy.

Let's change the signature of the `filterBy()` function so it catches these bugs at compile time. The new version of `filterBy()` is shown in the following listing.

Listing 5.17 A better version of `filterBy()`

```
function filterBy<T, P extends keyof T>(     <-- Checks that the provided property, P, belongs to the union [keyof T]
    property: P,                             <-- The property to filter by
    value: T[P],                             <-- A value for filtering must be of the type of the provided property, P
    array: T[]) {

    return array.filter(item => item[property] === value);
}
```

First of all, the fragment `<T, P extends keyof T>` tells us that our function accepts two generic values: `T` and `P`. We also added a restriction that `P extends keyof T`. In other words, `P` must be one of the properties of the provided type `T`. If the concrete type of `T` is `Person`, then `P` can be either `name` or `age`.

The function signature in listing 5.17 has yet another restriction, `value: T[P]`, which means the provided value must be of the same type as that declared for `P` in type `T`. That's why the following lines will give compile errors.

Listing 5.18 These lines won't compile

```
filterBy('lastName', 'John', persons)     <-- Non-existing lastName property
filterBy('age', 'twenty', persons)        <-- The value of age must be a number.
```

As you see, introducing `keyof` and a lookup type in the function signature allows you to catch possible errors at compile time. You can see this code sample in action in the TypeScript Playground at http://mng.bz/XpXa.

5.2.2 Declaring your own mapped types

Listing 5.13 shows the transformation function for the built-in `Readonly` mapped type. You can define your own transformation functions using similar syntax.

Let's try to define a `Modifiable` type—the opposite of `Readonly`. In the previous section, we took a `Person` type and made all of its properties read-only by applying the `Readonly` mapped type: `Readonly<Person>`. Now suppose the properties of the `Person` type were originally declared with the `readonly` modifier as follows:

```
interface Person {
  readonly name: string;
  readonly age: number;
}
```

How could you remove the `readonly` qualifiers from the `Person` declaration if you needed to? There's no built-in mapped type for that, so let's declare one.

Listing 5.19 Declaring a custom mapped type, `Modifiable`

```
type Modifiable<T> = {
  -readonly[P in keyof T]: T[P];
};
```

The minus sign in front of the `readonly` qualifier removes it from all properties of the given type. Now you can remove the `readonly` restriction from all properties by applying the `Modifiable` mapped type.

Listing 5.20 Applying the `Modifiable` mapped type

```
interface Person {
  readonly name: string;
  readonly age: number;
}

const worker1: Person = {name: "John", age: 25};

worker1.age = 27;              <—— Results in a compiler error

const worker2: Modifiable<Person> = {name: "John", age: 25};

worker2.age = 27;              <—— No errors here
```

You can see this code in the Playground at http://mng.bz/yzed.

5.2.3 Other built-in mapped types

You know that if a property name in a type declaration ends with the modifier `?`, the property is optional. Say we have the following declaration of the `Person` type:

```
interface Person {
  name: string;
  age: number;
}
```

Since none of the property names end with a question mark, providing values for `name` and `age` is mandatory. What if you need a type that has the same properties as `Person`, but all of its properties should be optional? This is what the mapped type `Partial<T>` is for. Its mapping function is declared in lib.es5.d.ts as follows.

Listing 5.21 The declaration of the `Partial` mapped type

```
type Partial<T> = {
    [P in keyof T]?: T[P];
};
```

Have you spotted the question mark there? Basically, we create a new type by appending the question mark to each property name of the given type. The mapped type `Partial` makes all properties in the given type optional.

Figure 5.3 shows a screenshot taken while hovering the mouse over the declaration of the `worker1` variable. It shows an error message because the `worker1` variable has the type `Person`, where each property is required, but the value for `age` was not provided. There are no errors in initializing `worker2` with the same object because the type of this variable is `Partial<Person>`, so all its properties are optional.

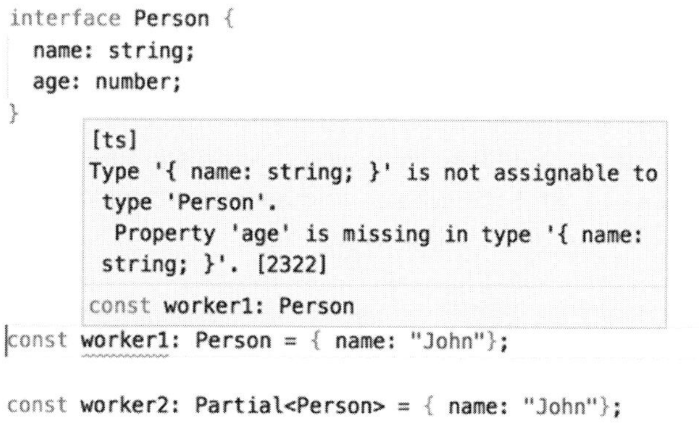

```
interface Person {
  name: string;
  age: number;
}
        [ts]
        Type '{ name: string; }' is not assignable to
         type 'Person'.
          Property 'age' is missing in type '{ name:
         string; }'. [2322]
        const worker1: Person
const worker1: Person = { name: "John"};

const worker2: Partial<Person> = { name: "John"};
```

Figure 5.3 Applying the `Partial` type

You can now make all properties of a type optional, but can you do the opposite? Can you take a type that was declared with some optional properties, and make all of them required? You bet! This can be done with the `Required` mapped type, which is declared as follows:

```
type Required<T> = {
    [P in keyof T]-?: T[P];
};
```

The `-?` means it's removing the modifier `?`.

Figure 5.4 shows a screenshot taken while hovering the mouse over the declaration of the `worker2` variable. The properties `age` and `name` were optional in the `Person`

```
interface Person {
  name?: string;
  age?: number;
}

const worker1: Person = { name: "John"};

    [ts] 'worker2' is declared but its value is n
    ever read. [6133]
    [ts] Property 'age' is missing in type '{ nam
    e: string; }' but required in type 'Required<
    Person>'. [2741]
    • main.ts(92, 3): 'age' is declared here.
    const worker2: Required<Person>
const worker2: Required<Person> = { name: "John"};
```

Figure 5.4 Applying the `Required` type

base type but they're required in the `Required<Person>` mapped type. Hence the error about the missing age.

> **TIP** The `Required` type was introduced in TypeScript 2.8. If your IDE doesn't recognize this type, make sure it uses the proper version of the TypeScript language service. In Visual Studio Code you can see the version in the bottom-right corner. Click on it to change to a newer version if you have one installed.

You can apply more than one mapped type to a given type. In the following listing, we apply `Readonly` and `Partial` to the `Person` type. The former will make each property read-only, and the latter will make each property optional.

Listing 5.22 Applying more than one mapped type

```
interface Person {
   name: string;
   age: number;
}

const worker1: Readonly<Partial<Person>>
                             = {name: "John"};

worker1.name = "Mary"; // compiler's error
```

- worker1 is still a Person, but its properties are read-only and optional. (`const worker1: Readonly<Partial<Person>>`)
- Initializes the property name but not the optional age (`= {name: "John"};`)
- name is read-only and can be initialized only once. (`worker1.name = "Mary";`)

TypeScript offers yet another useful mapped type called `Pick`. It allows you to declare a new type by picking a subset of properties of the given type. Its transformation function looks like this:

```
type Pick<T, K extends keyof T> = {
    [P in K]: T[P];
};
```

The first argument expects an arbitrary type, `T`, and the second expects a subset, `K`, of the properties of `T`. You can read it as "from `T`, pick a set of properties whose keys are in the union `K`." The next listing shows the `Person` type, which has three properties. With the help of `Pick`, we declare a `PersonNameAddress` mapped type that has two string properties: `name` and `address`.

Listing 5.23 Using the `Pick` mapped type

```
interface Person {          ⊲ Declares the Person type
  name: string;               with three properties
  age: number;
  address: string;
}

type PersonNameAddress<T, K> = Pick<Person, 'name' | 'address' >;   ⊲ Declares the PersonNameAddress mapped type with two properties
```

You may be thinking, "The discussion of built-in mapped types is good, and they do seem to be useful, but do I need to know how to implement my own?" The answer is yes, and you'll see examples of using the `Pick` mapped type to define a custom mapped type shortly in figure 5.5 and later on in chapter 10 in the sidebar titled "Examples of conditional and mapped types."

Mapped types allow you to modify existing types, but TypeScript offers yet another way of changing a type based on some condition. We'll look at this next.

5.3 Conditional types

With mapped types the transformation function is always the same, but with conditional types the transformation depends on a specific condition.

Many programming languages, including JavaScript and TypeScript, support conditional (ternary) expressions:

```
a < b ? doSomething() : doSomethingElse()
```

If the value of a is less than b, this code line invokes the function `doSomething()`, otherwise it invokes `doSomethingElse()`. This expression *checks the values* and conditionally executes different code. A conditional type would similarly use a conditional expression, but it would *check the expression's type.*

A conditional type will always be declared in the following form:

```
T extends U ? X : Y
```

Here, `extends U` means "inherits from U" or "is U." As with generics, these letters can represent any types.

In object-oriented programming, the declaration `class Cat extends Animal` means that `Cat` is `Animal` and `Cat` has the same (or more) features as `Animal`. Another way to put it is that a cat is a more specific version of an animal. This also means that the `Cat` object can be assigned to a variable of type `Animal`.

But can an `Animal` object be assigned to a variable of type `Cat`? No, it can't. Every cat is an animal, but not every animal is a cat.

Similarly, the expression `T extends U ?` checks if `T` is assignable to `U`. If this is true, we'll use type `X`, and otherwise type `Y`. The expression `T extends U` means that the value of type `T` can be assigned to a variable of type `U`.

> **TIP** We already mentioned *assignable* types while discussing listings 2.20 and 3.6. Look back to those discussions if you need a refresher.

Let's consider a function that can have different return types based on some condition. Specifically, we want to write a `getProducts()` function that should return the type `Product` if a numeric product ID was provided as an argument. Otherwise, this function has to return a `Product[]` array. Using conditional types, the signature of this function could look like this:

```
function getProducts<T>(id?: T):
  T extends number ? Product : Product[]
```

If the type of the argument is `number`, then the return type of this function is `Product`; otherwise `Product[]`.

The following listing includes a sample implementation of such a function. If the provided optional `id` is a number, we return one product; if not, we return an array of two products.

Listing 5.24 A function with a conditional return type

```
class Product {
  id: number;
 }

const getProducts = function<T>(id?: T):
          T extends number ? Product : Product[] {     ⇽ Declares a conditional return type

     if (typeof id === 'number') {            ⇽ Checks the type of the provided argument
       return { id: 123 } as any;
     } else {
       return [{ id: 123 }, {id: 567}] as any;
     }
}

const result1 = getProducts(123);    ⇽ Invokes the function with a numeric argument

const result2 = getProducts();    ⇽ Invokes the function with no arguments
```

The type of the `result1` variable is `Product`, and the type of `result2` is `Product[]`. You can see it for yourself by hovering the mouse pointer over these variables in the Playground at http://mng.bz/MOqB.

In listing 5.24, we used the `as` type assertion, which tells TypeScript that it shouldn't be inferring the type because you know about this type better than TypeScript does. The `as any` means "TypeScript, don't complain about this type." The problem is that the narrowed type of `id` is not picked up by the conditional type, so the function can't evaluate the condition and narrow the return type to `Product`.

Section 3.1.6 had a similar example, where we implemented a `getProducts()` function that could be invoked with or without an argument (see listing 3.9). There, `getProducts()` was implemented using method overloading.

Conditional types can be used in many different scenarios. Let's discuss another use case.

TypeScript has a built-in conditional `Exclude` type, which allows you to discard the specified types. `Exclude` is declared in the lib.es5.d.ts file as follows:

```
type Exclude<T, U> = T extends U ? never : T;
```

This type excludes types that are assignable to `U`. Note the use of the type `never`, which means "this should never exist; filter it out." If the type `T` is not assignable to `U`, then keep it.

Let's say we have a `Person` class, and we use this class in multiple places in the app for the popular TV show *The Voice*:

```
class Person {
  id: number;
  name: string;
  age: number;
}
```

All the vocalists must go through blind auditions, where the judges can't see them and know nothing about them. For these auditions, we want to create another type, which is the same as `Person` except it won't have their names or ages. In other words, we want to exclude the `name` and `age` properties from the `Person` type.

From the previous section, you remember that the `keyof` lookup type can give you a list of all properties from a type. Hence, the following type will contain all the properties of `T` except those that belong to the given type `K`:

```
type RemoveProps<T, K> = Exclude<keyof T, K>;
```

Let's create a new type that will be like `Person` minus `name` and `age`:

```
type RemainingProps = RemoveProps<Person, 'name' | 'age'>;
```

In this example, the type `K` is represented by the union `'name' | 'age'`, and the `RemainingProps` type represents the union of the remaining properties, which is only `id` in our example.

Now we can construct a new type that will contain just the `RemainingProperties` with the help of the `Pick` mapped type (which was illustrated previously in listing 5.24).

```
type RemainingProps = RemoveProps<Person, 'name' | 'age'>;
type PersonBlindAuditions = Pick<Person, RemainingProps>;
```

Figure 5.5 shows a screenshot taken while hovering the mouse pointer over the `PersonBlindAuditions` type. You can also see it in the TypeScript Playground at http://mng.bz/adGm.

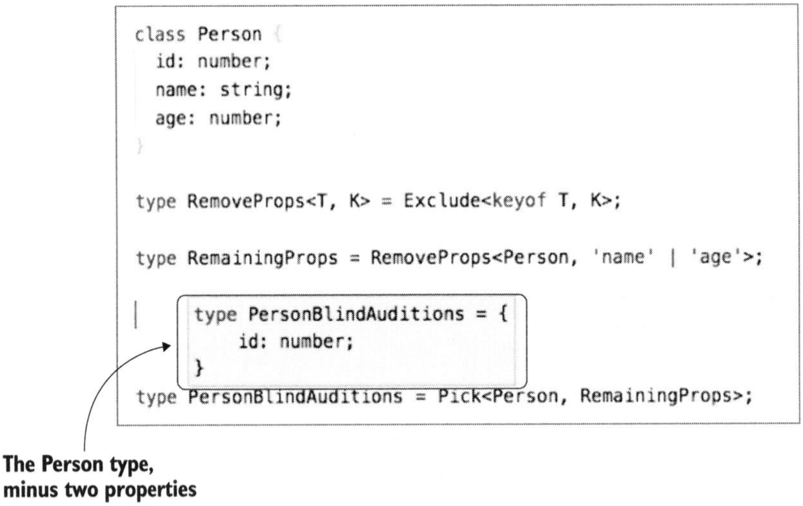

```
class Person {
  id: number;
  name: string;
  age: number;
}

type RemoveProps<T, K> = Exclude<keyof T, K>;

type RemainingProps = RemoveProps<Person, 'name' | 'age'>;

type PersonBlindAuditions = {
    id: number;
}
type PersonBlindAuditions = Pick<Person, RemainingProps>;
```

The Person type, minus two properties

Figure 5.5 Combining `Pick` and `Exclude`

You might say "Wouldn't it be easier to create a separate `PersonBlindAuditions` type that has just the `id` property?" This might be true in this simple case, where the `Person` type has just 3 properties. But a person could be described by 30 properties, and we might want to use it as a base class and create more descriptive conditional types based on it.

Even with our 3-property class, using conditional types can be beneficial. What if some time down the road a developer decides to replace the `name` property with `firstName` and `lastName` in the `Person` class? If you used the `PersonBlindAuditions` conditional type, its declaration would start giving you a compile error, and you'd fix it. But if you didn't declare `PersonBlindAuditions` as a conditional type, and simply created an independent `PersonBlindAuditionsIndie` class, the developer who renamed the properties in `Person` would need to *remember* to replicate the changes in the `PersonBlindAuditionsIndie` class.

Besides, the `RemoveProperties` type is generic. You can use it to remove any properties from any types.

5.3.1 *The infer keyword*

Our next challenge is to try to find the return type of a function and replace it with another one. Let's say we have an interface that declares some properties and methods, and we need to wrap each of the methods into a `Promise` so they run asynchronously. For simplicity, we'll consider a `SyncService` interface, which declares one property, `baseUrl`, and one method, `getA()`:

```
interface SyncService {
    baseUrl: string;
    getA(): string;
}
```

There's nothing to do with the `baseUrl` property as it is, but we want to *promisify* the `getA()` method. Here are the challenges:

- How can we differentiate properties from methods?
- How can we reach out to the original return type of the method before wrapping it into a `Promise`?
- How can we preserve the existing argument types of the methods?

Since we need to differentiate properties from methods, we'll use conditional types; mapped types will help us with modifying method signatures. Our goal is to create a `Promisify` type and apply it to `SyncService`. This way the implementation of `getA()` will have to return a `Promise`. We want to be able to write code as in the following listing.

Listing 5.25 Promisifying synchronous methods

```
class AsyncService
 implements Promisify<SyncService> {     // Maps SyncService to Promisify
    baseUrl: string;                     // No need to modify properties from SyncService

    getA(): Promise<string> {            // The original return type must be wrapped in Promise.
        return Promise.resolve('');
    }
}
```

We want to declare a new `Promisify` mapped type that will loop through all properties of a given type `T` and convert the signatures of its methods so they become asynchronous. The conversion will be done by a conditional type, with the condition being that the type `U` (the supertype of `T`) has to be a function that can take any number of arguments of any types and may return any value:

```
T extends (...args: any[]) => any ?
```

After the question mark, you provide the type to use if `T` is a function; you provide another type after the colon if `T` isn't a function (not shown).

The type `T` must be assignable to a type that looks like a function signature. If the provided type is a function, we want to wrap the return of this function into a `Promise`. The problem is that if we use the type `any`, we'll lose the type information for function arguments as well as the return type.

Let's assume that a generic type `R` represents the return type of the function. Then we can use the `infer` keyword with this variable `R`:

```
T extends (...args: any[]) => infer R ?
```

By writing `infer R`, we instruct TypeScript to check the provided concrete return type (for example, `string` for the `getA()` method) and replace `infer R` with this concrete type. Similarly, we can replace the `any[]` type in the function arguments with `infer A`:

```
T extends (...args: infer A) => infer R ?
```

Now we can declare our conditional type as follows:

```
type ReturnPromise<T> =
    T extends (...args: infer A) => infer R ? (...args: A) => Promise<R> : T;
```

This instructs TypeScript: "If a concrete type for `T` is a function, wrap its return type: `Promise<R>`. Otherwise, just preserve its type `T`." The conditional `ReturnPromise<T>` type can be applied to any type, and if we want to enumerate all the properties of a class, interface, and so on, we can use the `keyof` lookup type to get ahold of all the properties.

If you read section 5.2 on mapped types, the syntax of the next snippet should be familiar to you:

```
type Promisify<T> = {
    [P in keyof T]: ReturnPromise<T[P]>;
};
```

The `Promisify<T>` mapped type will iterate through the properties of `T` and apply to them the conditional `ReturnPromise` type. In our example, we'll do `Promisify<SyncService>`, which won't do anything to the `baseUrl` property, but will change the return type of `getA()` to `Promise<string>`.

Figure 5.6 shows the entire script, which you can also see in the Playground at http://mng.bz/gVWv.

```
type ReturnPromise<T> =
    T extends (...args: infer A) => infer R ? (...args: A) => Promise<R> : T;

type Promisify<T> = {
    [P in keyof T]: ReturnPromise<T[P]>;
};

interface SyncService {
    baseUrl: string;
    getA(): string;
}

class AsyncService implements Promisify<SyncService> {
    baseUrl: string;

    getA(): Promise<string> {
        return Promise.resolve('');
    }
}

let service = new AsyncService();

    let result: Promise<string>
let result = service.getA();
```

Hover over result: it's a type of Promise<string>.

Figure 5.6 Combining conditional and mapped types

Summary

- Using TypeScript decorators, you can add metadata to a class, function, property, or parameter.
- Decorators allow you to modify the type declaration or a behavior of a class, method, property, or parameter. Even if you don't write your own decorators, you need to understand their use if one of the frameworks uses them.
- You can create a type based on another one.
- Mapped types allow you to create apps that have a limited number of basic types and many derived types based on the basic ones.
- Conditional types allow you to postpone making a decision about what type to use; the decision is made at runtime based on some condition.
- These language features are not simple to understand, but they show the power of the language. When we discuss the code of the blockchain app in chapter 10, you'll see the practical use of mapped and conditional types.

6 Tooling

This chapter covers

- Debugging TypeScript code with the help of source maps
- The role of linters
- Compiling and bundling TypeScript apps with Webpack
- Compiling TypeScript apps with Babel
- How to compile TypeScript with Babel and bundle it with Webpack

TypeScript is one of the most loved languages. Yes, people love its syntax. But probably the main reason why it's loved is the tooling. TypeScript developers appreciate autocompletion, those squiggly lines indicating errors as you type, and the refactoring offered by IDEs.

And the best part is that most of these features are implemented by the TypeScript team and not by IDE developers. You'll see the same autocomplete and error messages in the online TypeScript Playground, in Visual Studio Code, or in WebStorm. When you install TypeScript, its bin directory includes two files: tsc and tsserver. The latter is the TypeScript Language Service that IDEs use to support these productivity features. When you type your TypeScript code, the IDEs communicate with tsserver, which compiles the code in memory.

With the help of source map files, you can debug your TypeScript code right in the browser. There are tools called linters; they allow you to enforce the coding styles in your organization.

Type declaration files (.d.ts files) allow tsserver to offer context-sensitive help showing the signatures of available functions or of object properties. Thousands of type declaration files for popular JavaScript libraries are available publicly, and they allow you to be more productive even with code that's not written in TypeScript.

All these conveniences add up and explain why people like TypeScript. But just having a great compiler is not enough for real-world projects, which consist of a diverse set of assets like JavaScript code, CSS, images, and so on. We'll take a look at some essential tools for modern web development: Webpack bundler and Babel. We'll also briefly review the emerging tools ncc and Deno.

6.1 Source maps

Code written in TypeScript gets compiled into the JavaScript, which is executed in a browser or a standalone JavaScript engine. To debug a program, you need to provide its source code to the debugger, but we have two versions of the source code: the executable code is in JavaScript, and the original is in TypeScript. We'd like to debug the TypeScript code, and source map files allow us to do this.

Source map files have .map extensions, and they contain JSON-formatted data that maps the corresponding code in the generated JavaScript to the original language, which in our case is TypeScript. If you decide to debug a running JavaScript program that was written in TypeScript, just have the browser download the source map files generated during compilation, and you'll be able to place breakpoints in the TypeScript code even though the engine runs JavaScript.

Let's take a simple TypeScript program, shown in the following listing, and compile it with the `--sourceMap` generation option turned on. After that, we'll peek inside the generated source map.

Listing 6.1 The greeter.ts file

```
class Greeter {

    static sayHello(name: string) {
        console.log (`Hello ${name}`);     <-- Prints the name on the console
    }
}

Greeter.sayHello('John');     <-- Invokes the sayHello() method
```

Let's compile this file, generating the source map file:

```
tsc greeter.ts --sourceMap true
```

After the compilation is complete, you'll see the files greeter.js and greeter.js.map. The latter is a source map file, a fragment of which is shown in the following listing.

Listing 6.2 The generated source map file, greeter.js.map

```
{"file":"greeter.js",
 "sources":["greeter.ts"],
 "mappings":"AAAA;IAAA;IAMA,CAAC;IAJU,gBAAQ,..."
}
```

This file is not expected to be read by humans, but you can see that it has a `file` property with the name of the generated JavaScript file and a `sources` property with the name of the source TypeScript file. The `mappings` property contains mappings of code fragments in the JavaScript and TypeScript files.

How does the JavaScript engine guess that the name of the file that contains the mapping is greeter.js.map? No guesses are needed. The Typescript compiler simply adds the following line at the end of the generated greeter.js file:

```
//# sourceMappingURL=greeter.js.map
```

Now let's run our little greeter app in the browser and see if we can debug its TypeScript code. First, let's create an HTML file that loads greeter.js:

Listing 6.3 An index.html file that loads greeter.js

```
<!DOCTYPE html>
<html>
  <body>
    <script src="greeter.js"/>      <-- Loads the JavaScript file here, not the TypeScript
  </body>
</html>
```

Next we need a web server that will serve the preceding HTML document to the browser. You can download and install a convenient live-server npm package as follows:

```
npm install -g live-server
```

Finally, start this server in the Terminal window from the directory where the greeter files are located:

```
live-server
```

It'll open the Chrome browser at localhost:8080 and will load the code from index.html (listing 6.3). You'll see a blank page. Open the Chrome Dev Tools in the Sources tab and select the greeter.ts file. In the source code, click to the left of line 5 to place a breakpoint there. The Sources panel should look similar to the one in figure 6.1.

Figure 6.1 Setting a breakpoint in the TypeScript code

Refresh the page, and the execution of this code will stop at the breakpoint, as shown in figure 6.2. You'll be able to use familiar debugger controls, like step forward, step into, and so on.

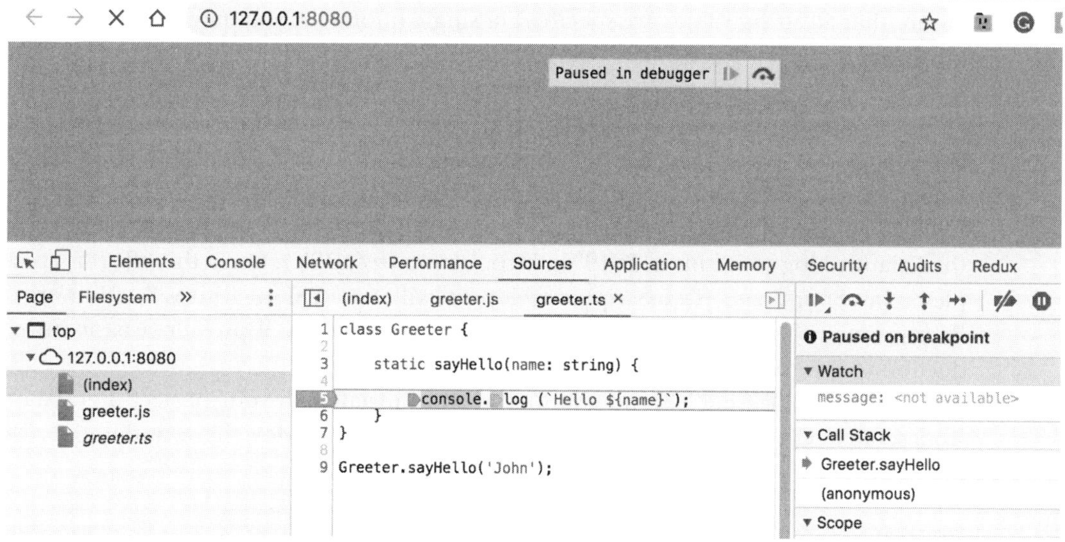

Figure 6.2 The execution paused in the debugger

> **NOTE** Although each IDE comes with its own debugger, we prefer debugging the source code in Chrome Dev Tools. You can even debug code that runs as a standalone Node.js app in Chrome, and we'll explain how to do that in the sidebar "Debugging Node.js code in the browser" at the end of section 10.6.1. (We cover debugging Node.js apps in chapter 10, where you can see a Node.js server used in the blockchain app.)

Now we'll show you the `--inlineSources` Typescript compiler option, which affects the process of generating source maps. With this option, the .js.map file will also include the TypeScript source code of your app. Try compiling the greeter.ts file as follows:

```
tsc greeter.ts  --sourceMap true --inlineSources true
```

It still produces the greeter.js and greeter.js.map files, but the latter now also includes the code from greeter.ts. This option eliminates the need to deploy separate .ts files under your web server, but you can still debug the TypeScript code.

NOTE Deploying files with the .js.map extension in production servers doesn't increase the size of the code downloaded by the browser. The browser downloads the source map files only if the user opens the browser's Dev Tools. The only reason not to deploy the source maps in a production server is if you want to prevent users from reading the source code of your app.

6.2 The TSLint linter

Linters are tools that check and enforce coding style. For example, you may want to ensure that all string values are specified in single quotes, or you may want to disallow unnecessary parentheses. Such restrictions are rules that you can configure in text files.

JavaScript developers use several linters: JSLint, JSHint, and ESLint. TypeScript developers use the TSLint linter, which is an open source project maintained by Palantir (https://palantir.github.io/tslint). There is also a plan to merge TSLint and ESLint to ensure a unified linting experience—you can read more about this effort on the Palantir blog ("TSLint in 2019" at http://mng.bz/eD9V). Once this effort is complete, JavaScript and TypeScript developers will use ESLint (https://eslint.org). Because many TypeScript teams continue to use TSLint, we'll provide a basic introduction to this tool here.

To get started using TSLint, you first need to install it in your project. Let's start from scratch. Create a new directory, open the Terminal window there, and initialize a new npm project with the following command:

```
npm init -y
```

The -y option will silently accept all the default options while creating the package .json file there.

Then install TypeScript and ts-lint there as follows:

```
npm install typescript tslint
```

This will create a node_modules directory and install TypeScript and tslint in it. The tslint executable will be located in the node_modules/.bin directory.

Now create a tslint.json configuration file using the following command:

```
./node_modules/.bin/tslint --init
```

TIP Starting from version 5.2, npm comes with an npx command line that can run executables from node_modules/.bin; for example, `npx tslint --init`. You can read more about this useful command on the npm site at www.npmjs.com/package/npx.

That command will create the tslint.json file with the following content.

Listing 6.4 The generated tslint.json file

```
{
    "defaultSeverity": "error",
    "extends": [
        "tslint:recommended"
    ],
    "jsRules": {},
    "rules": {},
    "rulesDirectory": []
}
```

- "tslint:recommended" — Uses the recommended rules
- "rules": {} — Optional custom rules go here
- "rulesDirectory": [] — An optional directory with custom rules

This configuration file states that tslint should extend the preset recommended rules, which you can find in the node_modules/tslint/lib/configs/recommended.js file. Figure 6.3 shows a snapshot of the recommended.js file.

```
"ordered-imports": {
    options: {
        "import-sources-order": "case-insensitive",
        "module-source-path": "full",
        "named-imports-order": "case-insensitive",
    },
},
"prefer-const": true,
"prefer-for-of": true,
quotemark: {
    options: ["double", "avoid-escape"],
},
radix: true,
semicolon: { options: ["always"] },
"space-before-function-paren": {
    options: {
        anonymous: "never",
        asyncArrow: "always",
        constructor: "never",
        method: "never",
        named: "never",
    },
},
"trailing-comma": {
    options: {
        esSpecCompliant: true,
        multiline: "always",
        singleline: "never",
    },
```

Figure 6.3 A fragment from recommended.js

The rule in lines 126–128 looks like this:

```
quotemark: {
    options: ["double", "avoid-escape"],
},
```

This enforces the use of double quotes around strings. The `"avoid-escape"` rule allows you to use the "other" quote mark in cases where escaping would normally be required. For double quotes, "other" would mean single quotes.

Figure 6.4 shows a screenshot of the WebStorm IDE, showing a linting error on the first line. Although using single quotes around strings is fine with the Typescript compiler, the `quotemark` rule states that in this project you should use single quotes.

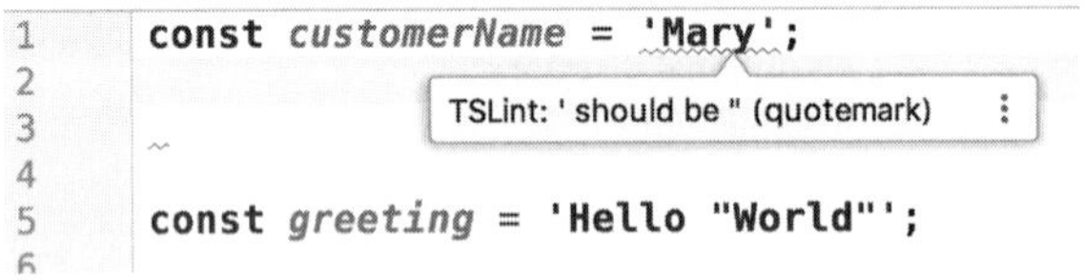

```
1  const customerName = 'Mary';
2                        TSLint: ' should be " (quotemark)
3  ~
4
5  const greeting = 'Hello "World"';
6
```

Figure 6.4 TSLint reports errors

> **TIP** Hover over the TSLint error, and the IDE may offer you an auto-fix.

To avoid using escape characters for a string inside another string in figure 6.4, on line 5 we surrounded "World" with double quotes, and the linter didn't complain because of the `avoid-escape` option.

> **TIP** To enable TSLint in VS Code, install its TSLint extension. Click on the Extension icon on the sidebar, and search for TSLint in the Marketplace. Make sure that VS Code uses the current version of TypeScript (the version number is shown at the bottom-right corner in the status bar). Changing the TypeScript version is described in the VS Code documentation (http://mng.bz/pynK).

In figure 6.4 you may notice a short squiggly line in the empty line 3. If you hover your mouse over this squiggly line, you'll see another linter error: "TSLint: Consecutive blank lines are forbidden (no-consecutive-blank-lines)." The name of the rule is shown in parentheses here, and you can find the following rule in the recommended.js file:

```
"no-consecutive-blank-lines": true,
```

> **TIP** You can see a description of the TSLint core rules on the TSLint site at https://palantir.github.io/tslint/rules/.

Let's override the `no-consecutive-blank-lines` rule in the tslint.json file shown in listing 6.4. We'll add a rule there allowing consecutive blank lines.

Listing 6.5 Overriding a rule in tslint.json

```
{
    "defaultSeverity": "error",
    "extends": [
        "tslint:recommended"
    ],
    "jsRules": {},
    "rules": {"no-consecutive-blank-lines": false},      <-- We added this line.
    "rulesDirectory": []
}
```

By assigning the value `false` to the `no-consecutive-blank-lines` rule, we've overridden its value from the recommended.js file. Now that little squiggly line in figure 6.4 will disappear.

You can override the recommended rules or add new ones that comply with your coding style or the style accepted by your project team.

6.3 Bundling code with Webpack

When a browser makes requests to a server, it gets HTML documents, which may include additional files like CSS, images, videos, and so on. In part 2 of this book, we'll be working with a sample blockchain app that has multiple files. Often you'll also be using one of the popular JavaScript frameworks, which could add hundreds of files to your app. If all these app files were deployed separately, the browser would need to make hundreds of requests to load them. The size of your app could be several megabytes.

Real-world applications consist of hundreds and even thousands of files, and we want to minimize, optimize, and bundle them together during deployment. Figure 6.5 shows how various files are given to Webpack, which produces a smaller number of files for deployment.

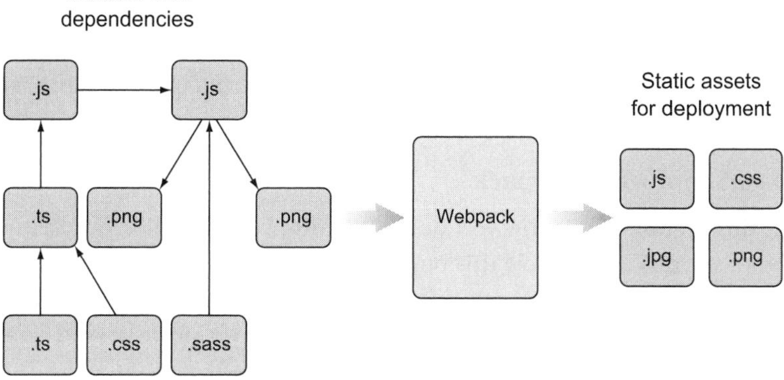

Figure 6.5 Bundling sources with Webpack

Bundling multiple files into one can offer better performance and faster downloads. Technically, you can specify one output file in tsconfig.json, and tsc can place the generated code of multiple .ts file into a single output file, but this only works if the compiler's `module` option is `System` or `AMD`; the output file generated by the bundler won't include third-party dependencies like JavaScript libraries.

Also, you want to be able to configure development and production builds differently. For production, you'll add optimization and minimization, whereas in development you'll just be bundling files together.

Several years ago, JavaScript developers were mostly using general task runners like Grunt and Gulp for orchestrating the build process. Today they use such bundlers as Webpack, Rollup, and Browserify. With the help of plugins, bundlers can also wear the hats of compilers if need be.

In this section, we'll introduce the Webpack bundler (https://github.com/webpack), which was created for web applications running in a browser. Webpack supports many typical tasks required to prepare web application builds, and it requires minimal configuration.

You can install Webpack either globally or locally (in the node_modules subdirectory of your project). Webpack also has a command-line interface (CLI) tool, webpack-cli (https://github.com/webpack/webpack-cli). Prior to Webpack 4, properly configuring a Webpack project wasn't easy, but the webpack-cli scaffolding tool greatly simplifies Webpack configuration.

To install Webpack and its CLI globally on your computer, run the following command (`-g` is for global):

```
npm install webpack webpack-cli -g
```

> **NOTE** Installing Webpack (or any other tool) globally allows you to use it with multiple projects. This is great, but in your organization, the production build might be done on a dedicated computer with restrictions as to what software can be installed globally. That's why we'll use locally installed Webpack and Webpack CLI.

Webpack is probably the most popular bundler in the JavaScript ecosystem, and in the next section we'll bundle a simple JavaScript app.

6.3.1 *Bundling JavaScript with Webpack*

The goal of this section is to show you how to configure and run Webpack for a basic JavaScript app, so you can see how this bundler works and what to expect as its output.

The source code that comes with this chapter has several projects, and we'll start with the project called webpack-javascript. This is an npm project, and you need to install its dependencies by running the following command:

```
npm install
```

In this project we have a tiny JavaScript file that uses a third-party library called Chalk (www.npmjs.com/package/chalk), which is listed in the dependencies section of package.json for this project.

Listing 6.6 The package.json of the webpack-javascript project

```
{
   "name": "webpack-javascript",
   "description": "Code sample for chapter 6",
   "homepage": "https://www.manning.com/books/typescript-quickly",
   "license": "MIT",
   "scripts": {
       "bundleup": "webpack-cli"          <-- Defines a command to run Webpack
   },
   "dependencies": {
       "chalk": "^2.4.1"      <-- The chalk library
   },
   "devDependencies": {
       "webpack": "^4.28.3",              <-- The Webpack bundler
       "webpack-cli": "^3.1.2"            <-- The Webpack command-line interface
   }
}
```

The Webpack packages are located in the `devDependencies` section because we need them only on the developer's computer. We'll be running this app by entering the command `npm run bundleup`, which will run the webpack-cli executable located in the node_modules/.bin directory.

The Chalk package paints the Terminal window's text in different colors, but what this package does is irrelevant for us here. Our goal is to bundle our JavaScript code (index.js) with a library. The code of index.js is shown in the next listing.

Listing 6.7 index.js: the source code of the webpack-javascript app

```
const chalk = require('chalk');                   <-- Loads the library
const message = 'Bundled by the Webpack';
console.log(chalk.black.bgGreenBright(message));  <-- Uses the library
```

Typically, developers use the webpack.config.js file for creating custom configurations, even though it's optional as of Webpack version 4. This is where you configure the build for the project. The following listing shows the webpack.config.js file for this project.

Listing 6.8 webpack.config.js: Webpack's config file

```
const { resolve } = require('path');

module.exports = {
    entry: './src/index.js',        <-- The source filename to bundle
    output: {
```

```
        filename: 'index.bundle.js',
        path: resolve(__dirname, 'dist')
    },
    target: 'node',
    mode: 'production'
};
```

The location of the output bundle

The name of the output bundle

We'll run this app under Node.js; don't inline built-in Node.js modules.

Optimizes the file size of the output bundle

To create a bundle, Webpack needs to know the main module (the entry point) of your application, which may have dependencies on other modules or third-party libraries. Webpack loads the entry point module and builds a memory tree of all dependent modules, if any.

In this config file, we use Node's `path` module, which can resolve the absolute path of a file with the help of the `__dirname` environment variable. Webpack runs under Node, and the `__dirname` variable will store the directory where the executable JavaScript module (webpack.config.js) is located. The fragment `resolve(__dirname, 'dist')` thus instructs Webpack to create a subdirectory named dist in the root of the project, and the bundled app will be located in the dist directory.

> **TIP** Storing the output files in a separate directory will allow you to configure your version control system to exclude the generated files. If you use Git, just add the dist directory to the .gitignore file.

We specified `production` as the value of the `mode` property so Webpack would minimize the size of the bundle.

Starting with Webpack 4, configuring a project became much easier because it introduced the default modes `production` and `development`. In `production` mode, the size of the generated bundles is small, the code is optimized for runtime, and the development-only code is removed from the sources. In `development` mode, the compilation is incremental and you can debug the code in the browser.

The webpack-cli tool allows you to bundle your app files providing the `entry`, `output`, and other parameters right on the command line. It can also generate a configuration file for your project.

Let's run Webpack to see how it will bundle up our app. You'll be running the local version of Webpack installed in the node_modules directory of your project. In listing 6.6, we defined the npm command `bundleup` so we can run the locally installed webpack-cli:

```
npm run bundleup
```

The bundling will finish in several seconds, and your console may look similar to figure 6.6.

From this output we can see that Webpack built the bundle named index.bundle.js, and its size is about 22 KB. This is the main chunk (a.k.a. bundle). In our simple example we have only one bundle, but larger apps are usually split into modules, and Webpack can be configured to build multiple bundles.

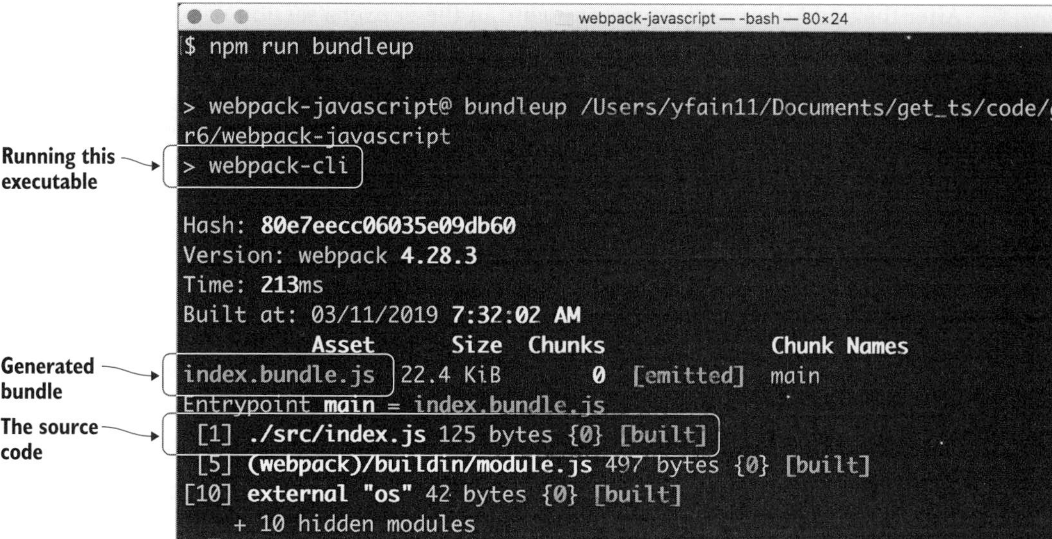

Figure 6.6 The console output of `npm run bundleup`

Note that the size of the original src/index.js file was only 125 bytes. The size of the bundle is much larger because it includes not only the three lines of our index.js file, but also the Chalk library and all its transitive dependencies. Webpack also adds its own code to keep track of the bundle content.

Change the value of the `mode` property in webpack.config.js to be `development`, and rerun the bundling. Under the hood, Webpack will apply different predefined configuration settings, and the size of the generated file will be more than 56 KB (as opposed to 22 KB in production mode).

Open the dist/index.bundle.js file in any plain text editor. In the production version, you'll just see one very long optimized line, whereas the development bundle will have readable content with comments.

The generated index.bundle.js file is a regular JavaScript file, and you can use it in an HTML `<script>` tag or any other place where JavaScript filenames are allowed. This particular app is not intended to run in a browser—it's for Node.js, and you can run it with the following command:

```
node dist/index.bundle.js
```

Figure 6.7 shows the console output, where the Chalk library displayed the message "Bundled by the Webpack" on a bright green background.

```
$ node dist/index.bundle.js
Bundled by the Webpack
```

Figure 6.7 Running your first bundle

We ran this example using the Node.js runtime, but for web apps, Webpack offers a development server that can serve your web pages. It has to be installed separately:

```
npm install webpack-dev-server -D
```

After that, add the `start` npm command in the `scripts` section of package.json. It'll look like this:

```
"scripts": {
  "bundleup": "webpack-cli --watch",        <-- Run webpack in watch mode so it rebuilds the bundle on code changes.
  "start": "webpack-dev-server"
}
```

Now let's create a super-simple index.js JavaScript file:

```
document.write('Hello World!');
```

We'll ask Webpack to generate a bundle for this file and save it in dist/bundle.js. The webpack.config.js file will be similar to the one shown in listing 6.8 with two changes: we'll add the `devServer` property and change the mode to `development`.

Listing 6.9 Adding the `devServer` property

```
const { resolve } = require('path');

module.exports = {
    entry: './src/index.js',
    output: {
        filename: 'index.bundle.js',
        path: resolve(__dirname, 'dist')
    },
    target: 'node',
    mode: 'development',        <-- Configuring Webpack for dev mode
    devServer: {                <-- Adding a section for webpack-dev-server
      contentBase: '.'
    }
};
```

In `devServer` you can configure any options that webpack-dev-server allows on the command line (see the Webpack documentation at https://webpack.js.org/configuration/dev-server/). We use `contentBase` to specify that the files should be served from the current directory.

Accordingly, our HTML file, index.html, can refer to index.bundle.js.

Listing 6.10 The index.html file that loads the bundled JavaScript

```
<!DOCTYPE html>
<html>
<body>
  <script src="dist/index.bundle.js"></script>
</body>
</html>
```

We're now ready to build the bundle and start the web server. Building the bundle comes first:

```
npm run bundleup
```

To start the server using webpack-dev-server, just run the following command:

```
npm start
```

You can find this app in the webpack-devserver directory. Open your browser to localhost:8080 and it will greet the world as seen in figure 6.8.

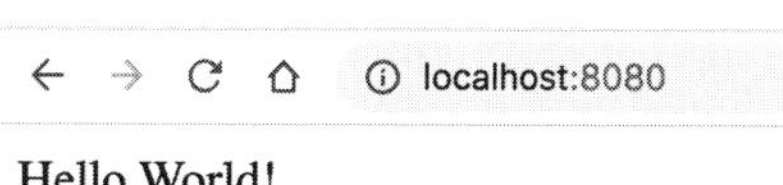

Hello World!

Figure 6.8 The browser rendering the index.html document

When you serve your application with webpack-dev-server, it'll run on the default port 8080. Because we started Webpack in `watch` mode, it will recompile the bundle each time you modify the code.

Now that you've seen how to bundle a pure JavaScript project, let's see how to use Webpack with TypeScript code.

6.3.2 Bundling TypeScript with Webpack

The source code that comes with this chapter has several projects, and in this section we'll work with the one in the webpack-typescript directory. This project is almost the same as the one in the previous section. It includes a three-line TypeScript index.ts file (in the previous section it was index.js) that uses the same JavaScript Chalk library.

Let's highlight the differences, starting with the index.ts file.

Listing 6.11 index.ts: the source code of the webpack-typescript app

```
import chalk from 'chalk';                                  // Imports the default object to access this library
const message: string = 'Bundled by the Webpack';           // The type of the message variable is declared explicitly.
console.log(chalk.black.bgGreenBright(message));            // Uses the library
```

The Chalk library explicitly exposes a default export. That's why, instead of writing `import * as chalk from 'chalk'`, we wrote `import chalk from chalk`. We didn't have to explicitly declare the type of `message`, but we wanted to make it obvious that this is TypeScript code.

In this project, the package.json file has two additional lines in the `devDependencies` section (compared to listing 6.6). We've added `ts-loader` and `typescript`.

Listing 6.12 The `devDependencies` section in package.json

```
"devDependencies": {
    "ts-loader": "^5.3.2",      // Added the TypeScript loader
```

```
    "typescript": "^3.2.2",          <-- Added the Typescript compiler
    "webpack": "^4.28.3",
    "webpack-cli": "^3.1.2"
}
```

Usually build-automation tools provide developers with a way to specify additional tasks that need to be performed during the build process, and Webpack offers *loaders* and *plugins* that allow you to customize builds. Webpack loaders preprocess one file at a time, whereas plugins can operate on a group of files.

> **TIP** You can find a list of loaders in the Webpack docs on GitHub at http://mng.bz/U0Yv.

Webpack loaders are transformers that take a source file as input and produce another file as output (in memory or on disk). For example, `json-loader` takes an input file and parses it as JSON. For compiling TypeScript to JavaScript, `ts-loader` uses the Typescript compiler, which explains why we added it to the `devDependencies` section in package.json. The Typescript compiler uses tsconfig.json, which has the following content.

Listing 6.13 tsconfig.json: the compiler's config options

```
{
  "compilerOptions": {
      "target": "es2018",          <-- Specifies compiling into the JavaScript syntax described in the ECMAScript 2018 spec
      "moduleResolution": "node"   <-- Uses the Node.js module resolution
  }
}
```

The `moduleResolution` option tells tsc how to resolve modules if the code includes import statements. If your app includes an `import { a } from "moduleA"` statement, tsc needs to know where to look for `moduleA`.

There are two strategies for module resolution: `Classic` and `Node`. In the `Classic` strategy, tsc will look for the definition of `moduleA` in the moduleA.ts file and in the moduleA.d.ts type definition file. In the `Node` strategy, module resolution will also try to find the module in files located in the node_modules directory, which is exactly what we need, because the third-party `chalk` library is installed in node_modules.

> **TIP** To read more about module resolution, visit the TypeScript documentation at www.typescriptlang.org/docs/handbook/module-resolution.html.

The following listing shows how we added `ts-loader` in the `rules` section of webpack .config.js.

Listing 6.14 webpack.config.js: the Webpack configuration file

```
const { resolve } = require('path');

module.exports = {
  entry: './src/index.ts',
  output: {
     filename: 'index.bundle.js',
     path: resolve(__dirname, 'dist')
  },
  module: {
    rules: [                          <-- Rules for modules (configure loaders, parser options, etc.)
       {
         test: /\.ts$/,               <-- Applies to files with the .ts extension
         exclude: /node_modules/,     <-- Rules for modules (configure loaders, parser options, etc.)
         use: 'ts-loader'             <-- Compiles TypeScript using options from the existing tsconfig.json
       }
    ]
  },
  resolve: {
      extensions: [ '.ts', '.js' ]    <-- Adds the .ts extension to the resolve property so it can import TypeScript files
  },
  target: 'node',
  mode: 'production'
};
```

In short, we say to Webpack, "If you see a file with the name extension .ts, use ts-loader to preprocess them. Ignore the .ts files located under the node_modules directory—there's no need to compile them."

In this simple example, the `rules` array has just one loader configured—`ts-loader`. In a real-world project, it usually includes multiple loaders. For example, `css-loader` is used for processing CSS files; `file-loader` resolves `import/require()` in a source file into a URL and emits it into the output bundle (it's used for handling images or other files that have specified name extensions).

> **TIP** There's an alternative Webpack loader for TypeScript called `awesome-typescript-loader` (see https://github.com/s-panferov/awesome-typescript-loader), which may show better performance on large projects.

Now you can build the index.bundle.js bundle just as we did in the previous section by running the following command:

```
npm run bundleup
```

To make sure that the bundled code works, just run it:

```
node dist/index.bundle.js
```

What Webpack plugins are for

Webpack loaders transform files one at a time, but plugins have access to multiple files, and they can process them before or after the loaders kick in. You can find a list of available Webpack plugins at https://webpack.js.org/plugins.

For example, the SplitChunksPlugin plugin allows you to break a bundle into separate chunks. Say your app code is split into two modules, `main` and `admin`, and you want to build two corresponding bundles. Each of these modules uses a framework, such as Angular. If you just specify two entry points (`main` and `admin`), each bundle will include the application code as well as its own copy of Angular's code.

To prevent this from happening, you can process the code with the SplitChunkPlugin. With this plugin, Webpack won't include any of the Angular code in the `main` and `admin` bundles; it will create a separate shareable bundle with only the Angular code. This will lower the total size of your application, because it shares one copy of Angular between two application modules. In this case, your HTML file should include the vendor bundle first (for example, the code of the Angular framework), followed by the application bundle.

The UglifyJSPlugin plugin performs code minification of all compiled files. It's a wrapper for the popular UglifyJS minifier, which takes the JavaScript code and performs various optimizations. For example, it compresses the code by joining consecutive `var` statements, removes unused variables and unreachable code, and optimizes `if` statements. Its mangler tool renames local variables to single letters.

The TerserWebpackPlugin also performs code minification using `terser` (a special JavaScript parser), mangler, optimizer, and the beautifier toolkit for ES6.

Using the `mode: "production"` option in the webpack.config.js file, you can implicitly engage a number of Webpack plugins that will optimize and minimize your code bundles. If you're interested in which specific plugins are being used in `production` mode, see the Webpack documentation at https://webpack.js.org/concepts/mode/#mode-production.

The configuration file presented in listing 6.14 is rather small and simple; in real-world projects, the webpack.config.js file can be complex and include multiple loaders and plugins. We just used the TypeScript loader in our tiny app, but you'll likely also be using loaders for HTML, CSS, images, and others.

Your project may have multiple `entry` files, and you might want to use special plugins to create bundles in a special way. For example, if your app will be deployed as 10 bundles, Webpack can extract the common code (from the framework you use) into a separate bundle so 9 others won't duplicate it.

As the complexity of the bundling process increases, the webpack.config.js JavaScript file grows too, and it becomes more difficult to write and maintain. Providing a value of a wrong type can result in errors during the bundling process, and the error description may not be easy to understand. The good news is that you can write the Webpack configuration file in TypeScript (webpack.config.ts), getting help from the static type analyzer as with any other TypeScript code. You can read about using

TypeScript for configuring Webpack in the Webpack documentation at https://webpack.js.org/configuration/configuration-languages.

In this section, we presented a project where the TypeScript code uses the Chalk JavaScript library. In chapter 7, we'll provide a more detailed discussion of mixed TypeScript-JavaScript projects. Meanwhile, let's see how we can use TypeScript with another popular tool called Babel.

6.4 Using the Babel compiler

Babel is a popular JavaScript compiler that offers a remedy for a well-known issue: not every browser supports every language feature declared in ECMAScript. We're not even talking about the full implementation of a specific ECMAScript version. At any given time, one browser may implement a specific subset of ECMAScript 2019, while another still understands only ECMAScript 5. Visit the caniuse.com site and search for "arrow functions." You'll see that Internet Explorer 11, Opera Mini, and some others do not support them.

If you're developing a new web app, you'll want to test it against all the browsers your users may have. Babel allows you to write modern JavaScript and compile it down to older syntaxes. Although tsc allows you to specify a particular ECMAScript spec as a target for compiling (such as ES2019), Babel is more fine-grained. It allows you to selectively pick language features that should be transformed to the JavaScript supported by older browsers.

Figure 6.9 shows a fragment of a browser compatibility table (from http://mng.bz/O9qw). At the top, you'll see the names of the browsers and compilers. On the left is a list of features. A browser, compiler, or server's runtime may fully or partially support some of the features, and Babel plugins allow you to specify that only certain features should be transformed into the older code. The complete list of plugins is available in the Babel documentation at https://babeljs.io/docs/en/plugins.

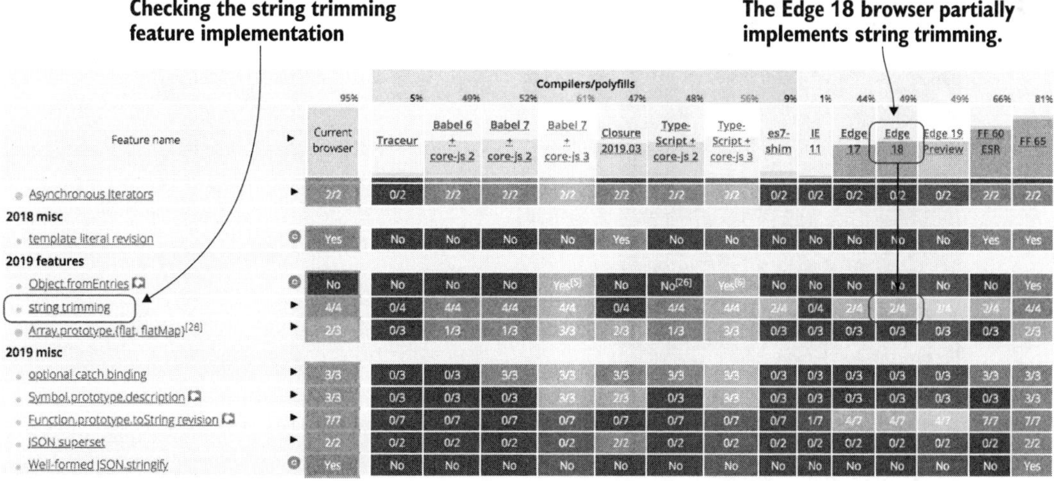

Feature name	Current browser	Traceur	Babel 6 + core-js 2	Babel 7 + core-js 2	Babel 7 + core-js 3	Closure 2019.03	TypeScript + core-js 2	TypeScript + core-js 3	es7-shim	IE 11	Edge 17	Edge 18	Edge 19 Preview	FF 60 ESR	FF 65
	95%	5%	49%	52%	61%	47%	48%	56%	9%	1%	44%	49%	49%	66%	81%
Asynchronous Iterators	2/2	0/2	2/2	2/2	2/2	2/2	2/2	2/2	0/2	0/2	0/2	0/2	0/2	2/2	2/2
2018 misc															
template literal revision	Yes	No	No	No	No	Yes	No	No	No	No	No	No	No	Yes	Yes
2019 features															
Object.fromEntries	No	No	No	No	Yes[5]	No	No[26]	Yes[6]	No	No	No	No	No	No	Yes
string trimming	4/4	0/4	4/4	4/4	4/4	0/4	4/4	4/4	2/4	0/4	2/4	2/4	2/4	2/4	4/4
Array.prototype.{flat, flatMap}[28]	2/3	0/3	1/3	1/3	3/3	2/3	1/3	3/3	0/3	0/3	0/3	0/3	0/3	0/3	2/3
2019 misc															
optional catch binding	3/3	0/3	0/3	3/3	3/3	3/3	3/3	3/3	0/3	0/3	0/3	0/3	0/3	3/3	3/3
Symbol.prototype.description	3/3	0/3	0/3	0/3	3/3	2/3	0/3	3/3	0/3	0/3	0/3	0/3	0/3	0/3	3/3
Function.prototype.toString revision	7/7	0/7	0/7	0/7	0/7	0/7	0/7	0/7	0/7	1/7	4/7	4/7	4/7	7/7	7/7
JSON superset	2/2	0/2	0/2	0/2	0/2	2/2	0/2	0/2	0/2	0/2	0/2	0/2	0/2	0/2	2/2
Well-formed JSON.stringify	Yes	No	No	No	No	No	No	No	No	No	No	No	No	No	Yes

Figure 6.9 A fragment of a browser compatibility table

For the sake of discussion, we picked the "string trimming" feature from the ES2019 spec (see the black arrow on the left of figure 6.9). Let's say our app needs to work in the Edge browser. Follow the vertical arrow, and you'll see that Edge 18 only partially (2/4) implements string trimming at this time.

We can use the string trimming feature in our code, but we'll need to ask Babel to compile this feature into the older syntax. Sometime later, when Edge fully supports this feature and no compiling is needed, Babel will be flexible enough to help you with this.

Babel consists of many plugins, each compiling a particular feature of the language, but trying to find and map features to plugins would be a time-consuming task. That's why Babel plugins are combined into *presets*, which are lists of plugins that you'll want to apply for compiling. In particular, `preset-env` allows you to specify the ECMAScript features and the browsers that your app should support.

In section A.12 of the appendix, we include a screenshot from http://babeljs.io illustrating Babel's REPL tool. Take a look at Babel's Try It Out menu, shown in figure 6.10, concentrating on the left navigation bar that allows you to configure presets.

Each preset is just a group of plugins, and if you want to compile your code into the ES2015 syntax, just select the es2015 check box. Instead of using ECMAScript spec names, you can configure specific versions of the browsers or other runtimes using the ENV PRESET option. The white arrow in figure 6.10 shows the editable box with the suggested values for the ENV preset: `>2%, ie 11, safari > 9`. This means that you

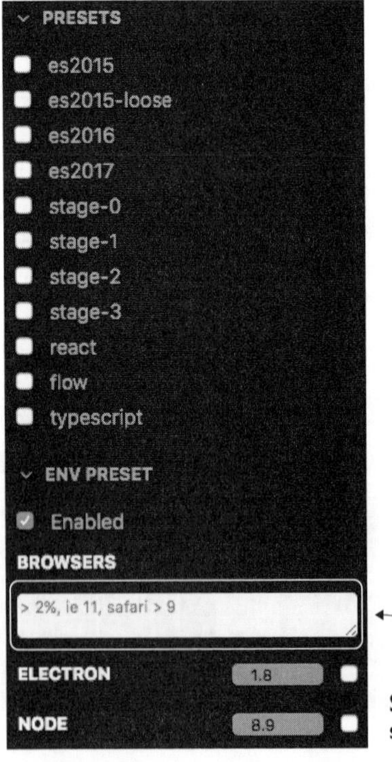

Figure 6.10 Configuring the ENV preset

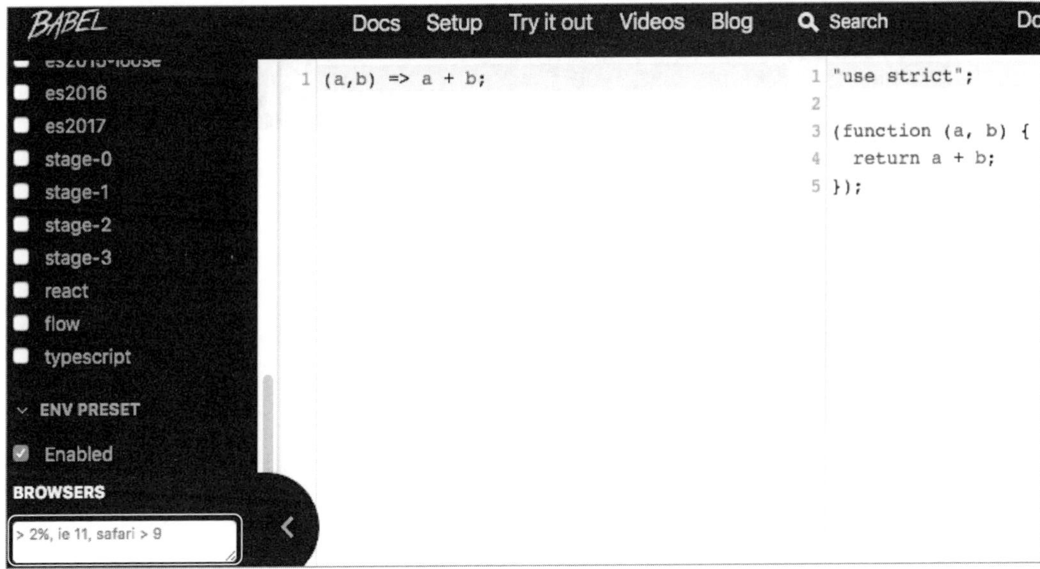

Figure 6.11 Applying the `ie` and `safari` presets

want Babel to compile the code so it'll run in all browsers with a market share of 2% or more, and also in Internet Explorer 11 and Safari 9.

Neither IE 11 nor Safari 9 support arrow functions, and if you enter `(a,b) ? a + b;`, Babel will transform it to JavaScript that these browsers understand, as shown in figure 6.11 on the right.

> **TIP** If you see errors after entering the names of the browsers, uncheck the Enabled check box after entering the browsers and versions. This seems like a bug, but it may be fixed by the time you read this.

Now let's change the preset to be "last 2 chrome versions," as shown in figure 6.12. Babel is smart enough to understand that the last two versions of Chrome support arrow functions and there's no need to do any transformation.

The ENV preset comes with a list of browsers, and you need to use proper names and phrases to specify the constraints (for example, `last 2 major versions`, `Firefox >= 20`, or `> 5% in US`). These phrases are listed in the `browserslist` project available at https://github.com/browserslist/browserslist.

> **NOTE** We used the ENV preset in the Babel REPL to play with target environments, but these options can be configured and used in Babel from a command line. In listing 6.15, we'll add `@babel/preset-env` to the .babelrc configuration file. In listing 6.17, you'll see the .browserslistrc file, where you can configure specific browsers and versions as we did in the Babel REPL. You can read more about `preset-env` in the Babel documentation at https://babeljs.io/docs/en/next/babel-preset-env.html.

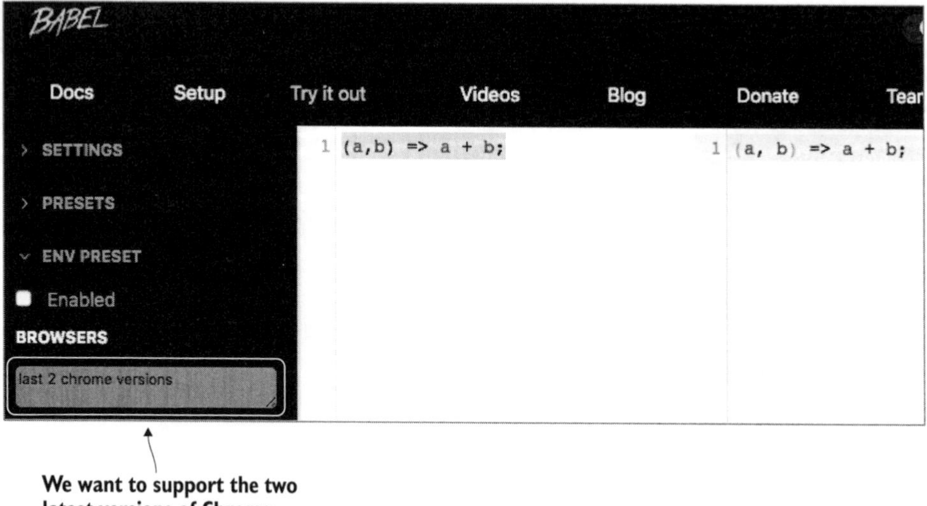

Figure 6.12 Applying the Chrome preset

Babel can be used to compile such programming languages as JavaScript, TypeScript, CoffeeScript, Flow, and more. For example, the React framework uses the JSX syntax, which is not even standard JavaScript, and Babel understands it. In chapter 12, we'll use Babel with a React app.

When Babel compiles TypeScript, it doesn't perform type checking, unlike tsc. Babel's creators didn't implement the full-featured Typescript compiler. Babel just parses the TypeScript code and generates the corresponding JavaScript syntax.

You may be thinking, "I'm pretty happy with the Typescript compiler. Why include this section on a JavaScript-to-JavaScript compiler in the TypeScript book?" The reason is that you may join a project where some of the modules were written in JavaScript and some in TypeScript. In such projects, Babel may well already be part of the development-deployment workflow. For example, Babel is popular among developers who use the React framework, which only recently started supporting TypeScript.

Like any npm package, you can install Babel either locally or globally (with the `-g` option). Installing it locally within the project directory makes your project self-sufficient because, after running `npm install`, you can use Babel without expecting that the computer has it installed elsewhere (someone may work with your project using a different computer).

```
npm install @babel/core @babel/cli @babel/preset-env
```

Here, `@babel/core` is the Babel compiler, `@babel/cli` is the command-line interface, and `@babel/preset-env` is the ENV preset discussed earlier.

NOTE In the npmjs.org registry, JavaScript packages can be organized as *organizations*. For example, `@babel` is the organization for Babel-related packages. `@angular` is the organization for packages that belong to the Angular framework. `@types` is the place for TypeScript type definition files for various popular JavaScript libraries.

In the following sections, we'll introduce you to three small projects. The first uses Babel with JavaScript, the second uses Babel with TypeScript, and the third uses Babel, TypeScript, and Webpack.

6.4.1 Using Babel with JavaScript

In this section, we'll review a simple project that uses Babel with JavaScript, located in the babel-javascript directory. We'll continue working with the three-line index.js script introduced in listing 6.7 that uses the Chalk JavaScript library. The only change in the following listing is that the message now reads "Compiled with Babel."

Listing 6.15 index.js: the source code of the babel-javascript app

```
const chalk = require('chalk');
const message = 'Compiled with Babel';
console.log(chalk.black.bgGreenBright(message));
```

The following listing shows the npm script that we'll use to run Babel and the dependencies that should be installed on the developer's machine.

Listing 6.16 A fragment from babel-javascript/package.json

```
"scripts": {
    "babel": "babel src -d dist"        <-- The npm script to compile
},                                          the code from src to dist
"dependencies": {
    "chalk": "^2.4.1"
},
"devDependencies": {                  <-- Locally installed
    "@babel/cli": "^7.2.3",               dev dependencies
    "@babel/core": "^7.2.2",
    "@babel/preset-env": "^7.2.3"
}
```

Babel is configured in the .babelrc file, and our configuration file will be very simple. We just want to use `preset-env` for compiling.

Listing 6.17 The file .babelrc

```
{
  "presets": [
      "@babel/preset-env"
  ]
}
```

We didn't configure any specific browser versions here, and without any configuration options `@babel/preset-env` behaves exactly the same as `@babel/preset-es2015`, `@babel/preset-es2016`, and `@babel/preset-es2017`. In other words, all language features introduced in ECMAScript 2015, 2016, and 2017 will be compiled to ES5.

> **TIP** We've configured Babel in the .babelrc file, which is fine for static configurations like ours. If your project needs to create Babel configurations programmatically, you'll need to use the babel.config.js file (see the Babel documentation for details: https://babeljs.io/docs/en/config-files#project-wide-configuration). If you'd like to see how Babel compiles our src/index.js file, install the dependencies of this project by running `npm install`, and then run the npm script from package.json: `npm run babel`.

The next listing shows the compiled version of index.js that's created in the dist directory. It will have the following content (compare with listing 6.15).

Listing 6.18 dist/index.js: a compiled version of src/index.js

```
"use strict";                                        // Babel added this line.
var chalk = require('chalk');                        // Babel replaced
var message = 'Compiled with Babel';                 // const with var.
console.log(chalk.black.bgGreenBright(message));
```

> **NOTE** The compiled file still invokes `require('chalk')` and this library is located in a separate file. Keep in mind that Babel is not a bundler. We'll use Webpack with Babel in section 6.4.3.

You can run the compiled version as follows:

```
node dist/index.js
```

The console output will look similar to figure 6.13.

```
$ node dist/index.js
Transpiled with Babel
```

Figure 6.13 Running the program compiled by Babel

If we wanted to ensure that Babel generates code that works in specific browser versions, we'd need to add an additional .browserslistrc config file. For example, imagine that we wanted our code to work only in the two latest versions of Chrome and Firefox. We could create the following file in the root of our project.

Listing 6.19 A sample .browserslistrc file

```
last 2 chrome versions
last 2 firefox versions
```

Now running Babel won't convert `const` to `var` as in listing 6.18 because both Firefox and Chrome have supported the `const` keyword for awhile. Try it out and see for yourself.

6.4.2 Using Babel with TypeScript

In this section, we'll review a simple project that uses Babel with TypeScript; it's located in the babel-typescript directory. We'll continue working with the three-line script introduced in listing 6.11 that uses the Chalk JavaScript library. The only change is that the message now reads "Compiled with Babel."

Listing 6.20 index.ts: the source code of the babel-typescript app

```
import chalk from 'chalk';
const message: string = 'Compiled with Babel';
console.log(chalk.black.bgGreenBright(message));
```

Compared to the package.json from the pure JavaScript project (see listing 6.16), our TypeScript project adds the `preset-typescript` dev dependency that strips TypeScript types from the code, so Babel can treat it as plain JavaScript. We'll also add an `--extensions '.ts'` option to the npm script that runs Babel as in listing 6.21. Now Babel will read .ts files.

Listing 6.21 A fragment from package.json

```
"scripts": {
    "babel": "babel src -d dist --extensions '.ts'"     <-- Instructs Babel to process files with .ts extensions
},
"dependencies": {
    "chalk": "^2.4.1"
},
"devDependencies": {
    "@babel/cli": "^7.2.3",
    "@babel/core": "^7.2.2",
    "@babel/preset-env": "^7.2.3",
    "@babel/preset-typescript": "^7.1.0"     <-- Adds the preset-typescript dependency
}
```

Typically presets include a number of plugins, but `preset-typescript` includes just one, `@babel/plugin-transform-typescript`. That plugin internally uses `@babel/plugin-syntax-typescript` to parse TypeScript and `@babel/helper-plugin-utils` for general utilities for plugins.

Although `@babel/plugin-transform-typescript` turns TypeScript code into ES.Next syntax, it's not a Typescript compiler. As strange as it sounds, Babel simply erases TypeScript. For example, it'll turn `const x: number = 0` into `const x = 0`. `@babel/plugin-transform-typescript` is a lot faster than the Typescript compiler because it does not type-check the input files.

NOTE `@babel/plugin-transform-typescript` has several minor limitations listed in the documentation at https://babeljs.io/docs/en/babel-plugin-transform-typescript (for example, it doesn't support `const enum`). For better TypeScript support, consider using the `@babel/plugin-proposal-class-properties` and `@babel/plugin-proposal-object-rest-spread` plugins.

You've read the first five chapters of this book, and started liking the type checking and compile-time errors that the real Typescript compiler offers, and now are we really suggesting you use Babel to erase the TypeScript-related syntax? Not really. During development, you can continue using tsc (with tsconfig.json) and an IDE with full TypeScript support. At the deployment stage, though, you may still introduce Babel and its ENV preset. (You've already started to like the flexibility the ENV preset offers in configuring target browsers, haven't you?)

In your build process, you can even add an npm script (in package.json) that runs tsc:

```
"check_types": "tsc --noEmit src/index.ts"
```

Now you can sequentially run `check_types` and `babel`, assuming you have tsc installed locally:

```
npm run check_types && npm run babel
```

The `--noEmit` option ensures that tsc won't output any files (such as index.js) because this will be done by the `babel` command that runs right after `check_types`. If there are compile errors in index.ts, the build process will fail and the `babel` command won't even run.

TIP If you use `&&` (double ampersand) between two npm scripts, they'll run sequentially. Use `&` (single ampersand) for parallel execution. See the sidebar "Using ampersands in npm scripts on Windows" in chapter 10 for more details.

In this project, the .babelrc config file includes `@babel/preset-typescript`.

Listing 6.22 The file .babelrc

```
{
  "presets": [
     "@babel/preset-env",
     "@babel/preset-typescript"
  ]
}
```

Compared to the babel-javascript project, we made the following TypeScript-related changes:

- Added the `--extensions '.ts'` option to the command that runs Babel
- Added TypeScript-related dev dependencies to package.json
- Added `@babel/preset-typescript` to the .babelrc config file

To compile our simple index.ts script, run the following npm script from package .json:

```
npm run babel
```

You'll find the compiled version of index.js in the dist directory. You can run the compiled code the same way we did in the previous section:

```
node dist/index.js
```

Now let's add Webpack to our workflow to bundle together the index.js script and the Chalk JavaScript library.

6.4.3 Using Babel with TypeScript and Webpack

Babel is a compiler, but it's not a bundler, which is required for any real-world app. There are different bundlers to choose from (such as Webpack, Rollup, and Browserify), but we'll stick to Webpack. In this section, we'll look at a simple project that uses Babel with TypeScript and Webpack. It's located in the webpack-babel-typescript directory.

In section 6.3.2, we reviewed the TypeScript-Webpack setup, and we'll continue using our three-line source code from that project.

Listing 6.23 index.ts: the source code of the webpack-babel-typescript app

```
import chalk from 'chalk';
const message: string = 'Built with Babel bundled with Webpack';
console.log(chalk.black.bgGreenBright(message));
```

The `devDependency` section from package .json is shown in the following listing.

Listing 6.24 The `devDependencies` section in package.json

```
"devDependencies": {
   "@babel/core": "^7.2.2",
   "@babel/preset-env": "^7.2.3",
   "@babel/preset-typescript": "^7.1.0",
   "babel-loader": "^8.0.5",              <-- Adding the Webpack
   "webpack": "^4.28.3",                      Babel loader
   "webpack-cli": "^3.1.2"
}
```

Compare the Babel dependencies in listings 6.24 and 6.21. There are three changes in listing 6.24:

- We added `babel-loader`, which is a Webpack loader for Babel.
- We removed `babel-cli` because we won't be running Babel from the command line.
- Instead of `babel-cli`, Webpack will use `babel-loader` as a part of the bundling process.

As you'll remember from section 6.3, Webpack uses the webpack.config.js configuration file. While configuring TypeScript with Webpack, we used `ts-loader` (see listing 6.14). This time we want `babel-loader` to handle the files with the .ts extension. The following listing shows the Babel-related section from webpack.config.js.

Listing 6.25 A fragment from webpack-babel-typescript/webpack.config.js

```
module: {
  rules: [
    {
      test: /\.ts$/,                  <-- Applies this rule for files ending with .ts.
      exclude: /node_modules/,
      use: 'babel-loader'             <-- Processes .ts files with babel-loader
    }
  ]
},
```

The .babelrc file will look exactly the same as in the previous section (see listing 6.20).

After we've installed the dependencies with `npm install`, we're ready to build the bundle by running the `bundleup` command from package.json:

```
npm run bundleup
```

This command will build index.bundle.js in the dist directory. That file will contain the compiled (by Babel) version of index.ts plus the code from the Chalk JavaScript library. You can run this bundle as usual:

```
node dist/index.bundle.js
```

The output shown in figure 6.14 will look familiar as well.

```
$ node dist/index.bundle.js
Built with Babel bundled with Webpack
```

Figure 6.14 Running the program compiled by Babel

As you can see, you don't have to select either Babel or tsc for generating JavaScript. They can live happily together in the same project.

> **NOTE** People who don't like TypeScript often use this argument: "If I write in plain JavaScript, I wouldn't need to use a compiler. I can run my JavaScript program as soon as it's written." This is plain wrong. Unless you're ready to ignore the newer JavaScript syntax introduced since 2015, you'll need a process that can compile the code written in modern JavaScript to code that all browsers can understand. Most likely, you'll introduce a compiler in your project anyway, whether it's Babel, TypeScript, or something else.

6.5 Tools to watch

In this section, we'd like to mention a couple of tools that were not officially released when we were writing, but that could become useful additions to the toolbox of a TypeScript developer.

6.5.1 Introducing Deno

Every JavaScript developer knows about the Node.js runtime. We also use it in this book for running apps outside browsers. Everybody likes Node.js . . . except for its original creator, Ryan Dahl. In 2018 he delivered a presentation titled "10 Things I

Regret About Node.js" (on YouTube at http://mng.bz/Yeyz) and he started working on Deno, a secure runtime environment that's built on top of the V8 engine (just like Node) and that has a built-in Typescript compiler.

NOTE At the time of writing, Deno is still an experimental piece of software. You can check its current status at https://deno.land.

Some of Ryan Dahl's regrets were that Node apps need package.json, node_modules .npm for module resolution, and a central repository for distributing packages. Deno doesn't need any of these. If your app needs a package, it should be able to get it directly from the source code repository of that package. We'll show you how this works in a small project named deno, which comes with this chapter's code.

Deno can run both JavaScript and TypeScript code, and our project has just one index.ts script as seen in the following listing.

Listing 6.26 index.ts: the source code of the app to run under Deno

```
import { bgGreen, black } from 'https://deno.land/std/colors/mod.ts';   // Includes the colors library
const message: string = 'Ran with deno!';   // Uses the TypeScript type string
console.log(black(bgGreen(message)));   // Uses the API from the colors library
```

Note that we're importing a library named *colors* right from the source. There is no package.json that would list this library as a dependency, and no `npm install` is required to get the package from a central repository. It uses only ES6 modules, and you just need to know its URL to import it into your app.

You might ask, "Isn't it dangerous using a direct link to a third-party library? What if their code changes, breaking your app?" That's not going to happen, because Deno locally caches each third-party library when it's loaded for the first time. Every subsequent run of your app will reuse the same version of each library unless you specify a special `--reload` option.

NOTE We couldn't use the Chalk library for this example, because it's not packaged for being consumed by Deno.

All you need for this script to run is the Deno executable, which can be downloaded from https://github.com/denoland/deno/releases. Just pick the latest release and get the zip file for the platform you use. For example, for macOS download and unzip the deno_osx_x64.gz file.

For simplicity, download the app in the deno directory. You can use the following command to launch the app once you have Deno downloaded:

```
./deno_osx_x64 index.ts
```

TIP In macOS you may need to add a permission to execute this file: `chmod +x ./deno_osx_x64`.

TIP If you run this on Windows, make sure you have at least version 6 of PowerShell and Windows Management Framework. Otherwise you may see the following error: "TS5009: Cannot find the common subdirectory path for the input files."

As you'll see, Deno runs a TypeScript program out of the box, and it doesn't require npm or package.json. The first time you run this app, it'll produce the following output:

```
Compiling file: ...chapter6/deno/index.ts
Downloading https://deno.land/std/colors/mod.ts...
Compiling https://deno.land/std/colors/mod.ts
```

Deno compiled index.ts and then downloaded and compiled the colors library. After that, it ran our app producing the output shown in figure 6.15.

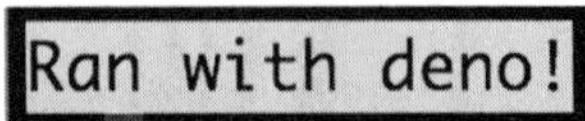

Figure 6.15 Running an app under Deno

Deno cached the compiled colors library so it won't need to download and compile colors the next time you run the app. As you can see, we didn't need to configure project dependencies, and there was nothing to install or configure prior to running the app.

Deno doesn't understand the format of npm packages, but if it gains traction, maintainers of the popular JavaScript libraries will be packaging their products in a format acceptable by Deno. Let's keep an eye on this tool.

6.5.2 Introducing ncc

The second tool to watch is ncc (https://github.com/zeit/ncc). It's a command-line interface for compiling a Node.js module into a single file, together with all its dependencies. This tool can be used by TypeScript developers who write apps that run on the server side.

Just to give you some background on ncc, it's a product of a company named Zeit, which is a serverless cloud provider. You may have heard of their product Now (https://zeit.co/now), which offers super-easy serverless deployment of web apps.

Zeit also develops software that allows you to split any app into as many small pieces as possible. For example, if you're writing an app that uses the Express framework, they'll want to represent each endpoint by a separate bundle that contains only the code needed for the functionality of that endpoint.

This allows them to avoid running live servers. If the client hits an endpoint, it returns the serverless bundle in a miniature container, and the response time is only 100 milliseconds, which is pretty impressive. And ncc is the tool that can package a server-side app into a small bundle.

ncc can take any JavaScript or TypeScript as an input and produce a bundle as output. It requires either minimal configuration or no configuration at all. The only requirement is that your code should use ES6 modules or `require()`.

We'll look at a small app, ncc-typescript, that has minimal configuration because we use TypeScript. If we wrote this app in JavaScript, no configuration would be needed. This app is located in the ncc-typescript directory, which contains the package.json file in the following listing, tsconfig.json, and index.ts, which uses the Chalk library.

Listing 6.27 A fragment of ncc/package.json

```
{
  "name": "ncc-typescript",
  "description": "A code sample for the TypeScript Quickly book",
  "homepage": "https://www.manning.com/books/typescript-quickly",
  "license": "MIT",
  "scripts": {
      "start": "ncc run src/index.ts",                    <-- Uses ncc in run mode
      "build": "ncc build src/index.ts -o dist -m"        <-- Compiles TypeScript with ncc (-m is for prod optimization)
  },
  "dependencies": {
      "chalk": "^2.4.1"
  },
  "devDependencies": {
      "@zeit/ncc": "^0.16.1"      <-- The ncc tool
  }
}
```

You won't see tsc as a dependency in this package.json file because the Typescript compiler is an internal dependency of ncc. Still, you can list the compiler's options in tsconfig.json if needed. From the development perspective, ncc allows you to compile and run your TypeScript code in one process.

Note the `scripts` section, where we defined two commands: `start` and `build`. This allows TypeScript developers to use two ncc modes:

- *Run mode*—ncc runs the TypeScript code without explicit compilation (it'll compile it internally).
- *Build mode*—The TypeScript is compiled into JavaScript.

The good part is that you don't need to use a bundler like Webpack, because ncc will build the bundle for you. Try it for yourself by doing `npm install` and running the sample app located in index.ts:

```
npm run start
```

As specified in the package.json shown in listing 6.27, the `start` command will run ncc that to compile and run index.ts, and the console output is shown in figure 6.16.

Our `start` command compiled index.ts with the generation of source maps (the default). In run mode, the compiled file was not generated. If you run the `build`

```
> ncc run src/index.ts

ncc: Using typescript@3.2.2 (ncc built-in)
 46kB  index.js
 58kB  index.js.map
121kB  sourcemap-register.js
167kB  [1880ms] - ncc 0.16.1
Built with ncc
```

Figure 6.16 Running the app with ncc

command, ncc will generate the index.js bundle in the dist directory, but the app won't run:

```
npm run build
```

The console output of the `build` command will look similar to this:

```
ncc: Using typescript@3.2.2 (ncc built-in)
24kB  dist/index.js
24kB  [1313ms] - ncc 0.16.1
```

The size of the optimized bundle is 24 KB (ncc uses Webpack internally). The ncc-generated bundle contains the code we wrote as well as the code of the Chalk library, and you can run it app as usual:

```
node dist/index.js
```

The output shown in figure 6.17 is as expected.

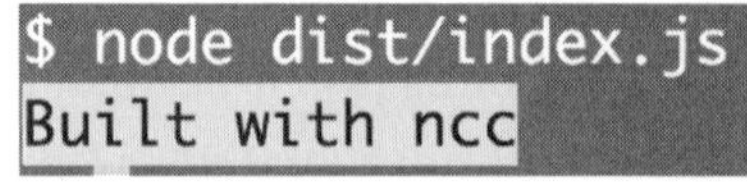

Figure 6.17 Running the app with ncc

To summarize, ncc has a few benefits:

- There's zero configuration for building and running apps.
- You can use either the run or build modes. Run mode spares you from explicitly compiling the TypeScript code.
- It supports hybrid projects where some code is written in JavaScript and some in TypeScript.

In this section, we mentioned two interesting tools, Deno and ncc, but the TypeScript ecosystem is evolving fast, and you should be watching for new tools that will make you more productive, your apps more responsive, and build and deployment processes more straightforward.

> **NOTE** We didn't mention yet another useful package called ts-node, which can run both tsc and Node.js runtime as a single process. We'll use it in section 10.4.2 in chapter 10 while starting a server written in TypeScript.

Summary

- Source maps allow you to debug your TypeScript code even though the browser runs the JavaScript version.
- Linters are used to check and enforce coding styles. We introduced TSLint too, but it's going to be merged with ESLint soon.
- To deploy a web app, we usually bundle up the source files to decrease the number of files the browser needs to download. Webpack is one of the most popular bundlers.
- JavaScript developers use Babel to compile code that uses a newer ECMAScript syntax into code that's supported by specific versions of web browsers. In some cases it make sense to use both TypeScript and Babel compilers.
- Knowing the syntax of any programming language is important, but understanding the process of how your program could be turned into a working runnable app is equally important.

7 Using TypeScript and JavaScript in the same project

This chapter covers

- Enjoying TypeScript's benefits when working with a JavaScript library
- The role of type definition files
- Upgrading an existing JavaScript app to TypeScript

In this chapter, we'll show how you can benefit from TypeScript features such as getting compilation errors and autocomplete even while using third-party libraries written in JavaScript. We'll start by explaining the role of type definition files, and then we'll discuss a concrete use case where an app written in TypeScript uses a JavaScript library. Finally, we'll discuss the things you should consider before implementing a gradual upgrade of your app from JavaScript to TypeScript.

7.1 Type definition files

The JavaScript language was created in 1995, and gazillions of lines of code have been written in this language since then. Developers from around the globe have released thousands of libraries written in JavaScript, and the chances are that your TypeScript app could benefit from using one of these libraries.

It would be naïve to expect creators of JavaScript libraries to invest time rewriting their libraries or frameworks in TypeScript, but we still want to be able to use JavaScript's heritage in our TypeScript apps. Moreover, we're spoiled by TypeScript conveniences like the static type analyzer, autocomplete, and immediate reports on compilation errors. Can we continue enjoying these features while working with the APIs of JavaScript libraries? Yes, we can, with the help of *type definition files*.

> **NOTE** In section 6.3.2, you already saw a project where the TypeScript code used a JavaScript library called Chalk. The goal of that example was to show how to *bundle* TypeScript and JavaScript together, so we didn't discuss how the code interacts and if the TypeScript code analyzer was able to help with the proper use of the Chalk library. We didn't use type definition files in chapter 6, but we will in this one.

7.1.1 Getting familiar with type definition files

The purpose of type definition files is to let the Typescript compiler know which types are expected by the APIs of specific JavaScript libraries or runtimes. Type definition files just include the names of the variables (with types) and function signatures (with types) used by a particular JavaScript library.

In 2012, Boris Yankov created a Github repository for type definition files (see https://github.com/DefinitelyTyped/DefinitelyTyped). Other people started contributing, and currently more than 10,000 contributors work with this project. Then the DefinitelyTyped.org site was created, and when TypeScript 2.0 was released, the `@types` organization was created at npmjs.org, which became another repository for type definition files. All declaration files from DefinitelyTyped.org are published automatically to the `@types` organization.

Definition filenames have a d.ts suffix, and you can find these files for more than 7,000 JavaScript libraries at www.npmjs.com/~types. Just go there and search for the JavaScript library you're interested in. For example, you can find information on jQuery type definitions at www.npmjs.com/package/@types/jquery—figure 7.1 shows a screenshot of this web page.

At the top right of figure 7.1, you can see the command that installs the type definition files for jQuery, but we like adding the `-D` option so that npm adds `@types/jquery` to the `devDependencies` section of the project's package.json file:

```
npm install @types/jquery -D
```

> **NOTE** The preceding command doesn't install the jQuery library; it just installs the type definitions for jQuery members.

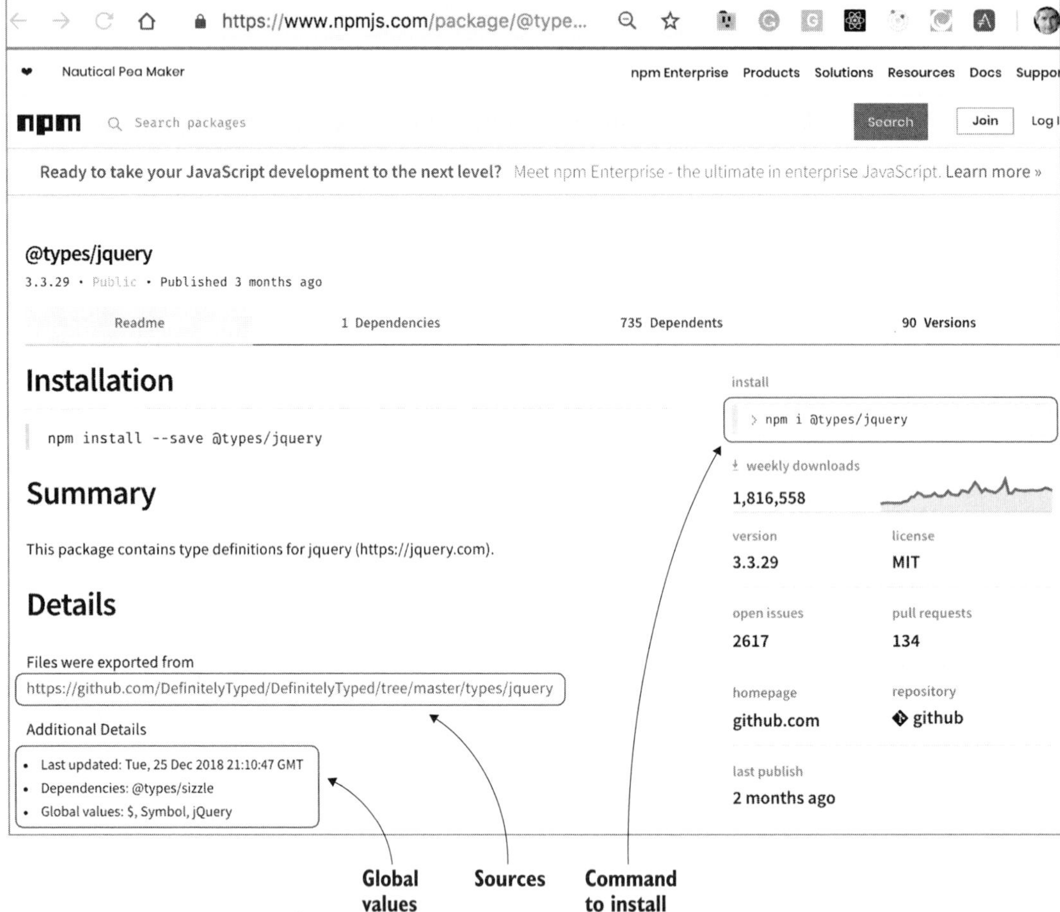

Figure 7.1 jQuery type definitions at npmjs.org

In general, you install type definitions from npmjs.org, specifying the `@types` organization name followed by the name of the package. Once you've installed `@types/jquery`, you can find several files with d.ts extensions, such as jQuery.d.ts and jQueryStatic.d.ts, located in the node_modules/@types/jquery directory of your project. The Typescript compiler (and static analyzer) will use them to help you with autocomplete and type errors.

In the middle of figure 7.1, you'll see the URL for the sources of the jQuery type definitions, and at the bottom are the names of global values offered by jQuery. For example, you can use `$` for accessing the jQuery API when it's installed.

You can create a new directory and turn it into an npm project by running the command `npm init -y` there. This command creates the package.json file, and then you can install the type definition for jQuery:

```
npm install @types/jquery -D
```

Let's see if, after installing type definition files, the static type analyzer and your IDE will start helping you with jQuery API.

7.1.2 *Type definition files and IDEs*

To see how IDEs use type definition files, open the npm project created in the previous section in your IDE, create and open main.ts, enter `$.`, and press Ctrl-Space. If you use the WebStorm IDE, you'll see the available jQuery APIs, as seen in figure 7.2. VS Code will show the available jQuery APIs as well.

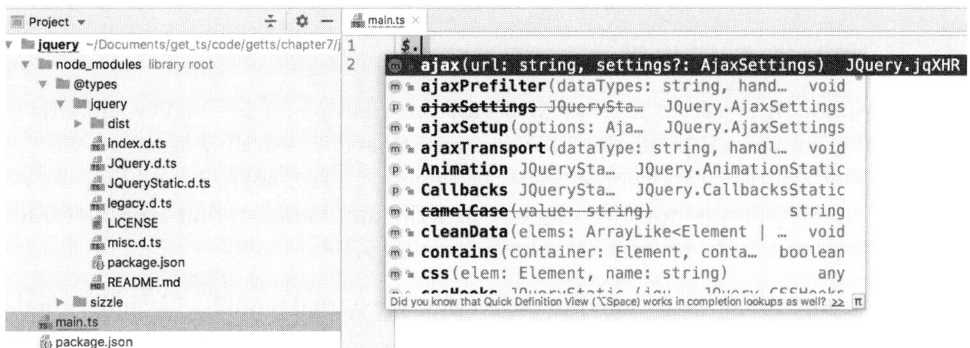

Figure 7.2 WebStorm's autocomplete for jQuery

At the top of figure 7.2, you can see JQuery's `ajax()` method with a strongly typed argument, just like in any TypeScript program. Keep in mind that we didn't even install jQuery (which is written in JavaScript anyway); we just have the type definitions.

This is great, but let's open the same project in VS Code. You may not see any autocomplete, as in figure 7.3. The reason is that the WebStorm IDE automatically shows all the definitions it can find in the project, whereas VS Code prefers us to explicitly configure which d.ts files to use.

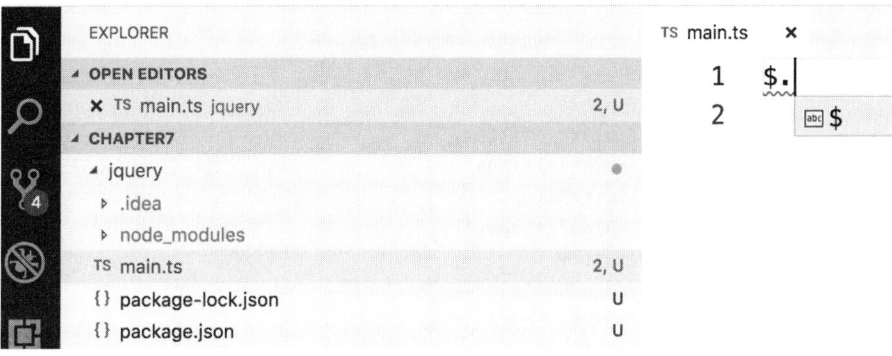

Figure 7.3 VS Code can't find type definitions for jQuery.

Let's play by the VS Code rules and create a tsconfig.json file with the compiler's `types` option. In this array, you can specify which type definitions to use for autocomplete (using the names of the directories under node_modules/@types). The following listing shows the tsconfig.json file that we added to the project.

Listing 7.1 The TypeScript config file, tsconfig.json

```
{
  "compilerOptions": {
      "types" : ["jquery"]
  }
}
```

Although `types: [jquery]` works for this example, if you had to add type definition files for several JavaScript libraries, you'd need to list all of them in the `types` compiler option (for example, `types: [jquery, lodash]`). But adding the compiler's `types` option is not the only way to help the compiler find type definitions—we'll show you the `reference` directive in section 7.1.4.

> **NOTE** Your project may need to refer to external modules like jquery, lodash, or others. The process the compiler goes through to figure out what an import refers to is called *module resolution*. For details on this process, refer to the TypeScript documentation at www.typescriptlang.org/docs/handbook/module-resolution.html.

Now enter `$.` and press Ctrl-Space. The autocomplete should start working properly. Click on the `ajax()` function, and VS Code will show its program documentation, as seen in figure 7.4. No matter what IDE you use, having a d.ts file for JavaScript code gives you intelligent help from the Typescript compiler and static analyzer.

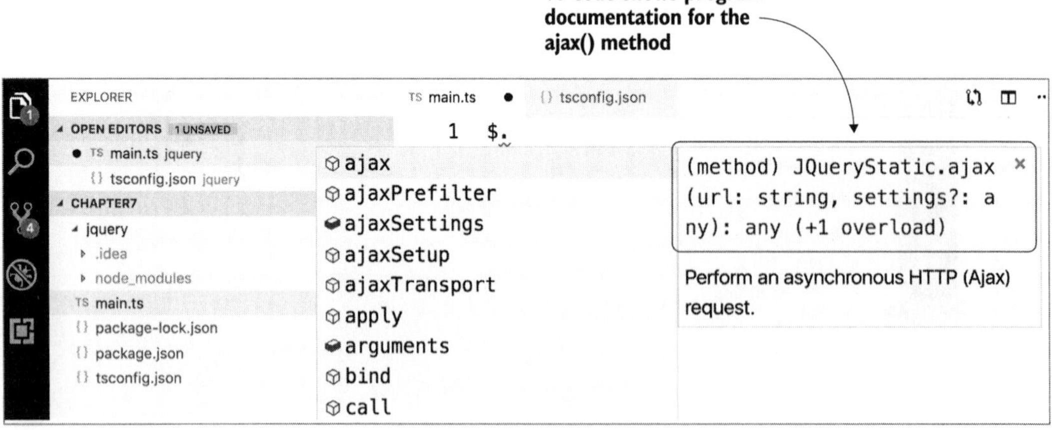

Figure 7.4 VS Code shows autocomplete and documentation for JQuery's ajax() method.

NOTE In WebStorm, to see program documentation for an item selected in the autocomplete list, select it and press Ctrl-J.

Let's peek inside a type definition file. The arrow in figure 7.4 points at the interface name where TypeScript found the type definitions for the `ajax()` function. Coincidentally, it's defined in the file called JQueryStatic.d.ts, located in the node_modules/@types/jquery directory. Hover your mouse pointer over the name of the function, `ajax()`, and Ctrl-click. Both VS Code and WebStorm will open the following fragment of `ajax()` type definitions.

Listing 7.2 A fragment from JQueryStatic.d.ts

Description of the ajax() function

Description of the ajax() parameters

```
/**
 * Perform an asynchronous HTTP (Ajax) request.
 * @param url A string containing the URL to which the request is sent.
 * @param settings A set of key/value pairs that configure the Ajax request.
➥ All settings are optional.
 * A default can be set for any option with $.ajaxSetup(). See jQuery.ajax(
➥ settings ) below
 * for a complete list of all settings.
 * @see \`{@link https://api.jquery.com/jQuery.ajax/ }\`
 * @since 1.5
 */
ajax(url: string, settings?: JQuery.AjaxSettings): JQuery.jqXHR;
```

Signature of ajax() with types

Type definition files can contain only type declarations. In the case of jQuery, its type declarations are wrapped in an interface with multiple properties and method declarations, as you can see for `ajax()` in the preceding listing.

In some d.ts files, you'll see the use of the word `declare`:

```
declare const Sizzle: SizzleStatic;

export declare function findNodes(node: ts.Node): ts.Node[];
```

We're not declaring `const Sizzle` or the function `findNodes()` here; we're just stating that we're going to use a JavaScript library that contains the declarations of `const Sizzle` and `findNodes()`. In other words, this line tries to calm down tsc: "Don't scream if you see `Sizzle` or `findNodes()` in my TypeScript code. At runtime my app will include the JavaScript library that has these types." Such declarations are known as `ambient declarations`—this is how you say to the compiler that the variable in question will exist at runtime. If you don't have type definitions for jQuery, you can simply write `declare var $: any` in your TypeScript code and use the variable `$` to access the jQuery API. Just don't forget to load jQuery along with your app.

As you can see, type definition files allow us to kill two birds with one stone: use the existing JavaScript libraries and enjoy the benefits of a strongly typed language.

NOTE Some JavaScript libraries include d.ts files, and there's no need to install them separately. A good example is the moment.js library, which is used for validating, manipulating, and formatting dates. Visit its repository at https://github.com/moment/moment, and you'll see the moment.d.ts file there.

Using JavaScript libraries without type definition files

Although type definition files are the preferable way of using JavaScript libraries in a TypeScript app, you can use these libraries even without having type definition files. If you know the global variable of the selected JavaScript framework (such as `$` in jQuery), you can use it as-is. Modern JavaScript libraries may use module systems, and instead of offering a global variable, they may require that a particular module member be imported in your code. Refer to the product documentation for the library of your choice.

Let's take jQueryUI, which is a set of UI widgets and themes built on top of jQuery. Let's assume that the type definition file for jQueryUI doesn't exist (even though it does).

JQueryUI's Getting Started guide (http://learn.jquery.com/jquery-ui/getting-started) states that to use this library in a web page, you need to install it locally and add the following code to the HTML document.

```
<link rel="stylesheet" href="jquery-ui.min.css">          <-- Adds CSS
<script src="external/jquery/jquery.js"></script>         <-- Adds jQuery
<script src="jquery-ui.min.js"></script>                  <-- Adds jQueryUI
```

After this is done, you can add jQueryUI widgets to the TypeScript code.

To get access to jQueryUI, you'd still use `$` (the global variable from jQuery). For example, if you have an HTML `<select id="customers">` dropdown, you can turn it into a jQueryUI `selectMenu()` dropdown like this:

```
$("#customers").selectMenu();
```

The preceding code will work, but without the type definition file you won't get any help from TypeScript, and your IDE will highlight jQueryUI API as erroneous.

Of course, you can "fix" all the tsc errors with the following ambient type declaration:

```
declare const $: any;
```

It's always better to use the type definition file, if it's available.

7.1.3 Shims and type definitions

A *shim* is a library that intercepts API calls and transforms the code so the old environment (such as IE 11) can support a newer API (such as ES6). For example, ES6 introduced the `find()` method for arrays, which finds the first element that meets the provided criteria. In the following listing, the value of `index` will be 4 because it's the first value that's greater than 3.

Listing 7.3 Using the find() method on an array

```
const data = [1, 2, 3, 4, 5];

const index = data.find(item => item > 3);  // index = 4
```

If your code has to run in IE 11, which doesn't support the ES6 API, you'd add the `"target": ES5` compiler option in tsconfig.json. As a result, your IDE would underline the `find()` method with a squiggly line as an error, because ES5 didn't support it. The IDE won't even offer the `find()` method in the autocomplete list, as shown in figure 7.5.

```
1
2 const data = [1, 2, 3, 4, 5];
3
4 data.
  concat          (methc
  every           cat(..
  filter          number
  forEach
  indexOf         Combin
  join
  lastIndexOf
  length
```

Figure 7.5 No find() method in ES5 arrays

Can you still use the newer API and see it in the autocomplete list? You can, if you install the es6-shim.d.ts type definition file and add it to the `types` compiler option in tsconfig.json:

```
npm install @types/es6-shim -D
```

Add this shim to your tsconfig.json file (`"types" : ["jquery", "es6-shim"]`), and your IDE won't complain and will display the `find()` method in the autocomplete list, as seen in figure 7.6.

NOTE There is a newer shim called core-js (www.npmjs.com/package/core-js), which can be used not only for the ES6 syntax, but for newer versions of the ECMAScript specs as well.

```
2 const data = [1, 2, 3, 4, 5];
3
4 const array2 = data.find( item => item > 3 );
  concat          (method) Array<number>.fin ×
  copyWithin      d(predicate: (value: numbe
  entries         r, index: number, obj: num
  every           ber[]) => boolean, thisAr
  fill            g?: any): number
  filter
  find            Returns the value of the first element in
  findIndex       the array where predicate is true, and
  forEach         undefined otherwise.
```

Figure 7.6 es6-shim helps with the ES6 API.

7.1.4 Creating your own type definition files

Let's say some time ago you created a `greeting()` JavaScript function, which is located in the hello.js file, as follows.

Listing 7.4 The JavaScript hello.js file

```
function greeting(name) {
    console.log("hello " + name);
}
```

You want to continue using this excellent function (with autocomplete and type checking) in your TypeScript project. In the src directory, create a typings.d.ts file with the following content.

Listing 7.5 The ./src/typings.d.ts file

```
declare function greeting(name: string): void;
```

Finally, you need to let TypeScript know where this type definition file is located. Because this `greeting()` function is not overly useful for the JavaScript community, it's not published at npmjs.org, and no one has created a d.ts file in the `@types` organization either. In this case, you can use a special TypeScript `reference` directive (a *triple-slash directive*), which has to be placed at the top of the .ts file that uses `greeting()`. Figure 7.7 shows a screenshot taken while we were typing `greeti` in the main.ts file in VS Code.

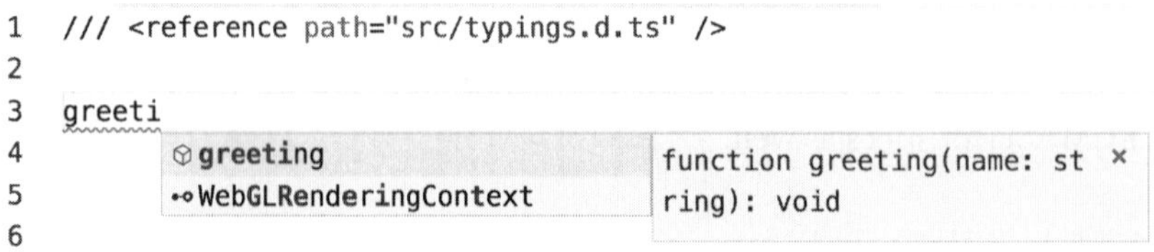

```
/// <reference path="src/typings.d.ts" />

greeti
        greeting                    function greeting(name: st ×
        WebGLRenderingContext       ring): void
```

Figure 7.7 Getting autocomplete in main.ts

As you see, autocomplete prompts us with the argument and return types of the `greeting()` JavaScript function. Figure 7.7 shows a triple-slash directive that uses the path to the type definition file, but if you have the type definition file for some library installed with npm, you can use `types` instead of `path`:

```
/// <reference types="some-library" />
```

> **NOTE** If you want to write a type definition file for a JavaScript library, read the TypeScript documentation at http://mng.bz/E1qq. You can read more about triple-slash directives in the documentation at http://mng.bz/NeqE.

7.2 A sample TypeScript app that uses JavaScript libraries

In this section, we'll look at an app that's written in TypeScript and that uses the jQuery UI JavaScript library. This simple app will display three shapes: a rectangle, a circle, and a triangle, as shown in figure 7.8.

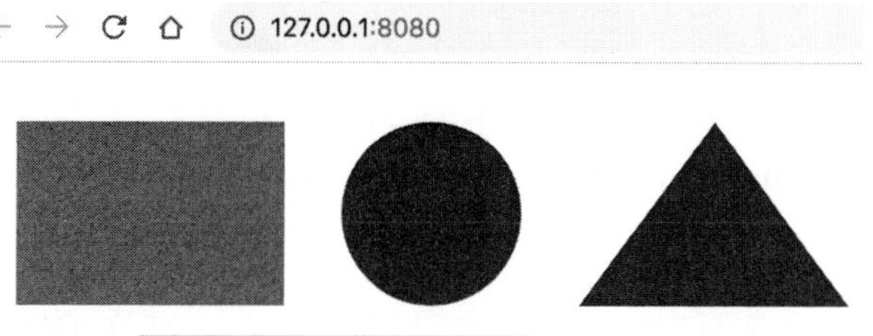

Figure 7.8 Three shapes rendered by jQuery UI

If you read the printed version of this book, you'll need to know that the rectangle is blue, and both the circle and triangle are green. The user can enter a valid CSS selector, and the input field will render a dropdown list with the shape names that have the provided selector.

Figure 7.9 shows a screenshot taken after the user entered `.green` in the input field and selected the triangle in the dropdown; the triangle was surrounded with a red border.

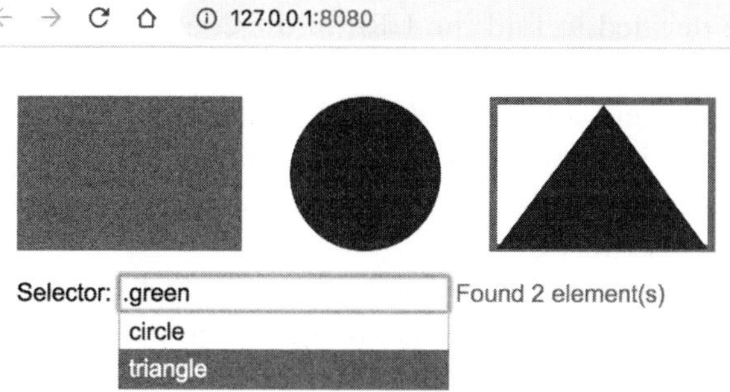

Figure 7.9 Finding an element that has the CSS class `.green`

In this app, we use jQuery to find the HTML elements that have one of the specified selectors; the rendering of shapes is done by jQuery UI. This sample project is located in the chapter7/jquery-ui-example directory, and it includes four files: package.json, tsconfig.json, index.ts, and index.html. The content of the package.json file is shown in the following listing.

Listing 7.6 package.json includes type definition files for jQuery and jQuery UI

```
{
  "name": "jquery-ui-example",
  "description": "Code sample for the TypeScript Quickly book",
```

```
  "homepage": "https://www.manning.com/books/typescript-quickly",
  "license": "MIT",
  "devDependencies": {
    "@types/jquery": "^3.3.29",          <- Type definitions for jQuery
    "@types/jqueryui": "^1.12.7",        <- Type definitions for jQueryUI
    "typescript": "^3.4.1"               <- The Typescript compiler
  }
}
```

As you can see, we didn't add the jQuery and jQuery UI libraries to package.json because we added the three lines shown in the following listing to the <head> section of index.html.

Listing 7.7 Adding jQuery and jQueryUI to index.html

```
<link rel="stylesheet"                                    <- Adds the jQuery UI styles
➥ href="//code.jquery.com/ui/1.12.1/themes/base/jquery-ui.css">
<script src="//code.jquery.com/jquery-3.3.1.min.js"></script>          <- Adds the jQuery library
<script src="//code.jquery.com/ui/1.12.1/jquery-ui.min.js"></script>   <- Adds the jQuery UI library
```

You may ask, why didn't we add a `dependencies` section to package.json as we do with all other npm packages? The locally installed jQuery UI didn't include the bundled version of this library, and we didn't want to complicate this app by adding Webpack or another bundler. So we decided to find the URL of the content delivery network (CDN) for these libraries.

The jQuery home page (jQuery.com) includes a Download button that takes you to the Download page (http://jquery.com/download), which includes the required URLs of the CDN. If you need to include a JavaScript library in your project, you'll need to go through a similar discovery process.

The <head> section of our index.html file also includes the styles shown in listing 7.8. In our TypeScript code we'll use jQuery to get references to the HTML elements with the IDs `#shapes`, `#error`, and `#info`.

> **NOTE** In this demo app, we use jQuery selectors to find elements on the page, but those selectors are already supported by the standard `document.querySelector()` and `document.querySelectorAll()` methods. We use jQuery just for the sake of showing how TypeScript code can work with JavaScript libraries.

The user will be able to enter in the input field any valid CSS style within the DOM element with an ID of `#shapes`. They'll see the results in the autocomplete list, as shown earlier in figure 7.9.

Listing 7.8 A fragment from the `<style>` tag in index.html

```
<style>
    #shapes {
      display: flex;
      margin-bottom: 16px;
    }

    #shapes > *:not(:last-child) {
      margin-right: 32px;
    }

    @media (max-width: 640px) {      <-- Changes the page layout for devices narrower than 640 pixels
      #shapes {
        flex-direction: column;
        align-items: center;
      }

      #shapes > *:not(:last-child) {
        margin-bottom: 16px;
        margin-right: 0;
      }
    }

    #rectangle {
      background-color: blue;      <-- The rectangle is blue.
      height: 100px;
      width: 150px;
    }

    #circle {
      background-color: green;     <-- The circle and triangle are green.
      border-radius: 50%;
      height: 100px;
      width: 100px;
    }

    #triangle {
      color: green;                <--
      height: 100px;
      width: 150px;
    }
  </style>
```

The `@media (max-width: 640px)` media query instructs the browser to change the layout on small devices (less than 640 pixels in width). The `flex-direction: column` style will render the shapes vertically, and `align-items: center;` will center the shapes on the page, as shown in figure 7.10.

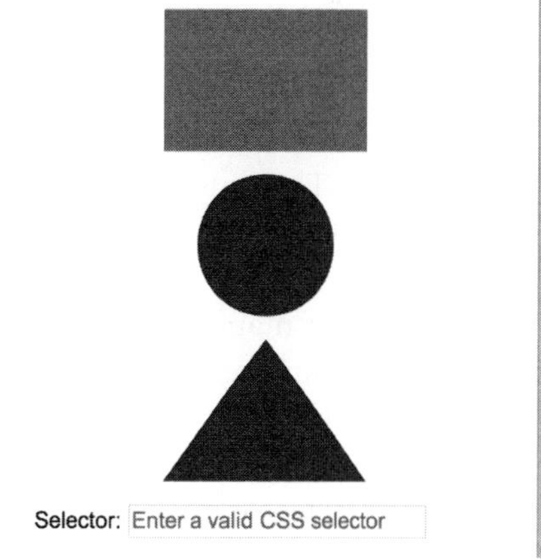

Figure 7.10 Finding the DOM element that has the CSS class `.green`

The <body> section of index.html has two containers implemented as <div> tags. The first one, `<div id="shapes">`, has child `<div>` tags that represent the shapes. The last container includes the input field for entering search criteria and two areas for displaying an error or info message (for example, "Found 2 element(s)" as in figure 7.9).

Listing 7.9 The body section of index.html

```
<body>
  <div id="shapes">                          <-- The container with shapes
    <div id="rectangle"
         class="blue"                        Any of these CSS attributes can be
         hasAngles>                          used for finding a shape with our UI.
    </div>

    <div id="circle"
         class="green"></div>

    <div id="triangle"
         class="green"
         hasAngles>
      <svg viewBox="0 0 150 100">
        <polygon points="75, 0, 150, 100, 0, 100" fill="currentColor"/>
      </svg>
    </div>
  </div>

  <div class="ui-widget">
    <label for="selector">Selector:</label>
    <input id="selector" placeholder="Enter a valid CSS selector">
    <span id="error"></span>                 <-- An error message will be rendered here.
    <span id="info"></span>                  <-- An info message will be rendered here.
  </div>

  <script src="dist/index.js"></script>      <-- This script is a compiled version of index.ts.
</body>
```

Any of the valid selectors, such as `div`, `.green`, `hasAngles`, can be entered in the input field. The only reason we added the `hasAngles` attribute to the rectangle and triangle was to allow searching for these shapes by entering the `[hasAngles]` selector in the input field.

The main goal of this app is to illustrate the use of jQuery UI's Autocomplete widget from the TypeScript code. It enables users to quickly find and select from a prepopulated list of values as they type, leveraging searching and filtering as you saw in figure 7.9. If the user enters `.green`, the app displays the DOM elements that have this CSS selector and will add them to the source list of values in the Autocomplete widget.

The Autocomplete widget is described in the jQuery UI documentation at http://api.jqueryui.com/autocomplete, and it requires an `options` object with a mandatory `source` property that defines the data to use.

Listing 7.10 Using the Autocomplete widget

```
$('#selector')                          // Our <input> field has id="#selector"
    .autocomplete({                     // Appends the jQuery UI Autocomplete widget
    source: (request,                   // A function that gets the data and returns a callback
      response) => {...}});             // A callback to invoke when a value from the list is selected
```

The code in listing 7.10 has no types, but since we have the jQuery UI type definition file installed, VS Code leads us through the autocomplete API as shown in figure 7.11. Note the digit 9 with the up and down arrows. jQuery UI offers many different ways of invoking `autocomplete()`, and by clicking on the arrows, you can pick the API you like.

```
                   autocomplete(options:
                   JQueryUI.AutocompleteOptions):
                 9 JQuery<HTMLElement>
$('#selector').autocomplete({})
```

Figure 7.11 The first prompt by VS Code

The prompt in figure 7.11 indicates that the type of the `option` object is `JQueryUI.AutocompleteOptions`. You can always press the Ctrl-Space keys, and the IDE will continue helping you. According to the widget's documentation, we need to provide the source of the autocomplete values, and VS Code lists the `source` option among others, as shown in figure 7.12.

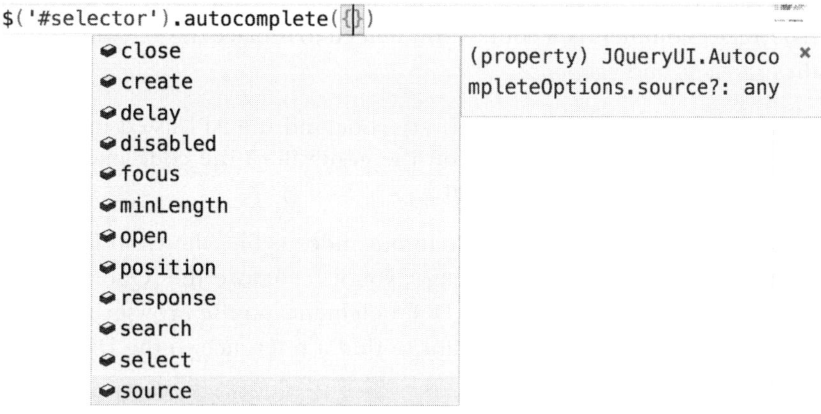

Figure 7.12 VS Code continues prompting

```
interface AutocompleteOptions extends AutocompleteEvents {
    appendTo?: any; //Selector;
    autoFocus?: boolean;
    delay?: number;
    disabled?: boolean;
    minLength?: number;
    position?: any; // object
    source?: any; // [], string or ()
    classes?: AutocompleteClasses;
}
```

This type declaration can be improved.

Figure 7.13 The JQueryUI.AutocompleteOptions type definitions

Cmd-click on Mac (or Ctrl-click on Windows) on the `autocomplete` list, and it'll open the index.d.ts file with all the possible options. Cmd-click on `JQueryUI.AutocompleteOptions` and you'll see its type definitions, as shown in figure 7.13.

The IDE's typeahead help may not be perfect; it's only as good as the provided type definition file. Take another look at the `source` property in figure 7.13. It's declared as `any`, and the comment states that it could be an array, string, or function. This declaration could be improved by declaring a union type that would allow only these types:

```
type arrayOrFunction = Array<any> | string | Function;

let source: arrayOrFunction = (request, response) => 123;
```

Introducing the `arrayOrFunction` type would eliminate the need for writing the `// [], string, or ()` comment. Of course, you'd need to replace the `123` with some code that handles `request` and `response`.

> **NOTE** As you can imagine, the library code and the API listed in its d.ts file may go out of sync. We depend on the goodwill of the code maintainers to keep the type definitions up to date.

Now let's review the TypeScript code in our index.ts file, shown in listing 7.11. If you were developing web apps 10 years ago, you'll recognize the jQuery style of coding: we start by getting references to the DOM elements on the browser's page. For example, `$('#shapes')` means that we want to find a reference to the DOM element with `id="shapes"`.

Listing 7.11 index.ts: the source code of our app

```
const shapesElement = $('#shapes');
const errorElement = $('#error');
const infoElement = $('#info');

$('#selector')
    .autocomplete({
    source: (request: { term: string },
             response: ([]) => void) => {
      try {
        const elements = $(request.term, shapesElement);
        const ids = elements.map((_index, dom) => ({ label: $(dom).attr('id'),
                    value: request.term })).toArray();

        response(ids);

        infoElement.text(`Found ${elements.length} element(s)`);
        errorElement.text('');
      } catch (e) {
        response([]);
        infoElement.text('');
        errorElement.text('Invalid selector');
        $('*', shapesElement).css({ border: 'none' });
      }
    },
    focus: (_event, ui) => {
      $('*', shapesElement).css({ border: 'none' });
      $(`#${ui.item.label}`, shapesElement).css({ border: '5px solid red' });
    }
});

$('#selector').on('input', (event: JQuery.TriggeredEvent<HTMLInputElement>)
➥ => {
  if (!event.target.value) {
    $('*', shapesElement).css({ border: 'none' });
    errorElement.text('');
    infoElement.text('');
  }
});
```

Annotations:
- Uses jQuery to find references to DOM elements
- The first parameter of the function is the search criterion.
- The second parameter is a callback to modify the DOM.
- Finds the elements with the shapes that meet the search criterion
- Finds the IDs of shapes that meet the criterion
- Invokes the callback, passing the autocomplete values
- Handles the event fired when the focus moves to one of the IDs
- Removes the borders from the shapes, if any
- Adds a red border to the DOM element with the selected ID
- Resets all previous selections and messages

We pass the Autocomplete widget an object with two properties: `source` and `focus`. Our `source` property is a function that takes two parameters:

- `request`—An object with the search criterion, such as `{term: '.green'}`
- `response`—A callback that finds the IDs of the DOM elements that meet the search criterion. In our case, we pass a callback function that contains one `try/catch` block.

The `focus` property is also a function. It's an event handler that will be invoked when you move the mouse over one of the items in the rendered list. There we clear previously bordered shapes and add a border to the currently selected one.

Before running this app, we need to compile our TypeScript to JavaScript. The Typescript compiler will use the following compiler options.

Listing 7.12 tsconfig.json: the compiler configuration

```
{
  "compilerOptions": {
    "outDir": "dist",        <- Where to place the compiled JavaScript
    "target": "es2018"       <- Compiles into JavaScript compatible with the ES2018 spec
  }
}
```

In previous chapters, we created an npm script command in package.json to run the locally installed version of the executable we wanted to run. For example, adding the command `"tsc": "tsc"` to the `scripts` section in package.json would allow us to run the locally installed compiler as follows:

```
npm run tsc
```

This time we were lazy and didn't configure this command. Actually, we wanted to illustrate the npx tool (which comes with npm). It runs the locally installed program if it exists or installs the requested program temporarily and runs it. Here's how you can compile the index.ts file using the locally installed tsc with the npx tool:

```
npx tsc
```

After running this command, you'll see the index.js file in the dist directory. This file is used in index.html as follows:

```
<script src="dist/index.js"></script>
```

We're almost there. The only missing player is a web server that can serve our app to the browser. One of the simplest web servers you can install is live-server (www.npmjs.com/package/live-server). Let's install it:

```
npm i live-server -g
```

NOTE Instead of installing live-server manually, you can run it as `npx live-server`. If live-server isn't found in the project's node_modules, npx will download it from npmjs.com, cache it globally on your computer, and run the live-server binary.

To run the server, enter the following command in the Terminal window in the root directory of your project:

```
live-server
```

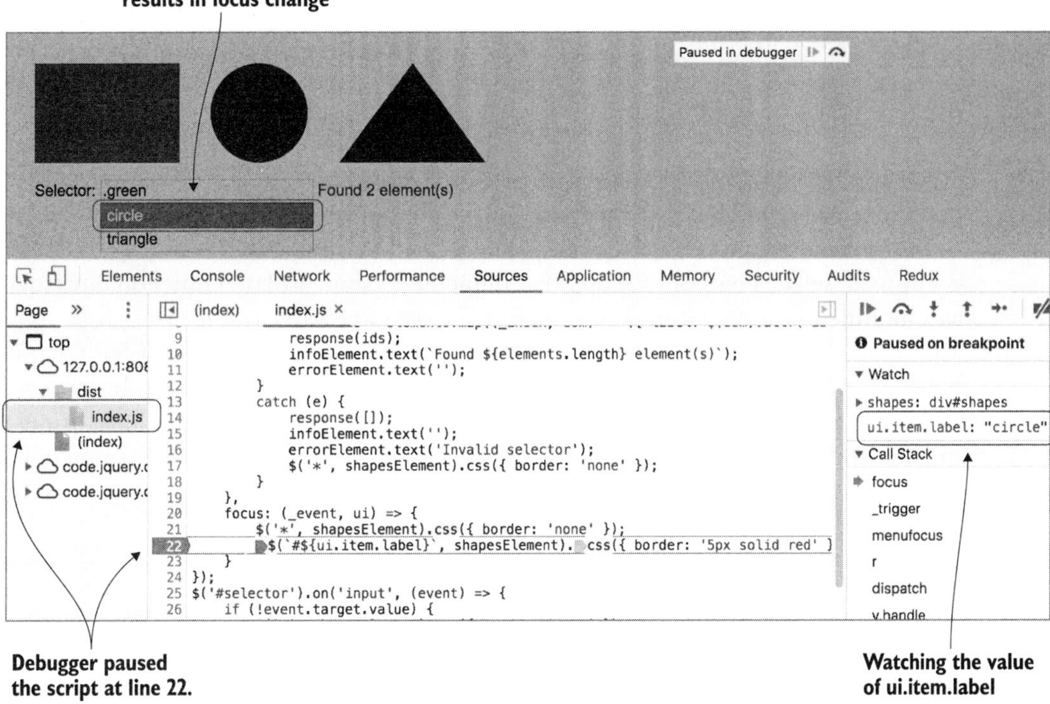

Figure 7.14 Hitting a breakpoint in dist/index.js

Point your browser to localhost:8080, and you'll see the app running. The best way to understand how the code works is by running it through a debugger; figure 7.14 shows the app running in Chrome. It paused in the running script, dist/index.js, at the breakpoint placed on line 22, which is invoked when the `focus` event is fired. In the Watch panel on the right, we've added `ui.item.label`, and it has the value `circle`, matching the selection in the UI.

> **NOTE** In section 6.1, we explained that having source map files allows you to debug the TypeScript code. Just add the line `"sourceMap": true` to the tsconfig.json file, and you'll be able to debug index.ts while running index.js.

Now that we've discussed using third-party JavaScript libraries with your TypeScript code, let's consider another scenario: you already have an app written in JavaScript, and you're considering switching to TypeScript.

7.3 Introducing TypeScript in your JavaScript project

In an ideal world, you always work with the latest languages and technologies, but in reality, you generally have a mix of old and new. Suppose you're an enterprise developer, and your team has been working on a JavaScript app for the last several years, but after reading this book you have a strong desire to write code in TypeScript. You can always come up with some pet project and develop it in TypeScript after hours, but is it possible to bring TypeScript to your main JavaScript project at work?

TypeScript supports optional typing, which means you don't have to modify your JavaScript code to declare types for each variable or function parameter, so why not use the Typescript compiler on your JavaScript app? Well, the code base of your JavaScript app may have tens of thousands of lines of code, and using tsc to compile all of them may reveal hidden bugs and slow down the deployment process. That may not be the best way to start.

Instead, select a part of your app that implements some isolated functionality (such as a module for adding a new customer or for shipping) and run it through tsc as-is. Most likely, your app already has a build process that uses tools such as Grunt, Gulp, Babel, Webpack, and so on. Find the right place, and incorporate tsc into this process.

You don't even need to rename JavaScript files to give them .ts extensions. Just use the `"allowJs": true` Typescript compiler option, which tells tsc, "Please compile not only the .ts files but the .js files as well, and don't perform type checking—just compile it according to the setting in the compiler's `target` option."

> **NOTE** If you don't change the file extensions from .js to .ts, your IDE will still highlight the types in the JavaScript files as erroneous, but tsc will compile the files if you use the `"allowJs": true` option.

You may wonder, "Why ask tsc to skip type checking if types are optional anyway?" One of the reasons is that tsc might not be able to fully infer all the type info from your JavaScript code, and it may report errors. Another reason is that your existing code can be buggy (even if the bugs aren't showstoppers), and allowing tsc to work at its fullest may reveal lots of compile errors that you don't have time or resources to fix. If it ain't broke, don't fix it, right?

Of course, you may have a different approach: "If it ain't broke, improve it." If you're confident that your JavaScript code is written well, opt in to type checking by adding the `"checkJs": true` tsc compiler option to tsconfig.json. Some of your JavaScript files may still generate errors, and you can skip checking them by adding a `//@ts-nocheck` comment to these files. Conversely, you can choose to check only a few .js files by adding a `//@ts-check` comment to them without setting `"checkJs": true`. You can even turn off type checking for a specific line of code by adding `//@ts-ignore` on the preceding line.

To illustrate the effect of type-checking existing JavaScript code, we randomly selected the OpenAjax.js file from the GitHub repository of the Dojo framework (https://github.com/dojo/dojo/blob/master/OpenAjax.js). Let's pretend we want to start turning this code into TypeScript, and so we added the `//@ts-check` comment to the top of this file. You'll see some of the lines with squigglies in VS Code, as shown in figure 7.15.

```
1  //@ts-check
2  import { isMoment } from './constructor';
3  import { normalizeUnits } from '../units/aliases';
4  import { createLocal } from '../create/local';
5  import isUndefined from '../utils/is-undefined';
6
7  if (!window["OpenAjax"]){
8      OpenAjax = new function(){
9          // summary:
10         //      the OpenAjax hub
11         // description:
12         //      see http://www.openajax.org/member/wiki/OpenAjax_Hub_Specif
13
14         var libs = {};
15         var ooh = "org.openajax.hub.";
16
17         var h = {};
18         this.hub = h;
19         h.implementer = "http://openajax.org";
20         h.implVersion = "0.6";
21         h.specVersion = "0.6";
22         h.implExtraData = {};
23         h.libraries = libs;
```

Type check errors

Figure 7.15 Adding the `//@ts-check` comment to the top of a JavaScript file

Let's ignore the errors on the import statements at the top; we wouldn't see them if all these files were present. It looks like the error in line 8 is not an error either. It seems that the `OpenAjax` object will be present at runtime. Adding `//@ts-ignore` above line 8 would remove that squiggly.

But to fix the errors in lines 19–23 we'd need to declare a `type` or an `interface` with all these properties. (Note that if you were changing this code to TypeScript, you might want to rename the variable `h` with a more meaningful name.)

Let's consider another piece of JavaScript code, shown in figure 7.16. We want to get the price of a product, and if it's less than $20, we'll buy it. The IDE doesn't complain and the code seems legitimate.

```
const getPrice = () => Math.random()*100;

if (getPrice < 20) {
    console.log("Buying!");
}
```

Figure 7.16 Buggy JavaScript code

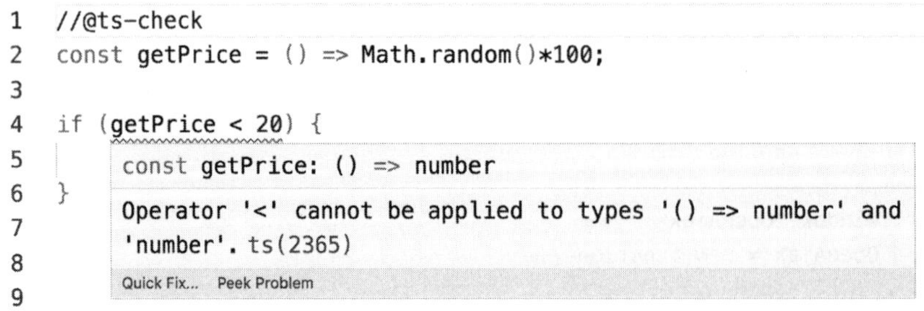

```
//@ts-check
const getPrice = () => Math.random()*100;

if (getPrice < 20) {

}
```

```
const getPrice: () => number
Operator '<' cannot be applied to types '() => number' and
'number'. ts(2365)
Quick Fix...   Peek Problem
```

Figure 7.17 `@ts-check` found a bug.

Let's add the `//@ts-check` comment at the top so the static type analyzer can check this code for validity, as shown in figure 7.17.

Oops! Our JavaScript code had a bug—we forgot to add parentheses after `getPrice` in the `if` statement (so we never invoked this function). If you were wondering why this code never gave you the OK to buy the product, now you know the reason: the expression `getPrice < 20` was never evaluated to `true`! Simply adding the `//@ts-check` at the top helped us find a runtime bug in a JavaScript program.

There's another tsc option, `noImplicitAny`, that could help you with JavaScript-to-TypeScript migration. If you're not planning to specify the types of function parameters and return types, tsc may have a hard time inferring the right types, and you may temporarily have to keep the compiler's `"noImplicitAny": false` option (the default). In this mode, if tsc cannot infer the variable type based on how it's used, the compiler silently defaults the type to `any`. That's what is meant by *implicit any*. But ideally, `noImplicitAny` should be set to `true`, so don't forget to turn it back on when the migration to TypeScript is complete.

> **NOTE** After turning on `noImplicitAny`, add another option, `strictNullChecks`, to catch all possible cases that may contain `null` or `undefined` where other values are expected.

The Typescript compiler will go easy on your .js files. It'll allow properties to be added to a class or a function after their declaration. The same applies to object literals in .js files: you can add properties to the object literal even if they were not defined originally. TypeScript supports the CommonJS module format and will recognize the `require()` function calls as module imports. All function parameters are optional by default, and calls with fewer arguments than the declared number of parameters are allowed.

You can also help tsc with type inference by adding the JSDoc annotations (such as `@param` and `@return`) to your JavaScript code. Read more on the subject in the document "JSDoc support in JavaScript" on GitHub at http://mng.bz/DNqy.

> **NOTE** The type-coverage CLI tool (www.npmjs.com/package/type-coverage) allows you to count all the identifiers in your app that are declared with an explicit type (except `any`) and report the type-coverage percentage.

The process of upgrading your JavaScript project to TypeScript is not overly complicated, and we've given you a high-level overview of one approach to doing it gradually. For more details, read the document "Migrating from JavaScript" in the TypeScript documentation at http://mng.bz/lolj. There you can find specifics on integrating with Gulp and Webpack, converting a React.js app to TypeScript, and more.

Once again: Why TypeScript?

TypeScript isn't the first attempt at creating an alternative to JavaScript that can run either in a browser or in a standalone JavaScript engine. TypeScript is only seven years old, but it's already in the top-10 programming languages in various ratings. Why don't top-10 language lists include older languages like CoffeeScript or Dart that were supposed to become alternative ways of writing JavaScript?

In our opinion, there are three major forces that make TypeScript stand out:

- TypeScript strictly follows the ECMAScript standards. If a proposed feature made it to the stage 3 of the TS39 process, it'll be included in TypeScript today.
- TypeScript IDEs work with the same static type analyzer, offering you consistent help as you're writing code.
- TypeScript easily interoperates with JavaScript code, which means that you can use thousands of existing JavaScript libraries in your TypeScript apps (and you learned how to do that in this chapter).

This concludes part 1 of this book, where we introduced the TypeScript language. We didn't cover each and every feature of the language, and we didn't plan to. The book's title is *TypeScript Quickly*, isn't it?

If you understand all the material from part 1, you'll easily be able to pass a TypeScript technical interview. But to become a really productive TypeScript developer, we encourage you to study and run all the sample apps described in part 2.

Summary

- You can use thousands of existing JavaScript libraries in your TypeScript project.
- Type definition files allow you to enjoy the type-checking and autocomplete features in libraries that were written in JavaScript. These files make you more productive in writing code.
- You can create type definition files for any proprietary JavaScript code.
- Even if a JavaScript library doesn't have a type definition file, you can still use it in your TypeScript project.
- There are well-defined steps that allow you to gradually upgrade your existing JavaScript code to TypeScript.

Part 2

Applying TypeScript in a blockchain app

Part 2 includes a number of applications written with the help of popular frameworks. Each of these apps uses TypeScript as a programming language. We start by explaining the concept of the blockchain technology, which is used for various versions of the sample app presented in Part 2.

We'll introduce such frameworks and libraries as Angular, React.js, and Vue.js, and you'll see how to develop a sample blockchain app with their help. The materials included in this part will help you to understand how TypeScript is being used in today's real-world projects. While you don't have to read each chapter of Part 2, getting familiar with the materials of chapters 8 and 10 is required for understanding of the apps presented in chapters 12, 14, and 16.

8 Developing your own blockchain app

This chapter covers

- The principles of blockchain apps
- What the hashing functions are for
- What block mining is
- Developing a simple blockchain-based app

In this chapter, we'll introduce a sample app that uses TypeScript and blockchain technology. Most of the subsequent chapters will include different versions of a blockchain app, as we introduce popular libraries and frameworks that can be used with TypeScript.

Using a non-trivial technology to develop a sample app for this book might surprise you, but there are several reasons why you might want to learn about blockchain:

- There's a need to improve confidence, fidelity, and transparency in workflows where multiple parties are involved. Blockchain is a great fit for these tasks, and TypeScript can be used to implement them.

- We are hearing about new data breaches daily. Are you 100% sure that no one can transfer a thousand dollars from your bank account without your approval? Only if you don't have a thousand dollars in your account. Blockchain eliminates the single point of failure. In blockchains, there is no single authority (like a bank) that owns your data; modifying your data requires approval by most of the blockchain members.
- New cryptocurrencies are being announced almost daily, and the need for software developers who understand the underlying technologies will increase.
- New well-paid jobs are being created in organizations that implement blockchains in their operations, such as in financial transactions, voting, logistics, establishing internet identity, ride sharing, internet advertising, and so on.

Because the whole idea of blockchains is still new, we'll start by explaining the basics of how blockchains operate and what they're for.

8.1 Blockchain 101

Blockchains can be used for various types of applications, but financial apps made blockchain a buzzword. Most likely, you've heard about cryptocurrencies in general and Bitcoin in particular. Often you'll see the words "Bitcoin" and "blockchain" in the same sentence, but whereas blockchain is a special decentralized way of storing immutable data, Bitcoin is a specific cryptocurrency that uses a concrete implementation of a blockchain. In other words, Bitcoin is to blockchain as your app data is to a DBMS.

A cryptocurrency has no physical bills or coins, but it can be used to buy or sell things or services. Also, transactions made using a cryptocurrency don't use brick and mortar institutions for their record keeping.

But if there are no bills, and banks aren't involved, how can one party be sure that the other paid for the provided services or goods? In a blockchain, transactions are combined into blocks, which then are validated and linked into a chain. Hence the term *blockchain*.

Try visualizing a bicycle chain: figure 8.1 depicts a blockchain that consists of three blocks (chain links). If a record of new transactions has to be added to a blockchain, an app creates a new block, which is given to the blockchain nodes (computers) for validation using one of the algorithms (for example, calculating a special hash code) used in blockchain systems. If the block is valid, it's added to the blockchain; otherwise it's rejected.

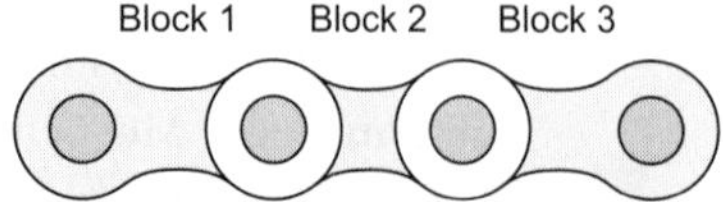

Figure 8.1 A blockchain of three blocks

Where is the data about transactions stored, and what's the meaning of the word *decentralized* in this context? A typical blockchain is decentralized because no single person or company controls or owns the data. Being decentralized also means that there is no single point of failure.

Imagine a server that has information about the available seats on some airlines. Multiple travel agencies connect to the same server to browse and book the air tickets.

Some agencies (nodes) are small and have only one computer connected to the server. Some have two, three, or even more computers in the same node, but they all depend on the data from that single server. This is *centralized data processing*, as illustrated in figure 8.2. If the server is down, no one can book air tickets.

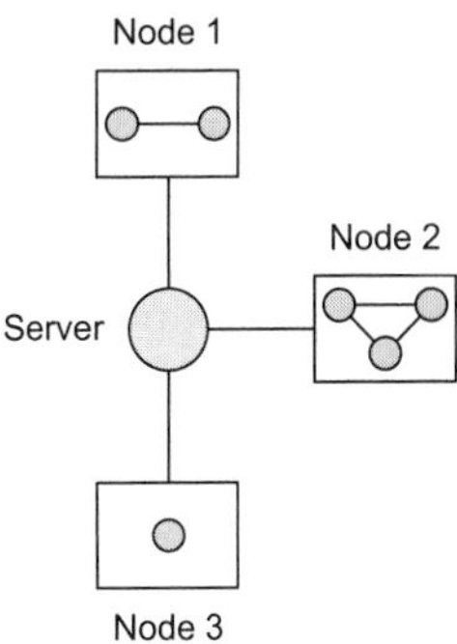

Figure 8.2 Centralized data processing

In the case of decentralized data processing, as in most blockchains, there is no central data server. Full copies of the blockchain are stored on the nodes of a *peer-to-peer* network, which could include your computers if you decide to join a blockchain. A single node doesn't mean one computer—you may be the owner of a computer cluster that represents one node. Figure 8.3 illustrates a decentralized network. If any of the nodes are down, the system remains operational as long as at least one node is running.

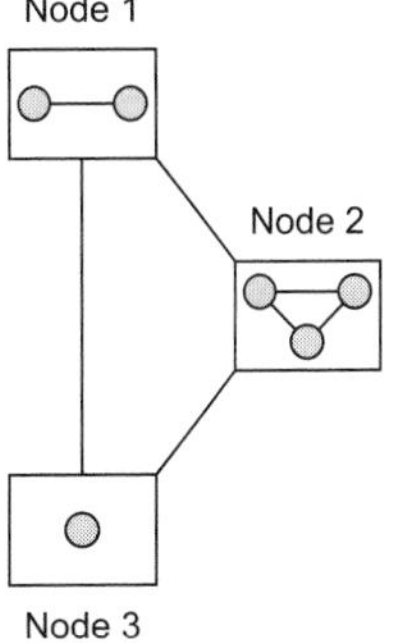

Figure 8.3 Decentralized data processing

> **NOTE** An ability to pass the digital currency from peer to peer without a central authority became crucial to the popularity of blockchain technology. Now blockchains are being used in other types of applications, like logistics, real-estate transactions, ticket reservation, voting, and so on.

Is it secure to store copies of transactions on multiple computers that belong to other people or organizations? What if one of these computer owners (a bad guy) modifies my transaction, changing the paid amount to 0? The good news is that this isn't possible. After a block is added to the chain, its data can't be changed—the data in a blockchain is immutable.

Think of a blockchain as storage where the data is "written in stone." Once a piece of data is added to the store, you can neither remove nor update it. A new block can only be inserted after some node in the network solves a math problem. This may well sound like magic—the best way to understand how a blockchain works is to build one, and we'll start doing so in next section.

Basically, a blockchain is a decentralized immutable ledger represented by a collection of blocks. Each block can store any type of data, such as information about financial transactions, voting results, medical records, and so on. Each block is linked to the previous one by storing the hash value of the previous block in the chain.

In the next section, we'll give you a mini primer on hashing.

8.1.1 Cryptographic hash functions

As defined on Wikipedia, a hash function "is a mathematical algorithm that maps data of arbitrary size (often called the 'message') to a bit string of a fixed size (the 'hash value,' 'hash,' or 'message digest') and is a one-way function, that is, a function which is practically infeasible to invert" (https://en.wikipedia.org/wiki/Cryptographic_hash_function). It also states that hash functions are suitable for use in cryptography.

A cryptographic hash function allows one to easily verify that some input data maps to a given hash value, but if the input data is unknown, it is deliberately difficult to reconstruct it (or any equivalent alternatives) by knowing the stored hash value.

Encryption involves a bidirectional function that takes a value and applies a secret key to return an encrypted value. Using the same key, the encrypted value can be decrypted.

In contrast, a *hashing* utility uses a unidirectional function. The process can't be reversed to reveal the original value. A hash function always produces the same hash value if provided the same input value, and complex hashing algorithms are used to minimize the probability that more than one input will provide the same hash value.

Let's consider a very basic and not overly secure hash function to understand the unidirectional nature of hashes. Suppose an app has numbers-only passwords, and we don't want to store them in clear in the database. We want to write a hash function that applies the modulo operator to the provided password and then adds 10 to it.

Listing 8.1 A very simple hash function

```
function hashMe(password: number): number{

  const hash =  10 + (password % 2);          <— Creates a modulo-based hash

  console.log(`Original password: ${password}, hashed value: ${hash}`);

  return hash;
}
```

For any even number, the expression `input % 2` will produce 0. Now let's invoke the `hashMe()` function several times, providing different even numbers as input parameters:

```
hashMe (2);
hashMe (4);
hashMe (6);
hashMe (800);
```

Each of these invocations will produce a hash value of 10, and the output will look like this:

```
Original password: 2, hashed value: 10
Original password: 4, hashed value: 10
Original password: 6, hashed value: 10
Original password: 800, hashed value: 10
```

You can see this function in action on CodePen at http://mng.bz/BYqv.

When a hashing function generates the same output for more than one input, it's called a *collision*. In cryptography, various Secure Hash Algorithms (SHA) offer more or less secure ways for creating hashes, and they are created to be *collision resistant*, making it extremely hard to find two inputs that will produce the same hash value.

A block in a blockchain is represented by a hash value, and it's very important that cyber criminals can't replace one block with another by preparing fraudulent content that produces the same hash as the legitimate block. Our simple hash function in listing 8.1 has no resistance to collision attacks. Blockchains, in contrast, use collision-resistant hashing algorithms, such as SHA-256, which takes a string of any length and produces a hash value of 256 bits or 64 hexadecimal characters. Even if you decided to generate a SHA-256 hash for the entire text of this book, its length would be 64 hexadecimal numbers. There are 2^{256} possible combinations of bits in SHA-256 hashes, which is more than the number of grains of sand in the world.

TIP To learn more about the SHA-256 algorithm, see the Wikipedia article at https://en.wikipedia.org/wiki/SHA-2.

To calculate a SHA-256 hash on a Unix-based OS, you can use the shasum utility. On Windows, you can use the program certUtil. There are multiple online SHA-256 generators as well. For creating hashes programmatically, you can use the `crypto` module in Node.js apps or the `crypto` object in modern browsers.

Here's how you can calculate the SHA-256 hash for the text "hello world" on macOS:

```
echo -n 'hello world' | shasum -a 256
```

This command produces the following hash:

```
b94d27b9934d3e08a52e52d7da7dabfac484efe37a5380ee9088f7ace2efcde9
```

No matter how many times you repeat the preceding command for the string "hello world" you'll always get the same hash value, but changing any character in the input string will produce a completely different SHA-256 hash. Applying functional-programming terminology, we can say that a hash function is a *pure function* because it always returns the same value for a given input.

TIP If you're interested in hashing methodologies and algorithms, see Arash Partow's discussion of hashing algorithms (www.partow.net/programming/hashfunctions) or read the Wikipedia article at https://en.wikipedia.org/wiki/Hash_function.

We've stated already that blocks in a blockchain are linked using hashes, and in the next section we'll get familiar with the block internals.

8.1.2 What a block is made of

You can think of a block as a record in a ledger. Each block in a blockchain contains app-specific data, and it also has a timestamp, its own hash value, and the hash value of the previous block. In a very simple (and easy to hack) blockchain, an app could perform the following actions to add a new block to the chain:

1. Find the hash of the most recently inserted block, and store it as a reference to the previous block.
2. Generate a hash value for the newly created block.
3. Submit the new block to the blockchain for validation.

Let's discuss these steps. At some point the blockchain was created, and the very first block was inserted into this chain. The very first block in a chain is called a *genesis block*. Obviously there are no blocks before this first one, so the previous block's hash doesn't exist.

Figure 8.4 shows a sample blockchain, where each block has a unique index, a timestamp, its data, and two hashes—its own and the previous block's. Note that the genesis block has an empty string instead of the previous block's hash.

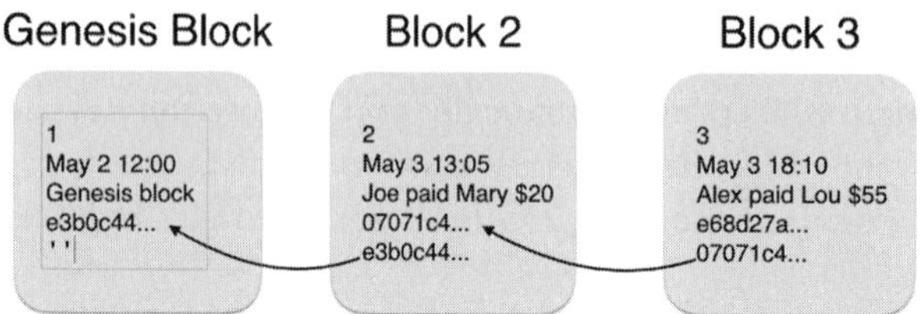

Figure 8.4 A sample blockchain

In figure 8.4, we used empty quotes in the genesis block to show the lack of the previous block's hash. Our data is represented by the text describing a transaction, such as "Joe paid Mary $20." In a real-world blockchain, Joe and Mary would be represented by long and encrypted account numbers.

> **TIP** You can think of a blockchain as a special type of a linked list, where each node has a reference only to the previous one. It's not a classical singly-linked list, where each node has a reference to the next one.

Now let's imagine that there is a bad guy named Rampage, and he found out that the hash of some block in our blockchain is "e68d27a..." Can he modify its data, stating that he paid Mary $1,000, and then regenerate the other blocks so the hash values play well? To prevent this from happening, a blockchain requires algorithms to be solved, taking time and resources. That's why blockchain members are required to spend time and resources to mine a block, rather than quickly generating a hash value.

8.1.3 What's block mining

Everyone understands what gold mining is—you perform some work to get gold, which can then be exchanged for real money or goods. The more people who mine gold, the more gold that exists in the world. In the past, the gold and other precious commodities were the basis for the value of paper money.

In the USA, the money supply is managed by the Federal Reserve, which consists of a number of commercial banks and has a board of directors. The Federal Reserve *has the authority* to manipulate paper currency, coins, funds in checking and savings accounts, and other legally accepted forms of exchange.

The money in cryptocurrencies (such as Bitcoin) is "produced" as the incentive for people (miners) to solve the math problems required by a particular blockchain. Since every new block has to be approved by other miners, more miners means a more secure blockchain.

In our distributed blockchain, we want to make sure that only the blocks that have certain hashes can be added. For example, our blockchain may require each hash to start with `0000`. The hash is calculated based on the content of the block, and it won't start with four zeros unless someone finds an additional value to add to the block's content to produce such a hash. Finding such a value is called block mining.

Before a new block is added to the blockchain, it is given to all nodes on the network for processing, and these nodes will start calculating the special value that produces a valid hash. The first one to find this value wins. Wins what? A blockchain may offers rewards—in the Bitcoin blockchain, a successful data miner may earn Bitcoins.

Let's assume that our blockchain requires the hash of each block to start with `0000`; otherwise the block will be rejected. Suppose an app wants to add a new block (number 4) to our blockchain, and it has the following data:

```
4
June 4 15:30?
Simon refunded Al $200
```

Prior to adding any block, its hash must be calculated, so we'll concatenate the preceding values into one string and generate the SHA-256 hash by running the following command:

```
echo -n '4June 4 15:30?Simon refunded Al $200' | shasum -a 256
```

The generated hash will look like this:

```
d6f9255c5fc579594bef56403778d475ab441abbd56bff788d597ae1e8d4ad22
```

This hash doesn't start with `0000`, so it will be rejected by our blockchain. We need to do some data mining to find a value that, if added to our block, will result in the generation of a hash that starts with `0000`. Brute force to the rescue! We can write a program that will be adding sequential numbers (1, 2, 3, etc.) to the end of our input string until the generated hash starts with `0000`.

After trying for a while, we found that secret value for our block—it's 236499. Let's append this value to our input string and recalculate the hash:

```
echo -n '4June 4 15:30?Simon refunded Al $200236499' | shasum -a 256
```

Now the generated hash starts with four zeros:

```
0000696c2bde5add287a7b6ccf9a7e57c9d69dad8a6a93922b0451a5150e6696
```

Perfect! We know the number to include in the block's content, so the generated hash will conform to the blockchain requirements. This number can be used just once with this particular input string. Changing any character in the input string will generate a hash that won't start with `0000`.

In cryptography, a number that can be used just once is called a *nonce*, and the value 236499 is such a nonce for our specific block. How about this: we'll add a property called `nonce` to the block object, and we'll let the data miners calculate its value for each new block.

A miner has to spend some computational resources to calculate the nonce, which is used as a *proof of work*, which is a must-have for any block to be considered for adding to a blockchain. We'll write a program to calculate nonces while developing our own little blockchain in the next section. Meanwhile, let's agree on the following structure of a block.

Listing 8.2 A sample block type

```
interface Block {
  index: number;                  // A sequential block number
  timestamp: number;              // The first parameter of the function is the search criterion.
  data: string;                   // Data about one or more app-specific transactions
  nonce: number;                  // A number to be figured out by miners
  hash: string;                   // This block's hash
  previousBlockHash: string;      // The hash value of the previous block in the blockchain
}
```

Please note that we used the TypeScript `interface` to declare the `Block` custom type. In the next section, we'll decide if it should remain an `interface` or become a `class`.

> **Bitcoin mining**
>
> Now that you've seen how the new block can be verified and added to a blockchain, you can understand how Bitcoin data mining works. Say there's a new transaction in Bitcoins between Joe and Mary, and this transaction needs to be added to the Bitcoin blockchain (the ledger). This transaction has to be placed into a block, and the block has to be verified first.
>
> Anyone who participates in the Bitcoin blockchain can become a data miner—a person (or a firm) who wants to use their hardware to be the first to solve the computationally difficult puzzle. This puzzle will require a lot more computational resources than our puzzle with four zeros.

Over time the number of miners grows, the computational resources increase, and the Bitcoin blockchain may increase the difficulty of the puzzle used for block mining. This is done so that the time required to mine a block remains the same, perhaps ten minutes, which may require finding hashes with 15–20 leading zeros.

The first person (say, the Bitcoin miner Peter) who solves the puzzle for a specific transaction (such as "Joe pays Mary five Bitcoins") will earn a newly released Bitcoin. Peter may also earn money from the transaction fees associated with adding transactions to the Bitcoin blockchain. But what if Peter likes Mary, and he decides to do her a "favor" by committing fraud, increasing the transaction amount from five to fifty? That's not possible, because Joe's transaction will be digitally signed using public-private key cryptography.

Earlier in this section, we concatenated the block number, the time, and a single transaction's text to calculate a hash. Bitcoin's blockchain stores blocks with multiple transactions (about 2,500) per block. There is no particular significance to the size of the block or number of transactions. Increasing the number of leading zeros required in a hash code makes it harder to solve the puzzle.

Bitcoins can be used to pay for services and can be bought and sold using conventional money or other crypto currencies. But Bitcoin mining is the only process that results in releasing new Bitcoins into circulation.

Ledgers, and cooking the books

Every business has to keep track of its transactions. In the past, these transactions would be manually recorded and categorized in a book: sales, purchases, and so on. These days, such records are stored in files, but the concept of a *ledger* remains unchanged. For our purposes, you can think of a blockchain as a representation of a ledger.

Cooking the books is a phrase that refers to falsifying financial statements. But if a ledger is implemented as a blockchain, cooking the books becomes nearly impossible. (More than 50% of the blockchain nodes would need to conspire to approve the illegal modification of the block, which is more of a theoretical possibility than a practical one.)

8.1.4 A mini project with hash and nonce

Modern browsers come with the `crypto` object to support cryptography. In particular, you can use the `crypto.subtle.digest()` API to generate hashes (see the Mozilla documentation for the method at http://mng.bz/dxKD).

We'd like to give you a little assignment to work on. After the assignment, we'll provide you with a solution, but without much explanation. Try to understand the code on your own:

1. Write a `generateHash(input: string)` function that takes a `string` input and finds its SHA-256 hash using the browser's `crypto` API.
2. Write a `calculateHashWithNonce(nonce: number)` function that will concatenate the provided nonce with an input string and will invoke `generateHash()`.
3. Write a `mine()` function that will invoke `calculateHashWithNonce()` in a loop until the generated hash starts with `0000`.

The `mine()` function should print the generated hash and the calculated nonce like this:

```
"Hash: 0000bfe6af4232f78b0c8eba37a6ba6c17b9b8671473b0b82305880be077edd9,
➥ nonce: 107105"
```

The following listing shows our solution to this assignment. We used the JavaScript keywords `async` and `await`, which are explained in the appendix. Read the code—you should be able to understand how it works.

Listing 8.3 The solution to the hash and nonce project

```
import * as crypto from 'crypto';

let nonce = 0;

async function generateHash(input: string): Promise<string> {    // Generates the SHA-256 hash from the provided input

    const msgBuffer = new TextEncoder().encode(input);    // Encodes as UTF-8

    const hashBuffer = await crypto.subtle.digest('SHA-256', msgBuffer);    // Hashes the message

    const hashArray = Array.from(new Uint8Array(hashBuffer));    // Converts ArrayBuffer to Array

    const hashHex = hashArray.map(b =>
➥ ('00' + b.toString(16)).slice(-2)).join('');    // Converts bytes to a hex string
    return hashHex;
}

async function calculateHashWithNonce(nonce: number): Promise<string> {    // Adds the nonce to the string and then calculates the hash
    const data = 'Hello World' + nonce;
    return generateHash(data);
  }

async function mine(): Promise<void> {    // Comes up with the nonce that will result in a hash that starts with four zeros
  let hash: string;
    do {
      hash = await this.calculateHashWithNonce(++nonce);    // Uses await because this function is asynchronous
    } while (hash.startsWith('0000') === false);

    console.log(`Hash: ${hash}, nonce: ${nonce}`);
}

mine();
```

You can see this solution in action in CodePen at http://mng.bz/rP4g. Initially the console panel will be empty, but after several seconds of work it will print the following:

```
Hash: 0000bfe6af4232f78b0c8eba37a6ba6c17b9b8671473b0b82305880be077edd9,
➥ nonce: 107105
```

If you change the code of the `mine()` method, replacing four zeros with five, the calculation may take minutes. Try it with ten zeros, and the calculation may take hours.

Calculating the nonce is time-consuming, but verification is fast. To check if the program in listing 8.3 calculated the nonce (107105) correctly, we used the macOS utility shasum as follows:

```
echo -n 'Hello World107105' | shasum -a 256
```

This utility printed the same hash as our program:

```
0000bfe6af4232f78b0c8eba37a6ba6c17b9b8671473b0b82305880be077edd9
```

In the `mine()` method in listing 8.3, we hardcoded the required number of zeros as `0000`. To make this method more useful, we could add an argument to it:

```
mine(difficulty: number): Promise<void>
```

The value of `difficulty` could be used to represent the number of zeros at the beginning of the hash value. Increasing the `difficulty` would substantially increase the time required to find the nonce.

In the next section, we'll start applying our TypeScript skills and build a simple blockchain app.

8.2 Developing your first blockchain

Reading and understanding the previous section is a prerequisite for understanding the content of this section, where we'll create two blockchain apps: one without a proof of work, and one with.

The first app (without the proof of work) will create a blockchain and provide an API for adding blocks to it. Prior to adding a block to the chain, we'll calculate the SHA-256 hash for the new block (no algorithm solving), and we'll store a reference to the hash of the previous block. We'll also add an index, timestamp, and some data to the block.

The second app (with the proof of work) won't accept blocks with arbitrary hashes, but it will require mining to calculate nonces that produce hashes starting with `0000`.

Both programs will run from the command line using the node.js runtime, and they'll use the crypto module (https://nodejs.org/api/crypto.html) to generate SHA-256 hashes.

8.2.1 The project's structure

Each chapter in part 2 of this book is a separate project with its own package.json file(s) (dependencies) and tsconfig.json file(s) (Typescript compiler options). You can find the source code for this chapter's project at https://github.com/yfain/getts.

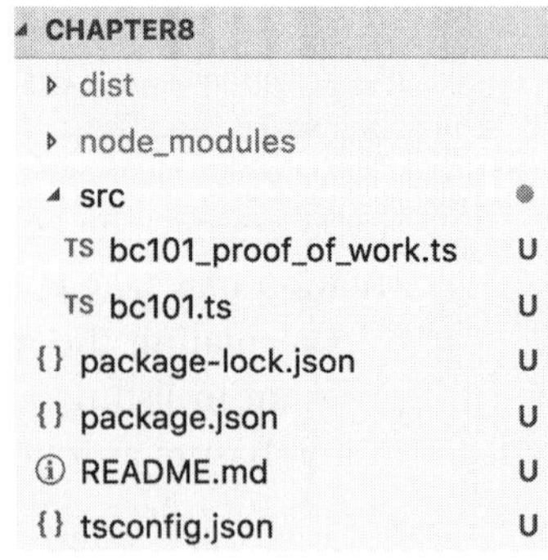

Figure 8.5 The blockchain project structure

Figure 8.5 shows a screenshot of the VS Code IDE after we opened the project for chapter 8, ran `npm install`, and compiled the code with the tsc compiler. This project has two apps, and their source code is located in the src/bc101.ts and src/bc101_proof_of_work.ts files.

Running the tsc compiler will create the dist directory and the JavaScript code. Running the `npm install` command from the project's root directory installs all the project dependencies in the node_modules directory. This project's dependencies are listed in the following package.json file.

Listing 8.4 The project's package.json file

```
{
  "name": "chapter8_blockchain",
  "version": "1.0.0",
  "license": "MIT",
  "scripts": {
    "tsc": "tsc"          <-- The npm script command that runs the locally installed tsc compiler
  },
  "devDependencies": {
    "@types/node": "^10.5.1",     <-- The type definition file for Node.js
    "typescript": "~3.0.0"        <-- The Typescript compiler
  }
}
```

The `tsc` compiler is one of the dependencies of this project, and we defined a custom npm command to run it in the `scripts` section. npm scripts allow you to redefine some npm commands or to define your own. You can define a command of any name and ask npm to run it by entering `npm run command-name`.

As per the content of the `scripts` section of our project, you can run the tsc compiler as follows:

```
npm run tsc
```

You may ask, why not just run the `tsc` command from the command line? You can do that if the tsc compiler is installed globally on the computer where you run it, and this may be the case if you run this command on your computer, where you have full control over the globally installed tools.

This may not be the case if your firm has a dedicated team responsible for building and deploying projects on their computers. They may require you to provide the application code as well as the build utilities in one package. When you run any program using the `npm run` command, npm will look for the specified program in the node_modules/bin directory.

In our project, after running `npm install`, the tsc compiler will be installed locally in node_modules/bin, so our package includes the tooling required to build our app.

> **A type definition file in action**
>
> We introduced type definition files in chapter 6. These files include type declarations for public JavaScript APIs, and in this project we use the file describing the Node.js API. Type definition files have *.d.ts extensions.
>
> Type definition files allow the TypeScript type checker to warn you if you're trying to use the API incorrectly, such as if a function expects a numeric argument and you're trying to invoke it with a string. This type checking wouldn't be possible if you were just using the JavaScript library, which has no type annotations. If type definition files for a JavaScript library or module are present, IDEs can offer context-sensitive help.
>
> The following screenshot shows the VS Code editor after we entered the word `crypto.`, and the IDE offered context-sensitive help for the crypto module's API, which comes with Node.js. 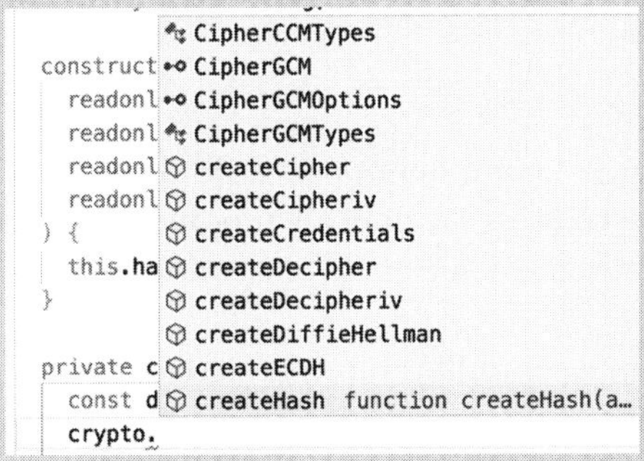
>
> ```
>            CipherCCMTypes
> construct  CipherGCM
>   readonl  CipherGCMOptions
>   readonl  CipherGCMTypes
>   readonl  createCipher
>   readonl  createCipheriv
> ) {        createCredentials
>   this.ha  createDecipher
> }          createDecipheriv
>            createDiffieHellman
> private c  createECDH
>   const d  createHash  function createHash(a…
>   crypto.
> ```
>
> **Autocomplete for the crypto module**
>
> If we hadn't installed the @types/node type definition file, we wouldn't get this help. The npmjs.org repository has a special `@type` section (or "organization") that stores thousands of type definition files for popular JavaScript libraries.

Our project also includes the following tsconfig.json configuration file with the TypeScript compiler options.

Listing 8.5 tsconfig.json: the configuration for the tsc compiler

```
{
  "compilerOptions": {
    "module": "commonjs",
```

How to generate code for JavaScript modules

```
      "outDir": "./dist",       <-- The directory where compiled
      "target": "es2017",       <--   JavaScript is stored
      "lib": [
        "es2017"     <--               Compiles into the ES2017 syntax
      ]
    }
  }                         This project will use the API
                            described in the library es2017.
```

While the `outDir` and `target` compiler options are self-explanatory, `module` and `lib` require additional explanation.

Prior to ES6, JavaScript developers were using different syntax for splitting code into modules. For example, the AMD format was popular for browser-based apps, and CommonJS was used by Node.js developers. ES6 introduced the `import` and `export` keywords, so a script from one module could import whatever was exported from another.

In TypeScript, we always use ES6 modules, and if a script needs to load some code from a module, we use the `import` keyword. For example, to use code from the Node.js crypto module, we could add the following line to our script:

```
import * as crypto from 'crypto';
```

But the Node.js runtime implements the CommonJS spec for modules, which requires you to write the JavaScript as follows:

```
const crypto = require("crypto");
```

By specifying the `"module": "commonjs"` compiler option in listing 8.5, we instruct tsc to turn the `import` statement into `require()`, and all module members with the `export` qualifier will be added to the `module.exports={…}` construct as prescribed by the CommonJS spec.

As for `lib`, TypeScript comes with a set of libraries that describe APIs provided by browsers and JavaScript specs of different versions. You can selectively make these libraries available to your program via the `lib` compiler option. For example, if you want to use a `Promise` (introduced in ES2015) in your program, and run it in the target browsers that support promises, you can use the following compiler option:

```
{
  "compilerOptions": {
    "lib": [ "es2015" ]
  }
}
```

The `lib` option includes only type definitions; it doesn't provide the actual implementation of the API. Basically, you tell the compiler, "Don't worry when you see `Promise` in this code—the runtime JavaScript engine natively implements this API." But you have to either run your code in an environment that natively supports `Promise` or include a polyfill library that provides a `Promise` implementation for older browsers.

> **TIP** You can find a list of available libraries at https://github.com/Microsoft/TypeScript/tree/master/lib.

Now that we've gone through the configuration files for our project, let's review the code in the two TypeScript files in the src directory, as seen earlier in figure 8.5.

8.2.2 *Creating a primitive blockchain*

The chapter8/src/bc101.ts script is the first version of our blockchain. It contains the classes `Block` and `Blockchain` as well as a short script that uses the API of `Blockchain` to create a blockchain of three blocks. In this chapter, we won't use web browsers—our scripts will run under the Node.js runtime. Let's look at the code of bc101.ts, starting with the `Block` class.

The `Block` class declares the properties required for each block (such as the index, and hash values of the current and previous blocks) as well as the method to calculate its hash using the Node.js crytpo module. During the instantiation of the `Block` object, we calculate its hash based on the concatenated values of all of its properties.

Listing 8.6 The `Block` class from bc101.ts

```
import * as crypto from 'crypto';

class Block {
  readonly hash: string;                              // The hash of this block

  constructor (
    readonly index: number,                           // The sequential number of this block
    readonly previousHash: string,                    // The hash of the previous block
    readonly timestamp: number,                       // The time of the block's creation
    readonly data: string                             // The app-specific data
  ) {
    this.hash = this.calculateHash();                 // Calculates the hash of this block on its creation
  }

  private calculateHash(): string {
    const data = this.index + this.previousHash + this.timestamp + this.data;
    return crypto
           .createHash('sha256')                      // Creates an instance of the Hash object for generating SHA-256 hashes
           .update(data)                              // Computes and updates the hash value inside the Hash object
           .digest('hex');                            // Converts the hash value into a hexadecimal string
  }
};
```

The constructor of the `Block` class invokes the `calculateHash()` method, which starts by concatenating the values of the block's properties: `index`, `previousHash`, `timestamp`, and data. This concatenated string is given to the crypto module, which calculates its hash in the form of a string of hexadecimal characters. This hash is assigned to the hash property of the newly created Block object, which will be given to the Blockchain object to be added to the chain.

The block's transaction data is stored in the data property, which in our Block class has the string type. In a real-world application, the data property would have a custom type that describes the structure of the data, but in our primitive blockchain, using the string type is fine.

Now let's create a Blockchain class that uses an array to store blocks and has an addBlock() method that does three things:

1. Creates an instance of the Block object
2. Gets the hash value of the most recently added block and stores it in the new block's previousHash property
3. Adds the new block to the array

When the Blockchain object is instantiated, its constructor will create the genesis block, which won't have a reference to a previous block.

Listing 8.7 The Blockchain class

```
class Blockchain {
  private readonly chain: Block[] = [];    <-- Our blockchain is stored here.

  private get latestBlock(): Block {    <-- The getter to get a reference to the most recently added block
    return this.chain[this.chain.length - 1];
  }

  constructor() {    <-- Creates the genesis block and adds it to the chain
    this.chain.push(
       new Block(0, '0', Date.now(),
       'Genesis block'));
  }

  addBlock(data: string): void {    <-- Creates a new instance of Block and populates its properties
    const block = new Block(
      this.latestBlock.index + 1,
      this.latestBlock.hash,
      Date.now(),
      data
    );

    this.chain.push(block);    <-- Adds the block to the array
  }
}
```

Now we can invoke the Blockchain.addBlock() method to mine blocks. The following code creates an instance of Blockchain and invokes addBlock() twice, adding two blocks with the data "First block" and "Second block" respectively. The genesis block is created in the constructor of Blockchain.

Listing 8.8 Creating a 3-block blockchain

```
console.log('Creating the blockchain with the genesis block...');
const blockchain = new Blockchain();          // Creates a new blockchain

console.log('Mining block #1...');
blockchain.addBlock('First block');           // Adds the first block

console.log('Mining block #2...');
blockchain.addBlock('Second block');          // Adds the second block

console.log(JSON.stringify(blockchain, null, 2));   // Prints the content of the blockchain
```

The bc101.ts file includes the scripts shown in listings 8.6–8.8. To run this script, compile it and run its bc101.js JavaScript version under the Node.js runtime:

```
npm run tsc
node dist/bc101.js
```

The bc101.js script will print the content of our blockchain on the console, as shown in the following listing. The `chain` array stores three blocks of our primitive blockchain.

Listing 8.9 The console output produced by bc101.js

```
Creating the blockchain with the genesis block...
Mining block #1...
Mining block #2...
{
  "chain": [
    {
      "index": 0,
      "previousHash": "0",
      "timestamp": 1532207287077,
      "data": "Genesis block",
      "hash": "cc521dd5bbf1786977b14d16ce5d7f8da0e9f3353b3ebe0762ad9258c8ab1a
     04"
    },
    {
      "index": 1,
      "previousHash": "cc521dd5bbf1786977b14d16ce5d7f8da0e9f3353b3ebe0762ad92
     58c8ab1a04",
      "timestamp": 1532207287077,
      "data": "First block",
      "hash": "52d40c33a8993632d51754c952fdb90d61b2c8bf13739433624bbf6b04933e
     52"
    },
    {
      "index": 2,
      "previousHash": "52d40c33a8993632d51754c952fdb90d61b2c8bf13739433624bbf
     6b04933e52",
```

```
      "timestamp": 1532207287077,
      "data": "Second block",
      "hash": "0d6d43368772e2bee5da8a1cc92c0c7f28a098bfef3880b3cc8caa5f40c597
     76"
    }
  ]
}
```

NOTE When you run the bc101.js script, you won't see the same hash values as in listing 8.9 because we use the timestamp for hash generation. It will be different for each reader.

Notice that the `previousHash` of each block (except the genesis block) has the same value as the `hash` property of the previous block in the chain. This program runs very quickly, but a real-world blockchain would require data miners to spend some CPU cycles and solve an algorithm so that the generated hashes conform to certain requirements, as described in section 8.1.3.

Let's make the block-mining process a bit more realistic by introducing problem solving.

8.2.3 Creating a blockchain with proof of work

The next version of our blockchain is located in the bc101_proof_of_work.ts file. This script has a lot of similarities to bc101.ts, but it has some extra code to force data miners to provide proof of work, so that their blocks can be considered for addition to the blockchain.

The bc101_proof_of_work.ts script also has the `Block` and `Blockchain` classes, but although the latter is exactly the same as listing 8.7, the `Block` class has additional code.

In particular, the `Block` class has a `nonce` property that is calculated in the new `mine()` method. The nonce will be concatenated to other properties of the block to produce a hash that starts with five zeros.

The process of calculating a nonce that meets our requirements will take some time. This time, we want hashes that start with five zeros. The `mine()` method will invoke `calculateHash()` multiple times with different nonce values until the generated hash starts with `00000`. The new version of the `Block` class is shown in the following listing.

Listing 8.10 The `Block` class from bc101_proof_of_work.ts

```
class Block {
  readonly nonce: number;          ◁— The new nonce property
  readonly hash: string;

  constructor (
    readonly index: number,
    readonly previousHash: string,
    readonly timestamp: number,
    readonly data: string
```

```
  ) {
    const { nonce, hash } = this.mine();        ◁ Calculates nonce
    this.nonce = nonce;                            and hash
    this.hash = hash;
  }

  private calculateHash(nonce: number): string {
    const data = this.index + this.previousHash + this.timestamp +
➥ this.data + nonce;                                    ◁
    return crypto.createHash('sha256').update(data).digest('hex');
  }
                                          Nonce is part of the input
  private mine(): { nonce: number, hash: string } {    for calculating the hash
    let hash: string;
    let nonce = 0;
                                                 Uses brute force
    do {                                         for data mining
      hash = this.calculateHash(++nonce);    ◁
    } while (hash.startsWith('00000') === false);    ◁ Runs this loop until the
                                                        hash starts with 00000
    return { nonce, hash };
  }
};
```

Note that the `calculateHash()` method is almost identical to the method from listing 8.6. The only difference is that we append the value of the nonce to the input string used for calculating the hash. The `mine()` method keeps calling `calculateHash()` in a loop, providing the sequential numbers 0, 1, 2, … as the `nonce` argument. Sooner or later, the calculated hash will start with `00000`, and the `mine()` method will return the hash as well as the calculated nonce.

We'd like to bring your attention to the line that invokes the `mine()` method:

```
const { nonce, hash } = this.mine();
```

The curly braces on the left of the equal sign represent JavaScript destructuring (see the appendix). The `mine()` method returns the object with two properties, and we extract their values into two variables: `nonce` and `hash`.

We've reviewed only the `Block` class from the bc101_proof_of_work.ts script because the rest of the script is the same as in bc101.ts. You can run this program as follows:

```
node dist/bc101_proof_of_work.js
```

This script won't end as quickly as bc101.ts. It may take several seconds to complete, as it spends time doing block mining. The output of this script is shown in the following listing.

Listing 8.11 The console output produced by bc101_proof_of_work.ts

```
Creating the blockchain with the genesis block...
Mining block #1...
Mining block #2...
{
  "chain": [
    {
      "index": 0,
      "previousHash": "0",
      "timestamp": 1532454493124,
      "data": "Genesis block",
      "nonce": 2832,
      "hash": "000005921a5611d92cdc81f89d554743d7e33af2b35b4cb1a0a52cd4664445
     ca"
    },
    {
      "index": 1,
      "previousHash": "000005921a5611d92cdc81f89d554743d7e33af2b35b4cb1a0a52c
     d4664445ca",
      "timestamp": 1532454493140,
      "data": "First block",
      "nonce": 462881,
      "hash": "000009da95386579eee5e944b15eab2539bc4ac223398ccef8d40ed83502d4
     31"
    },
    {
      "index": 2,
      "previousHash": "000009da95386579eee5e944b15eab2539bc4ac223398ccef8d40e
     d83502d431",
      "timestamp": 1532454494233,
      "data": "Second block",
      "nonce": 669687,
      "hash": "0000017332a9321b546154f255c8295e4e805417e50b78609ff59a10bf9c23
     7c"
    }
  ]
}
```

Once again, the `chain` array stores the blockchain of three blocks, but this time each block has a different value in its `nonce` property, and the hash value of each block starts with `00000`, which serves as proof of work: we did the block mining and solved the algorithm for the block!

Take another look at the code in listing 8.10 and identify the familiar TypeScript syntax elements. Each of the six class properties has a type and is marked as `readonly`. The properties `nonce` and `hash` were explicitly declared on this class, and four more properties were created by the Typescript compiler because we used the `readonly` qualifier with each argument of the constructor.

Both class methods explicitly declare the types of their arguments and return values. Both methods were declared with the `private` access level, which means that they can be invoked only within the class.

The return type of the `mine()` method is declared as `{ nonce: number, hash: string }`. Because this type is used only once, we didn't create a custom data type for it.

Summary

- The big idea of a blockchain is that it offers decentralized processing of transactions without relying on a single authority.
- In a blockchain, each block is identified by a hash value and is linked to the previous block by storing the hash value of the previous block.
- Before inserting a new block into the blockchain, a mathematical problem is offered to each node of the blockchain interested in calculating an acceptable hash value for a reward. When we use the term "node," we mean a computer, network, or farm that represents one member of a blockchain.
- In cryptography, a number that can be used just once is called a "nonce," and a miner has to spend some computational resources to calculate the nonce—this is how they will get proof of work, which is a must-have for any block to be considered for addition to the blockchain.
- In our sample blockchain app, the acceptable hash value had to start with five zeros, and we calculated the nonce to ensure that the hash of the block indeed started with five zeros. Calculating such a nonce takes time, which delays the insertion of the new block into the blockchain, but it can be used as the proof of work needed to award the blockchain node that did it faster than others.

9 Developing a browser-based blockchain node

This chapter covers

- Creating a web client for a blockchain
- Creating a small library for hash generation
- Running the blockchain web app and debugging TypeScript in the browser

In chapter 8, we developed an app that would create a blockchain, and we provided a script for adding blocks to it. We launched that app from the command line, and it ran under the Node.js runtime.

In this chapter, we'll modify the blockchain app so that it runs in the browser. We won't use a web framework here, so it will have a pretty basic UI. We'll use standard browser API methods, like `document.getElementById()` and `addEventListener()`.

In this app, each block will store data about several transactions. They won't be simple strings as in chapter 8 but will be implemented as TypeScript custom types. We'll accumulate several transactions and then create the block to be inserted in the blockchain. Also, we created a small library that contains the code for mining blocks and generating the proper hash; this library can be used in a browser as well as in the Node.js environment.

This chapter's app includes practical examples of the following TypeScript (and JavaScript) syntax elements covered in part 1 of this book:

- Using `private` and `readonly` keywords
- Using TypeScript interfaces and classes for declaring custom types
- Cloning objects using the JavaScript spread operator
- Using the `enum` keyword
- Using `async`, `await`, and a `Promise`

We'll start by looking at the project structure and running our blockchain web app. After that, we'll review the code in detail.

9.1 Running the blockchain web app

In this section, we'll start by showing you how this blockchain project will be configured. Then you'll see the commands to compile and deploy it, and finally you'll see how the user can work with this app in the browser.

9.1.1 The project structure

You can find the source code for this project at https://github.com/yfain/getts. Figure 9.1 shows how this project is structured.

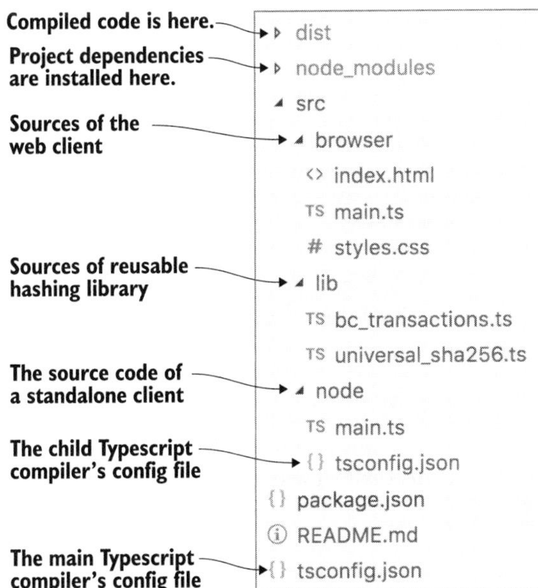

Figure 9.1 Project structure for the blockchain app

The sources (TypeScript, HTML, and CSS) are located in the subdirectories called browser, lib, and node. The main machinery for creating the blockchain is implemented in the lib directory, but we provided two demo apps—one for the web browser and another for the Node.js runtime. Here's what the subdirectories of src contain:

- *lib*—The lib directory implements blockchain creation and block mining. It also has a universal function for generating hashes for both the browser and Node.js environments.
- *browser*—The browser directory contains code that implements the UI of the blockchain web app. This code uses the code in the lib directory.
- *node*—The node directory contains a small app that you can run independently; it also uses the code from the lib directory.

This project will have some dependencies you haven't seen yet in the package.json file (listing 9.1). Since this is a web app, we'll need a web server, and in this chapter, we'll use the package called "serve," available on npmjs.org. From a deployment perspective, this app will have not only JavaScript files but also HTML and CSS files copied into the dist deployment directory. The copyfiles package will do this job.

Finally, to avoid manually invoking the copyfiles script, we'll add a couple of commands to the npm scripts section of package.json. We started using npm scripts in section 8.2.1, but the `scripts` section in this chapter's package.json file will have more commands.

Listing 9.1 The package.json file

```
{
  "name": "TypeScript_Quickly_chapter9",
  "version": "1.0.0",
  "license": "MIT",
  "scripts": {
    "start": "serve",
    "compileDeploy": "tsc && npm run deploy",
    "deploy": "copyfiles -f src/browser/*.html src/browser/*.css dist"
  },
  "devDependencies": {
    "@types/node": "^10.5.1",
    "serve": "^10.0.1",
    "copyfiles": "^2.1.0",
    "typescript": "~3.0.0"
  }
}
```

- The npm start command will start the web server. (annotates `"start": "serve"`)
- Combines two commands: tsc and deploy (annotates `"compileDeploy"`)
- The deploy command will copy HTML and CSS files. (annotates `"deploy"`)
- The serve package is a new dev dependency. (annotates `"serve"`)
- The copyfiles package is a new dev dependency. (annotates `"copyfiles"`)

After you run the `npm install` command, all the project dependencies will be installed in the node_modules directory, and the serve and copyfiles executables will be installed in node_modules/.bin. The sources of this project are located in the src directory, and the deployed code will be saved in dist.

Note that this project has two tsconfig.json files that are used by the Typescript compiler. The base tsconfig.json is located in the project's root directory, and it defines compiler options for the whole project, such as the JavaScript target and which libraries to use.

Listing 9.2 The base tsconfig.json file

```
{
  "compilerOptions": {
    "sourceMap": true,          // Generates source maps files
    "outDir": "./dist",         // Compiled JavaScript files go to the dist directory.
    "target": "es5",
    "module": "es6",            // Uses the ES6 modules syntax
    "lib": [
      "dom",                    // Uses type definitions for the browser's DOM API
      "es2018"                  // Uses type definitions supported by ES2018
    ]
  }
}
```

For the code that runs in the browser, we want the Typescript compiler to generate JavaScript that uses modules (as explained in section A.11 of the appendix).

Also, we want to generate source map files that map the lines in the TypeScript code to the corresponding lines in the generated JavaScript. With source maps, you can debug your TypeScript code while you run the web app in the browser, even though the browser executes JavaScript. We'll show you how to do this in section 9.5. If the browser's Developer Tools panel is open, it will load the source map file along with the JavaScript file, and you can debug your TypeScript code there.

The other tsconfig.json is in the src/node directory. This file inherits all the properties from the tsconfig.json file in the root of the project, as specified in the `extends` option. tsc will load the base tsconfig.json file first, and then the inherited ones, overriding or adding properties.

Listing 9.3 The src/node/tsconfig.json child config file

```
{
  "extends": "../../tsconfig.json",     // Inherits properties from this file
  "compilerOptions": {
    "module": "commonjs"
  }
}
```

In the base tsconfig.json file, the `module` property has a value of `es6`, which is fine for generating JavaScript that runs in the browser. The child configuration file in the node directory overrides the `module` property with the value `commonjs`, so the TypeScript compiler will generate module-related code as per the CommonJS rules.

TIP You can find a description of all the options allowed in tsconfig.json in the TypeScript documentation at www.typescriptlang.org/docs/handbook/tsconfig-json.html.

9.1.2 Deploying the app using npm scripts

To deploy our web app, we need to compile the TypeScript files into the dist directory, and copy index.html and styles.css there as well.

The `scripts` section of package.json (see listing 9.1) has three commands: `start`, `compileDeploy`, and `deploy`.

```
"scripts": {
  "start": "serve",
  "compileDeploy": "tsc && npm run deploy",
  "deploy": "copyfiles -f src/browser/*.html src/browser/*.css dist"
},
```

- Starts the web server
- Runs the commands tsc and deploy
- Copies the HTML and CSS files from the src/browser directory to dist

The `deploy` command just copies the HTML and CSS files from the src/browser directory to dist.

The `compileDeploy` command runs two commands: `tsc` and `deploy`. In npm scripts, the double ampersand (`&&`) is used to specify command sequences, so to compile the TypeScript files and copy index.html and styles.css to the dist directory, we need to run the following command:

```
npm run compileDeploy
```

After we run this command, the dist directory will contain the files shown in figure 9.2.

NOTE The source code of a real-world app contains hundreds of files, and prior to deploying them in a web server, you'd use tools to optimize and bundle the code as a smaller number of files. One of the most popular bundlers is Webpack, which we introduced in section 6.3.

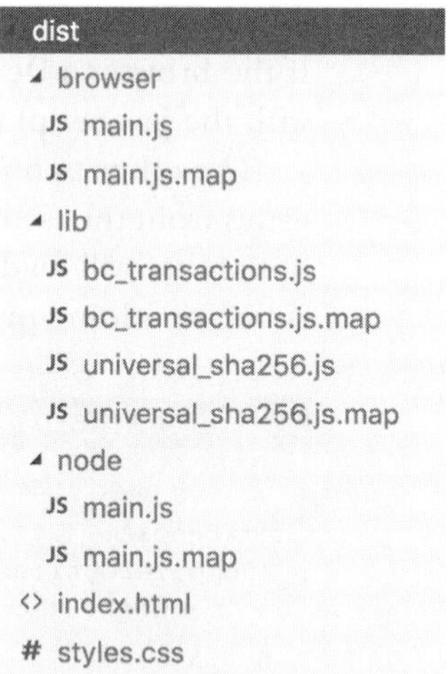

Figure 9.2 The files for our web app deployment

Now you can start the web server by running the following command:

```
npm start
```

This command will start the web server on localhost on port 5000. The console will show the output you can see in figure 9.3.

```
Serving!

- Local:            http://localhost:5000
- On Your Network:  http://10.0.0.6:5000

Copied local address to clipboard!
```

Figure 9.3 Running the web server

TIP npm supports a limited number of scripts, and `start` is one of them (see the npm documentation at https://docs.npmjs.com/misc/scripts). With these scripts, you don't have to use the `run` option, and that's why we didn't use the `run` command, as in `npm run start`. However, custom scripts like `compileDeploy` require the `run` command.

NOTE In chapter 10, we'll create an app that will have separate code for the client and server; we'll be starting the server using an npm package called nodemon.

9.1.3 Working with the blockchain web app

Open your browser to http://localhost:5000/dist, and the web server will send dist/index.html to the browser. The index.html file will load the compiled JavaScript files, and after a couple of seconds spent on genesis block mining, the UI of the blockchain web app will look like figure 9.4.

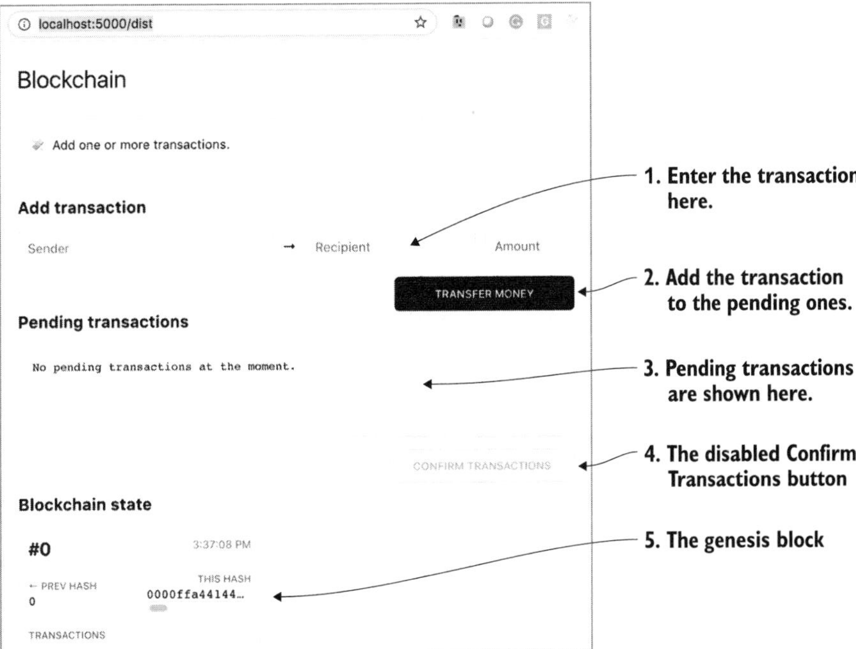

Figure 9.4 Running the web server

The landing page of this app shows the initial state of our blockchain with a single genesis block. The user can add transactions and click on the Transfer Money button after each transaction, which will add the transaction to the Pending Transactions field. The Confirm Transactions button is enabled, and the browser's window will look like figure 9.5.

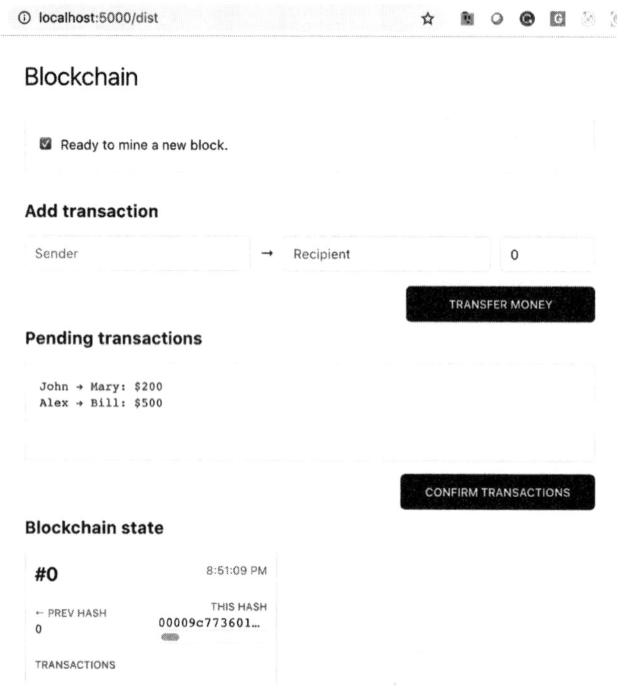

Figure 9.5 Creating pending transactions

As you can see, we've added two pending transactions, and we've neither created nor submitted a new block to our blockchain yet. This is what the Confirm Transactions button is for. Figure 9.6 shows the browser window after we clicked this button and the app spent some time performing data mining.

> **NOTE** For simplicity, we've assumed that if John pays Mary a certain amount of money, he has this amount. In real-world apps, the account balance is checked first, and only afterwards is the pending transaction created.

As in chapter 8, the new block, #1, was created with a hash value that starts with four zeros. But now the block includes *two* transactions: one between John and Mary, and the other between Alex and Bill. The block has also been added to the blockchain. As you see, no pending transactions are left.

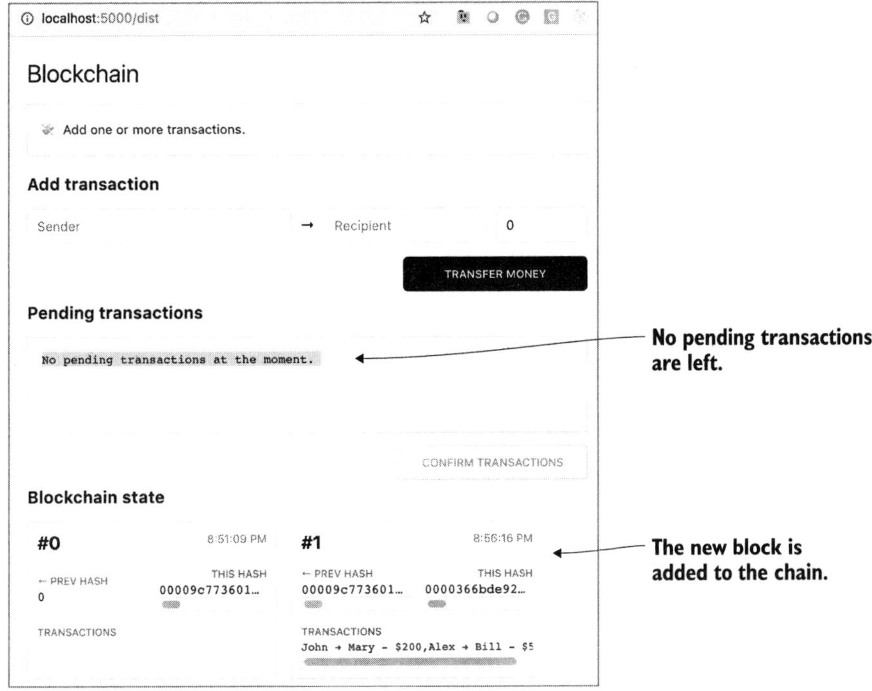

Figure 9.6 Adding a new block to the blockchain

You may be wondering why seemingly unrelated transactions are placed in the same block. That's because adding a block to the blockchain is a slow operation, and creating a new block for each transaction would slow down the process even more.

To add some context to our blockchain, let's imagine that this blockchain has been created for a large real estate agency. John is buying an apartment from Mary and needs to provide proof that he paid for it. Similarly, Alex is paying Bill for a house, and this is another transaction. While these transactions are in a pending state, they are not considered proof of payment. But once they have been added to the block and the block is added to the blockchain, it's considered a done deal.

Now that you've seen the app running, let's review the code, starting with UI.

9.2 The web client

The browser directory has three files: index.html, main.ts, and styles.css. We'll review the code of the first two files, starting with index.html.

Listing 9.4 browser/index.html: the script that loads the web app

```
<!DOCTYPE html>
<html lang="en">
<head>
  <meta charset="UTF-8">
```

```
    <meta name="viewport" content="width=device-width, initial-scale=1.0">
    <title>Blockchain</title>
    <link rel="stylesheet" href="dist/styles.css">                    ◁ Includes CSS
    <script type="module" src="dist/browser/main.js"></script>    ◁ Includes the main module of our app
  </head>
  <body>
    <main>
      <h1>Blockchain</h1>
      <aside>
        <p id="status">⌛ Initializing the blockchain, creating the genesis
➥ block...</p>
      </aside>
                                  This section is for
      <section>               ◁  adding transactions.
        <h2>Add transaction</h2>
        <form>
          <input  id="sender"    type="text"   autocomplete="off" disabled
➥ placeholder="Sender">
          <span>•</span>
          <input  id="recipient" type="text"   autocomplete="off" disabled
➥ placeholder="Recipient">
          <input  id="amount"    type="number" autocomplete="off" disabled
➥ placeholder="Amount">
          <button id="transfer"  type="button" class="ripple" disabled>
              TRANSFER MONEY</button>               ◁ Adds transaction to the list of pending ones
        </form>
      </section>

Pending transactions are displayed in this section. ▷
      <section>
        <h2>Pending transactions</h2>
        <pre id="pending-
     transactions">No pending transactions at the moment.</pre>
        <button id="confirm" type="button" class="ripple" disabled>
              CONFIRM TRANSACTIONS</button>         ◁ Starts mining a new block with pending transactions
        <div class="clear"></div>
      </section>

The content of the blockchain is rendered here. ▷
      <section>
        <h2>Blockchain state</h2>
        <div class="wrapper">
          <div id="blocks"></div>
          <div id="overlay"></div>
        </div>
      </section>
    </main>
  </body>
</html>
```

The <head> section of index.html includes the tags to load styles.css and main.js. The latter is a compiled version of main.ts, which is not the only TypeScript file in our app, but since we modularized our app, the main.ts script starts by importing members of the lib/bc_transactions.ts JavaScript module, as shown in the following listing.

NOTE Note that we use the `type="module"` attribute in the `<script>` tag that loads main.ts. You can learn more about the `module` type in section A.11 of the appendix.

Listing 9.5 The first part of browser/main.ts

```
import { Blockchain, Block } from '../lib/bc_transactions.js';    <- Imports the Block and Blockchain classes

enum Status {                                                      <- Declares possible statuses of the app
  Initialization = '⌛ Initializing the blockchain, creating the genesis
➥ block...',
  AddTransaction = '✉ Add one or more transactions.',
  ReadyToMine    = '✅ Ready to mine a new block.',
  MineInProgress = '⌛ Mining a new block...'
}

// Get HTML elements                                               <- Gets references to all the important HTML elements
const amountEl              = document.getElementById('amount')
➥ as HTMLInputElement;
const blocksEl              = document.getElementById('blocks') as
➥ HTMLDivElement;
const confirmBtn            = document.getElementById('confirm')
➥ as HTMLButtonElement;
const pendingTransactionsEl =
➥ document.getElementById('pending-transactions') as HTMLPreElement;
const recipientEl           = document.getElementById('recipient')
➥ as HTMLInputElement;
const senderEl              = document.getElementById('sender')
➥ as HTMLInputElement;
const statusEl              = document.getElementById('status')
➥ as HTMLParagraphElement;
const transferBtn           = document.getElementById('transfer')
➥ as HTMLButtonElement;
```

In chapter 4, we explained enums, which are named constants. In listing 9.5, we use enums to declare a finite number of statuses for our app: `Initialization`, `AddTransaction`, `ReadyToMine`, and `MineInProgress`. The `statusEl` constant represents the HTML element where we want to display the current status of the app.

NOTE The little icons that you see in the `enum` strings are emoji symbols. You can insert them into strings on macOS by pressing Cmd-Ctrl-Space and on Windows 10 by pressing Win-. (Win and a period) or Win-; (Win and a semicolon).

The rest of listing 9.5 shows code that gets references to various HTML elements that either store the values entered by the user or display the blocks of our blockchain. Each of these HTML elements has a unique `id` (see listing 9.4), and we use the browser API's `getElementById()` method to get a hold of these DOM objects.

Listing 9.6 shows the immediately invoked function expression (IIFE) `main()`, and we use the `async/await` keywords here (see section A.10.4 in the appendix). This function creates a new blockchain with an initial genesis block, and it assigns event listeners to the buttons that add pending transactions and initiate new block mining.

Listing 9.6 The second part of browser/main.ts

```
(async function main(): Promise<void> {

  transferBtn.addEventListener('click', addTransaction);     // Adds event listeners to buttons
  confirmBtn.addEventListener('click', mineBlock);

  statusEl.textContent = Status.Initialization;     // Shows the initial status using enum

  const blockchain = new Blockchain();     // Creates an instance of Blockchain
  await blockchain.createGenesisBlock();     // Creates the genesis block
  blocksEl.innerHTML = blockchain.chain.map((b, i) =>
➥ generateBlockHtml(b, i)).join('');     // Generates HTML for rendering block(s)

  statusEl.textContent = Status.AddTransaction;
  toggleState(true, false);

  function addTransaction() {     // Adds a new pending transaction
    blockchain.createTransaction({
      sender: senderEl.value,
      recipient: recipientEl.value,
      amount: parseInt(amountEl.value),
    });

    toggleState(false, false);
    pendingTransactionsEl.textContent =
➥ blockchain.pendingTransactions.map(t =>
      `${t.sender} • ${t.recipient}: $${t.amount}`).join('\n');     // Renders pending transactions as strings
     statusEl.textContent = Status.ReadyToMine;

    senderEl.value = '';     // Resets the form's values
    recipientEl.value = '';
    amountEl.value = '0';
  }

  async function mineBlock() {     // Mines the block and renders it on the web page
    statusEl.textContent = Status.MineInProgress;
    toggleState(true, true);
    await blockchain.minePendingTransactions();     // Creates a new block, calculates the hash, and adds it to the blockchain

    pendingTransactionsEl.textContent = 'No pending transactions at
➥ the moment.';
    statusEl.textContent = Status.AddTransaction;
    blocksEl.innerHTML = blockchain.chain.map((b, i) =>
➥ generateBlockHtml(b, i)).join('');     // Renders the newly inserted block on the web page
    toggleState(true, false);
  }
})();
```

In listing 9.6, we use the `Blockchain` class (discussed in section 9.3), which has an array called `chain` that stores the content of our blockchain. The `Blockchain` class has a `minePendingTransactions()` method that adds transactions to the new block.

This mining process starts when the user clicks on the Confirm Transactions button. In a couple of places, we invoke `blockchain.chain.map()` to convert the blocks into text or HTML elements for rendering on the web page. This workflow is shown in figure 9.7.

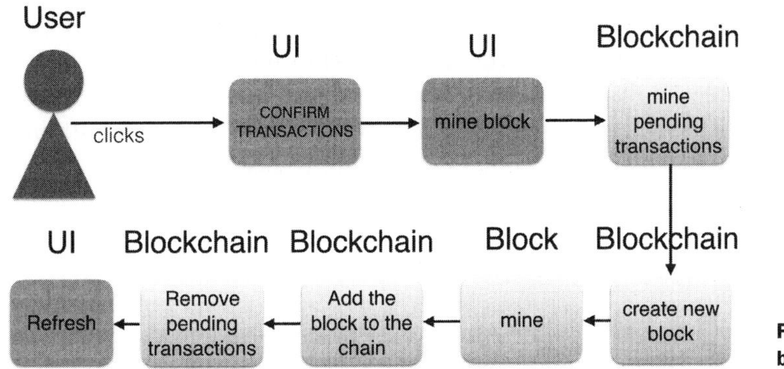

Figure 9.7 The user-blockchain workflow

Whenever we invoke an asynchronous function, we change the content of the HTML element `statusEl` to keep the user informed about the current status of the web app.

Listing 9.7 shows the remaining part of main.ts, which contains two functions: `toggleState()` and `generateBlockHtml()`.

Listing 9.7 The third part of browser/main.ts

```
function toggleState(confirmation: boolean, transferForm: boolean): void {
  transferBtn.disabled = amountEl.disabled = senderEl.disabled =
➥ recipientEl.disabled = transferForm;
  confirmBtn.disabled = confirmation;
}

function generateBlockHtml(block: Block, index: number) {
  return `
    <div class="block">
      <span class="block__index">#${index}</span>
      <span class="block__timestamp">${new
➥ Date(block.timestamp).toLocaleTimeString()}</span>
      <div class="prev-hash">
        <div class="hash-title">• PREV HASH</div>
        <div class="hash-value">${block.previousHash}</div>
      </div>
      <div class="this-hash">
        <div class="hash-title">THIS HASH</div>
        <div class="hash-value">${block.hash}</div>
      </div>
      <div class="block__transactions">
```

Disables/enables the form and the confirm button

Generates the block's HTML

```
        <div class="hash-title">TRANSACTIONS</div>
        <pre class="transactions-
      value">${block.transactions.map(t => `${t.sender} •
➥ ${t.recipient} - $${t.amount}`)}</pre>
      </div>
    </div>
  `;
}
```

The `toggleState()` function has two `boolean` parameters. Depending on the value of the first parameter, we either enable or disable the form, which consists of the Sender, Recipient, and Amount input fields and the Transfer Money button. The second parameter enables or disables the Confirm Transactions button.

The `generateBlockHtml()` function returns the `<div>` container with information on each block, as seen at the bottom of figure 9.6. We use several CSS `class` selectors, which are defined in the browser/styles.css file (not shown here).

To summarize, the code in the browser/main.ts script is responsible for the user interaction, and it performs the following:

1. Gets access to all HTML elements
2. Sets listeners for the buttons, which add pending transactions and create a new block
3. Creates the instance of the blockchain with the genesis block
4. Defines the method that creates pending transactions
5. Defines the method that mines the new block with pending transactions
6. Defines a method that generates HTML for rendering the blocks of the blockchain

Now that you've seen how the browser's UI is implemented, let's review the code that creates the blockchain, adds the blocks, and handles hashes.

9.3 Mining blocks

Our project contains the lib directory, which is a small library that supports creating blocks with multiple transactions. This library also checks if our blockchain app runs in the browser or in the standalone JavaScript engine, so the appropriate API for generating SHA-256 hashes is used.

This library consists of two files:

- bc_transactions.ts—Implements the creation of blocks with transactions
- universal_sha256.ts—Checks the environment and exports the proper `sha256()` function, which will use either the browser's or Node's API for generating SHA-256 hashes.

In chapter 8 (listing 8.6), we used Node's `crypto` API to synchronously invoke three functions:

```
crypto.createHash('sha256').update(data).digest('hex');
```

Now we'd like to generate hashes in Node.js as well as in browsers. But the browser's crypto API is async, unlike the package we use with Node.js, so the hash-generation code needs to be wrapped into asynchronous functions. For example, the `mine()` function that invokes the `crypto` API returns a `Promise` and is marked as `async`:

```
async mine(): Promise<void> {...}
```

Basically, instead of simply returning the value from a function, we'll wrap it in a `Promise`, which will make the `mine()` function asynchronous.

We'll review the code of bc_transactions.ts in two parts. Listing 9.8 shows the code that imports the SHA-256 generating function and declares the `Transaction` interface and the `Block` class. A block may contain more than one transaction, and the `Transaction` interface declares the structure of one transaction.

Listing 9.8 The first part of lib/bc_transactions.ts

```
import {sha256} from './universal_sha256.js';     ◁ Imports the function for hash generation

export interface Transaction {     ◁ A custom type representing a single transaction
  readonly sender: string;
  readonly recipient: string;
  readonly amount: number;
}

export class Block {     ◁ A custom type representing a single block
  nonce: number = 0;
  hash: string;

  constructor (
    readonly previousHash: string,
    readonly timestamp: number,
    readonly transactions: Transaction[]     ◁ Passes an array of transactions to the newly-created block
  ) {}

  async mine(): Promise<void> {     ◁ The asynchronous function to mine the block
    do {     ◁ Uses brute force to find the proper nonce
      this.hash = await this.calculateHash(++this.nonce);
    } while (this.hash.startsWith('0000') === false);
  }

  private async calculateHash(nonce: number): Promise<string> {     ◁ The asynchronous wrapper function for hash generation
    const data = this.previousHash + this.timestamp +
➥ JSON.stringify(this.transactions) + nonce;
    return sha256(data);     ◁ Invokes the function that uses the crypto API and generates the hash
  }
}
```

The UI of our blockchain allows the user to create several transactions using the Transfer Money button (see figure 9.5), and only clicking the Confirm Transactions button creates the `Block` instance, passing the `Transaction` array to its constructor.

In chapter 2, we showed you how to declare TypeScript custom types using classes and interfaces. In listing 9.8, you can see both: the Transaction type is declared as an interface but the Block type as a class. We couldn't make Block an interface, because we wanted it to have a constructor so we could use the new operator, as you'll see in listing 9.9. The Transaction type is a TypeScript interface, which will prevent us from making type errors during development, but the lines that declare Transaction won't make it into the compiled JavaScript.

Our Transaction type is rather simple; in a real-world blockchain we could introduce more properties in the Transaction interface. For example, buying real estate is a multistep process that requires several payments over time (an initial deposit, a payment for the title search, a payment for property insurance, and so on). In a real-world blockchain, we could introduce a propertyID to identify the property (house, land, or apartment) and a type to identify the transaction type.

Every transaction will include properties that describe the business domain of a particular blockchain—you'll always have a transaction type. A block will also have properties required by the blockchain implementation, such as creation date, hash value, and previous block's hash value. Also, a block type may include some utility methods, such as mine() and calculateHash() in listing 9.8.

NOTE We already had a Block class in chapter 8 (see listing 8.6), which stored its data as a string in the data property. This time the data is stored in a more structured way in a property of type Transaction[]. You may have also noticed that three of the properties of the Block class were declared implicitly via the constructor's arguments.

Our Block class has two methods: mine() and calculateHash(). The mine() method keeps increasing the nonce and invoking calculateHash() until it returns a hash value that starts with four zeros.

As specified in its signature, the mine() function returns a Promise, but where's the return statement of this function? We don't really want this function to return anything—the loop should simply end when the proper hash is generated. But any function marked with the async keyword must return a Promise, which is a generic type (explained in chapter 4) and must be used with a type parameter. By using Promise<void>, we specify that this function returns a Promise with an empty value, so a return statement is not required.

Since the method calculateHash() shouldn't be used by scripts external to Block, we declared it as private. This function invokes sha256(), which takes a string and generates a hash. Note that we use JSON.stringify() to turn an array of type Transaction into a string. The sha256() function is implemented in the universal_sha256.ts script, and we'll discuss it in section 9.4.

NOTE For simplicity, our calculateHash() function concatenates multiple transactions into a string and then calculates the hash. In real-world blockchains, a more efficient algorithm called *Merkle Tree* (https://en.wikipedia

.org/wiki/Merkle_tree) is used for calculating the hashes of multiple transactions. Using this algorithm, a program can build a tree of hashes (one per two transactions), and if someone tries to tamper with one transaction, there's no need to traverse all the transactions to recalculate and verify the final hash.

The first line in listing 9.8 imports from the ./universal_sha256.js JavaScript file, even though the lib directory only has the TypeScript version of this file. TypeScript doesn't allow us to use .ts extensions to reference imported filenames. This ensures that references to external scripts won't change after compilation, where all files have .js extensions. This import statement looks like we're importing a single function, `sha256()`, but under the hood it'll import different functions that use different crypto APIs, depending on the environment the app runs in. We'll show you how it's done in section 9.4 where we'll review the code of universal_sha256.ts.

In the second part of the bc_transactions.ts file, we declare the `Blockchain` class.

Listing 9.9 The second part of lib/bc_transactions.ts

```
export class Blockchain {
  private readonly _chain: Block[] = [];
  private _pendingTransactions: Transaction[] = [];

  private get latestBlock(): Block {        <-- The getter for the latest block in the blockchain
    return this._chain[this._chain.length - 1];
  }

  get chain(): Block[] {        <-- The getter for all blocks in the blockchain
    return [ ...this._chain ];
  }

  get pendingTransactions(): Transaction[] {        <-- The getter for all pending transactions
    return [ ...this._pendingTransactions ];
  }

  async createGenesisBlock(): Promise<void> {        <-- Creates the genesis block
    const genesisBlock = new Block('0', Date.now(), []);
    await genesisBlock.mine();        <-- Creates the hash for the genesis block
    this._chain.push(genesisBlock);        <-- Adds the genesis block to the chain
  }

  createTransaction(transaction: Transaction): void {        <-- Adds a pending transaction
    this._pendingTransactions.push(transaction);
  }

  async minePendingTransactions(): Promise<void> {        <-- Creates a block with pending transactions and adds it to the blockchain
    const block = new Block(this.latestBlock.hash,
          Date.now(), this._pendingTransactions);        <-- Creates the hash for the new block
    await block.mine();        <-- Adds the new block to the blockchain
    this._chain.push(block);
    this._pendingTransactions = [];
  }
}
```

Adding a new block to the blockchain intentionally takes time to prevent *double-spending attacks* (see the "Double-spending attacks" sidebar). For example, Bitcoin keeps this time at around 10 minutes by controlling the complexity of the algorithm that needs to be solved by the blockchain nodes. Creating a new block for each transaction would make the blockchain extremely slow, which is why a block can contain multiple transactions. We accumulate pending transactions in the `pendingTransactions` property and then create a new block that stores all of them. For example, one Bitcoin block contains about 2,500 transactions.

Double-spending attacks

Let's say you have only two $1 bills in your pocket, and you want to buy a cup of coffee that cost $2. You hand two $1 bills to the barista, he gives you the coffee, and you have no money in your pocket, which means that you can't buy anything else, unless you steal or counterfeit more. Counterfeiting money takes time and can't be done on the spot in the coffee shop.

The digital currency could be subject to counterfeiting. For example, a dishonest person might try to pay a given amount of money to multiple recipients. Suppose Joe has only one Bitcoin and he pays it to Mary (creating a block with the transaction "Joe Mary 1"), and then he immediately pays one Bitcoin to Alex (creating another block with the transaction "Joe Alex 1"). This is an example of a *double-spending attack.*

Bitcoin and other blockchains implement mechanisms for preventing such an attack, and they have a consensus process for validating each block and resolving conflicts. In section 10.1, we'll explain the longest chain rule, which can be used to prevent the insertion of invalid blocks.

When a user adds transactions using the UI shown in figure 9.5, we invoke the `createTransaction()` method for each transaction, and it adds one transaction to the `pendingTransactions` array (see listing 9.9). At the end of the `minePendingTransactions()` method, when the new block is added to the blockchain, we remove all pending transactions from this array.

Note that we declared the `_pendingTransactions` class variable as `private`, so it can only be modified via the `createTransaction()` method. We also provided a public getter that returns an array of pending transactions. It looks like this:

```
get pendingTransactions(): Transaction[] {
  return [ ...this._pendingTransactions ];
}
```

This method has just one line that creates a clone of the `_pendingTransactions` array (using the JavaScript spread operator explained in section A.7 of the appendix). By creating a clone, we make a copy of the transactions' data. Also, each property of the `Transaction` interface is `readonly`, so any attempt to modify the data in this array will result in a TypeScript error. This getter is used in the browser/main.ts file, which displays pending transactions on the UI as seen in listing 9.6. The same cloning technique is used with the `chain()` getter, which returns a clone of the blockchain.

The genesis block is created by invoking the `createGenesisBlock()` method (in listing 9.9), and the browser/main.ts script does this (see listing 9.6). The genesis block has an empty transactions array, and invoking `mine()` on this block calculates its hash. Mining the block may take some time, and we don't want the UI to freeze, so this method is asynchronous. Also, we added `await` to the invocation of the `mine()` method to ensure that the block is added to the blockchain only after the mining is complete.

Our blockchain app was created for educational purposes, so every time the user launches our app, the blockchain will contain only the genesis block. The user starts creating pending transactions, and at some point they'll click on the Confirm Transactions button. This will invoke the `minePendingTransactions()` method, which creates a new `Block` instance, calculates its hash, adds the block to the blockchain, and resets the `_pendingTransactions` array.

> **TIP** After mining a new block, the miner should be rewarded. We'll take care of this in the blockchain app in chapter 10.

You may want to take another look at the code of the `mineBlock()` method in listing 9.6 to get a better understanding of how the results of block mining are rendered on the UI.

Whether you're mining the genesis block or a block with transactions, the process invokes the `mine()` method in the `Block` class (see listing 9.8). The `mine()` method runs a loop invoking `calculateHash()`, which in turn invokes `sha256()`, discussed next.

9.4 Using crypto APIs for hash generation

Because we wanted to create a blockchain that could be used by both web and standalone apps, we needed to use two different crypto APIs to generate SHA-256 hashes:

- For web apps, we can invoke the API of the `crypto` object supported by all browsers.
- Standalone apps will run under the Node.js runtime, which comes with the crypto module (https://nodejs.org/api/crypto.html). We'll use it for generating hashes just like we did in listing 8.6.

We want our little library to make the decision about which API to use at runtime, so the client apps will use one function without knowing which specific crypto API will be used. The lib/universal_sha256.ts file in the following listing declares three functions: `sha256_node()`, `sha256_browser()`, and `sha256()`. Note that only the last one is exported.

Listing 9.10 lib/universal_sha256.ts: a wrapper for crypto APIs

```
function sha256_node(data: string): Promise<string> {      // The function to be used in the Node.js runtime
    const crypto = require('crypto');
    return Promise.resolve(crypto.createHash('sha256').update(data)
➥ .digest('hex'));                                          // Generates a SHA-256 hash
}

async function sha256_browser(data: string): Promise<string> {   // The function to be used in browsers

    const msgUint8Array = new TextEncoder().encode(data);    // Encodes the provided string as UTF-8

    const hashByteArray = await crypto.subtle.digest('SHA-256',
    msgUint8Array);                                          // Hashes the data

    const hashArray = Array.from(new Uint8Array(hashByteArray));   // Converts the ArrayBuffer to Array

    const hashHex = hashArray.map(b => ('00' +
➥ b.toString(16)).slice(-2)).join('');                     // Converts bytes to a hexadecimal string
    return hashHex;
}

export const sha256 = typeof window === "undefined" ?       // Checks if the runtime has a global variable window
                        sha256_node :                        // Exports the hashing function for Node
                        sha256_browser;                      // Exports the hashing function for browsers
```

When a JavaScript file contains import or export statements, it becomes an ES6 module (see the appendix for a discussion of this). The universal_sha256.ts module declares the functions `sha256_node()` and `sha256_browser()`, but it doesn't export them. These functions become private and can be used only inside the module.

The `sha256()` function is the only one that is exported and can be imported by other scripts. This function has a very simple mission—to find out if the module is running in the browser or not. Depending on the result, we want to export either `sha256_browser()` or `sha256_node()`, but under the name `sha256()`.

We came up with a simple solution: if the runtime environment has a global `window` variable, we assume that this code is running in the browser, and we export `sha256_browser()` under the name `sha256()`. Otherwise we export `sha256_node()` under the same name of `sha256()`. In other words, this is an example of a dynamic export.

We already used the Node.js crypto API in chapter 8, but here we've wrapped this code in a `Promise`:

```
Promise.resolve(crypto.createHash('sha256').update(data).digest('hex'));
```

We did this to align the signatures of the functions `sha256_node()` and `sha256_browser()`.

The `sha256_browser() function` runs in the browser and uses the asynchronous crypto API, which makes this function asynchronous as well. As per the browser's crypto API requirements, we start by using the Web Encoding API's `TextEncoder.encode()` method (see the Mozilla documentation at http://mng.bz/1wd1), which encodes the string as UTF-8 and returns the result in a special JavaScript typed array of unsigned 8-bit integers (see http://mng.bz/POqY). Then the browser's crypto API generates a hash in the form of an array-like object (an object with a `length` property and indexed elements). After that, we use the `Array.from()` method to create a real array.

Figure 9.8 shows a screenshot taken in Chrome's debugger. It shows fragments of data in the `hashByteArray` and `hashArray` variables. The breakpoint was placed right before calculating the value of the `hashHex` variable. (We'll explain how to debug your TypeScript code in the browser in section 9.6.)

Finally, we want to turn the calculated hash into a string of hexadecimal values, and this is done in the following statement:

```
const hashHex = hashArray.map(
                b => ('00' + b.toString(16)).slice(-2))
                .join('');
```

We convert each element of the `hashArray` into a hexadecimal value with the `Array.map()` method. Some hexadecimal values are represented by one character, while others need two. To ensure that one-character values are prepended with a zero, we concatenate `00` and the hexadecimal value, and then use `slice(-2)` to take just the two characters at the right. For example, the hexadecimal value `a` becomes `00a` and then `0a`.

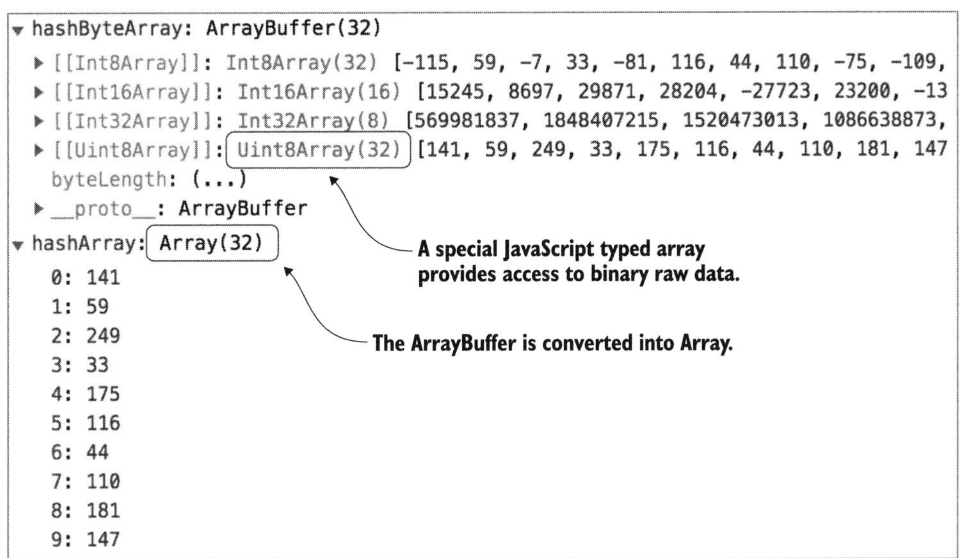

Figure 9.8 The `hashByteArray` and `hashArray` variables in the debugger

The `join('')` method concatenates all the converted elements of `hashArray` into a `hashHex` string, specifying an empty string as a separator (such as no separator). Figure 9.9 shows a fragment of the result of applying `map()`, along with the final hash in the `hashHex` variable.

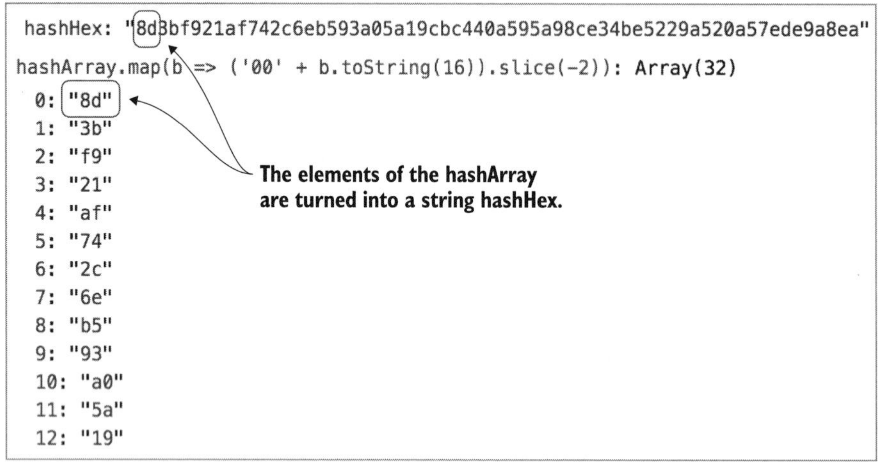

Figure 9.9 Applying `map()` and `join()`

You may ask why the signature of the `sha256_browser()` function declares the return type `Promise`, but it actually returns a string. We declared this function as `async`, so it automatically wraps its returned value into a `Promise`.

By now, you should understand the code in the lib directory and how the web client uses it. The last piece to review is the standalone client that can be used instead of the web client.

9.5 The standalone blockchain client

The directory node of this project has a little script that can create a blockchain without the web UI, but we wanted to show you that the code in the lib directory is reusable, and that if the app runs under Node.js, the proper crypto API will be engaged. The following listing shows a script that doesn't need a browser but runs under the Node runtime. The first line imports the Blockchain class, which hides the details of the specific crypto API.

Listing 9.11 node/main.ts: a standalone script for block mining

```
import { Blockchain } from '../lib/bc_transactions';

(async function main(): Promise<void> {
    console.log('? Initializing the blockchain, creating the genesis
➥ block...');

    const bc = new Blockchain();     <—— Creates a new blockchain
```

```
    await bc.createGenesisBlock();     <-- Creates the genesis block

    bc.createTransaction({ sender: 'John', recipient: 'Kate', amount: 50 });
    bc.createTransaction({ sender: 'Kate', recipient: 'Mike', amount: 10 });

    await bc.minePendingTransactions();   4((CO12-5))

    bc.createTransaction({ sender: 'Alex', recipient: 'Rosa', amount: 15 });
    bc.createTransaction({ sender: 'Gina', recipient: 'Rick', amount: 60 });

    await bc.minePendingTransactions();

    console.log(JSON.stringify(bc, null, 2));
})();
```

Creates the genesis block

Creates a pending transaction

Creates a new block and adds it to the blockchain

Prints the content of the blockchain

This program starts by printing a message stating that the new blockchain is being created. The process of creating the genesis block can take some time, and the first `await` waits for it to complete.

What would happen if we didn't use `await` in the line that invokes `bc.createGenesisBlock()`? The code would proceed with mining blocks before the genesis block was created, and the script would fail with runtime errors.

After the genesis block is created, the script proceeds with creating two pending transactions and mining a new block. Again, `await` will wait for this process to complete, and then we create two more transactions and mine another block. Finally, the program prints the content of the blockchain.

> **TIP** Node.js supports `async` and `await` starting with version 8.

Remember that the directory node has its own tsconfig.json file, as was shown in figure 9.1. Its content was shown in listing 9.3.

To launch this program, make sure that the code is compiled by running tsc. It's important that you run tsc from the src/node directory, to ensure that the compiler picks up the options from the whole hierarchy of tsconfig.json files. As specified in the base tsconfig.json file, the compiled code will be saved in the dist directory.

> **TIP** The compiler's `-p` option allows you to specify the path to a valid JSON configuration file. For example, you could compile the TypeScript code by running the following command: `tsc -p src/node/tsconfig.json`.

Now you can ask Node.js to launch the JavaScript version of the code shown in listing 9.11. If you're still in the src/node directory, you can run the app as follows:

```
node ../../dist/node/main.js
```

Listing 9.12 shows the console output of this command.

Listing 9.12 Creating the blockchain in a standalone app

```
? Initializing the blockchain, creating the genesis block...
{
  "_chain": [
    {                                          <-- The genesis block
      "previousHash": "0",
      "timestamp": 1540391674580,
      "transactions": [],
      "nonce": 239428,
      "hash": "0000d1452c893a79347810d1c567e767ea55e52a8a5ffc9743303f780b6c30
➥ 8f"
    },
    {                                          <-- The second block
      "previousHash": "0000d1452c893a79347810d1c567e767ea55e52a8a5ffc9743303f
➥ 780b6c308f",
      "timestamp": 1540391675729,
      "transactions": [
        {
          "sender": "John",
          "recipient": "Kate",
          "amount": 50
        },
        {
          "sender": "Kate",
          "recipient": "Mike",
          "amount": 10
        }
      ],
      "nonce": 69189,
      "hash": "00006f79662bde59ff46cd57cff928977c465d931b2ba2d11e05868afcfee8
➥ 36"
    },
    {                                          <-- The third block
      "previousHash": "00006f79662bde59ff46cd57cff928977c465d931b2ba2d11e0586
➥ 8afcfee836",
      "timestamp": 1540391676138,
      "transactions": [
        {
          "sender": "Alex",
          "recipient": "Rosa",
          "amount": 15
        },
        {
          "sender": "Gina",
          "recipient": "Rick",
          "amount": 60
        }
      ],
      "nonce": 33462,
      "hash": "0000483b745526f48afde33435c21517dd72ea0a25407bc35be3f921029a32
➥ 09"
    }
  ],
  "_pendingTransactions": []      <-- The array of pending transactions is empty
}
```

Whereas the web version of this app is more interactive, the standalone version runs the entire process in batch mode. Still, the main focus of this chapter was developing a web app. Now we'll show you how to debug the TypeScript code of a web app in the browser.

9.6 Debugging TypeScript in the browser

Writing code in TypeScript is fun, but web browsers don't understand this language. They load and run only the JavaScript version of the app. Moreover, the executable JavaScript may be optimized and compressed, which makes it unreadable. But there is a way to load the original TypeScript code into the browser as well.

For that, you need to generate source map files, which map the executable lines of code back to the corresponding source code, which is TypeScript in our case. If the browser loads the source map files, you can debug the original sources! In the tsconfig.json file shown in listing 9.2, we asked the compiler to generate source maps, which are files with the extension .js.map, as shown in figure 9.2.

When a browser loads the JavaScript code of a web app, it loads only the .js files, even if the deployed app includes the .js.map files. But if you open the browser's dev tools, the browser will then load the source maps as well.

> **TIP** If your browser doesn't load the source map files for your app, check the settings of the dev tools. Ensure that the JavaScript source maps option is enabled.

Now let's load our web client (as explained in section 9.1) in the Chrome browser and open dev tools from the Sources tab. This will split the screen into three parts, as shown in figure 9.10.

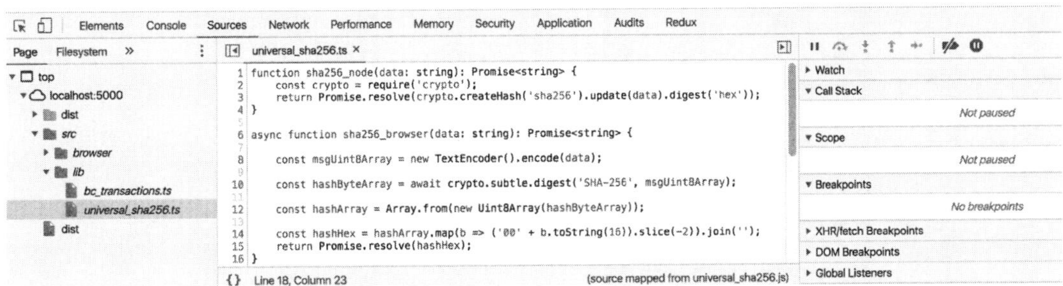

Figure 9.10 The Sources panel of Chrome's dev tools

On the left you can browse and select a source file from your project. We've selected universal_sha256.ts, and its TypeScript code is shown in the middle. On the right, you see the debugger panel.

Let's set a breakpoint at line 12 by clicking to the left of the line number, and then refresh the browser window. The app will stop at the breakpoint, and the browser window will look like the one in figure 9.11.

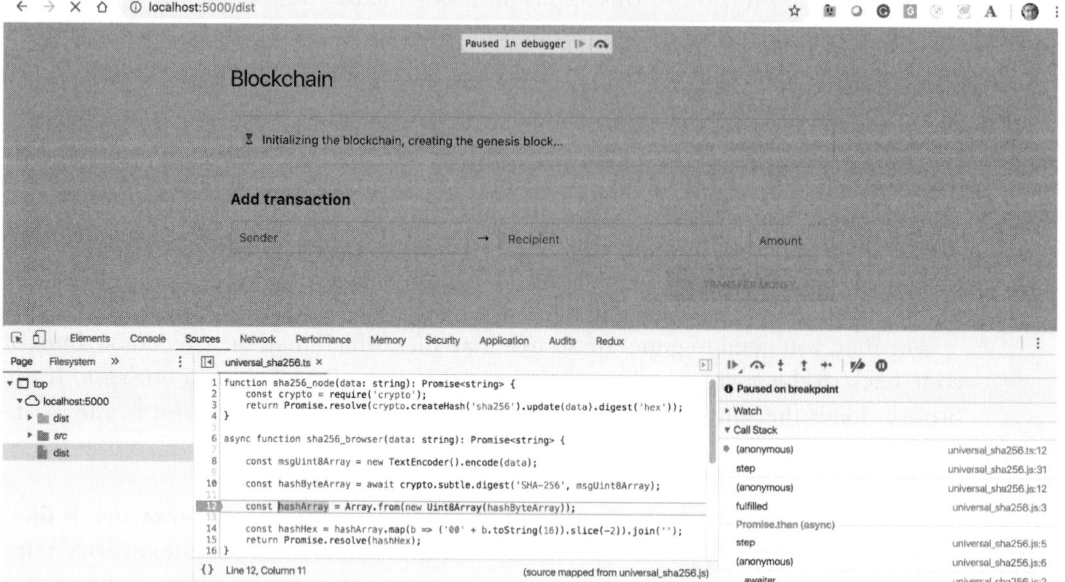

Figure 9.11 The program paused at the breakpoint

You can see the values of the variables by hovering your mouse over a variable name. Figure 9.12 shows the values of the msgUint8Array variable as we hovered our mouse over its name in line 8.

```
Sources  Netwo   Uint8Array(17)                    on  Audits  Redux
         universal_s  0: 48
                      1: 49
 1 function           2: 53
 2     cons           3: 52
 3     retu           4: 48        .update(data).digest('hex'));
 4 }                  5: 51
 5
 6 async fu                        tring> {
 7
 8     const msgUint8Array = new TextEncoder().encode(data);
 9
10     const hashByteArray = await crypto.subtle.digest('SHA-256', msgUint8Array);
11
12     const hashArray = Array.from(new Uint8Array(hashByteArray));
13
14     const hashHex = hashArray.map(b => ('00' + b.toString(16)).slice(-2)).join('');
15     return Promise.resolve(hashHex);
16 }
```

Figure 9.12 Viewing a variable's values by hovering the mouse on its name

You can also view the values of any variable or expression by adding it to the Watch area in the debugger panel on the right. Figure 9.13 shows the program paused at line 15. We've added a couple of variable names and one expression by clicking on the plus sign in the Watch area on the right.

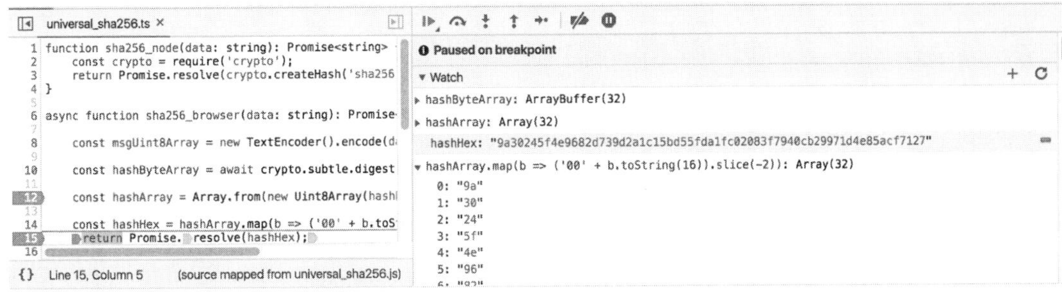

Figure 9.13 Watching variables in the Watch area

If you want to remove a watched variable, click on the minus sign to the right of the variable or expression you want to remove. In figure 9.13, you can see this minus sign to the right of the `hashHex` variable in the Watch area.

The Chrome browser comes with a full-featured debugger. To learn more about it, watch the video "Debugging JavaScript - Chrome DevTools 101" on YouTube at http://mng.bz/JzqK. With source maps, you'll be able to debug your TypeScript even if the JavaScript was optimized, minimized, or uglified.

NOTE IDEs also come with debuggers, and in chapter 10, we'll use VS Code's debugger to debug a standalone TypeScript server. But when it comes to web apps, we prefer debugging right in the browser because we may need to know more about the execution context (network requests, application storage, session storage, and so on) to figure out a problem.

Summary

- Typically, a TypeScript app is a project that consists of multiple files. Some contain configuration options for the Typescript compiler and the bundler, and others contain the source code.
- You can organize the source code of a project by splitting the code into several directories. In our app, the lib directory was reused by two different client apps—a web app (in the browser directory) and the standalone app (in the node directory).
- You can use npm scripts to create custom commands for app deployment, starting the web server, and so on.

10 Client-server communications using Node.js, TypeScript, and WebSockets

This chapter covers

- Why a blockchain may need a server
- The longest chain rule
- How to create a Node.js WebSocket server in TypeScript
- Practical use of TypeScript interfaces, abstract classes, access qualifiers, enums, and generics

In the previous chapter, you learned that each block miner can take a number of pending transactions, create a valid block that includes the proof of work, and add the new block to the blockchain. This workflow is easy to follow when there is only one miner creating the proof of work. Realistically, there could be thousands of miners around the world trying to find the valid hash for a block with the same transactions, which may cause conflicts.

In this chapter, we'll use TypeScript to create a server that uses the WebSocket protocol to broadcast messages to the blockchain's nodes. The web clients can also make requests of this server.

While writing code in TypeScript remains our main activity, we'll use several JavaScript packages for the first time in this book:

- *ws*—A Node.js library that supports the WebSocket protocol
- *express*—A small Node.js framework offering HTTP support
- *nodemon*—A tool that restarts Node.js-based apps when script file changes are detected
- *lit-html*—HTML templates in JavaScript for rendering to the browser's DOM

These packages are included in the package.json file as dependencies (see section 10.4.2).

Before discussing the TypeScript code of this chapter's blockchain app, we need to cover the following subjects:

- The blockchain concept known as the *longest chain rule*
- How to build and run a blockchain app emulating more than one block miner

We'll also need to go over these infrastructure-related subjects:

- The project structure, its configuration files, and npm scripts.
- The WebSocket protocol—what it's about and why it's better than HTTP for implementing a notification server. As an illustration, we'll create a simple WebSocket server that can push messages to a web client.

Let's start with the longest chain rule.

10.1 Resolving conflicts using the longest chain rule

In chapter 9, we had a simplified way to start block mining—the user would click the Confirm Transaction button to create a new block. In this chapter, let's consider a more realistic example of a blockchain that has already 100 blocks and a pool of pending transactions. Multiple miners could grab pending transactions (such as 10 transactions each) and start mining blocks.

> **NOTE** While reading about block mining in this chapter, keep in mind that we're talking about a decentralized network. The blockchain nodes work in parallel, which may result in conflict situations if more than one node claims to have mined the next block. That's why a consensus mechanism is required to resolve conflicts.

Let's pick three arbitrary miners, M1, M2, and M3, and assume they've found the proper hash (the proof of work) and broadcast their versions of the new block, number 101, as a candidate for adding to the blockchain. Each of their candidate blocks may contain different transactions, but each wants to become block number 101.

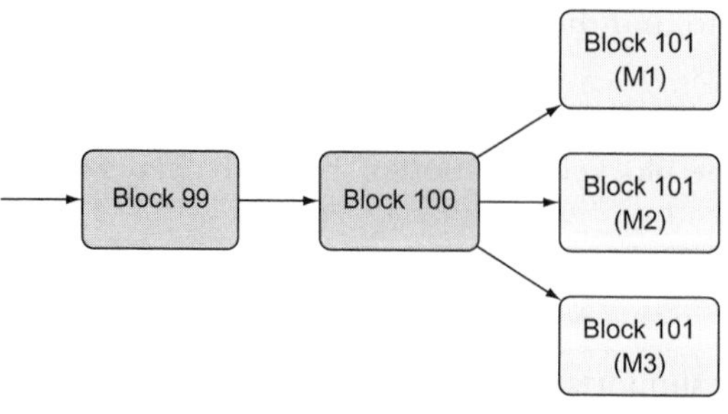

Figure 10.1 A forked blockchain

The miners are located on different continents, and forks are created in these miners' nodes as shown in figure 10.1. Temporarily, three forks exist—they're identical to the first 100 blocks, but block 101 is different in each fork. At this point, each of these three blocks is validated (they have the right hashes), but they're not confirmed yet.

How can we decide which of these three should be added to the blockchain? We'll use the *longest chain rule*. A multinode chain may have multiple blocks that are candidates for being added to the network, but the blockchain is like a living, growing organism that keeps adding nodes all the time. By the time all of the miners have finished mining, one of their chains will have been used by some miner to add more blocks, and that will have become the longest chain.

For simplicity, we'll consider just our three miners, though there could be hundreds of thousands of them at the same time. Our miners are mining blocks 102, 103, and so on, based on one of the versions of block 101. Suppose some other miner, M4, already requested the longest chain and picked block 101 from M2's fork, and M4 already calculated the hash for the next candidate block, 102. Let's assume that M2 had a more powerful CPU than M1 and M3, so the M2's fork was the longest (it had the extra block 101) at some point. That's why miner M4 linked it to block 101, as shown in figure 10.2.

Now, even though we have three forks that include block 101, the longest chain is the one that ends with block 102, and it will be adopted by all other nodes. The forks created by miners M1 and M3 will be discarded, and their transactions will be placed back into the pool of pending transactions so other miners can pick them up while creating other blocks.

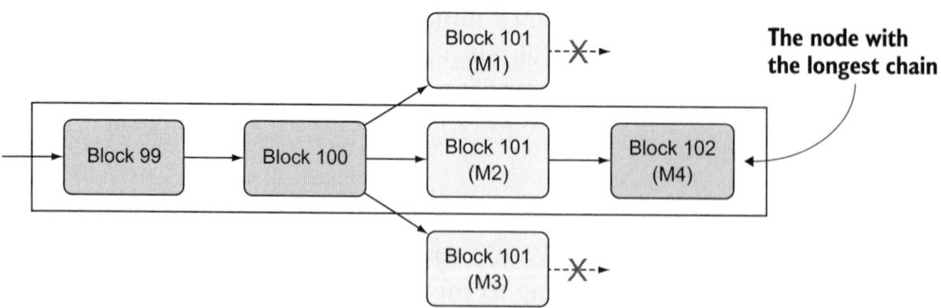

Figure 10.2 M2 has the longest chain.

M2 will get the reward for mining block 101; miners M1 and M3 just wasted electricity calculating the hash for their versions of block 101. M4 was similarly risking useless work when it selected M2's block with an unconfirmed, but valid, hash.

NOTE Blockchains implement a mechanism to ensure that if a transaction is included in a valid block by any node, it isn't placed back in the pool of pending transactions when blocks are discarded.

We've used a small number of blocks in this example for simplicity, but public blockchains may have many thousands of nodes. In our scenario, there was a moment when the fork of miner M2 had a longest chain that was just one block longer than the other forks. In real-world blockchains, there could be multiple forks of different lengths. Since the blockchain is a distributed network, blocks are being added on multiple nodes, and each node may have a chain of a different length. The longest chain is considered to be the correct one.

TIP Later in this chapter, we'll go over the process of requesting the longest chain and getting responses. Figures 10.5–10.8 show the communication between two nodes while requesting the longest chain and announcing newly mined blocks.

Now let's see how the longest chain rule helps in preventing the *double-spending* problem, and other fraud. Let's say one miner has a friend, John, who has $1,000 in his account. One of the transactions in block 99 is: "John paid Mary $1,000." What if the miner decides to commit fraud by forking the chain and adding another transaction, "John paid Alex $1,000," in block 100? Technically, this criminal miner is trying to cheat the blockchain by making it appear that John spent the same $1,000 twice—once in a transaction to Mary, and again in a transaction to Alex. Figure 10.3 shows an attempt by the criminal miner to convince others that the correct view of the blockchain is the fork that contains the John-to-Alex transaction.

Remember, the block's hash value is easy to check, but it's time-consuming to calculate, so our criminal miner has to calculate the hashes for blocks 100, 101, and 102. Meanwhile, other miners continue mining new blocks (103, 104, 105, and so on) adding them to the chain shown at the top of figure 10.3. There's no way that the criminal miner can recalculate all the hashes and create a longer chain faster than all the other nodes. The chain with the most work done (the longest chain) wins. In other words, the chances of modifying the content of the existing block(s) is close to zero, which makes a blockchain immutable.

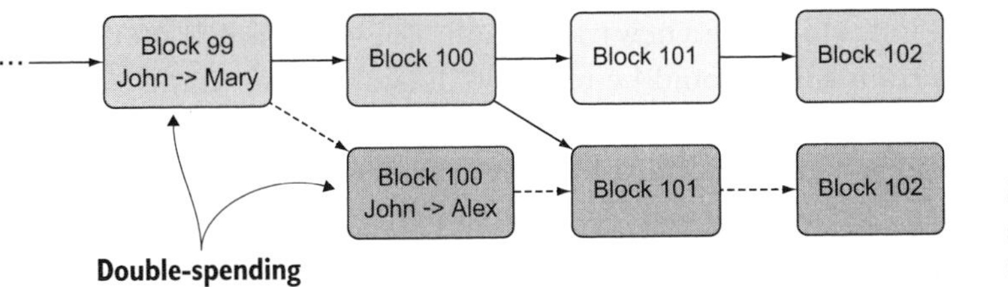

Figure 10.3 An attempt to double-spend

What's a consensus?

Any decentralized system needs to have rules allowing all the nodes to agree that a valid event happened. What if two nodes calculated the hash of a new block at the same time? Which block would be added to the chain, and which node would be rewarded? All nodes of the blockchain have to come to a general agreement—a *consensus*—about who the winner is.

Consensus is required from all members because there is no system administrator who could modify or delete a block. Blockchains use different rules (*consensus protocols*), and in our app we'll use proof of work combined with the longest chain to reach consensus on the true state of the blockchain. The aim of the consensus protocol is to guarantee that a single chain is used.

So far we haven't discussed how blockchain nodes communicate with each other. We'll do that in the next section.

10.2 Adding a server to the blockchain

As you'll recall, we've praised blockchain technology for being completely decentralized without a server. The server we add here won't be a central authority for creating, validating, and storing blocks. The blockchain can remain decentralized and still use a server for utility services, such as caching hashes, broadcasting new transactions, requesting the longest chain, or announcing newly created blocks. Later in this chapter (section 10.6.1), we'll review the code of such a server. In this section we'll discuss the process of communication between clients via this server.

> **TIP** Anton Moiseev has implemented our blockchain app using a peer-to-peer technology called WebRTC (see https://github.com/antonmoiseev/blockchain-p2p), and you can experiment with it on your own.

Suppose the M1 node has mined a block and requested the longest chain from the server, which broadcasts this request to all other nodes on the blockchain. Each of the nodes responds with their chains (just the block headers), and the server forwards these responses to M1.

The M1 node receives the longest chain and validates it by checking the hashes of each block. Then M1 adds its newly mined block to this longest chain, and this chain is saved locally. For some time, M1's node will enjoy the status of "the source of truth," because it will have the longest chain until someone else mines one or more new blocks.

Let's say M1 wants to create a new transaction: "Joe sent Mary $1,000." Creating a new block for each transaction would be too slow (lots of hashes would need to be calculated) and expensive (the electricity cost). Typically, one block includes multiple transactions, and M1 can simply broadcast its new transaction to the rest of the blockchain members. Miners M2 and M3 and any others will do the same with their transactions.

All broadcast transactions go into the pool of pending transactions, and any node can pick a group of transactions (say, 10 of them) from there and start mining.

> **TIP** For our version of blockchain, we'll use Node.js to create a server that implements broadcasting via a Websocket connection. As an alternative, you could go completely serverless by implementing broadcasting using some peer-to-peer technology like WebRTC (https://en.wikipedia.org/wiki/WebRTC).

10.3 The project structure

The blockchain app that comes with this chapter consists of two parts, the server and the client, both of which are implemented using TypeScript. We'll show you the project structure and explain how to run this app first. Then we'll discuss selected parts of the code that illustrate the practical use of particular TypeScript syntax constructs.

In your IDE, open the project in the chapter10 directory, and run `npm install` in the terminal window. The structure of this project is shown in figure 10.4.

The public directory is created during the build process, and the public/index.html file loads the compiled version of the client/main.ts file, along with all its imported scripts. This is the web client that we'll use to illustrate the blockchain node.

The server/main.ts file contains the code that imports additional scripts and starts the WebSocket and the blockchain notification servers.

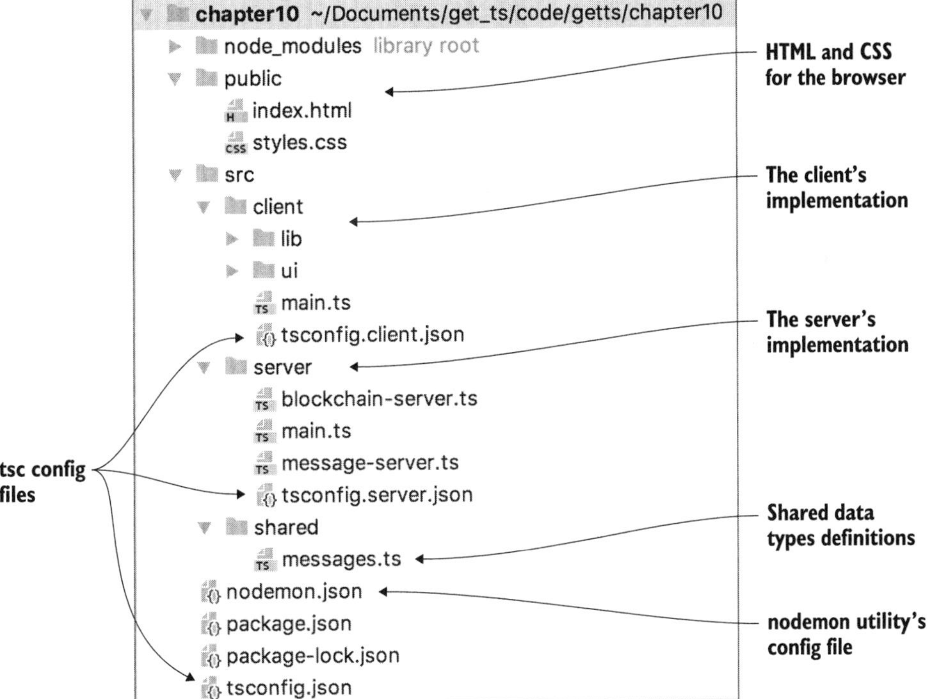

Figure 10.4 The project structure

NOTE In section 10.4.4, we'll explain how to build and run the client and the server.

Have you noticed that there are three config files for the Typescript compiler? The tsconfig.json file in the root directory contains the compiler options that are common to both the client and server. The tsconfig.client.json and tsconfig.server.json files extend tsconfig.json and add compiler options specific to the client and server respectively. We'll review their content in the next section.

Our server runs under the Node.js runtime, and its compiled code will be stored in the build/server directory. You can start the server with the following command:

```
node build/server/main.js
```

However, the `node` executable doesn't support live reload (it won't restart if you change and recompile the TypeScript code of the server). That's why we use the nodemon utility (https://nodemon.io), which monitors the Node.js app's codebase and restarts the Node.js server on file changes. If you have the nodemon utility installed, you can use it instead of `node`. For example, this is how you can start the Node.js runtime and run the code using the globally installed nodemon:

```
nodemon build/server/main.js
```

If you don't have nodemon, run it as follows:

```
npx nodemon build/server/main.js
```

In our project, we'll be starting the server with `nodemon`, which will be configured in the nodemon.json file discussed in the next section. The package.json file includes the npm scripts section, and we'll review it in the next section as well.

10.4 The project's configuration files

The project that comes with this chapter includes several JSON configuration files that we'll review in this section.

10.4.1 Configuring the TypeScript compilation

A tsconfig.json file can inherit configurations from another file using the `extends` config property. In our project, we have three config files:

- tsconfig.json contains the common tsc compiler options for the entire project.
- tsconfig.client.json contains the options for compiling the client portion of the project.
- tsconfig.server.json includes the options for compiling the server portion of the project.

The following listing shows the content of the base tsconfig.json file.

Listing 10.1 tsconfig.json—common tsc options

```
{
  "compileOnSave": false,
  "compilerOptions": {
    "target": "es2017",
    "sourceMap": true,
    "plugins": [
      {
        "name": "typescript-lit-html-plugin".
      }
    ]
  }
}
```

- Doesn't autocompile on each modification of the TypeScript files
- Compiles into JavaScript using the syntax supported by ECMAScript 2017
- Generates source map files
- This plugin enables HTML autocompletion for template strings tagged with html.

We specified `es2017` as the compilation target because we're sure that the users of this app will use modern browsers that support all the features in the ECMAScript 2017 specification.

The next listing shows the tsconfig.client.json file, which contains the tsc options we want to use for compiling the client's portion of the code. This file is located in the src/client directory.

Listing 10.2 tsconfig.client.json—tsc options for the client

```
{
  "extends": "../../tsconfig.json",
  "compilerOptions": {
    "module": "es2015",
    "outDir": "../../public",
    "inlineSources": true
  }
}
```

- Inherits the config options from this file
- Uses import/export statements in the generated JavaScript
- Places the compiled code in the public directory
- Emits the original TypeScript code and source maps within a single file

Source maps allow you to debug TypeScript while the browser executes JavaScript. They work by instructing the browser's dev tools which lines of the compiled code (JavaScript) correspond to which lines of the source (TypeScript). However, the source code needs to be available to the browser, and you can either deploy TypeScript along with JavaScript to the web server, or use the `inlineSources` option as we did here, which embeds the original TypeScript right inside the source maps files.

> **TIP** If you don't want to reveal the source of your app to users, don't deploy source maps in production.

The following listing shows the tsconfig.server.json file, which contains tsc options for compiling the server's code. This file is located in the src/server directory.

Listing 10.3 tsconfig.server.json—tsc options for the server

```
{
  "extends": "../../tsconfig.json",          // Inherits config options from this file
  "compilerOptions": {
    "module": "commonjs",                     // Converts import/export statements to commonjs-compliant code
    "outDir": "../../build"                   // Places compiled code in the build directory
  },
  "include": [
    "**/*.ts"                                 // Compiles all .ts files from all subdirectories
  ]
}
```

TIP In a perfect world, you would never see the same compiler option in the base and inherited config files. But sometimes IDEs don't handle tsc configuration inheritance properly, and you may need to repeat an option in more than one file.

Now that we have more than one tsc config file, how do we let the Typescript compiler know which one to use? We use the `-p` option. The following command compiles the web client code using the options from tsconfig.client.json:

```
tsc -p src/client/tsconfig.client.json
```

The next command compiles the server code using tsconfig.server.json:

```
tsc -p src/server/tsconfig.server.json
```

NOTE If you introduce tsc configuration files named other than tsconfig.json, you need to use the `-p` option and specify the path to the file you want to use. For example, if you ran the `tsc` command in the src/server directory, it wouldn't use the options from the tsconfig.server.json file, and you might experience unexpected compilation results.

Now let's take a look at the dependencies and the npm scripts for this project.

10.4.2 What's in package.json

Listing 10.4 shows the content of package.json. The `scripts` section contains custom npm commands, and the `dependencies` section lists only three packages that are required to run our app (both the client and server):

- *ws*—A Node.js library that supports WebSocket protocol
- *express*—A small Node.js framework offering HTTP support
- *lit-html*—HTML templates in JavaScript for rendering to the browser's DOM

The web part of this app uses lit-html (https://github.com/Polymer/lit-html). It's a templating library for JavaScript, and typescript-lit-html-plugin will enable autocomplete (IntelliSense) in your IDE.

The `devDependencies` section includes packages that are needed only during development.

Listing 10.4 package.json: dependencies of our web app

```
{
  "name": "blockchain",
  "version": "1.0.0",
  "description": "Chapter 10 sample app",
  "license": "MIT",
  "scripts": {                                          <- Our custom npm script commands
    "build:client": "tsc -p src/client/tsconfig.client.json",
    "build:server": "tsc -p src/server/tsconfig.server.json",
    "build": "concurrently npm:build:*",
    "start:client": "tsc -p src/client/tsconfig.client.json --watch",   <- Runs tsc for the client in a watch mode
    "start:server": "nodemon --inspect src/server/main.ts",
    "start": "concurrently npm:start:*",
    "now-start": "NODE_ENV=production node build/server/main.js"
  },
  "dependencies": {
    "express": "^4.16.3",      <- The web framework for Node.js
    "lit-html": "^0.12.0",     <- The templating library for the client
    "ws": "^6.0.0"             <- The package to support WebSocket in Node.js apps
  },
  "devDependencies": {
    "@types/express": "^4.16.0",   <- Type definition files
    "@types/ws": "^6.0.1",
    "concurrently": "^4.0.1",      <- The package to run multiple commands concurrently
    "nodemon": "^1.18.4",          <- The utility for the live reload of the Node.js runtime
    "ts-node": "^7.0.1",           <- Runs both tsc and node as a single process
    "typescript": "^3.1.1",
    "typescript-lit-html-plugin": "^0.6.0"   <- The plugin to enable IntelliSense for the lit-html tags
  }
}
```

ts-node launches a single Node process. After Node is launched, it registers a custom extension/loader pair using the Node's `require.extensions` mechanism. When Node's `require()` call resolves to a file with the extension `.ts`, Node invokes a custom loader, which compiles TypeScript into JavaScript on the fly using tsc's programmatic API, without launching a separate tsc process.

Note that the `start:client` command runs tsc in watch mode (using the `--watch` option). This ensures that as soon as you modify and save any TypeScript code on the client, it'll get recompiled. But what about recompiling the server's code?

10.4.3 Configuring nodemon

We could start the tsc compiler in watch mode on the server as well, and the JavaScript would be regenerated when the TypeScript code is modified. But having fresh JavaScript code is not enough on the server—we'll need to restart the Node.js runtime on each code change. That's why we've installed the nodemon utility, which will start the Node.js process and monitor the JavaScript files in the specified directory.

The package.json file (listing 10.4) includes the following command:

```
"start:server": "nodemon --inspect src/server/main.ts"
```

TIP The `--inspect` option allows you to debug the code that runs in Node.js in Chrome's dev tools (see Node's "Debugging Guide" for details: http://mng.bz/wlX2). Nodemon just passes the `--inspect` option to Node.js, so it will be started in debug mode.

It might seem that the `start:server` command requests nodemon to start the main.ts TypeScript file, but since our project has the nodemon.json file, nodemon will use the options from there. Our nodemon.json file contains the following configuration options for nodemon.

Listing 10.5 nodemon.json: the config file for the nodemon utility

```
{
  "exec": "node -r ts-node/register/transpile-only",   <-- How to start the node
  "watch": [ "src/server/**/*.ts" ]   <-- Watches all .ts files located in all server's subdirectories
}
```

The `exec` command allows us to specify the options for starting Node.js. In particular, the `-r` option is a shortcut for `--require module`, which is used for preloading modules on startup. In our case, it asks the ts-node package to preload TypeScript's faster transpile-only module, which simply converts the code from TypeScript to JavaScript without performing type-checking. This module will automatically run the Typescript compiler for each file with the extension `.ts` loaded by Node.js.

By preloading the `transpile-only` module, we eliminate the need to start a separate tsc process for the server. Any TypeScript file will be loaded and autocompiled as part of the single Node.js process.

NOTE You can use the ts-node package in different ways. For example, you can use it to start Node.js with TypeScript compilation: `ts-node myScript.ts`. See the ts-node page on npm for more details: www.npmjs.com/package/ts-node.

You've seen a high-level overview of the blockchain app's configuration. The next step is to see it in action.

10.4.4 Running the blockchain app

In this section, we'll show you how to run both the server and two clients emulating blockchain nodes. To start the processes we'll be using npm scripts, so let's take a closer look at the scripts section of the package.json file.

Listing 10.6 The `scripts` section of package.json

```
"scripts": {
  "build:client": "tsc -p src/client/tsconfig.client.json",
  "build:server": "tsc -p src/server/tsconfig.server.json",
  "build": "concurrently npm:build:*",
  "start:tsc:client": "tsc -p src/client/tsconfig.client.json --watch",
  "start:server": "nodemon --inspect src/server/main.ts",
  "start": "concurrently npm:start:*",
}
```

- Compiles the client's code
- Compiles the server's code
- Concurrently runs all commands that start with npm:build
- Starts tsc in watch mode for the client's code
- Starts the server with nodemon
- Concurrently runs all commands that start with npm:start

The first two `build` commands start the tsc compiler for the client and server respectively. These processes compile TypeScript to JavaScript. The compilation of the client and server code can be done in parallel, so the third command uses the npm package called "concurrently" (www.npmjs.com/package/concurrently), which allows you to run multiple commands concurrently.

The `start:tsc:client` command compiles the client's code in watch mode, and `start:server` starts the server using nodemon, as described in the previous section. The third `start` command runs both `start:tsc:client` and `start:server` concurrently.

In general, you can start more than one npm command by simply adding an ampersand between commands. For example, you could define two custom commands, `first` and `second`, and then run them concurrently with `npm start`. In npm scripts, the ampersand means "run these commands concurrently."

Listing 10.7 Concurrent execution with the ampersand

```
"scripts": {
    "first": "sleep 2; echo First",
    "second": "sleep 1; echo Second",
    "start": "npm run first & npm run second"
},
```

- Sleeps for 2 seconds and prints "First"
- Sleeps for 1 second and prints "Second"
- Runs the first and second commands concurrently

If you run `npm start`, it'll print "Second" and then "First," which proves that the commands ran concurrently. Replacing `&` with `&&` will print "First" and then "Second," indicating sequential execution.

Using the concurrently package rather than an ampersand gives you a clean separation of the messages printed by each concurrent process.

Using ampersands in npm scripts on Windows

A single ampersand (`&`) doesn't run npm commands in parallel on Windows. To start running them at the same time, you can use the npm-run-all package (www.npmjs.com/package/npm-run-all).

Here is what the code from listing 10.7 would look like on Windows:

```
"scripts": {
  "first": "timeout /T 2 > nul && echo First",
  "second": "timeout /T 1 > nul && echo Second",
  "start": "run-p first second"
}
```

timeout is a Windows alternative for the sleep command on Unix systems.

run-p is a command installed along with the npm-run-all package.

Instead of `sleep` we use `timeout` and specify how long the process should be inactive in seconds, using the `/T` parameter. While running, the `timeout` command prints to the console how many seconds are still left to wait. To avoid these messages interfering with the "First" and "Second" output, we redirect `timeout`'s output to `nul`, which throws messages away.

`run-p` is a command that comes with the `npm-run-all` package. It runs npm scripts with the specified names in parallel.

To start the blockchain app, run the `npm start` command in the Terminal window. The following listing shows the terminal output. We're running two commands concurrently: `start:tsc:client` and `start:server`. Each line in the terminal output starts with the name of the process (in square brackets) that produced this message.

Listing 10.8 Starting the blockchain app

```
> blockchain@1.0.0 start /Users/yfain11/Documents/get_ts/code/getts/chapter10
10:47:18 PM - Starting compilation in watch mode...
[start:tsc:client]
[start:server] [nodemon] 1.18.9
[start:server] [nodemon] to restart at any time, enter `rs`
[start:server] [nodemon] watching: src/server/**/*.ts
[start:server] [nodemon] starting `node -r ts-node/register/transpile-only
➥ --inspect src/server/main.ts`
[start:server] Debugger listening on
➥ ws://127.0.0.1:9229/2254fc00-3640-4390-8302-1e17285d0d23
[start:server] For help, see: https://nodejs.org/en/docs/inspector
[start:server] Listening on http://localhost:3000
[start:tsc:client] 10:47:21 PM - Found 0 errors. Watching for file changes.
```

The output of the start:tsc:client process (points to `[start:tsc:client]`)

The output of the start:server process (points to the "For help" line)

The Node.js debugger runs locally on port 9229.

The server is up and running on port 3000.

The output of the start:tsc:client process (points to the last line)

NOTE The URL of the Node.js debugger is ws://127.0.0.1. It starts with "ws," indicating that the dev tools connect to the debugger using the WebSocket protocol, which we'll introduce in the next section. When the Node.js debugger is running, you'll see a green hexagon on the Chrome dev tools toolbar. Read more about the Node.js debugger in Paul Irish's article "Debugging Node.js with Chrome Dev Tools" on Medium, at http://mng.bz/qX6J.

The server is up and running, and entering `localhost:3000` will start the first client of our blockchain. After a couple of seconds, the genesis block will be generated, and you'll see a web page as in figure 10.5.

We'll show you what's happening under the hood in section 10.6, after we explain how the clients communicate with each other via the WebSocket server. At this point, suffice it to say that before creating any blocks, the client makes a request to the server to find the longest chain.

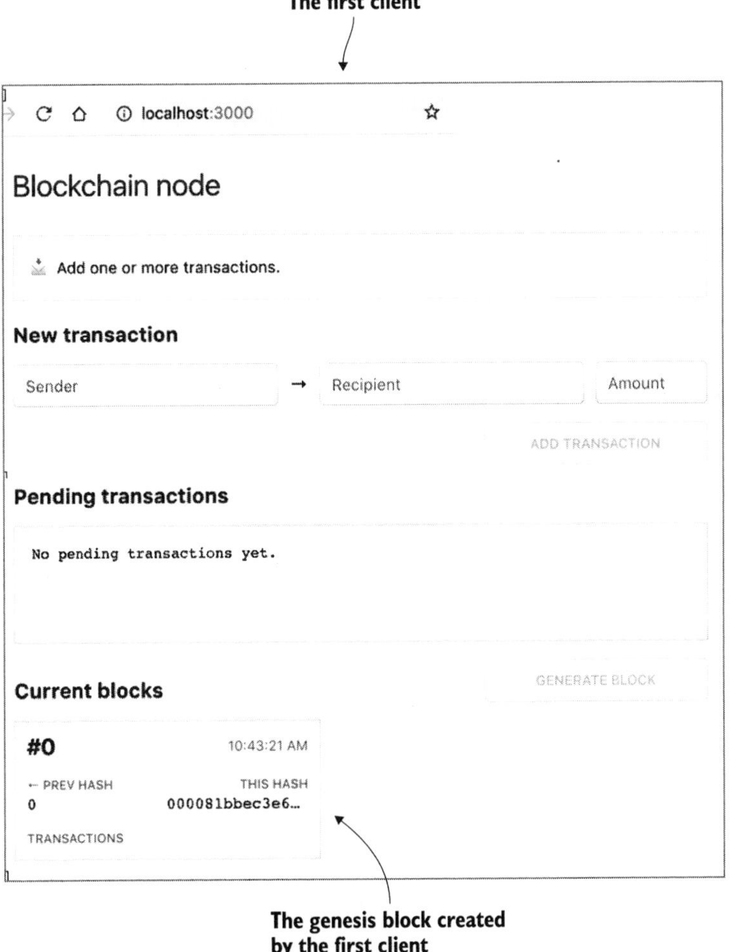

Figure 10.5 The view of the very first blockchain client

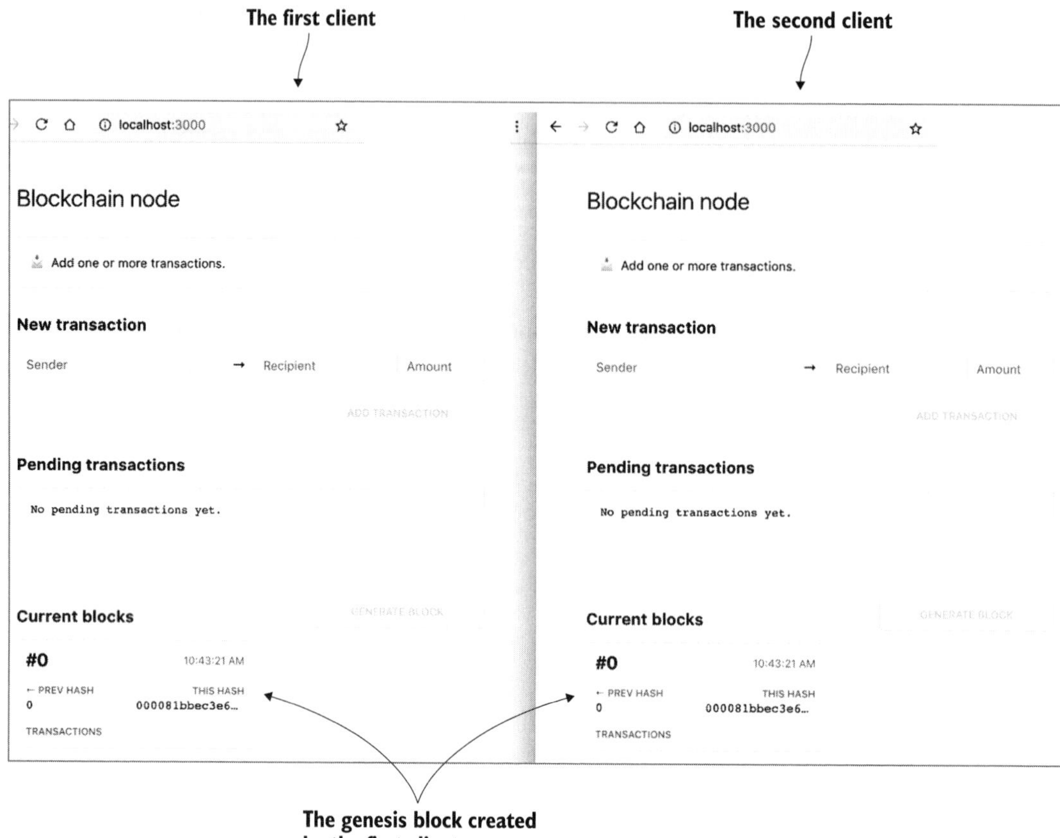

Figure 10.6 The view of the first two blockchain clients

Start the second client by opening a separate browser window at localhost:3000, as shown in figure 10.6.

Now let's discuss the use case when only the first client adds pending transactions, starts block mining, and invites other nodes to do the mining too. By this time, our blockchain has a genesis block, and the server broadcast it to all connected clients (to the client on the right in figure 10.6). Note that both clients see the same block that was mined by the first client. Then the first client enters two transactions, as shown in figure 10.7. No requests for the new block's generation have been made yet.

> **NOTE** While a client is adding pending transactions, there are no communications with other clients, and the messaging server is not being used.

Now the first client starts mining by clicking on the GENERATE BLOCK button. Under the hood, the first client sends a message with the block's content to the server, announcing that the first client started mining this block. The server broadcast this message to all connected clients, and they start mining the same block as well.

Figure 10.7 One client created pending transactions.

One of the clients will be faster, and its new block is added to the blockchain and is broadcast to other connected clients so they can add this block to their versions of the blockchain. After the blocks are accepted in the blockchain, all clients will contain the same blocks, as shown in figure 10.8.

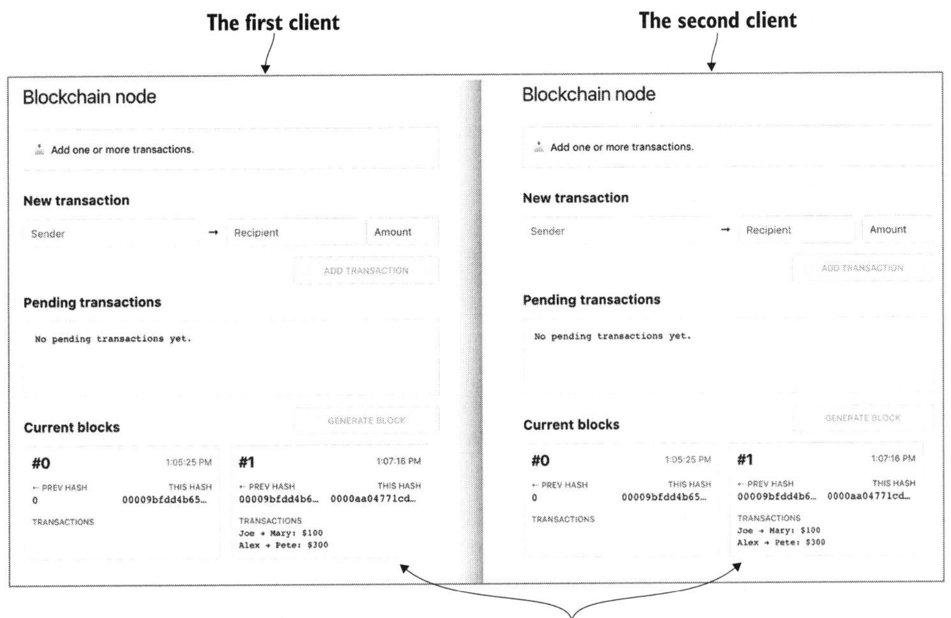

Figure 10.8 Each client adds the same block.

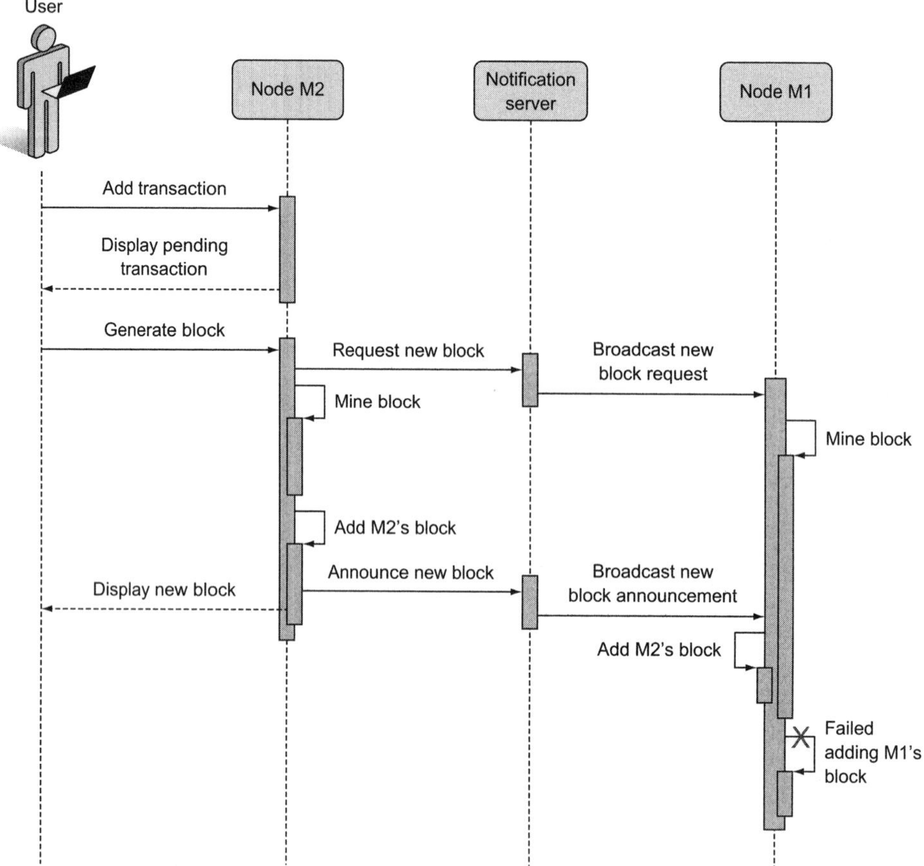

Figure 10.9 The mining process in a two-node blockchain

In section 10.6, we'll discuss the messages that go over the sockets while the blocks are being mined, so the process of mining in a multinode network won't look like magic. For now, figure 10.9 shows a sequence diagram that should help you follow the messaging exchange, assuming that there are just two nodes: M1 and M2.

In this example, the user works with the M2 node. When pending transactions are created, no messages are being sent to other nodes. The messaging starts when the user initiates the generate-block operation. The M2 node sends a "request new block" message and starts mining at the M2 node. The server broadcasts this message to other nodes (M1 in this case), which also starts mining, competing with M2.

In this diagram, the M2 node is faster and is the first to announce the new block, and the server broadcasts this message across the blockchain. The M1 node added M2's block to its local blockchain. A bit later, M1 finished mining too, but the addition of M1's block failed because it had already accepted and added M2's block, and the existing chain is longer. In other words, M2's block was approved as the winning block by consensus between M1 and M2. Finally, the new block is rendered on the user's UI.

The code that corresponds to the failed attempt of adding the new node will be shown later in this chapter (in the sidebar titled, "When the new block is rejected").

NOTE In our simplified blockchain, the UI and the block-creation logic are implemented in the same web app. A real-world app that uses blockchain technology would have separate apps for adding transactions and mining blocks.

Now that you've seen how the app works, let's get familiar with the client-server communications over WebSockets. If you're familiar with WebSockets, you can skip ahead to section 10.6.

10.5 A brief introduction to WebSockets

The blockchain app in this chapter will be pushing notifications using the WebSocket protocol (https://en.wikipedia.org/wiki/WebSocket), so we'd like to give you a brief overview of this low-overhead binary protocol supported by all modern web browsers as well as all web servers written in Node.js, .Net, Java, Python, and so on.

The WebSocket protocol allows bidirectional message-oriented streaming of text and binary data between browsers and web servers. In contrast to HTTP, WebSocket is not a request-response based protocol, and both the server and client apps can initiate the data push to the other party as soon as the data becomes available, in real time. This makes the WebSocket protocol a good fit for various apps:

- Live trading, auctions, and sports notifications
- Controlling medical equipment over the web
- Chat applications
- Multiplayer online games
- Real-time updates in social streams
- Blockchain

All of these apps have one thing in common: there's a server (or a device) that may need to send an immediate notification to the user because some important event happened elsewhere. This is different from the use case when the user decides to send a request for fresh data to the server.

For example, you could use WebSockets to send a notification immediately to all users when a stock trade happens on the stock exchange. Or a server could broadcast notifications from one blockchain node to others. It's important to understand that the WebSocket server can push a notification to a client without needing to receive a request from the client for data.

In our blockchain example, miner M1 may start or finish mining a block, and all other nodes must know about it right away. M1 sends the message to the WebSocket server announcing the new block, and the server can push this message to all other nodes immediately.

10.5.1 Comparing HTTP and WebSocket protocols

With the request-based HTTP protocol, a client sends a request over a connection and waits for a response to come back. Both requests and responses use the same browser-server connection. First the request goes out, and then the response comes back via the same "wire." Think of a narrow bridge over a river, where cars from both sides have to take turns crossing the bridge. Cars on the server side can only go over the bridge after a car from the client side passes. In the web realm, this type of communication is called *half-duplex*.

In contrast, the WebSocket protocol allows data to travel in both directions simultaneously (*full-duplex*) over the same connection, and any party can initiate the data exchange. It's like a two-lane road. Another analogy is a phone conversation, where two callers can speak and be heard at the same time. The WebSocket connection is kept alive continuously, which has an additional benefit: low latency in the interaction between the server and the client.

A typical HTTP request/response adds several hundred bytes (HTTP headers) to the application data. Say you want to write a web app that reports the latest stock prices every second. With HTTP, such an app would need to send an HTTP request (about 300 bytes) and receive a stock price that would arrive with an additional 300 bytes of an HTTP response object.

With WebSockets, the overhead is as low as a couple of bytes. Besides, there's no need to keep sending requests for a new price quote every second. A particular stock may not be traded for a while. Only when the stock price changes will the server push the new value to the client.

Every browser supports a `WebSocket` object for creating and managing a socket connection to the server (see Mozilla's WebSocket documentation: http://mng.bz/1j4g). Initially the browser establishes a regular HTTP connection with the server, but then your app requests a connection upgrade, specifying the server's URL that supports the WebSocket connection. After that, the communication goes on without the need of HTTP. The URLs of WebSocket endpoints start with "ws" instead of "http"—for instance, ws://localhost:8085. Similarly, for secure communications, you'd use "wss" instead of "https."

The WebSocket protocol is based on events and callbacks. For example, when your browser app establishes a connection with the server, it receives a `connection` event, and your app invokes a callback to handle this event. To handle the data that the server may send over this connection, the client's code expects a `message` event providing the corresponding callback. If the connection is closed, the `close` event is dispatched, so your app can react accordingly. In case of an error, the `WebSocket` object gets an `error` event.

On the server side, you'll have to process similar events. Their names may be different, depending on the WebSocket software you use on the server. In the blockchain app that comes with this chapter, we use the Node.js runtime to implement notifications using a WebSocket server.

10.5.2 Pushing data from a Node server to a plain client

To get you familiar with WebSockets, let's consider a simple use case: the server pushes data to a tiny browser client as soon as the client connects to the socket. Our client won't need to send a request for data—the server will initiate the communications.

To enable WebSocket support, we'll use the npm package called "ws" (www.npmjs.com/package/ws) as you saw in package.json in listing 10.4. The `@types/ws` type definitions are needed, so that the Typescript compiler won't complain when we use the API from the ws package.

This section shows a pretty simple WebSocket server: it will push the message "This message was pushed by the WebSocket server" to a plain HTML/JavaScript client as soon as the client connects to the socket. We purposely don't want the client to send any requests to the server so you can see that the server can push data without any request ceremony.

This example app creates two servers. The HTTP server (implemented with the Express framework) runs on port 8000 and is responsible for sending the initial HTML page to the browser. When this page is loaded, it immediately connects to the WebSocket server that runs on port 8085. This server will push the message with the greeting as soon as the connection is established.

The code of this app is located in the server/simple-websocket-server.ts file, and it's shown in the following listing.

Listing 10.9 simple-websocket-server.ts: a simple WebSocket server

```
import * as express from "express";
import * as path from "path";
import { Server } from "ws";

const app = express();

// HTTP Server
app.get('/', (req, res) => res.sendFile(
    path.join(__dirname, '../../public/simple-websocket-client.html')));

const httpServer = app.listen(8000, 'localhost', () => {
    console.log('HTTP server is listening on localhost:8000');
});

// WebSocket Server
const wsServer = new Server({port: 8085});
console.log('WebSocket server is listening on localhost:8085');

wsServer.on('connection',
         wsClient => {
            wsClient.send('This message was pushed by the WebSocket server');

            wsClient.onerror = (error) =>
                console.log(`The server received: ${error['code']}`);
         }
);
```

- We'll use Server from the ws module to instantiate a WebSocket server. (`import { Server } from "ws";`)
- Instantiates the Express framework (`const app = express();`)
- When the HTTP client connects with the root path, the HTTP server sends back this HTML file. (`app.get('/', ...)`)
- Starts the HTTP server on port 8000 (`const httpServer = app.listen(8000, ...)`)
- Starts the WebSocket server on port 8085 (`const wsServer = new Server({port: 8085});`)
- Listens to the connection event from clients (`wsServer.on('connection', ...)`)
- Pushes the message to the newly connected client (`wsClient.send(...)`)
- Handles connection errors (`wsClient.onerror = ...`)

NOTE We could start two server instances on the same port, and we'll do that later, in listing 10.12. For now, to simplify the explanations, we'll keep the HTTP and WebSocket servers on different ports.

Resolving paths in Node.js

The following code line starts with `app.get()`, and it maps the URL of an HTTP request to a specific endpoint in the code or a file on disk (in this case it's `GET`, but it could be `POST` or another request). Let's consider this code fragment:

```
app.get('/',                                          // Server receives an HTTP GET with the base URL
        (req, res) => res.sendFile(                   // Sends the file back to the client via the HTTP response object
                path.join(__dirname, '../../public/simple-websocket-
➥ client.html')));                                   // Builds an absolute path to the HTML file
```

The `path.join()` method uses the Node.js `_dirname` environment variable as a starting point and then builds the full absolute path. `_dirname` represents the directory name of the main module.

Suppose we start the server with the following command:

```
node build/server/simple-websocket-server.js
```

In this case, the value of `__dirname` will be the path to the build/server directory. Accordingly, the following code will go two levels up and one level down into public from the build/server directory, to where the simple-websocket-client.html file is located.

```
path.join(__dirname,'../../public/simple-websocket-client.html')
```

To make this line 100% cross-platform, it's safer to write it without using the forward slash as a separator:

```
path.join(__dirname, '..', '..', 'public', 'simple-websocket-
➥ client.html')
```

As soon as any client connects to our WebSocket server via port 8085, the connection event is dispatched on the server, and the server will also receive a reference to the object that represents this particular client. Using the `send()` method, the server sends the greeting to this client. If another client connects to the same socket on port 8085, it'll also receive the same greeting.

NOTE As soon as a new client connects to the server, a reference to this connection is added to the `wsServer.clients` array, so you can broadcast messages to all connected clients if needed: `wsServer.clients.forEach (client ? client.send('…'));`.

The content of the public/simple-websocket-client.html file is shown in the following listing. This is a plain HTML/JavaScript client that uses the browser's `WebSocket` object.

Listing 10.10 simple-websocket-client.html: a simple WebSocket client

```
<!DOCTYPE html>
<html>
  <head>
    <meta charset="UTF-8">
  </head>
  <body>
    <span id="messageGoesHere"></span>

    <script type="text/javascript">
      const ws = new WebSocket("ws://localhost:8085");   <- Establishes the socket connection

      const mySpan = document.getElementById("messageGoesHere");   <- Gets a reference to the DOM element for showing messages

      ws.onmessage = function(event){   <- The callback for handling messages
        mySpan.textContent = event.data;   <- Displays the message in the <span> element
    };

    ws.onerror = function(event) {   <- In case of an error, the browser logs the error message on the console.
        console.log(`Error ${event}`);
    }
   </script>
  </body>
</html>
```

When the browser loads simple-websocket-client.html, its script connects to your WebSocket server at ws://localhost:8085. At this point, the server upgrades the protocol from HTTP to WebSocket. Note that the protocol is `ws` and not `http`.

To see this sample in action, run `npm install` and compile the code by running the custom command defined in package.json:

```
npm run build:server
```

The compiled version of all TypeScript files from the server directory will be stored in the build/server directory. Run this simple WebSocket server as follows:

```
node build/server/simple-websocket-server.js
```

You'll see the following messages on the console:

```
WebSocket server is listening on localhost:8085
HTTP server is listening on localhost:8000
```

Open the Chrome browser and its dev tools to http://localhost:8000. You'll see the message, as shown in figure 10.10 at the top left. Under the Network tab on the right,

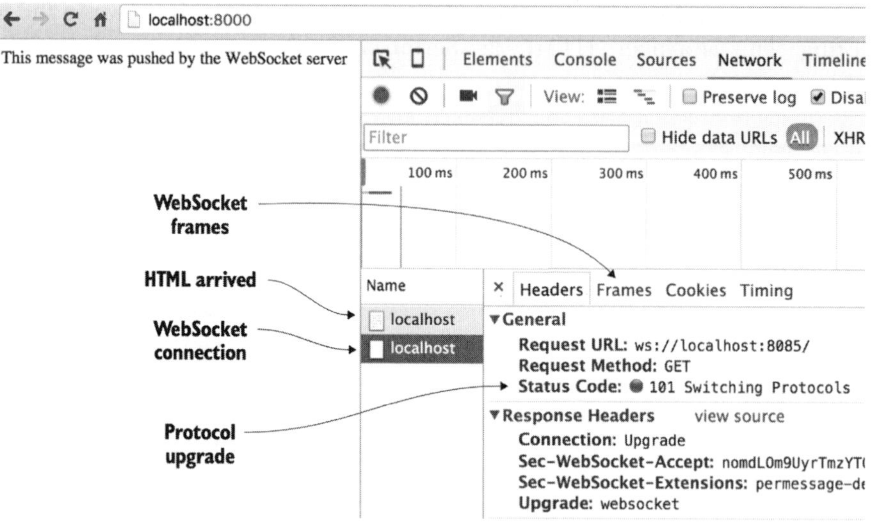

Figure 10.10 Getting the message from the socket

you'll see two requests made to the servers running on localhost. The first one loads the simple-websocket-client.html file via HTTP, and the second request goes to the socket opened on port 8085 on our server.

In this example, the HTTP protocol is used only to initially load the HTML file. Then the client requests the protocol upgrade to WebSocket (status code 101), and from then on this web page won't use HTTP.

Click on the Frames tab, and you'll see the content of the message that arrived over the socket connection from the server: "This message was pushed by the WebSocket server" (see figure 10.11).

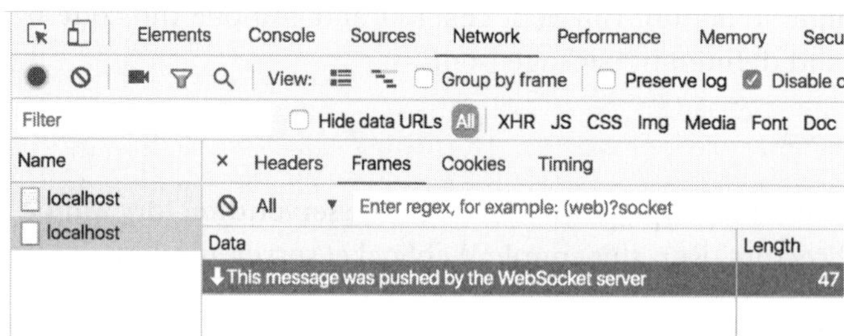

Figure 10.11 Monitoring the frame content

Note the arrow pointing down beside the message in the Frames tab. It denotes incoming socket messages. Up arrows mark messages sent by the client.

To send a message from the client to the server, invoke the `send()` method on the browser's `WebSocket` object:

```
ws.send("Hello from the client");
```

Actually, before sending messages, you should always check the status of the socket connection to ensure that it's still active. The `WebSocket` object has a `readyState` property, which can have one of the values shown in table 10.1.

Table 10.1 Possible values of `WebSocket.readyState`

Value	State	Description
0	CONNECTING	Socket has been created. The connection is not yet open.
1	OPEN	The connection is open and ready to communicate.
2	CLOSING	The connection is in the process of closing.
3	CLOSED	The connection is closed or couldn't be opened.

You'll see the `readyState` property used later, in the code of the message server in listing 10.17.

> **TIP** If you keep looking at this table with its limited set of constants, sooner or later TypeScript enums will come to mind, right?

In the next section, we'll go over the process of block mining, and you'll see how the WebSocket server is used there.

10.6 Reviewing notification workflows

In this section, we'll review only the parts of the code that are crucial for understanding how the server communicates with the blockchain clients. We'll start with the scenario of two clients communicating that we looked at earlier in this chapter, but this time we'll keep the Chrome dev tools panel open, so we can monitor the messages going over the WebSocket connections between the clients and server.

Once again, we'll launch the server on port 3000 using the `npm start` command. Open the first client in the browser and connect to localhost:3000, having the tabs Network > WS opened in the Chrome dev panel, as shown in figure 10.12. Click on the name "localhost" at the bottom left, and you'll see the messages sent over the socket. The client connects to the server and makes a request to find the longest chain by sending a message of type `GET_LONGEST_CHAIN_REQUEST` to the server.

> **TIP** In the Frames panel, an arrow on the left pointing up means the message went up to the server. An arrow pointing down means that the message arrived from the server.

This client happened to be the very first one on this blockchain, and it received the message `GET_LONGEST_CHAIN_RESPONSE` from the server with an empty payload, because the blockchain doesn't exist, and there are no other nodes just yet. If there were other nodes, the server would have broadcast the request to other nodes, collected their responses, and sent them to the original node-requestor—the client that requested the longest chain.

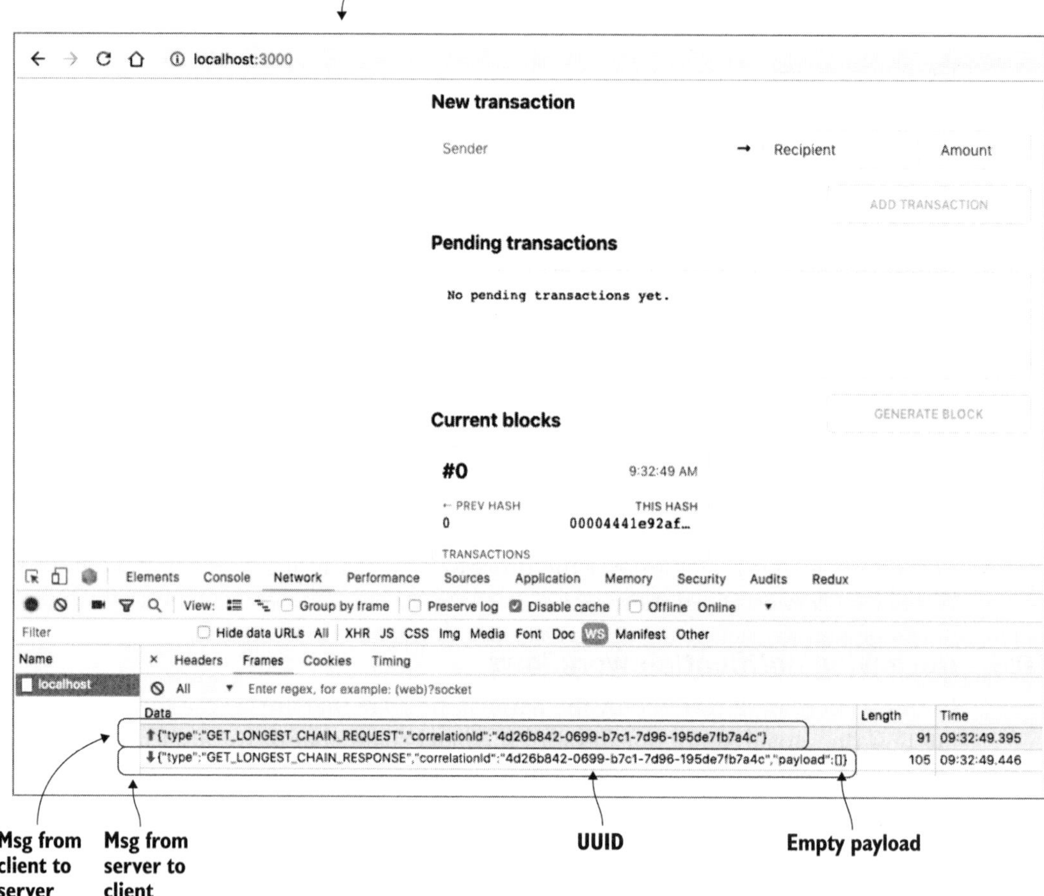

Figure 10.12 The very first client connected

The message format is defined in the shared/messages.ts file shown in the following listing. Note that we define custom types using the `type`, `interface`, and `enum` TypeScript keywords.

Listing 10.11 shared/messages.ts: defining the message types

```
export type UUID = string;     <— Declares an alias type for UUID

export interface Message {
  correlationId: UUID;     <— Declares a custom Message type
  type: string;
  payload?: any;     <— The payload is optional
}

export enum MessageTypes {     <— Declares an enum with a set of constants
```

```
  GetLongestChainRequest   = 'GET_LONGEST_CHAIN_REQUEST',
  GetLongestChainResponse = 'GET_LONGEST_CHAIN_RESPONSE',
  NewBlockRequest          = 'NEW_BLOCK_REQUEST',
  NewBlockAnnouncement     = 'NEW_BLOCK_ANNOUNCEMENT'
}
```

The messages are being sent asynchronously, and we added a `correlationId` property so we can match the outgoing and arriving messages. If the client sends the message `GET_LONGEST_CHAIN_REQUEST` to the server, it'll contain a unique correlation ID. Sometime later, the server sends a `GET_LONGEST_CHAIN_RESPONSE` message, which will also contain the correlation ID. By comparing the correlation IDs of outgoing and incoming messages, we can find matching requests and responses. We use universally unique identifiers (UUIDs) as the values for `correlationId`.

Generating UUIDs

As per specification RFC 4122 (www.ietf.org/rfc/rfc4122.txt), "A UUID is an identifier that is unique across both space and time, with respect to the space of all UUIDs. Since a UUID is a fixed size and contains a time field, it is possible for values to rollover (around A.D. 3400, depending on the specific algorithm used)."

A UUID is a fixed-length string of ASCII characters in the following format: `"xxxxxxxx-xxxx-xxxx-xxxx-xxxxxxxxxxxx"`, and you can see an example in the messages in figure 10.12. We borrowed the code for generating UUIDs from StackOverflow (http://mng.bz/7z6e).

In our app, all requests are initiated by the client, so UUIDs are generated in the client's code. You can find the `uuid()` function in the client/lib/cryptography.ts script.

Because a UUID is a string of characters, we could declare the `Message.correlationId` property to be of type `string`. Instead, we created a `UUID` type alias using the `type` keyword (see listing 10.11), and declared `correlationId` to be of type `UUID`, which increased the code's readability.

When a client (a blockchain node) starts mining, it sends the message `NEW_BLOCK_REQUEST`, inviting other nodes to do the same. A node announces that the mining is complete by sending the message `NEW_BLOCK_ANNOUNCEMENT` to other nodes, and its block becomes a candidate for adding to the blockchain.

10.6.1 Reviewing the server's code

We start the server by loading the server/main.ts script (listing 10.12) in the Node.js runtime. In this script, we import the Express framework for configuring the HTTP endpoints and the directory where the web client's code is deployed. We also import the `http` object from Node.js, and the ws package for WebSocket support. The server/main.ts script starts two server instances on the same port: `httpServer`, which supports HTTP, and `wsServer`, which supports the WebSocket protocol.

Listing 10.12 server/main.ts: the script to start HTTP and WebSocket servers

```
import * as express from 'express';
import * as http from 'http';
import * as path from 'path';
import * as WebSocket from 'ws';                    ◁ Enables our script with WebSocket support
import { BlockchainServer } from './blockchain-server';   ◁ Imports the BlockchainServer class

const PORT = 3000;
const app = express();     ◁ Instantiates Express
app.use('/', express.static(path.join(__dirname, '..', '..', 'public')));   ◁ Specifies the location of the client's code
app.use('/node_modules', express.static(path.join(__dirname, '..', '..',
➥ 'node_modules')));     ◁ Specifies the location of node_modules used by the client

const httpServer: http.Server = app.listen(PORT, () => {
  if (process.env.NODE_ENV !== 'production') {
    console.log(`Listening on http://localhost:${PORT}`);
  }
});          ◁ Starts the HTTP server

const wsServer = new WebSocket.Server({ server: httpServer });   ◁ Starts the WebServer
new BlockchainServer(wsServer);     ◁ Starts the blockchain notification server
```

The lines that start with `app.use()` map the URLs that come from the client to the specific resources on the server. This was discussed in the "Resolving paths in Node.js" sidebar in the previous section.

> **TIP** The fragment `'..', '..', 'public'` will resolve to `'../../public'` in Unix-based systems and to `'..\..\public'` on Windows.

While instantiating `WebSocket.Server`, we pass the instance of the existing HTTP server to it. This allows us to run both HTTP and WebSocket servers on the same port. Finally, we instantiate the `BlockchainServer` TypeScript class, which uses WebSockets. Its code is located in the blockchain-server.ts script. The `BlockchainServer` class is a subclass of `MessageServer`, which encapsulates all the work related to WebSocket communications. We'll review its code later in this section.

The first part of the blockchain-server.ts script is shown in the following listing.

Listing 10.13 The first part of server/blockchain-server.ts

```
import * as WebSocket from 'ws';
import { Message, MessageTypes, UUID } from '../shared/messages';
import { MessageServer } from './message-server';

type Replies = Map<WebSocket, Message>;     ◁ Replies from the blockchain nodes

export class BlockchainServer extends MessageServer<Message> {   ◁ This class extends MessageServer.
    private readonly receivedMessagesAwaitingResponse = new Map<UUID,
➥ WebSocket>();     ◁ A collection of clients' messages waiting for responses
```

```
    private readonly sentMessagesAwaitingReply = new Map<UUID, Replies>();
➥ // Used as accumulator for replies from clients.

    protected handleMessage(sender: WebSocket, message: Message): void {    ◁ A handler for all message types
        switch (message.type) {                                              ◁ Invokes the appropriate handler based on the message type
            case MessageTypes.GetLongestChainRequest :
                return this.handleGetLongestChainRequest(sender, message);
            case MessageTypes.GetLongestChainResponse :
                return this.handleGetLongestChainResponse(sender, message);
            case MessageTypes.NewBlockRequest :
                return this.handleAddTransactionsRequest(sender, message);
            case MessageTypes.NewBlockAnnouncement :
                return this.handleNewBlockAnnouncement(sender, message);
            default : {
                console.log(`Received message of unknown type:
➥ "${message.type}"`);
            }
        }
    }

    private handleGetLongestChainRequest(requestor: WebSocket, message:
➥ Message): void {
        if (this.clientIsNotAlone) {
          this.receivedMessagesAwaitingResponse.set(message.correlationId,
➥ requestor);                                   ◁ Stores the client's request using the correlation ID as a key
          this.sentMessagesAwaitingReply.set(message.correlationId,
➥ new Map());                                   ◁ This map accumulates replies from clients.
          this.broadcastExcept(requestor, message);    ◁ Broadcasts the message to other nodes
        } else {
            this.replyTo(requestor, {
              type: MessageTypes.GetLongestChainResponse,
              correlationId: message.correlationId,
              payload: []          ◁ There are no longest chains in a single-node blockchain.
            });
        }
    }
```

The `handleMessage()` method serves as a dispatcher for messages received from the clients. It has a `switch` statement to invoke the appropriate handler based on the received message. For example, if one of the clients sends a `GetLongestChainRequest` message, the `handleGetLongestChainRequest()` method is invoked. First it stores the request (the reference to the open WebSocket object) in a map using the correlation ID as a key. Then it broadcasts the message to other nodes, requesting their longest chains. The `handleGetLongestChainRequest()` method can return an object with an empty payload only if the blockchain has just one node. The `handleMessage()` method was declared as `abstract` in the `MessageServer` superclass; we'll review it later in this section.

NOTE The method signature of `handleMessage()` includes the `void` keyword, which means that it doesn't return a value, so why does its body have a number of return statements? Typically, every `case` clause in a JavaScript `switch` statement has to end with `break`, so the code doesn't "fall through" and execute the code in the next `case` clause. Using `return` statements in every `case` clause allows us to avoid these `break` statements and still guarantee that the code doesn't fall through.

Listing 10.14 shows the second part of blockchain-server.ts. It has the code that handles responses from other nodes sending their longest chains.

Listing 10.14 The second part of server/blockchain-server.ts

```
private handleGetLongestChainResponse(sender: WebSocket, message: Message):
➥ void {
        if (this.receivedMessagesAwaitingResponse.has(message.correlationId)) {   // Finds the client that requested the longest chain
            const requestor =
➥ this.receivedMessagesAwaitingResponse.get(message.correlationId);   // Gets the reference to the client's socket object

        if (this.everyoneReplied(sender, message)) {
            const allReplies =
➥ this.sentMessagesAwaitingReply.get(message.correlationId).values();
            const longestChain =
➥ Array.from(allReplies).reduce(this.selectTheLongestChain);   // Finds the longest chain
            this.replyTo(requestor, longestChain);   // Relays the longest chain to the client that requested it
        }
    }
}

private handleAddTransactionsRequest(requestor: WebSocket, message:
➥ Message): void {
    this.broadcastExcept(requestor, message);
}

private handleNewBlockAnnouncement(requestor: WebSocket, message:
➥ Message): void {
    this.broadcastExcept(requestor, message);
}

private everyoneReplied(sender: WebSocket, message: Message): boolean {   // Checks if every node replied to the request
    const repliedClients = this.sentMessagesAwaitingReply
        .get(message.correlationId)
        .set(sender, message);

    const awaitingForClients =
➥ Array.from(this.clients).filter(c => !repliedClients.has(c));

    return awaitingForClients.length === 1;   // Have all nodes except the original requestor replied?
}
```

```
    private selectTheLongestChain(currentlyLongest: Message,
                        current: Message, index: number) {
        return index > 0 && current.payload.length >
➥ currentlyLongest.payload.length ?
                        current : currentlyLongest;
    }

    private get clientIsNotAlone(): boolean {
        return this.clients.size > 1;
    }
}
```

This method is used while reducing the array of longest chains.

Checks if there is more than one node in the blockchain

When nodes send their `GetLongestChainResponse` messages, the server uses the correlation ID to find the client who requested the longest chain. When all nodes have replied, the `handleGetLongestChainResponse()` method turns the `allReplies` set into an array and uses the `reduce()` method to find the longest chain. Then it sends the response back to the requesting client using the `replyTo()` method.

This is all good, but where's the code that supports the WebSocket protocol and defines such methods as `replyTo()` and `broadcastExcept()`? All this machinery is located in the abstract `MessageServer` superclass, shown in listings 10.15 and 10.16.

Listing 10.15 The first part of server/message-server.ts

```
import * as WebSocket from 'ws';

export abstract class MessageServer<T> {

  constructor(private readonly wsServer: WebSocket.Server) {
    this.wsServer.on('connection', this.subscribeToMessages);
    this.wsServer.on('error', this.cleanupDeadClients);
  }

  protected abstract handleMessage(sender: WebSocket, message: T): void;

  protected readonly subscribeToMessages = (ws: WebSocket): void => {
    ws.on('message', (data: WebSocket.Data) => {
      if (typeof data === 'string') {
        this.handleMessage(ws, JSON.parse(data));
      } else {
        console.log('Received data of unsupported type.');
      }
    });
  };

  private readonly cleanupDeadClients = (): void => {
    this.wsServer.clients.forEach(client => {
      if (this.isDead(client)) {
        this.wsServer.clients.delete(client);
      }
    });
  };
```

Subscribes to messages from a newly connected client

Cleans up references to disconnected clients

This method is implemented in the BlockchainServer class.

The message from the client has arrived.

Passes the message to the handler

Purges the disconnected clients

While reading the code of `MessageServer`, you'll recognize many of the TypeScript syntax elements covered in part 1 of this book. First of all, this class is declared as `abstract` (see section 3.1.5):

```
export abstract class MessageServer<T>
```

You can't instantiate an abstract class; you have to declare a subclass that will provide a concrete implementation of all abstract members. In our case, the `BlockchainServer` subclass implements the only abstract member, `handleMessage()`. Also, the class declaration uses the generic type `T` (see section 4.2), which is also used as an argument type in the `handleMessage()`, `broadcastExcept()`, and `replyTo()` methods. In our app, the concrete type `Message` (see listing 10.11) replaces the generic `<T>`, but in other apps it could be a different type.

By declaring the `handleMessage()` method as `abstract`, we state that any subclass of `MessageServer` is free to implement this method any way it likes, as long as the signature of the method looks like this:

```
protected abstract handleMessage(sender: WebSocket, message: T): void;
```

Because we enforced this method signature in the abstract class, we know how the `handleMessage()` method should be invoked when implemented. We do that in `subscribeToMessages()` as follows:

```
this.handleMessage(ws, JSON.parse(data));
```

Strictly speaking, we can't invoke an abstract method, but at runtime the `this` keyword will refer to the instance of the `BlockchainServer` concrete class where the `handleMessage` method won't be abstract any longer.

The following listing shows the second part of the `MessageServer` class. These methods implement broadcasting and replying to clients.

Listing 10.16 The second part of server/message-server.ts

```
protected broadcastExcept(currentClient: WebSocket, message: Readonly<T>):
➥ void {                                                      ◁ Broadcasts to all other nodes
    this.wsServer.clients.forEach(client => {
      if (this.isAlive(client) && client !== currentClient) {
        client.send(JSON.stringify(message));
      }
    });
  }

  protected replyTo(client: WebSocket, message: Readonly<T>): void {   ◁ Sends a message to a single node
    client.send(JSON.stringify(message));
  }
```

```
  protected get clients(): Set<WebSocket> {
    return this.wsServer.clients;
  }

  private isAlive(client: WebSocket): boolean {
    return !this.isDead(client);
  }

  private isDead(client: WebSocket): boolean {      <-- Checks if a particular
    return (                                            client is disconnected
      client.readyState === WebSocket.CLOSING ||
      client.readyState === WebSocket.CLOSED
    );
  }
}
```

In the last line of the server/main.ts script (see listing 10.12), we passed the instance of the WebSocket server to the constructor of the `BlockchainServer`. This object has a `clients` property, which is a collection of all active WebSocket clients. Whenever we need to broadcast a message to all clients, we iterate through this collection as in the `broadcastExcept()` method. If we need to remove a reference to a disconnected client, we also use the `clients` property in the `cleanupDeadClients()` method.

The signatures of the `broadcastExcept()` and `replyTo` methods have an argument of a `Readonly<T>` mapped type, which we covered in section 5.2. It takes a `T` type and marks all of its properties as `readonly`. We use the `Readonly` to avoid accidental modifications being made to the value within the method. You can see more examples in the sidebar titled "Examples of conditional and mapped types," later in this chapter.

Now let's continue discussing the workflow started in figure 10.12 by the first client. The second client joins the blockchain and sends a message to the WebSocket server requesting the longest chain, which is just the genesis block at the moment. Figure 10.13 shows the messages transferred over the WebSocket connections. We numbered the messages so it's easier to understand their sequence:

1. The second client (on the right in the figure) connects to the messaging server, requesting the longest chain. The server broadcasts this request to other clients.
2. The first client (on the left) receives this request. This client has a single genesis block, which is its longest chain.
3. The first client (on the left) sends a message back with its longest chain in the message payload.
4. The second client (on the right) receives the longest chain in the message payload.

In this example, we have only two clients, but the WebSocket server broadcasts the messages to all connected clients, so all of them would respond.

Next, the first client (on the left in figure 10.14) creates two pending transactions, as shown in figure 10.14. This is a local event and no messages are being sent to the WebSocket server.

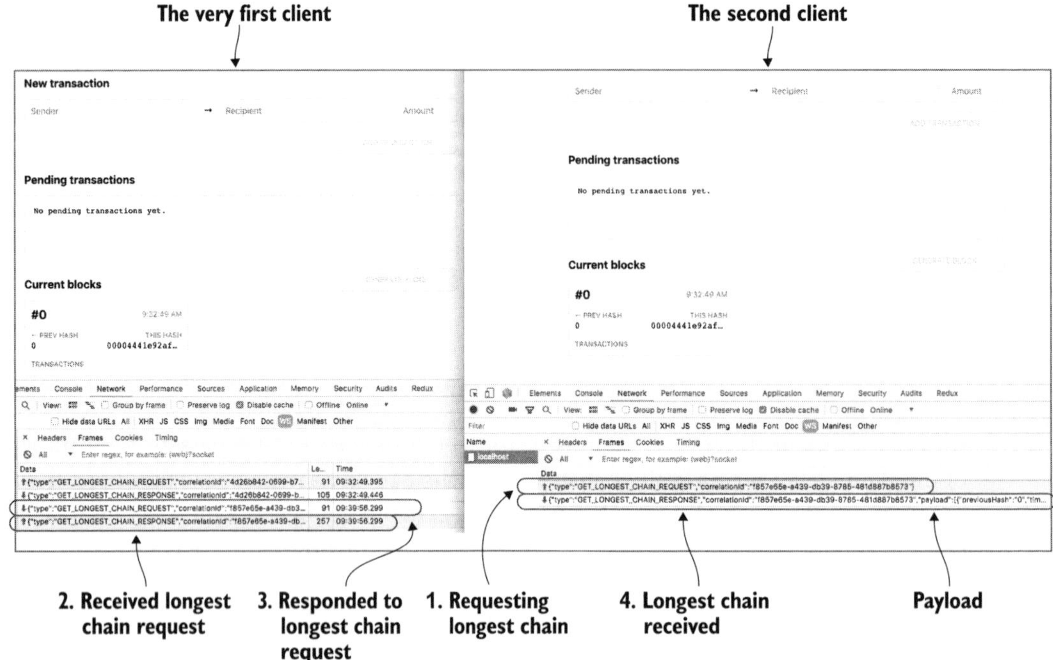

Figure 10.13 The second client connected

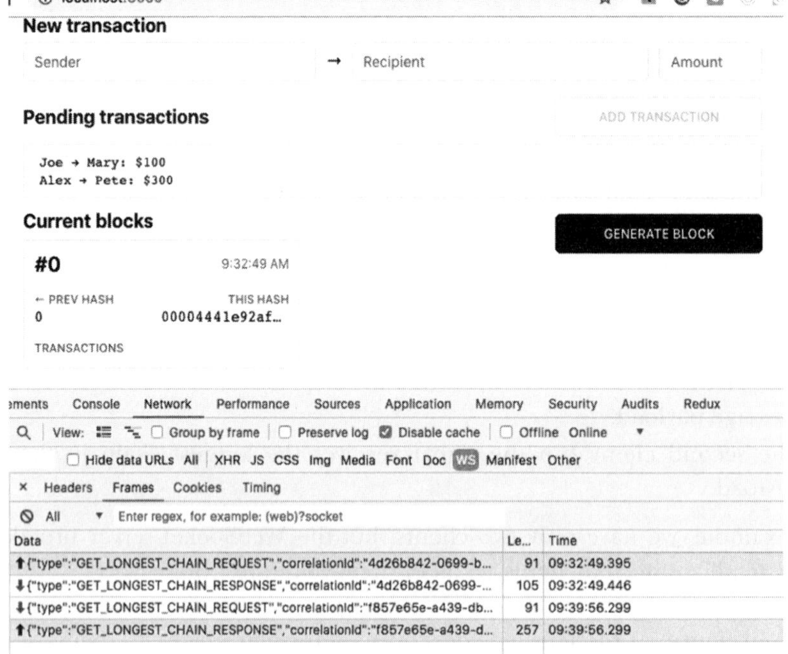

Figure 10.14 Adding transactions doesn't send messages.

Now the first client clicks on the GENERATE BLOCK button, starting the block mining and requesting other nodes to do the same. The `NEW_BLOCK_REQUEST` message is this invitation to mining. Some time later, the mining is complete (in our case the first miner finished first), and the first client announces the new candidate block by sending a `NEW_BLOCK_ANNOUNCEMENT` message. Figure 10.15 shows the messages related to block mining, and the content of the `NEW_BLOCK_ANNOUNCEMENT` message.

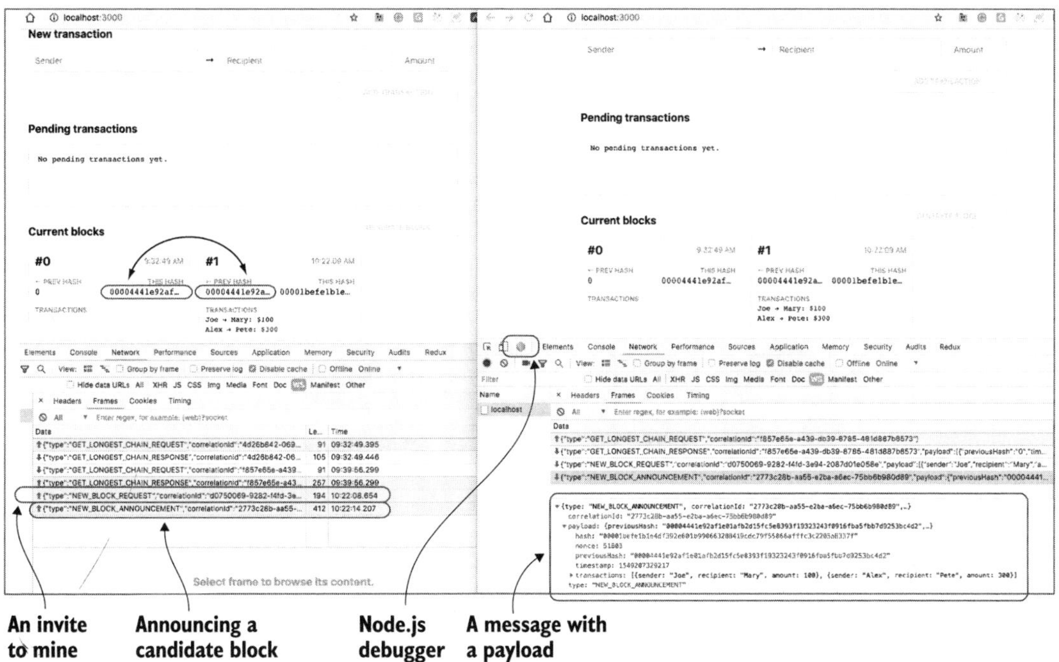

Figure 10.15 New block messaging

Both clients now show the same two blocks: `#0` and `#1`. Note that the `hash` value of block #0 and the `previousHash` value of block #1 are the same.

The following listing shows the content of the `NEW_BLOCK_ANNOUNCEMENT` message. We shortened the hash values to improve readability.

Listing 10.17 A message containing the new block

```
correlationId: "2773c28b-aa55-e2ba-a6ec-75bb6b980d89"
payload: {previousHash: "00004441e92af1",…}
  hash: "00001befe1b1e4df392e601..."
  nonce: 51803
  previousHash: "00004441e92a..."
  timestamp: 1549207329217
  transactions: [{sender: "Joe", recipient: "Mary", amount: 100},
  {sender: "Alex", recipient: "Pete", amount: 300}]
type: "NEW_BLOCK_ANNOUNCEMENT"
```

- **The correlation ID (UUID)**
- **The hash value of block #1**
- **The calculated nonce (the proof of work)**
- **The hash value of block #0**
- **The block's transactions**
- **The message type**

Revisit listing 10.11 to find the definitions of custom data types used in this message. The next question is: Who sent the message with the payload containing the newly mined block? The web client did, and in the next section we'll review the relevant code from the web client.

Debugging Node.js code in the browser

We started Node.js with the `--inspect` option, so when you open Chrome's dev tools you'll see a green octagon to the left of the Elements tab (see figure 10.15). That octagon represents the Node.js debugger—click it to open a detached window of the Node.js dev tools.

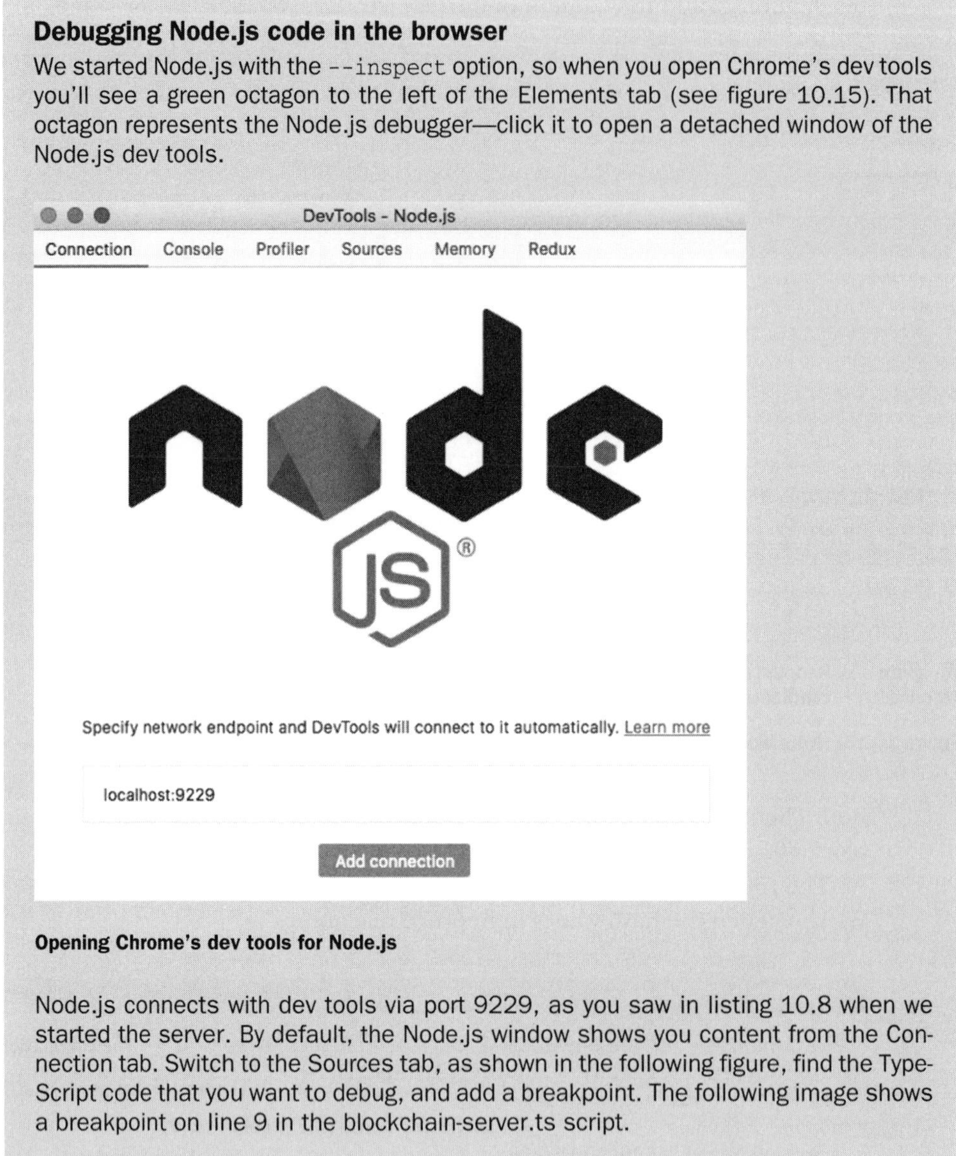

Opening Chrome's dev tools for Node.js

Node.js connects with dev tools via port 9229, as you saw in listing 10.8 when we started the server. By default, the Node.js window shows you content from the Connection tab. Switch to the Sources tab, as shown in the following figure, find the TypeScript code that you want to debug, and add a breakpoint. The following image shows a breakpoint on line 9 in the blockchain-server.ts script.

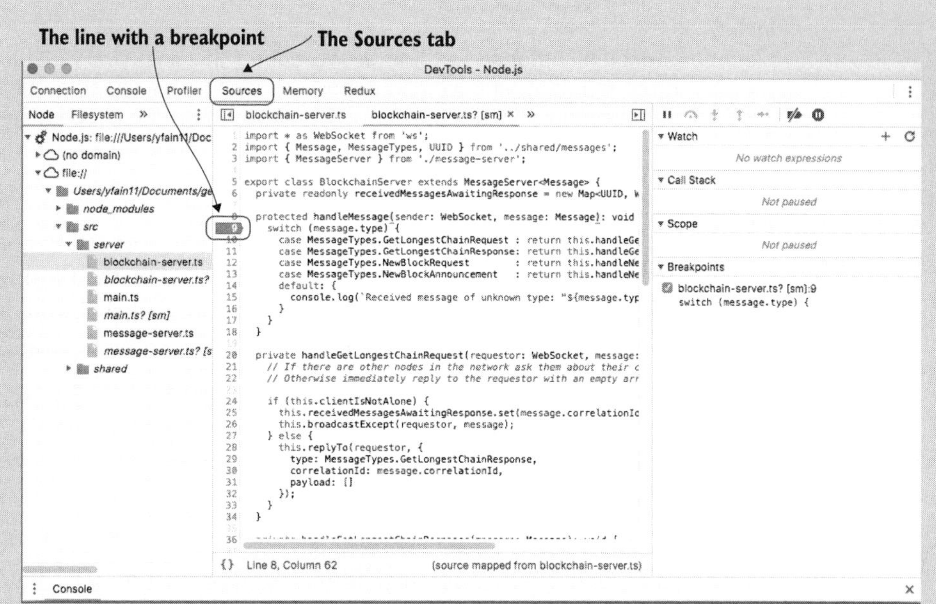

Selecting the Sources tab

We want to intercept the moment when the client sends a message to the server. The following screenshot was taken after the client created an "Alice -> Julie -> $200" transaction and clicked the GENERATE BLOCK button.

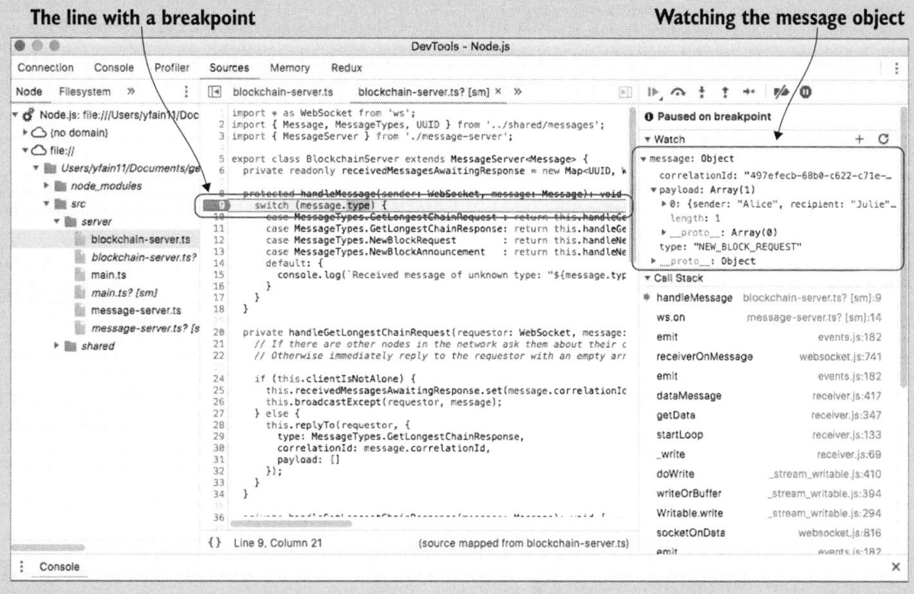

Debugging Node.js in the Chrome browser

(continued)
The execution obediently stopped at line 9. We added the `message` variable to the Watch panel at the top right, and we can debug or monitor this variable. All the features of Chrome's dev tools' debugger are available for the Node.js code.

10.6.2 Reviewing the client's code

We've been using the word "client" because in this app we're discussing communications between a client web app and a server. But "node" would be the right word here. Our node's code is implemented as a web app, but in a real blockchain the nodes that mine blocks and the UI where users can add transactions would be separate apps.

NOTE The main subject of this chapter is introducing the messaging server. We're not going to review each and every line of the code, but we will show you the parts of the code that are crucial for understanding the client's implementation.

The code that runs in the web browser is located in the src/client directory. For HTML rendering we use a small library called lit-html (www.npmjs.com/package/lit-html), which allows you to write HTML templates with JavaScript template literals. This library uses tagged templates, which are plain JavaScript functions combined with HTML (as explained in section A.3.1 of the appendix). In short, this library can take a string with HTML markup, create a browser DOM node, and re-render it when its data changes.

The lit-html library efficiently renders the content from string templates to the DOM by updating only those nodes that need to display updated values. Listing 10.18 is from the lit-html documentation (http://mng.bz/m4D4); it defines a tagged template with the `${name}` expression, and then it passes "Steve" as a name to render: `<div> Hello Steve</div>`. Then, when the value of the `name` variable changes to "Kevin," it updates only the name in that `<div>`.

Listing 10.18 How lit-html renders HTML

```
import {html, render} from 'lit-html';                     // Imports the functions html and render

const helloTemplate = (name) => html`<div>Hello ${name}!</div>`;   // Declares the tagged template
render(helloTemplate('Steve'), document.body);      // Renders the <div> greeting Steve
render(helloTemplate('Kevin'), document.body);      // Replaces the name Steve with Kevin in the <div>
```

NOTE The main idea of lit-html is that it parses HTML and builds the DOM node once, and after that it only renders new values for the embedded variables when they change. It doesn't create a virtual DOM like React.js, and it doesn't use change detectors like Angular. It just updates the variable values.

When you're reading the scripts in the client/ui directory, you won't see HTML files there, but rather invocations of the `render()` function similar to the preceding example. If you're familiar with the Angular or React libraries, think of a class that has the `render()` function as a UI component. The main API of lit-html is `html`, and you'll see that every `render()` function uses it.

Let's consider the small `PendingTransactionsPanel` class that renders the panel with pending transactions. Listing 10.19 shows the ui/pending-transactions-panel.ts file that implements the `render()` function.

Listing 10.19 pending-transaction-panel.ts: the Pending Transactions panel

```
import { html, TemplateResult }
➥ from '../../../node_modules/lit-html/lit-html.js';
import { BlockchainNode } from '../lib/blockchain-node.js';
import { Callback, formatTransactions, Renderable, UI } from './common.js';

export class PendingTransactionsPanel implements
➥ Renderable<Readonly<BlockchainNode>> {

  constructor(readonly requestRendering: Callback) {}    ◁ Provides the callback function to the constructor

  render(node: Readonly<BlockchainNode>): TemplateResult {    ◁ The argument type of the render() function is defined in blockchain-node.ts.
    const shouldDisableGenerate = node.noPendingTransactions || node.isMining;
    const formattedTransactions = node.hasPendingTransactions
      ? formatTransactions(node.pendingTransactions)
      : 'No pending transactions yet.';

    return html`    ◁ lit-html needs the html tagged template.
      <h2>Pending transactions</h2>
      <pre class="pending-transactions__list">${formattedTransactions}</pre>
      <div class="pending-transactions__form">${UI.button('GENERATE BLOCK',
➥ shouldDisableGenerate)}</form>
      <div class="clear"></div>
    `;
  }
}
```

The `PendingTransactionsPanel` class implements the `Renderable` interface, which requires it to have the `requestRendering` property and the `render()` method, both defined in the common.ts file as follows.

Listing 10.20 A fragment from ui/common.ts

```
// other type definition go here
export type Callback = () => void;    ◁ Defines the custom type of a callback function

export interface Renderable<T> {    ◁ Defines a generic interface
  requestRendering: Callback;    ◁ A callback function
  render(data: T): TemplateResult;    ◁ The function to render HTML using lit-html
}
```

You'll find multiple render() functions in the client's code, but all of them work in a similar way: they insert the values of JavaScript variables into HTML templates and refresh the corresponding portion of the UI when the values in these variables change.

The client's top-level class is called Application, and it also implements the Renderable interface, so lit-html knows how to render it. The client/main.ts file creates an instance of the Application class and passes a callback to it that invokes its render() function.

Listing 10.21 ui/main.ts: the script that creates the top-level component

```
import { render } from '../../node_modules/lit-html/lit-html.js';
import { Application } from './ui/application.js';

let renderingIsInProgress = false;
let application = new Application(async () => {

  if (!renderingIsInProgress) {
    renderingIsInProgress = true;
    await 0;
    renderingIsInProgress = false;
    render(application.render(), document.body);
  }
});
```

- A flag to prevent double rendering (`let renderingIsInProgress = false;`)
- Passes a callback to the Application instance (`let application = new Application(...)`)
- Invokes the render() function (`render(application.render(), document.body);`)

TIP Even though the render() function takes document.body as an argument, the lit-html library doesn't re-render the entire page—only the values in the templates' placeholders that have changed.

When the Application class is instantiated, it receives the callback function (the constructor's argument is called requestRendering), which invokes the render() function. We'll show you two fragments of the Application class, and where you see this.requestRendering(), it invokes this callback. The first fragment of the application.ts script follows.

Listing 10.22 The first fragment of ui/application.ts

```
export class Application implements Renderable<void> {
  private readonly node: BlockchainNode;
  private readonly server: WebsocketController;

  private readonly transactionForm = new
➥ TransactionForm(this.requestRendering);
  private readonly pendingTransactionsPanel =
➥ new PendingTransactionsPanel(this.requestRendering);
  private readonly blocksPanel = new BlocksPanel(this.requestRendering);

  constructor(readonly requestRendering: Callback) {
```

- This object is responsible for the WebSocket communications. (`private readonly server: WebsocketController;`)
- Passes the top-level callback to each UI component (the `transactionForm`, `pendingTransactionsPanel` and `blocksPanel` declarations)
- The callback reference will be stored in the requestRendering property. (`constructor(readonly requestRendering: Callback) {`)

```
    this.server = new WebsocketController(this.handleServerMessages);   <-- Connects to the WebSocket server
    this.node = new BlockchainNode();   <-- All blockchain and node creation logic is here.

    this.requestRendering();
    this.initializeBlockchain();   <-- Initializes the blockchain
  }

  private async initializeBlockchain() {
    const blocks = await this.server.requestLongestChain();   <-- Requests the longest chain from all nodes
    if (blocks.length > 0) {
      this.node.initializeWith(blocks);
    } else {
      await this.node.initializeWithGenesisBlock();
    }

    this.requestRendering();
  }

  render(): TemplateResult {   <-- Renders the UI components
    return html`
      <main>
        <h1>Blockchain node</h1>
        <aside>${this.statusLine}</aside>
        <section>${this.transactionForm.render(this.node)}</section>   <-- Re-renders the child component
        <section>
          <form @submit="${this.generateBlock}">
            ${this.pendingTransactionsPanel.render(this.node)}
          </form>
        </section>
        <section>${this.blocksPanel.render(this.node.chain)}</section>
      </main>
    `;
  }
```

The initial rendering is initiated from the constructor by invoking `this.requestRendering()`. After several seconds, the second rendering is done from the `initializeBlockchain()` method. Child UI components get the reference to the `requestRendering` callback, and they can decide when to refresh the UI.

The `initializeBlockchain()` method is invoked after the initial rendering of the UI, and this method requests the longest chain from the WebSocket server. If this node is not the first and only one, the longest chain is returned and is rendered in the block panel at the bottom of the screen. Otherwise the genesis block is generated and rendered. Both `requestLongestChain()` and `initializeWithGenesisBlock()` are asynchronous operations, and the code waits for their completion by using the `await` JavaScript keyword.

Listing 10.23 shows two methods from application.ts. The `handleServerMessages()` method is invoked when the WebSocket server sends a message to the client. Using the `switch` statement, it invokes the appropriate handler based on the message type. The `handleGetLongestChainRequest()` method is invoked when the client receives a request to send its longest chain.

Listing 10.23 The second fragment of ui/application.ts

```
private readonly handleServerMessages = (message: Message) => {    // Handles messages from the WebSocket server
    switch (message.type) {                                          // Dispatches the message to the right handler
      case MessageTypes.GetLongestChainRequest: return
                          this.handleGetLongestChainRequest(message);
      case MessageTypes.NewBlockRequest :
➥ return this.handleNewBlockRequest(message);
      case MessageTypes.NewBlockAnnouncement : return
➥ this.handleNewBlockAnnouncement(message);
      default: {
        console.log(`Received message of unknown type: "${message.type}"`);
      }
    }
  }

  private handleGetLongestChainRequest(message: Message): void {     // The node sends its own chain to the server.
    this.server.send({
      type: MessageTypes.GetLongestChainResponse,
      correlationId: message.correlationId,
      payload: this.node.chain
    });
```

Examples of conditional and mapped types

In chapter 5, we introduced conditional and mapped types. Here, you'll see how we use them in the blockchain app. We're not going to review the entire client/lib/blockchain-node.ts script; you can read up on generics and the mapped type `Pick` in the TypeScript documentation at http://mng.bz/5AJa.

Prior to version 3.5, TypeScript didn't include the `Omit` type, and we had to declare our own custom `Omit` type. Recently, `Omit` became a built-in utility type, but we decided to keep this sidebar's code sample as-is for illustration purposes. Let's discuss the `Omit`, `WithoutHash`, and `NotMinedBlock` custom types presented in the following code.

```
export interface Block {     // Declares the Block type
  readonly hash: string;
  readonly nonce: number;
  readonly previousHash: string;
  readonly timestamp: number;
  readonly transactions: Transaction[];
}

export type Omit<T, K> = Pick<T, Exclude<keyof T, K>>;   // A helper type that uses Pick
export type WithoutHash<T> = Omit<T, 'hash'>;            // Declares a type similar to Block but without a hash
export type NotMinedBlock = Omit<Block, 'hash' | 'nonce'>;   // Declares a type similar to Block but without a hash and nonce
```

The `Omit` type in the following line allows us to declare a type that will have all the properties of type `T` except `hash`:

```
type WithoutHash<T> = Omit<T, 'hash'>;
```

The process of generating the block's hash value takes time, and until we have it, we can use the `WithoutHash<Block>` type, which won't have the `hash` property.

You can specify more than one property to be excluded:

```
type NotMinedBlock = Omit<Block, 'hash' | 'nonce'>;
```

You could use this type as follows:

```
let myBlock: NotMinedBlock;

myBlock = {
    previousHash: '123',
    transactions: ["Mary paid Pete $100"]
};
```

Our `NotMinedBlock` type will always be `Block` minus `hash` and `nonce`. If at some point, someone adds another required `readonly` property to the `Block` interface, the assignment to the variable `myBlock` won't compile, complaining that the newly added property must be initialized. In JavaScript, we'd get a runtime error in the same scenario.

The interface defines a custom `Block` type with five properties, and all of them are required and `readonly`, meaning they can be initialized only during the instantiation of the block. But creating a block takes some time, and not all the values for these properties are available during instantiation. We'd like to benefit from strong typing, but we'd also like to have the freedom to initialize some properties after the `Block` instance is created.

TypeScript comes with a `Pick` mapped type and a conditional `Exclude` type, and we can use them to define a new type that excludes some of the properties of existing ones. `Exclude` enumerates the remaining properties. The `Pick` type allows you to create a type from the provided list of properties.

The following line means that we want to declare a generic type, `Omit`, that can take a type `T` and a key `K`, and exclude from `T` the properties that match `K`:

```
type Omit<T, K> = Pick<T, Exclude<keyof T, K>>;
```

The generic `Omit` type can be used with any type `T`, and `keyof T` returns a list of properties of the concrete type. For example, if we provide `Block` as type `T`, the `keyof T` construct will represent the list of properties defined in the `Block` interface. Using `Exclude<keyof T, K>` allows us to remove some of the properties from the list, and `Pick` will create a new type from that new list of properties.

Listings 10.22 and 10.23 show most of the application.ts file, where the client communicates with the WebSocket server via the `WebsocketController` class, which gets a callback to handle messages via its constructor. Let's get familiar with the code of the `WebsocketController` class by reviewing the workflow when the user clicks on the GENERATE BLOCK button. That should result in the following actions:

1. Broadcast the `GET_LONGEST_CHAIN_REQUEST` message to other nodes via the WebSocket server.
2. Broadcast the `NEW_BLOCK_REQUEST` message to other nodes via the WebSocket server.
3. Mine the block.
4. Process all `GET_LONGEST_CHAIN_RESPONSE` messages received from other nodes.
5. Broadcast the `NEW_BLOCK_ANNOUNCEMENT` message to other nodes, and save the candidate block locally.

In listing 10.22, the `render()` method contains a form that looks like this:

```
<form @submit="${this.generateBlock}">
    ${this.pendingTransactionsPanel.render(this.node)}
</form>
```

The UI element with pending transactions and the GENERATE BLOCK button are implemented in the `PendingTransactionsPanel` class. We use the `@submit` directive from lit-html, and when the user clicks on the GENERATE BLOCK button, the `generateBlock()` async method is invoked.

Listing 10.24 The `generateBlock()` method of the `Application` class

```
private readonly generateBlock = async (event: Event): Promise<void> => {
    event.preventDefault();                                              // Prevents a page refresh

    this.server.requestNewBlock(this.node.pendingTransactions);          // Lets all other nodes know that this one has started mining
    const miningProcessIsDone =
  this.node.mineBlockWith(this.node.pendingTransactions);                // Starts the block mining

    this.requestRendering();                                             // Refreshes the status on the UI

    const newBlock = await miningProcessIsDone;                          // Waits for the mining to complete
    this.addBlock(newBlock);                                             // Adds the block to the local blockchain
};
```

When we announce that we're starting block mining, we provide a list of pending transactions, `this.node.pendingTransactions`, so other nodes can compete and try to mine the block for the same transactions faster. Then this node starts mining as well.

When the new block is rejected

The `Application.addBlock()` method invokes the `addBlock()` method in the `BlockchainNode` class. We already discussed the process of block mining, in chapters 8 and 9, but we'd like to highlight the code that rejects an attempt to add a new block:

```
const previousBlockIndex = this._chain.findIndex(b => b.hash ===
➥ newBlock.previousHash);
    if (previousBlockIndex < 0) {                          <-- Does the new block contain an existing previousHash?
      throw new Error(`${errorMessagePrefix} - there is no block in the
➥ chain with the specified previous hash "${newBlock.previousHash
➥ .substr(0, 8)}".`);
    }

const tail = this._chain.slice(previousBlockIndex + 1);
if (tail.length >= 1) {                                    <-- Does the chain already have at least one extra block?
    throw new Error(`${errorMessagePrefix} - the longer tail of the
➥ current node takes precedence over the new block.`);
}
```

This code is related to the failed attempt of adding a block, shown at the bottom-right corner of figure 10.10. First we check whether the new block's value of `previousHash` even exists in the blockchain. It may exist, but not in the last block.

The second `if` statement checks if there is at least one block after the one that contains this `previousHash`. This would mean that at least one new block has already been added to the chain (received from other nodes). In this case, the longest chain takes precedence and the newly generated block is rejected.

Now let's review the code related to WebSocket communications. If you read the code of the `addBlock()` method, you'll see the following line there:

```
this.server.announceNewBlock(block);
```

This is how the node asks the WebSocket server to announce the fresh-from-the-oven block candidate. The `Application` class also has a `handleServerMessages()` method, which handles messages arriving from the server. It's implemented in the client/lib/websocket-controller.ts file, which declares the `PromiseExecutor` interface and `WebsocketController` class.

The `Application` class creates an instance of `WebsocketController`, which is our only contact for all communications with the server. When the client needs to send a message to the server, it'll use such methods as `send()` or `requestLongestChain()`, but sometimes the server will be sending messages to the clients. That's why we pass a callback method to the constructor of `WebsocketController`.

Listing 10.25 websocket-controller.ts: the WebsocketController class

```
export class WebsocketController {
  private websocket: Promise<WebSocket>;
  private readonly messagesAwaitingReply = new Map<UUID,
➥ PromiseExecutor<Message>>();    // A map of WebSocket clients waiting for responses

  constructor(private readonly messagesCallback: (messages: Message) =>
➥ void) {    // Passes the callback to the constructor
    this.websocket = this.connect();    // Connects to the WebServer
  }

  private connect(): Promise<WebSocket> {
    return new Promise((resolve, reject) => {
      const ws = new WebSocket(this.url);
      ws.addEventListener('open', () => resolve(ws));
      ws.addEventListener('error', err => reject(err));
      ws.addEventListener('message', this.onMessageReceived);    // Assigns callbacks to WebSocket messages
    });
  }

  private readonly onMessageReceived = (event: MessageEvent) => {    // Handles incoming messages
    const message = JSON.parse(event.data) as Message;

    if (this.messagesAwaitingReply.has(message.correlationId)) {
      this.messagesAwaitingReply.get(message.correlationId).resolve(message);
      this.messagesAwaitingReply.delete(message.correlationId);
    } else {
      this.messagesCallback(message);
    }
  }

  async send(message: Partial<Message>, awaitForReply: boolean = false):
➥ Promise<Message> {
    return new Promise<Message>(async (resolve, reject) => {
      if (awaitForReply) {
        this.messagesAwaitingReply.set(message.correlationId, { resolve,
➥ reject });    // Stores messages that need a response
      }
      this.websocket.then(
        ws => ws.send(JSON.stringify(message)),
        () => this.messagesAwaitingReply.delete(message.correlationId)
      );
    });
  }
```

TIP The `Partial` type is covered in chapter 5.

The `connect()` method connects to the server and subscribes to the standard WebSocket messages. These actions are wrapped in a `Promise`, so if this method returns, we can be sure that the WebSocket connection is established and all handlers are assigned. An additional benefit is that now we can use the `async` and `await` keywords with these asynchronous functions.

The `onMessageReceived()` method handles messages coming from the server—it's essentially the message router. In that method, we deserialize the message and check its correlation ID. If the incoming message is a response to another message, the following code will return `true`:

```
messagesAwaitingReply.has(message.correlationId)
```

Every time the client sends a message out, we store its correlation ID mapped to the `PromiseExecutor` in `messagesAwaitingReply`. The `PromiseExecutor` knows which client waits for the response.

Listing 10.26 The `PromiseExecutor` interface from websocket-controller.ts

```
interface PromiseExecutor<T> {
  resolve: (value?: T | PromiseLike<T>) => void;
  reject: (reason?: any) => void;
}
```

- This type is used by tsc internally to initialize the promise.
- Enforces the signature of the resolve() method
- Enforces the signature of the reject() method

To construct a `Promise`, the `PromiseConstructor` interface (see the declaration in lib.es2015.promise.d.ts) uses the `PromiseLike` type. TypeScript has a number of types that end with "Like" (such as `ArrayLike`), and they define subtypes that have fewer properties than the original type. Promises may have various constructor signatures; for example, all of them have `then()`, but they may or may not have `catch()`. `PromiseLike` tells tsc, "I don't know what the implementation of this thing is, but at least it's *thenable*."

When the client sends a message that requires a response, it uses the `send()` method shown in listing 10.25, which stores a reference to the client's messages using the correlation ID and an object of type `PromiseExecutor`:

```
this.messagesAwaitingReply.set(message.correlationId, { resolve, reject });
```

The response is asynchronous, and we don't know when it will arrive. In such scenarios, a JavaScript caller can create a `Promise`, providing the `resolve` and `reject` callbacks as explained in section A.10.2 of the appendix. That's why the `send()` method wraps the code sending a message in a `Promise`, and we store the references to the object containing `resolve` and `reject` along with the correlation ID in `messagesAwaitingReply`.

For messages expecting replies, we need a way to push the reply when it arrives. We could use a `Promise`, which could be resolved (or rejected) using the callbacks that we pass to the constructor as `Promise(resolve, reject)`. To preserve the references to this pair of resolve/reject functions until the moment we get a reply, we create a `PromiseExecutor` object that has exactly these two properties, `resolve` and `reject`, and puts them aside. In other words, `PromiseExecutor` is just a container for two callbacks.

The `PromiseExecutor` interface just describes the type of object that we're storing in the `messagesAwaitingReply` map. When the response arrives, the `onMessageReceived()` method finds the `PromiseExecutor` object by the correlation ID, it invokes `resolve()`, and it deletes this message from the map:

```
this.messagesAwaitingReply.get(message.correlationId).resolve(message);
this.messagesAwaitingReply.delete(message.correlationId);
```

Now that you understand how the `send()` method works, you should be able to understand the code that invokes it. The following listing shows how the client can request the longest chain.

Listing 10.27 Requesting the longest chain in websocket-controller.ts

```
async requestLongestChain(): Promise<Block[]> {
  const reply = await this.send(        // Invokes the send() method and waits for the response
    {                                   // The first argument is a Message object.
      type: MessageTypes.GetLongestChainRequest,
      correlationId: uuid()
    }, true);                           // true means "waiting for a reply."
  return reply.payload;                 // Returns the payload from the response
}
```

The `WebsocketController` class has several other methods that deal with other types of messages. They are implemented much like `requestLongestChain()`. Look at the client/lib/websocket-controller.ts file to see the complete code of `WebsocketController`.

To see this app in action, run `npm install` and then `npm start`. Open a couple of browser windows and try to mine some blocks.

Summary

- In a blockchain, multiple nodes may be mining a block containing the same transaction. The longest chain rule can help to find the winning node and reach a consensus amongst nodes.
- If you want to develop an app where the client and the server portions are written in TypeScript, create two separate node-based projects. Each project will have its own package.json file and all the required configuration scripts.
- If you need to arrange client-server communication where each party can initiate the data exchange, consider using the WebSocket protocol. Whereas HTTP is a request-based protocol, WebSocket is not, which makes it a good choice when a server needs to push data to a client.
- Node.js and most other technologies used in the backend support the WebSocket protocol, and you can implement a Node.js server in TypeScript.

11 Developing Angular apps with TypeScript

This chapter covers

- A quick intro to the Angular framework
- How to generate, build, and serve a web app written in Angular and TypeScript
- How Angular implements dependency injection

In October of 2014, a team of Google developers was considering creating a new language, AtScript, which would extend TypeScript and be used for developing the all new Angular 2 framework. In particular, AtScript would support decorators, which were not in TypeScript back then.

Then one of the Googlers suggested meeting with the TypeScript team from Microsoft to see if they would be willing to add decorators to TypeScript itself. The Microsoft folks agreed, and the Angular 2 framework was written in TypeScript, which also became a recommended language for developing Angular apps. Today, more than a million developers use Angular with TypeScript for developing web apps, and this gave a tremendous boost to TypeScript's popularity.

At the time of writing, Angular has 56,000 stars and 1,000 contributors on GitHub. Let's pay respect to this framework and see how we can use TypeScript to develop Angular apps. This chapter will provide a brief introduction to the Angular framework. Chapter 12 contains a code review of the blockchain app written in Angular.

Today, the main players in the market for developing web apps (besides the super-popular jQuery) are Angular and React.js, with Vue.js getting more and more traction every month. Angular is a framework, whereas React.js is a library that does one thing really well: rendering the UI in the browser's DOM. Chapter 13 will get you started with developing web apps using React.js and TypeScript. In chapter 14, we'll use React to develop another version of the blockchain client. Chapter 15 will cover the basics of Vue.js, and in chapter 16, we'll write yet another version of the blockchain client in Vue.

NOTE It's difficult to provide detailed coverage of Angular development with TypeScript in a single chapter. If you're serious about learning Angular, read our book, *Angular Development with TypeScript*, second edition (Manning, 2018).

The difference between a framework and library is that a framework forces you to write your apps in a certain way, whereas a library offers you certain features that you can use in any way you like. In this sense, Angular is definitely a framework, or even more than a framework—it's an opinionated platform (a framework that can be extended) that has everything you need to develop a web app:

- Support for dependency injection
- Angular Material—a library of modern-looking UI components
- A router for arranging the user's navigation in the app
- A module to communicate with HTTP servers
- A means for splitting the app into deployable modules that can be loaded either eagerly or lazily
- Advanced forms support
- A library of reactive extensions (RxJS) to handle data streams
- A development web server that supports live code reloads
- Build tools for optimizing and bundling for deployment
- A command-line interface for quickly scaffolding an app, a library, or smaller artifacts like components, modules, services, and the like

Let's quickly create and run a simple web app that will allow us to demonstrate some of Angular's features.

11.1 Generating and running a new app with Angular CLI

CLI stands for command-line interface, and the Angular CLI is a tool that can generate and configure a new Angular project in less than a minute. To install Angular CLI on your computer, run the following command:

```
npm install @angular/cli -g
```

Now you can run the CLI from the terminal window using the `ng` command with parameters. This command can be used for generating a new workspace, application, library, component, service, and more. The parameters for the `ng` command are described in Angular's CLI documentation (https://angular.io/cli), and you can also see what's available by running `ng help` in the terminal window. To get help for a specific parameter, run `ng help` followed by the name of the parameter you need help with, such as `ng help new`.

> **NOTE** In this chapter, we used Angular CLI 7.3. To see which version is installed on your computer, run `ng version`.

This chapter comes with four sample projects that were generated by Angular CLI. Even though these projects are ready to be reviewed and run, we'll describe the process of generating and running the hello-world project so you can try it on your own.

To generate a new minimalistic project, run the `ng new` command followed by the name of the project (a.k.a. workspace). To generate a simple hello-world project, run the following command in the terminal window:

```
ng new hello-world --minimal
```

It will ask you, "Would you like to add Angular routing? (y/N)," and let's answer N. Then you'll need to select the style sheets format; press Enter for CSS (the default). In a second, you'll see the names of the generated files in the new hello-world directory, and one of them will be package.json. In the next 30 seconds, it will run npm and install all required dependencies. Figure 11.1 shows what your terminal window may look like once the project is ready.

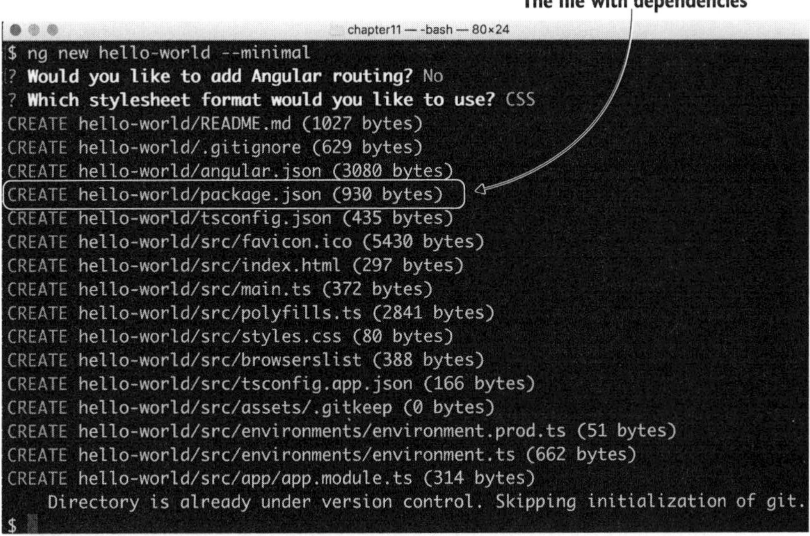

Figure 11.1 Generating a minimal project

In the terminal window, switch to the newly generated hello-world directory and run the app in the browser with the `ng serve -o` command (`-o` means "open the browser for me at the default host and port"):

```
cd hello-world
ng serve -o
```

The `ng serve -o` command builds the bundles for this app in memory, starts the web server with your app, and opens the browser. It will produce the console output shown in figure 11.2. At the time of writing, the `ng serve` command uses Webpack to bundle your apps and Webpack DevServer to serve it. By default, your app is served at localhost:4200.

```
$ cd hello-world
$ ng serve -o
** Angular Live Development Server is listening on localhost:4200, open your browser on h
ttp://localhost:4200/ **
                                                                          u Date: 201
9-04-10T10:35:12.530Z
Hash: 617767a50a6f77b8c833
Time: 7615ms
chunk {es2015-polyfills} es2015-polyfills.js, es2015-polyfills.js.map (es2015-polyfills)
284 kB [initial] [rendered]
chunk {main} main.js, main.js.map (main) 9.11 kB [initial] [rendered]
chunk {polyfills} polyfills.js, polyfills.js.map (polyfills) 236 kB [initial] [rendered]
chunk {runtime} runtime.js, runtime.js.map (runtime) 6.08 kB [entry] [rendered]
chunk {styles} styles.js, styles.js.map (styles) 16.3 kB [initial] [rendered]
chunk {vendor} vendor.js, vendor.js.map (vendor) 3.52 MB [initial] [rendered]
i 「wdm」: Compiled successfully.
```

The app bundle

The bundle with Angular's code

Figure 11.2 The app bundles are created

If you read chapter 6, you'll recognize the Webpack bundles and source map files. The app code is located in the main.js chunk, and the code from the Angular framework is located in the chunk called vendor.js. Don't be scared by the size of vendor.js (3.52 MB) because `ng serve` builds the bundles in memory without optimization. Running the production build, `ng serve --prod`, would produce bundles with a total size of just over 100 KB.

Congratulations! Your first Angular app is up and running, rendering a page with the message "Welcome to hello-world!" At the time of writing, it looks like figure 11.3.

Figure 11.3 Running hello-world

Although this is not the UI that your app needs, this project contains the basic TypeScript code, tsconfig.json, the HTML file that renders this UI, package.json with all the required dependencies, a preconfigured bundler, and some other files. Having a bundled and running app within a couple of minutes, without spending any time studying Angular, is pretty impressive, but you'll still need to learn this framework to develop your own app, so we'll help you get started with Angular.

First, terminate the running hello-world app by pressing Ctrl-C in the terminal window. Next, open the hello-world directory in VS Code, which offers a lot more convenient development environment than a terminal window and a plain text editor.

11.2 Reviewing the generated app

Figure 11.4 is a VS Code screenshot showing the structure of the generated hello-world project. All these files were generated by Angular CLI. We won't go through each file, but we will describe the files that are crucial for understanding how an Angular app works and what the main players of any Angular app are. We've marked those files with arrows in figure 11.4.

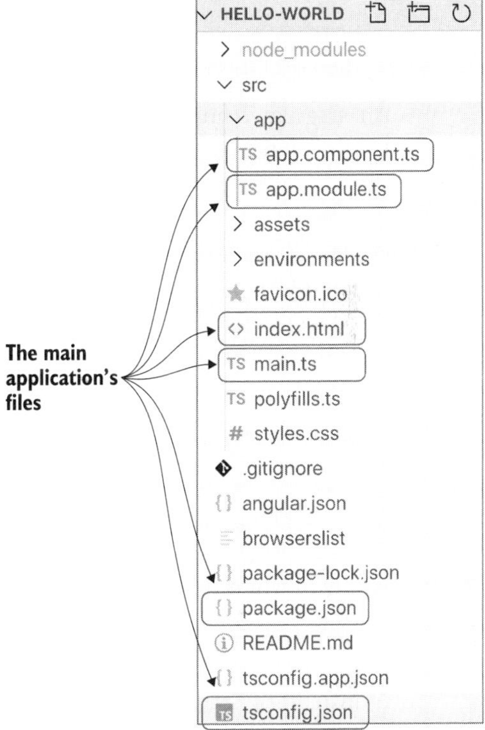

Figure 11.4 Looking at the hello-world workspace in VS Code

The source code of our app is located in the src folder, and at the very minimum it will have one component (app .component.ts) and one module (app .module.ts). The content of app.component.ts is shown in the following listing.

Listing 11.1 app.component.ts: the top-level component

```
import { Component } from '@angular/core';

@Component({
  selector: 'app-root',
  template: `
    <div style="text-align:center">
      <h1>
        Welcome to {{title}}!
      </h1>
      <img width="300" src="data:image/svg+xml;base64,PHN2ZyB4b...">
```

- Imports the Component decorator
- Decorates the class with @Component
- In other templates, you can refer to this component as <app-root>
- The template (UI) of this component
- Binds the value of the title class property

```
    </div>
    <h2>Here are some links to help you start: </h2>
    <!-- We removed the ul tag due to book space constraints -->
  `,
  styles: []
})
export class AppComponent {
  title = 'hello-world';
}
```

CSS goes here

The decorated component class

Declares and initializes the title class property

NOTE We've removed the links shown in figure 11.3 from the HTML part of the code to make the important code more visible.

An Angular component is a class decorated with `@Component()`; we covered decorators in section 5.1. The UI of any component is declared in the object that we pass to the `@Component()` decorator, namely in its `selector`, `template`, or `styles` properties, or a few others.

The `selector` property contains a value that can be used in HTML files that have to include this component. In listing 11.1, the CLI generated the value `app-root` as the selector for the app component, and if you open the index.html file, you'll see a <body> section that includes opening and closing tags that match that selector:

```
<body>
  <app-root></app-root>
</body>
```

The UI elements of any component are placed in the `template` property of the `@Component()` decorator. Note the backticks that allow multiline strings, which comes handy in when formatting HTML.

TIP Angular allows you to separate HTML from TypeScript code. If you prefer to keep the HTML in a separate file, use the `templateURL` property instead of `template`; for example, `templateUrl: "app.component.html"`.

Now let's look at the line of listing 11.1 that reads `Welcome to {{title}}!`. Double curly braces represent *interpolation*—embedding expressions into text. It's also a way *to bind* a value into a string. Binding is about keeping the values of your TypeScript class members and the UI in sync. So where is this `title` coming from? It's a property of the `AppComponent` class.

The value of the `title` class property is `hello-world`, which explains why the UI in figure 11.2 rendered "Welcome to hello-world!" Modify the value of the `title` property while the app is running, and the UI will be immediately updated.

NOTE Double curly braces are used to bind values from a variable to a string in a template. Square brackets, on the other hand, are used to bind a value to a property of a component: `<CustomerComponent [name]=lastName>`. Here we bind the value of the `lastName` variable to the `name` property of the `CustomerComponent`. You'll see more examples of property binding syntax in listings 11.26 and 11.32.

In listing 11.1, the `styles` property points at the empty array. If we wanted to add CSS styles, we could either add them inline or specify the filenames of one or more CSS files in the `styleUrls` property, such as `styleUrls: [app.component.css]`.

But declaring a component class is not enough, because your app must have at least one Angular module (not to be confused with ECMAScript modules). An Angular module is a TypeScript class decorated with the `@NgModule()` decorator. It's like a registry of components, services, and possibly other modules that belong together. Typically the code of the class is empty, and the list of module members is specified in the decorator's properties.

Let's look at the code generated in the app.module.ts file.

Listing 11.2 The src/app/app.module.ts file

```
import { BrowserModule } from '@angular/platform-browser';
import { NgModule } from '@angular/core';

import { AppComponent } from './app.component';

@NgModule({
  declarations: [
    AppComponent
  ],
  imports: [
    BrowserModule
  ],
  providers: [],
  bootstrap: [AppComponent]
})
export class AppModule { }
```

- **BrowserModule is needed for a web app.** (import { BrowserModule })
- **We need the implementation of the NgModule() decorator.** (import { NgModule })
- **This is our app's only component.** (import { AppComponent })
- **Applies the NgModule() decorator** (@NgModule)
- **Declares all components that belong to this module** (declarations)
- **Imports other modules if needed** (BrowserModule)
- **Declares providers for Angular services, if any** (providers)
- **Specifies the root component that has to be loaded** (bootstrap)

The `@NgModule()` decorator requires you to list all the components and modules used in the app. In the `declarations` property we have only one component, but if we had several of them (such as `CustomerComponent` and `OrderComponent`), we'd have to list them as well:

```
declarations: [ AppComponent, CustomerComponent, OrderComponent ]
```

Of course, if you mention a class, interface, variable, or function name, they have to be imported at the top of the module's file, just like we did for `AppComponent`. By the way, did you notice the `export` keyword in listing 11.1? If we didn't have it there, we wouldn't be able to import `AppComponent` in the app.module.ts file, or any other file for that matter.

The `imports` property is the place for listing other required modules. Angular itself is split into modules, and your real-world app will likely be modularized as well.

Listing 11.1 has only `BrowserModule` in `imports`—it must be included in the root module of any app that runs in the browser. The following listing shows another example of an `imports` property, illustrating what can be included there.

Listing 11.3 Importing other modules

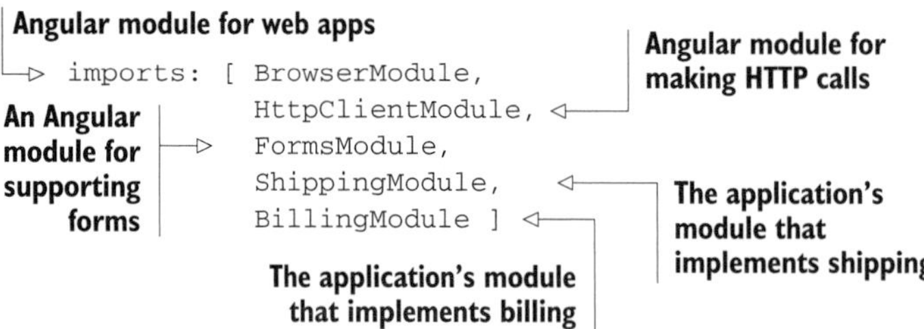
Angular module for web apps
imports: [BrowserModule,
HttpClientModule,
FormsModule,
ShippingModule,
BillingModule]
Angular module for making HTTP calls
An Angular module for supporting forms
The application's module that implements shipping
The application's module that implements billing

NOTE Besides listing the modules in the `imports` property of the `@NgModule()` decorator, you need to add an ES6 import statement for each of these modules to point at the files where they are implemented.

In the next section, we'll talk about services and dependency injection. We'll also discuss about service providers that can be listed in the module's `providers` property.

The `bootstrap` property names the top-level component (the root component) that the module must load first. The root component may use child components, which Angular will recognize and load, and those child components may have their own children—Angular will find and load all of them. The Angular module in listing 11.2 has only one component in the `declaration` section, so it's listed in the `bootstrap` as well, but if it had several components, you'd need to specify one to bootstrap when the module is loaded.

And where's the code that bootstraps the module with its `AppComponent` (shown earlier in listing 11.1)? It's located in the CLI-generated main.ts file.

Listing 11.4 The src/main.ts file

```
import { enableProdMode } from '@angular/core';
import { platformBrowserDynamic } from '@angular/platform-browser-dynamic';

import { AppModule } from './app/app.module';
import { environment } from './environments/environment';

if (environment.production) {          // Checks the production environment variable
  enableProdMode();
}

platformBrowserDynamic()               // Creates the entry point to the app
  .bootstrapModule(AppModule)          // Bootstraps the root module
  .catch(err => console.error(err));   // Catches errors, if any
```

First, the code in main.ts reads one of the files in the environments directory to check the value of the `environment.production` Boolean variable. Without going into details, we'll just state that this value affects how many times Angular's change detector will pass the app components tree to see what has to be updated on the UI. The change detector monitors each and every variable bound to the UI and gives a signal to the rendering engine about what to update.

Second, the `platformBrowserDynamic()` API creates a *platform*, which is an entry point to the web app. Then it bootstraps the module, which in turn loads the root and all child components required to render the module. It'll also render other modules listed in the `imports` property, and it will create an injector that knows how to inject the services listed in the `providers` property of the `@NgModule()` decorator.

OK, we've gone through the TypeScript code, we've built the bundles, and you might guess that the index.html file shown in figure 11.4 will use the bundle, right? Wrong! That was the initial version of index.html, and it only included the selector of our root component, as seen in the following listing.

Listing 11.5 src/index.html: the HTML file that loads the app

```
<!doctype html>
<html lang="en">
<head>
  <meta charset="utf-8">
  <title>HelloWorld</title>
  <base href="/">

  <meta name="viewport" content="width=device-width, initial-scale=1">
  <link rel="icon" type="image/x-icon" href="favicon.ico">
</head>
<body>
  <app-root></app-root>          <— The root component of our app
</body>
</html>
```

In this file, you won't see `<script>` tags pointing at the JavaScript bundles shown in figure 11.2. But when you run the app with `ng serve`, Angular will add the `<script>` tags to the HTML file, and you can see them at runtime in the Chrome dev tools, as shown in figure 11.5.

> **NOTE** The `ng serve` command builds and rebuilds the bundles in memory to speed up the development process, but if you'd like to see the actual files, run the `ng build` command, and it will create the index.html file and all the bundles in the dist directory.

> **TIP** The CLI-generated angular.json file contains all the project configurations, and you can change the output directory as well as many other default options there.

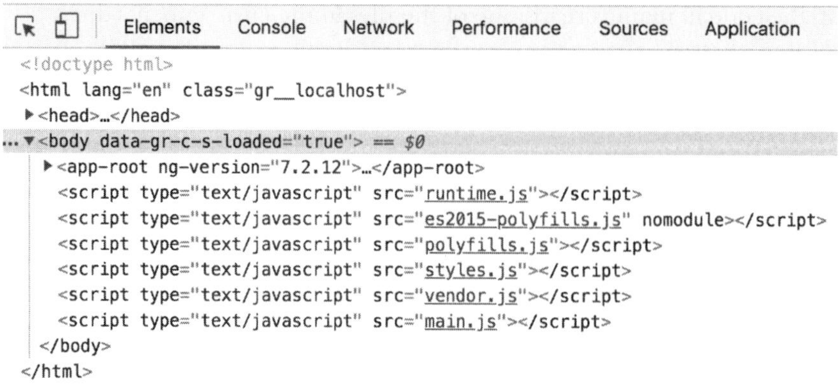

```
Elements   Console   Network   Performance   Sources   Application
<!doctype html>
<html lang="en" class="gr__localhost">
 ▶<head>…</head>
…▼<body data-gr-c-s-loaded="true"> == $0
   ▶<app-root ng-version="7.2.12">…</app-root>
    <script type="text/javascript" src="runtime.js"></script>
    <script type="text/javascript" src="es2015-polyfills.js" nomodule></script>
    <script type="text/javascript" src="polyfills.js"></script>
    <script type="text/javascript" src="styles.js"></script>
    <script type="text/javascript" src="vendor.js"></script>
    <script type="text/javascript" src="main.js"></script>
  </body>
</html>
```

Figure 11.5 The runtime version of the HTML doc has `<script>` tags

That was a high-level overview of a project generated by the `ng new hello-world --minimal` CLI command. If we didn't use the `--minimal` option, CLI would also generate some boilerplate code for unit and end-to-end testing.

You can use the simple generated project as a base for this chapter's app, which will require more components and services, and Angular CLI can help you in generating the boilerplate code for various artifacts in your app, like components and services. Let's get familiar with the role of services in an Angular app.

11.3 Angular services and dependency injection

If a component is a class with a UI, a service is just a class that implements the business logic of your app. You can create a service that calculates shipping costs, and another may encapsulate all HTTP communications with the server. What all these services have in common is that they don't have a UI. Angular can instantiate and *inject* a service into your application's components or another service.

What dependency injection is all about

If you've ever written a function that takes an object as an argument, you've already written a program that instantiates this object and *injects* it into the function.

Imagine a fulfillment center that ships products. An application that keeps track of shipped products could create a product object and invoke a function that creates and saves a shipment record:

```
var product = new Product();
createShipment(product);
```

The `createShipment()` function depends on the existence of an instance of the `Product` object. In other words, the `createShipment()` function has a dependency: `Product`. But the function itself doesn't know how to create `Product`. The calling script should somehow create and give (think *inject*) this object as an argument to the function.

Technically, you're decoupling the creation of the `Product` object from its use. But both of the preceding lines of code are located in the same script, so it's not real decoupling, and if you need to replace `Product` with `MockProduct`, it's a small code change in this simple example.

What if the `createShipment()` function had three dependencies (such as product, shipping company, and fulfillment center), and each of those dependencies had their own dependencies? In that case, creating a different set of objects for the `createShipment()` function would require many more manual code changes. Would it be possible to ask someone to create instances of the dependencies (with their dependencies) for you?

This is what the dependency injection (DI) pattern is about: if object A depends on an object identified by token (a unique ID) B, object A won't explicitly use the `new` operator to instantiate the object that B points at. Rather, it will have B *injected* from the operational environment.

Object A just needs to declare, "I need an object known as B; could someone please give it to me?" Object A doesn't request a specific object type (such as `Product`) but rather delegates to the framework the responsibility of what to inject into the token B. It seems that object A doesn't want to be in control of creating instances and is ready to let the framework control this process, doesn't it? We're talking about the *inversion of control (IoC)* principle here. "Hey framework, instantiate the object I need now and give it to me, will you?"

Another good use of DI is writing unit tests, where the real services need to be replaced with mocks. In Angular, you can easily configure which objects (mocks or real ones) have to be injected into your test scripts as shown in the following image.

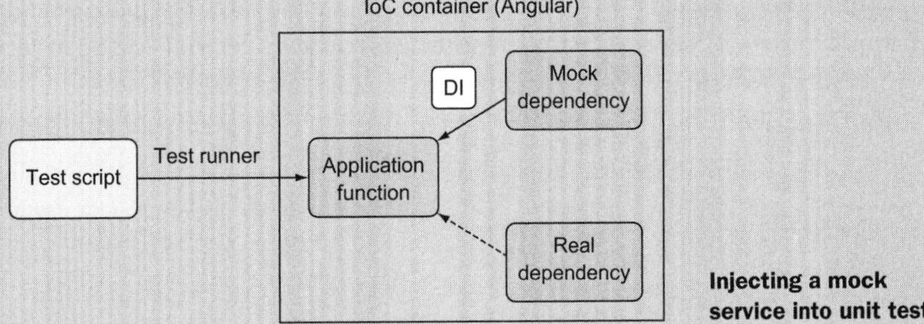

Injecting a mock service into unit tests

The Angular framework implements the DI pattern and offers you a simple way of replacing one object with another, if need be.

Let's ask Angular CLI to generate the `ProductService` class in our hello-world project. For this we'll use the `ng generate` CLI command, which can generate services, components, modules, and so on. To generate a service, you need to use the command ng generate service (or ng g s) followed by the name of the service. The following command will generate a new product.service.ts file in the src/app directory:

```
ng generate service product --skip-tests
```

TIP To see all the arguments and options of the ng generate command, run ng --help generate in the terminal window.

If we didn't specify the --skip-tests option, the CLI would also generate a file with the boilerplate code for testing the product service. The following listing shows the content of the product.service.ts file.

Listing 11.6 The generated product.service.ts file

```
import { Injectable } from '@angular/core';

@Injectable({                          // This decorator marks the class as injectable.
  providedIn: 'root'                   // The instance of service must be available for all members of the root module.
})
export class ProductService {

  constructor() { }
}
```

The @Injectable() decorator will instruct Angular to generate additional metadata required to instantiate and inject the service. The providedIn property allows you to specify where this service has to be available. The value root means that we want this service to be *provided* on the app level and to be a singleton, meaning that all other components and services will use a single instance of the ProductService object. If your app consists of several feature modules, you can restrict the service to be available only in a particular module, such as providedIn: ShippingModule.

An alternative to using the providedIn property is specifying the provider in the module's providers property in @NgModule:

```
@NgModule({
  ...
  providers: [ProductService]
})
```

Say you have a ProductComponent that gets product details using the ProductService class. Without DI, your ProductComponent needs to know *how* to instantiate the ProductService class. This can be done in multiple ways, such as using the new operator, calling getInstance() on a singleton object, or invoking some createProductService() factory function. In any case, ProductComponent becomes *tightly coupled* with ProductService, because replacing ProductService with another implementation of this service requires a code change in ProductComponent.

If you want to reuse `ProductComponent` in another application that uses a different service to get product details, you must modify the code, perhaps as `productService = new AnotherProductService()`. DI allows you to decouple the application's components and services by sparing them from knowing how to create their dependencies.

Angular's documentation uses the concept of a *token*, which is an arbitrary key representing an object to be injected. You map tokens to values for DI by specifying providers; a *provider* is an instruction to Angular about *how* to create an instance of an object for future injection into a target component or another service.

We already mentioned that a provider can be specified in a module declaration (if you need a singleton service), but you can also specify a provider on a component level as shown in listing 11.7, where `ProductComponent` gets the `ProductService` injected.

Angular instantiates and injects any class used in the constructor's arguments. If you declared a provider in a `@Component()` decorator, the component would get its own instance of the service, which would be destroyed as soon as the component is destroyed.

Listing 11.7 `ProductService` injected into `ProductComponent`

```
@Component({
  providers: [ProductService]          <-- Specifies the ProductService
})                                         token as a provider for injection
class ProductComponent {
  product: Product;
                                                        Injects the object represented
  constructor(productService: ProductService) {    <--  by the ProductService token

    this.product = productService.getProduct();   <--  Uses the API of the injected object,
  }                                                    assuming that getProduct() exists
}                                                      in the service
```

Often the token name matches the type of the object to be injected. The preceding code snippet uses a shorthand, `[ProductService]`, to instruct Angular to provide a `ProductService` token by instantiating the class of the same name. The long version would look like this: `providers:[{provide: ProductService, useClass: ProductService}]`. You say to Angular, "If you see a class with a constructor that uses the token `ProductService`, inject an instance of the `ProductService` class."

`ProductComponent` doesn't need to know which concrete implementation of the `ProductService` type to use—it'll use whatever object is specified as a provider. The reference to the `ProductService` object will be injected via the constructor argument, and there's no need to explicitly instantiate `ProductService` in `ProductComponent`. Just use it as in the preceding code, which calls the `getProduct()` service method on the `ProductService` instance magically created by Angular.

If you need to reuse the same `ProductComponent` with a different implementation of the `ProductService` type, change the providers line like this: `providers: [{provide:`

ProductService, useClass: AnotherProductService}]. Now Angular will instantiate AnotherProductService, but the code of the ProductComponent that uses Product-Service doesn't require modification. In this example, using DI increases the reusability of ProductComponent and eliminates its tight coupling with ProductService.

11.4 An app with ProductService injection

This chapter comes with a sample di-products project that shows how you can inject (and use) ProductService into ProductComponent. The following listing shows the code of ProductService.

Listing 11.8 The product.service.ts file from the di-products project

```
import { Injectable } from '@angular/core';
import { Product } from './product';

@Injectable({
  providedIn: 'root'                    <-- Creates a singleton instance of ProductService
})
export class ProductService {

  getProduct(): Product {               <-- Returns the hardcoded product data
    return { id: 0,
            title: "iPhone XI",
            price: 1049.99,
            description: "The latest iPhone" };
  }
}
```

In this service, we have a getProduct() method that returns hardcoded data of Product type, shown in the following listing, but in real-world apps, we'd make an HTTP request to the server to get the data.

Listing 11.9 The product.ts file

```
export interface Product {
  id: number,
  title: string,
  price: number,
  description: string
}
```

NOTE We declared the Product type as an interface, which enforces type checking in getProduct() but leaves no footprint in the compiled JavaScript. We could have declared the Product type as a class, but that would have resulted in generating JavaScript code (such as a class or function depending on the value in the target compiler's option). For declaring custom types, it's better to use interfaces than classes if possible.

Now let's look at the product component, which we generated with the following CLI command:

```
ng generate component product --t --s --skip-tests
```

The `--t` option specifies that we don't want to generate a separate HTML file for the component's template. The `--s` option specifies that we'll use inline styles instead of generating a separate CSS file. And `--skip-tests` generates the file without the boilerplate unit-test code.

The following listing shows our `ProductComponent` after adding the template and injecting `ProductService`.

Listing 11.10 product.component.ts: the product component

```
import {Component} from '@angular/core';
import {ProductService} from "../product.service";
import {Product} from "../product";

@Component({
  selector: 'di-product-page',
  template: `<div>
  <h1>Product Details</h1>
  <h2>Title: {{product.title}}</h2>                    <- Binds title to the UI
  <h2>Description: {{product.description}}</h2>        <- Binds description to the UI
  <h2>Price: \${{product.price}}</h2>                  <- Binds price to the UI
</div>`
})

export class ProductComponent {
  product: Product;                  <- This object's properties are bound to the UI.

  constructor( productService: ProductService) {       <- Injects ProductService

    this.product = productService.getProduct();        <- Uses the API of ProductService
  }
}
```

When Angular instantiates `ProductComponent`, it will also inject `ProductService` into the component because it's a constructor argument. Then the constructor will invoke `getProduct()`. The component's `product` property will be populated, and the UI will be updated using binding.

> **NOTE** Please don't curse us for invoking `getProduct()` from the component's constructor. In a real-word project we'd use a special `ngOnInit()` callback for this, but we wanted to show you the simplest possible code.

Finally, our `AppComponent` specifies `ProductComponent` as a child by using its selector in the template.

Listing 11.11 app.component.ts: the top-level component

```
import { Component } from '@angular/core';

@Component({
  selector: 'app-root',
  template: `<h1> Basic Dependency Injection Sample</h1>
            <di-product-page></di-product-page>`    ◁ Adds ProductComponent to the template
})
export class AppComponent {}
```

Build the bundle and start the dev server using the `ng serve -o` command, and the browser will render the UI as shown in figure 11.6.

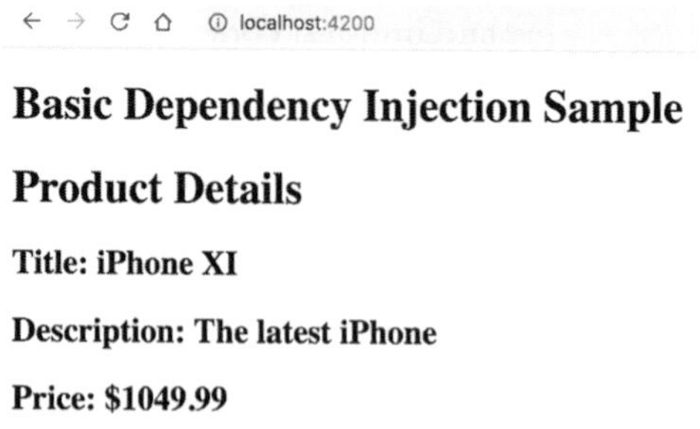

> **TIP** In the unlikely event that you don't like the UI of our component, shown in figure 11.6, you can add a `styles` property to its `@Component()` decorator and use whatever styles you like.

Figure 11.6 Rendering the product data

State management in Angular

State management is one of the most important parts of any app. It deserves a chapter on its own, but we only have room for a sidebar. We've placed this sidebar in our discussion of DI because, in Angular, DI is widely used for implementing state management.

In a web app, one component can change the value of one or more variables used in another component. This can result from the user's actions or from new server-generated data. For example, you're on Facebook and the top toolbar (one component) shows that you have three unread messages. When you click on the digit 3, it opens Messenger (another component), which shows you these three messages.

Something besides the toolbar and Messenger components stores and maintains the message counter during the user's session. This is an example of *app state management*, and it plays a very important role in any app.

Angular injectable services (combined with RxJS) offer you a straightforward way to implement state management. If you create an `AppState` service and declare its provider in the `@NgModule()` decorator, Angular will create an `AppState` singleton, and you can inject it in any components or services that need to have access to the current app state.

The `AppState` service may have a `messageCounter` property, and the `MessengerComponent` could increment it every time a new message arrives. The `ToolbarComponent` would thus get the current value of the `AppState.messageCounter` and render it in the UI. This way, `AppState` becomes a *single source of truth* for storing and providing app state values. Moreover, when one component updates the message counter, `AppState` can broadcast its new value to other components that are interested in getting the new state.

Although injectable services offer a clean solution for state management, some people prefer using third-party libraries (such as NGRX or NGXS) for implementing state management in Angular apps. These libraries may require you to write a lot of additional boilerplate code, and you should think twice before making a decision about the implementation of state management in your app. Poorly implemented state management can make your app buggy and costly to maintain.

Yakov Fain has posted a video titled "Angular: When ngrx is an overkill," where he compares using a singleton service to using the NGRX library for implementing state management in a simple app. You can find it on YouTube (http://mng.bz/6w5A).

11.5 Programming to abstractions in TypeScript

In section 3.2.3, we recommended that you program to interfaces (a.k.a. abstractions). Since Angular DI allows you to replace injectable objects, it would be nice if you could declare a `ProductService` interface and specify it as a provider. The injection point would look like `constructor( productService: ProductService)`, and you'd write several concrete classes that implement this interface and switch them in the provider's declaration as needed.

You could do this in Java, C#, and other object-oriented languages. In TypeScript, the problem is that after compiling the code into JavaScript, the interfaces are removed, because JavaScript doesn't support them. In other words, if `ProductService` were declared as an interface, the constructor `constructor(productService: ProductService` would turn into `constructor(productService`, and Angular wouldn't know anything about `ProductService`.

The good news is that TypeScript supports abstract classes, which can have some methods implemented and some abstract—declared but not implemented (see section 3.1.5 for details). Then you'd need to implement concrete classes that extend the abstract ones, and implement all the abstract methods. For example, you could have the classes in the following listing.

Listing 11.12 Declaring an abstract class and two descendants

```
export abstract class ProductService{          <-- Declares an abstract class
  abstract getProduct(): Product;          <-- Declares an abstract method
}

export class MockProductService extends ProductService{   <-- Creates the first concrete implementation of the abstract class
  getProduct(): Product {
    return new Product('Samsung Galaxy S10');
  }
}

export class RealProductService extends ProductService{   <-- Creates the second concrete implementation of the abstract class
  getProduct(): Product {
```

```
    return new Product('iPhone XII');
  }
}
```

The good news is that you can use the name of the abstract class in the constructors, and during the JavaScript code generation, Angular will use a specific concrete class based on the provider declaration. Having the `ProductService`, `MockProductService`, and `RealProductService` classes declared as in listing 11.12 will allow you to write something like the following.

Listing 11.13 Using an abstract class as a provider

```
// A fragment from app.module.ts
@NgModule({
  providers: [{provide: ProductService, useClass: RealProductService}],   <-- Maps a concrete type to an abstract token
  ...
})
export class AppModule { }

// A fragment from product.component.ts
@Component({...})
export class ProductComponent {
  constructor(productService: ProductService) {...};   <-- Uses an abstract token at the injection point
  }
  ...
}
```

Here we use a `ProductService` abstraction in declaring the provider and as a constructor argument. This was not the case in listing 11.8, where `ProductService` was a concrete implementation of certain functionality. You can replace the providers the same way as described earlier, or switch from one concrete implementation of the service to another.

If you didn't use abstract classes, you'd need to be very careful in declaring the `ProductService` and `MockProductService` classes so that they'd have exactly the same `getProducts()` API. If you use the abstract class approach, the Typescript compiler will give you an error if you try to implement a concrete class but miss implementing one of the abstract methods. Program to abstractions!

> **TIP** There is another way to use DI and make sure that several classes have the same APIs. In TypeScript, a class can implement another class, such as `class MockProductService implements ProductService`. This syntax allows the type analyzer to ensure that the `MockProductService` class implements all public methods defined in `ProductService` and to use any of these classes with DI.

11.6 Getting started with HTTP requests

Angular applications can communicate with any web server that supports HTTP, and in this section, we'll show you how you can start making HTTP requests. This will help you understand the code of the blockchain app presented in the next chapter.

Browser-based web apps run HTTP requests asynchronously, so the UI remains responsive. The user can continue working with the application while HTTP requests are being processed by the server. In Angular, asynchronous HTTP is implemented using a special *observable* object offered by the RxJS library that comes with Angular.

If your app requires HTTP communications, you need to add `HttpClientModule` to the `imports` section of the `@NgModule()` decorator. After that, you can use the injectable service `HttpClient` to invoke `get()`, `post()`, `put()`, `delete()`, and other requests. Each of these requests returns an `Observable` object.

In the context of client-server communications, you can think of `Observable` as a stream of data that can be pushed to your web app by the server. This concept is easier to grasp if used with WebSocket communications—the server keeps pushing the data into the stream over the open socket. With HTTP, you always get back just a single result set, but you can think of it as a stream of one piece of data.

> **TIP** Yakov Fain has published a series of blogs about RxJS and observable streams. The series is available on his website at http://mng.bz/omBp.

Let's see how a web client could make a request to the server's `/product/123` end-point to retrieve the `Product` with an ID of 123. The following listing illustrates one way of invoking the `get()` method of the `HttpClient` service, passing a URL as a `string`.

Listing 11.14 Making an HTTP `GET` request

```
interface Product {          <-- Defines the Product type
    id: number,
    title: string
}
...
class ProductService {
constructor(private httpClient: HttpClient) { }   <-- Injects the HttpClient service

ngOnInit() {   <-- This callback method is invoked by Angular.
  this.httpClient.get<Product>('/product/123')    <-- Declares a get() request
      .subscribe(
        data => console.log(`id: ${data.id} title: ${data.title}`),   <-- Subscribes to the result of get()
        (err: HttpErrorResponse) => console.log(`Got error: ${err}`)   <-- Logs an error, if any
      );
  }
}
```

The `HttpClient` service is injected in the constructor, and since we added a `private` qualifier, `httpClient` becomes a property of the `ProductService` object instantiated by Angular. We placed the code that makes the HTTP request inside a so-called `hook` method, `ngOnInit()`, which is invoked by Angular when a component is instantiated and all its properties are initialized.

In the `get()` method, we didn't specify the full URL (such as http://localhost:8000/product/123). We're assuming that the Angular app makes the request to the same server where it is deployed, so the base portion of the URL can be omitted. Note that in `get<Product>()` we use the `<Product>` type assertion (equivalent to `as Product`) to specify the type of data expected in the body of the HTTP response. This type assertion tells the static type analyzer something like this: "Dear TypeScript, you're having a hard time inferring the type of the data returned by the server. Let me help you—it's `Product`."

The returned result is always an RxJS `Observable` object, which has the `subscribe()` method. We specified two callbacks as its arguments:

- The first will be invoked if the data is received; it prints the data on the browser's console.
- The second will be invoked if the request returns an error.

The `post()`, `put()`, and `delete()` methods are used in a similar fashion. You invoke one of these methods and subscribe to the results.

> **NOTE** We stated earlier that every injectable service requires a provider declaration, but the providers for `HttpClient` are declared inside `HttpClientModule`, which is included in the `imports` of `@NgModule`, so you don't need to explicitly declare them in your app.

By default, `HttpClient` expects the data in JSON format, and the data is automatically converted into JavaScript objects. If you expect non-JSON data, use the `responseType` option. For example, you can read arbitrary text from a file as shown in the following listing.

Listing 11.15 Specifying `string` as a returned data type

```
let someData: string;

this.httpClient
    .get<string>('/my_data_file.txt', {responseType: 'text'})    <- Specifies string as a response body type
    .subscribe(
        data => someData = data,    <- Assigns the received data to a variable
        (err: HttpErrorResponse) => console.log(`Got error: ${err}`)    <- Logs errors, if any
    );
```

Now let's see how we can read some data from a JSON file using `HttpClient`. This chapter comes with a read-file project that illustrates using `HttpClient.get()` to read a file containing JSON-formatted product data. This app has a data directory that contains the products.json file shown in the following listing.

Listing 11.16 The data/products.json file

```
[
  { "id": 0, "title": "First Product", "price": 24.99 },
  { "id": 1, "title": "Second Product", "price": 64.99 },
  { "id": 2, "title": "Third Product", "price": 74.99}
]
```

The data directory contains project assets (the products.json file) and needs to be included in the project bundles, so we'll add this directory to the app's `assets` property in the angular.json file.

Listing 11.17 A fragment from angular.json

```
"assets": [
  "src/favicon.ico",
  "src/assets",
  "src/data"
]
```

Default assets generated by Angular CLI (`"src/favicon.ico"`, `"src/assets"`)

The name of the assets directory that we've added to the project (`"src/data"`)

Typically, you'll be specifying the server's URL when you use the `HttpClient` service, but in our sample app, the URL will point to the local data/products .json file. Our app will read this file and will render the products as shown in figure 11.7.

`ApplicationComponent` will use `HttpClient.get()` to issue an HTTP `GET` request, and we'll declare a `Product` interface defining the structure of the expected product data.

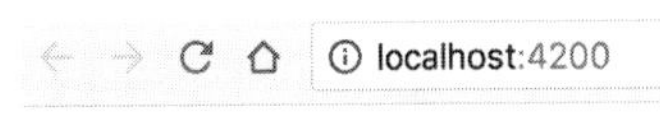

Products

- First Product: $24.99
- Second Product: $64.99
- Third Product: $74.99

Figure 11.7 Rendering the content of products.json

Listing 11.18 src/product.ts: a custom `Product` type

```
export interface Product {
    id: string;
    title: string;
    price: number;
}
```

The app.component.ts file is shown in listing 11.19, and it's where we'll implement a simpler way of subscribing to the `HttpClient` responses. This time you won't see the explicit `subscribe()`. We'll use the `async` pipe instead.

> **NOTE** Angular pipes are special converter functions that can be used in the component's template and are represented by a vertical bar followed by the pipe name. For example, the `currency` pipe converts a number into currency; `123.5521 | currency` will render `$123.55` (dollar is the default currency sign).

Listing 11.19 app.component.ts: the top-level component

```
import {HttpClient} from '@angular/common/http';
import {Observable} from 'rxjs';
import {Component, OnInit} from "@angular/core";
import {Product} from "./product";

@Component({
  selector: 'app-root',
  template: `<h1>Products</h1>
  <ul>
    <li *ngFor="let product of products$ | async">
      {{product.title }}: {{product.price | currency}}
    </li>
  </ul>
  `})
export class AppComponent implements OnInit{
  products$: Observable<Product[]>;

  constructor(private httpClient: HttpClient) {}

  ngOnInit() {
    this.products$ = this.httpClient
                      .get<Product[]>('/data/products.json');
  }
}
```

- Imports Observable from the RxJS library
- Iterates through the observable products and autosubscribes to them with the async pipe
- Renders the product title and the price formatted as currency
- Declares a typed observable for products
- Injects the HttpClient service
- Makes an HTTP GET request specifying the type of the expected data

The observable returned by `get()` will be unwrapped in the template by the `async` pipe, and each product's title and price will be rendered by the following code:

```
<li *ngFor="let product of products$ | async">
  {{product.title }}: {{product.price | currency}} 1((CO17-1))
</li>
```

`*ngFor` is an Angular structural directive that iterates through every item emitted by the `products$` observable and renders the `<li>` element. Each element will show the product title and price using binding. The dollar sign at the end of `products$` is just a naming convention for variables that represent observables.

To see this app in action, run `npm install` in the client directory, and then run the following command:

```
ng serve -o
```

11.7 Getting started with forms

HTML provides basic features for displaying forms, validating entered values, and submitting data to the server. But HTML forms may not be good enough for real-world applications, which need a way to programmatically process the entered data, apply custom validation rules, display user-friendly error messages, transform the format of the entered data, and choose the way data is submitted to the server.

Angular offers two APIs for handling forms:

- *Template-driven API*—With the template-driven API, forms are fully programmed in the component's template using directives, and the model object is created implicitly by Angular. Because you're limited to the HTML syntax while defining the form, the template-driven approach suits only simple forms.
- *Reactive API*—With the reactive API, you explicitly create the model object in the TypeScript code, and then link the HTML template elements to that model's properties using special directives. You construct the form model object explicitly using the `FormControl`, `FormGroup`, and `FormArray` classes.

For nontrivial forms, the reactive approach is a better option. In this section, we'll give you a brief overview of using reactive forms, which will also be used in our blockchain app.

To enable reactive forms, you need to add `ReactiveFormsModule` from `@angular/forms` to the `imports` list of the `@NgModule()` decorator, as follows.

Listing 11.20 Adding support for reactive forms

```
import { ReactiveFormsModule } from '@angular/forms';

@NgModule({
  ...
  imports: [
    ...
    ReactiveFormsModule        <-- Importing the module that supports reactive forms
  ],
  ...
})
```

Now let's look at creating a form model, which is a data structure that holds the form's data. It can be constructed out of `FormControl`, `FormGroup`, and `FormArray` classes. For example, the following listing declares a class property of type `FormGroup` and initializes it with a new object that will contain instances of the form controls for your form.

Listing 11.21 Creating a form model object

```
myFormModel: FormGroup;

  constructor() {
    this.myFormModel = new FormGroup({     <-- Creates an instance of the form model
      username: new FormControl(''),       | Adds form controls
      ssn: new FormControl('')             | to the form model
    });
  }
```

`FormControl` is an atomic form unit, which typically corresponds to a single `<input>` element, but it can also represent a more complex UI component like a calendar or a slider. A `FormControl` instance stores the current value of the HTML element it corresponds to, the element's validity status, and whether it's been modified.

Here's how you can create a control and pass its initial value as the first argument of the constructor:

```
city = new FormControl('New York');
```

You can also create a `FormControl` and attach one or more built-in or custom validators, which can be attached to a form control or to the entire form. The following listing shows how you can add two built-in Angular validators to a form control.

Listing 11.22 Adding validators to a form control

```
city = new FormControl('New York',
                  [Validators.required,
                   Validators.minLength(2)]);
```

- Creates a form control with an initial value of New York
- Adds a required validator to a form control
- Adds a minLength validator to a form control

`FormGroup` is a collection of `FormControl` objects, and it represents either the entire form or a part. `FormGroup` aggregates the values and validity of each `FormControl` in the group. If one of the controls in a group is invalid, the entire group becomes invalid.

The injectable `FormBuilder` service is one way of creating form models. Its API is terser and saves you from the repetitive instantiation of new `FormControl` objects as in listing 11.21. In the following listing, Angular injects the `FormBuilder` object that's used to declare the form model.

Listing 11.23 Creating a `formModel` with `FormBuilder`

```
constructor(fb: FormBuilder) {
  this.myFormModel = fb.group({
    username: [''],
    ssn: [''],
    passwordsGroup: fb.group({
      password: [''],
      pconfirm': ['']
    })
  });
}
```

- Injects the FormBuilder service
- FormBuilder.group() creates a FormGroup using a configuration object passed to it.
- Each FormControl is instantiated using an array that may contain an initial control's value and its validators.
- Like FormGroup, FormBuilder allows you to create nested groups.

The `FormBuilder.group()` method accepts an object with extra configuration parameters as the last argument. You can use it to specify group-level validators there if needed.

The reactive approach requires you to use directives in the component templates. These directives are prefixed with `form`, such as `formGroup` (note the small `f`) as in the following listing.

Listing 11.24 Binding `FormGroup` to the HTML `form` tag

```
@Component({
  selector: 'app-root',
  template: `
    <form [formGroup]="myFormModel">      <- Binds the instance of the form model to the formGroup directive of the <form>
    </form>
  `
})
class AppComponent {
  myFormModel = new FormGroup({       <- Creates an instance of the form model
                username: new FormControl(''),
                ssn: new FormControl('')
              });
}
```

The reactive directives `formGroup` and `formControl` bind DOM elements like `<form>` and `<input>` to the model object (such as `myFormModel`) using the property-binding syntax with square brackets:

```
<form [formGroup]="myFormModel">
   ...
 </form>
```

The directives that link DOM elements to the TypeScript model's properties by name are `formGroupName`, `formControlName`, and `formArrayName`. They can only be used inside an HTML element marked with the `formGroup` directive.

The `formGroup` directive binds an instance of the `FormGroup` class that represents the entire form model to a top-level form's DOM element, usually a `<form>`. In the component template, use `formGroup` (with a lowercase `f`), and in TypeScript, create an instance of the class `FormGroup` (with a capital `F`).

The `formControlName` directive must be used in the scope of the `formGroup` directive. It links an individual `FormControl` instance to a DOM element. Let's continue adding code to the example of the `dateRange` model from the previous section. The component and form model remain the same. You only need to add HTML elements with the `formControlName` directive to complete the template.

Listing 11.25 Completed form template

```
<form [formGroup]="myFormModel">
  <div formGroupName="dateRange">
    <input type="date" formControlName="from">    <- from is a property name in the model's dateRange nested group.
    <input type="date" formControlName="to">      <- to is a property name in the model's dateRange nested group.
  </div>
</form>
```

As in the `formGroupName` directive, you specify the name of a `FormControl` you want to link to the DOM element. Again, these are the names you chose while defining the form model.

The `formControl` directive is used with individual form controls or single-control forms. It's useful when you don't want to create a form model with `FormGroup` but still want to use Forms API features, like validation and the reactive behavior provided by the `FormControl.valueChanges` property, which is of type `Observable` (that is, you can subscribe to `valueChanges` and receive the form field's data each time the user enters a character there).

The following code snippet looks up the weather in the city entered on the form and then prints it on the console.

Listing 11.26 A weather component that uses `FormControl`

```
@Component({
    ...
    template: `<input type="text" [formControl]="weatherControl">`
})
class FormComponent {
  weatherControl: FormControl = new FormControl();

  constructor() {
    this.weatherControl.valueChanges
        .pipe(
          switchMap(city => this.getWeather(city))
        )
        .subscribe(weather => console.log(weather));
  }
}
```

- Uses formControl with the property binding
- Instead of defining a form model, creates a standalone instance of a FormControl
- Uses the valueChanges observable to get the value from the form
- Uses the RxJS operator to switch to another observable returned by getWeather()
- Subscribes to valueChanges and prints the weather received from this observable

RxJS comes with dozens of operators that can be applied to the data item emitted by the observable before it's given to the `subscribe()` method. Without going into details, we'll just say that in the preceding code snippet, the `getWeather()` method makes an HTTP request to the weather server and returns an observable. The `switchMap` operator takes the data from the `valueChanges` observable and passes them to `getWeather()`, which also returns an observable.

In chapter 12, we'll use the reactive Forms API in the `AppComponent` class for handling the form with the blockchain transactions:

```
this.transactionForm = fb.group({
  sender    : ['', Validators.required],
  recipient: ['', Validators.required],
  amount    : ['', Validators.required]
});
```

This code will render a form with three input controls: `sender`, `recipient`, and `amount`. Each of these controls will get an empty string as its initial value and will have `Validators.required` attached to it.

11.8 Router basics

In a single-page application (SPA), the web page won't be reloaded, but its parts may change. We want to add navigation to an application like this, so that it will change the content area of the page based on the user's actions. The Angular router allows you to configure and implement such navigation without performing a full page reload.

The landing page of a SPA will have some parts that always stay on the page, whereas some other parts will render different components based on user actions or other events. Figure 11.8 shows a sample web page where the navigation bar on top, the search panel on the left, and the footer will always be rendered on the page. But the large area marked with the `<router-outlet>` tag is where different components can be rendered, one at a time. Initially, the router outlet could display `HomeComponent`, and when the user clicks on a link, the router could show `ProductComponent` there.

Every application has one router object, and to arrange navigation you need to configure the routes of your app. Angular includes many classes supporting navigation,

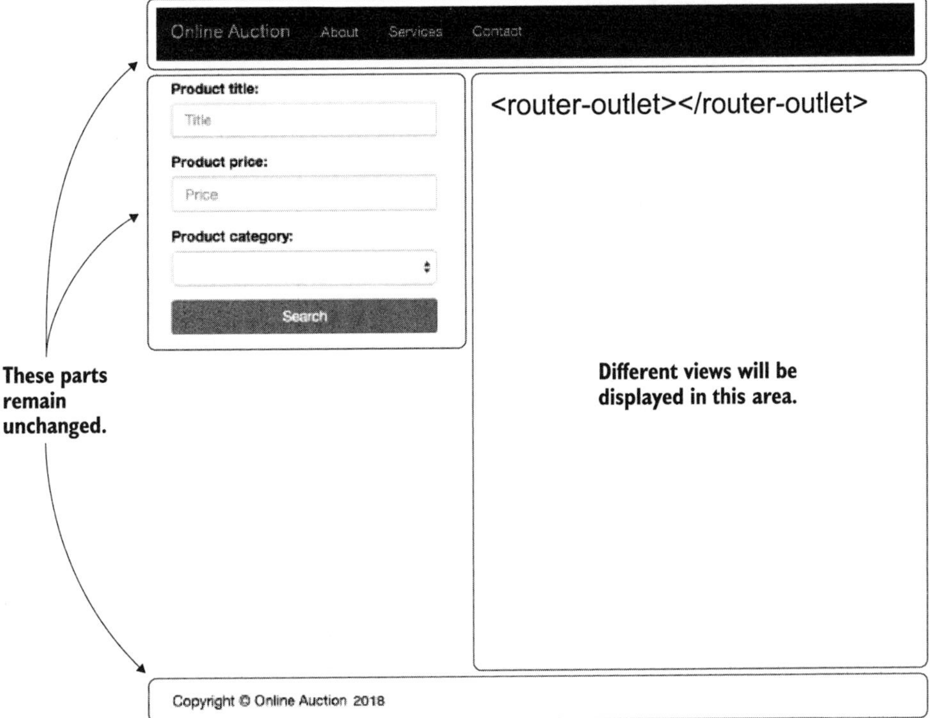

Figure 11.8 A page with the `router-outlet` area

such as Router, Route, Routes, ActivatedRoute, and others. You configure routes in an array of objects of type Route.

Listing 11.27 A sample routes configuration

```
const routes: Routes = [
    {path: '',        component: HomeComponent},
    {path: 'product', component: ProductDetailComponent}
];
```

An empty path indicates that the HomeComponent is rendered by default.

If the URL contains the product segment, render ProductDetailComponent.

Because routes configuration is done on the module level, you need to let the app module know about the routes in the @NgModule() decorator. If you declare routes for the root module, use the forRoot() method as in the following listing.

Listing 11.28 Letting the root module know about the routes

```
import { BrowserModule } from '@angular/platform-browser';
import { RouterModule } from '@angular/router';
...
@NgModule({
  imports: [BrowserModule,
            RouterModule.forRoot(routes)],
    ...
})
```

Create a router module and a service for the app root module.

Let's review a simple app located in the router directory. We generated it using the command ng new router --minimal. When it asked, "Would you like to add Angular routing?", we selected the "Yes" option, and CLI generated the app-routing.module.ts file.

The AppComponent has two links, Home and Product, at the top of the page. The application renders either HomeComponent or ProductDetailComponent depending on which link the user clicks. HomeComponent renders the text "Home Component," and ProductDetailComponent renders "Product Detail Component." Initially the web page displays HomeComponent, as shown in figure 11.9.

After the user clicks the Product link, the router should display ProductDetailComponent, as shown in figure 11.10. See what the URLs for these routes look like in figures 11.9 and 11.10.

Figure 11.9 Rendering HomeComponent

Figure 11.10 Rendering ProductDetailComponent

The main goal of this basic app is to become familiar with the router, so the components are very simple. The following listing shows the code of `HomeComponent`.

Listing 11.29 home.component.ts: the `HomeComponent` class

```
import {Component} from '@angular/core';

@Component({
    selector: 'home',
    template: '<h1 class="home">Home Component</h1>',
    styles: ['.home {background: red}']})
export class HomeComponent {}
```

Renders this component with a red background

The code of `ProductDetailComponent` looks similar, as you can see in the following listing, but it uses a cyan background.

Listing 11.30 product-detail.component.ts: the `ProductDetailComponent` class

```
import {Component} from '@angular/core';

@Component({
    selector: 'product',
    template: '<h1 class="product">Product Detail Component</h1>',
    styles: ['.product {background: cyan}']})
export class ProductDetailComponent {}
```

Renders this component with a cyan background

Angular CLI generated a separate module for routing in the app-routing.module.ts file. The root module will import the configured `RouterModule` from this file, shown in the following listing. We pass to the `forRoot()` method a config object with declared routes. In this use, just two properties are defined in the `Routes` interface: `path` and `component`.

Listing 11.31 app-routing.module.ts: a module with configured routes

```
import { NgModule } from '@angular/core';
import { Routes, RouterModule } from '@angular/router';
import { HomeComponent } from './home.component';
import { ProductDetailComponent } from './product-detail.component';

const routes: Routes = [
  { path: '',        component: HomeComponent },
  { path: 'product', component: ProductDetailComponent }
];

@NgModule({
  imports: [RouterModule.forRoot(routes)],
  exports: [RouterModule]  )
})
export class AppRoutingModule { }
```

HomeComponent is mapped to a path containing an empty string, which makes it the default route.

If the URL has the product segment, renders ProductDetailComponent in the router outlet

Makes routes available in RouterModule

Exports the configured RouterModule so it can be imported by the root module

The next step is to create a root component that will contain the links for navigating between the Home and Product views.

Listing 11.32 app.component.ts: the top-level component

```
import {Component} from '@angular/core';

@Component({
    selector: 'app-root',
    template: `
      <a [routerLink]="['/']">Home</a>
      <a [routerLink]="['/product']">Product Details</a>
      <router-outlet></router-outlet>
    `
})
export class AppComponent {}
```

- Creates a link that binds routerLink to the empty path
- Creates a link that binds routerLink to the /product path
- <router-outlet> specifies the area on the page where the router will render the components (one at a time).

The square brackets around `routerLink` denote property binding, whereas the brackets to the right on the same line represent an array with one element (for example, `['/']`). The second anchor tag has the `routerLink` property bound to the component configured for the `/product` path.

The path is provided as an array because it may include parameters that are passed during the navigation. For example, `['/product', 123]` could instruct the router to go to the component that will render information about the product with the ID 123. The matched components will be rendered in the area marked with `<router-outlet>`, which in this app is located below the anchor tags. None of the components are aware of the router configuration, because it's done at the module level, as shown in the following listing.

Listing 11.33 app.module.ts: the root module

```
...
@NgModule({
  declarations: [
    AppComponent, HomeComponent, ProductDetailComponent
  ],
  imports: [
    BrowserModule,
    AppRoutingModule
  ],
  bootstrap: [AppComponent]
})
export class AppModule { }
```

- Declares components that belong to this module
- Imports the module with preconfigured routes

To run the app described in this section, install dependencies by running `npm install` in the directory router. Then the `ng serve -o` command will start the server and open the browser at localhost:4200. The browser will render the window shown earlier in figure 11.8.

We just showed you a very basic app that uses Angular's router, but it offers a lot more features:

- Passing parameters during navigation
- Subscribing to changing parameters of the parent component
- Guarding (protecting) routes: applying business logic that may prevent the user from navigating to the routes
- Lazy loading of modules during navigation
- The ability to define more than one router outlet in a component

Angular is a very solid solution for developing single-page apps, and the router plays a main role in client-side navigation.

This concludes our brief introduction to the Angular framework. It won't make you an Angular expert, but you'll be ready to read and understand the code of the new version of the blockchain client presented in chapter 12.

Due to space limitations, we didn't explain the principles of reactive programming supported by the RxJS library, which is included in Angular. We didn't show you Angular Material—a set of modern-looking UI components. These topics are explained in our 500-page book, *Angular Development with TypeScript*, second edition (Manning, 2018).

Summary

- Angular is a framework that has everything needed for developing single-page apps. It includes a router and supports dependency injection, working with forms, and much more.
- With the help of Angular CLI, you can generate your first Angular app in about a minute. This app will be fully configured and runnable.
- Angular uses TypeScript decorators for various reasons, such as declaring components, declaring injectable services, declaring input and output properties.
- Angular CLI comes with a build tool that allows you to build optimized bundles for production or non-optimized ones for dev mode.
- Angular itself was written in TypeScript, which is also a recommended language for developing web apps with this framework.

12 Developing the blockchain client in Angular

This chapter covers

- Reviewing the code of the blockchain web client in Angular
- How to run an Angular client that communicates with a WebSocket server

In this chapter, we'll review a new version of the blockchain app, where the client portion is written in Angular. The source code is located in two directories: client and server. But these are two different projects now, with separate package.json files, whereas in chapter 10, these directories were part of the same project. In real-world apps, the front- and backend apps typically are separate projects.

The code of the messaging server is the same as in chapter 10, and the functionality of this version of the blockchain app is the same as well. The only difference is that the implementation of the frontend was completely rewritten in Angular. Let's see this app in action.

> **TIP** You may want to review chapter 10 to refresh your memory of the functionality of the blockchain client and messaging server.

12.1 Launching the Angular blockchain app

The code of this app consists of the messaging server and the web client. To start the server, open the terminal window in the server directory, run `npm install` to install the server's dependencies, and then run the `npm start` command. You'll see the message "Listening on http://localhost:3000." Keep the server running while you start the client.

To start the Angular client, open another terminal window in the client directory, run `npm install` to install Angular and its dependencies, and then run the `npm start` command. In the client's package.json, the `start` command is an alias to a familiar `ng serve` command. It'll build the bundles the same way as in every app reviewed in chapter 11, and you can open the browser to localhost:4200.

At this point, you'll have two servers running: the dev server that was installed by Angular CLI and the WebSocket messaging server that runs under Node.js, as seen in figure 12.1.

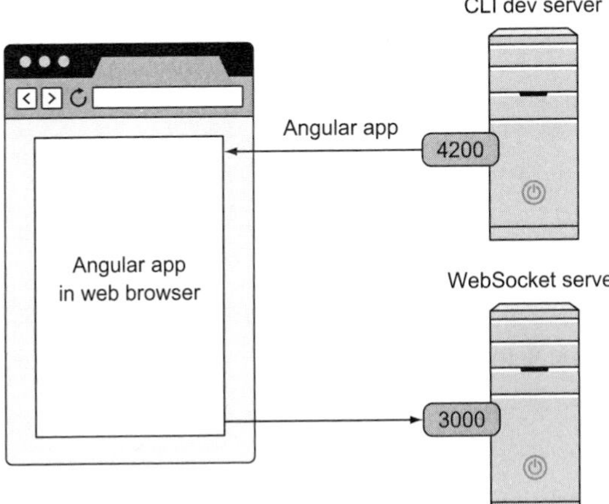

Figure 12.1 One app, two servers

If instead of the WebSocket server you were running an HTTP server, you'd have to configure a proxy to overcome the restrictions imposed by the same origin policy. You can read more about proxying to a backend server in the Angular documentation at http://mng.bz/nvl2.

> **NOTE** If you had to deploy this app in production, you'd need a WebServer that would host the bundles of the blockchain client, and you'd run the WebSocket server on the same port too. You can build the optimized bundles for deployment by running the command `ng build --prod`. The process of deployment is described in the Angular documentation at https://angular.io/guide/deployment.

The app will spend some time generating the genesis block, and then you'll see a familiar window, as shown in figure 12.2.

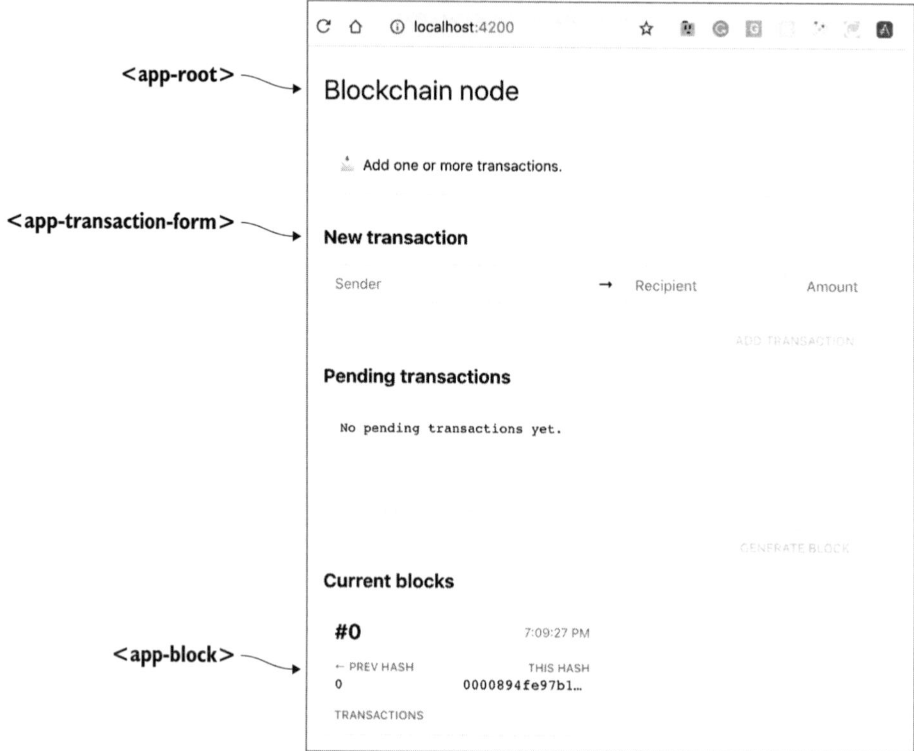

Figure 12.2 Running the blockchain client written in Angular

This app has three components:

- `AppComponent`—The top level component; its selector is `app-root`.
- `TransactionFormComponent`—The component that renders transactions. Its selector is `app-transaction-form`, and this component is a form containing three input fields and the ADD TRANSACTION button.
- `BlockComponent`—The component that renders the block data; its selector is `app-block`.

The structure of the Angular project is shown in figure 12.3, and the arrows point to the files or directories where you'll find the source code of the blockchain client.

The files representing `BlockComponent` are located in the block directory. The files of the `TransactionFormComponent` are in the transaction-form directory. The shared directory contains the reusable services `BlockchainNodeService`, `CryptoService`, and `WebsocketService`.

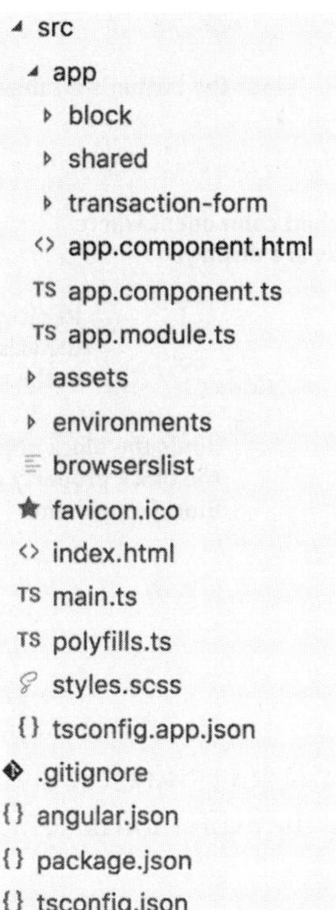

Figure 12.3 Angular project structure

12.2 Reviewing AppComponent

We won't be reviewing the code specific to the blockchain functionality, because we already did that in chapters 8–10. Here, we'll review only the code that shows how things are done in Angular.

The code for the root component is located in two files: app.component.html and app.component.ts. The following listing shows the template of the top-level component.

Listing 12.1 The template of `AppComponent`: app.component.html

```
<main>
  <h1>Blockchain node</h1>
  <aside><p>{{ statusLine }}</p></aside>
  <section>
    <app-transaction-form></app-transaction-form>
  </section>
  <section>
    <h2>Pending transactions</h2>
    <pre class="pending-transactions__list">{{ formattedTransactions }}</pre>
    <div class="pending-transactions__form">
      <button type="button"
          class="ripple"
          (click)="generateBlock()"
```

The child component where the user enters transactions (annotation on the `<app-transaction-form>` line)

Adds the click event handler for the button that generated blocks

```
        [disabled]="node.noPendingTransactions || node.isMining">    <-- Binds the button's disabled attribute
        GENERATE BLOCK
      </button>
    </div>
    <div class="clear"></div>
  </section>
  <section>
    <h2>Current blocks</h2>
    <div class="blocks">
      <div class="blocks__ribbon">
        <app-block                                                    <-- The child component where blocks are displayed
          *ngFor="let blk of node.chain; let i = index"               <-- Iterates through the existing blocks in the chain
                  [block]="blk"                                        <-- Binds the block object to the block property of the BlockComponent
                  [index]="i">                                         <-- Binds the iterator's index to the BlockComponent's input property
        </app-block>
      </div>
      <div class="blocks__overlay"></div>
    </div>
  </section>
</main>
```

In this template, we use data binding three times:

- In listing 12.1, the `disable` property of the GENERATE BLOCK button will be either `true` or `false`, depending on the value of the expression `node.noPendingTransactions || node.isMining`.
- The `block` property of the `<app-block>` component gets a value from the current `blk` as the `ngFor` directive iterates through the `node.chain` array, which is a property of the `AppComponent` class (shown in listings 12.2, 12.3, and 12.4).
- The `index` property of the `<app-block>` component gets a value from the `index` variable offered by the `ngFor` directive. This value represents the current value of the loop iterator.

The line `(click)="generateBlock()"` declares the event handler for the click event. In Angular templates you use parentheses to specify an event handler.

The template in listing 12.1 is included in the `@Component()` decorator of the `AppComponent` TypeScript class. Its first part is shown in the following listing.

Listing 12.2 The first part of app.component.ts

```
import {Component} from '@angular/core';
import {Message, MessageTypes} from './shared/messages';
import {Block, BlockchainNodeService, formatTransactions, Transaction,
➥ WebsocketService}
        from './shared/services';    <-- Uses the directory services (not a file) in the import statement

@Component({
  selector: 'app-root',
  templateUrl: './app.component.html',
})
export class AppComponent {
```

```
constructor(private readonly server: WebsocketService,
            readonly node: BlockchainNodeService) {
  this.server.messageReceived.subscribe(message =>
                this.handleServerMessages(message));
  this.initializeBlockchain();
}

private async initializeBlockchain() {
  const blocks = await this.server.requestLongestChain();
  if (blocks.length > 0) {
    this.node.initializeWith(blocks);
  } else {
    await this.node.initializeWithGenesisBlock();
  }
}
```

Injects two services

Subscribes to service messages

Creates an instance of the blockchain

Revisit the template of the app component in listing 12.1; if the user clicks on the GENERATE BLOCK button, it will invoke the `generateBlock()` method declared in the `AppComponent` TypeScript class. The following listing shows several methods from the `AppComponent` class.

Listing 12.3 The second part of app.component.ts

```
get statusLine(): string {
    return (
      this.node.chainIsEmpty           ? '⌛ Initializing the blockchain...' :
      this.node.isMining               ? '⌛ Mining a new block...' :
      this.node.noPendingTransactions ? '✉ Add one or more transactions.' :
                                         '✅ Ready to mine a new block.'
    );
  }

  get formattedTransactions() {
    return this.node.hasPendingTransactions
      ? formatTransactions(this.node.pendingTransactions)
      : 'No pending transactions yet.';
  }

  async generateBlock(): Promise<void> {
     this.server.requestNewBlock(this.node.pendingTransactions)
    const miningProcessIsDone =
➥ this.node.mineBlockWith(this.node.pendingTransactions);

    const newBlock = await miningProcessIsDone;
    this.addBlock(newBlock);
  };

  private async addBlock(block: Block, notifyOthers = true): Promise<void> {
    try {
      await this.node.addBlock(block);
      if (notifyOthers) {
        this.server.announceNewBlock(block);
      }
```

The click event handler for the GENERATE BLOCK button

This function attempts to add the new block to the blockchain.

The new block was accepted by the blockchain.

```
    } catch (error) {
      console.log(error.message);
    }
  }
```

The new block was rejected by the blockchain.

Note how using the `async` and `await` keywords allows us to write code that looks as if it's being executed synchronously, even though every function call prepended with `await` is an asynchronous execution.

Organizing imports with index.ts

Note that the `AppComponent` class imports several classes specifying the name of the directory instead of having several import statements pointing at different files. This is possible because we introduced a special index.ts TypeScript file in the shared/services directory. The content of index.ts is shown in the following snippet:

```
export * from './blockchain-node.service';
export * from './crypto.service';
export * from './websocket.service';
```

In this file, we re-export all the members exported from the three files listed in this file. If a directory includes a file named index.ts, you can simplify your import statements by just using the directory name, and tsc will find the members for imports in the files included in index.ts:

```
import {Block, BlockchainNodeService, formatTransactions, Transaction,
  ➥ WebsocketService}
        from './shared/services';
```

Without this index.ts file, we'd need to write five import statements pointing at different files.

The third part of the code in app.component.ts, in the following listing, shows the methods in the `AppComponent` class that handle server messages pushed over the WebSocket. They handle the longest chain requests and new block requests. This functionality was explained in chapter 10.

Listing 12.4 The third part of app.component.ts

```
handleServerMessages(message: Message) {
    switch (message.type) {
      case MessageTypes.GetLongestChainRequest: return
➥ this.handleGetLongestChainRequest(message);
      case MessageTypes.NewBlockRequest       : return
➥ this.handleNewBlockRequest(message);
      case MessageTypes.NewBlockAnnouncement  : return
➥ this.handleNewBlockAnnouncement(message);
      default: {
        console.log(`Received message of unknown type: "${message.type}"`);
```

Handles WebSocket server's messages

```
      }
    }
  }
                                                          Handles the longest
                                                               chain requests
  private handleGetLongestChainRequest(message: Message): void {  <-
    this.server.send({
      type: MessageTypes.GetLongestChainResponse,
      correlationId: message.correlationId,
      payload: this.node.chain
    });
  }

  private async handleNewBlockRequest(message: Message): Promise<void> {
    const transactions = message.payload as Transaction[];
    const newBlock = await this.node.mineBlockWith(transactions);
    this.addBlock(newBlock);
  }                                                    Handles the new block
                                                              announcement
  private async handleNewBlockAnnouncement(message: Message): Promise<void> {<-
    const newBlock = message.payload as Block;
    this.addBlock(newBlock, false);
  }
}
```

Revisit the AppComponent template shown in listing 12.1, and you'll find the reference to the <app-transaction-form> child component. We'll review that component next.

12.3 Reviewing TransactionFormComponent

The template of AppComponent hosts two child components: TransactionFormComponent and BlockComponent. The template of TransactionFormComponent is a three-control form with an ADD TRANSACTION button, as shown in the next listing. We took a regular HTML <form> tag and added to it the [formGroup]="transactionForm" directive to enable the reactive forms API offered by Angular.

Listing 12.5 transaction-form.component.html: TransactionFormComponent's UI

```
Binds the transactionForm class property
to the Angular formGroup directive
  <h2>New transaction</h2>
  <form class="add-transaction-form"                   Invokes enqueueTransaction()
->      [formGroup]="transactionForm"                  when the Submit button is
        (ngSubmit)="enqueueTransaction()">        <-   clicked
    <input type="text"
           name="sender"
           autocomplete="off"
           placeholder="Sender"
           formControlName="sender">     <-  The name of the
                                             corresponding property
    <span class="hidden-xs">•</span>         in the form model

    <input type="text"
           name="recipient"
```

```
         autocomplete="off"
         placeholder="Recipient"
         formControlName="recipient">    <-- The name of the corresponding property in the form model

  <input type="number"
         name="amount"
         autocomplete="off"
         placeholder="Amount"
         formControlName="amount">

  <button type="submit"
          class="ripple"
          [disabled]="transactionForm.invalid || node.isMining">    <-- Uses property binding to conditionally disable the Submit button
          ADD TRANSACTION
  </button>
</form>
```

In section 11.7, we gave you a brief intro to Angular reactive forms, and listing 12.5 uses the directives of this API as well. Note that we start by binding the `transactionForm` model object (defined in the `BlockComponent` class) to the `formGroup` attribute. Also, each form control has a `formControlName` attribute, which corresponds to the `transactionForm` object's property with the same name. The code of the `TransactionFormComponent` is shown in the following listing.

Listing 12.6 transaction-form.component.ts: `TransactionFormComponent` class

```
import { Component } from '@angular/core';
import { FormBuilder, FormGroup, Validators } from '@angular/forms';
import { BlockchainNodeService } from '../shared/services';

@Component({
  selector: 'app-transaction-form',
  templateUrl: './transaction-form.component.html'
})
export class TransactionFormComponent {
  readonly transactionForm: FormGroup;

  constructor(readonly node: BlockchainNodeService,
                         fb: FormBuilder) {    <-- Injects services
    this.transactionForm = fb.group({    <-- Declares the transactionForm model object
      sender   : ['', Validators.required],
      recipient: ['', Validators.required],
      amount   : ['', Validators.required]    <-- Each form control has the required validator attached and no initial value.
    });
  }

  enqueueTransaction() {    <-- This method is invoked when you add a new transaction to the list of pending ones.
    if (this.transactionForm.valid) {
      this.node.addTransaction(this.transactionForm.value);
      this.transactionForm.reset();
    }
  }
}
```

Once again, revisit the template of the AppComponent, shown in listing 12.1, and you'll see a *ngFor loop that renders the <app-block> child components. We'll review that next.

12.4 Reviewing the BlockComponent

BlockComponent is responsible for rendering one block, and its template is shown in the following listing. This template is pretty straightforward; it contains a bunch of <div> and <span> tags, and the Block properties are inserted using binding, represented by double curly braces.

Listing 12.7 block.component.html: BlockComponent's UI

```
<div class="block">
  <div class="block__header">
    <span class="block__index">#{{ index }}</span>
    <span class="block__timestamp">{{ block.timestamp |
➥ date:'mediumTime' }}</span>
  </div>
  <div class="block__hashes">
    <div class="block__hash">
      <div class="block__label">• PREV HASH</div>
      <div class="block__hash-value">{{ block.previousHash }}</div>
    </div>
    <div class="block__hash">
      <div class="block__label">THIS HASH</div>
      <div class="block__hash-value">{{ block.hash }}</div>
    </div>
  </div>
  <div>
    <div class="block__label">TRANSACTIONS</div>
    <pre class="block__transactions">{{ formattedTransactions }}</pre>
  </div>
</div>
```

Inserts the values of the Block property in the template

Inserts the formatted transactions

At the top of the template, we used the date pipe to format the date, block.timestamp | date:'mediumTime', which will render the date in the form h:mm:ssa. The rendered block is shown in figure 12.4. You can read about the date pipe in the Angular documentation at https://angular.io/api/common/DatePipe.

Figure 12.4 A block rendered in the browser

The BlockComponent TypeScript class is shown in the next listing. It's a presentation component that just receives values from its parent and displays them. No application logic is applied here.

Listing 12.8 block.component.ts: the BlockComponent class

```
import { Component, Input } from '@angular/core';
import { Block, formatTransactions } from '../shared/services';

@Component({
  selector: 'app-block',
  templateUrl: './block.component.html'
})
export class BlockComponent {
  @Input() index: number;          // Gets the index from the parent component
  @Input() block: Block;           // Gets the Block from the parent component

  get formattedTransactions(): string {
    return formatTransactions(this.block.transactions);   // Formats transactions using the function from the blockchain-node.service.ts file
  }
}
```

Once more, let's revisit listing 12.1 where the parent component's template uses the `*ngFor` directive to loop through all the blocks in the blockchain and pass data to the each `BlockComponent` instance, as shown again here.

Listing 12.9 A fragment from app.component.html

```
<app-block
   *ngFor="let blk of node.chain; let i = index"
    [block]="blk" [index]="i">
</app-block>
```

The instance of the block object (`blk`) and the current index (`i`) are passed to the `BlockComponent` instance via bindings through the `@Input()` properties. The user sees the values of `block` and `index` as shown in figure 12.4.

Any Angular component can receive data from its parent using properties marked with the `@Input()` decorator, and our `BlockComponent` has two such properties. The preceding code snippet may look a little confusing, so let's imagine that a parent component needs to display just one block. The following listing shows how such a parent could pass data to `BlockComponent`.

Listing 12.10 A parent passing data to a child

```
@Component({
  selector: 'app-parent',
  template: ` Meet my child
  <app-block
         [block]="blk"               // Binds the value of blk to the block property of the child
         [index]="blockNumber">      // Binds the value of blockNumber to the index property of the child
  </app-block>

  `

})
```

```
export class ParentComponent {
  blk: Block =
      { hash: "00005b1692f26",
              nonce: 2634,
              previousHash: "0000734b922d",
              timestamp: 25342683;
              transactions: ["John to Mary $100",
                             "Alex to Nina $400"];
      };

  blockNumber: 123;
}
```

Initializes the values in the parent

TIP The child can pass data to the parent via the properties marked with the `@Output()` decorator. You can read about that in Yakov Fain's blog "Angular 2: Component communication with events vs callbacks" at http://mng.bz/vlQ4.

So far we've been reviewing the components (classes with UIs) of our blockchain app. Now let's review the services (classes with app logic).

12.5 Reviewing services

In chapter 10, the blockchain app came with the class `WebsocketController`, which was instantiated with the `new` keyword. Here, the same functionality is wrapped into a service instantiated and injected by Angular. In this project, services are located in the shared/services directory.

The following listing shows a fragment of the `WebsocketService` responsible for all communications with our WebSocket server.

Listing 12.11 A fragment from websocket.service.ts

```
interface PromiseExecutor<T> {
  resolve: (value?: T | PromiseLike<T>) => void;
  reject: (reason?: any) => void;
}

@Injectable({
  providedIn: 'root'
})
export class WebsocketService {
  private websocket: Promise<WebSocket>;
  private readonly messagesAwaitingReply = new Map<UUID,
➥ PromiseExecutor<Message>>();
  private readonly _messageReceived = new Subject<Message>();

  get messageReceived(): Observable<Message> {
    return this._messageReceived.asObservable();
  }

  constructor(private readonly crypto: CryptoService) {
    this.websocket = this.connect();
  }
```

- PromiseExecutor knows which client waits for the response.
- This service is a singleton available to all components and other services.
- Creates an instance of the RxJS Subject
- Gets the observable portion of the Subject
- Connects to the WebSocket server

```
  private get url(): string {
    const protocol = window.location.protocol === 'https:' ? 'wss' : 'ws';
    const hostname = environment.wsHostname;          <-- Gets the URL of
    return `${protocol}://${hostname}`;                   the server from the
  }                                                       environment variable

  private connect(): Promise<WebSocket> {
    return new Promise((resolve, reject) => {
      const ws = new WebSocket(this.url);
      ws.addEventListener('open', () => resolve(ws));
      ws.addEventListener('error', err => reject(err));
      ws.addEventListener('message', this.onMessageReceived);
    });
  }
```

TIP The `PromiseExecutor` type was introduced in listing 10.26.

The `WebsocketService` object is injected into the `AppComponent`:

```
export class AppComponent {
   constructor(private readonly server: WebsocketService,
               readonly node: BlockchainNodeService) {
this.server.messageReceived.subscribe(message =>
                   this.handleServerMessages(message));
 ...
   }
 ...
}
```

The `AppComponent` subscribes to and handles messages coming from the server or sends messages to the server, such as requesting the longest chain or announcing a new block.

The `WebsocketService` service gets the URL of the WebSocket server from the `environment.wsHostname` environment variable, which is defined in each of the files located in the environments directory of the project. Since our client starts in dev mode (`ng serve`), it uses the setting from the environments.ts file, shown in the following listing.

Listing 12.12 The environments/environment.ts file

```
export const environment = {
  production: false,            <-- The code runs in dev mode.
  wsHostname: 'localhost:3000'  <-- This is the URL for the
};                                  dev WebSocket server.
```

RxJS: Observable, Observer, and Subject

The RxJS library offers different ways of handling streams of data. If you have an instance of an `Observable` object, you can invoke `subscribe()` on it, providing the `Observer` instance knows what to do with the data. Every time the `Observable` emits new data, the `Observer` will process it.

The RxJS `Subject` encapsulates an `Observable` and `Observer`. One `Subject` can have multiple observers, and each of them represents one subscriber. To broadcast the data to all subscribers, we invoke the `next(someData)` method on the `Subject`. To subscribe to the data, we invoke `subscribe()` on the `Subject`.

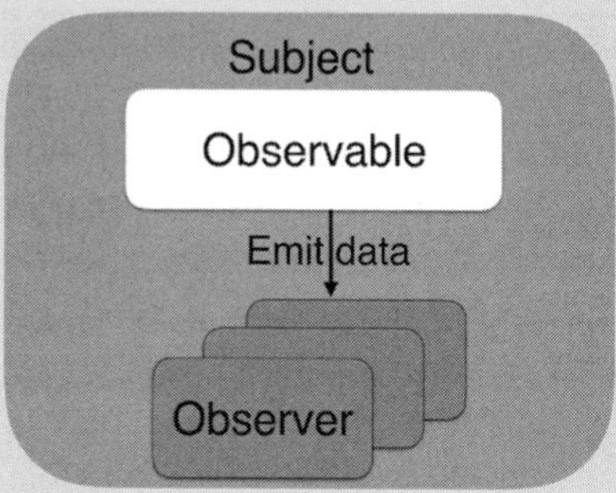

Broadcasting with the RxJS Subject

The following code snippet creates one `Subject` instance and two subscribers. In the last line, the code emits `123`, and each subscriber will get this value.

```
const mySubject = new Subject();     <— Creates a Subject
...
const subscription1 = mySubject.subscribe(...);?     <— Creates the first subscriber
const subscription2 = mySubject.subscribe(...);?     <— Creates the second subscriber
...
?mySubject.next(123);     <— Broadcasts 123 to subscribers
```

If you want to restrict a piece of code so it can only subscribe (but not emit) to the subject, give this code only the observable portion of the `Subject` using the `asObservable()` method, as shown in the `messageReceived` getter in listing 12.11.

If you started the client with `ng serve --prod` or built the files with `ng build --prod`, your app would use the environment.prod.ts file, which can have a different value of `wsHostname`.

The shared/services directory also has the following files:

- *blockchain-node.service.ts*—This code creates a block. In the app from chapter 10, this functionality was implemented in the blockchain-node.ts file.
- *crypto.service.ts*—This file has the `sha256()` method, which knows how to calculate the hash value.

This concludes our code review of the Angular version of the blockchain client app.

> **NOTE** If you like Angular's syntax for developing the client side of a web app, take a look at the server-side framework called NestJS (see https://github.com/nestjs). It runs under Node.js and its syntax will look very familiar to any Angular developer. Nest.js supports TypeScript, it comes with the CLI tool, and it even has a TypeORM module that allows you to work with relational databases from server-side TypeScript.

Summary

- In dev mode, we usually run Angular apps with two web servers: one that serves the data, and the other that serves the web app. The latter comes with the Angular framework.
- Typically, all communication with the server is implemented in services that are injected into components. In our blockchain client, the web client implements communication with the WebSocket server in the `WebSocketService` TypeScript class.
- The `Subject` RxJS class offers broadcasting capabilities, which in our blockchain app are used for sending messages to multiple blockchain nodes.

13 Developing React.js apps with TypeScript

This chapter covers

- A quick intro to the React.js library
- How React components use props and state
- How React components communicate with each other

The React.js library (a.k.a. React) was created by a Facebook engineer, Jordan Walke, in 2013, and today it has 1,300 contributors and 140,000 stars on GitHub! According to the Stack Overflow Developer Survey of 2019, it's the second-most popular JavaScript library (jQuery remains the most broadly used library). React is not a framework but a library responsible for rendering views in the browser (think of the letter V in the MVC design pattern). In this chapter, we'll show you how to start developing web apps in React using TypeScript.

The main players in React are components, and the UI of a web app consists of components having parent-child relations. But where Angular takes control of the entire root element of the web page, React allows you to control a smaller page element (such as a `<div>`) even if the rest of the page is implemented with another framework or in pure JavaScript.

You can develop React apps either in JavaScript or in TypeScript and deploy them using tools like Babel and Webpack (described in chapter 6). Without further ado, let's start by writing the simplest version of the Hello World app using React and JavaScript; we'll switch to TypeScript in section 13.2.

13.1 Developing the simplest web page with React

In this section, we'll show you two versions of a simple web page written with React and JavaScript. Each of these pages renders "Hello World," but the first version will use React with no additional tooling; the second version will engage Babel.

In real-world apps, a React app is a project with configured dependencies, tools, and a build process, but to keep things simple, our first web page will just have a single HTML file that loads the React library from CDN. This version of the Hello World page is located in the hello-world-simplest/index.html file, and its content is shown in the following listing.

Listing 13.1 hello-world-simplest/index.html: the Hello World app

```
<!DOCTYPE html>
<html>
   <head>
     <meta charset="utf-8">
     <script
       crossorigin src="https://unpkg.com/react@16/umd/react.development.js">    <- Loads the React package from CDN
     </script>
     <script
       crossorigin src="https://unpkg.com/react-dom@16/umd/
       react-dom.development.js">    <- Loads the ReactDOM package from CDN
     </script>
   </head>
   <body>
     <div id="root"></div>    <- Adds the <div> with the id "root"

     <script >
         const element = React.createElement('h1',    <- Creates the <h1> element using the createElement function
                                             null,    <- We don't pass any data (a props object) to the <h1> element.
                                             'Hello World');    <- The text of the <h1> element
          ReactDOM.render(element,
                          document.getElementById('root'));    <- Renders the <h1> inside the <div>
       </script>

   </body>
</html>
```

The processes of declaring the page content (`React.createElement()`) and rendering it to the browser's DOM (`ReactDOM.render()`) are decoupled. The former is supported by the `React` object's API, whereas the latter is done by `ReactDOM`. That's why we loaded those two packages in the <head> section of the page.

In React, UI elements are represented as a tree of components that always has a single root element. This web page has a `<div>` with the ID `root` that serves as such an element for the content rendered by React. In the script in listing 13.1, we prepare the element to be rendered using `React.createElement()`, and then we invoke `ReactDOM.render()`, which finds the element with the `root` ID and renders it in this element.

> **TIP** In Chrome, right-click on the Hello World web page and select the Inspect menu option. It will open the dev tools showing the `<div>` with the `<h1>` element inside.

The `createElement()` method has three arguments: the name of the HTML element, its *props* (immutable data to be passed to the element), and content. In this case, we didn't need to provide any props (think *attributes*) and used `null` here; we'll explain what props are for in section 13.4.3. The content of `h1` is "Hello World," but it can contain child elements (such as a `ul` with nested `li` elements), which could be created with the nested `createElement()` calls.

Open the index.html file in your browser, and it will render the text "Hello World" as shown in figure 13.1.

Figure 13.1 Rendering the hello-world-simplest/index.html file

Invoking `createElement()` on a page that has only one element is fine, but for a page that has dozens of elements, this would be tedious and annoying. React allows you to embed the UI markup into JavaScript code, which looks like HTML but is JSX, as we'll discuss in the "JSX and TSX" sidebar a little later in this chapter.

Let's see what our Hello World page could look like if we used JSX. Note the line `const myElement = <h1>Hello World</h1>` in the following listing—we use it instead of invoking `createElement()`.

Listing 13.2 index_jsx.html: a JSX version of Hello World

```
<!DOCTYPE html>
  <head>
    <meta charset="utf-8">
    <script
       src="https://unpkg.com/react@16/umd/react.development.js"></script>
    <script
       src="https://unpkg.com/react-dom@16/umd/
➥ react-dom.development.js"></script>

    <script src="https://unpkg.com/babel-standalone/
➥ babel.min.js"></script>                  ⟵ Adds Babel from CDN
  </head>
  <body>
    <div id="root"></div>
     <script type="text/babel">             ⟵ The type of the script is text/babel.
```

```
        const myElement = <h1>Hello World</h1>;     <— Assigns a JSX value
                                                        to a variable
        ReactDOM.render(          <— Initiates the rendering of myElement to the <div>
              myElement,
              document.getElementById('root')
        );

        console.log(myElement);    <— Monitors the JavaScript
      </script>                        object that was rendered

  </body>
</html>
```

This app renders the same page you saw in figure 13.1, but it's written differently. The JavaScript code has an embedded `<h1>Hello World!</h1>` string that looks like HTML, but it's actually JSX. Browsers can't parse this, so we need a tool to turn JSX into a valid JavaScript. Babel to the rescue!

The `<head>` section in listing 13.2 has an additional `<script>` tag that loads Babel from a CDN. Also, we changed the type of the script to `text/babel`, which makes browsers ignore it but tells Babel to transform the content of this `<script>` tag into JavaScript.

> **NOTE** In a real-world project we wouldn't use CDN to add Babel to a Node-based project (as we did in listing 13.2), but it suffices for demo purposes. In Node-based apps, Babel would be installed locally in the project, and it would be a part of the build process.

Figure 13.2 shows a screenshot with the browser's console open. Babel converted the JSX value to a JavaScript object that was rendered inside the `<div>`, and we printed this object in the console.

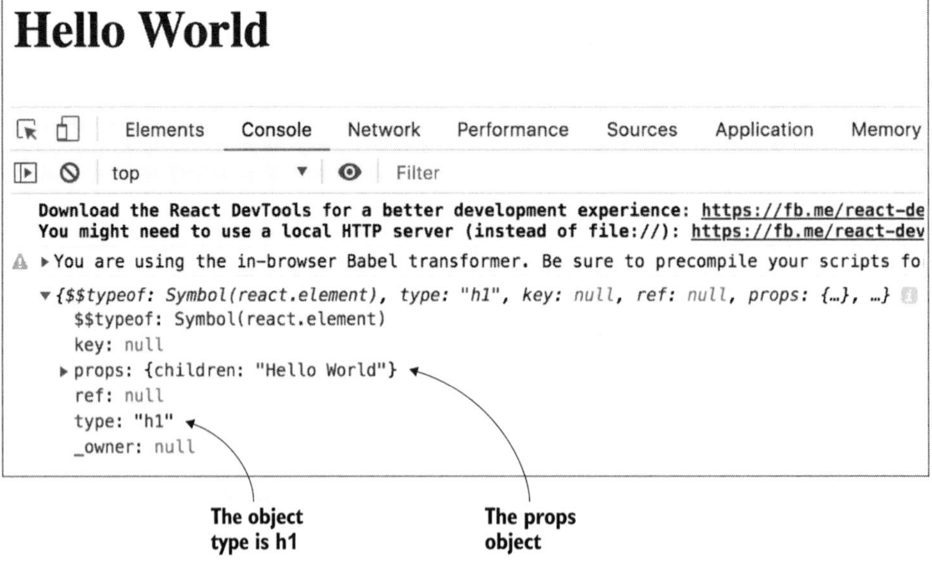

Figure 13.2 The rendered JavaScript object

Now that you have a fair understanding of how very basic pages use React, we'll switch to Node-based projects and component-based apps. Let's see some tooling that React developers use in the real world.

13.2 Generating and running a new app with Create React App

If you want to create a React app that includes a transpiler and a bundler, you'll need to add configuration files to your app. This process is automated by the command-line interface (CLI) called Create React App (see www.npmjs.com/package/create-react-app). This tool generates all the required configuration files for Babel and Webpack, so you can concentrate on writing your app instead of wasting time configuring the tooling. To install the create-react-app package globally on your computer, run the following command in the terminal window:

```
npm install create-react-app -g
```

Now you can generate either a JavaScript or a TypeScript version of the app. To generate the TypeScript app, run the command `create-react-app` followed by the app name and the `--typescript` option:

```
create-react-app hello-world --typescript
```

In a minute or so, all required files will be generated in the hello-world directory, and the project dependencies will be installed. In particular, it installs the following React packages:

- *react*—A JavaScript library for creating user interfaces
- *react-dom*—The React package for working with the DOM
- *react-scripts*—Scripts and configurations used by Create React App; for TypeScript support, you need react-scripts version 2.1 or higher

Besides the preceding packages, the CLI installs Webpack, Babel, TypeScript, their type definition files, and other dependencies.

To launch the generated web app, switch to the hello-world directory and run `npm start`, which in turn runs `react-scripts start`. Webpack will bundle the app, and webpack-dev-server will serve the app on localhost:3000, as shown in figure 13.3. This functionality is provided by the Webpack DevServer.

TIP For bundling, Webpack uses the config options from the webpack.config.js file located in the node_modules/react-scripts/config directory.

Figure 13.3 Running the hello-world app

The UI of the generated app tells us to edit the src/App.tsx file, which is the main TypeScript file of the generated app. Open the directory in VS Code, and you'll see the project files as shown in figure 13.4.

The source code of your app is located in the src directory, and the public directory is for assets of your app that shouldn't be included in the app bundles. For example, your app has thousands of images and needs to dynamically reference their paths—they go in the public directory, along with other files that don't require any processing before deployment.

The index.html file contains a `<div id="root"></div>` element, which serves as a container for the generated React app. You won't find any `<script>` tags for loading the React library code there; they'll be added during the build process when the app's bundles are ready.

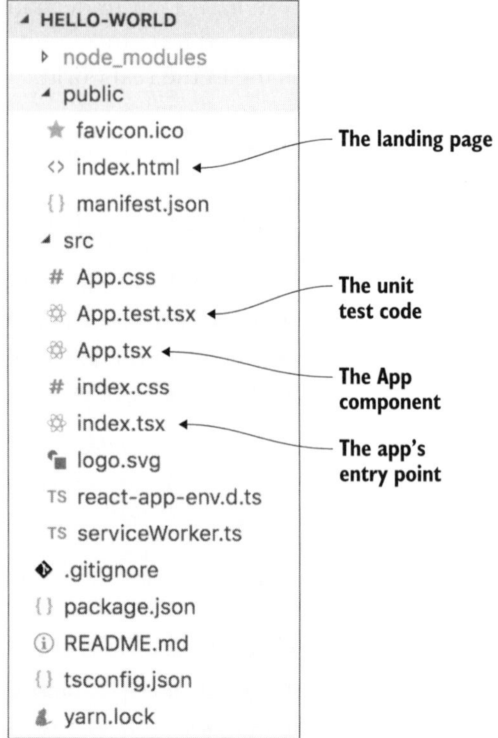

Figure 13.4 The generated files and directories

TIP Run the app and open the Chrome dev tools under the Elements tab to see the runtime content of index.html.

NOTE The serviceWorker.ts file is generated just in case you want to develop a progressive web app (PWA) that can be started offline using cached assets. We won't use it in our sample apps.

As you can see, some of the files have an unusual extension: .tsx. If we were writing the code in JavaScript, the CLI would generate the app file with the extension .jsx (not .tsx). JSX and TSX are explained in the "JSX and TSX" sidebar.

JSX and TSX

The draft of the JSX specification (https://facebook.github.io/jsx) offers the following definition: "JSX is an XML-like syntax extension to ECMAScript without any defined semantics. It's NOT intended to be implemented by engines or browsers."

JSX stands for JavaScript XML. It defines a set of XML tags that can be embedded inside JavaScript code. These tags can be parsed and turned into regular HTML tags for rendering by the browser, and React includes such a parser. In chapter 6, we demonstrated Babel's REPL (https://babeljs.io/repl), and the following figure shows a screenshot of this REPL with some sample JSX.

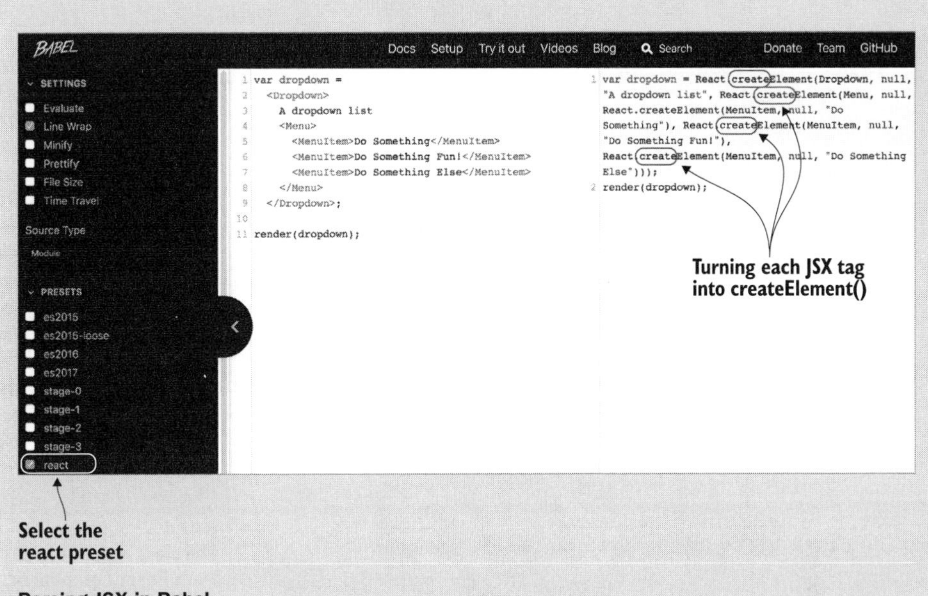

Parsing JSX in Babel

On the left, we selected the React preset and pasted some sample code from the JSX spec. This preset specifies that we want to turn each JSX tag into a `React.createElement()` invocation. The sample code should render a dropdown menu containing three items. On the right, you can see how the JSX was parsed into JavaScript.

Every React app has at least one component, the *root component*, and our generated app has only the root component `App`. The file with the `App` function code has the extension .tsx, which tells the Typescript compiler that it contains JSX. But just having the .tsx extension is not enough for tsc to handle it: you need to enable JSX by adding the `jsx` compiler option. Open the tsconfig.json file, and you'll find the following line:

```
"jsx": "preserve"
```

The `jsx` option only affects the emit stage—type checking is unaffected. The `preserve` value tells tsc to copy the JSX portion into the output file, changing its extension to .jsx, because there will be another process (such as Babel) parsing it. If that value was `react`, tsc would turn the JSX tags to `React.createElement()` invocations, as seen in the previous image on the right.

A React component can be declared either as a function or a class. A functional (function-based) component is implemented as a function and is structured as follows (types are omitted).

Listing 13.3 A functional component

```
const MyComponent = (props) => {     <-- props is used to pass data to the components.

  return (
    <div>...</div>     <-- Returns the component's JSX
  )

  // other functions may go here
}

export default MyComponent;
```

Developers who prefer working with classes can create class-based components, which are implemented as subclasses of `React.Component`. They are structured like the following example.

Listing 13.4 A class-based component

```
class MyComponent extends React.Component {     <-- The class must inherit from React.Component.

  render() {     <-- The render() method is invoked by React.
    return (     <-- Returns JSX for rendering
      <div>...</div>
    );
  }

  // other methods may go here
}

export default MyComponent;
```

A functional component simply returns JSX, but a class-based component has to include the `render()` method, which returns JSX. We prefer using functional components, which have several benefits over class-based ones:

- A function requires less code to write, and there is no need to inherit the component's code from any class.
- A functional component generates less code during Babel compiling, and code minifiers better infer unused code and can shorten variables names more aggressively since all of them are local to the function, unlike class members, which are considered a public API and cannot be renamed.
- Functional components have no need for the `this` reference.
- Functions are easier to test than classes; assertions simply map props to the returned JSX.

NOTE You should use class-based components only if you have to use a React version older than 16.8. In those older versions, only class-based components will support state and life cycle methods.

If you use the current version of Create React App with the `--typescript` option, the generated App.tsx file file will already include the boilerplate code for a functional component (a function of type `React.FC`), as shown in the following listing.

Listing 13.5 The App.tsx file

```
import React from 'react';                     // Imports the React library
import logo from './logo.svg';
import './App.css';

const App: React.FC = () => {                  // Specifies a functional component
  return (                                     // Returns the component's template as a JSX expression (it's not a string)
    <div className="App">                      // In JSX, use className instead of the "class" CSS selector to avoid conflicts with the JavaScript "class" keyword.
      <header className="App-header">
        <img src={logo} className="App-logo" alt="logo" />
        <p>
          Edit <code>src/App.tsx</code> and save to reload.
        </p>
        <a
          className="App-link"
          href="https://reactjs.org"
          target="_blank"
          rel="noopener noreferrer"
        >
          Learn React
        </a>
      </header>
    </div>
  );
}

export default App;                            // Exports the App component declaration so it can be used in other modules
```

NOTE We used version 3.0 of Create React App. Older versions of this tool would generate a class-based `App` component.

The generated `App` function returns the markup (or template) that React uses to render this component's UI, shown earlier in figure 13.3. During the build process, Babel will convert the markup into a pure JavaScript object, `JSX.element`, with a `<div>` container that will update the Virtual DOM and the browser's DOM (we'll discuss Virtual DOM in section 13.5). This `App` component didn't have a separate place for storing its data (its state), so we'll add that in the next section.

13.3 Managing a component's state

A component's state is a datastore that contains data that should be rendered by the component. The data in the component's `state` is preserved even if React re-renders the component. If you have a Search component, its state could store the last search criteria and the last search result. Whenever the code updates the component's state,

React updates the component's UI to reflect changes caused by the user's actions (such as button clicks or typing in input fields) or other events.

NOTE Do not confuse an individual component's state with the application's state. The application state stores data that may come from multiple components, functions, or classes.

How can you define and update the component's state? This depends on how the component was created in the first place. We're going to move back to class-based components for a minute so that you can understand the difference in dealing with state in class-based and functional components. Then we'll return to functional components, which we recommend using.

13.3.1 Adding state to a class-based component

If you have to work with a class-based component, you can define a type representing the state, create and initialize an object of this type, and then update it as needed by invoking `this.setState(…)`.

Let's consider a simple class-based component that has a state object with two properties: the user name and the image to be displayed. To serve images, we'll use the Lorem Picsum website, which returns random images of a specified size. For example, if you enter the URL https://picsum.photos/600/150, the browser will show a random image with a width of 600 px and a height of 150 px. The following listing shows such a class-based component with a two-property state object.

Listing 13.6 A class-based component with state

```
interface State {                    ◁─ Defines the type for the
  userName: string;                     component's state
  imageUrl: string;
}
+
export default class App extends Component {

  state: State = { userName: 'John',              ◁─ Initializes the State object
           imageUrl: 'https://picsum.photos/600/150' };

  render() {
    return (
      <div>
        <h1>{this.state.userName}</h1>          ◁─ Renders the userName here
        <img src={this.state.imageUrl} alt=""/>  ◁─ Renders the imageUrl here
       </div
    );
  }
}
```

Based on the code of the `render()` method, you can probably guess that this component will render "John" and an image. Note that we embedded the values of the state properties into JSX by placing them inside curly braces: `{this.state.userName}`.

Any class-based component is inherited from the `Component` class, which has a `state` property and the `setState()` method. If you need to change the value of any state property, you must do it using this method:

```
this.setState({userName: "Mary"});
```

By invoking `setState()`, you let React know that a UI update may be required. If you update the state directly (such as with `this.state.userName='Mary'`), React won't call the `render()` method to update the UI. As you might have guessed, the `state` property is declared on the base class `Component`.

In section 13.2, we listed the benefits of functional components over class-based ones, and we won't use class-based components any longer. In functional components, we manage state by using *hooks*, which were introduced in React 16.8.

13.3.2 Using hooks to manage state in functional components

In general, hooks allow you to "attach" behavior to a functional component without the need to write classes, create wrappers, or use inheritance. It's as if you said to a functional component, "I want you to have additional functionality while remaining a plain old function."

The names of hooks must start with the word "use"—this is how Babel detects them and distinguishes them from regular functions. For example, `useState()` is the hook for managing the component's state, and `useEffect()` is used to add a side-effect behavior (such as fetching data from a server). In this section, we'll focus on the `useState()` hook, using the same example as in the previous section: a component whose state is represented by a user name and an image URL, but this time it'll be a functional component.

The `useState()` hook can create a primitive value or a complex object and preserve it between the functional component invocations. The following line shows how you can define a state for the user name.

```
const [userName, setUserName] = useState('John');
```

The `useState()` function returns a pair: the current state value and a function that lets you update it. Do you remember the syntax for array destructuring introduced in ECMAScript 6? (If not, take a look at section A.8.2 in the appendix.) The preceding line means that the `useState()` hook takes the string `'John'` as an initial value and returns an array, and we use destructuring to get the two elements of this array into two variables: `userName` and `setUserName`. The syntax of array destructuring allows you to give any names to these variables. If you need to update the value of `userName` from "John" to "Mary" and make React update the UI (if needed), you can do it as follows:

```
setUserName('Mary');
```

TIP In your IDE, Cmd-Click or Ctrl-Click on `useState()`, and it will open the type definition of this function, which will declare that the function returns a stateful value and a function to update it. The `useState()` function is not a pure function because it stores the component's state somewhere inside React. It's a function with side effects.

The following listing shows a functional component that stores its state in two primitives, `userName` and `imageUrl`, and displays their values using JSX.

Listing 13.7 A functional component using primitives to store state

```
import React, {useState} from 'react';          <— Imports the useState hook

const App: React.FC = () => {

  const [userName, setUserName] = useState('John');     <— Defines the userName state
  const [imageUrl, setImageUrl] = useState('https://picsum.photos/600/150');  <— Defines the imageUrl state

  return (
    <div>
      <h1>{userName}</h1>          <— Renders the value of the userName state variable
      <img src={imageUrl} alt=""/>   <— Renders the value of the imageUrl state variable
    </div>
  );
}

export default App;
```

Now let's rewrite the preceding component so that instead of two primitives, it declares its state as an object with two properties: `userName` and `imageUrl`. The following listing declares a `State` interface and uses the `useState()` hook to work with the object of type `State`.

Listing 13.8 Using an object to store state

```
import React, {useState} from 'react';

interface State {          <— Defines the type for the component state
  userName: string;
  imageUrl: string;
}

const App: React.FC = () => {

  const [state, setState] = useState<State>({    <— Defines and initializes the state object
    userName: 'John',
    imageUrl: 'https://picsum.photos/600/150'
  });

  return (
    <div>
```

```
      <h1>{state.userName}</h1>                    <-- Renders the value of the userName state property
      <img src={state.imageUrl} alt=""/>           <-- Renders the value of the imageUrl state property
    </div>
  );
}

export default App;
```

Note that `useState()` is a generic function, and during its invocation we provided the concrete type `State`.

The source code of this sample app is located in the hello-world directory. Run the `npm start` command, and the browser will render a window that looks similar to figure 13.5 (the image may be different, though).

Figure 13.5 Rendering a user name and an image

The user name and image are too close to the left border of the window, but that's easy to fix with CSS. The generated app shown in listing 13.5 had a separate app.css file with CSS selectors applied in the component using the `className` attribute (you can't use `class` because it would conflict with the JavaScript's reserved `class` keyword). This time, we'll add a `margin` by declaring a JavaScript object with styles and using it in JSX. In the following listing, we've added the `myStyles` variable and used it in the component's JSX.

Listing 13.9 Adding styles to the component

```
const App: React.FC = () => {

  const [state, setState] = useState<State>({
    userName: 'John',
    imageUrl: 'https://picsum.photos/600/150'
  });

  const myStyles = {margin: 40};   <-- Declares the styles

  return (
```

```
    <div style ={myStyles}>        <—— Applies the styles
      <h1>{state.userName}</h1>
      <img src={state.imageUrl} alt=""/>
    </div>
  );
}
```

Note that the `style` property is strongly typed, which helps in validating CSS properties. This is one of JSX's advantages over plain HTML—JSX will be turned into JavaScript, and TypeScript will add strong typing to HTML and CSS elements via type definition files.

With this margin, the browser will render the `<div>` with an additional 40 px of space around it, as shown in figure 13.6.

Figure 13.6 Adding a margin

Our first React app works and looks good! It has one functional component that stores hardcoded data in the state object and renders that data using JSX. It's a good start, and in the next section, we'll start writing a new app with more functionality.

13.4 Developing a weather app

In this section, we'll develop an app that will let the user enter the name of a city and get the current weather there. We'll develop this app gradually:

1. We'll add an HTML form to the `App` component where the user can enter the name of the city.
2. We'll add code to fetch the real weather data from the weather server, and the `App` component will display the weather.
3. We'll create another component, `WeatherInfo`, which will be a child of the `App` component. The `App` component will retrieve the weather data and will pass it to `WeatherInfo`, which will display the weather.

We'll be getting real weather data from the weather service at http://openweathermap.org, which provides an API for making weather requests for many cities around the world. This service returns the weather information as a JSON-formatted string. For example, to get the current temperature in London in Fahrenheit (`units=imperial`), the URL would look like this: http://api.openweathermap.org/data/2.5/find?q=London&units=imperial&appid=12345. (The creators of this service require you to apply for an application ID, which is a simple process. If you want to run our weather app, apply for one and replace 12345 in the preceding URL with the APPID you receive.)

The sample code for this chapter includes the weather app, located in the weather directory, which was initially generated with the following command:

```
create-react-app weather --typescript
```

Then we replaced the JSX code in the app.tsx file with a simple HTML form where the user could enter the name of the city and press the Get Weather button. Also, the entered city represents the state of this component, and the `App` component will update its state as the user enters the city name.

13.4.1 Adding a state hook to the App component

The first version of our `App` component defines its state with the `useState()` hook as follows:

```
const [city, setCity] = useState('');
```

The value in the `city` variable has to be updated with the `setCity()` function. Our `useState()` hook initializes the `city` variable with an empty string, so TypeScript will infer the type of `city` as `string`. Listing 13.10 shows the `App` component with the declared state, and the form defined in the JSX section. This code also has an event handler, `handleChange()`, which is invoked each time the user enters or updates any character in the input field.

Listing 13.10 The App.tsx file in the weather app

```
import React, { useState, ChangeEvent } from 'react';

const App: React.FC = () => {

  const [city, setCity] = useState('');          <-- Declares the city state

  const handleChange = (event: ChangeEvent<HTMLInputElement>) => {    <-- Declares the function to handle input field events
    setCity(event.target.value);          <-- Updates the state by invoking setCity()
  }

  return (
    <div>
      <form>
```

```
        <input type="text" placeholder="Enter city"
               onChange = {handleChange} />            <—— Assigns the handler to
        <button type="submit">Get weather</button>         the onChange attribute
        <h2>City: {city}</h2>    <—— Displays the current
      </form>                        state value
    </div>
  );
}

export default App;
```

The input field defines the event handler: `onChange = {handleChange}`. Note that we didn't invoke `handleClick()` here; we just provided the name of this function. React's `onChange` behaves as `onInput` and is fired as soon as the content of the input field changes. As soon as the user enters (or changes) a character in the input field, the `handleChange()` function is invoked, which updates the state and thus causes the UI update.

> **TIP** There is no documentation about which types of React events you can use with specific JSX elements. To avoid using `event: any` as the argument in event handler functions, open the index.d.ts file in the node_modules/@types/react directory and search for "Event Handler Types." This should help you figure out that the proper type for the `onChange` event is a generic `ChangeEvent<T>` that takes the type of a specific element as a parameter, such as `ChangeEvent<HTMLInputElement>`.

To illustrate the state updates, we've added an <h2> element that displays the current value of the state: `<h2>Entered city: {city}</h2>`. Note that for re-rendering the current value of `city`, we didn't need to write any jQuery-like code to find the reference to this <h2> element and change its value directly. The invocation of `setCity(event.target.value)` forces React to update the corresponding node in the DOM.

In general, if you need to update a functional component's state, do it only using the appropriate `setXXX()` function that's returned by the `useState()` hook. By invoking `setXXX()`, you let React know that the UI update may be required. If you update the state directly (such as with `city="London"`), React won't update the UI. React may batch the UI updates before reconciling the Virtual DOM with the browser's DOM. Figure 13.7 shows a screenshot taken after the user entered *Londo* in the input field.

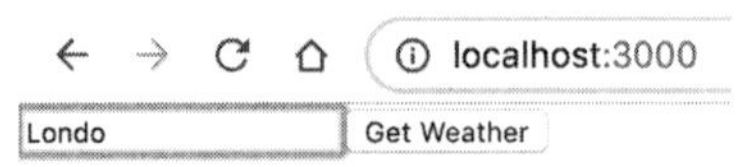

City: Londo

Figure 13.7 After the user entered Londo

> **TIP** To see that React updates only the <h2> node in the DOM, run this app (using `npm start`) with the Chrome dev tools open to the Elements tab. Expand the DOM tree so the content of the <h2> element is visible, and start typing in the input field. You'll see that the browser changes only the content of the <h2> element, while all other elements remain unchanged.

Redux and app state management

The `useState()` hook in functional components (or the `setState()` method in class-based components) is used to store the component's internal data and synchronize that data with the UI, but the entire app may also need to store and maintain data used by multiple components or about the current state of UI (for example, the user selected product X in component Y). In React apps, the most popular state-management JavaScript library is Redux (you could also choose to use MobX, another popular library). Redux is based on the following three principles:

- *Single source of truth*—There is a single *data store*, which contains the state of your app.
- *State is read-only*—When an action is emitted, the *reducer* function clones the current state and updates the cloned object based on the action.
- *State changes are made with pure functions*—Reducer functions take an action and the current state object, and they return a new state.

In Redux, the data flow is unidirectional:

1. The app component dispatches the action on the store.
2. The reducer (a pure function) takes the current state object and then clones, updates, and returns it.
3. The app component subscribes to the store, receives the new state object, and updates the UI accordingly.

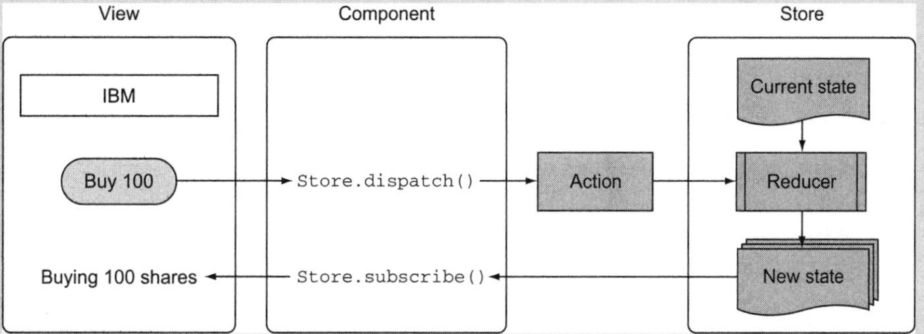

The Redux data flow

The following image shows the unidirectional Redux data flow.

The user clicks on the button to buy 100 shares of IBM stock. The click handler function invokes the `dispatch()` method, emitting an *action*, which is a JavaScript object that has a `type` property describing what happened in your app (for example, the user wants to buy the IBM stock). Besides the `type` property, an action object can optionally have another property with a payload of data to be stored in the app state:

```
{
  type: 'BUY_STOCK',                            <-- The type of action
  stock: {symbol: 'IBM', quantity: 100}         <-- The action's payload
}
```

(continued)

This object only describes the action and provides the payload, but it doesn't know how the state should be changed. Who does? The reducer does—it's a *pure function* that specifies how the app state should be changed. The reducer never changes the current state, but creates a new version and returns a new reference to it. As you can see in the preceding image, the component subscribes to the state changes and updates the UI accordingly.

The reducer function doesn't implement any app logic that requires working with external services (such as placing an order). Reducers just update and return the app state based on the action and its payload, if any. Implementing the app logic would require interacting with the environment outside the reducer, causing side effects, and pure functions can't have side effects. For more details, read the Redux documentation on GitHub at http://mng.bz/QOlv.

Working with the component's state is an internal function of the component. But at some point, the component may need to start working with external data, and this is where the `useEffect()` hook comes in.

13.4.2 Fetching data with the useEffect hook in the App component

You learned how to store the city name in the state of the `App` component, but our ultimate goal is finding the weather in the given city by fetching data from an external server. Using terminology from functional programming, we need to write a function with *side effects*. Unlike *pure functions*, functions with side effects use external data, and every invocation may produce different results even if the function arguments remain the same.

In React's functional components, we'll be using the `useEffect()` hook to implement functionality with side effects. By default, React automatically invokes the callback function passed to `useEffect()` after every DOM rendering. Let's add the following function to the `App` component from listing 13.10:

```
useEffect(() => console.log("useEffect() was invoked"));
```

If you run the app with the browser console open, you'll see the message "useEffect() was invoked" each time you enter a character in the input field and the UI is refreshed. Every React component goes through a set of life cycle events, and if you need your code to be executed after the component is added to the DOM, or each time it is re-rendered, the `useEffect()` hook is the right place for such code. But if you want the code in `useEffect()` to be executed only once, after the initial rendering, specify an empty array as the second argument:

```
useEffect(() => console.log("useEffect() was invoked"), []);
```

The code in the preceding hook will be executed only once, right after the component has been rendered, which makes it a good place to perform the initial data fetch.

Let's assume you live in London and would like to see the weather in London as soon as this app is launched. Start by initializing the `city` state with "London:"

```
const [city, setCity] = useState('London');
```

Now you need to write a function that will fetch the data for the specified city. The URL will include the following static parts (replace `12345` with your APPID).

```
const baseUrl = 'http://api.openweathermap.org/data/2.5/weather?q=';
const suffix = "&units=imperial&appid=12345";
```

In between, you need to place the name of the city, so the complete URL might look like this:

```
baseUrl + 'London' + suffix
```

For making Ajax requests, we'll use the browser's Fetch API (see the Mozilla documentation at http://mng.bz/Xp4a). The `fetch()` function returns a `Promise`, and we'll use the `async` and `await` keywords (see section A.10.4 in the appendix) in our `getWeather()` method.

Listing 13.11 Fetching the weather data

```
const getWeather = async (city: string) => {
  const response = await fetch(baseUrl + city + suffix);   <-- Makes an async call to the weather server
  const jsonWeather = await response.json();   <-- Converts the response to JSON format
  console.log(jsonWeather);   <-- Prints the weather JSON on the console
}
```

NOTE We prefer using the `async` and `await` keywords for asynchronous code, but using promises with chained `.then()` invocations would also work here.

When you use a standard browser's `fetch()` method, getting the data is a two-step process: you get the response first, and then you call the `json()` function on the response object to get to the actual data.

TIP JavaScript developers often use third-party libraries for handling HTTP requests. One of the most popular ones is a promise-based library called Axios (www.npmjs.com/package/axios).

Now you can use this function for the initial data fetch in `useEffect()`:

```
useEffect( () => getWeather(city), []);
```

If you want the code in `useEffect()` to be executed only if a specific state variable changes, you can attach the hook to that state variable. For example, you could specify that `useEffect()` should run only if the `city` is updated:

```
useEffect(() => console.log("useEffect() was invoked"),
                ['city']);
```

The current version of the `App` component is shown in the following listing.

Listing 13.12 Fetching the London weather in `useEffect()`

```
import React, { useState, useEffect, ChangeEvent } from 'react';

const baseUrl = 'http://api.openweathermap.org/data/2.5/weather?q=';
const suffix = "&units=imperial&appid=12345";

const App: React.FC = () => {

 const [city, setCity] = useState('London');

 const getWeather = async (city: string) => {     ◁ Asynchronously fetches weather data for the specified city
      const response = await fetch(baseUrl + city + suffix);
      const jsonWeather = await response.json();
      console.log(jsonWeather);
  }

  useEffect( { () => getWeather(city) }, []);     ◁ An empty array means run this hook once.

 const handleChange = (event: ChangeEvent<HTMLInputElement>) => {
    setCity( event.target.value );          ◁ Updates the state
}

  return (
    <div>
      <form>
        <input type="text" placeholder="Enter city"
               onInput = {handleChange} />
        <button type="submit">Get Weather</button>
        <h2>City: {city}</h2>
      </form>
    </div>
  );
}

export default App;
```

The second argument of `useEffect()` is an empty array, so `getWeather()` will be invoked only once, when the `App` component is initially rendered.

NOTE If you run this app, the browser's console will show the following warning: "React Hook useEffect has a missing dependency: 'city'. Either include it or remove the dependency array react-hooks/exhaustive-deps." That's because inside this hook we use the state variable `city`, which is a dependency and should be listed in the array. This is not an error, and for simplicity, we'll keep this code as-is, but you should keep this in mind while designing your hooks.

TIP For in-depth coverage of the `useEffect()` hook, read "A complete guide to useEffect," by Dan Abramov, available on his *Overreacted* blog at https://overreacted.io/a-complete-guide-to-useeffect.

Run this app with the browser console open, and it'll print the retrieved JSON with the London weather, as shown in figure 13.8.

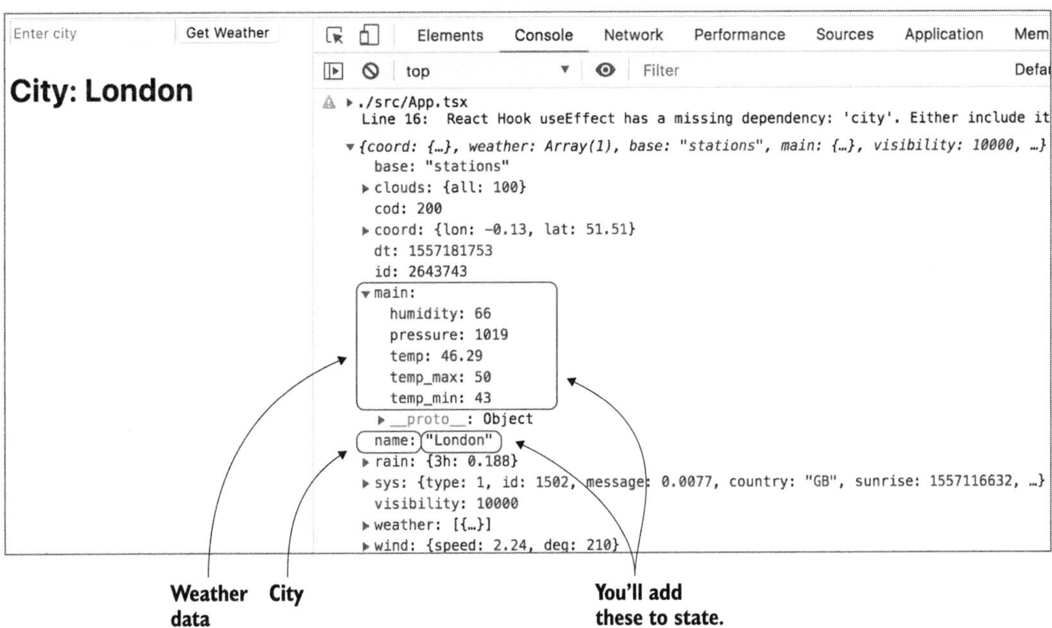

Figure 13.8 The London weather in the console

The initial data fetch for the default city is complete, and it looks like a good idea to store the retrieved weather data in the component's state. Let's define a new `Weather` type for storing the content of the `name` and `main` properties, both marked in figure 13.8.

Listing 13.13 The weather.ts file

```
export interface Weather {
  city: string;
  humidity: number;
  pressure: number;
```

- `city`: This property corresponds to the name property in figure 13.8.
- `humidity`, `pressure`: These values come from the main property in figure 13.8.

```
  temp: number;
  temp_max: number;
  temp_min: number;
}
```

These values come from the main property in figure 13.8.

In the App component, we'll add a new weather state variable and a function to update it, as follows:

```
const [weather, setWeather] = useState<Weather | null>(null);
```

Note that the useState() hook allows you to use a generic parameter for better type safety.

Now we need to update the getWeather() function so it saves the retrieved weather and city name in the component's state.

Listing 13.14 Saving state in getWeather

```
async function getWeather(location: string) {
  const response = await fetch(baseUrl + location + suffix);
  if (response.status === 200){
    const jsonWeather = await response.json();
    const cityTemp: Weather = jsonWeather.main;
    cityTemp.city=jsonWeather.name;
    setWeather(cityTemp);
  } else {
     setWeather(null);
  }
}
```

Stores the content of the main property

Stores the city name

Saves the weather in the component's state

The weather retrieval failed.

This code takes the jsonWeather.main object and the city name from jsonWeather .name, and saves them in the weather state variable.

So far, our getWeather() function has been invoked by the useEffect() hook for the initial retrieval of the London weather. The next step is to add code to invoke getWeather() when the user enters any other city and clicks on the Get Weather button. As you saw in listing 13.12, this button is part of the form (its type is submit), so we'll add an event handler to the <form> tag. The handleSubmit() function and the first version of the JSX are shown in the following listing.

Listing 13.15 Handling the button click

When the Submit button is clicked, the FormEvent is dispatched.

```
const handleSubmit = (event: FormEvent) => {
    event.preventDefault();
    getWeather(city);
  }

return (
```

Prevents the default behavior of the form's submit button

Invokes getWeather() for the entered city

```
    <div>
      <form onSubmit = {handleSubmit}>          <-- Attaches the event
         <input type="text" placeholder="Enter city"    handler to the form
                onInput = {handleChange} />
        <button type="submit">Get Weather</button>
        <h2>City: {city}</h2>
        {weather &&  <h2>Temperature: {weather.temp}F</h2>}   <-- Displays
      </form>                                                     the retrieved
    </div>                                                        temperature
);
```

In React, event handlers get instances of `SyntheticEvent`, which is an enhanced version of the browser's native events (see https://reactjs.org/docs/events.html for details). `SyntheticEvent` has the same interface as the browser's native events (such as `preventDefault()`), but the events work identically across all browsers (unlike native browser events).

To provide the parameter's value to `getWeather(city)`, we don't have to find a reference to the `<input>` field on the UI. The component's `city` state was updated when the user typed the name of the city, so the `city` variable already has its value displayed in the `<input>` field. Figure 13.9 shows a screenshot of the page after a user entered Miami and clicked the Get Weather button.

Figure 13.9 It's hot in Miami.

NOTE In our book *Angular Development with TypeScript*, second edition (Manning, 2018), we also used this weather service. You can find the Angular version of this app on GitHub at http://mng.bz/yzMd.

What if the user enters a city that doesn't exist or that's not supported by openweathermap.org? The server returns 404, and we should add the appropriate error handling. So far we have the following line to prevent displaying the temperature if the `weather` state is falsy:

```
{ weather &&  <h2>Temperature: {weather.temp}F</h2> }
```

In the next version of this app, we'll create a type guard to check if the weather for the provided city was received or not.

For now, let's take a breather and recap what we've done so far, while developing the weather app:

1. Applied for the APPID at openweathermap.org
2. Generated a new app and replaced the JSX with a simple `<form>`.
3. Declared the `city` state using the `useState()` hook.
4. Added the `handleChange()` function that updates `city` on each change in the input field.
5. Added the `useEffect()` hook, which will be invoked only once on app startup.

6 Ensured that `useEffect()` invokes the `getWeather()` function, which uses the `fetch()` API to retrieve the weather in London.
7 Declared the `weather` state to store the retrieved temperature and humidity, which are some of the properties of the retrieved weather object.
8 Added the `handleSubmit()` event handler to invoke `getWeather()` after the user enters the city name and clicks the Get Weather button.
9 Modified the `getWeather()` function to save the retrieved weather in the `weather` state.
10 Displayed the retrieved temperature on the web page under the form.

This is all good, but we shouldn't put all the app logic in one `App` component. In the next section, we'll create a separate component that will be responsible for displaying the weather data.

13.4.3 Using props

A React app is a tree of components, and you need to decide which are going to be the *container* components, and which the *presentation* ones. A container (a.k.a. smart) component contains application logic, communicates with external data providers, and passes data to its child components. Typically, container components are stateful and have little or no markup.

A presentation (a.k.a. dumb) component just receives data from its parent and displays it. A typical presentation component is stateless and has lots of markup. A presentation component gets the data to be displayed via its *props* JavaScript object.

> **TIP** In section 14.4, we'll look at the UI components of the React version of the blockchain app. There you'll see one container component and three presentation components.

> **TIP** If you use a library for managing the state of an entire app (such as Redux), only the container components will communicate with such a library.

In our weather app, `App` is a container component that knows how to receive weather data from the external server. So far our `App` component also displays the received temperature, as shown in figure 13.9, but we should delegate the weather rendering functionality to a separate presentation component, such as `WeatherInfo`. Any app consists of multiple components, and having a separate `WeatherInfo` component will allow us to illustrate how a parent component can send data to its child. Besides, having a separate `WeatherInfo` component that just knows how to display the data passed via props makes it reusable.

The `App` component (the parent) will contain the `WeatherInfo` component (the child), and the parent will need to pass the received weather data to the child. Passing data to a React component works similarly to passing data to HTML elements.

We'll start getting familiar with the role of props by using JSX elements as an example. Any JSX element can be rendered differently depending on the data it gets. For example, the JSX of a red disabled button can look like this:

```
<button className="red" disabled />
```

This code instructs React to create a `button` element and pass it certain values via the `className` and `disabled` attributes. React will start by transforming the preceding JSX into an invocation of `createElement()`:

```
React.createElement("button", {
  className: "red",
  disabled: true
});
```

Then, the preceding code will produce a JavaScript object that looks like this:

```
{
  type: 'button',
  props: { className: "red", disabled: true }
}
```

As you can see, `props` contains the data being passed to the React element. React uses props for data exchange between parent and child components (the previous button was a part of a parent element too).

Suppose you created a custom `Order` component and added it to the parent's JSX. You could pass the data to it via `props` as well. For example, an `Order` component may need to receive the values of such props as `operation`, `product`, and `price`:

```
<Order operation="buy" product="Bicycle" price={187.50} />
```

Similarly, we'll add the `WeatherInfo` component to the `App` component's JSX, passing the received weather data. Also, we promised to add a user-defined type guard to ensure that the `WeatherInfo` component won't render anything if the weather for the city is not available. The following listing shows the code from the `App` component that defines and uses the type guard called `has`.

Listing 13.16 Adding the `has` type guard

```
const has = (value: any): value is boolean => !!value;    ◁ Declares the has type guard

...

return (                    An empty JSX tag can be used as a container.
  <>                   ◁
    <form onSubmit = {handleSubmit}>
      <input type="text" placeholder="Enter city"
             onInput = {handleChange} />
```

```
      <button type="submit">Get Weather</button>
    </form>
    {has(weather) ? (                                  
      <WeatherInfo weather={weather} />
    ) : (
      <h2>No weather available</h2>
    )}
  </>
);
```

Applies the type guard has

Passes the weather to WeatherInfo and renders it

Renders the text message instead of WeatherInfo

Closes the empty JSX tag

As you can see, the `App` component hosts the form and the `WeatherInfo` component, which should render the weather data. All JSX tags have to be wrapped into a single container tag. Earlier, we used `<div>` as a parent tag. In listing 13.16, we use an empty tag instead, which is a shortcut for a special tag container, `<React.Fragment>`, that doesn't add an extra node to the DOM.

In section 2.3, we introduced TypeScript's user-defined type guards. In listing 13.16, we declared the `has` type guard as a function whose return type is a type predicate:

```
const has = (value: any): value is boolean => !!value;
```

It takes a value of `any` type and applies to it the JavaScript double bang operator to check if the provided value is truthy. Now the expression `has(weather)` will check if the weather is received (as you can see in the JSX in listing 13.17). The received weather is given to the `WeatherInfo` component via its `weather` props:

```
<WeatherInfo weather={weather} />
```

Now let's discuss how we created the `WeatherInfo` component that receives and renders the weather data. In VS Code, we created a new weather-info.tsx file and declared the `WeatherInfo` component there. As in the `App` functional component, we used the arrow function notation for `WeatherInfo`, but this time our component accepts an explicit `props`. Hover the mouse over `FC`, and you'll see its declaration, as shown in figure 13.10.

Generic type with default parameter

```
import * as React from 'react';
                        type React.FC<P = {}> = React.FunctionComponent<P>
const WeatherInfo: React.FC = (props) => {
    return (
      <div>

      </div>
    );
}
```

Figure 13.10 A generic type with default parameter

React.FC is a generic type that takes P (for props) as a type parameter. So why didn't the Typescript compiler complain when we declared the App component without using the generic notation and a concrete type? The P = {} part did the trick. This is how you can declare a generic type with a default value (see the sidebar titled "Default values of generic types" in section 4.2.2). Our App component didn't use props, and by default, React assumed that props was an empty object.

Each component has a property called props, which can be an arbitrary JavaScript object with properties specific to your app. In JavaScript you can't specify the type of the props content, but TypeScript generics allow you to let the component know that it's going to get the props containing the Weather, as shown in the following listing.

Listing 13.17 WeatherInfo.tsx: the WeatherInfo functional component

Our component is a generic function with an argument of type Weather.

```
import * as React from 'react';
import {Weather} from './weather';

const WeatherInfo: React.FC<{weather: Weather} >=
  ({ weather }) => {

    const {city, humidity, pressure, temp, temp_max, temp_min} = weather;

    return (
      <div>
        <h2>City: {city}</h2>
        <h2>Temperature: {temp}</h2>
        <h2>Max temperature: {temp_max}</h2>
        <h2>Min temperature: {temp_min}</h2>
        <h2>Humidity: {humidity}</h2>
        <h2>Pressure: {pressure}</h2>
      </div>
    );
}

export default WeatherInfo;
```

The fat arrow function has one argument—the weather object.

Destructures the weather object

Renders the city

Renders the weather data

The WeatherInfo component is a generic function with one parameter, <P>, as shown in figure 13.10, and we used the {weather: Weather} type as its argument. To render the data, we could access each property of the weather object by using dot notation (such as weather.city), but the fastest way to extract the values of these properties into local variables is destructuring (discussed in section A.8 of the appendix) as shown in the following line:

```
const {city, humidity, pressure, temp, temp_max, temp_min} = weather;
```

Now all these variables can be used in the JSX returned by this component; for example, <h2>City: {city}</h2>.

Passing a markup to the child component

`props` can be used not only for passing data to a child component, but also for passing JSX fragments. If you place a JSX fragment between the opening and closing tags of the component, as shown in the following snippet, this content will be stored in the `props.children` property, and you can render it as needed.

```
<WeatherInfo weather = {weather} >
   <strong>Hello from the parent!</strong>
</WeatherInfo>
```

Passes this markup to WeatherInfo

Here, the `App` component passes the HTML element `<strong>Hello from the parent!</strong>` to the `WeatherInfo` child component, and it could have passed any other React component the same way.

The `WeatherInfo` component also has to declare its interest in receiving not only the `Weather` object (shown earlier in listing 13.13), but also the content of `props.children` from `React.FC` as follows:

```
const WeatherInfo: React.FC<{weather: Weather} >=
➥ ({ weather, children }) =>...
```

This line tells React, "We'll give your React.FC component the object with the property `weather`, but we'd like to use the `children` property as well." Now the local `children` variable contains the markup provided by the parent, which can be rendered along with the weather data:

```
return (
   <div>
     {children}
     <h2>City: {city}</h2>
     <h2>Temperature: {temp}</h2>
     { /* The rest of the JSX is omitted */ }
   </div>
 );
```

Renders the markup received from the parent

After embedding the `{children}` expression, the `WeatherInfo` component will be rendered, as follows.

This came from the parent.

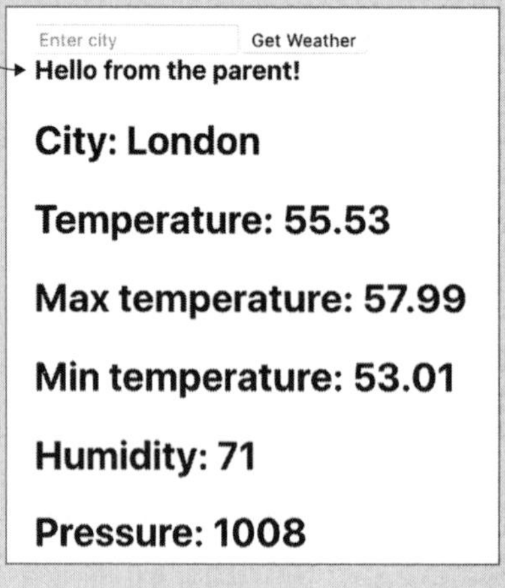

Enter city
Get Weather
Hello from the parent!
City: London
Temperature: 55.53
Max temperature: 57.99
Min temperature: 53.01
Humidity: 71
Pressure: 1008

Displaying the content received via props.children

To visualize the props and state of each component, install the Chrome extension called React Developer Tools and run a React app with the Chrome dev tools open. You'll see an extra React tab that shows rendered elements on the left and the props and state (if any) of every component on the right (figure 13.11). Our `WeatherInfo` component is stateless; otherwise you'd see the content of the state as well.

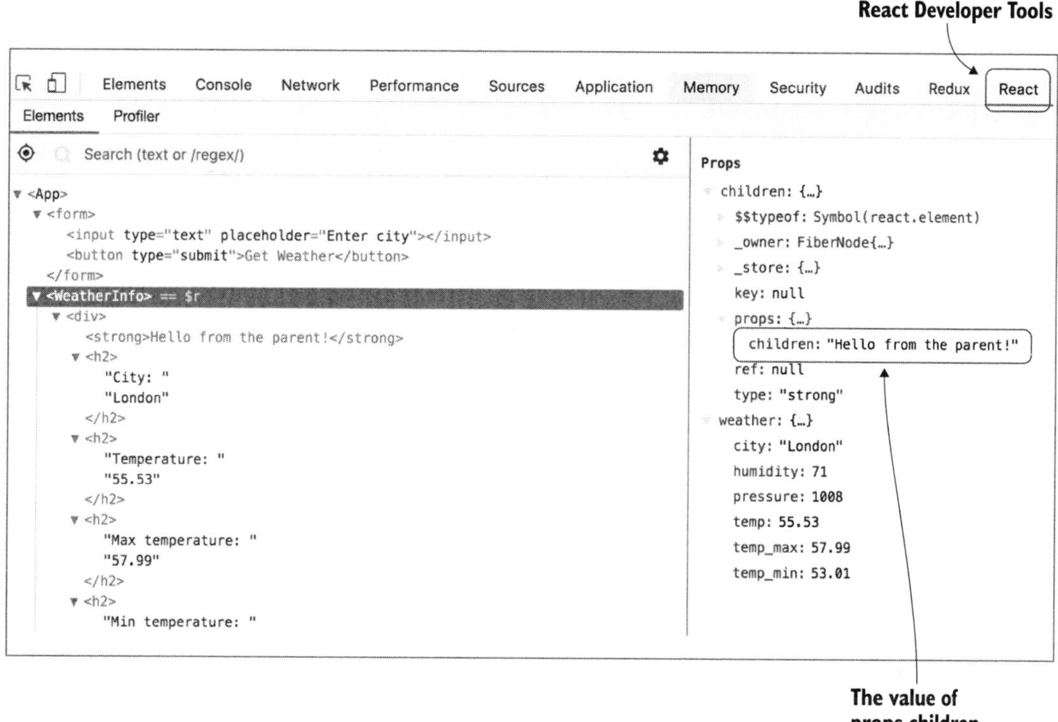

Figure 13.11 React Developer Tools

It's great that a parent component passes data to its child via props, but what about sending data in the opposite direction?

13.4.4 How a child component can pass data to its parent

There are scenarios when a child component needs to send data to its parent, and this is also done via props. Imagine a child component that's connected to a stock exchange, and it receives the latest stock prices every second. If its parent is responsible for handling that data, the child needs to be able to pass the data to its parent.

For simplicity, we'll just illustrate how the `WeatherInfo` component could send some text to its parent. This will require some coding on both the parent's and the child's ends. Let's start with the parent.

If a parent expects to get some data from the child, it has to declare a function that knows how to handle this data. Then, in the parent's JSX where it embeds the child component, we add an attribute to the child's tag containing a reference to this function. In the weather app, the `App` component is the parent, and we want it to be able to receive text messages from its child, `WeatherInfo`. The following listing shows what we need to add to the code of the `App` component developed in the previous section.

Listing 13.18 Adding code to the `App` component for receiving data

```
const [msgFromChild, setMsgFromChild] = useState('');     // Declares the msgFromChild state variable to store the child's message

const getMsgFromChild = (msg: string) => setMsgFromChild(msg);     // Declares the function to store the child's message in the msgFromChild state

return (
<>
  /* The rest of the JSX is omitted */

  {msgFromChild}          // Displays the child's message
  {has(weather) ? (
    <WeatherInfo weather = {weather} parentChannel = {getMsgFromChild}>     // Adds the parentChannel property to the child
</>
```

Here we added the `msgFromChild` state variable to store the message received from the child. The `getMsgFromChild()` function gets the message and updates the state using the `setMsgFromChild()` function, which results in re-rendering `{msgFromChild}` in the UI of the `App` component.

Finally, we need to give the child a reference for invoking the message handler. We decided to call this reference `parentChannel`, and we passed it to `WeatherInfo` as follows:

```
parentChannel = {getMsgFromChild}
```

`parentChannel` is an arbitrary name that the child will use to invoke the `getMsgFromChild()` message handler.

The modifications to the parent's code are complete, so let's take care of the `WeatherInfo` child component. The following listing shows the additions to the child's code.

Listing 13.19 Adding code to `WeatherInfo` for sending data to parent

```
const WeatherInfo: React.FC<{weather: Weather, parentChannel:
   (msg: string) => void}> =          // Adds parentChannel to the type of the generic function
  ({weather, children, parentChannel}) => {     // Adds parentChannel to the function argument
```

```
/* The rest of the WebInfo code is omitted */

return (
<div>
   <button
     onClick ={() => parentChannel ("Hello from child!")}>     ⊲ Invokes the parent's function on the button click, using parentChannel as a reference
     Say hello to parent
   </button>

/* The rest of the JSX code is omitted */
</div>
);
```

Since the parent gives the child the `parentChannel` reference to invoke the message-handler function, we need to modify the type parameter of the component to include this reference:

```
<{weather: Weather, parentChannel: (msg: string) => void}>
```

The type of `parentChannel` is a function that takes a string parameter and returns no value. Our `WeatherInfo` component will process `props`, which is now an object with three properties: `weather`, `children`, and `parentChannel`.

The `onClick` button handler returns a function that will invoke `parentChannel()`, passing the message text to it:

```
() => parentChannel ("Hello from child!")
```

Run this version of the weather app, and if you click on the button at the bottom of the `WeatherInfo` component, the parent will receive the message and render it as shown in figure 13.12.

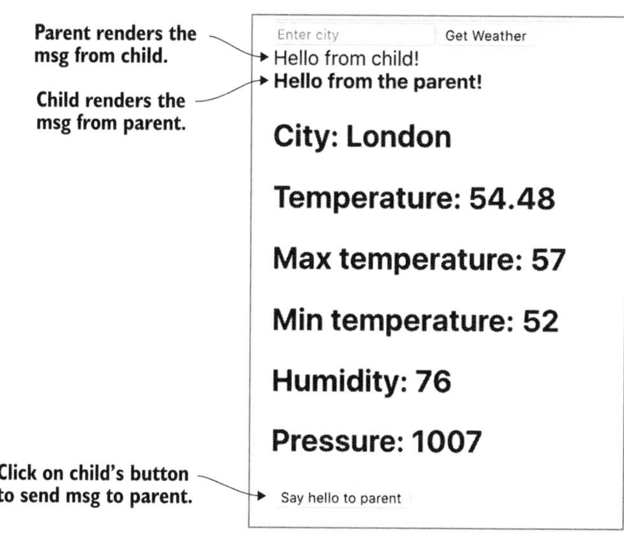

Figure 13.12 Message from child

NOTE The code in listing 13.19 can be optimized, and this is your homework. This code works, but it recreates the function `() ? parentChannel("Hello from child!")` on each re-rendering of the UI. To keep this from happening, read about `useCallback()` in the React documentation at http://mng.bz/MO8B, and wrap the `parentChannel()` function in this hook.

Now that we have introduced both `state` and `props`, we'd like to stress that they serve different purposes:

- `state` stores a private component's data; `props` is used for passing data to child components or back to the parent.
- A component may use the received `props` to initialize its `state`, if any.
- Direct modifications of `state` properties' values is prohibited; you must use the function returned by the `useState()` hook in functional components, or the `setState()` method in class-based components, to ensure that the changes are reflected on the UI.
- `props` are immutable, and a component can't modify the original data received via props.

NOTE State and props serve different purposes, but the UI in React is a function of both state and props.

In our brief overview of the React framework, we discussed components, state, and props, but even the shortest overview of React must include one more topic: Virtual DOM.

13.5 What's Virtual DOM?

A unique feature of React is *Virtual DOM*, a layer between the component and the browser's DOM. Each component consists of UI elements, and Virtual DOM optimizes the process of rendering these elements to the browser's DOM, as illustrated in figure 13.13.

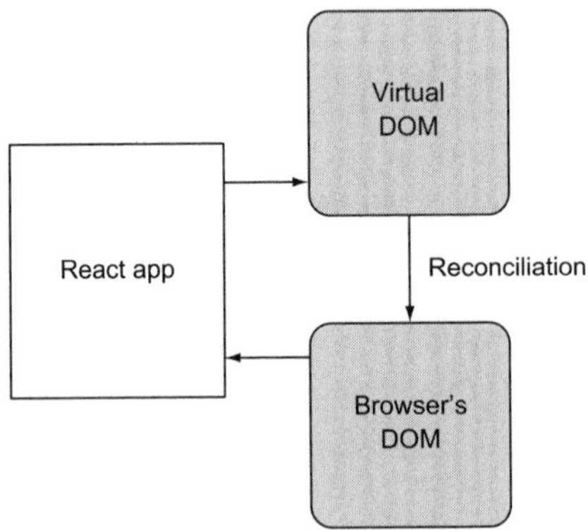

Figure 13.13 React's Virtual DOM

When you start the app, React creates a tree of UI components in its own Virtual DOM, and it renders this tree to the browser's DOM. As the user works with the React app, the browser's DOM triggers events to the app. If the event is handled by JavaScript, and if the handler code updates the component's state, then React re-creates the Virtual DOM, diffs its new version with the previous one, and syncs the differences with the browser's DOM. Applying this *diffing* algorithm is called *reconciliation* (see more in React's documentation at https://reactjs.org/docs/reconciliation.html).

NOTE The term "Virtual DOM" is a bit of a misnomer, because the React Native library uses the same principles for rendering the iOS and Android UIs, which don't have DOMs.

In general, the rendering of the UI from the browser's DOM is a slow operation, and to make it faster, React doesn't re-render all the elements of the browser's DOM every time an element changes. You may not see much of a difference in the speed of rendering a web page that has a handful of HTML elements, but in a page that has thousands of elements, the difference in rendering performed by React versus regular JavaScript will be noticeable.

If you can't imagine a web page with thousands of HTML elements, think of a financial portal showing the latest trading activity in tabular form. If such a table contains 300 rows and 40 columns, it has 12,000 cells, and each cell consists of several HTML elements. A portal may need to render several such tables.

The Virtual DOM spares developers from working with the browser DOM API like jQuery does—just update the component's state, and React will update the corresponding DOM elements in the most efficient manner. This is basically all the React library does, which means you'll need other libraries for implementing such functionality as making HTTP requests, routing, or working with forms.

This concludes our brief introduction to developing web apps using the React.js library and TypeScript. In chapter 14, we'll review the code of a new version of the blockchain client written in React.js.

Summary

- React.js is a great library for rendering UI components. You can use React.js in any part of an existing app that uses other frameworks or just JavaScript. In other words, you can develop a non-single-page-app with React if need be.
- You can generate a TypeScript-React app with the Create React App command-line tool in about a minute. This app will be fully configured and runnable.
- A React component is typically implemented either as a class or as a function.
- The UI portion of a component is typically declared using the JSX syntax. React components written in TypeScript are stored in files with the .tsx extension, which tell the tsc compiler that it contains JSX.
- A React component usually has *state*, which can be represented as one or more properties of the component. Whenever a state property is modified, React re-renders the component.
- Parent and child components can exchange data using props.
- React uses in-memory Virtual DOM, which is a layer between the component and the browser's DOM. Each component consists of UI elements, and Virtual DOM optimizes the process of rendering these elements to the browser's DOM.

14

Developing a blockchain client in React.js

This chapter covers

- Reviewing a blockchain web client written with React.js
- How the React.js web client communicates with the WebSocket server
- Running a React app that works with two servers in dev mode
- Splitting the UI of a blockchain client into components, and arranging their communications

In the previous chapter, you learned the basics of React, and now we'll review a new version of the blockchain app with the client portion written in React. The source code of the web client is located in the blockchain/client directory, and the messaging server is located in the blockchain/server directory.

The code of the server remains the same as in chapters 10 and 12, and the functionality of this version of the blockchain app is the same as well, but the UI portion of the app was completely rewritten in React.

In this chapter, we won't be reviewing the blockchain functionality, because it was covered in the previous chapters, but we will review the code that's specific to the React.js library. You may want to look back at chapter 10 to refresh your memory about the functionality of the blockchain client and messaging server.

First, we'll start the blockchain messaging server and the React client. Then, we'll introduce the code of the UI components, highlighting the difference between smart and presentation components. You'll also see multiple code samples that demonstrate intercomponent communications via props.

14.1 Starting the client and the messaging server

To start the server, open the terminal window in the blockchain/server directory, run `npm install` to install the server's dependencies, and then run the `npm start` command. You'll see the message "Listening on http://localhost:3000;" keep the server running.

To start the React client, open another terminal window in the blockchain/client directory, run `npm install` to install React and its dependencies, and then run the `npm start` command.

The blockchain client will start on port 3001, and after a short delay, the genesis block will be generated. Figure 14.1 shows a screenshot of the React client, with labels pointing to the UI files of the app, with the App.tsx file containing the code of the root component called `App`.

The `start` command is defined in package.json as an alias to the `react-scripts start` command, and it engages Webpack to build the bundles and use webpack-dev-server to launch the app. We went through a similar workflow when starting the Angular blockchain client in chapter 12.

However, apps generated by the Create React App CLI are preconfigured to start the webpack-dev-server on the port 3000, so we had a ports conflict, because port 3000 was already taken by our messaging server. We had to find a way to configure a different port for the client, and we'll explain how we did it shortly.

Projects that are generated by the Create React App tool are also preconfigured to read custom environment variables from the .env.development file (shown in the following listing) in the dev mode, or from .env.production in prod.

> **TIP** To prepare an optimized production build, run the `npm run build` command and you'll find index.html and the app bundles in the directory build. This command uses the environment variables from the .env.production file.

Listing 14.1 env.development: environment variables are defined here

```
PORT=3001
REACT_APP_WS_PROXY_HOSTNAME=localhost:3000
```

In the preceding listing, we first declared port 3001 to be used when webpack-dev-server starts the app, and this will resolve the conflict with the server, which runs on port 3000. Then we declared a custom `REACT_APP_WS_PROXY_HOSTNAME` environment variable that

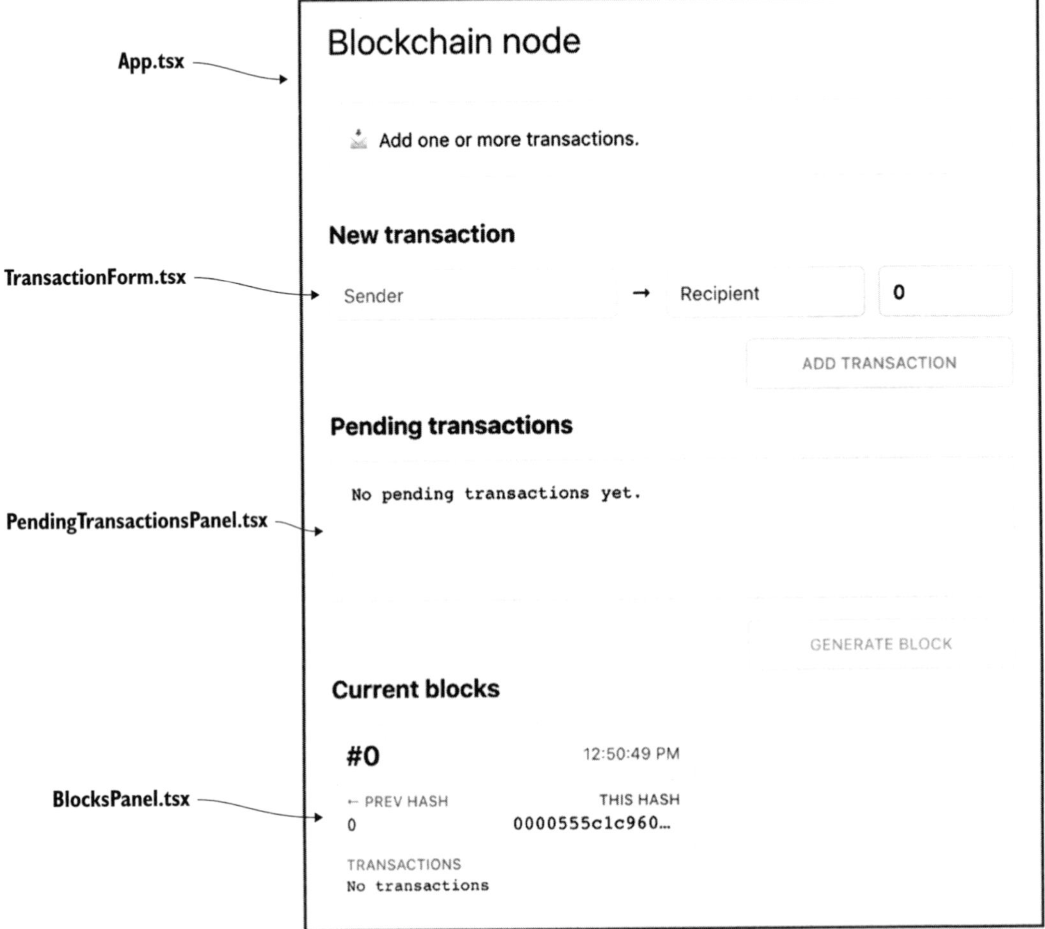

Figure 14.1 The blockchain client is launched.

can be used to proxy the client's requests to the server running on localhost:3000. This variable will be used in the websocket-controller.ts script. You can read more about adding custom environment variables in Create React App projects in the documentation, at http://mng.bz/adOm.

Figure 14.2 shows how our blockchain client runs in dev mode. The CLI dev server (currently, it's webpack-dev-server) serves the React app on port 3001, which then connects to another server that runs on port 3000.

> **NOTE** The Create React App CLI allows you to add the `proxy` property to package.json and specify a URL to be used if the dev server doesn't find the requested resource (for example, `"proxy": "http://localhost:3000"`). But this property doesn't work with the WebSocket protocol, so we had to use a custom environment variable to specify the URL of our messaging server.

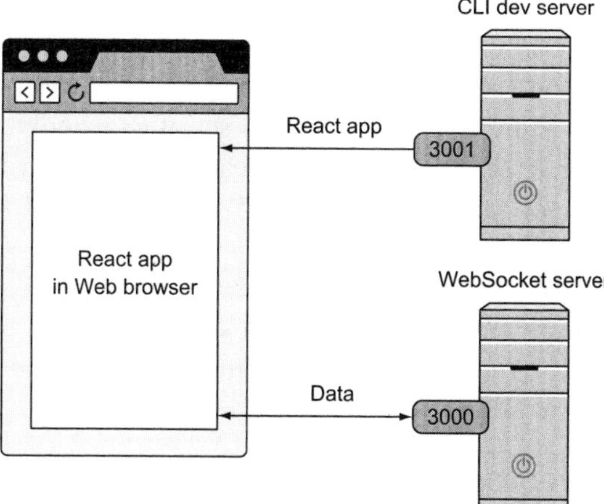

Figure 14.2 One app, two servers

Both Angular and React projects have similar file structures and launching procedures. But because our React app uses Babel in its workflow, the configuration of the supported browsers is different than for tsc. Listing 14.2 shows that we list specific browser versions that our app should support.

In section 6.4, we showed you how Babel can use presets to specify which versions of specific browsers the app has to support. The Create React App tool adds a default `browserslist` section to package.json. Open this file and you'll find the following default browser configuration.

Listing 14.2 A fragment from package.json

```
"browserslist": {
    "production": [          <-- Browsers that must be
      ">0.2%",                   supported in prod builds
      "not dead",
      "not op_mini all"
    ],
    "development": [         <-- Browsers that must be
      "last 1 chrome version",   supported in dev builds
      "last 1 firefox version",
      "last 1 safari version"
    ]
  }
```

TIP Even though we don't use tsc to compile the code and emit JavaScript, we still specified the option `"target": "es5"` in tsconfig.json to ensure that TypeScript doesn't complain about the TypeScript syntax from our blockchain app. Remove the `target` option or change its value to `es3`, and the `get url()` getter from listing 14.5 will be underlined by a red squiggly line with the error message, "Accessors are only available when targeting ECMAScript 5 and higher."

In section 6.4, we explained the use of `browserslist` (see https://browserl.ist), which allows you to configure tsc to emit JavaScript that runs in specific browsers. The Create React App supports it as well, and the settings from package.json are used when you create a production build by running the npm `build` script or when you create dev bundles by running the `start` script. Copy and paste each entry from your app's `browserslist` to the https://browserl.ist web page, and it'll show you which browsers are covered by this entry.

As in previous versions of the blockchain app, the code is divided into a UI part and the supporting scripts that implement the blockchain's algorithms. In the React version, the UI components are located in the components directory, and the supporting scripts are in lib.

14.2 What changed in the lib directory

As a reminder, the lib directory contains the code that generates new blocks, requests the longest chain, notifies other nodes about newly generated blocks, and invites other members of the blockchain to start generating new blocks for the specified transactions. These processes were described in sections 10.1 and 10.2.

We slightly modified the websocket-controller.ts file, which contains the script for communicating with the WebSocket server. In chapter 10, we didn't use JavaScript frameworks and simply instantiated the `WebsocketController` class using the `new` operator. We passed `messageCallback` to the constructor to handle messages coming from the server.

In listing 12.2, we used Angular's dependency injection, and this framework instantiated and injected the `WebsocketService` object into `AppComponent`. We could rely on Angular to instantiate the service first, and only after create the App component.

> **TIP** If you have an Angular background and are accustomed to creating singleton services that can be injected into components, learn about React's `Context` (https://reactjs.org/docs/context.html), which can be used as common storage for data that should be passed from one component to another. In other words, props is not the only way to pass data between components.

In the React version of the blockchain app, we'll manually instantiate `WebsocketController`. The App.tsx script starts as shown in the following listing.

Listing 14.3 Instantiating classes before the component

```
const server = new WebsocketController();     // First, instantiates WebsocketController
const node = new BlockchainNode();            // Second, instantiates BlockchainNode

const App: React.FC = () => {                 // Third, declares the root UI component
   // The code of the App component is omitted
   // We'll review it later in this chapter
}
```

To ensure that `WebsocketController` and `BlockchainNode` are global objects, we start the script by instantiating them. But `WebsocketController` needs a callback method from the `App` component to handle server messages changing the component's state. The problem is that the `App` component is not instantiated yet, so we can't provide such a callback to the component's constructor.

That's why we created the `connect()` method in `WebsocketController`. This method takes the callback as its parameter. The complete code of the `connect()` method is shown in the following listing.

Listing 14.4 The `connect()` method from `WebsocketController`

Passes the callback to the controller

```
connect(messagesCallback: (messages: Message) => void):
                                          Promise<WebSocket> {
  this.messagesCallback = messagesCallback;
  return this.websocket = new Promise((resolve, reject) => {
    const ws = new WebSocket(this.url);
    ws.addEventListener('open', () => resolve(ws));
    ws.addEventListener('error', err => reject(err));
    ws.addEventListener('message', this.onMessageReceived);
  });
}
```

Wraps the socket creation in a Promise

The `App` component will invoke `connect()` passing the proper callback (as we'll discuss in the next section, and you'll see in listing 14.10). What's the value of `this.url`, which is supposed to point at the WebSocket server? In section 14.1, we stated that the server's domain name and port will be taken from the environment variables. The following listing shows the code of the `url` getter in `WebsocketController`.

Listing 14.5 The `url` getter

Gets the host name and port from the environment variable

```
private get url(): string {
  const protocol = window.location.protocol === 'https:' ? 'wss' : 'ws';
  const hostname = process.env.REACT_APP_WS_PROXY_HOSTNAME
                             || window.location.host;
  return `${protocol}://${hostname}`;
}
```

If the host name is not found in process.env, uses the current app host

The `REACT_APP_WS_PROXY_HOSTNAME` variable was defined in the env.development file shown in listing 14.1. The `env` property of the `process` Node.js global variable is where your code can access all the available environment variables. You might object and say that our app runs in the browser and not in the Node.js runtime! This is correct, but during the bundling, Webpack reads the values of the variables available in `process.env` and inlines them into the bundles of the web app.

TIP The values of custom environment variables are inlined into the bundles. Run the command `npm run build` and open the main bundle from the build/static directory. Then search for the value of one of the variables from the .env.production file, such as localhost:3002.

After adding the `connect()` method, we decided to add the `disconnect()` method, which will close the socket connection:

```
disconnect() {
  this.websocket.then(ws => ws.close());
}
```

In our version of the blockchain client, the WebSocket connection is established by the `App` component, so when the `App` component is destroyed, the entire app is destroyed, including the socket connection. But this may not always be the case, so it's nice to have a separate method that will close the socket. This allows other components to establish and destroy the connection if need be.

14.3 The smart App component

The UI of this version of blockchain consists of five React components located in the .tsx files in the components directory:

- `App`
- `BlocksPanel`
- `BlockComponent`
- `PendingTransactionsPanel`
- `TransactionForm`

The App.tsx file contains the root `App` component. The other .tsx files contain the code of its children, `TransactionForm`, `PendingTransactionsPanel`, and `BlocksPanel`, which is also a parent of one or more `BlockComponent` instances as shown in figure 14.3.

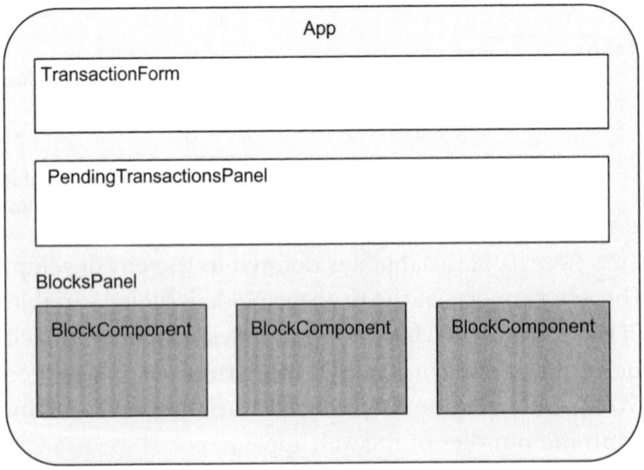

Figure 14.3 Parent and child components

In section 13.4.3, we introduced the concept of container (smart) and presentation (dumb) components. `App` is a smart component that contains a reference to the blockchain node instance and all related algorithms. The `App` component also performs all communications with the messaging server.

A typical presentation component either displays data, or, based on the user's actions, sends its data to other components. Presentation components don't implement complex application logic. For example, if a `PendingTransactionsPanel` component needs to initiate the creation of a new block, it simply invokes the proper callback on the `App` component, which will start the block generation process. In our blockchain client, the presentation components are `TransactionForm`, `PendingTransactionPanel`, and `BlocksPanel`.

The smart `App` component is implemented in the App.tsx file, which also creates instances of `BlockchainNode` and `WebsocketController`. To give you a big picture view of how the `App` component communicates with its children, the following listing shows the JSX part of the `App` component.

Listing 14.6 The `App` component's JSX

```
const App: React.FC = () => {

  // Other code is omitted for brevity

  return (
    <main>
      <h1>Blockchain node</h1>
      <aside><p>{status}</p></aside>
      <section>
        <TransactionForm                                  ◁ The first child component
          onAddTransaction={addTransaction}               ◁ This child can invoke addTransaction() on the App component.
          disabled={node.isMining || node.chainIsEmpty}
        />
      </section>
      <section>
        <PendingTransactionsPanel                         ◁ The second child
          formattedTransactions={formatTransactions(node.pendingTransactions)}
          onGenerateBlock={generateBlock}                 ◁ This child can invoke generateBlock() on the App component.
          disabled={node.isMining || node.noPendingTransactions}
        />
      </section>
      <section>
        <BlocksPanel blocks={node.chain} />               ◁ The third child
      </section>
    </main>
  );
}
```

14.3.1 Adding a transaction

The JSX of the `App` component includes child components, which can invoke callback methods on `App`. We discussed how a React child component can interact with its parent in section 13.4.4. In listing 14.6, you saw that the `App` component passes the `onAddTransaction` callback to `TransactionForm` via props.

Accordingly, when the user clicks on the ADD TRANSACTION button on the `TransactionForm` component, it'll invoke its `onAddTransaction()` method, which will result in the invocation of the `addTransaction()` method on the `App` component. This is what the word "implicitly" means in figure 14.4, which shows a screenshot of VS Code with the outline of the App component.

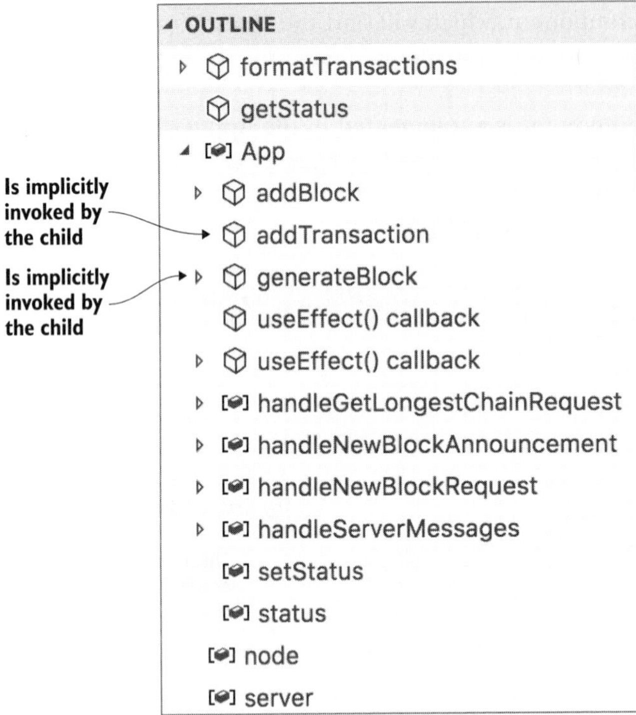

Figure 14.4 The `App` component has methods that will be invoked by its children.

To complete our discussion of the add transaction workflow, let's see what triggers the UI change when a new transaction is added. In React, we change the state of the component to update the UI, and we do this by invoking the function returned by the `useState()` hook. In the `App` component, the name of this function is `setStatus()`.

Listing 14.7 The App code that adds a transaction

```
const node = new BlockchainNode();                        <-- The node instance

const App: React.FC = () => {
  const [status, setStatus] = useState<string>('');       <-- Declares the status state
                                                              of the App component
  function addTransaction(transaction: Transaction): void {
```

```
    node.addTransaction(transaction);      <-- Adds the transaction received
    setStatus(getStatus(node));                from the child component
  }                                        <-- Updates the state

  // the rest of the code is omitted for brevity
}

function getStatus(node: BlockchainNode): string {     <-- This function is
  return node.chainIsEmpty            ? '⌛ Initializing the blockchain...' :    implemented outside
         node.isMining                ? '⌛ Mining a new block...' :             the App component.
         node.noPendingTransactions ? '✉ Add one or more transactions.' :
                                        '✓ Ready to mine a new block.';
}
```

We reviewed the blockchain node implementation and identified operations that change the internal state of the node. We added the helper properties `chainIsEmpty`, `isMining`, and `noPendingTransactions` to probe the node's internal state. After each operation that may change the internal node's state, we verify the UI state against the node's internal state, and React applies any required changes. If any of these values change, we need to update the UI of the `App` component. But what can we use in the `App` component to trigger the invocation of `setStatus()`?

The `getStatus()` function returns the text describing the current blockchain node's status, and the `App` component will render the corresponding message (see listing 14.7). Initially the status value is "Initializing the blockchain..." If the user adds a new transaction, `getStatus()` will return "Add one or more transactions," and the `setStatus(getStatus(node));` line will change the component's state, resulting in the UI being re-rendered. Figure 14.5 shows the app's status (or state): "Add one or more transactions."

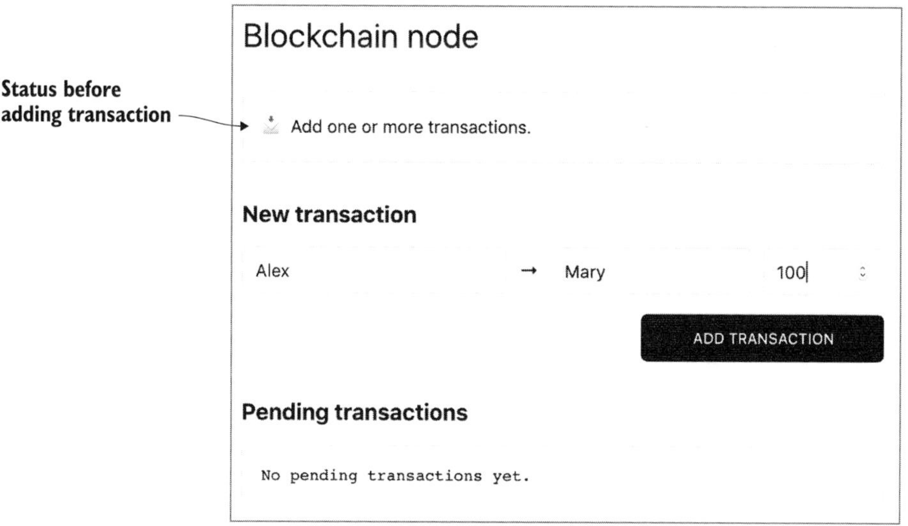

Figure 14.5 The user is ready to add a transaction.

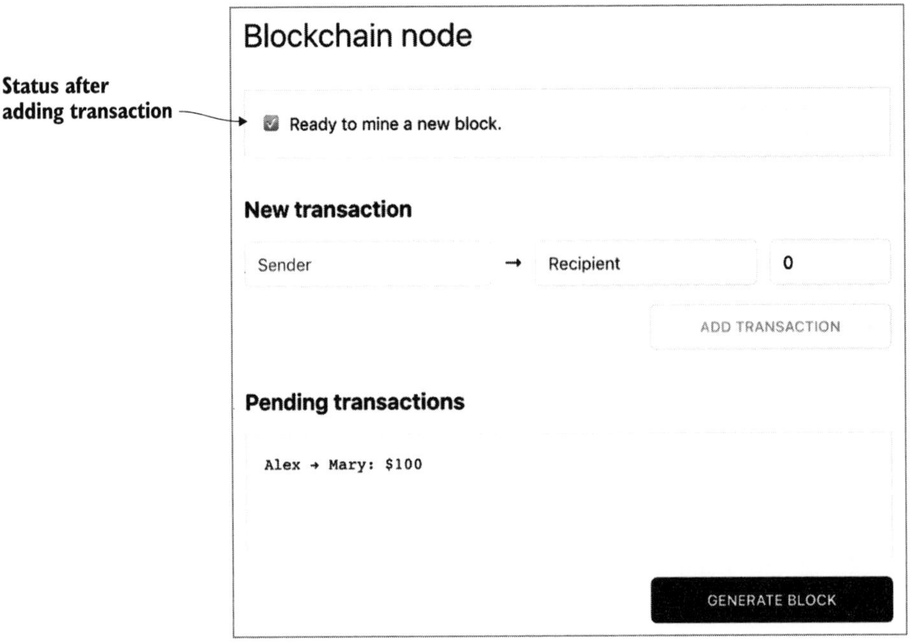

Figure 14.6 The user is ready to mine a new block.

Figure 14.6 shows a screenshot taken after the user clicked the ADD TRANSACTION button. The `App` component's state is "Ready to mine a new block," and the GENERATE BLOCK button is enabled.

While testing this app, we noticed an issue: if the user adds more than one transaction, it will still show only the first one in the Pending Transactions field. But after clicking the GENERATE BLOCK button, the new block will include all pending transactions. For some reason, React didn't re-render the UI for any new transactions except the first one.

The problem was that after adding the first transaction, the state of the `App` component contained "Ready to mine a new block," and this value didn't change after adding other transactions. Accordingly, the `setStatus(getStatus(node));` line didn't change the component's state and React didn't see any reason for UI re-rendering!

This issue was easy to fix. We slightly modified the `getStatus()` function by adding a transaction counter to the status line. Now instead of keeping the "Ready to mine new block" status, the status includes a changing part:

```
`Ready to mine a new block (transactions:
➥ ${node.pendingTransactions.length}).`;
```

Now every invocation of `addTransaction()` will change the component's state.

TIP Making the node immutable would be a better solution to this issue. For an immutable object, whenever its state changes, a new instance (and a reference) would be created, and the hack with the transaction counter wouldn't be necessary.

14.3.2 Generating a new block

Let's take another look at listing 14.6. The `App` component passes the `onGenerateBlock()` callback to `PendingTransactionsPanel` using props. When the user clicks on the GENERATE BLOCK button, the `PendingTransactionsPanel` component invokes `onGenerateBlock()`, which in turn invokes the `generateBlock()` method on the `App` component. This method is shown in the following listing.

Listing 14.8 The `generateBlock()` method

```
async function generateBlock() {

    server.requestNewBlock(node.pendingTransactions);
    const miningProcessIsDone = node.mineBlockWith(node. pendingTransactions);

    setStatus(getStatus(node));

    const newBlock = await miningProcessIsDone;
    addBlock(newBlock);
}
```

Annotations:
- Invites other nodes to start generating a new block for the pending transactions (server.requestNewBlock line)
- Declares an expression for block mining (const miningProcessIsDone line)
- Changes the component's state (setStatus line)
- Starts the block mining and waits for completion (const newBlock line)
- Adds the new block to the blockchain (addBlock line)

NOTE By providing the parent's method references to child components, we control what the child can access in the parent. In this app, neither the `TransactionForm` nor `PendingTransactionsPanel` components have access to the `BlockchainNode` and `WebsocketController` objects. These children are strictly presentational components; they can display data or notify the parent about some events.

14.3.3 Explaining the useEffect() hooks

In the `App` component's code, you can find two `useEffect()` hooks. As you'll recall, `useEffect()` hooks can be automatically invoked when a specified variable has changed. The `App` component has two such hooks. The following listing shows the first `useEffect()` hook, which works only once on app startup.

Listing 14.9 The first `useEffect()` hook

```
useEffect(() => {
  setStatus(getStatus(node));
}, []);
```

The goal of this effect is to initialize the component's state with the message "Initializing the blockchain..." If you commented out this hook, the app would still work, but there wouldn't be any status message when the app starts.

Listing 14.10 shows the second `useEffect()` hook, which connects to the WebSocket server, passing it the `handleServerMessages` callback that handles messages pushed by the server.

Listing 14.10 The `useEffect()` hook attached to `handleServerMessages`

```
useEffect(() => {
    async function initializeBlockchainNode() {       // Declares the initializeBlockchainNode() function
      await server.connect(handleServerMessages);     // Connects to the WebSocket server providing the callback
      const blocks = await server.requestLongestChain();   // Requests the longest chain
      if (blocks.length > 0) {
        node.initializeWith(blocks);                  // The blockchain already has some blocks.
      } else {
        await node.initializeWithGenesisBlock();      // No blocks exist yet; creates the genesis block
      }
      setStatus(getStatus(node));                     // Updates the App state
    }

    initializeBlockchainNode();                       // Invokes the initializeBlockchainNode() function

    return () => server.disconnect();                 // Disconnects from WebSocket when the App component is destroyed

  }, [handleServerMessages]);                         // This hook is attached to handleServerMessages.
```

If a function is used only inside the effect, it's recommended that you declare it inside the effect. Because `initializeBlockchainNode()` is used only by the preceding `useEffect()`, we declared it inside this hook.

This `useEffect()` hook makes the initial connection to the server and initializes the blockchain, so we want it to be invoked only once. To ensure this, we tried to use an empty array for the second argument, as the documentation prescribes. An empty array means that this effect doesn't use any values that could participate in the React data flow, so it's safe to invoke only once.

But React noticed that this hook uses the component-scoped `handleServerMessages()` function, which, being a closure, could potentially capture a component's state variable. This might become outdated on the next rendering, but our effect would keep the reference to `handleServerMessages()`, which captured the old state. Because of this, React forced us to replace the empty array with `[handleServerMessages]`. However, because we won't be changing state inside this callback, this `useEffect()` will be invoked only once.

Note the `return` statement at the end of the `useEffect()` shown in listing 14.10. Returning a function from `useEffect()` is optional, but if it's there, React guarantees that it will call that function when the component is about to be destroyed. If we established the WebSocket connection in other components (not in the root component), it would be good practice to have a return statement in `useEffect()` to avoid memory leaks.

While we were wrapping the asynchronous function inside the effect in listing 14.10, we initially tried to just add the `async` keyword as follows:

```
useEffect(async () => { await ...})
```

But because any `async` function returns a `Promise`, TypeScript started complaining that "Type 'Promise<void>' is not assignable to type '() ? void | undefined'." The `useEffect()` hook didn't like a function that would return a `Promise`. That's why we changed the signature a little bit:

```
useEffect(() => {
    async function initializeBlockchainNode() {...}
    initializeBlockchainNode();
   }
)
```

We declared the asynchronous function first, and then invoked it. This made TypeScript happy, and we were able to reuse the same code as in chapters 10 and 12 inside the React's `useEffect()`.

14.3.4 Memoization with the useCallback() hook

Now let's talk about yet another React hook, `useCallback()`, which returns a *memoized* callback. Memoization is an optimization technique that stores the results of function calls and returns the cached result when the same inputs occur again.

Suppose you have a function, `doSomething(a,b)`, that performs some long-running calculations on the supplied arguments. Let's say the calculations take 30 seconds, and that this is a pure function that always returns the same result if the arguments are the same. The following code snippet should run 90 seconds, right?

```
let result: number;
result = doSomething(2, 3);  // 30 sec
result = doSomething(10, 15);  // 30 sec
result = doSomething(2, 3);  // 30 sec
```

But if we saved the results for each pair of arguments in a table, we wouldn't need to invoke `doSomething(2, 3)` for the second time, because we already have the result for this pair. We'd just need to do a quick lookup in our table of results. This is an example where memoization could optimize the code so it would run for a little more than 60 seconds instead of 90 seconds.

In React components you don't need to implement memoization for each function manually—you can use the provided `useCallback()` hook. Listing 14.11 shows a `useCallback()` hook that returns a memoized version of the `doSomething()` function.

Listing 14.11 Wrapping a function in a `useCallback()` hook

```
const memoizedCallback = useCallback(    <-- The useCallback() hook
  () => {
    doSomething(a, b);    <-- The memoized doSomething() function
  },
  [a, b], <-- Dependencies of doSomething()
);
```

If the `doSomething()` function is a part of the React component, memoization will prevent this function from being unnecessarily re-created during each UI rendering unless its dependencies, `a` or `b`, change.

In our `App` component, we wrapped all the functions that handle messages from the WebSocket server, such as `handleServerMessages()`, inside the `useCallback()` hook. Figure 14.7 shows a screenshot of the `App` component's code with the collapsed bodies of the functions wrapped inside `useCallback()`.

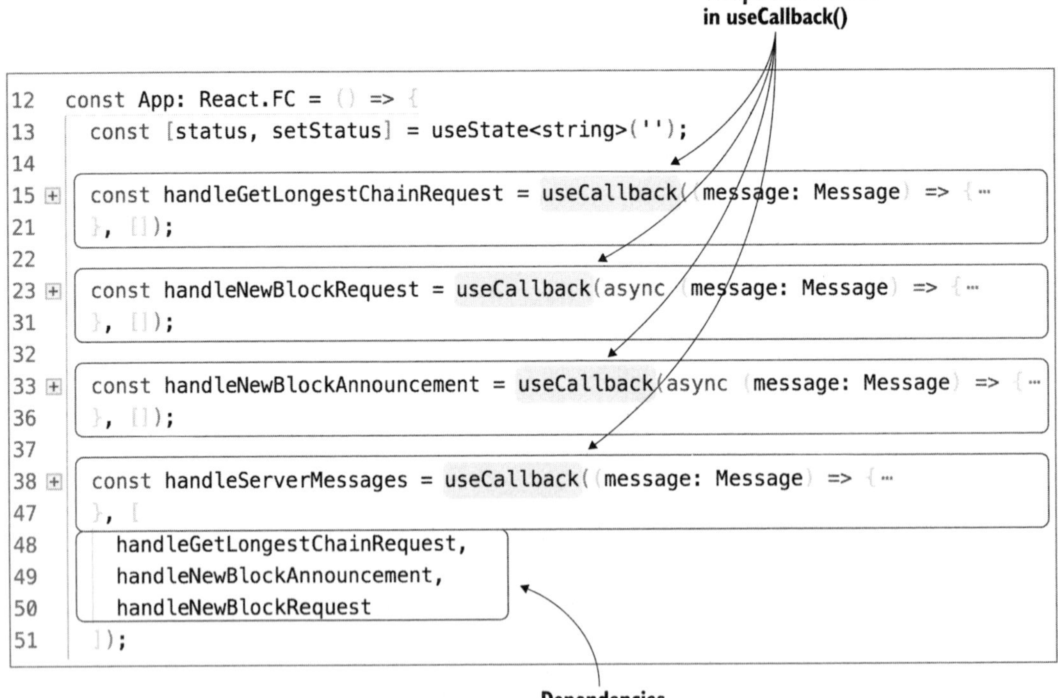

Figure 14.7 Memoized functions in the `App` component

In figure 14.7, each of the variables declared in lines 15, 23, 33, and 38 is local to the App component, so React assumes that their values (the function expressions) can change. By wrapping the bodies of these functions in `useCallback()` hooks, we instruct React to reuse the same function instance on each rendering, which makes it more efficient.

Look at the last line of listing 14.10—`handleServerMessages` is a dependency of `useEffect()`. Technically, if instead of the function expression `const handleNewBlockRequest = useCallback()` we used `function handleNewBlockRequest()`, the app would still work, but each function would be recreated on each rendering.

In lines 21, 31, and 36 in figure 14.7, the array of dependencies is empty, which tells us that these callbacks can't have any stale values, and there's no need for any dependencies. In lines 48–49, we listed the variables `handleGetLongestChainRequest`, `handleNewBlockAnnouncement`, and `handleNewBlockRequest` as dependencies, which are used inside the `handleServerMessages()` callback, as seen in the following listing. Didn't we state in the previous paragraph that these callbacks won't create a stale state situation? We did, but React can't peek inside these callback to see this.

Listing 14.12 The `handleServerMessages()` callback

```
const handleServerMessages = useCallback((message: Message) => {
    switch (message.type) {
      case MessageTypes.GetLongestChainRequest:
           return handleGetLongestChainRequest(message);
      case MessageTypes.NewBlockRequest        :
           return handleNewBlockRequest(message);
      case MessageTypes.NewBlockAnnouncement   :
           return handleNewBlockAnnouncement(message);
      default: {
        console.log(`Received message of unknown type: "${message.type}"`);
      }
    }
  }, [
    handleGetLongestChainRequest,
    handleNewBlockAnnouncement,
    handleNewBlockRequest
  ]);
```

Uses a dependency inside useCallback()

Declares a dependency of useCallback()

Besides the functions that communicate with the WebSocket server, the App component has three functions that communicate with the `BlockchainNode` instance. The next listing shows the `addTransaction()`, `generateBlock()`, and `addBlock()` functions. We didn't change the logic of these operations, but each of these functions now ends with an invocation of the React-specific `setState()`, which requests re-rendering.

Listing 14.13 Three more functions from the App component

```
function addTransaction(transaction: Transaction): void {
    node.addTransaction(transaction);
    setStatus(getStatus(node));
  }

  async function generateBlock() {

    server.requestNewBlock(node.pendingTransactions);
    const miningProcessIsDone = node.mineBlockWith(node.pendingTransactions);

    setStatus(getStatus(node));

    const newBlock = await miningProcessIsDone;
    addBlock(newBlock);
  }

  async function addBlock(block: Block, notifyOthers = true): Promise<void> {
    try {
      await node.addBlock(block);
      if (notifyOthers) {
        server.announceNewBlock(block);
      }
    } catch (error) {
      console.log(error.message);
    }

    setStatus(getStatus(node));
  }
```

The invocation of this function is initiated by the child component.

Updates the component's status

NOTE The invocation of the `addTransaction()` and `generateBlock()` functions is driven by the `TransactionForm` and `PendingTransactionsPanel` child components respectively. We'll review the relevant code in the next section.

The `addTransaction()` function accumulates pending transactions, which are handled by the `generateBlock()` function, and when one of the nodes completes the mining first, the `addBlock()` function attempts to add it to the blockchain. If our node was the first in mining, this function would add the new block and notify others; otherwise, the new block will arrive from the server via the `handleNewBlockAnnouncement()` callback.

The `getStatus()` function is located in the App.tsx file, but it's implemented outside of the `App` component.

Listing 14.14 The getStatus() function from App.tsx

```
function getStatus(node: BlockchainNode): string {
  return node.chainIsEmpty           ? '⌛ Initializing the blockchain...' :
         node.isMining               ? '⌛ Mining a new block...' :
         node.noPendingTransactions ? '✉ Add one or more transactions.' :
                                      '✅ Ready to mine a new block.';
}
```

When the App component invokes `setStatus(getStatus(node));`, there are two possible outcomes: either `getStatus()` will return the same status as before, or it will return a new one. If the status didn't change, calling `setStatus()` won't result in re-rendering the UI, and vice versa.

We've now covered the React specifics for the smart App component. Let's now get familiar with the code of the presentation components.

14.4 The TransactionForm presentation component

Figure 14.8 shows the UI of the `TransactionForm` component, which allows the user to enter the names of the sender and recipient, as well as the transaction amount. When the user clicks the ADD TRANSACTION button, this information has to be sent to the parent App component (the smart component), because it knows how to process this data.

New transaction

Sender → Recipient 0

ADD TRANSACTION

Figure 14.8 The UI of the `TransactionForm` component

The JSX of the App component that communicates with `TransactionForm` is shown in the following listing.

Listing 14.15 The App component's JSX for rendering TransactionForm

```
<TransactionForm
  onAddTransaction={addTransaction}
  disabled={node.isMining || node.chainIsEmpty}
/>
```

- `onAddTransaction={addTransaction}` — Child's onAddTransaction() results in parent's addTransaction()
- `disabled=...` — Conditionally enables or disables the child

From this JSX, we can guess that when the `TransactionForm` component invokes its `onAddTransaction()` function, the App component will invoke its `addTransaction()` (shown earlier in listing 14.13). We can also see that the child component has the `disabled` props, driven by the status of the `node` variable, which holds the reference to the `BlockchainNode` instance.

The following listing shows the first half of the code in the TransactionForm.tsx file.

Listing 14.16 The first part of TransactionForm.tsx

```
import React, { ChangeEvent, FormEvent, useState } from 'react';
import { Transaction } from '../lib/blockchain-node';

type TransactionFormProps = {
  onAddTransaction: (transaction: Transaction) => void,
```

- `onAddTransaction: ...` — Props for sending data to the parent

```
  disabled: boolean                    <-- Props for getting data from the parent
};

const defaultFormValue = {recipient: '', sender: '', amount: 0};   <-- The object with the default values for the form

const TransactionForm: React.FC<TransactionFormProps> =
➥ ({onAddTransaction, disabled}) => {            <-- This component accepts two props.
  const [formValue, setFormValue] = useState<Transaction>(defaultFormValue);   <-- The component's state
  const isValid = formValue.sender && formValue.recipient &&
➥ formValue.amount > 0;   <-- The isValid flag specifies whether the button can be enabled.

  function handleInputChange({ target }: ChangeEvent<HTMLInputElement>) {   <-- One event handler for all input fields
    setFormValue({
      ...formValue,
      [target.name]: target.value
    });
  }

  function handleFormSubmit(event: FormEvent<HTMLFormElement>) {
    event.preventDefault();
    onAddTransaction(formValue);          <-- Passes the formValue object to the parent
    setFormValue(defaultFormValue);       <-- Resets the form
  }

  return (
    // The JSX is shown in listing 14.17
  );
}
```

When the user clicks the ADD TRANSACTION button, the `TransactionForm` component has to invoke some function on the parent. Since React doesn't want the child to know the internals of the parent, the child just gets the `onAddTransaction` props, but it has to know the correct signature of the parent's function that corresponds to `onAdd-Transaction`. The following line maps the name of the `onAddTransaction` props to the signature of the function to be called on the parent:

```
onAddTransaction: (transaction: Transaction) => void,
```

In listing 14.13, you saw that the parent's `addTransaction()` function has the signature `(transaction: Transaction) => void`. In listing 14.6, you can easily find the line that maps the parent's `addTransaction` to the child's `onAddTransaction`.

The `TransactionForm` component renders a simple form and defines only one state variable, `formValue`, which is the object containing the current form's values. When the user types in the input fields, the `handleInputChange()` event handler is invoked and saves the entered value in `formValue`. In listing 14.17, you'll see that this event handler is assigned to each input field of the form.

In the `handleInputChange()` handler, we use destructuring to extract the `target` object, which points at the input field that triggered this event. We get the name and value of the DOM element dynamically from the `target` object. The `target.name` property will contain the name of the field, and `target.value` contains its value. In Chrome dev tools, put a breakpoint in the `handleInputChange()` method to see how this works. By invoking `setFormValue()`, we change the component's state to reflect the current values of the input fields.

> **TIP** While invoking `setState()`, we use object cloning with the spread operator. This technique is described in section A.7 of the appendix.

The default values for the transaction form are stored in the `defaultFormValue` variable, and they are used for the initial form rendering as well as resetting the form after the ADD TRANSACTION button is clicked. When the user clicks on this button, the `handleFormSubmit()` function invokes `onAddTransaction()`, passing the `formValue` object to the parent (the `App` component).

The following listing shows the JSX of the `TransactionForm` component. It's a form with three input fields and a submit button.

Listing 14.17 The second part of TransactionForm.tsx

```
return (
  <>
    <h2>New transaction</h2>
    <form className="add-transaction-form" onSubmit={handleFormSubmit}>
      <input
        type="text"
        name="sender"
        placeholder="Sender"
        autoComplete="off"
        disabled={disabled}                    ← Enables the button only when the form is valid
        value={formValue.sender}               ← Binds the value from the corresponding state property
        onChange={handleInputChange}           ← Invokes handleInputChange on every state mutation
      />
      <span className="hidden-xs">•</span>
      <input
        type="text"
        name="recipient"
        placeholder="Recipient"
        autoComplete="off"
        disabled={disabled}                    ← Binds the disable attribute to the disabled props
        value={formValue.recipient}            ← Binds the value from the corresponding state property
        onChange={handleInputChange}           ← Invokes handleInputChange on every state mutation
      />
      <input
        type="number"
        name="amount"
        placeholder="Amount"
        disabled={disabled}                    ← Binds the disable attribute to the disabled props
        value={formValue.amount}               ← Binds the value from the corresponding state property
        onChange={handleInputChange}           ← Invokes handleInputChange on every state mutation
      />
      <button type="submit"
```

```
                disabled={!isValid || disabled}              ◁——  Enables the button only
                className="ripple">ADD TRANSACTION</button>       when the form is valid
      </form>
    </>
  );
```

React handles HTML forms differently than other elements because a form has an internal state—an object with all the form fields' values. In React, you can turn a regular form field into a *controlled component* by binding the state object's property (such as `formValue.sender`) to its attribute `value` and adding an `onChange` event handler.

Our form has three controlled components (input fields), and every state mutation will have an associated handler function. In the `TransactionForm` component, `handleInputChange()` is such a handler function. As you can see in listing 14.16, we're just cloning the state object in `handleInputChange()`, but you can put any app logic in such a handler.

We'd like to stress again that `TransactionForm` is a presentation component that only knows how to present its values and which function to invoke when the form is submitted. It has no knowledge about its parent and doesn't communicate with any external services, which makes it 100% reusable.

14.5 The PendingTransactionsPanel presentation component

Each time the user clicks the ADD TRANSACTION button in the `TransactionForm` component, the entered transaction should be passed to the `PendingTransactionsPanel`. Figure 14.9 shows this component rendered with two pending transactions. These two components don't know about each other, so the `App` component can play the role of mediator in passing the data from one component to another.

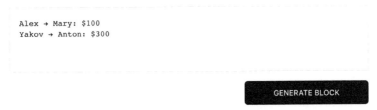

Figure 14.9 The UI of the `PendingTransactionsPanel` component

Listing 14.18 shows a snippet of the `App` component's JSX that renders the `PendingTransactionsPanel` component. The `App` component communicates with `PendingTransactionsPanel` much like it does with `TransactionForm`. This component gets three props from `App`.

Listing 14.18 The App component's JSX for rendering PendingTransactionsPanel

```
<PendingTransactionsPanel
  formattedTransactions={formatTransactions(node.pendingTransactions)}
  onGenerateBlock={generateBlock}
  disabled={node.isMining || node.noPendingTransactions}
/>
```

- **Formats the transaction and passes it to this component** (annotates `formattedTransactions`)
- **The child's onGenerateBlock() results in the parent's generateBlock().** (annotates `onGenerateBlock`)
- **This child has to be disabled initially.** (annotates `disabled`)

The first props is `formattedTransactions`, and the `App` component passes it in to `PendingTransactionsPanel` for rendering. While reviewing the code from the App.tsx file, we left out its `formatTransactions()` utility function, which simply creates a nicely formatted message about this transaction. The following listing shows the code of the self-explanatory `formatTransactions()` function, located in the App.tsx file outside of the `App` component. Figure 14.9 shows what the formatted transactions look like.

Listing 14.19 The formatTransactions() function

```
function formatTransactions(transactions: Transaction[]): string {
  return transactions.map(t =>`${t.sender} • ${t.recipient}: $${t.amount}`)
  .join('\n');
}
```

The second props, `onGeneratedBlock`, is a reference to the function that should be called on the parent of `PendingTransactionsPanel` when the user clicks the GENERATE BLOCK button.

The following listing shows the code of the `PendingTransactionsPanel` component. It's pretty straightforward because it doesn't contain any forms and doesn't need to handle user input, except for clicking the GENERATE BLOCK button.

Listing 14.20 The PendingTransactionsPanel.tsx file

```
import React from 'react';

type PendingTransactionsPanelProps = {
  formattedTransactions: string;
  onGenerateBlock: () => void;
  disabled: boolean;
}

const PendingTransactionsPanel: React.FC<PendingTransactionsPanelProps> =
          ({formattedTransactions, onGenerateBlock, disabled}) => {
  return (
    <>
      <h2>Pending transactions</h2>
      <pre className="pending-transactions__list">
```

- **The props for formatted transactions**
- **The onGenerateBlock props must use this method signature.**
- **Aligns everything (including subsequent sibling elements) to the right side of the parent container** (annotates the `<pre>` line)

```
        {formattedTransactions || 'No pending transactions yet.'}     ◁─┐
      </pre>                                          Displays either a provided
      <div className="pending-transactions__form">    transaction or the default text
        <button disabled={disabled}
                onClick={() => onGenerateBlock()}     ◁─┐ Invokes the
                className="ripple"                      │ onGenerateBlock() props
                type="button">GENERATE BLOCK</button>
      </div>
      <div className="clear"></div>     ◁── Clears the right-alignment
    </>
  );
}

export default PendingTransactionsPanel;
```

When the user clicks the GENERATE BLOCK button, we invoke the `onGenerateBlock()` props, which in turn invokes the `generateBlock()` function on the `App` component.

In the `.pending-transactions__form` style selector (in index.css), we use `float: right`, which forces everything to be aligned to the right side of the parent container, including subsequent sibling elements. The `clear` style is defined as `clear: both`, and it stops the right-alignment rule so we don't break the following Current Blocks section.

The last component we have to review is the one that shows the blockchain at the bottom of the window.

14.6 The BlocksPanel and BlockComponent presentation components

When the user clicks the GENERATE BLOCK button in the `PendingTransactions-Panel` component, all active blocks in the blockchain start the mining process, and after the consensus, a new block will be added to the blockchain and rendered in the `BlocksPanel` component, which can parent one or more `BlockComponent` components. Figure 14.10 shows the rendering of `BlocksPanel` with a two-block blockchain.

Figure 14.10 The UI of the `BlocksPanel` component

During the process of block mining and getting the consensus, the instances of `BlockchainNode` and `WebsocketController` are involved, but because it's a presentation component, `BlocksPanel` doesn't directly communicate with either of these objects. That work is delegated to the smart `App` component. The `BlockPanel` component doesn't send any data to its parent; its goal is to render the blockchain provided via the `block` props:

```
<BlocksPanel blocks={node.chain} />
```

The BlocksPanel.tsx file contains the code of two components: `BlocksPanel` and `BlockComponent`. The following listing shows the code of `BlockComponent`, which renders a single block in the blockchain. Figure 14.10 showed two instances of `BlockComponent`.

Listing 14.21 The `BlockComponent`

```
const BlockComponent: React.FC<{ index: number, block: Block }> =
➥ ({ index, block }) => {
  const formattedTransactions = formatTransactions(block.transactions);    // The formattedTransaction() function is the same as in the App component.
  const timestamp = new Date(block.timestamp).toLocaleTimeString();

  return (
    <div className="block">
      <div className="block__header">
        <span className="block__index">#{index}</span>    // The block number
        <span className="block__timestamp">{timestamp}</span>
      </div>
      <div className="block__hashes">
        <div className="block__hash">
          <div className="block__label">• PREV HASH</div>
          <div className="block__hash-value">{block.previousHash}</div>    // The previous block's hash
        </div>
        <div className="block__hash">
          <div className="block__label">THIS HASH</div>
          <div className="block__hash-value">{block.hash}</div>    // This block's hash
        </div>
      </div>
      <div>
        <div className="block__label">TRANSACTIONS</div>
        <pre className="block__transactions">{formattedTransactions
                                        || 'No transactions'}</pre>    // The block's transactions
      </div>
    </div>
  );
}
```

TIP We use the symbols __ and – in naming some styles, as recommended by the Block Element Modifier (BEM) methodology described on the Get BEM website, at http://getbem.com.

The following listing shows the `BlocksPanel` component, which serves as a container for all `BlockComponent` components.

Listing 14.22 The `BlocksPanel` component

```
import React from 'react';
import { Block, Transaction } from '../lib/blockchain-node';

type BlocksPanelProps = {
```

```
  blocks: Block[]          <-- An array of Block instances
};                             is the only props here.

const BlocksPanel: React.FC<BlocksPanelProps> = ({blocks}) => {
  return (
    <>
      <h2>Current blocks</h2>
      <div className="blocks">                     Uses Array.map() to turn
        <div className="blocks__ribbon">           the data into components
          {blocks.map((b, i) =>                <--
                <BlockComponent key={b.hash} index={i} block={b}>
➥ </BlockComponent>)}                          <-- Passes key, index,
        </div>                                      and block props to
        <div className="blocks__overlay"></div>     BlockComponent
      </div>
    </>
  );
}
```

The `BlocksPanel` gets an array of `Block` instances from the `App` component and applies the `Array.map()` method to convert each `Block` object into a `BlockComponent`. The `map()` method passes the key (the hash code), the unique index of the block, and the `Block` object to each instance of `BlockComponent`.

The props of `BlockComponent` are `index` and `block`. Note that we're assigning the block hash as a `key` props to each instance of the `BlockComponent`, even though the `key` props was never mentioned in its code in listing 14.21. That's because when you have a collection of rendered objects (such as list items or multiple instances of the same component), React needs a way to uniquely identify each component during its reconciliation with the Virtual DOM, to keep track of the data associated with each DOM element.

If you don't use a unique value for the `key` props on each `BlockComponent`, React will print a warning in the browser console stating that "Each child in array or iterator should have a unique key props." In our app, this won't mess up the data, because we are only adding new blocks to the end of the array, but if the user could add or remove arbitrary elements from a collection of UI components, not using a unique `key` props could create a situation where a UI element and the underlying data wouldn't match.

This concludes our code review of the React version of our blockchain app.

Summary

- In development, our React web app was deployed under a Webpack dev server, but it was communicating with another (messaging) server as well. To accomplish this, we declared custom environment variables with the messaging server's URL. For a WebSocket server, this was enough, but if you used other HTTP servers, you'd have to proxy the HTTP requests as described in the Create React App documentation at http://mng.bz/gV9v.

- Typically, the UI of a React app consists of smart and presentation components. Don't place the application logic in the presentation components, which are meant for presenting the data received from other components. The presentation components can also implement the interaction with the user and send the user's input to other components.
- A child component should never call an API from its parent directly. Using props, the parent component should give the child a name that's mapped to a function that should be called as the result of a child's action. The child will invoke the provided function reference without knowing the real name of the parent's function.
- To prevent unnecessarily re-creating function expressions located in React components, consider using memoization with the `useCallback()` hook.

15 Developing Vue.js apps with TypeScript

This chapter covers

- A quick intro to the Vue.js framework
- How to jumpstart a new project with Vue CLI
- How to work with class-based components
- How to arrange client-side navigation using the Vue Router

Angular is a framework, React.js is a library, and Vue.js (a.k.a. Vue) feels like a "library plus plus." Vue (https://vuejs.org) was created by Evan You in 2014 as an attempt to create a lighter version of Angular. At the time of this writing, Vue.js has 155,000 stars and 285 contributors on GitHub. The numbers are high, but Vue is not backed by any large corporation like Angular (Google) or React.js (Facebook).

Vue is a progressive, incrementally adoptable JavaScript framework for building UIs on the web, so if you already have a web app written with or without any JavaScript libraries, you can introduce Vue to just a small portion of your app and keep adding Vue to other parts of the app as needed. Much like React, you can attach a

Vue instance to any HTML element (such as a `<div>`), and only this element will be controlled by Vue.

Vue is a component-based library that's focused on the app's *View* part (the *V* in the MVC pattern). The core Vue library focuses on declarative rendering of UI components, and like React.js, Vue uses the Virtual DOM under the hood. Besides the code library, Vue comes with other modules for client-side routing, state management, and so on.

> **NOTE** The first two versions of Vue were written in JavaScript, but Vue 3.0 is being rewritten in TypeScript from scratch. We wrote this chapter in the fall of 2019, and the creators of Vue announced that the upcoming Vue 3 will have a number of major changes—a built-in reactivity API, a hooks-like API, and improved TypeScript integration. A new function-based composition API is in the works (https://github.com/vuejs/rfcs/pull/78), as well as flattening the internal structure of the node in the Virtual DOM. The creators of the new version of Vue state that the new API will be 100% compatible with current syntax and will be purely additive, but for breaking changes they will offer a version-updater tool that should automatically upgrade your existing code base to Vue 3.

Having learned something about Angular and React, you should be comfortable with the concept of web components, which can be represented by custom tags like `<transaction-form-component>` or `<BlocksPanel>`. Such components can have their own state, and they can take data in or send it out so components can communicate with each other. A component can have child components, and in that sense Vue works the same way as Angular or React, although Vue uses a different syntax for declaring components.

As with React and Angular, you can scaffold a Vue project using a CLI tool, but we'd like to start in the simplest possible way. In the next section, you'll see how to create a Hello World web app without using any tooling.

15.1 Developing the simplest web page with Vue

In this section, we'll show you a very simple web page written with Vue and JavaScript. This page renders the message "Hello World" inside an HTML `<div>` element. We'll add the Vue library to this HTML page by using a `<script>` tag pointing to the URL of a Vue CDN.

Listing 15.1 Adding Vue to index.html

```
<!DOCTYPE html>
  <body>
    <div id="one"></div>
    <div id="two"></div>

    <script src="https://cdn.jsdelivr.net/npm/vue/dist/vue.js></script>
  </body>
</html>
```

Adds Vue from a CDN

This web page contains two empty <div> tags and a <script> tag to load the code of the Vue library. We purposely added two <div> tags to illustrate how you can attach the Vue instance just to a specific HTML element.

By loading Vue in a web page, we make all its APIs available to the scripts of this page. The next step is to create an instance of the `Vue` object and attach it to a specific HTML element. Note that our <div> elements have different IDs, so we can tell Vue, "Please start controlling the <div> that has the ID `one`." The second <div> could contain the content of an existing app written using different technology, so we wouldn't want Vue to control it.

The constructor of the `Vue` object requires an argument of type `ComponentOptions`, and you can find the names of all its optional properties in the options.d.ts type definition file. We'll just specify the `el` property (short for "element") containing the ID of the HTML element to be controlled by Vue, along with the `data` property, which will store the data to be rendered. The following listing shows the script that creates and attaches the `Vue` instance to the first `div`, passing the greeting "Hello World" as data.

Listing 15.2 Attaching the Vue instance to the first div

```
<!DOCTYPE html>
  <body>
    <div id="one">                 // This div will be controlled by Vue.
        <h1>{{greeting}}</h1>      // Data binding will show the value of the greeting variable.
    </div>
    <div id="two">                 // This div is not controlled by Vue.
        <h1>{{greeting}}</h1>      // No data binding here; the browser will render the text {{greeting}}.
    </div>

    <script src="https://cdn.jsdelivr.net/npm/vue/dist/vue.js"></script>

    <script type="text/javascript">
      const myApp = new Vue({      // Creates the Vue instance
          el: "#one",              // Attaches the Vue instance to the element with the ID "one"
          data: {                  // Passes the data to the element
              greeting: "Hello World"
          }
      })
    </script>
  </body>
</html>
```

Open the index.html file in the Chrome browser with its dev tools showing the Elements tab, and you'll see a web page as shown in figure 15.1. In this web page, the bottom <div> is just a regular HTML element and the browser renders "{{expression}}" as text. While instantiating Vue, we passed in a JavaScript object providing the ID of the

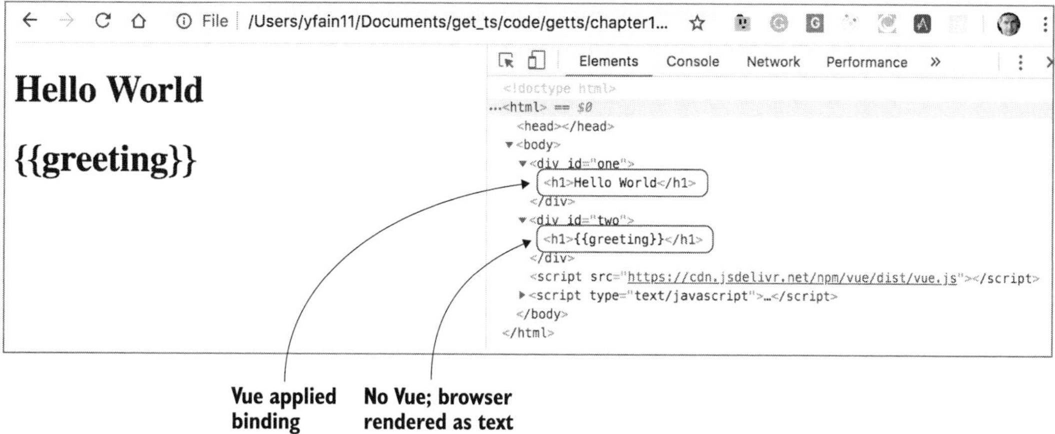

Figure 15.1 Rendering divs with and without Vue

top <div> element ("one"), so the Vue instance started it and applied binding to the `greeting` variable, rendering its "Hello World" value.

When an HTML element uses the "double mustache" notation, `{{expression}}`, Vue understands that it needs to render the evaluation of this expression. The UI of this app becomes *reactive*, and as soon as the value of the `greeting` variable changes, the new value is rendered inside the top <div> (with an ID of "one"). Because the `Vue` instance is scoped to a particular DOM element, nothing stops you from creating multiple `Vue` instances bound to different DOM elements.

You can access all the properties defined in the `data` object through the `myApp` reference variable. Figure 15.2 shows a screenshot taken after we entered `myApp.greeting = "Hello USA!"`. The new value is rendered in the top `div`.

TIP Enter the URL of the CDN in the browser, and you'll see the version of the Vue library it hosts. At the time of writing, the version was 2.6.10.

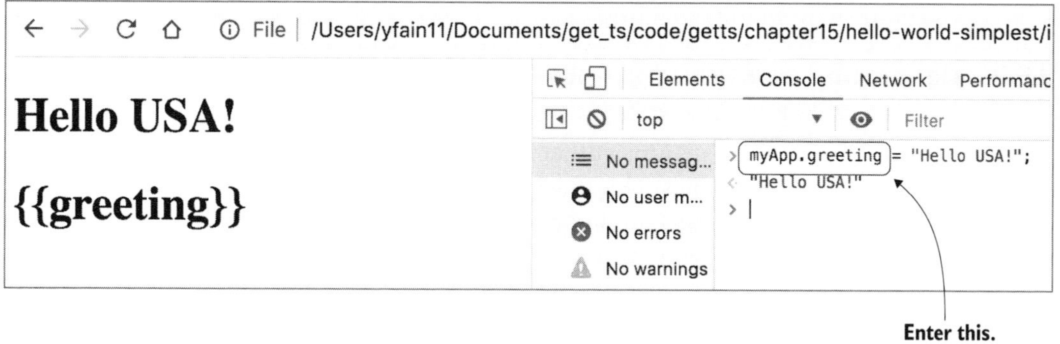

Figure 15.2 Changing the greeting's value in the browser's console

A `Vue` instance contains one or more UI components. In listing 15.2, we passed to the `Vue` instance an object literal with two properties, but we could provide an object with a `render()` function to render a top-level component:

```
new Vue({
  render: h => h(App) // App is a top-level component
})
```

You'll see this syntax starting from the next section in the apps generated by Vue CLI. Here the letter `h` stands for a script that generates HTML structures, such as the `createElement()` function. It's a shorter way of writing the following code:

```
render: function (createElement) {
    return createElement(App);
}
```

So `h` is a `createElement()` function described in the Vue documentation at http://mng.bz/5AJO.

TIP `h` stands for *hyperscript*: a script that generates HTML structures.

In our very simple app shown in listing 15.2, we just used the `<div>` DOM element to play the role of a UI component, but in the next section you'll see how to declare a Vue component that will have three sections:

- A declarative template
- A script
- Styles

The `data` property in listing 15.2 played the role of the component's state. If we added an input element so the user could enter data (such as a name), the Vue instance would update the component's state, and the `render()` function would re-render the component with the new state.

Let's switch to the Node-based project setup to see how a Vue app can be split into UI components in the real world.

15.2 Generating and running a new app with Vue CLI

The command-line interface called Vue CLI (https://cli.vuejs.org/) automates the process of creating a Vue project that has a compiler, a bundler, scripts for reproducible builds, and config files. This tool generates all the required configuration files for Webpack, so you can concentrate on writing your app instead of wasting time configuring tooling.

To install the Vue CLI package globally on your computer, run the following command in the terminal window:

```
npm install @vue/cli -g
```

TIP To see which version of the Vue CLI was installed, enter the `vue --version` command. We used CLI version 3.9.2 in writing this book.

Now you can run the `vue` command in your terminal window to generate a new project. To generate a TypeScript app, run the `vue create` command followed by the app name:

```
vue create hello-world
```

This command will open a dialog asking you to select options for your project. The default configuration is Babel and ESLint, but to work with the Typescript compiler, select the Manually Select Features option. Then you'll see a list of options, shown in figure 15.3, and you can select or unselect project options by using the up and down arrows and the space bar.

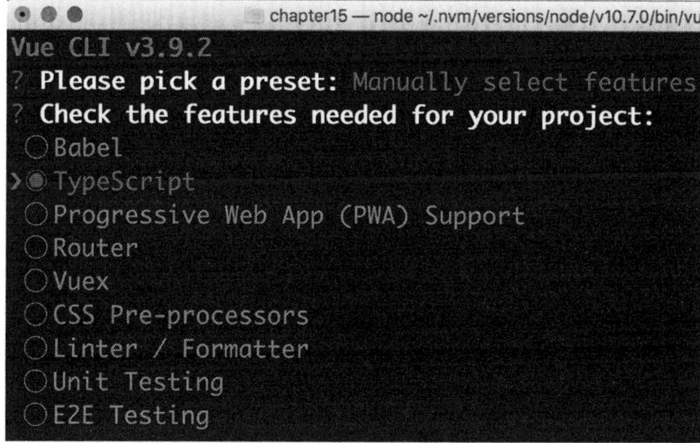

Figure 15.3 Manually selecting project features

For our hello-world project, we selected only TypeScript and pressed the Enter key. The next question is "Use class-style component syntax?" Agree to this. The next question is whether you want to use Babel alongside TypeScript (we rejected this option). In the remaining questions, we selected keeping separate config files for Babel and other tools, we didn't save these answers for future projects, and we selected npm as the default package manager.

Vue CLI generated a new Node-based project in the hello-world directory and installed all the required dependencies. Are you ready to run this app? Just enter the following commands in your terminal window:

```
cd hello-world
npm run serve
```

The code of the generated project will be compiled, and Webpack DevServer will serve the app at localhost:8080, as shown in figure 15.4.

Welcome to Your Vue.js + TypeScript App

For a guide and recipes on how to configure / customize this project,
check out the vue-cli documentation.

Installed CLI Plugins

typescript

Essential Links

Core Docs Forum Community Chat Twitter News

Ecosystem

vue-router vuex vue-devtools vue-loader awesome-vue

Figure 15.4 Running the initially generated project

The procedure for generating and running a Vue project is similar to using CLI for generating Angular and React projects. Under the hood, Vue CLI also uses Webpack for bundling and its webpack-dev-server for serving the app in the dev mode. When Webpack builds the bundles for deployment, it uses a special Vue plugin to transform the code of each component to JavaScript, so web browsers can parse and render it.

The following listing shows the package.json file, which includes the npm script commands `serve` and `build` to start the dev server and to build bundles with Webpack.

Listing 15.3 The generated package.json file

```
{
  "name": "hello-world",
  "version": "0.1.0",
```

```
"private": true,
  "scripts": {
    "serve": "vue-cli-service serve",
    "build": "vue-cli-service build"
  },
  "dependencies": {
    "vue": "^2.6.10",
    "vue-class-component": "^7.0.2",
    "vue-property-decorator": "^8.1.0"
  },
  "devDependencies": {
    "@vue/cli-plugin-typescript": "^3.9.0",
    "@vue/cli-service": "^3.9.0",
    "typescript": "^3.4.3",
    "vue-template-compiler": "^2.6.10"
  }
}
```

Starts the app using Webpack's dev server

Builds app bundles with Webpack

The CLI TypeScript plugin

The Typescript compiler

TIP Installing Vue using npm gives you TypeScript type declaration files, and the IDE will offer you autocomplete and help with static types without the need to use any additional tooling.

Let's open the generated project in VS Code and get familiar with the structure of the generated project, shown in figure 15.5. It's structured as a typical Node.js project with all dependencies listed in package.json and installed under node_modules. Since we write in TypeScript, the compiler's options are listed in the file tsconfig.json. The file main.ts loads the top-level component from the file App.vue. All UI components are located in the directory components.

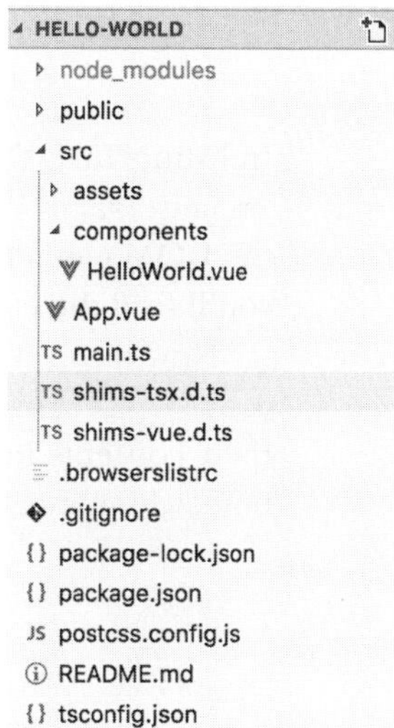

Figure 15.5 The project structure of the CLI-generated Hello World

The public folder contains the index.html file, which has the markup, including the HTML element that will be controlled by Vue. The build process will modify this file to include the scripts with the app bundles. You're free to add more directories and files containing app logic, and we'll do this in chapter 16 when we work on a Vue version of the blockchain client.

Listing 15.4 shows the content of the main.ts file, which creates the `Vue` instance and bootstraps the app. This time the script uses the options object with the `render` property, which stores a function (`h => h(App)`) that creates an instance of the `App` component and renders it in the DOM element with the ID `app`.

Listing 15.4 main.ts

```
import Vue from 'vue'
import App from './App.vue'

Vue.config.productionTip = false

new Vue({                          // Instantiates Vue and passes the options object
  render: h => h(App),             // Starts the rendering of the components tree
}).$mount('#app')                  // Attaches the Vue instance to the DOM element with the "app" ID
```

TIP If VS Code is your IDE, install the extension called Vetur (https://vuejs.github.io/vetur), which offers Vue-specific syntax highlighting, linting, autocompletion, formatting, and more.

In listing 15.2, we *mounted* Vue on a specific HTML element via a configuration object with the `el` property:

```
const myApp = new Vue({
          el: "#one"
          ...
          }
      })
```

In listing 15.4, the Vue instance didn't receive the `el` property. Instead, invoking the `$mount('#app')` method starts the mounting process and attaches the `Vue` instance to the DOM element with the `app` ID. If you open the generated public/index.html file, you'll find the element `<div id="app"></div>` there.

Now let's review the code in the App.vue file. It consists of three sections: `<template>`, `<script>`, and `<style>`. Figure 15.6 shows these sections after we collapsed their contents in VS Code. Note that the `<script>` section has a `lang = "ts"` attribute, which means TypeScript.

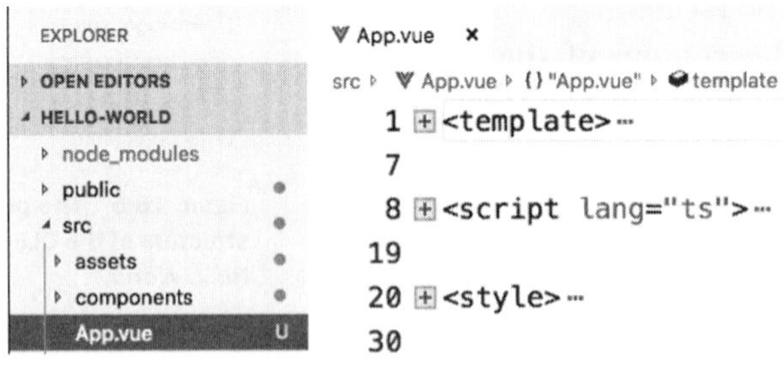

Figure 15.6 Three sections of the App.vue file

Listing 15.5 shows the content of the Vue CLI-generated `<template>` section. Having seen how Angular and React represent custom web components, you should easily spot the child component's `<HelloWorld>` tag here.

Listing 15.5 The `<template>` section of the `App` component

```
<template>
  <div id="app">
    <img alt="Vue logo" src="./assets/logo.png">
    <HelloWorld msg="Welcome to Your Vue.js + TypeScript App"/>
  </div>
</template>
```

The child HelloWorld component (annotation on the `<HelloWorld>` line)

From this template, you might also have correctly guessed that the `HelloWorld` component takes the `msg` property, and the `App` component passes the welcome message to it. Most of the content of the generated app is rendered by the `HelloWorld` component.

Listing 15.6 shows the `<script>` section of the `App` component. As with Angular, when you write Vue apps in TypeScript, you can use decorators. An example is `@Component()`, which takes an optional argument of the `ComponentOptions` type that has such properties as `el`, `data`, `template`, `props`, `components`, and more.

Listing 15.6 The `<script>` section of the `App` component

```
<script lang="ts">
import { Component, Vue } from 'vue-property-decorator';
import HelloWorld from './components/HelloWorld.vue';

@Component({
  components: {
    HelloWorld,
  },
})
export default class App extends Vue {}
</script>
```

Applies the Component decorator to the App class (annotation on the `@Component({` line)

Passes the ComponentOptions argument with the components property (annotation on the `components: {` line)

The App component is a class that extends Vue.

TIP To support TypeScript decorators, the compiler's `experimentalDecorators` option must be set to `true` in tsconfig.json.

During code generation, the CLI added two dependencies in package.json: `vue-class-component` and `vue-property-decorator`. The vue-class-component package allows us to write a Vue component as a class that extends `Vue`, but starting from Vue 3.0, class-based components will be supported natively. The vue-property-decorator package allows us to use a variety of decorators like `@Component()`, `@Prop()`, and others.

Without these packages, we could have used the object literal notation and exported the object instead of a class in the <script> section of the App.vue file:

```
import HelloWorld from './components/HelloWorld.vue';

export default {
  name: 'app',
  components: {
     HelloWorld
  }
}
```

The `HelloWorld` child component has a large <template> section with multiple <a> tags, but on top of the template you'll see the bound value `{{ msg }}`, as shown in listing 15.7.

Listing 15.7 A fragment of the `HelloWorld` component's template

```
<template>
  <div class="hello">
    <h1>{{ msg }}</h1>          <-- Binds the value of the msg property to the view
    <p>
    <!-- The rest of the content is omitted for brevity-->
</template>
```

The <script> section of the `HelloWorld` component is shown in the next listing. You can see two TypeScript decorators there: `Component()` and `Prop()`. In chapter 13, we introduced React.js props; in Vue they play the same role—passing data from parent to child.

Listing 15.8 The `<script>` section of HelloWorld.vue

```
<script lang="ts">
import { Component, Prop, Vue } from 'vue-property-decorator';

@Component                     <-- Uses the @Component() class decorator without any arguments
export default class HelloWorld extends Vue {
  @Prop() private msg!: string;     <-- Uses the @Prop() property decorator
}
</script>
```

Have you noticed the exclamation point after `msg`? It's a non-null assertion operator. By adding the exclamation point to the property name, you say to TypeScript's type checker, "Don't complain about the possibility of `msg` being `null` or `undefined`, because it won't be. Take my word for it!"

You can also provide a default value for msg as follows:

```
@Prop({default: "The message will go here"}) private msg: string;
```

Vue CLI generated the code with a `@Prop()` property-level decorator to declare that the `HelloWorld` component takes one property, `msg`. The other way to do this is by using the `props` property of the `@Component()` decorator. The following code snippet shows an alternative way of passing the `msg` props via the property of `@Component()`:

```
@Component({
   props: {
     msg: {
       default: "The message will go here"
     }
   }
}
export default class HelloWorld extends Vue { }
```

The default property value will be rendered if the parent component won't assign a value to the `msg` attribute, for example, `<HelloWorld />`.

Using props you can send data from parent to child, but to pass data from child to parent, use the `$emit()` method. For example, the `<order-component>` child component can send a `place-order` event with `orderData` as the payload to the parent as follows:

```
this.$emit("place-order", orderData);
```

The parent can receive this event like this:

```
<order-component @place-order = "processOrder">

...

processOrder(payload) {

// handle the payload, i.e. the orderData received from the order component

}
```

> **TIP** You'll see an example of using `$emit()` in listing 16.6. There, the `Pending-TransactionsPanel` component sends the `generate-block` event to its parent.

Now that you understand how a basic Vue app works, we'll introduce you to navigation with the client-side router offered by Vue.

15.3 Developing single-page apps with router support

In chapter 11, we developed a simple Angular app that read and rendered data from the products.json file. In this section, we'll create a single-page Vue app that will also read this file and display the list of products. Through this app, we'll introduce the Vue Router, and we'll show you how to use some of the Vue directives to render the list of products. Then we'll go over another app, illustrating how you can pass parameters while navigating to the route that shows the product details view.

The first app is located in the router-product-list directory and the second is in router-product-details.

NOTE In chapter 11, we introduced the Angular router. The vue-router package implements client-side navigation using similar concepts.

The landing page of the router-product-list single-page app (SPA) will show the list of products in the `Home` component, as shown in figure 15.7. The user will be able to click on the selected product so the app can process it as needed. The About link will navigate to the `About` view without making any requests to the server.

Figure 15.7 A product list with the second product selected

The point of using the Vue Router is to support user navigation on the client side and persist state in the address bar. It creates a bookmarkable location that can be shared and opened directly without the need to go through multiple steps to see a desired view. Also, the router allows you to avoid loading separate web pages from the server—the page remains the same, but the user can navigate *on the client* from one view to another without asking the server to load a different page. This is possible because the code of all UI components is already downloaded by the browser.

In single-page apps, we don't use the original `<a href="…">` HTML tags for links, as they would result in server requests and page reloads. A framework that supports client-side routing produces anchor tags that include click handlers to invoke functions on the client and update the address bar.

In Vue, the router offers the `<router-link>` tag, which doesn't send the request to the server. For the `about` route, the Vue Router will form the URL `localhost:8080/about`, and then it'll read the mapping for the `/about` segment and render the `About` component in the `<router-view>` area. If the user clicks the About link for the first time, Vue will lazily load the `About` component before rendering it. For all subsequent clicks on this link, only the `About` component will be rendered.

The Vue Router is implemented in the package called "vue-router," and you'll find it in the list of dependencies in the package.json file.

15.3.1 Generating a new app with the Vue Router

We used the CLI again to generate the router-product-list project, but this time we also selected Router in the list of CLI options. The CLI also asked if this app should use the history mode for router, and we agreed to this.

The History API is implemented by browsers that support the HTML5 API, so if your app has to support really old browsers, don't select history mode. Without history mode, all the URLs in your app will include hash sign to separate the server and client portions of the URL.

For example, without history mode, the URL of the client's resource might look like http://localhost:8080/#about, with the segment to the left of the hash sign being handled by the server. The URL segment to the right of the hash sign is handled by the client app. If you select history mode, the URL for the same resource would look like http://localhost:8080/about. You can read more about the HTML5 history mode in Mozilla's documentation at http://mng.bz/6w5e.

Change to the router-product-list directory and run the command `npm run serve`. You'll see the landing page of the generated app. It will look similar to figure 15.4 but with a small addition: there will be two links, Home and About, at the top of the window, as shown in figure 15.8.

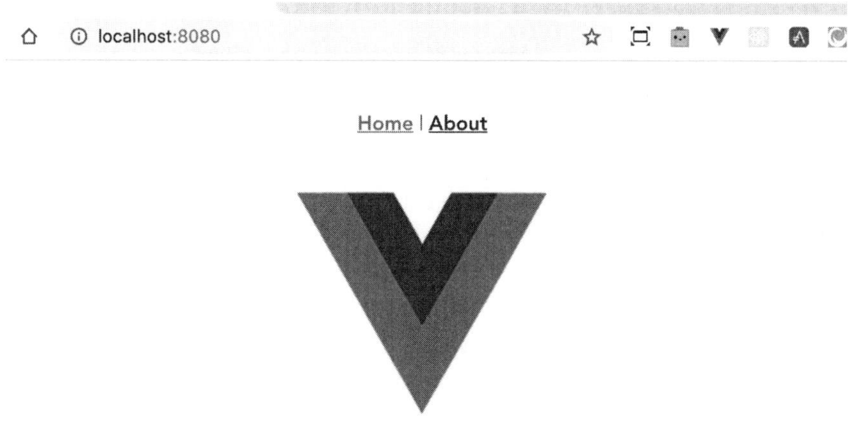

Figure 15.8 The generated App component with two links on top

CLI generated the src/views directory with two files: Home.vue and About.vue. These components are controlled by the Vue Router. Note the URL in figure 15.8—it's just the protocol (not shown), domain name, and port. There is no client segment in this URL. We can guess that the router was configured to render the `Home` component by default if the URL doesn't contain a client segment. If the user clicks on the About link, the browser renders the `About` component, as shown in figure 15.9.

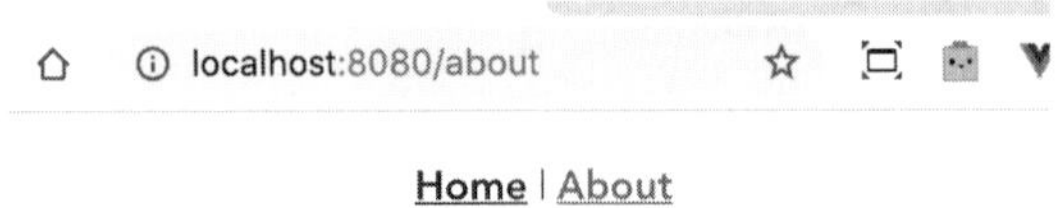

Figure 15.9 The generated `About` component

This time, the URL contains the client segment `/about`, and again we can guess that the router was configured to render the `About` component for this segment. Pretty soon you'll see that our guesses are correct.

The generated main.ts file imports the `Router` object and adds it to the `Vue` instance.

Listing 15.9 The main file imports the router configuration

```
import Vue from 'vue';
import App from './App.vue';
import router from './router';

Vue.config.productionTip = false;

new Vue({
  router,
  render: (h) => h(App),
}).$mount('#app');
```

Annotations:
- `import router from './router';` — Imports the routes configuration from router.ts
- `router,` — Adds the Router object with configured routes to the Vue instance

TIP In listing 15.9, we pass an object literal to the Vue instance, and ES6 allows us to use a shortcut syntax: we can just specify the property name if it's the same as the variable name that contains the value. That's why instead of writing `router: router` we wrote `router` here.

The `Vue` instance includes a reference to the `Router` object that contains configured routes, so it knows which component to render if the user clicks on Home or About. The initial routes configuration was generated in the router.ts file, and its content is shown in the following listing. In general, when you design a single-page app, you need to think about the user's navigation on the client and create an array that maps URL segments to UI components. In the following listing, this array is called `routes`.

Listing 15.10 The CLI-generated router.ts

```
import Vue from 'vue';
import Router from 'vue-router';
import Home from './views/Home.vue';

Vue.use(Router);

export default new Router({
```

Annotations:
- `Vue.use(Router);` — Enables the use of the Router package
- `export default new Router({` — Creates the Router object

```
  mode: 'history',                          ◁ Supports the HTML5 History
▷ base: process.env.BASE_URL,                 API (no # in the URL)
  routes: [              ◁ Configures an array of routes
    {
      path: '/',                  Uses the server's URL as a base
      name: 'home',
      component: Home,          ◁ Renders the Home component
    },                            for the default / path
    {
      path: '/about',
      name: 'about',
      component: () => import(/* webpackChunkName: "about" */
➥ './views/About.vue'),        ◁ Renders the About component
    },                            for the /about path
  ],
});
```

When you create an instance of the Router object, you are passing an object of type RouterOptions to its constructor. We didn't use the linkActiveClass property here, but if you don't like the green color of the active link, you can change it using this property.

By enabling the Router package, we get the access to a special $route variable, and we'll use it in the next section to get the parameters passed during navigation. Note the mode property: its value is history because we selected history mode during app generation. The '/ path is mapped to the Home component, and CLI didn't forget to import this component from the Home.vue file. But instead of mapping the /about path to the About component, it's mapped to the following fat arrow expression:

```
() => import(/* webpackChunkName: "about" */ './views/About.vue')
```

This line states that the router has to lazy-load the About component when the route is visited. For this to happen, the code instructs Webpack that when it generates production bundles, that it should split the code and generate a separate chunk (about.[hash].js) for this route. The import is done dynamically only if the user decides to navigate to the About view.

> **TIP** To see that Webpack does split the code, run the production build with npm run build and check the content of the dist directory. There you'll find a separate file with a name similar to about.8027d92e.js. In prod, this file won't be loaded unless the router navigates to the About view.

Our top-level component, App.vue, has links that will display one view or another, and listing 15.11 shows the template section of the App.vue, which contains the tags <router-link> and <router-view>. The <router-view> tag defines the area where the changing content (the Home or About component) will be rendered.

Each <router-link> has a to attribute, telling Vue which component to render based on the configured routes. The to attribute in the <router-link> tag is where you specify where to navigate, and the router uses the value of the to attribute to decide which component to render. For example, `to="/"` specifies where to navigate if the URL has no client-side segments.

Listing 15.11 The `<template>` section of the App.vue

```
<template>
  <div id="app">
    <div id="nav">
      <router-link to="/">Home</router-link>          <-- Renders the default component
      <router-link to="/about">About</router-link>    <-- Renders the component configured for the /about URL segment
    </div>
    <router-view/>      <-- The router has to render Home or About here.
  </div>
</template>
```

NOTE In listing 15.11, both `<router-link>` tags have static values in the `to` attribute. This doesn't have to be the case. You can bind a variable to the `:to` attribute (note the colon in front of `to`).

In the next section, we'll replace the code generated in the Home.vue file so it reads and renders the list of products. We'll also replace the code in About.view so it displays the details of the selected product. While doing this, we'll look at how you can pass data while navigating to the product details view.

15.3.2 Displaying a list of products in the Home view

In this section, we'll look at the products.json file in the public directory. It has the following content:

```
[
  { "id":0, "title": "First Product", "price": 24.99 },
  { "id":1, "title": "Second Product", "price": 64.99 },
  { "id":2, "title": "Third Product", "price": 74.99}
]
```

This file contains JSON-formatted product data of a rather simple structure, and it's easy to write a TypeScript interface to represent a product. But you can also generate the corresponding TypeScript interface by using a third-party tool like MakeTypes (https://jvilk.com/MakeTypes). Figure 15.10 shows a screenshot of the MakeTypes website. You just paste the JSON data in the text area on the left, and it'll generate the corresponding TypeScript interface in the field on the right. We used MakeTypes to generate the `Product` interface, which is located in the product.ts file.

Our app should read this file as soon as the user navigates to the Home route, which is the default route. But where in the `Home` component should we put the code for fetching data? Do we know exactly when the creation of the `Home` component is complete? Yes, we do. Vue offers a number of callbacks that are invoked at different stages of the component's life cycle. In the TypeScript file-declarations file, options.d.ts,

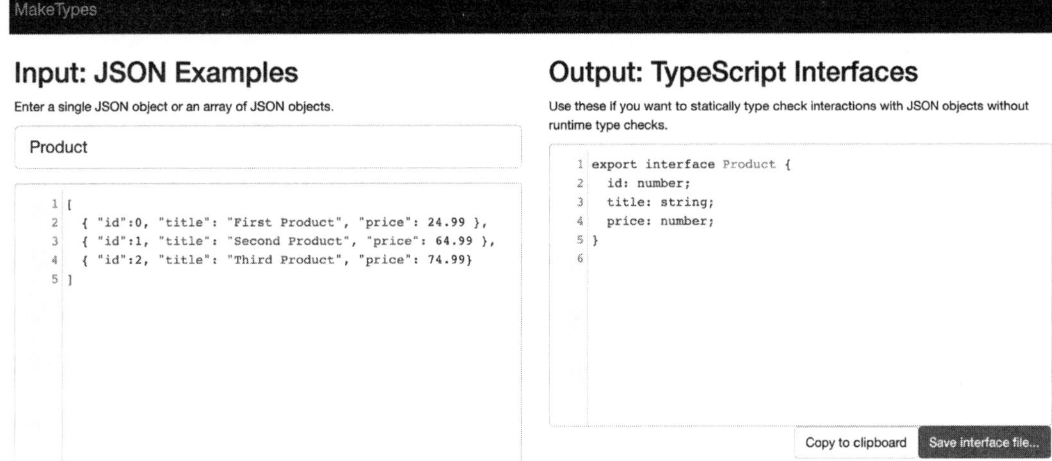

Figure 15.10 Generating a TypeScript interface from JSON using MakeTypes

located in node_modules/vue/types, you'll find the declaration of the `ComponentOptions` interface. It contains the declarations of all the life cycle hooks.

Listing 15.12 Component life cycle hooks

```
beforeCreate?(this: V): void;
created?(): void;
beforeDestroy?(): void;
destroyed?(): void;
beforeMount?(): void;
mounted?(): void;
beforeUpdate?(): void;
updated?(): void;
activated?(): void;
deactivated?(): void;
errorCaptured?(err: Error, vm: Vue, info: string): boolean | void;
serverPrefetch?(this: V): Promise<void>;
```

You can find a description of each of these methods in the Vue.js documentation (http://mng.bz/omBZ), but we'll just say that the `created()` method fits our needs. It's invoked when the component is initialized and is ready to receive data and handle events.

Life cycle hooks are invoked by Vue, so we just need to put our data-fetching code inside the `created()` method. The following listing shows the first modified version of the `Home` component.

Listing 15.13 Adding the component's created() life cycle hook

```
<template>
  <div class="home">
    <h1>I'm the Home component</h1>
  </div>
</template>

<script lang="ts">
import { Component, Vue } from 'vue-property-decorator';

@Component
export default class Home extends Vue {

  created() {                              <-- This life cycle hook
    console.log("Home created!");              is invoked by Vue.
  }
}

</script>
```

TIP The Vue Router has its own life cycle hooks and guards that allow you to intercept important events during navigation to a route. They are described in the vue-router documentation at https://router.vuejs.org/guide/.

Run the app, and you'll see the message "Home created!" on the browser's console. Now that we're sure that the `created()` hook is invoked, we'll make it fetch products.

Listing 15.14 Fetching products

```
<template>
  <div class="home">
    <h1>I'm the Home component</h1>
  </div>
</template>

<script lang="ts">
import { Component, Vue } from 'vue-property-decorator';
import { Product } from '@/product';          <-- Imports the
                                                  Product interface
@Component
export default class Home extends Vue {

  products: Product[]=[];                     Initiates the data
                                              fetch using Promise
  created() {
    fetch("/products.json")                   <--
    .then(response => response.json())        <-- Converts the response
                                                  to JSON format
    .then(json => {
      this.products=json;    <-- Populates the products array with the data

      console.log(this.products);             <-- Prints the retrieved data
    },                                            on the browser console
```

```
      error => {
         console.log('Error loading products.json:', error);
      });
   }
}
</script>
```

In this version of the `Home` component, we used the browser's Fetch API to read the products.json file and simply print the retrieved data on the browser's console. Here we used the Promise-based syntax, and later, in the router-product-detail app, we'll use the `async` and `await` keywords, so you can compare the two.

In listing 15.14, there is an `import` statement that uses the `@` sign as a shortcut for `./src`. This is possible because the tsconfig.json file specifies the `paths` option as follows:

```
"paths": {
  "@/*": [
    "src/*"
  ]
}
```

The `@` sign can also be a shortcut for the Vue directive `v-on`, which is used for handling events. For example, instead of writing `<button v-on:click="doSomething()">` you can write `<button @click="doSomething()">`.

The next step is to add the `<ul>` tag to display the list of products in the `Home` component. Vue comes with a number of directives that tell the `Vue` instance what to do with the DOM element. Directives can be used in the template and look like a prefixed HTML attribute: `v-if`, `v-show`, `v-for`, `v-bind`, `v-on`, and others.

Here we'll use the directive `v-for` to iterate through the `products` array, rendering `<li>` for each element of the array. Vue needs to be able to track each element of the list, so you need to provide a unique key attribute for each item, and we'll use the `v-bind:key` directive, specifying the product ID as a unique key. The following listing shows the next version of the `Home` component, which renders the list of products.

Listing 15.15 Displaying the list of products in the `Home` component

```
<template>
  <div class="home">
    <h1>Products</h1>
    <ul id="prod">
       <li v-for="product in products"      <-- Iterates products with the v-for directive
           v-bind:key="product.id">        <-- Assigns a unique key to each <li> element
         {{ product.title }}     <-- Renders only the product title
       </li>
    </ul>
  </div>
</template>

<style>
```

```
  ul {
    text-align: left;      ⊲— Aligns the text of the list elements
  }
</style>

<script lang="ts">
import { Component, Vue } from 'vue-property-decorator';
import {Product} from '@/product';

@Component
export default class Home extends Vue {

  products: Product[]=[];

  created() {
    fetch("/products.json")
    .then(response => response.json())
    .then(json => {
      this.products=json;
    },
    error => {
       console.log('Error loading products.json:', error);
    });
  }
}

</script>
```

Running the app will render the `Home` component, as shown in figure 15.11.

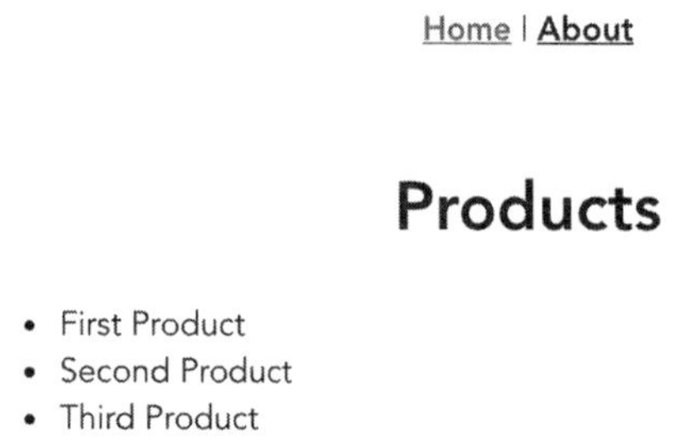

Home | About

Products

- First Product
- Second Product
- Third Product

Figure 15.11 Rendering products

We'll implement one more feature in this app—the user should be able to select a product from the list, and the app should know which one was selected. In the next version of the `Home` component, we'll handle the click event and highlight the selected product with a light blue background. The following listing shows the template with an added `v-on:click` directive, and we used the `@` shortcut for `v-on`.

Listing 15.16 The new template of the `Home` component

```
<template>
  <div class="home">
    <h1>Products</h1>
```

```
    <ul id="prod">
       <li v-for="product in products"
           v-bind:key="product.id"
           v-bind:class="{selected: product === selectedProduct}"
           @click = "onSelect(product)">
          {{ product.title }}
       </li>
    </ul>
  </div>
</template>
```

Uses binding to dynamically apply a different style to the selected item

Calls the onSelect method, passing the selected product's data

The template in listing 15.16 has two additions. First, we've added the `v-bind` directive to bind the `selected` CSS selector to the `<li>` element that has the same value as the `selectedProduct` class property. Second, we've added a click event handler to call the `onSelect()` method, where we'll set the value for `selectedProduct` so the binding mechanism can highlight the corresponding list item.

The following listing shows the `<style>` section of the `Home` component, where the `selected` class is defined.

Listing 15.17 The new style of the `Home` component

```
<style>

.home {
  display: flex;
  flex-direction: column;
}
  ul {
    text-align: left;
    display: inline-block;
    align-self: start;
  }

  .selected {
    background-color: lightblue
  }
</style>
```

Declares the style for highlighting the selected product

The next listing shows the content of the `<script>` section of the `Home` component, which has the new `selectedProduct` property.

Listing 15.18 The `<script>` section of the `Home` component

```
<script lang="ts">
import { Component, Vue } from 'vue-property-decorator';
import {Product} from '@/product';

@Component
export default class Home extends Vue {

  products: Product[]=[];
```

```
  selectedProduct: Product | null = null;      <-- The selectedProduct property stores the selected product.

  created() {
    fetch("/products.json")
    .then(response => response.json())
    .then(json => {
      this.products=json;
    },
    error => {
       console.log('Error loading products.json:', error);
    });
  }

  onSelect(prod: Product): void {              <-- The handler function for the click event
    this.selectedProduct = prod;               <-- Sets the value of the selectedProduct
    }
}
</script>
```

Note the type of the `selectedProduct` property of the `Home` class. We had to initialize this property, or TypeScript would complain that "Property 'selectedProduct' has no initializer and is not definitely assigned in the constructor." This check can either be disabled for the entire project in tsconfig.json with `strictPropertyInitialization: false`, or it can be suppressed on the property level with an exclamation mark right after the property name:

```
selectedProduct!: Product;
```

Declaring this property as `selectedProduct: Product = null` wouldn't work either, because TypeScript would complain that you can't assign `null` to the `Product` type. That's why we explicitly allowed `selectedProduct` to be `null` by applying the union type `selectedProduct: Product | null = null;`. We need to initialize `selectedProduct` with a value, because otherwise property won't exist in the generated code, Vue won't make it reactive, and we won't be able to use it in the component's template.

Now when the user clicks on the product, the `onSelect()` method is invoked, setting the value of the `selectedProduct` property, which is used in the `v-bind:class` directive for changing the CSS selector of the selected list item. When we set the value of `selectedProperty`, the entire UL is rendered (this happens when the value of any class property changes), clearing the style on the previously selected item. Figure 15.12 shows the rendered product list with the second product selected.

- First Product
- Second Product
- Third Product

Figure 15.12 A product is highlighted when it's clicked on.

Earlier in this chapter, you saw how a parent component can pass data to its child by using props. In the next section, we'll show you how to pass data while navigating to a route.

15.3.3 *Passing data with the Vue Router*

When the user navigates to a route, your app can pass data to the destination component using the route parameters. In this section, we'll review yet another version of our app that renders a list of products. In this case, when the user selects a product, the app navigates to a product details view, showing info about the selected product.

This app is located in the router-product-detail directory. Run `npm install` and then `npm run serve`, and the list of products will be displayed. Click on a product, and the app will navigate to the product details. Figure 15.13 shows a screenshot taken after the user clicks on Second Product in the list. The text "Second Product" displays in green.

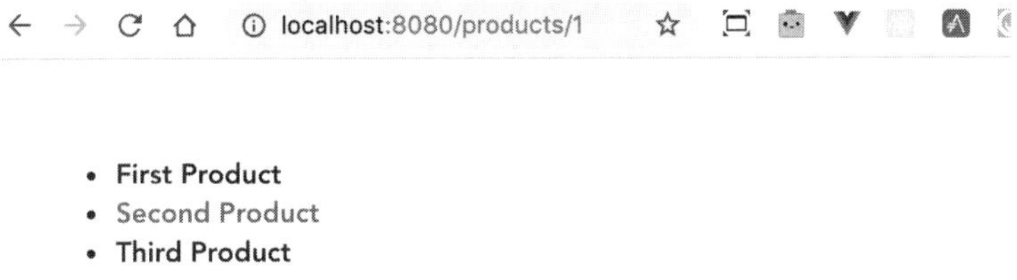

Figure 15.13 Showing details for the second product

This app has only two components: `App` and `ProductDetail`. The top part of the image is the UI of the `App` component, and the bottom part is `ProductDetails`. Note the URL segment `/products/1`. The route that navigates to the product details view is configured as the path `'/products/:productId'`, as shown in the following listing.

Listing 15.19 The router.ts file: the route for /products/:productId

```
import Vue from 'vue';
import Router from 'vue-router';
import ProductDetails from './views/ProductDetails.vue';

Vue.use(Router);

export default new Router({
  base: process.env.BASE_URL,
  mode: 'history',
  routes: [
    {
      path: '/products/:productId',
```

Configures the navigation for the URL "products" followed by the value

```
      component: ProductDetails,      ◁─ Navigates to ProductDetail,
    },                                   passing the :productId
  ],                                     value as productId
});
```

It's not obvious from figure 15.13, but the product list items are represented by HTML anchor tags, and each link has a URL that includes the selected product ID. The following listing shows the template of the `App` component that renders a link for each product.

Listing 15.20 The template of the `App` component

```
<template>
  <div id="app">
    <div id="nav">
      <ul>                                            Forms a link that includes
        <li v-for="product in products"                the selected product ID
            v-bind:key="product.id">
            <router-link v-bind:to="'/products/' + product.id">     ◁
              {{ product.title }}
            </router-link>
        </li>
      </ul>
      <p>Click on a product to see details</p>
    </div>
    <router-view/>    ◁─ The ProductDetail component
  </div>                 will be rendered here.
</template>
```

Compare the content of the dynamically generated `<li>` element here with the version from listing 15.16. There, we just rendered the text `product.title`, but here we render the following:

```
<router-link v-bind:to="'/products/' + product.id">
  {{ product.title }}
</router-link>
```

The code displays the title but adds the product ID to the URL. During compilation, Vue will replace `<router-link>` with a regular anchor tag, `<a>`, and the entire list will be shown in the area identified by the `<router-view>` tag.

The `<script>` section in App.vue has only the code to read the products.json file, as shown in the following listing. We explained this code earlier.

Listing 15.21 The `<script>` section in App.vue

```
<script lang="ts">
import { Component, Vue } from 'vue-property-decorator';
import { Product } from '@/product';

@Component
```

```
export default class App extends Vue {
  private products: Product[] = [];

  private created() {
    fetch('/products.json')
      .then((response) => response.json())
      .then(
        (data) => this.products = data,
        (error) => console.log('Error loading products.json:', error),
      );
  }
}
</script>
```

The fact that the products property of the App component is declared as private but can be used in the template anyway shows that Vue needs to improve its TypeScript support. Angular wouldn't let you access private class variables from the template.

Now let's review the code of the ProductDetail component, which needs to extract the value of the productId from the router and render the product details. The following listing shows the <template> section of the ProductDetails component.

Listing 15.22 The <template> section of ProductDetails.vue

```
<template>
  <div>
    <h1>Product details</h1>
    <ul v-if="product">          <-- Conditional rendering of the <ul>
      <li>ID: {{ product.id }}</li>
      <li>Title: {{ product.title }}</li>
      <li>Price: {{ product.price }}</li>
    </ul>
  </div>
</template>
```

Here we use the v-if directive, which allows us to control the rendering of the DOM element based on some condition. Here the v-if="product" expression means "render this <ul> only if the product variable has a truthy value." The product property is declared in the ProductDetails class, and it'll have a value only after the data for the product is fetched. For this to happen, the user has to select a product in the App component. When that happens, the router will navigate to ProductDetails, passing the product ID as a router parameter. Then the fetchProductByID() method will populate the product property, and its info will be rendered using the component template.

The following listing shows the code of the ProductDetails class, which has the product property and three methods: beforeRouteEnter(), beforeRouteUpdate(), and fetchProductByID().The first two are the router's hooks (navigation guards), and the last one finds the product by ID.

Listing 15.23 The <script> section of ProductDetails.vue

```
<script lang="ts">
import { Component, Vue } from 'vue-property-decorator';
import { Route } from 'vue-router';
import { Product } from '@/product';

@Component({
  async beforeRouteEnter(to: Route, from: Route, next: Function) {     // The beforeRouterEnter navigation guard
    const product = await fetchProductByID(to.params.productId);       // Fetches the data for the provided product ID
    next((component) => component.product = product);                  // Resolves the navigation guard
  },

  async beforeRouteUpdate(to: Route, from: Route, next: Function) {    // The beforeRouterUpdate navigation guard
     this.product = await fetchProductByID(to.params.productId);
    next();
  },
})
export default class ProductDetails extends Vue {
  private product: Product | null = null;                              // Declares the product property
}

async function fetchProductByID(id: string): Promise<Product> {        // The method that fetches the product details
  const productId = parseInt(id, 10);
  const response = await fetch('/products.json');
  const products = await response.json();
  return products.find((p) => p.id === productId);
}
</script>
```

The `beforeRouteEnter()` hook is called before the route that renders this component is confirmed. Vue provides three arguments for this hook:

- `to`—The target `Route` object being navigated to
- `from`—The current `Route` being navigated from
- `next`—The function that must be called to continue navigation

The `to` argument contains the `params` property that stores the value of the parameter passed to the route. In our case, we used the name `productId` in the router.ts file, so we have to use the same name to get the value of this parameter in the destination route.

The `beforeRouteEnter()` hook doesn't have access to the `this` component instance because it has not been created yet when this guard is called. However, you can access the instance by passing a callback to `next()`. The callback will be invoked when the navigation is confirmed, and the component instance will be passed to the callback as the argument:

```
next((component) => component.product = product);
```

Here we initialize the `product` property of the component's instance. The `before-RouteUpdate()` hook is invoked when the route that renders this component changes. In our app, this happens when the `ProductDetails` component is already rendered, but the user clicks on another product in the list. This hook has access to the `this` component instance, so we can simply assign the product's value to `this.product`, and the `next()` callback doesn't need any arguments.

For simplicity, we find the product details info with the `fetchProductByID()` method. It uses the Fetch API to read the entire products.json file and then it finds just one object with a matching product ID. We use the `async` and `await` keywords, and you can compare this syntax with the Promise-based one shown in listing 15.14.

This concludes our introduction to the Vue library/framework. In the next chapter, we'll create yet another version of the blockchain UI, this time using Vue.

Summary

- Vue is a library that allows you to create UI components for rendering, and it also includes a client-side router for arranging the user's navigation and tooling to generate a new project and create dev or prod bundles for deployment.
- If you prefer developing UI components that have HTML, styles, and the code in one file, Vue will fit the bill. A single file contains three sections: `<template>` for markup, `<script>` for code, and `<style>` for CSS.
- Learning Vue is easier than React or Angular, and Vue offers similar features.
- JavaScript developers work with Vue using the object-based API, but TypeScript developers may find using class-based components more natural than creating components as JavaScript objects. In Vue 3, we'll also have the option to create functional components, just as we do in the React framework.
- Vue 3 is in the works, and it will offer a new Composition API that will allow you to develop functional UI components. At the time of writing, the Composition API is at the Request For Comments stage, but the core Vue team promises that upgrades from Vue 2 to 3 will be a simple and mostly automated process. The Composition API will be an addition to the existing object-based API.
- Like React.js, Vue doesn't force you to turn an existing app into a SPA. You can gradually introduce Vue to existing frontend code without rewriting the entire code base at once.

16 Developing the blockchain client in Vue.js

This chapter covers

- Reviewing the Vue.js version of the blockchain web client
- Running a Vue app that works with two servers in dev mode
- The flow of data, from entering a transaction to generating a block
- Arranging communications between the blockchain's client components

In the previous chapter, you learned the basics of Vue, and now we'll review a new version of the blockchain app with the client portion written in Vue. The source code of the web client is located in the blockchain/client directory, and the messaging server located in the blockchain/server directory.

The code for the server side remains the same as in chapter 14, and the functionality of this version of the blockchain app is the same as well. The UI portion of the app, however, has been completely rewritten in Vue and TypeScript.

We won't be reviewing the functionality of the blockchain app in this chapter, because we covered that in previous chapters, but we will review the code that's specific to the Vue library. You may want to look back at chapter 10 to refresh your memory of the functionality of the blockchain client and messaging server.

To recap, when the user of any node clicks on the GENERATE BLOCK button, the client's code announces the start of the mining process, which doesn't mean that this node will be the first to finish the mining. Other nodes may also start mining the block with the same transactions, and all these nodes will use the messaging server to exchange their longest chains and come to a consensus as to which node is the winner.

First we'll show you how to start the messaging server and the Vue client for the blockchain app. Then we'll introduce the code of the class-based Vue components.

16.1 Starting the client and the messaging server

To start the server, open the terminal window in the server directory, run `npm install` to install the server's dependencies, and then run the `npm start` command. You'll see the message "Listening on http://localhost:3000." Keep the server running.

To start the Vue client, open another terminal window in the client directory, run `npm install` to install Vue and its dependencies, and then run the `npm run serve` command. Open the browser to localhost:8080, and you'll see a familiar blockchain web page, shown in figure 16.1. The App.vue file contains the code for the top-level `App`

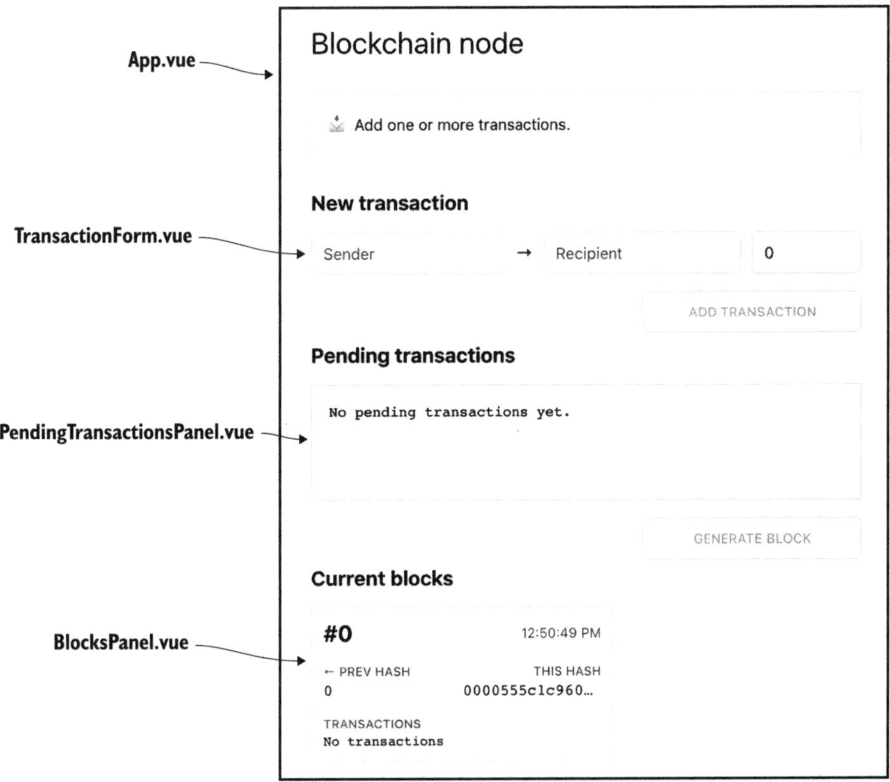

Figure 16.1 The blockchain client is launched.

component, and the other *.vue files contain the child components `TransactionForm`, `PendingTransactionsPanel`, and `BlocksPanel`.

The client portion of this app was generated by Vue CLI, and we selected Babel, TypeScript, and class-based components from the list of CLI options. Figure 16.2 shows the file structure of the client directory. UI components are located in the components subdirectory, and the lib subdirectory contains other scripts that create blockchain nodes and communicate with the messaging server. The public directory contains an incomplete index.html file (it'll be updated during the build process) and the styles.css file that contains all the styles for this app. We didn't use the Vue Router in this app.

During this project generation, we selected both TypeScript and Babel. You can see that the configuration file includes the `@vue/app` preset. Also, Babel comes with a TypeScript plugin, so our app has a single compile process controlled by Babel.

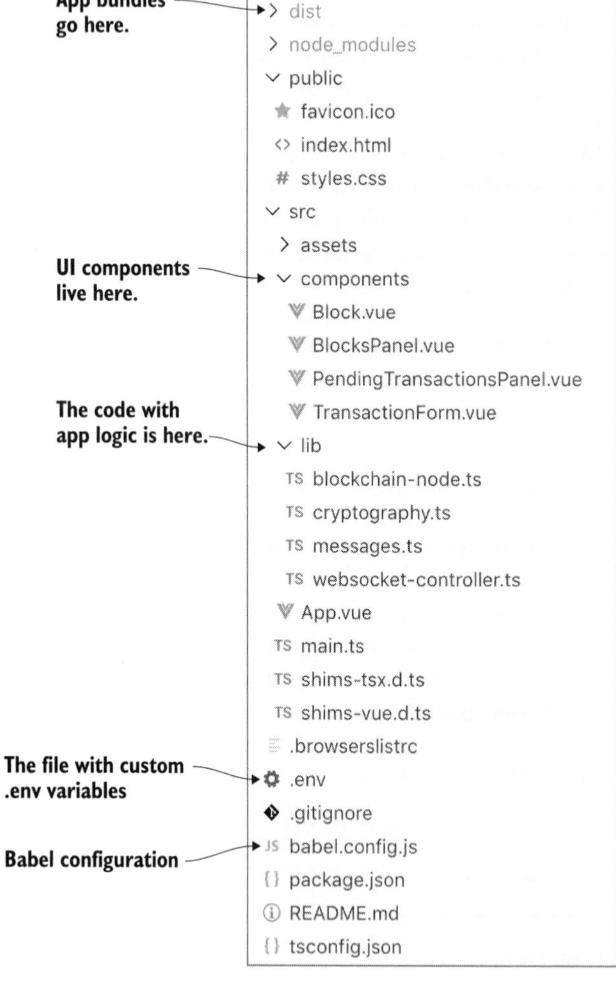

Figure 16.2 The project structure

You may want to consider using Babel for the following reasons:

- *Modern mode*—Basically this is feature-identical to Angular's differential loading. Two sets of bundles are generated: one in ES5 format and the other in ES2015. If the user's web browser supports the ES2015 syntax, only the corresponding bundles will be loaded.
- *Auto-detecting polyfills*—This is related to the previous point, but it's not the same. Modern mode is about JavaScript language features, whereas this feature is related to the browser's APIs. Babel automatically detects the polyfills needed based on the language features used in your source code. This ensures that the minimum number of polyfills are included in your final bundle.
- *JSX support*—Without Babel, we can use only HTML-based templates.

The lib directory has the code that generates new blocks, requests the longest chain, notifies the other nodes about newly generated blocks, and invites other members of the blockchain to start generating new blocks for the specified transactions. These processes were described in sections 10.1 and 10.2. Because the code in the lib directory doesn't have any UI components, it remains exactly the same as in the React blockchain client from chapter 14.

> **TIP** Compare figure 16.1 with figure 14.1. You'll see that the landing page of the blockchain client is split into UI components the same way in Vue and React.

When you run the CLI-generated app, it uses the vue-cli-service script. You can find these commands in the package.json file:

```
"scripts": {
    "serve": "vue-cli-service serve",
    "build": "vue-cli-service build"
  }
```

The vue-cli-service script always reads the .env file, which can be used for configuring custom environment variables, such as host names and port numbers. Figure 16.3 illustrates how the Webpack dev server (port 8080) proxies requests to the messaging server (port 3000). It's done much as it's done in React and Angular. The proxy is configured in the .env file as `VUE_APP_WS_PROXY_HOSTNAME=localhost:3000`.

The entry point to the blockchain client is the main.ts file, which mounts the `Vue` instance at the DOM element with the `app` ID.

```
new Vue({
  render: h => h(App),
}).$mount('#app')
```

Like React, Vue uses a Virtual DOM, and the `render()` function returns an instance of the `VNode` virtual node, which is actually a tree of `VNode` elements with a root element

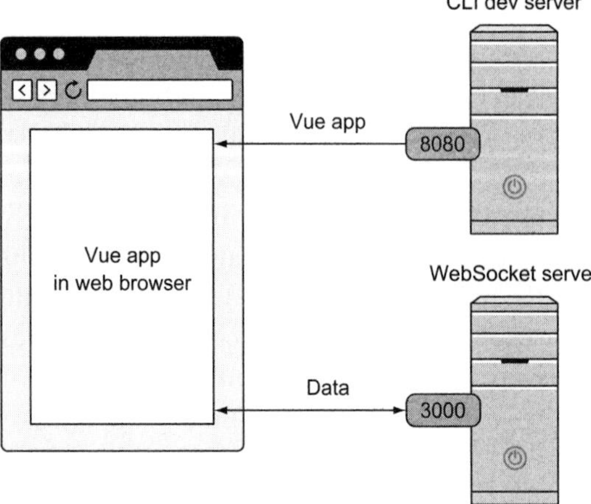

Figure 16.3 One app, two servers

having the ID app. This is where the top-level component of our app will be rendered, and we'll review its code in the next section.

16.2 The App component

The App.vue file contains the code of the class-based `App` component, and its `<template>` section contains three child components: `TransactionForm`, `PendingTransactionsPanel`, and `BlocksPanel`.

Listing 16.1 The `<template>` section of the App.vue file

```
<template>
  <main id="app">
    <h1>Blockchain node</h1>
    <aside><p>{{ status }}</p></aside>
    <section>
      <transaction-form                          // The TransactionForm component
        :disabled="shouldDisableForm()"          // Binds the disabled property
        @add-transaction="addTransaction">       // Handles the add-transaction event
      </transaction-form>
    </section>
    <section>
      <pending-transactions-panel                // The PendingTransactionsPanel component
        :transactions="transactions()"
        :disabled="shouldDisableGeneration()"
        @generate-block="generateBlock">
      </pending-transactions-panel>
    </section>
    <section>
      <blocks-panel :blocks="blocks()"></blocks-panel>    // The BlocksPanel component
    </section>
  </main>
</template>
```

The expression `:disabled="shouldDisableForm()"` is a shortcut for `v-bind:disabled ="shouldDisableForm()"`, and in this context it controls the `disabled` property of the `TransactionForm` component. The parentheses after the method name mean that we invoke the `shouldDisableForm()` method here. This method is declared in the `App` class (see listing 16.2). All the methods of the component's instance can be invoked from the template.

The expression `@add-transaction="addTransaction"` tells us that the `TransactionForm` component may dispatch an `add-transaction` event, and when that happens the `App` component's `addTransaction()` method has to be invoked. In this case, there were no parentheses after the method name—it's just a reference to the method that might be invoked later.

> **TIP** If a component class is named using camel-case notation, you can use it as-is in the template of another component, or use a dash as a separator. In listing 16.1, we used the `<transaction-form>` tag to represent the `TransactionForm` component, but we could have used the tag with a camel-case name, `<TransactionForm>`, as well.

The expression `@generate-block="generateBlock"` means that the `PendingTransactionsPanel` component may emit the `generate-block` event, and when that happens, the `App` component will invoke its `generateBlock()` method.

In the expression `:blocks="blocks()"`, we invoke the `block()` method, and whatever it returns is assigned to the `blocks` property of the `BlocksPanel` component, which is marked with the `@Prop` decorator (as you'll see in listing 16.7).

Listing 16.2 shows part of the code of the `<script>` section of the `App` component. We omitted the code of most of the methods because they contained blockchain-specific code that we've already explained in previous chapters. We'll just comment on some Vue-specific code.

Listing 16.2 Part of the `<script>` section from the App.vue file

```
<script lang="ts">
// imports are omitted for brevity
const node = new BlockchainNode();
const server = new WebsocketController();

@Component({
  components: {                          <-- Lists all child components in
                                             the @Component decorator
    BlocksPanel, PendingTransactionsPanel, TransactionForm
  }
})
export default class App extends Vue {
  status: string = '';

  blocks(): Block[] {          <-- This function is invoked
    return node.chain;             from the template
  }
```

```
  transactions(): Transaction[] {            ◁─┐
    return node.pendingTransactions;           │
  }                                            │
                                               │ This function is invoked
  shouldDisableForm(): boolean {             ◁─┤ from the template
    return node.isMining || node.chainIsEmpty; │
  }                                            │
                                               │
  shouldDisableGeneration(): boolean {       ◁─┘
    return node.isMining || node.noPendingTransactions;
  }

  created() {                      ◁─┐ The component's created()
    this.updateStatus();               │ life cycle callback
    server
      .connect(this.handleServerMessages.bind(this))
      .then(this.initializeBlockchainNode.bind(this));
  }
                                   ┌ The component's destroyed()
  destroyed() {                 ◁─┘ life cycle callback
    server.disconnect();
  }

  updateStatus() {          ◁── Updates the status property

   this.status = node.chainIsEmpty          ? '⌛ Initializing
➥ the blockchain...' :
                 node.isMining              ? '⌛ Mining a new block...' :
                 node.noPendingTransactions ? '✉ Add one or
➥ more transactions.' :
                                             `✅ Ready to mine a new block
➥ (transactions: ${node.pendingTransactions.length}).`;
  }

  async initializeBlockchainNode(): Promise<void> {...}
  addTransaction(transaction: Transaction): void {...}
  async generateBlock(): Promise<void> {...}
  async addBlock(block: Block, notifyOthers = true): Promise<void> {...}
  handleServerMessages(message: Message) {...}
  handleGetLongestChainRequest(message: Message): void {...}
  async handleNewBlockRequest(message: Message): Promise<void> {...}
  handleNewBlockAnnouncement(message: Message): void {...}
}
</script>
```

The parameter of the `@Component()` decorator is an object literal, and here we use the shorthand syntax introduced by ES6. If the property value in the object literal has the same name as the property identifier, you don't have to repeat them. The long version of the object representing the child component would look like this:

```
{
  BlocksPanel: BlocksPanel,
  PendingTransactionsPanel: PendingTransactionsPanel,
  TransactionForm: TransactionForm
}
```

TIP In listing 16.7 in the `BlocksPanel` component, we'll use the long notation and explain why.

Rather than declaring `node` and `server` as class properties, we keep them outside of the Vue component class to prevent Vue from augmenting objects with getters and setters required for Vue's change-detection process. We wanted to write a method that returns all nodes from the blockchain as a getter (for example, `get blocks() { return node.chain; }`), but Vue didn't allow component templates to work with getters, so we wrote it as a class method. The same applies to several other methods of the class `App`.

The component's `created()` life cycle hook is invoked by Vue when the data and events are ready to use, but the template is not rendered yet. In this method, we connect to the messaging server providing the `handleServerMessages()` callback. When the WebSocket connection is established, the code initializes the blockchain node (requesting the longest chain as explained in chapter 10), and either initializes the node with existing blocks or with a genesis block.

TIP There's also a `mounted()` life cycle hook, which is invoked after the component's template has been rendered.

The component's `destroyed()` life cycle hook is invoked by Vue when all the internals of the component have been destroyed and you just need to do some final cleanup. In our case, we disconnect from the WebSocket server to avoid having an orphan connection in memory that continues receiving messages from other blocks. The `beforeDestroy()` callback could be an alternative place for performing some data cleanup. When `beforeDestroy()` is invoked, the component is still fully functional, and you can apply some business logic regarding the cleanup procedure.

TIP The Vue documentation includes a diagram illustrating all the life cycle hooks. You can find it at http://mng.bz/9wnx.

The `updateStatus()` method is called from several other methods like `generateBlock()` and `addBlock()`. It updates the `status` property, which causes the UI to re-render because `status` is a property of the component. Vue wraps each component property in a getter and setter, which is how it knows that it's time to re-render the UI. The Vue documentation calls the properties of a component *reactive*, because all of them become setters and getters and can react to changes.

Once again about programming to interfaces

In chapter 3, we spent some time explaining the benefits of programming to interfaces, and now we'd like to illustrate what happens when you don't. Vue has a hook called `created()`, which is a callback invoked by the `Vue` object. Try misspelling the name of this hook by adding an extra `t`, as in `creatted()`. Your app won't work correctly, because the `created()` method, which communicates with the messaging server and updates the `status` class variable, won't exist.

(continued)

If such errors only show up at runtime, there's no benefit to using TypeScript. This particular case clearly shows that TypeScript support was added to Vue as an afterthought. What can be done differently?

Let's see how the component life cycle hooks are designed in Angular, where TypeScript was considered a primary language from the very beginning. Angular declares an interface for each life cycle hook. For example, there is an `OnInit` interface, which declares one method, `ngOnInit()`. If you want your component to implement this hook, you start by declaring that your class implements `OnInit`, and then you write the implementation of `ngOnInit()` in that class:

```
export class App implements OnInit() {OnInit

   ngOnInit() {...}

}
```

Try to misspell the name of the hook by adding an extra `t`, as in `ngOnInitt()`. The TypeScript static code analyzer will highlight it as an error, stating that you promised to implement all the methods declared in the `OnInit` interface, so where's `ngOnInit()`? Wouldn't you agree that programming to interfaces eliminates such bugs?

Now let's review the code of the child components, starting with `TransactionForm`.

16.3 The TransactionForm presentation component

Figure 16.4 shows the UI of the `TransactionForm` component, which allows the user to enter the names of the sender and recipient, as well as the transaction amount. When the user clicks on the ADD TRANSACTION button, this information has to be sent to the parent `App` component, which is a smart component because it knows how to process this data. This button will become enabled when the form is filled out.

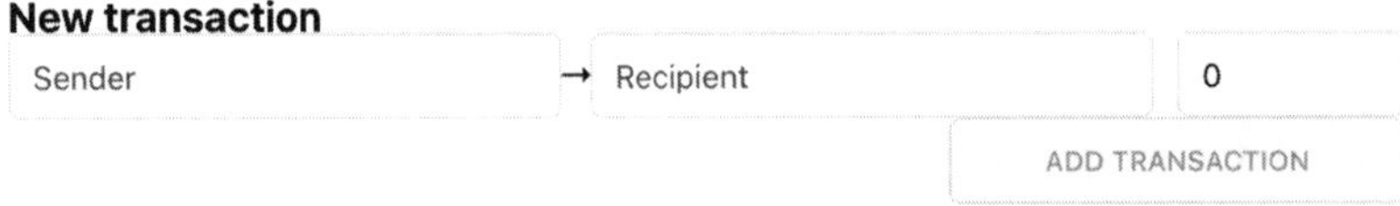

Figure 16.4 The UI of the `TransactionForm` component

The template of the top-level `App` component uses `TransactionForm` as follows:

```
<transaction-form
  :disabled="shouldDisableForm()"
  @add-transaction="addTransaction">
</transaction-form>
```

Listing 16.3 shows the template of `TransactionForm`, which is an HTML form where every input field uses the `disabled` property controlled by the parent's `shouldDisable-Form()` method. Revisit listing 16.2 and you'll see that `shouldDisableForm()` returns `true` if the node is being mined or if there are no blocks in the blockchain yet.

Behind this form is a data model object that stores all the values entered by the user. Vue comes with the `v-model` directive that's used to create two-way data bindings between the form's `input`, `textarea`, and `select` elements. "Two-way" means that if the user enters or changes the data in the form field, the new value will be assigned to the variable specified in the `v-model` directive of this field; if the value of that variable is changed programmatically, the form field will be updated as well.

Listing 16.3 The `<template>` section of the `TransactionForm` component

```
<template>
  <div>
    <h2>New transaction</h2>
    <form class="add-transaction-form"
          @submit.prevent="handleFormSubmit">
      <input
        type="text"
        name="sender"
        placeholder="Sender"
        autoComplete="off"
        v-model.trim="formValue.sender"
        :disabled="disabled">

      <span class="hidden-xs">•</span>

      <input
        type="text"
        name="recipient"
        placeholder="Recipient"
        autoComplete="off"
        :disabled="disabled"
        v-model.trim="formValue.recipient">

      <input
        type="number"
        name="amount"
        placeholder="Amount"
        :disabled="disabled"  3((CO3-6))
        v-model.number="formValue.amount">

      <button type="submit"
              class="ripple"
              :disabled="!isValid() || disabled">
        ADD TRANSACTION
      </button>
    </form>
  </div>
</template>
```

Prevents the default page reload of the form's submit event

formValue.sender is bound to this form field.

The disabled class variable controls this field.

formValue.recipient is bound to this form field.

formValue.amount is bound to this form field.

Conditionally enables the form's submit button

Vue offers several event modifiers, and here we use the one called `.prevent`. In Vue, the expression `@submit.prevent="handleFormSubmit"` means "Prevent the default handling of the form's submit button. Invoke the `handleFormSubmit()` method instead."

Each input field is bound to one of the properties of the `formValue` object, which plays the role of the form model and is defined in the script section of this component as `formValue: Transaction`. The `Transaction` type is defined like this:

```
export interface Transaction {
  readonly sender: string;
  readonly recipient: string;
  readonly amount: number;
}
```

For example, the following line uses the Vue directive `v-model` to map the sender field of the form to the `sender` property of the `formValue` object:

```
v-model="formValue.sender"
```

But the `v-model` directive supports *modifiers*, so we wrote it as follows:

```
v-model.trim="formValue.sender"
```

The `trim` modifier automatically trims whitespace from the user's input. We also used the `number` modifier in `v-model.number="formValue.amount"` to ensure that the input value is automatically typecast as a number while synchronizing the value from the `amount` field with the `formValue.amount` property.

Listing 16.4 shows the `<script>` section of the TransactionForm.vue file. It defines and initializes the `formValue` object. It also has the `isValid()` method to check if the form is valid, as well as the `handleFormSubmit()` method that's invoked when the user clicks the ADD TRANSACTION button.

Listing 16.4 The `<script>` section of the TransactionForm.vue file

```
<script lang="ts">
import { Component, Prop, Vue } from 'vue-property-decorator';
import { Transaction } from '../lib/blockchain-node';

@Component
export default class TransactionForm extends Vue {

  @Prop(Boolean) readonly disabled: boolean;        <-- The prop value is given by the parent.

  formValue: Transaction = this.defaultFormValue();  <-- Initializes the form model with default values

  isValid() {        <-- Is the form valid?
    return (
      this.formValue.sender &&
      this.formValue.recipient &&
```

```
      this.formValue.amount > 0
    );
  }

  handleFormSubmit() {                                    ◁ Handles the click on the ADD TRANSACTION button
      this.$emit('add-transaction', { ...this.formValue });   ◁ Emits the event on the parent

      this.formValue = this.defaultFormValue();   ◁ Resets the form
  }

  private defaultFormValue(): Transaction {   ◁ The default value of the form model
    return {
      sender: '',
      recipient: '',
      amount: 0
    };
  }
}
</script>
```

Here, we use the `@Prop` decorator with the `Boolean` argument telling Vue to typecast the provided value (HTML string data) to this type.

The `isValid()` method returns `true` only if the user entered all three values in the form. This will enable the form's ADD TRANSACTION button, and if the user clicks it, the `handleFormSubmit()` method emits the `add-transaction` event to the parent `App` component, which will invoke its `addTransaction()` method.

A child component can send the data to its parent using the `$emit()` method, and we invoke it with the payload `{...this.formValue}`. Here, we clone the `formValue` object using the JavaScript spread operator. The `addTransaction()` method in the `App` component will receive an object of type `Transaction` and will add it to the list of pending transactions maintained by the `PendingTransactionsPanel` component.

We encourage you to run this app through the browser's debugger, placing a breakpoint in the `handleFormSubmit()` method of `TransactionForm`. Figure 16.5 shows a screenshot taken after we entered "Alex," "Mary," and "100" as sender, recipient, and amount, and clicked the ADD TRANSACTION button in the form. Chrome's debugger stopped at the breakpoint in the `handleFormSubmit()` method. By default, the tsconfig .json file has the source map option turned on, so you can debug TypeScript.

To find the TypeScript sources in the debugger, open the Source panel of the Chrome dev tools and find the Webpack section in the left panel. Then find the image of the folder named with a period, and then find the src subfolder. You may see multiple files with the same name, ending with different numbers, as shown in figure 16.5. This is because of the hot module replacement: whenever you modify a file, Webpack pushes a new version of the file but with a different name suffix, so you may need to spend a couple of seconds finding the one with TypeScript.

The middle section of figure 16.5 shows the breakpoint at line 59. In the right panel, we've added `this.formValue` to the Watch section, and you can see the values

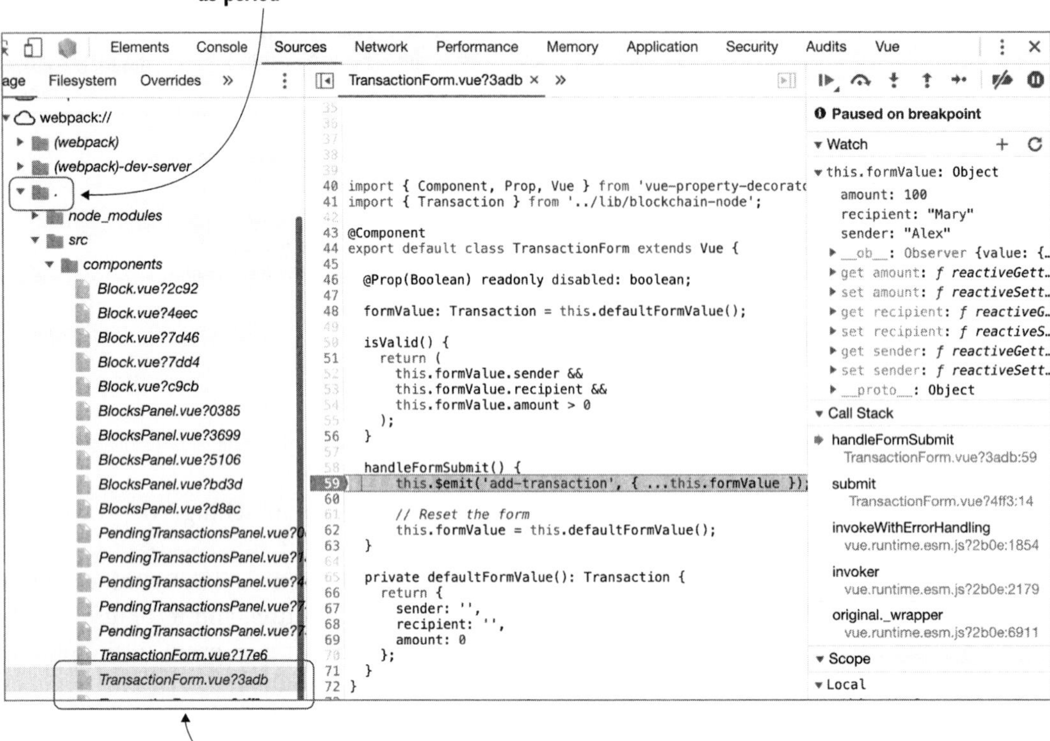

Figure 16.5 Debugging the `TransactionForm` component

`100`, `Mary`, and `Alex` there. Click the Step Over icon, and the debugger will take you to the `addTransaction()` method in the `App` component, where you'll see that the object with these values is received. After that, this transaction is added to the list of Node's pending transactions, as shown in the next listing.

Listing 16.5 The `addTransaction` method of the `App` component

```
addTransaction(transaction: Transaction): void {
  node.addTransaction(transaction);
  this.updateStatus();
}
```

Invoking the `this.updateStatus()` method modifies the `status` class variable, which causes the `PendingTransactionsPanel` component to be re-rendered, as we'll discuss next.

16.4 The PendingTransactionsPanel presentation component

PendingTransactionsPanel is a presentation component that has the transactions props. Its parent App component provides an array of transactions as follows:

```
<pending-transactions-panel
    :transactions="transactions()"          <—— Passes the transactions array
    :disabled="shouldDisableGeneration()"
@generate-block="generateBlock">
```

In the template of PendingTransactionsPanel, we invoke formattedTransactions() (see listing 16.6), which iterates over the Transactions[] array and formats and renders its elements as strings in a <pre> element.

The PendingTransactionsPanel component can also do one more thing—initiate block generation when the user clicks on the GENERATE BLOCK button. Since this is a presentation component, it doesn't know how to generate a block, but it can send the generate-block event to its parent, which will decide what to do with it. The following listing shows the code of the PendingTransactionsPanel component.

Listing 16.6 The PendingTransactionsPanel.vue file

```
<template>
  <div>
    <h2>Pending transactions</h2>
    <pre class="pending-transactions__list">{{
➥ formattedTransactions() || 'No pending transactions yet.' }}
    </pre>                          <—— Formatted transactions are shown here.
    <div class="pending-transactions__form">
      <button class="ripple"
              type="button"
              :disabled="disabled"
              @click="generateBlock()">     <—— Clicking on the GENERATE BLOCK button invokes generateBlock().
        GENERATE BLOCK
      </button>
    </div>
    <div class="clear"></div>
  </div>
</template>

<script lang="ts">
import { Component, Prop, Vue } from 'vue-property-decorator';
import { Transaction } from '@/lib/blockchain-node';

@Component
export default class PendingTransactionsPanel extends Vue {

  @Prop(Boolean) readonly disabled: boolean;      <—— The value for this props as Boolean
  @Prop({ type: Array, required: true }) readonly transactions: Transaction[];

  formattedTransactions(): string {         <—— Formats pending transactions
    return this.transactions
      .map((t: any) =>`${t.sender} • ${t.recipient}: $${t.amount}`)
```

```
      .join('\n');
  }

  generateBlock(): void {           <-- Emits the generate-block event
    this.$emit('generate-block');
  }
}
</script>
```

One of the `@Prop` decorators has the following parameter: `{ type: Array, required: true }`. This is how we tell Vue to parse the provided value as an array, and the value of this props is required.

Figure 16.6 shows the rendering of the `PendingTransactionsPanel` component with two pending transactions that came from the `TransactionForm` component.

Figure 16.6 The UI of the `PendingTransactionsPanel` component

Clicking on the GENERATE BLOCK button in `PendingTransactionsPanel` should start the process of block generation. Since the `App` component has access to the `Transactions[]` array, the `generateBlock()` method simply emits the event. The `App` component hosts `PendingTransactionsPanel` as follows:

```
<pending-transactions-panel
  :transactions="transactions()"
  :disabled="shouldDisableGeneration()"
  @generate-block="generateBlock">
</pending-transactions-panel>
```

When the `generate-block` event is dispatched, the `App` component's `generateBlock()` method is invoked, which in particular updates the status property. This results in the UI re-rendering because `status` is a property of the component. The `BlocksPanel` component gets the all the blocks via its `blocks` props.

Now let's see what's going on in `BlocksPanel`.

16.5 The BlocksPanel and Block presentation components

When the user clicks on the GENERATE BLOCK button in the `PendingTransactionPanel` component, all active nodes in the blockchain start the mining process. After the consensus, a new block will be added to the blockchain and rendered in the

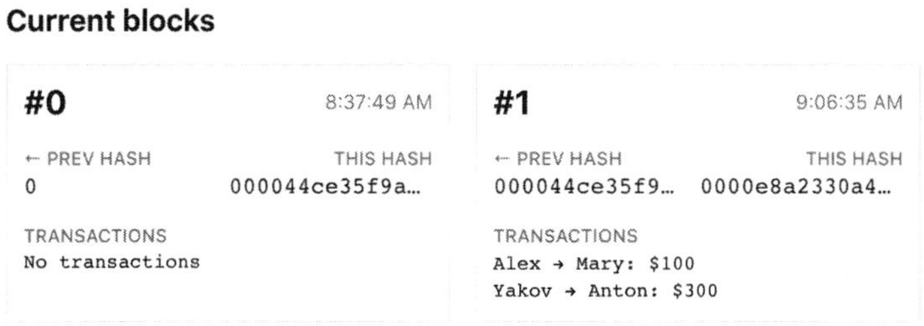

Current blocks

#0	8:37:49 AM	#1	9:06:35 AM
← PREV HASH	THIS HASH	← PREV HASH	THIS HASH
0	000044ce35f9a…	000044ce35f9…	0000e8a2330a4…
TRANSACTIONS		TRANSACTIONS	
No transactions		Alex → Mary: $100 Yakov → Anton: $300	

Figure 16.7 The UI of the `BlocksPanel` component

`BlocksPanel` component, which serves as a container of `Block` child components. Figure 16.7 shows `BlocksPanel` rendered with a two-block blockchain.

During block mining and getting the consensus, the instances of `BlockchainNode` and `WebsocketController` are involved, but because `BlockPanel` is a presentation component, it doesn't directly communicate with either of these objects. That work is delegated to the smart `App` component.

The `BlocksPanel` component doesn't send any data to its parent; its goal is to render the blockchain provided via the `blocks` props. The `App` component invokes its `blocks()` method and binds the returned value (the collection of existing blocks in the blockchain) to the `blocks` property of the `BlocksPanel` component (the colon is for binding):

```
<blocks-panel :blocks="blocks()"></blocks-panel>
```

The following listing shows the code of the `BlocksPanel` component. Note that the declaration of the `blocks` property is decorated with the `@Prop` decorator, which means that the values are coming from the parent.

Listing 16.7 BlocksPanel.vue

```
<template>
  <div>
    <h2>Current blocks</h2>
    <div class="blocks">
      <div class="blocks__ribbon">
        <block v-for="(b, i) in blocks"
               :key="b.hash"
               :index="i"
               :block="b">
        </block>
      </div>
      <div class="blocks__overlay"></div>
    </div>
  </div>
</template>

<script lang="ts">
import { Component, Prop, Vue } from 'vue-property-decorator';
import { Block } from '@/lib/blockchain-node';
```

Iterates over the blocks array and renders BlockComponents

Assigns a unique key to each rendered block (annotates `:key="b.hash"`)

Passes the value to the props of the Block component

Imports the Block interface (annotates `import { Block }`)

```
import BlockComponent from './Block.vue';      <-- Imports the Block component

@Component({
  components: {                                  Registers the child BlockComponent
    Block: BlockComponent                   <--  under the name Block
  }
})
export default class BlocksPanel extends Vue {
  @Prop({ type: Array, required: true }) readonly blocks: Block[];   <--
}
</script>                                    Declares the decorated property blocks
```

The `BlocksPanel` presentation component uses the `v-for` Vue directive to iterate over the `blocks` array, rendering one `Block` component for each element of the array. In the React version of the app, we used the `Array.map()` method to render the blocks (see listing 14.22 in chapter 14). Why did we use the special `v-for` attribute of the HTML element here to render blocks? The reason is that in React we used JSX, which allowed us to use the full power of JavaScript, but here the HTML-based templates only allow us to use special tag attributes. In other words, in React you can use JavaScript for rendering, whereas in Vue it's a static string.

TIP We didn't use JSX in this chapter so we could show you how to work with HTML-based templates, but Vue's documentation makes recommendations on how you can use JSX at http://mng.bz/j58z. Consider using JSX if you prefer JavaScript to HTML in templates.

Note that we didn't use the short object literal syntax for specifying the child component here:

```
components: {
  Block: BlockComponent
}
```

The property name on the left (`Block`) defines the name of the component you can use in the template: <block>. HTML is case-insensitive, and if the component's name in the script is `Block`, it can be referred to as `<block>` in HTML.

TIP The "HTML case sensitivity workaround" discussion on GitHub at http://mng.bz/WOv4 provides more details on referring to components in scripts and HTML.

We had to use the long syntax here because of the name conflict: we declared an interface named `Block` in the lib/blockchain-node directory, and the Block.vue file declares the component, which is also named `Block`, as you'll see in listing 16.8. First we tried the shorthand ES6 syntax for object literals:

```
components: {
  Block
}
```

Vue complained about not recognizing the `<block>` tag, but because we used the `default` keyword to export `class Block`, we could import it under any arbitrary name. We gave it the name `BlockComponent`, as you saw earlier in listing 16.7. We're saying to Vue, "We have a component called `Block`, but we imported its code under the name `BlockComponent`."

> **NOTE** A simpler solution to this naming conflict would be changing the template tag from `<block>` to `<block-component>`, but we wanted to use this conflict to present a use case where the shorthand syntax for object literals wouldn't work.

The following listing shows the code of the `Block` component.

Listing 16.8 Block.vue

```
<template>
  <div class="block">
    <div class="block__header">
      <span class="block__index">#{{ index }}</span>
      <span class="block__timestamp">{{ timestamp() }}</span>
    </div>
    <div class="block__hashes">
      <div class="block__hash">
        <div class="block__label">• PREV HASH</div>
        <div class="block__hash-value">{{ block.previousHash }}</div>
      </div>
      <div class="block__hash">
        <div class="block__label">THIS HASH</div>
        <div class="block__hash-value">{{ block.hash }}</div>
      </div>
    </div>
    <div>
      <div class="block__label">TRANSACTIONS</div>
      <pre class="block__transactions">{{ formattedTransactions() ||
➥ 'No transactions' }}</pre>
    </div>
  </div>
</template>

<script lang="ts">
import { Component, Prop, Vue } from 'vue-property-decorator';
import { Block as ChainBlock, Transaction }
➥ from '@/lib/blockchain-node';                <-- Imports, giving an alias name to Block

@Component
export default class Block extends Vue {
  @Prop(Number) readonly index: number;    <-- The block's sequential number
```

```
  @Prop({ type: Object, required: true }) readonly block: ChainBlock;     <-- The block's data

  timestamp() {
    return new Date(this.block.timestamp).toLocaleTimeString();
  }

  formattedTransactions(): string {
    return this.block.transactions
      .map((t: Transaction) =>`${t.sender} • ${t.recipient}: $${t.amount}`)
      .join('\n');
  }
}
</script>
```

In listing 16.8 we also had to resolve a naming conflict between the `Block` component class and the interface with the same name. Here, we use a different syntax:

```
import { Block as ChainBlock} from '@/lib/blockchain-node';
```

In this case, the `Block` interface was exported as a named export in the blockchain-node.ts file, so we couldn't just use any name. We had to write `import { Block as ChainBlock}` to introduce the alias name `ChainBlock`. Note the curly braces—you have to use them while importing named exports.

The `Block` component is the simplest component in this app. It just renders the data of one block, as you saw in figure 16.7. This concludes our review of the blockchain client written in Vue and TypeScript.

Summary

- Because Vue generates setters and getters for each component property, the process of change detection is greatly simplified. Changing a value of the component's property serves as a signal for UI re-rendering.
- As with React and Angular, the UI of a Vue app consists of smart and presentation components. Don't place your application logic in the presentation components, which are meant for presenting the data received from other components or for providing interaction with the user (sending the user's input to other components).
- In Vue, a parent component passes data to its child via props. The child sends the data to its parent by emitting events with or without a payload.
- Vue CLI generates projects that use Webpack under the hood for bundling. In development, the Webpack Dev Server supports auto-recompilation and hot module replacement, which pushes the new code to the browser without reloading the page.

Epilogue

In this book, we showed you the main syntax constructs of TypeScript as well as multiple applications that use this language. Major web frameworks support TypeScript, and you don't need to wait for a new project to start using it. You can gradually introduce this language into existing JavaScript projects. As an extra bonus, we explained the basics of blockchain technology, showing you multiple versions of TypeScript apps that use it.

We hope that after reading this book you understand why TypeScript is gaining popularity in leaps and bounds. We believe that TypeScript's ascendancy is here to stay. Enjoy TypeScripting!

appendix *Modern JavaScript*

ECMAScript is a standard for scripting languages, and the evolution of ECMAScript is governed by the TC39 committee. ECMAScript syntax is implemented in several languages, and the most popular implementation is JavaScript. Starting from the sixth edition (a.k.a. ES6 or ES2015), TC39 has been releasing a new specification of ECMAScript annually.

You can read the latest version of the spec at http://mng.bz/8zoZ, but ECMAScript 2015 introduced major additions to JavaScript. Most of the syntax covered in this appendix was introduced in the ES2015 spec, and most web browsers fully support the ES2015 specification (see http://mng.bz/ao59). Even if the users of your app have older browsers, you can develop in ES6/7/8/9 today and use transpilers like TypeScript or Babel to turn code that uses the latest ECMAScript syntax into an ES5 version.

We assume that the you know the ES5 syntax of JavaScript. We'll cover only selected features introduced in ECMAScript starting from 2015.

A.1 How to run the code samples

The code samples for this appendix come as JavaScript files with the .js extension, and we'll use a website called CodePen (https://codepen.io) to run the code samples. CodePen allows you to quickly write, test, and share apps that use HTML, CSS, and JavaScript. We'll provide CodePen links to most of the code samples so you can follow the link, see the selected code sample in action, and modify it if you choose to do so. If a code sample produces output on the console, just click the Console at the bottom of the CodePen window to see it.

Let's now review some of the features of ECMAScript as they are implemented in JavaScript.

A.2 The keywords let and const

The `let` or `const` keywords should be used as replacements for the `var` keyword. Let's start by reviewing the issues with the `var` keyword.

A.2.1 The var keyword and hoisting

In ES5 and older versions of JavaScript, you'd use the `var` keyword to declare a variable, and the JavaScript engine would move the declaration to the top of the execution context (for example, a function). This is called *hoisting* (see more on hoisting at http://mng.bz/3x9w).

Because of hoisting, if you declared a variable inside a code block (for example, inside the curly braces in an `if` statement), this variable would be visible outside the block as well. Look at the following example where we declare the variable `i` inside a `for` loop but use it outside as well:

```
function foo() {

    for (var i=0; i<10; i++) {

    }

  console.log("i=" + i);
}

foo();
```

Running this code will print `i=10`. The variable `i` is still available outside the loop, even though it seems like it was meant to be used only inside the loop. JavaScript automatically hoists the variable declaration to the top of the function.

In the preceding example, hoisting didn't cause any harm, because there was only one variable named `i`. If two variables with the same name are declared inside and outside the function, however, this may result in confusing behavior. Consider the following listing, which declares the `customer` variable on the global scope. A bit later we'll introduce another `customer` variable in the local scope, but for now let's keep it commented out.

Listing A.1 Hoisting a variable declaration

```
var customer = "Joe";
(function () {
    console.log("The name of the customer inside the function is "  +
➥ customer);
   /*  if (true) {
            var customer = "Mary";
       } */
})();
console.log("The name of the customer outside the function is "  + customer);
```

The global variable customer is visible inside and outside the function, and running this code will print the following:

```
The name of the customer inside the function is Joe
The name of the customer outside the function is Joe
```

Uncomment the if statement that declares and initializes the customer variable inside the curly braces. Now we have two variables with the same name—one on the global scope and another on the function scope. The console output is different now:

```
The name of the customer inside the function is undefined
The name of the customer outside the function is Joe
```

The reason is that in ES5, the variable declarations are hoisted to the top of the scope (in this case, it's the expression within the topmost parentheses), but the variable initializations aren't. When a variable is created, its initial value is undefined. The declaration of the second undefined customer variable was hoisted to the top of the function declaration, and console.log() printed the value of the variable declared inside the function, which has shadowed the value of the global customer variable.

NOTE See it on CodePen: http://mng.bz/cK9y.

Function declarations are hoisted as well, so you can invoke a function before it's declared:

```
doSomething();

function doSomething() {
   console.log("I'm doing something");
}
```

On the other hand, function expressions are considered variable initializations, so they aren't hoisted. The following code snippet will produce undefined for the doSomething variable:

```
doSomething();

var doSomething = function() {
   console.log("I'm doing something");
}
```

Now let's see how the let or const keyword can help you with scoping.

A.2.2 Block scoping with let and const

ES6 eliminates the hoisting confusion by introducing the keywords let and const. The let keyword is used when you need to declare a variable that may be initialized with one value and then get another value assigned. The const keyword is used if you can assign a value to the identifier only once and it can't be reassigned afterwards.

Don't assume that const represents immutable values. The const qualifier just means that it can be initialized only once. This doesn't mean that the property of an object assigned to a const identifier can't be changed. For example, the following const products represents an array of objects, and you can change individual properties of these objects after initializing const products:

```
const products = [
  { id: 1, description: 'Product 1' },
   {id: 2, description: 'Product 2'}
]

products[0].id = 111;
products[1].description = 'Product 222';
```

Declaring variables with the keywords let or const instead of var allows variables to have block scoping. The next listing shows an example.

Listing A.2 Variables with block scoping

```
const customer = "Joe";

  (function () {
      console.log("1. Inside the function " + customer);
      if (true) {
        const customer = "Mary";
        console.log("2. Inside the block " + customer);
      }
 })();

console.log("3. In the global scope "  + customer);
```

Now two customer variables have different scopes and values, and this program will print the following:

```
The name of the customer inside the function is Joe
The name of the customer inside the block is Mary
The name of the customer in the global scope is Joe
```

To put it simply, if you're developing a new application, don't use var. Use let or const instead.

TIP If you try to use a variable defined with let or const before its declaration, you'll get a ReferenceError runtime error. This is called a *temporal dead zone*, where you can't access the variable before it's defined.

In the preceding code sample, we should have used const instead of let, because we never reassigned the values for either customer identifier.

NOTE See it on CodePen: http://mng.bz/fkJd.

TIP If you need to declare an identifier, make it a const. It's never too late to change it to let if there is a need to assign a new value to it.

A.3 Template literals

String literals can now contain embedded expressions. This feature is known as *string interpolation*. In ES5, you'd use concatenation to create a string that contains string literals combined with the values of variables:

```
const customerName = "John Smith";
console.log("Hello" + customerName);
```

Now you can use template literals, which are strings surrounded with backtick symbols. You can embed expressions right inside the literal by placing them between the curly braces prefixed with a dollar sign. In the next code snippet, the value of the `customerName` variable is embedded in the string literal:

```
const customerName = "John Smith";
console.log(`Hello ${customerName}`);

function getCustomer() {
  return "Allan Lou";
}
console.log(`Hello ${getCustomer()}`);
```

The output of this code is shown here:

```
Hello John Smith
Hello Allan Lou
```

NOTE See it on CodePen: http://mng.bz/Ey30.

In the preceding example, we embedded the value of the `customerName` variable into the template literal, and then embedded the value returned by the `getCustomer()` function. You can use any valid JavaScript expression between the curly braces.

Strings can span multiple lines in your code. Using backticks, you can write multiline strings without the need to concatenate them:

```
const message = `Please enter a password that
               has at least 8 characters and
               includes a capital letter`;

console.log(message);
```

The resulting string will treat all spaces as part of the string, so the output will look like this:

```
Please enter a password that
               has at least 8 characters and
               includes a capital letter
```

NOTE See it on CodePen: http://mng.bz/1SSP.

A.3.1 *Tagged template strings*

If a template string is preceded with a function name, the string is evaluated first and then passed to the function for further processing. The string parts of a template are given to the function as an array, and all the expressions that were evaluated in the template are passed as separate arguments. The syntax looks a little unusual, because you don't use parentheses as in regular function calls.

In the following code snippet, the tag function `mytag` is followed by the template string:

```
mytag`Hello ${name}`;
```

The value of the variable `name` would be evaluated and provided to the function `mytag`.

Let's write a simple tagged template that would print an amount with a currency sign that depends on the `region` variable. If the value of `region` is 1, we keep the amount unchanged and prepend it with a dollar sign. If the value of `region` is 2, we need to convert the amount, applying 0.9 as an exchange rate, and prepend it with a euro sign. Our template string will look like this:

```
`You've earned ${region} ${amount}!`
```

Let's call the `currencyAdjustment` tag function. The tagged template string will look like this:

```
currencyAdjustment`You've earned ${region} ${amount}!`
```

Our `currencyAdjustment` function will take three arguments: the first will represent all the string parts from our template string, the second will get the region, and the third is for the amount. You can add any number of arguments after the first one. The complete example follows:

```
function currencyAdjustment(stringParts, region, amount) {
    console.log( stringParts);
    console.log( region );
    console.log( amount );

  let sign;
  if (region === 1){
    sign="$"
  } else{
    sign='\u20AC';       // the euro sign
    amount=0.9*amount;  // convert to euros using 0.9 as exchange rate
  }
  return `${stringParts[0]}${sign}${amount}${stringParts[2]}`;
}

const amount = 100;
const region = 2;  // Europe: 2, USA: 1

const message = currencyAdjustment`You've earned ${region} ${amount}!`
console.log(message);
```

The `currencyAdjustment` function will get a string with embedded `region` and `amount`, and it will parse the template, separating the string parts from these values (blank spaces are also considered string parts). We'll print these values first for illustration. Then this function will check the region, apply the conversion, and return a new string template. Running the preceding code will produce the following output:

```
["You've earned "," ","!"]
2
100
You've earned ?90!
```

NOTE See it on CodePen: http://mng.bz/E1Yo.

In section 10.6.2, we'll discuss the code of a web client that uses a lit-html, which itself uses tagged template strings.

A.4 Optional parameters and default values

You can specify default values for function parameters (arguments) that will be used if no value is provided during function invocation. Say you're writing a function to calculate tax that takes two arguments: the annual income and the state where the person lives. If the state value isn't provided, we want to use Florida as a default.

In ES5, we'd need to start the function body by checking whether the state value was provided; otherwise we'd use Florida:

```
function calcTaxES5(income, state) {

    state = state || "Florida";

    console.log("ES5. Calculating tax for the resident of " + state +
                                        " with the income " + income);
}

calcTaxES5(50000);
```

Here's what this code prints:

```
"ES5. Calculating tax for the resident of Florida with the income 50000"
```

Starting from ES6 you can specify the default value right in the function signature:

```
function calcTaxES6(income, state = "Florida") {

  console.log("ES6. Calculating tax for the resident of " + state +
                                  " with the income " + income);
}

calcTaxES6(50000);
```

NOTE See it on CodePen: http://mng.bz/U51z.

A.5 Arrow function expressions

Arrow function expressions (a.k.a. fat arrow functions) provide a shorter notation for anonymous functions and add lexical scope for the `this` variable. The syntax of arrow function expressions consists of arguments, the fat arrow sign (=>), and the function body. If the function body is just one expression, you don't even need curly braces. If a single-expression function returns a value, there's no need to write the `return` statement—the result is returned implicitly:

```
let sum = (arg1, arg2) => arg1 + arg2;
```

The body of a multiline arrow function expression has to be enclosed in curly braces and use the explicit `return` statement:

```
(arg1, arg2) => {
  // do something
  return someResult;
}
```

If an arrow function doesn't have any arguments, use empty parentheses:

```
() => {
  // do something
  return someResult;
}
```

If the function has just one argument, parentheses are not mandatory:

```
arg1 => {
  // do something
}
```

In the following code snippet, we pass arrow function expressions as arguments to the JavaScript `Array` method's `reduce()` to calculate a sum, and `filter()` to print even numbers:

```
const myArray = [1, 2, 3, 4, 5];

console.log( "The sum of myArray elements is " +
                myArray.reduce((a,b) => a+b));  // prints 15

console.log( "The even numbers in myArray are " +
                myArray.filter( value => value % 2 === 0)); // prints 2 4
```

Now that you're familiar with the syntax of arrow functions, let's see how they streamline working with the `this` object reference.

In ES5, figuring out which object is referred to by the `this` keyword isn't always a simple task. Search online for "JavaScript this and that" and you'll find multiple posts where people complain about `this` pointing to the "wrong" object. The `this` reference can have different values depending on how the function is invoked and on whether strict mode was used (see the documentation for "Strict Mode" on the Mozilla Developer Network at http://mng.bz/VNVL). We'll illustrate the problem first, and then we'll show you the solution offered by ES6.

Consider the code in the following listing that invokes the anonymous function every second. The function prints random generated prices for the stock symbol provided to the `StockQuoteGenerator()` constructor function.

Listing A.3 `this` points at different objects

```
function StockQuoteGenerator(symbol){
    this.symbol = symbol;                          // this.symbol is a property of StockQuoteGenerator().
    console.log(`this.symbol=${this.symbol}`);

    setInterval( function () {
        console.log(`The price of ${this.symbol}   // this.symbol is undefined here.
        is ${Math.random()}`);
    }, 1000);
}
const stockQuoteGenerator = new StockQuoteGenerator("IBM");
```

In the first occurrence, `this` was pointing at the function object, and `this.symbol` had a value of IBM. In the second occurrence, because of `setInterval()`, the value of `this.symbol` is `undefined`. You'll see the same behavior not only if a function is invoked inside `setInterval()`, but if a function is invoked in any callback. Inside the callback, if strict mode is off, `this` would point at the global object, which is not the same as `this` defined by the `StockQuoteGenerator()` constructor function. If strict mode is on, the `this` object would be `undefined`.

NOTE In the preceding code sample we could have just used `symbol` instead of `this.symbol`. But our goal was to show you how the `this` variable points at different objects. You can see it on CodePen: http://mng.bz/NeEN.

The other solution for ensuring that a function runs in a particular `this` object is to use the JavaScript `call()`, `apply()`, or `bind()` functions.

NOTE If you're not familiar with the `this` problem in JavaScript, check out Richard Bovell's article, "Understand JavaScript's 'this' with Clarity, and Master It" on his *JavaScript is Sexy* blog at http://mng.bz/ZQfz.

The following listing illustrates an arrow function solution that offers an unambiguous `this`. We just replaced the anonymous function given to `setInterval()` with a fat arrow function.

Listing A.4 Using a fat arrow function

```
function StockQuoteGenerator(symbol){
    this.symbol = symbol;    // this.symbol is undefined inside getQuote()
    console.log("this.symbol=" + this.symbol);
```

```
    setInterval(() =>
        console.log(`The price of ${this.symbol} is ${Math.random()}`)
    , 1000);
}
const stockQuoteGenerator = new StockQuoteGenerator("IBM");
```

The preceding code sample will properly resolve the `this` reference. An arrow function that's given as an argument to `setInterval()` uses the `this` value of the enclosing context, so it will recognize "IBM" as the value of `this.symbol`.

NOTE See it on CodePen: http://mng.bz/DNOn.

A.6 The rest operator

In ES5, writing a function with a variable number of parameters required using a special `arguments` object. This object is *similar* to an array, and it contains values corresponding to the arguments passed to a function.

Starting from ES6, you can use the rest operator for a variable number of arguments in a function. The ES6 rest operator is represented by three dots (...), and it has to be the last argument of the function. If the name of the function argument starts with the three dots, the function will get the rest of the arguments in an array.

For example, you can pass multiple customers to a function using a single variable name with a rest operator:

```
function processCustomers(...customers) {
  // implementation of the function goes here
}
```

Inside this function, you can handle the `customers` data the same way you'd handle any array.

Imagine that you need to write a function to calculate taxes that must be invoked with the first argument, `income`, followed by any number of arguments representing the names of the customers. Listing A.5 shows how you could process a variable number of arguments using first ES5 and then ES6 syntax. The `calcTaxES5()` function uses the object named `arguments`, and the function `calcTaxES6()` uses the ES6 rest operator.

Listing A.5 Using the rest operator

```
// ES5 and arguments object
  function calcTaxES5() {

      console.log("ES5. Calculating tax for customers with the income ",
                             arguments[0]);   // income is the first element

      // extract an array starting from 2nd element
      var customers = [].slice.call(arguments, 1);
```

```
        customers.forEach(function (customer) {
            console.log("Processing ", customer);
        });
    }

    calcTaxES5(50000, "Smith", "Johnson", "McDonald");
    calcTaxES5(750000, "Olson", "Clinton");

// ES6 and rest operator
    function calcTaxES6(income, ...customers) {
        console.log(`ES6. Calculating tax for customers with the income
➥ ${income}`);

        customers.forEach( (customer) => console.log(`Processing ${customer}`));
    }

    calcTaxES6(50000, "Smith", "Johnson", "McDonald");
    calcTaxES6(750000, "Olson", "Clinton");
```

Both functions, `calcTaxES5()` and `calcTaxES6()`, produce the same results:

```
ES5. Calculating tax for customers with the income 50000
Processing Smith
Processing Johnson
Processing McDonald
ES5. Calculating tax for customers with the income 750000
Processing Olson
Processing Clinton
ES6. Calculating tax for customers with the income 50000
Processing Smith
Processing Johnson
Processing McDonald
ES6. Calculating tax for customers with the income 750000
Processing Olson
Processing Clinton
```

NOTE See it on CodePen: http://mng.bz/I2zq.

There's a difference in handling customers, though. Because the `arguments` object isn't a real array, we had to create an array in the ES5 version by using the `slice()` and `call()` methods to extract the names of the customers starting from the second element in `arguments`. The ES6 version doesn't require us to use these tricks because the rest operator gives you a regular array of customers. Using the rest operator made the code simpler and more readable.

A.7 The spread operator

The ES6 spread operator is also represented by three dots (...) like the rest operator, but whereas the rest operator can turn a variable number of parameters into an array, the spread operator can do the opposite: turn an array into a list of values or function parameters.

Say you have two arrays and you need to add the elements of the second array to the end of the first one. With the spread operator it's one line of code:

```
let array1= [...array2];
```

Here the spread operator extracts each element of `array2` and adds it to the new array (the square brackets mean "create a new array" here). You can also create a copy of an array as follows:

```
array1.push(...array2);
```

Finding a maximum value in the array is also easy with the spread operator:

```
const maxValue = Math.max(...myArray);
```

In some cases you'll want to clone an object. Suppose you have an object that stores the state of your app, and you want to create a new object when one of the state properties changes. You don't want to mutate the original object, but you want to clone it and modify one or more properties. One way to implement immutable objects is by using the `Object.assign()` function. The following code listing creates a clone of the object first and then creates another clone, changing the value of `lastName` at the same time.

Listing A.6 Cloning with `assign()`

```
// Clone with Object.assign()
const myObject = {name: "Mary" , lastName: "Smith"};
const clone = Object.assign({}, myObject);
console.log(clone);

// Clone with modifying the lastName property
const cloneModified = Object.assign({}, myObject, {lastName: "Lee"});
console.log(cloneModified);
```

The spread operator offers a more concise syntax for achieving the same goal, as you can see in the following listing.

Listing A.7 Cloning with spread

```
// Clone with spread
const myObject = { name: "Mary" , lastName: "Smith"};
const cloneSpread = {...myObject};
console.log(cloneSpread);

// Clone with modifying the `lastName`
const cloneSpreadModified = {...myObject, lastName: "Lee"};
console.log(cloneSpreadModified);
```

Our `myObject` has two properties: `name` and `lastName`. The line that clones `myObject` while modifying `lastName` will work even if you or someone else adds more properties to `myObject`.

NOTE See it on CodePen: http://mng.bz/X2pL.

Cloning with `Object.assign()` or with the spread operator creates a shallow copy of the object. It copies all the property values that the object has at the time of cloning, but if some of the properties of an object are also objects, only references to the nested ones will be copied. If after a shallow cloning the values of the nested properties change in the original object, the clone will get the same changes.

Listing A.8 shows an object that has a nested object, `birth`. Initially, the birthdate is 18 Jan 2019. After cloning, the clone object will have the same birthdate. But if you change the birthdate on the original object, the clone will get the new value as well. This proves that only the reference to the nested object was copied, not its values.

Listing A.8 Shallow cloning

```
const myObject = { name: 'Mary', lastName: 'Smith', birth: { date:
➥ '18 Jan 2019' }};
const clone = {...myObject};                    // Clones myObject
console.log(clone.birth.date);                  // The clone's birthdate is 18 Jan 2019.
myObject.birth.date = '20 Jan 2019';            // Changes the birthdate on the original object
console.log(clone.birth.date);                  // The clone's birth date is changed to 20 Jan 2019.
```

A.8 Destructuring

Creating instances of objects means constructing them in memory. The term *destructuring* means changing the structure or taking objects apart. In ES5, you could deconstruct any object or a collection by writing a function to do it. ES6 introduced the destructuring assignment syntax that allows you to extract data from an object's properties or from an array in a simple expression by specifying a *matching pattern*. It's easier to explain by demonstrating an example, which we'll do next.

A.8.1 Destructuring objects

Let's say that a `getStock()` function returns a `Stock` object that has the attributes `symbol` and `price`. In ES5, if you wanted to assign the values of these attributes to separate variables, you'd need to create a variable to store the `Stock` object first, and then write two statements assigning the object attributes to the corresponding variables:

```
var stock = getStock();
var symbol = stock.symbol;
var price = stock.price;
```

Starting in ES6, you just need to write a matching pattern on the left and assign the `Stock` object to it:

```
let {symbol, price} = getStock();
```

It's a little unusual to see curly braces on the left of the equal sign, but this is part of the syntax of a matching expression. When you see curly braces on the left side, think of them as a block of code and not the object literal.

The following listing demonstrates getting the `Stock` object from the `getStock()` function and destructuring it into two variables.

Listing A.9 Destructuring an object

```
function getStock() {

    return {
        symbol: "IBM",
        price: 100.00
    };
}

let {symbol, price} = getStock();

console.log(`The price of ${symbol} is ${price}`);
```

Running that script will print the following:

```
The price of IBM is 100
```

In other words, we bind a set of data (object properties, in this case) to a set of variables (`symbol` and `price`) in one assignment expression. Even if the `Stock` object had more than two properties, the preceding destructuring expression would still work because `symbol` and `price` would have matched the pattern. The matching expression lists only the variables for the object attributes you're interested in.

NOTE See it on CodePen: http://mng.bz/CI47.

You can also destructure nested objects. The next code listing creates a nested object that represents Microsoft stock and passes it to the `printStockInfo()` function, which pulls the stock symbol and the name of the stock exchange from this object.

Listing A.10 Destructuring a nested object

```
const msft = {
     symbol: "MSFT",
     lastPrice: 50.00,
     exchange: {          <-- The nested object
         name: "NASDAQ",
         tradingHours: "9:30am-4pm"
     }
```

```
};

function printStockInfo(stock) {
    let {symbol, exchange: {name}} = stock;
    console.log(`The ${symbol} stock is traded at ${name}`);
}

printStockInfo(msft);
```

Destructures a nested object to get the name of the stock exchange

Running the preceding script will print the following:

```
The MSFT stock is traded at NASDAQ
```

NOTE See it on CodePen: http://mng.bz/Xauq.

Say you're writing a function to handle a browser DOM event. In the HTML part, you invoke this function, passing the event object as an argument. The event object has multiple properties, but your handler function only needs the `target` property to identify the component that dispatched this event. The destructuring syntax makes it easy:

```
<button id="myButton">Click me</button>
...
document
  .getElementById("myButton")
  .addEventListener("click", ({target}) =>
                              console.log(target));
```

Note the destructuring syntax `{target}` in the function argument.

NOTE See it on CodePen: http://mng.bz/Dj24.

Starting from ES2018, you can use syntax similar to the rest and spread operators while destructuring objects. For example, the following code will assign the value of `50` to the variable `lastPrice`, and the rest of the `msft` object properties will be placed in the `otherInfo` object.

Listing A.11 Combining destructuring and the rest operator

```
const msft = {
     symbol: "MSFT",
     lastPrice: 50.00,
     exchange: {
         name: "NASDAQ",
         tradingHours: "9:30am-4pm"
     }
};
const { lastPrice, ...otherInfo } = msft;

console.log(`lastPrice= ${lastPrice}`);
console.log(`otherInfo=`, otherInfo);
```

Destructuring and the rest operator

NOTE See it on CodePen: http://mng.bz/loN6.

A.8.2 Destructuring arrays

Array destructuring works much like object destructuring, but instead of using curly brackets, you'll need to use square ones. Whereas in destructuring objects you need to specify variables that match object properties, with arrays you specify variables that match array indexes.

The following code extracts the values of two array elements into two variables:

```
let [name1, name2] = ["Smith", "Clinton"];
console.log(`name1 = ${name1}, name2 = ${name2}`);
```

The output will look like this:

```
name1 = Smith, name2 = Clinton
```

If you just wanted to extract the second element of this array, the matching pattern would look like this:

```
let [, name2] = ["Smith", "Clinton"];
```

If a function returns an array, the destructuring syntax turns it into a function with a multiple-value return, as shown in the `getCustomers()` function:

```
function getCustomers() {
    return ["Smith", , , "Gonzales"];
}

let [firstCustomer, , , lastCustomer] = getCustomers();
console.log(`The first customer is ${firstCustomer} and the last one is
➥ ${lastCustomer}`);
```

Now let's combine array destructuring with rest parameters. Let's say we have an array of multiple customers, but we want to process only the first two. The following code snippet shows how to do it:

```
let customers = ["Smith", "Clinton", "Lou", "Gonzales"];

let [firstCust, secondCust, ...otherCust] = customers;

console.log(`The first customer is ${firstCust} and the second one is
➥ ${secondCust}`);
console.log(`Other customers are ${otherCust}`);
```

Here's the console output produced by that code:

```
The first customer is Smith and the second one is Clinton
Other customers are Lou, Gonzales
```

On a similar note, you can pass the matching pattern with a rest parameter to a function:

```
var customers = ["Smith", "Clinton", "Lou", "Gonzales"];

function processFirstTwoCustomers([firstCust, secondCust, ...otherCust]) {

  console.log(`The first customer is ${firstCust} and the second one is
➥ ${secondCust}`);
  console.log(`Other customers are ${otherCust}`);

}

processFirstTwoCustomers(customers);
```

The output will be the same:

```
The first customer is Smith and the second one is Clinton
Other customers are Lou,Gonzales
```

To summarize, the benefit of destructuring is that you can write less code when you need to initialize variables with data that's located in object properties or arrays.

A.9 Classes and inheritance

Although ES5 supports object-oriented programming and inheritance, ES6 classes make the code easier to read and write.

In ES5, objects can be created either from scratch or by inheriting from other objects. By default, all JavaScript objects inherit from `Object`. This object inheritance, *prototypal inheritance* in this case, is implemented via a special property called `prototype`, which points at an object's ancestor. In ES5, to create an `NJTax` object that inherits from the object `Tax`, you can write something like this:

```
function Tax() {
  // The code of the tax object goes here
}

function NJTax() {
  // The code of New Jersey tax object goes here
}

NJTax.prototype = new Tax();        <-- Inherits NJTax from Tax

var njTax = new NJTax();
```

ES6 introduced the keywords `class` and `extends` to bring the syntax into line with other object-oriented languages such as Java and C#. The ES6 equivalent of the preceding code is shown next:

```
class Tax {
  // The code of the tax class goes here
}

class NJTax extends Tax {
  // The code of New Jersey tax object goes here
}

let njTax = new NJTax();
```

The `Tax` class is an ancestor or *superclass*, and `NJTax` is a descendant or *subclass*. You can also say that the `NJTax` class has an "is a" relation with the `Tax` class: `NJTax` *is a* `Tax`. You can implement additional functionality in `NJTax`, but `NJTax` still "is a" or "is a kind of" `Tax`. Similarly, if you create an `Employee` class that inherits from `Person`, you can say that `Employee` is a `Person`.

You can create one or more instances of the objects, like this:

```
var tax1 = new Tax();    <-- First instance of the Tax object
var tax2 = new Tax();    <-- Second instance of the Tax object
```

NOTE In contrast to function declarations, class declarations aren't hoisted. You need to declare the class before you use it or you'll get a `ReferenceError`.

Each of these objects will have properties and methods that exist in the `Tax` class, but they will have different *state*. For example, the first instance could be created for a customer with an annual income of $50,000, and the second for a customer who earned $75,000. Each instance would share the same copy of the methods declared in the `Tax` class, so there's no duplication of code.

In ES5, you can also avoid code duplication by declaring methods not inside the objects but on their prototypes:

```
function Tax() {
  // The code of the tax object goes here
}

Tax.prototype = {
  calcTax: function() {
    // code to calculate tax goes here
  }
}
```

JavaScript remains a language with prototypal inheritance, but ES6 allows you to write more elegant code:

```
class Tax() {

  calcTax() {
    // code to calculate tax goes here
  }
}
```

> **Class member variables aren't supported**
>
> At the time of writing, JavaScript doesn't allow you to declare class member variables (a.k.a. class fields or class properties), as you can in Java, C#, or TypeScript.
>
> Currently, class fields are in stage 3 of the next ECMAScript proposal, and they are supported in Chrome v76 and in Babel. You can see how to declare member variables in TypeScript classes in section 2.2.2.

A.9.1 Constructors

During instantiation, classes execute the code placed in special methods called *constructors*. In languages like Java and C#, the name of the constructor must be the same as the name of the class, but in JavaScript you specify the class's constructor by using the `constructor` keyword:

```
class Tax {

  constructor(income) {
    this.income = income;
  }
}

const myTax = new Tax(50000);
```

A constructor is a special method that's executed only once: when the object is created. The `Tax` class doesn't declare a separate class-level `income` variable but creates it dynamically on the `this` object, initializing `this.income` with the values of the constructor's argument. The `this` variable points at the instance of the current object.

The next example shows how you can create an instance of an `NJTax` subclass, providing the income of 50,000 to its constructor:

```
class Tax {
    constructor(income) {
       this.income = income;
    }
}

class NJTax extends Tax {
    // The code specific to New Jersey tax goes here
}

const njTax = new NJTax(50000);

console.log(`The income in njTax instance is ${njTax.income}`);
```

The output of this code snippet is as follows:

```
The income in njTax instance is 50000
```

Because the `NJTax` subclass doesn't define its own constructor, the one from the `Tax` superclass is automatically invoked during the instantiation of `NJTax`. This wouldn't be the case if a subclass defined its own constructor. You'll see such an example in the next section.

> **NOTE** Until JavaScript supports class fields, you have to declare a constructor in the subclass if you need to add a new class member variable there. In the upcoming ECMAScript release, class fields should be supported, and you won't need to declare a subclass constructor just for this.

JavaScript classes are just syntactic sugar that increase code readability. Under the hood, JavaScript still uses prototypal inheritance, which allows you to replace the ancestor dynamically at runtime, whereas a class can have only one direct ancestor. Try to avoid creating deep inheritance hierarchies, because they reduce the flexibility of your code and complicate refactoring if it's needed.

A.9.2 The super keyword and the super function

The `super()` function allows a subclass (descendant) to invoke a constructor from a superclass (ancestor). The `super` keyword is used to call a method defined in a superclass.

The following listing illustrates both `super()` and `super`. The `Tax` class has a `calculateFederalTax()` method, and its `NJTax` subclass adds the `calculateStateTax()` method. Both of these classes have their own versions of the `calcMinTax()` method.

Listing A.12 Using `super()` and `super`

```
class Tax {
     constructor(income) {
        this.income = income;
     }

     calculateFederalTax() {
         console.log(`Calculating federal tax for income ${this.income}`);
     }

     calcMinTax() {
         console.log("In Tax. Calculating min tax");
         return 123;
     }
 }

 class NJTax extends Tax {
    constructor(income, stateTaxPercent) {
        super(income);
        this.stateTaxPercent=stateTaxPercent;
    }

    calculateStateTax() {
```

```
        console.log(`Calculating state tax for income ${this.income}`);
    }

    calcMinTax() {
        let minTax = super.calcMinTax();
        console.log(`In NJTax. Will adjust min tax of ${minTax}`);
    }
}

const theTax = new NJTax(50000, 6);

theTax.calculateFederalTax();
theTax.calculateStateTax();

theTax.calcMinTax();
```

Running this code produces the following output:

```
Calculating federal tax for income 50000
Calculating state tax for income 50000
In Tax. Calculating min tax
In NJTax. Will adjust min tax of 123
```

NOTE See it on CodePen: http://mng.bz/6e9S.

The `NJTax` class has its own explicitly defined constructor with two arguments, `income` and `stateTaxPercent`, which you provide while instantiating `NJTax`. To make sure the constructor of `Tax` is invoked (it sets the `income` attribute on the object), you explicitly call it from the subclass's constructor: `super(income)`. Without this line, the preceding script would report an error; you must call the constructor of a superclass from the derived constructor by calling the `super()` function.

The other way of invoking code in superclasses is by using the `super` keyword. Both `Tax` and `NJTax` have the `calcMinTax()` methods. The one in the `Tax` superclass calculates the base minimum amount according to federal tax laws, whereas the subclass's version of this method uses the base value and adjusts it. Both methods have the same signature, so you have a case of *method overriding*.

By calling `super.calcMinTax()`, you ensure that the base federal tax is taken into account for calculating state tax. If you didn't call `super.calcMinTax()`, the subclass's version of the `calcMinTax()` method would apply. Method overriding is often used to replace the functionality of a method in the superclass without changing its code.

A.9.3 Static class members

If you need a class property that's shared by multiple class instances, you have to declare it using the `static` keyword. Such a property will be created not on any particular instance, but on the class itself.

In listing A.13, you can access the static variable `counter` from both instances of the object `A` by invoking the `printCounter()` method. But if you try to access the `counter` variable directly using the reference to the object instance (for example, `a1.counter`), it'll be undefined.

Listing A.13 Sharing a class property

```
class A {
  static counter = 0;   ◁— Declares a static property

  printCounter(){
    console.log("static counter=" + A.counter);   ◁— Refers to a static property by class name
  };
}

const a1 = new A();   ◁— Creates the first instance of the class A
A.counter++;   ◁— Increments the static counter
a1.printCounter();    // prints 1

A.counter++;   ◁— Increments the static counter

const a2 = new A();   ◁— Creates the second instance of the class A
a2.printCounter();    // prints 2

console.log("On the a1 instance, counter is " + a1.counter);
console.log("On the a2 instance, counter is " + a2.counter);
```

In this code sample, we increment the counter outside the class instances by using the class names as a reference: `A.counter`. Both instances of the class `A` see the same value of the counter. Note that even if we invoke the `printCounter()` method on a particular instance, it still refers to the static property using the class name.

That code produces this output:

```
static counter=1
static counter=2
On the a1 instance, counter is undefined
On the a2 instance, counter is undefined
```

In the last two lines of this output, we try to access the `counter` property using the instance references `a1` and `a2`, but there is no such a property on either of the instances, so they are undefined.

NOTE See it on CodePen: http://mng.bz/BYQ0.

You can also create a static method by using the `static` keyword. Static methods are also invoked not on the instance of the class, but on the class itself. We often use static methods in a class that serves as a collection of utility functions and no instantiation is needed.

Listing A.14 The `Helper` class is collection of utility functions

```
class Helper {

  static convertDollarsToEuros() {   ◁— Declares the first static method
```

```
    console.log("Converting dollars to euros");
  }

  static convertCelsiusToFahrenheit() {     <-- Declares the second static method

    console.log("Converting Celsius to Fahrenheit");
  }

}

Helper.convertDollarsToEuros();         | Invokes the static method
Helper.convertCelsiusToFahrenheit();    | without instantiating the class
```

NOTE See it on CodePen: http://mng.bz/dxaN.

In listing 2.2, where we implement the singleton design pattern, you can see a practical use of static class members.

A.10 Asynchronous processing

To arrange asynchronous processing in ES5, you had to use *callbacks*—functions that are given as arguments to another function for invocation. Callbacks can be called synchronously or asynchronously.

For example, you can pass a callback to an array's `forEach()` method for synchronous invocation. In making AJAX requests to a server, you can pass a callback function to be invoked asynchronously when the result arrives from the server.

A.10.1 A callback hell

Let's consider an example of getting data about some ordered products from a server. It starts with an asynchronous call to the server to get the information about the customers, and then for each customer you'll need to make another call to get the orders. For each order, you need to get products, and the final call will get the product details. In asynchronous processing, you don't know when each of these operations will complete, so you need to write callback functions that are invoked when the previous one is complete.

Let's use the `setTimeout()` function to emulate delays, as if each operation requires one second to complete. Figure A.1 shows what this code might look like.

NOTE Using callbacks is considered an anti-pattern, also known as the pyramid of doom, as seen in figure A.1 on the left. The code in that figure had four callbacks, and this level of nesting makes the code hard to read. In real-world apps, the pyramid may quickly grow, making the code very hard to read and debug.

```
(function getProductDetails() {

    setTimeout(function () {
        console.log('Getting customers');
        setTimeout(function () {
            console.log('Getting orders');
            setTimeout(function () {
                console.log('Getting products');
                setTimeout(function () {
                    console.log('Getting product details')
                }, 1000);
            }, 1000);
        }, 1000);
    }, 1000);
})();
```

Asynchronous callbacks

Figure A.1 Callback hell or pyramid of doom

Running the code in figure A.1 will print the following messages with one-second delays:

```
Getting customers
Getting orders
Getting products
Getting product details
```

NOTE See it on CodePen: http://mng.bz/DAX5.

A.10.2 Promises

When you press the button on your coffee machine, you don't get a cup of coffee that very second. You get a promise that you'll get a cup of coffee sometime later. If you didn't forget to provide the water and the ground coffee, the promise will be *resolved*, and you can enjoy the coffee in a minute or so. If your coffee machine is out of water or coffee, the promise will be *rejected*. The entire process is asynchronous, and you can do other things while your coffee is being brewed.

JavaScript *promises* allow you to avoid nested calls and make the async code more readable. The `Promise` object represents the eventual completion or failure of an async operation. After the `Promise` object is created, it waits and listens for the result of an asynchronous operation and lets you know if it succeeds or fails so you can proceed with the next steps accordingly.

The `Promise` object represents the future result of an operation, and it can be in one of these states:

- *Fulfilled*—The operation successfully completed.
- *Rejected*—The operation failed and returned an error.
- *Pending*—The operation is in progress, neither fulfilled nor rejected.

You can instantiate a `Promise` object by providing two functions to its constructor: the function to be called if the operation is fulfilled, and the function to be called if the operation is rejected. Consider a script with a getCustomers() function, as shown in the following listing.

Listing A.15 Using a promise

```
function getCustomers() {

  return new Promise(
     function (resolve, reject) {

      console.log("Getting customers");
        // Emulate an async server call here
      setTimeout(function() {
        const success = true;
        if (success) {
          resolve("John Smith");     <— Got the customer
        } else {
          reject("Can't get customers");     <— This is invoked if
        }                                        an error occurs.
      }, 1000);

     }
  );
}                          This is invoked when the
                           promise is fulfilled.
getCustomers()                                   This is invoked if the
  .then((cust) => console.log(cust)) <—         promise is rejected.
  .catch((err) => console.log(err));     <—
console.log("Invoked getCustomers. Waiting for results");
```

The getCustomers() function returns a Promise object, which is instantiated with a function that has resolve and reject as the constructor's arguments. In the code, you invoke resolve() if you receive the customer information. For simplicity, setTimeout() emulates an asynchronous call that lasts one second. We also hardcoded the success flag to be true. In a real-world scenario, you could make a request with the XMLHttpRequest object and invoke resolve() if the result was successfully retrieved or reject() if an error occurred.

At the bottom of the preceding listing, we attached then() and catch() methods to the Promise() instance. Only one of these two will be invoked. When you call resolve("John Smith") from inside the function, it results in the invocation of the then() that received "John Smith" as its argument. If you change the value of success to false, the catch() method would be called with the argument containing "Can't get customers:"

```
Getting customers
Invoked getCustomers. Waiting for results
John Smith
```

Note that the message "Invoked getCustomers. Waiting for results" is printed before "John Smith." This proves that the `getCustomers()` function worked asynchronously.

NOTE See it on CodePen: http://mng.bz/5rf3.

Each promise represents one asynchronous operation, and you can chain them to guarantee a particular order of execution. Let's add a `getOrders()` function in the following listing that can find the orders for a provided customer, and chain `getOrders()` with `getCustomers()`.

Listing A.16 Chaining promises

```
function getCustomers() {

  return new Promise(
     function (resolve, reject) {

      console.log("Getting customers");
        // Emulate an async server call here
      setTimeout(function() {
        const success = true;
        if (success){
          resolve("John Smith");      <-- Invoked when the customer is successfully obtained
        }else{
          reject("Can't get customers");
        }
      }, 1000);

     }
  );
}

function getOrders(customer) {

  return new Promise(
     function (resolve, reject) {

        // Emulate an async server call here
      setTimeout(function() {
        const success = true;
        if (success) {
          resolve(`Found the order 123 for ${customer}`);   <-- Invoked when the order for a customer is successful
        } else {
          reject("Can't get orders");
        }
      }, 1000);
     }
  );
}
getCustomers()
  .then((cust) => {
          console.log(cust);
```

```
            return cust;
        })
  .then((cust) => getOrders(cust))      ⇐ Chains with getOrders()
  .then((order) => console.log(order))
  .catch((err) => console.error(err));             ⇐ Handles errors
console.log("Chained getCustomers and getOrders. Waiting for results");
```

This code not only declares and chains two functions but also demonstrates how you can print intermediate results on the console. The output of the preceding listing follows (note that the customer returned from `getCustomers()` was properly passed to `getOrders()`):

```
Getting customers
Chained getCustomers and getOrders. Waiting for results
John Smith
Found the order 123 for John Smith
```

NOTE See it on CodePen: http://mng.bz/6z5k.

You can chain multiple function calls using `then()` and have just one error-handling script for all chained invocations. If an error occurs, it will be propagated through the entire chain of `then`s until it finds an error handler. No `then`s will be invoked after the error.

Changing the value of the `success` variable to `false` in the preceding listing will result in printing the message "Can't get customers," and the `getOrders()` method won't be called. If you remove these console prints, the code that retrieves customers and orders looks clean and is easy to understand:

```
getCustomers()
  .then((cust) => getOrders(cust))
  .catch((err) => console.error(err));
```

Adding more `then`s doesn't make this code less readable (compare it with the pyramid of doom shown in figure A.1).

A.10.3 Resolving several promises at once

Another case to consider is asynchronous functions that don't depend on each other. Say you need to invoke two functions in no particular order, but you need to perform some action only after both of them are complete. The `Promise` object has an `all()` method that takes an iterable collection of promises and executes (resolves) all of them. Because the `all()` method returns a `Promise` object, you can add `then()` or `catch()` (or both) to the result.

Imagine a web portal that needs to make several asynchronous calls to get the weather, stock market news, and traffic information. If you want to display the portal page only after all of these calls have completed, `Promise.all()` is what you need:

```
Promise.all([getWeather(),
             getStockMarketNews(),
             getTraffic()])
.then( (results) => { /* render the portal's UI here */ })
.catch(err => console.error(err)) ;
```

Keep in mind that `Promise.all()` resolves only after all of the promises resolve. If one of them rejects, control goes to the `catch()` handler.

Compared to callback functions, promises make your code more linear and easier to read, and they represent multiple states of an application. On the negative side, promises can't be cancelled. Imagine an impatient user who clicks a button several times to get some data from the server. Each click creates a promise and initiates an HTTP request. There's no way to keep only the last request and cancel the uncompleted ones.

JavaScript code with promises is easier to read, but if you look at the `then()` function carefully, you still have to provide a callback function that will be called some time later. The `async` and `await` keywords are the next step in the evolution of JavaScript syntax for asynchronous programming.

A.10.4 async-await

The `async` and `await` keywords were introduced in ES8 (a.k.a. ES2017). They allow you to treat functions returning promises as if they're synchronous. The next line of code is executed only when the previous one completes, but the waiting for the asynchronous code to complete happens in the background and doesn't block the execution of other parts of the program:

- `async`—A keyword that marks an asynchronous function.
- `await`—A keyword that you place right before the invocation of the `async` function. This instructs the JavaScript engine to not proceed to the next line until the asynchronous function either returns the result or throws an error. The JavaScript engine will internally wrap the expression on the right of the `await` keyword into a promise and the rest of the method into a `then()` callback.

To illustrate the use of the `async` and `await` keywords, the following listing reuses the `getCustomers()` and `getOrders()` functions, which use promises inside to emulate asynchronous processing.

Listing A.17 Declaring two functions that use promises

```
function getCustomers() {

    return new Promise(
        function (resolve, reject) {

            console.log("Getting customers");
            // Emulate an async call that takes 1 second to complete
            setTimeout(function() {
```

```
                const success = true;
                if (success){
                    resolve("John Smith");
                } else {
                    reject("Can't get customers");
                }
            }, 1000);
        }
    );
}

function getOrders(customer) {

    return new Promise(
        function (resolve, reject) {

            // Emulate an async call that takes 1 second
            setTimeout(function() {
                const success = true;    // change it to false

                if (success){
                    resolve( `Found the order 123 for ${customer}`);
                } else {
                    reject(`getOrders() has thrown an error for ${customer}`);
                }
            }, 1000);
        }
    );
}
```

We want to chain these function calls, but this time we won't be using the `then()` calls as we did with promises. We'll create a new `getCustomersOrders()` function that internally invokes `getCustomers()`, and when that completes, `getOrders()`.

We'll use the keyword `await` in the lines where we invoke `getCustomers()` and `getOrders()` so the code will wait for each of these functions to complete before continuing execution. We'll mark the `getCustomerOrders()` function with the keyword `async` because it'll use `await` inside. The following listing declares and invokes the `getCustomerOrders()` function.

Listing A.18 Declaring and invoking an async function

```
(async function getCustomersOrders() {          // Declares the function with the async keyword
  try {
      const customer = await getCustomers();    // Invokes the asynchronous getCustomers() function with await so the code below won't be executed until the function completes
      console.log(`Got customer ${customer}`);
      const orders = await getOrders(customer); // Invokes the asynchronous getOrders() function with await so the code below won't be executed until the function completes
      console.log(orders);
  } catch(err) {                                // Handles errors
      console.log(err);
```

```
  }
})();
                                    This code runs outside of the async function.

console.log("This is the last line in the app. Chained getCustomers() and
➥ getOrders() are still running without blocking the rest of the app.");
```

As you can see, this code looks as if it's synchronous. It has no callbacks and is executed line by line. Error processing is done in a standard way, using the `try/catch` block.

Running this code will produce the following output:

```
Getting customers
This is the last line in the app. Chained getCustomers() and getOrders()
are still running without blocking the rest of the app.
Got customer John Smith
Found the order 123 for John Smith
```

Note that the message about the last line of code is printed before the name of the customer and the order number. Even though these values are retrieved asynchronously a bit later, the execution of this small app was not blocked, and the script reached the last line before the async functions `getCustomers()` and `getOrders()` finished their execution.

NOTE See the `async-await` code sample on CodePen: http://mng.bz/pSV8.

A.11 Modules

In any programming language, splitting code into modules helps organize the application into logical and possibly reusable units. Modularized applications allow programming tasks to be split between software developers more efficiently. Developers of modules get to decide which APIs should be exposed by the module for external use and which should be used internally.

ES5 doesn't have language constructs for creating modules, so we have to resort to one of these options:

- Manually implement a module design pattern as an immediately initialized function.
- Use third-party module implementations, such as the asynchronous module definition (AMD; http://mng.bz/JKVc) or CommonJS (http://mng.bz/7Lld) standard.

CommonJS was created for modularizing JavaScript applications that run outside the web browser (such as those written in Node.js and deployed under Google's V8 engine). AMD is primarily used for applications that run in a web browser.

You should split your app into modules to make your code more maintainable. Besides that, you should minimize the amount of JavaScript code loaded to the client on app startup. Imagine a typical online store. Do you need to load the code for processing payments when users open the application's home page? What if they never click the Place Order button? It would be nice to modularize the application so the code is loaded on an as-needed basis. RequireJS is probably the most popular third-party library that implements the AMD standard; it lets you define dependencies between modules and load them into the browser on demand.

Starting with ES6, modules have become part of the language. A script becomes a module if it uses the `import` or `export` keywords. For example, the following shipping.js script exports the `ship()` function, which can be imported by other scripts. The `calculateShippingCost()` function remains invisible for external scripts.

Listing A.19 The shipping.js module exports only its `ship()` member

```
export function ship() {
 console.log("Shipping products...");
}

function calculateShippingCost(){
 console.log("Calculating shipping cost");
}
```

The following main.js script imports and uses the `ship()` function from shipping.js.

Listing A.20 Importing the `ship` member from the main.js module

```
import {ship} from './shipping.js';

ship();
```

Syntax-wise this looks pretty clean and simple. In ES6, though, having the `import` statement doesn't load the module; load modules aren't standardized, and developers used third-party loaders like SystemJS or Webpack (see chapter 6 for details).

Now you can specify the type of the script as `module`, as in the following listing. All modern web browsers support `module` as a valid type in the `<script>` tag, so you can tell the browser to load the script as an ES6 module.

Listing A.21 index.html: using the script of the `module` type

```
<!DOCTYPE html>
<head>
    <title>My modules</title>
</head>
<body>
  <h1>Hello modules!</h1>
  <script type="module" src="./main.js"></script>      <-- Loading the first module
</body>
</html>
```

Note that even though we never mention the script located in the shipping.js file, it'll be loaded anyway because the script from main.js imports it. For older browsers, you can use the `nomodule` attribute and provide a fallback script:

```
<script type="module" src="./main.js"></script>
<script nomodule src="./main_fallback.js"></script>
```

If a browser supports the `module` type, it'll ignore the line with `nomodule`.

TIP In listing 9.4, you'll see an HTML file that uses the `<script>` tag with the attribute `type="module"`.

JavaScript modules and global scope

Say you have a multifile project, and one of the files has the following content:

```
class Person {}
```

Because we didn't export anything from this file, it's not an ES6 module, and the instance of the `Person` class will be created in the global scope. If you already have another script in the same project that also declares the `Person` class, the Typescript compiler will give you an error in the preceding code stating that you're trying to declare a duplicate of what already exists.

Adding the `export` statement to the preceding code changes the situation, and this script becomes a module:

```
export class Person {}
```

Now objects of type `Person` won't be created in the global scope; their scope will be limited to only those scripts (other ES6 modules) that import `Person`.

ES6 modules allow you to avoid polluting the global scope and restrict the visibility of the script and its members (classes, functions, variables, and constants) to those modules that import them.

A.11.1 Imports and exports

A *module* is just a JavaScript file that implements certain functionality and exports (or imports) a public API so other JavaScript programs can use it. There's no special keyword declaring that the code in a particular file is a module. Just by using the keywords `import` and `export` you turn the script into an ES6 module.

The `import` keyword enables one script to declare that it needs to use exported members from another script. Similarly, the `export` keyword lets you declare variables, functions, or classes that the module should expose to other scripts. In other words, by using the `export` keyword, you can make selected APIs available to other modules. The module's functions, variables, and classes that aren't explicitly exported remain private to the module.

ES6 offers two types of `export` usage: named and default. With named exports, you can use the `export` keyword in front of multiple members of the module (such as classes, functions, and variables). The code in the following tax.js file exports the `taxCode` variable and the `calcTaxes()` and `fileTaxes()` functions, but the `doSomethingElse()` function remains hidden from external scripts:

```
export let taxCode = 1;

export function calcTaxes() { }

function doSomethingElse() { }

export function fileTaxes() { }
```

> **ES6 vs. Node modules**
>
> It's important to note that ES6 modules are statically resolved, which is a serious advantage compared to Node's modules, which use a `require()` function. With ES modules, the path to a module must be a string literal. In the `require()` call, we can pass an expression that's evaluated into a string at runtime.
>
> In the case of expressions, tools such as IDEs, static analyzers, and bundlers cannot get rid of the unused code from the module that we import, because tools don't know which other code uses the module, and what's used from the module.
>
> But if we provide a string literal to the `require()` call (which we do in most cases), commonJS modules can also be tree-shaken, although not to the same extent as ES modules, which are explicitly marked with `export` and `import` keywords. Tools can clearly see which symbols can be imported by other modules and what we want to import. Tools can do a better job of analyzing and tree-shaking source code that uses ES6 modules than commonJS ones.

When a script imports named exported module members, the names of these members must be placed in curly braces. The following main.js file illustrates this:

```
import {taxCode, calcTaxes} from 'tax';

if (taxCode === 1) { // do something }

calcTaxes();
```

Here, `tax` refers to the filename of the module, minus the file extension. The curly braces represent destructuring. The module from the tax.js file exports three members, but we're interested in importing only `taxCode` and `calcTaxes`.

One of the exported module members can be marked as `default`, which means this is an anonymous export and another module can give it any name in its `import` statement.

The my_module.js file that exports a function might look like this:

```
export default function() { // do something }      ⇐ No semicolon

export let taxCode;
```

The main.js file imports both named and default exports while assigning the name `coolFunction` to the default one:

```
import coolFunction, {taxCode} from 'my_module';

coolFunction();
```

Note that you don't use curly braces around `coolFunction` (the default export) but you do around `taxCode` (a named export). A script that imports a class, variable, or function that was exported with the `default` keyword can give them new names without using any special keywords:

```
import aVeryCoolFunction, {taxCode} from 'my_module';

aVeryCoolFunction();
```

To give an alias name to a named export, however, you'll need to write something like this:

```
import coolFunction, {taxCode as taxCode2016} from 'my_module';
```

Module `import` statements don't copy the exported code. Imports serve as references. The script that imports modules or members can't modify them, and if the values in the imported modules change, the new values are immediately reflected in all places where they were imported.

A.12 Transpilers

If you're about to start a new JavaScript project, don't use a 10-year-old syntax; use the syntax from the latest ECMAScript specs. If the users of your apps have to work with older browsers that don't support the latest ECMAScript, you can *transpile* your code down to ES5 or another supported syntax.

Transpilers (often called "compilers") convert source code from one language to source code of another. In the context of this appendix, you may need to transpile your JavaScript code from ES6 (or later) to ES5 before deploying your app in production.

In the JavaScript ecosystem, the most popular transpiler is called Babel (http://babeljs.io). You can try any of the code samples from this appendix in Babel's REPL utility (http://babeljs.io/repl), which allows you to enter a code fragment in one of the newer versions of ECMAScript and compile it down to ES5. Figure A.2 shows a screenshot of the Babel Try it out tab that shows how the ES2015 code from listing

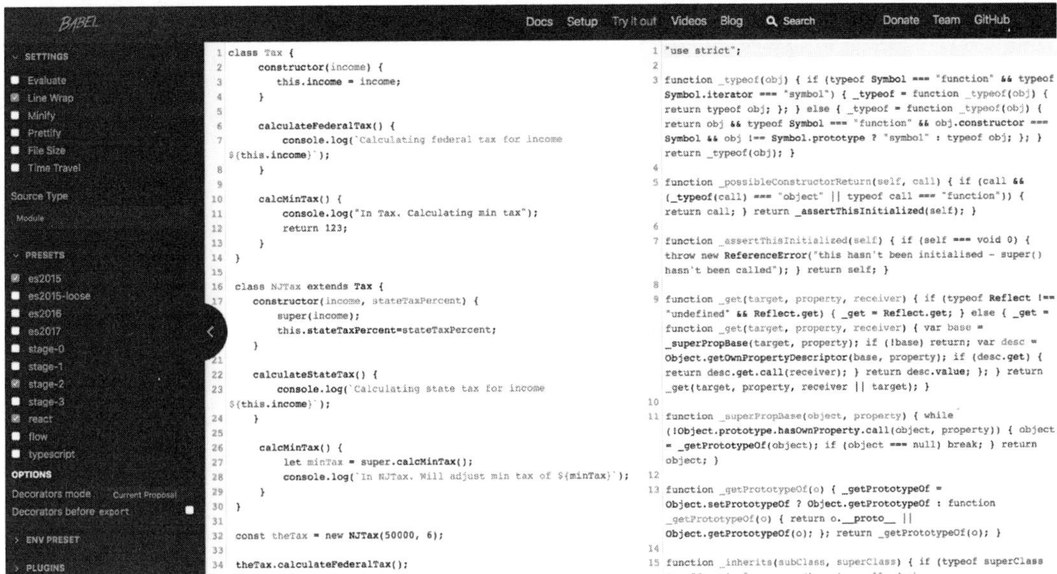

Figure A.2 Using Babel's REPL

A.12 (on the left) would be transpiled into ES5 (on the right). You can see it in action by copying the code sample from listing A.12 to http://babeljs.io/repl.

You can use Babel not only for transpiling newer JavaScript syntax into older versions, but also for converting TypeScript to JavaScript as well (as you can see in section 6.4). But typically you'll be transpiling TypeScript (to any version of JavaScript) using its own compiler, which is discussed in section 1.3.

This concludes our overview of some of the most important features introduced by the recent ECMAScript specs. The good news is that you can use all these features in your TypeScript programs without waiting until all the browsers support them.

index

A

J

K

L

M

N

O

P

S

T

Y